Maintaining Sustainable Accounting Systems in Small Business

Luísa Cagica Carvalho
Open University, Portugal & University of Évora, Portugal

Elisa Truant
University of Turin, Italy

A volume in the Advances in Finance, Accounting, and Economics (AFAE) Book Series

IGI Global
DISSEMINATOR OF KNOWLEDGE

Published in the United States of America by
IGI Global
Business Science Reference (an imprint of IGI Global)
701 E. Chocolate Avenue
Hershey PA, USA 17033
Tel: 717-533-8845
Fax: 717-533-8661
E-mail: cust@igi-global.com
Web site: http://www.igi-global.com

Library of Congress Cataloging-in-Publication Data

Names: Carvalho, Luisa Cagica, 1970- editor. | Truant, Elisa, 1982- editor.
Title: Maintaining sustainable accounting systems in small business / Luisa Cagica Carvalho and Elisa Truant, editors.
Description: Hershey : Business Science Reference, [2018]
Identifiers: LCCN 2017038398| ISBN 9781522552673 (hardcover) | ISBN 9781522552680 (ebook)
Subjects: LCSH: Small business--Accounting.
Classification: LCC HF5635 .M225 2018 | DDC 657/.9042--dc23 LC record available at https://lccn.loc.gov/2017038398

This book is published in the IGI Global book series Advances in Finance, Accounting, and Economics (AFAE) (ISSN: 2327-5677; eISSN: 2327-5685)

British Cataloguing in Publication Data
A Cataloguing in Publication record for this book is available from the British Library.

All work contributed to this book is new, previously-unpublished material. The views expressed in this book are those of the authors, but not necessarily of the publisher.

For electronic access to this publication, please contact: eresources@igi-global.com.

Advances in Finance, Accounting, and Economics (AFAE) Book Series

Ahmed Driouchi
Al Akhawayn University, Morocco

ISSN:2327-5677
EISSN:2327-5685

Mission

In our changing economic and business environment, it is important to consider the financial changes occurring internationally as well as within individual organizations and business environments. Understanding these changes as well as the factors that influence them is crucial in preparing for our financial future and ensuring economic sustainability and growth.

The **Advances in Finance, Accounting, and Economics (AFAE)** book series aims to publish comprehensive and informative titles in all areas of economics and economic theory, finance, and accounting to assist in advancing the available knowledge and providing for further research development in these dynamic fields.

Coverage

- Economics of Natural and Environmental Resources
- Microeconomics
- Environmental and Social Accounting
- Economics Geography
- Managerial Accounting
- Economics of Migration and Spatial Mobility
- Economic Policy
- Investments and Derivatives
- Borrowing and Lending
- Economic Theory

IGI Global is currently accepting manuscripts for publication within this series. To submit a proposal for a volume in this series, please contact our Acquisition Editors at Acquisitions@igi-global.com or visit: http://www.igi-global.com/publish/.

The Advances in Finance, Accounting, and Economics (AFAE) Book Series (ISSN 2327-5677) is published by IGI Global, 701 E. Chocolate Avenue, Hershey, PA 17033-1240, USA, www.igi-global.com. This series is composed of titles available for purchase individually; each title is edited to be contextually exclusive from any other title within the series. For pricing and ordering information please visit http://www.igi-global.com/book-series/advances-finance-accounting-economics/73685. Postmaster: Send all address changes to above address.

Titles in this Series

For a list of additional titles in this series, please visit: www.igi-global.com/book-series

Fractal Approaches for Modeling Financial Assets and Predicting Crises
Inna Nekrasova (Southern Federal University, Russia) Oxana Karnaukhova (Southern Federal University, Russia) and Bryan Christiansen (PryMarke, LLC, USA)
Business Science Reference • copyright 2018 • 306pp • H/C (ISBN: 9781522537670) • US $215.00 (our price)

Regulation and Structure in Economic Virtualization Emerging Research and Opportunities
Denis Ushakov (Suan Sunandha Rajabhat University, Thailand)
Business Science Reference • copyright 2018 • 238pp • H/C (ISBN: 9781522549666) • US $145.00 (our price)

Accountancy and the Changing Landscape of Integrated Reporting
Ioana Dragu (Babes-Bolyai University, Romania)
Business Science Reference • copyright 2018 • 303pp • H/C (ISBN: 9781522536222) • US $195.00 (our price)

Foreign Direct Investments (FDIs) and Opportunities for Developing Economies in the World Market
Venkataramanaiah Malepati (University of Gondar, Ethiopia) and C. Mangala Gowri (University of Gondar, Ethiopia)
Business Science Reference • copyright 2018 • 315pp • H/C (ISBN: 9781522530268) • US $215.00 (our price)

Economic Growth in Latin America and the Impact of the Global Financial Crisis
Mauricio Garita (Universidad del Valle de Guatemala, Guatemala) and Celso Fernando Cerezo Bregni (Universidad del Valle de Guatemala, Guatemala)
Business Science Reference • copyright 2018 • 240pp • H/C (ISBN: 9781522549819) • US $180.00 (our price)

Uncertainties and Risk Assessment in Trade Relations
Marianne Ojo (George Mason University, USA)
Business Science Reference • copyright 2018 • 385pp • H/C (ISBN: 9781522541318) • US $225.00 (our price)

Economic Reforms for Global Competitiveness
Denis Ushakov (International College Suan Sunandha Rajabhat University, Thailand & Russian Academy of National Economy and Public Administration–South, Russia)
Business Science Reference • copyright 2018 • 363pp • H/C (ISBN: 9781522538561) • US $235.00 (our price)

Alternative Decision-Making Models for Financial Portfolio Management Emerging Research and Opportunities
Narela Spaseski (International University of Sarajevo, Bosnia and Herzegovina)
Business Science Reference • copyright 2018 • 333pp • H/C (ISBN: 9781522532590) • US $175.00 (our price)

IGI Global
DISSEMINATOR OF KNOWLEDGE

701 East Chocolate Avenue, Hershey, PA 17033, USA
Tel: 717-533-8845 x100 • Fax: 717-533-8661
E-Mail: cust@igi-global.com • www.igi-global.com

Table of Contents

Detailed Table of Contents

Small and medium enterprises (SMEs) have a prominent role in both the European and the Italian economies, but their approach towards corporate social responsibility (CSR) and sustainability is still underdeveloped. The reasons are mainly related to perceived low economic returns, lack of enforced compliance of the legislation, limited financial and practical support. In overcoming these problems, the role of small and medium practices (SMPs) can be determinant due to the relationship between SMEs and their (not only accounting) consultants. This chapter focuses on SMPs' role in promoting SMEs' initiatives and also considers the academic debate about their sustainability reporting. The investigation of this stream of research and the results of a web survey (involving SMPs in the Northeast of Italy) emphasize how SMPs can support SMEs' sustainable practices and reporting.

Urban public transport seeks the mobility of citizens within the municipal area, and it is a service whose importance is on the increase as a consequence of the ever more dynamic changes in life and work. This chapter analyzes companies that provided services for Italian cities in 2010, estimating the environmental efficiency for the service, using DEA (data envelopment analysis) technique. In the Italian context, both large enterprises and SMEs operate, and this study compares whether the differences in efficiency levels can be explained in terms of the type of company.

practices to take root, a business ecosystem perspective is required. The chapter highlights the theoretical dimensions of energy management and emerging ecosystem of energy management through case studies of the Firozabad glass industry and the Morbi ceramic tiles industry.

Social economy has been a prominent topic among scholars, politicians, and practitioners. Social economy organizations are mission-driven with the purpose of creating social value, overcoming a social problem, and contributing to attain sustainable social development. In this chapter, a particular weakness underlying those organizations is addressed: lack of managerial skills and the importance of a well-structured process of strategic management and organizational innovation. Based on the analysis of a Portuguese case study, the goal is to increase the knowledge on the facilitating factors and barriers to the improvement of the quality of service and the efficiency of the management of a social economy organization, in order to understand how it creates and delivers social value and ensures its future sustainability. The findings highlight a number of best practices in the design of a structured innovation process which were supported by the Portuguese program Q3-qualifying the third sector, which may help similar organizations to improve their innovation and organizational processes.

In order to support family SMEs in developing more responsible, innovative, and competitive business models, this chapter proposes to study the role and interaction between sustainability control systems (SCSs) and management control systems (MCSs). The chapter will examine management control and family business literature with the purpose of discussing the following research issues: What are the interactions between different forms of social responsibility in family SMESs? How can we transfer the family firms' attitude to social responsibility in a sustainable business model? What are main elements of a sustainable business model that can leverage on family firms business model? The conceptual framework will be defined through literature review: the main aim is to convey the meaning of sustainability and investigating the integration between SCSs and MCSs in family SMEs.

This chapter addresses the issue of sustainability in small family firms, considering the relation between entrepreneurial orientation and family influence factors. The literature describes positive links between small firms and sustainability outlining their power in spreading good practices. Furthermore, the role

Preface

This book aims to provide relevant insights for academics, deepening the topic of sustainability accounting systems within small business. In particular, the book will aim to provide contributions about the features of sustainability accounting systems and, in particular, how the economic, social and environmental aspects are related to each other in the company's management and performance.

This comprehensive and timely publication aims to explore and discuss innovative studies and reports as key developments. At the same time providing practical implications and allowing managers a better understanding about the different sustainable accounting systems in the different perspective, such as the strategic, the organizational and the accounting.

This book addressing a range of approaches including, but not limited to aspects of, Small business, small and medium enterprises (SME) issues, Sustainability accounting and accountability, Strategic planning and management control systems, case studies, etc. It covers a wide range of topics, organised into 15 chapters.

In the next paragraphs, the book structure is detailed, with its chapters.

Chapter 1, "The Role of Small and Medium Practices in the Sustainability Reporting of Italian Small and Medium Enterprises", written by Agostini, Costa and Bagnolio focuses on SMPs' role in promoting SMEs' initiatives and also considers the academic debate about their sustainability reporting.

Chapter 2, "Environmental Efficiency Analysis of Bus Transport in Italy: SMEs vs. Large Companies" by Alfiero, Cane, Doronzo, and Esposito, addresses two related themes concerning "good" and "green" urban transport with particular reference to the provision of urban bus services in Italy.

Chapter 3 titled "Managing Small Business Social Responsibility (SBSR) in Formalized Network Using a Euclidean Perspective" by Corazza and Cisi aims deepening the knowledge of inter-firm collaborations to address sustainability issues between SMEs in the context of Italian SMEs

Chapter 4 entitled "Fostering Organic Farming Sustainability Throughout Alternative Food Networks (AFNs)" by De Bernardi, Tirabeni, and Scagnelli discusses the context of shorter organic supply-chains to provide environmental, social and economic benefits that can be better supported by giving a greater emphasis on Alternative Food Networks (AFNs).

Chapter 5, "Determinants of Sustainability Reporting in Medium Enterprises" by Paiva and Gavancha examines the determinants of sustainability reporting in 100 medium enterprises operating in Portugal with an excellent financial performance over the past three years. And concludes that sustainability accounting is in a relatively early phase of development and we hope that this study will further the understanding of the firm characteristics that explain sustainability in medium enterprises.

Chapter 6 with the title "SME and Sustainability: A Managerial Model to Enhance Relationships and Interactions Between Different Local Actors of the Territory" by Casalegno, Christian, and Büchi, presenting a managerial model with the local players and interactions (between public and private organizations) that able to analyze the how local small and medium enterprises create value for themselves by creating a common value made up of relationships, a deep and ongoing communication, and exchanges (of goods, services and ideas).

Chapter 7 entitled "An Innovative Company in a Smart City: A Sustainable Business Model" by Culasso and Mauro, analyzing the business model of an innovative company in the context of a smart city. Specifically, this research investigates key components and challenges concerning the operationalization of a business model originally conceived to be sustainable.

Chapter 8, "Energy Management and Auditing in Indian MSMEs: A Business Ecosystem Perspective" by Basak, Saha, and Shekhar, investigate the adoption of energy management by MSMEs in the Indian context where MSMEs account for 30 percent of exports in and contribute about 40 percent of the gross industrial value.

Chapter 9, titled "Innovation, Sustainability, and Organizational Change in a Social Portuguese Organization: A Strategic Management Perspective" by Barbosa, Romero, and Cunha, focuses on a particular weakness found in several social economy organizations the lack of entrepreneurial skills and the fact that social organizations managers and/or starting social entrepreneurs must be aware of the importance of a well-structured process of strategic management and innovation, in order to understand how the organization creates and delivers social value. This chapter aims to contribute to the empirical literature on the organizational sustainability of social economy organizations, based on the analysis of a Portuguese case study.

Chapter 10 with the title "Integration of Sustainability and Management Control Systems: A Challenge for Family SMEs" by Vola study the role and interaction between Sustainability Control Systems (SCSs) and Management Control Systems (MCSs) examining the management control and family business literature.

Chapter 11, "Entrepreneurial Orientation and Family Influence Factors for Sustainable Small Business: First Insights From the Leading Italian Craft Beer Producer" by Fiandrino, Civera, and Cortese, addresses the issue of sustainability in small family firms, considering the relation between entrepreneurial orientation and family influence factors. The aim of this chapter is firstly demonstrate the influence that family factors play on entrepreneurial orientation and, secondly, highlight how factors and orientations shape small family firms' sustainable approach.

Chapter 12, "The Family Company in Spain: Its Principal Activity, Its Human Capital, Its Challenge, Its Sustainability" by López-Arranz focuses on the importance that family businesses in Spain have in the current business environment, which is characterized by great instability.

Chapter 13 titled "Matching Sustainability Strategy and Results: A Successful Family Firm Case Study" by Broccardo and Truant, analysing the design and implementation of sustainability strategic goals in an Italian family firm operating in the beverage sector that was able to integrate the profit needs with a sustainability orientation. In particular, the research aims at investigating in the selected case how the economic, social and environmental goals are related to each other in order to guarantee high quality products, respectful of the environment and the local community's needs.

Chapter 14 entitled " 'Glocal' Small Business for Sustainability: What Reporting?" by Migliaccio, discusses the model of production and consumption that seems to fall between the extremes described, in which are simultaneously present the innovative aspects of globalization combined with local traditions, often factor in winning competitive strategy: this is "glocalization".

Chapter 15, "Sustainable Management Accounting Systems for Small and Medium-Sized Businesses" by Gunarathne and Cooray, provide a discussion on sustainability management accounting that can be used by small and medium-sized enterprises (SMEs). SMEs represent the majority of firms in the economic systems of both developed and developing countries and their economic contribution is significant in any country. The role of SMEs is evident on many economic fronts such as the creation of business, provision of employment and promotion of innovation and creativity.

Luísa Cagica Carvalho
Open University, Portugal & University of Évora, Portugal

Elisa Truant
University of Turin, Italy

Chapter 1
The Role of Small and Medium Practices in the Sustainability Reporting of Italian Small and Medium Enterprises

Marisa Agostini
Ca' Foscari University of Venice, Italy

Ericka Costa
University of Trento, Italy

Carlo Bagnoli
Ca' Foscari University of Venice, Italy

ABSTRACT

Small and medium enterprises (SMEs) have a prominent role in both the European and the Italian economies, but their approach towards corporate social responsibility (CSR) and sustainability is still underdeveloped. The reasons are mainly related to perceived low economic returns, lack of enforced compliance of the legislation, limited financial and practical support. In overcoming these problems, the role of small and medium practices (SMPs) can be determinant due to the relationship between SMEs and their (not only accounting) consultants. This chapter focuses on SMPs' role in promoting SMEs' initiatives and also considers the academic debate about their sustainability reporting. The investigation of this stream of research and the results of a web survey (involving SMPs in the Northeast of Italy) emphasize how SMPs can support SMEs' sustainable practices and reporting.

INTRODUCTION

Nowadays a considerable emphasis is placed on CSR, *i.e.* Corporate Social Responsibility (Ali *et al.*, 2017; Mio & Venturelli, 2013; Vázquez-Carrasco & López-Pérez, 2013; Venturelli *et al.*, 2017). The European Commission believes that CSR is important for sustainability, competitiveness, and innova-

DOI: 10.4018/978-1-5225-5267-3.ch001

tion in European enterprises and the European economy (European Commission, 2011). According to the European Commission, CSR should be company-led by integrating social, environmental, ethical, consumer, and human rights concerns into their business strategy and operations. This integration should also be applied to the sustainable initiatives and reporting of Small and Medium Enterprises (SMEs). The present chapter aims to investigate the incentives promoting sustainability for SMEs and the role of the main SMEs' accounting consultants (i.e. SMPs or Small and Medium Practices) in supporting SMEs' sustainable practices and their reporting of such practices. These research items are especially relevant given the data recently distributed by the Organization for Economic Cooperation and Development (OECD, 2016). It has recently emphasized the massive proliferation of SMEs and highlighted the key role of these firms in global economic development. SMEs make up 99.8% of all enterprises, 57.4% of value added, and 66.8% of employment. In 2015, just under 23 million SMEs in the non-financial business sector generated €3.9 trillion of added value and employed 90 million people. Moreover, start-ups are SMEs in most cases and they are key contributors to the innovation and growth dynamics of the European economy (European Commission, 2016). This is especially relevant in the Italian context: Italian SMEs are considered the engine of the national economy. They represent 99.9% of Italian enterprises and account for 80% of the industrial and service labor force (Eurostat, 2011; OECD, 2016). They share a number of common recurring features: almost half of them have a 'unicellular' structure, with a small number of employees, sole proprietorship and average turnover comparable to that of micro-firms (Unioncamere & Ufficio Studi di Mediobanca, 2016).

In parallel to these descriptive studies concerning the ubiquity and typology of SMEs, the latest report issued by the 'International Federation of Accountants' (2016, p. 10) emphasizes that SMPs are the main suppliers of accounting support to SMEs and are indeed themselves SMEs. The role of SMPs has been extremely important in the Italian economic system for a long time (Agostini et al., 2018), but it has not been deeply investigated in the literature. According to the International Federation of Accountants, SMPs are "practices that exhibit the following characteristics: their clients are mostly SMEs; they use external sources to supplement limited in-house technical resources; they employ a limited number of professional staff" (IFAC, 2010, p. 10). Moreover, SMPs "do not ordinarily audit the accounts of listed companies, and most of their work is the provision of non-assurance services (e.g., regulatory compliance, tax, advisory services)" (IFAC, 2016, p. 10). This definition highlights the strong professional/client relationship between SMPs and SMEs. Given their usual features as described above, SMEs often suffer from a lack of in-house specific expertise (Jarvis & Thompson, 2014). They resort to SMPs' services mainly to obtain accounting, legal and fiscal external support for both mandatory tasks and business advice. Such a supply relationship tends to go beyond the statutory service provision: it promotes the development of accountants' non-conventional services; it facilitates the understanding of mutual needs and the establishment of a relationship based on trust between SMPs and SMEs (Gooderham et al., 2004). In this way, SMPs can provide both accountancy-based services and other forms of value-adding business advisory services such as advice on strategic planning, financing, risk and sustainability.

This second category of SMPs' services is today especially relevant. Several European Directives (especially 2014/95/EU and 2003/51/EC) continue to push for disclosure on social and environmental matters. In particular, the 51/2003 European Directive had a deep impact in the Italian context (Agostini & Costa, 2018; Costa & Agostini, 2017). It introduced for the first time the consideration of "both financial and, where appropriate, non-financial key performance indicators relevant to the particular business, including information relating to environmental and employee matters" (2003/51/EC, 14) in order to enable a balanced and comprehensive analysis of the development and performance of the business in question. This European prescription was introduced in Italy by Legislative Decree 32/2007, which integrated it with Article 2428 of the Italian Civil Code requiring mandatory disclosure of environmental and employee matters in management commentary reporting (MC). Even though it does not provide operative suggestions about the disclosure of such non-financial information, it represents the definitive recognition that something more about corporate performance ought to be included in traditional financial reporting. It looks like the beginning of a path of convergence between sustainability and financial reports into a single 'narrative' (Agostini & Costa, 2018). This is relevant in the present chapter for two main reasons: the growing prominence of 'integrated reporting' in the Italian context during the last few years and the need of professional support for reporting/evaluating sustainability issues and initiatives. Starting from these considerations, the present work aims to answer the following research question: what is the role of Small and Medium Practices (SMPs) in supporting the sustainability practices of Italian Small and Medium Enterprises (SMEs)*?* A full discussion of its answer requires the study of SMEs' sustainability practices (in paragraphs 4 and 5), the investigation of the relationship between SMEs and SMPs (in paragraph 6 and 7), the analysis of further services that SMPs should offer given SMEs' recent needs (in paragraph 8). The chapter also presents the results (in paragraph 9) of a web survey about SMPs' actual and expected types of customers, services and work organization in the Northeast of Italy. The final concluding remarks try to answer the research question and to provide hints for future research into the topic.

BACKGROUND

The Importance of Small and Medium Sized Enterprises (SMEs) in Europe

SMEs have been defined in various different ways across the world, even if all definitions converge in adopting both employment, turnover and asset base as metrics of analysis. In Europe, SMEs are defined as companies which employ fewer than 250 persons (micro 1–9; small 10–49, medium 50–249) and which have an annual turnover not exceeding 50 million euro, and/or an annual balance sheet total not exceeding 43 million euro[1].

From an accounting perspective, the IFAC (International Federation of Accountants) defines SMEs as "entities considered to be of a small and medium size by reference to quantitative (for example assets, turnover/employees) and/or qualitative characteristics (for example, concentration of ownership and management among a small number of individuals)" (IFAC 2010).

As highlighted by Morgsen and Perrini (2009), SMEs play a significant role in the development of the European economy. The relevance of this sector is emphasized by the following factors:

1. SMEs are a key part of European industry, not least as they contribute up to 80% of employment in some industrial sectors.
2. SMEs are the predominant form of enterprise in the European Union (absolute numbers, contribution to GDP, and contribution to employment).
3. SMEs have more labour-intensive production processes than larger companies and they therefore punch above their weight in the labour market by providing around 76 million jobs in the European Union (EU).

4. SMEs are a major source of entrepreneurial skills and innovation, and they contribute to economic and social cohesion in niche markets that demand high flexibility and customized products.

SMEs are indispensable for the delivery of stronger, lasting growth and more and better jobs. Furthermore, to revitalise its economies, Europe needs more people willing to become entrepreneurs, hence the importance of promoting an entrepreneurial culture[2].

SMEs are the backbone of the EU economy. Their prosperity is a crucial factor for achieving more growth and more and better jobs in the EU. That is why SME policy has become a key element of the renewed Lisbon Partnership for Growth and Jobs since its relaunch in 2005.

SMEs and CSR/Sustainability Practices: An Overview

CSR and "sustainability" are two concepts adopted in discussing the social and environmental contributions and consequences of business activity. CSR relates to the managerial practices adopted by enterprises in order to contribute to the achievement of economic, social and environmental sustainability. Sustainability relates to an ultimate objective of maintaining and preserve the viability of our economies and societies in which enterprises operate (Jenkins, 2009).

In spite of the potential contribution of SMEs within the European economy, understanding them in terms of CSR and sustainability is still underdeveloped (Spence, 2016; 2014a, 2014b; Morsing & Perrini, 2009; Fassin, 2008). One explanation for this scant knowledge base could be linked to the problem of defining CSR behaviours and activities for SMEs (Murillo & Lozano, 2009) because of the difficulties of fully grasping the heterogeneous nature of the SME community and fully exploring potential alternative options (including measurement) in terms of engaging with CSR.

Therefore, an interest in understanding CSR and the contribution to sustainable development within SMEs is now well established (Spence, 2016; Morsing & Perrini, 2009). Beyond multinational companies, which pioneered in this field with relevant commitments to engage in CSR activities, SMEs are today developing new tools and approaches for managing social and environmental issues within the scope of their strategic and competitive activities (Spence, 2014a; 1999).

CSR has to be conceived not as a once-off gesture, but should be viewed as an integrated priority within the company's core business. The full integration of CSR and sustainable procedures into day-to day business practice can positively affect the company's performance and competitiveness by enhancing its developmental potential and reducing its risk profile.

Previous research has mainly investigated i) the rationale and motivation for SMEs' engaging in CSR activities, ii) the peculiarities of a CSR perspective in SMEs and iii) the development of appropriate theories for considering CSR in SMEs.

In terms of motivations, a traditional motivation for CSR activities has been found in the link between CSP (Corporate Social Performance) and CFP (Corporate Financial Performance). However, the motivation of increased social performance leading to economic and financial returns would appear to be less plausible for SMEs (Jenkins, 2009). What emerges from previous studies is that SMEs' rationales for instituting and pursuing CSR practices are linked to owners' and managers' concerns relating to societal and environmental impact, rather than economic and financial benefits. What emerges therefore is a 'voluntaristic' approach, according to which SMEs feel limited 'compliance' pressure and limited (or no) pressure from the suppliers of other stakeholders (Worthington *et al.*, 2006) and move towards CSR and sustainability, if at all, on a voluntary basis.

In terms of peculiarities, many studies have highlighted the relevance of ethical values and interpersonal relationships with the different stakeholders (Spence, 2016; 2014a; Morsing & Perrini, 2009). Specifically, openness, trust, religious-based references to ethics, considered relationships with suppliers, and honest dealings with employees have been recognized as important drivers in delivering CSR practices within SMEs (Spence, 2016). The cultivation of close relationships based on such values creates a fertile *humus* for survival in the increasingly competitive market arenas. Moreover, the adoption of value-based CSR practices may also enhance reputation and therefore relationships with multiple stakeholders, such as financial institutions, suppliers and other partners (Vyakarnam *et al.,* 1997). A focus on the internal dimension (i.e. the employees) is also relevant, because of the attitude of SMEs to ensuring employees' health and safety and to improve workplace climate and productivity (Murillo and Lozano 2006).

In terms of theories, the most important theory regarding CSR approaches has been recognised as the stakeholder theory (Freeman, 1984). Stakeholder theory is indeed arguably the business and society framework that has had most impact both from a theoretical/academic point of view and from an empirical one. Stakeholder theory posits that corporations have a responsibility to all those who affect or are affected by their actions—including, or in addition to, a fiduciary duty to their shareholders. While some scholars have proposed a generic list of stakeholders, it is not the intention of stakeholder theory to predetermine stakeholder groups; on the contrary, it is intended to be applicable to any organization, i.e. public, private, big company or SMEs.

In the SMEs setting, Spence (2016) has expanded the traditional approach to stakeholder theory and introduced a feminist perspective, in particular an ethic of care (Held, 2006), in order to include such emotions as sympathy, empathy, sensitivity, and responsiveness as enhancing a more moral perspective on the stakeholder-organisation relationship.

In summary, Brown and Fraser (2006) identify three potential views of the SMEs approaches to CSR and sustainability, as follows:

- **The Business Case Approach:** Where CSR is seen as an extension of existing management instruments aimed at enhancing shareholder value and improving the company's reputation. This approach focuses on identifying and pursuing forms of CSR and sustainability that result in 'win–win' outcomes for both business and wider stakeholders. CSR is thus primarily situated in the traditional context of 'creating value for the business (shareholders)' in order to improve reputation and enhanced business performance.
- **The Stakeholder Case Approach:** Where CSR is viewed as moral responsibility toward different stakeholders. CSR is thus based on accountability and transparency as central drivers of a democratic society. Shareholder primacy is not acknowledged because various stakeholders are recognized as having information rights which need to be fulfilled through CSR and sustainability practices.
- **The Critical Case Approach:** According to which CSR should bring about a fundamental change in the paradigm of the business system and of capitalism more generally, introducing an open and participatory process involving the multiple-stakeholders in a society. In this view, CSR is useless on its own without a radical change in capitalist society.

SMEs and CSR/Sustainability Frameworks

Moving the focus of the discussion to the formal tools for delivering CSR and sustainability, it is clear that much remains to be understood with reference to SMEs (Bürgi, 2010). While CSR practices are most closely related to the behaviours that SMEs and organisations in general adopt to deliver and pursue their socially responsible actions and values, when discussing CSR tools, the authors are referring to all the social and environmental management practices (Burgi, 2010; Jarvis & Rigby, 2012), such as codes, reports, and formal standards, that can foster the adoption of CSR practices within an organisation.

Previous literature has highlighted that SMEs still lack formal tools because they require an enormous investment of time, financial resources, human resources and competences for the implementation of new organizational routines that SMEs are not yet ready or able to provide (Jarvis & Rigby, 2012). Therefore, the analysis of motivations, process and content of CSR disclosure and reporting remains complex and challenging.

In terms of motivations, what has been found in business organisation is that companies disclosing CSR and sustainability practices are mainly driven by legitimacy and image-restoration concerns (Deegan, 2002, 2007). Companies would keep their stakeholders informed regarding their activities in order to gain, maintain or reinforce their legitimacy, and perhaps to obtain any (undefined) benefits that may accrue from their good corporate behaviour.

In terms of process and content, there is an increasing production of CSR reports across companies (KMPG, 2015), even if these are still lagging behind in the SMEs context. None the less, Stubbs *et al.*, (2012) estimated that among the over 60,000 multi-national corporations throughout the world, only 2,000 draw up formal CSR reports. Therefore, even if there is an increasing theoretical willingness to deliver CSR disclosure by providing formal metrics and estimates conforming to international standards (i.e. GRI – Global Reporting Initiative or IIRC International Integrated Reporting Council Framework), there is still a distinct lack of big companies producing them. Why, then, should SMEs do better in terms of formal reporting?

Rationales for non-reporting have been analysed as follows (Stubbs *et al.*, 2012):

- The delivery of CSR reports could not always be linked to CSR actions, and conversely the absence of CSR reports need not imply an absence of CSR actions;
- Limited benefits and stakeholder pressure perceived;
- Limited view of the benefits of sustainability and sustainable development;
- Not yet a regulatory requirement, thus entirely addressed on a voluntary basis. Organisation structures often are not capable of supporting the implementation of these processes because of the lack of specific skills and knowledge;
- Compliance culture, i.e. producing only what is legally required.

The absence of detailed regulation on SMEs' CSR formal reports has thus been found to be a specific reason for not adopting them. Jenkins (2009) highlighted the difficulties of regulating SMEs' CSR behaviour because they are not only reluctant to adopt voluntary regulation but are also distrustful of bureaucracy. However, SMEs are also very responsive to the changing environment and thus can quickly adapt to changing market opportunities and pressures; SMEs may therefore be able to rapidly take advantage of new niche markets for products and services that involve social and environmental requirements (Jenkins, 2006).

Changes to SMEs' regulation could therefore be seen as an obstacle by these enterprises, which are typically distrustful of social/environmental legislation as a main driving force in determining compliance with government requirements.

Wilson *et al.*, (2012) highlight that a traditional, although not universal, view of regulation is that it restricts companies' business. However, this traditional view has been widely discussed, and indeed questioned, in the literature. Williamson *et al.* (2006) suggested that there was no evidence of a negative impact of regulation on economic growth in SMEs. On the contrary, they showed that regulation plays an important role in bridging the gap between a firm's self-interest and the broader interests of society. SMEs are not always able to perceive the immediate impact of regulations, but they well understand the differential impact when one firm complies and another doesn't have to.

Key drivers in SME sustainability are (Wilson *et al.*, 2012):

- The lack of understanding by smes of current social/environmental legislation;
- The limited support available to help with compliance;
- The lack of compliance enforcement in connection with the legislation.

A failure to understand regulations is sometimes linked with the perceived effort required for compliance, so that some SMEs simply ignored a regulation or made no attempt to comply. A significant minority of SMEs assume that regulation will force them to make environmental improvements even though they have little knowledge of what legislation applies to them or any experience of regulation in practice. Some SMEs also have difficulty in distinguishing between health and safety regulators and environmental regulators.

Moreover, Baldwin (2004) reported that four out of five SMEs perceive the bureaucratic burdens as excessive. He argued that SMEs have to carry out their own administration and do not have the time and competencies to employ regulatory specialists, with the result that compliance-related work diverts the attention of key managers away from day-to-day business activities.

As a consequence, SMEs need to find viable solutions in order to potentially manage CSR/sustainable regulations which compel them to adopt new forms of evaluation or accounting metrics.

This issue is of some urgency for Italian SMEs, due to the changing regulatory environment (Costa & Agostini, 2016). Indeed, the 51/2003 European Directive required the consideration of "both financial and, where appropriate, non-financial key performance indicators relevant to the particular business, including information relating to environmental and employee matters" (Article 14) in consolidated annual reports in order to permit a balanced and comprehensive analysis of the development and performance of the business. The application of this European Directive has been Italy's first experience of a social and environmental regulatory framework. The impact of such regulation is thus new and under-investigated (Costa and Agostini, 2016), but it has undoubtedly opened up new challenges for all business enterprises.

Even if the framework is actually currently focused on corporate groups, there is an urgent call to think about its possible impact on SMEs, since they represent the majority of Italian economic enterprises (Eurostat, 2011; OECD, 2016).

How can Italian companies face up to these new challenges and be ready to conform to the government's 'sustainability agenda'? This is relevant for two main reasons: the growing prominence of 'integrated reporting' in the Italian context during the last few years and the need of professional support for reporting/evaluating sustainability issues and initiatives. Starting from these considerations, the present work aims to answer the following research question: what is the role of Small and Medium Practices (SMPs) in the sustainability reporting required of Italian Medium Enterprises (SMEs)? The IFAC (International Federation of Accountants) emphasizes that Small and Medium Practices (SMPs) are the main suppliers of accounting support to SMEs, and are besides themselves SMEs. Therefore, the authors expect that that there will be an increasing demand for assistance on sustainability issues from SMEs to SMPs due to the Italian 'sustainability agenda'. Are they ready for this new challenge and able to contribute to the sustainability debate? The following section will investigate the current state of SME-SMP relationships, and highlight future directions of change.

SMEs and SMPs' Relationship in Providing Services

'Small and medium-sized practices (SMPs)' is a less well-known term than the SME, even if they are considered the major providers of human resources and employment advice to SMEs (Jarvis and Rigby, 2012). SMPs could be easily defined as small professional accounting bodies which provide business support to SMEs. The SME-SMP relationship is thus regarded as a necessary one because SMEs need to produce documentation, audited financial reports for example, to comply with government regulations, and will turn to SMPs to produce these statements (Blackburn and Jarvis, 2010). The need to provide a detailed definition of SMP (IFAC, 2010) emerges from the idea of distinguishing them as far as possible from large accountancy organizations – *i.e.* the 'Big Four' (PriceWaterhouseCoopers, KMPG, Deloite and ErnstandYoung) – which do not focus their activities on SMEs'services. Despite the relevance of SMPs in daily assisting the SMEs' activities, little is known about the nature of their relationship and their degree of involvement.

What *have* been previously explored are the motivations that prompt SMEs to seek the support of SMPs. Indeed, a dynamic market with higher complexities and instability has made owners and managers of SMEs aware of the need to draw on external sources of advice and support services because of gaps in their internal resource base. Indeed, SMEs need to constantly develop new competencies in order to be competitive in a changing environment (Teece *et al.*, 1997) and often the lack of internal knowledge (Brown. *et al.*, 2006) pushes SMEs to look for advice and support in SMPs. SMPs have become therefore key business advisers for SMEs, even if the type, nature and future of this role is still an open question (Blackburn & Jarvis, 2010).

The nature of the SMP-SMEs relationship is continuously changing because of the dynamicity of the market. Both market conditions and the regulatory environment are in a state of constant flux and the demand for business advisory services will therefore continue to evolve over time.

Government regulatory changes in the requirements for statutory audits are probably the most pertinent issue, but other factors are also affecting the demand for advice and support (Blackburn & Jarvis, 2010).

Continuous market changes represent a big opportunity for the SMPs, because they are in a strong position to fulfil the needs of SMEs, but it is important that the advice and services they provide are fit for purpose, that is relevant, timely and of high quality.

From the SMEs' perspective (demand side) the majority of the services required concerns statutory audit and taxation matters (IFAC, 2008). However, these services are provided in a tailored way because of the multiple differences between SMEs, which vary considerably in terms of size, age, sector, location and growth profiles as well as being run by owner-managers with different capabilities and motivations (Johnson *et al.*, 2007). These characteristics inevitably influence the type of external service provision SMEs will seek and at the same time increase the complexity of SMPs' provision of services.

The Current State of the SMEs-SMPs Relationship

The literature covering the SMEs-SMPs relationship is variegated and covers academic, government and practitioner studies. The specific term SMP has been adopted (relatively) recently by the academic literature and it is more diffused amongst professional bodies. Blackburn and Jarvis (2010), in a study conducted in 2010, found that the specific term SMEs-SMP accountant appeared only 35 times in Google Scholar from 2006 to 2009. Beyond the specific terms, there are many more academic and practitioner studies which cover this relationship.

Following on their analysis, previous studies could be classified into two main categories:

- One stream of research focuses on the demand side for business advice by smes;
- Another stream of research investigates the kind of services and advices provided by SMPs.

From the SMEs perspective – i.e. the demand side – previous studies have investigated rationales and motivations which have driven the owners and managers of SMEs to seek business support for their activities. Broadly speaking this literature have highlighted the diffidence of owner and managers in readily seeking advice. Shaw (2006) and Curran and Blackburn (1994) agree that neither owners and managers like to expose their weaknesses to outsiders and therefore prefer to 'go it alone'. Alongside the need to avoid revealing problems there is also a certain caution regarding the quality of the advice – a fear that it may prove poor or irrelevant – and the unknown extent of the financial costs needing to be borne. Once initial scepticism has been overcome, SMEs generally appreciate the quality of the SMPs' business advice. More specifically, previous literature has highlighted three main issues particularly stressed by the SMEs regarding the SMP's services (Jarvis & Rigby, 2012): competency, trust, proximity and responsiveness.

These three elements have been investigated as major driver for SMEs-SMP relationship. In detail:

1. **Competency:** A main reason for using SMP business services is linked with their technical competencies and expertise for statutory audit and taxation services (Robson & Bennett, 2000; Collis & Jarvis, 2002; Gooderham *et al.*, 2004). The demonstration of technical competency is also relevant – more than any formal qualification – to the continuation of the SME-SMP relationship (Marriott *et al.*, 2008). Once SMP accountants have demonstrated their technical competency in compliance work, they may then be called upon for noncompliance advice and support (Gooderham *et al.*, 2004) because here other elements, such as trust, enter into the relationship.
2. **Trust:** Previous studies agree that 'trust' is a crucial underpinning of the SME-SMP relationship and this provides a platform for the potential take-up of business advices (Bennett & Robson, 2004; Berry *et al.*, 2006; Gooderham *et al.*, 2004, Blackburn *et al.*, 2011). Trust has then been better understood by separating institutional trust – which derives from being a member of a government regulated profession; relational trust – which is linked to the behavioural aspect of the relationship; and competence trust which can be developed when the owner-managers have been able to develop a more rational and critical assessment of the SMPs' competencies.
3. **Proximity and Responsiveness:** Geographical proximity of SMPs to SMEs and the speed of delivery of advice is crucial to many SMEs (Berry *et al.*, 2006). These factors have also been judged more significant than a demonstrated qualification or prior competency.

From the SMPs' perspective – i.e. the kind of services and advices provided by the professional accountants – previous studies have pointed out that traditionally accountants and SMPs provide compliance and monitoring services to meet regulations related to taxation and audit (Parker, 2001). These 'traditional' services typically focus on the preparation or interpretation of financial data within existing regulations and according to standardized principles and formats (Doving & Gooderham, 2008). Even if the bulk of the SMP accounting services remain anchored in traditional financial issues, in the last thirty years the range of services and advice has expanded in number and variety. Indeed, SMP' services now include monitoring and advisory activities aimed at various stakeholder in order to support a broader range of information requirements (Greenwood *et al.*, 2002).

However, the continuous changes in the marketplace and the regulatory framework imply the need for a new response by accountants and SMPs. Whether or not SMPs are able to meet these new demands and move from providing conventional audit and taxation services, to becoming more comprehensive business consultant and advisers is an ongoing challenge (Marriott *et al.*, 2008; Parker 2001).

In this light, there may well be further room for the development of new services beyond compliance advice.

MAIN FOCUS OF THE CHAPTER

Expanding the Services of SMPs to Answer SMEs' Needs

The previous paragraphs have emphasized the economic relevance of SMEs[3] and the importance of developing a sustainable approach for both internal dimensions (especially regarding employees) and market relationships. In spite of such relevance, SMEs are still not widely involved in CSR (Morsing & Perrini, 2009; Spence, 1999). According to legitimacy theory (Deegan, 2002; Rawls, 1999), sustainable approaches may correspond to mutually advantageous agreements between the organizations and the other members of society. They can be voluntary, and they do not necessarily need written legal documents. In order to help the involvement process, SMEs may find a valid support in their relationships with other more 'sustainability-conscious' organizations and/or with professional suppliers. In the first case, SMEs should use their territorial (local) rooting to network with other market actors that have already adopted sustainability approaches. In this context, it would be advantageous to promote specific projects and to create networks of stakeholders that can interact strategically with new collaborative, responsible and sustainable approaches. In this way, through large-scale network operations or production chains (Ciliberti *et al.*, 2008), bigger (not necessarily multinational) companies, which have already adopted sustainable practices either legally or voluntarily as outlined in the previous paragraphs, can play a role in promoting SMEs' sustainability through various supportive actions. The implementation of a sustainable approach is undoubtedly more expensive for SMEs; for this reason, public funding may be required (Schaltegger *et al.*, 2006). The suggested projects should firstly be based on direct supply chain relationships in order to involve SMEs in sustainability practices, demonstrating that such an approach can be diffused as effectively as for larger organizations once the cost barrier has been overcome. Such projects emphasize the "collective grandness of the actions" involving SMEs (Morsing & Perrini, 2009). In this way CSR becomes a social opportunity, a built-in activity and a value creation driver rather than a cost or a reactive-defensive strategy: SMEs can move from merely enacting CSR to being socially responsible (Clarkson, 1995; Grayson & Hodges, 2004; Midttun, 2009). In spite of the benefits deriving from supportive networks of stakeholders promoting sustainability, at the moment, Italian SMEs mainly use their territorial roots to entrust their activities (including their few sustainable practices) to professionals that are located in their own territory and are usually small accounting practices, as emphasized in the previous paragraphs. In Italy, these SMPs are mainly composed by various types of accounting professionals, such as chartered accountants, accounting experts or bookkeepers – these qualifications differ because of the legal requirements to enter the accounting professions[4]. This differentiation is typical of the Italian legal context, while the distinction illustrated by Carnegie and Napier (2010) concerns the international stereotypes of professional accountants. Such authors have analyzed the changing activities of accountants (including the rise of consulting) and have identified two different stereotypes: 'traditional accountants' and 'business professionals'. The typical 'traditional accountant' (DeCoster & Rhode, 1971; Bedeian et al., 1986; Friedman & Lyne, 2001; Granleese & Barrett, 1990) is a man[5], white and middle-aged. This stereotype has both negative and positive features: he is honest and trustworthy, careful with money, painstaking, reliable, polite and well-spoken on one hand, but also dull, boring and colourless, excessively fixated with money, pedantic, uncommercial and even shabby on the other. The second stereotype (i.e. 'business professionals') counters the unappealing features of the first type. It is of more recent introduction and emphasises the positive personal aspects of executives and managers. Canergie and Napier (2010) focus on the ability of "business professionals" to innovate and expand the range of services offered to their clients. Therefore, this second stereotype corresponds to young, dynamic and creative professionals. These are no longer boring and extremely cautious, but well-trained and creative. The main purpose of their activity is adding value to their customers' businesses and, secondarily, to serve the public interest. In the light of some famous financial scandals, such creativity has also been linked to negative actions such as earnings manipulation, off-balance-sheet financing manoeuvres and even corruption. On the other hand, the creativity of this stereotype, also called 'colourful accountant' (Jeacle, 2008; Canergie & Napier, 2010), may be positively related to the introduction and spread of innovative approaches such as sustainability and integrated reporting. This innovative approach should be adopted by SMPs, and traditional services be considered basic services, as the minimum to be offered to each customer. These basic services involve accounting, auditing and administration expertise: drafting and verifying of financial statements and any other accounting documents for the companies; administration and liquidation of companies and assets (also individual assets); appraisals and technical consultancy; inspections and administrative reviews; regulation and liquidation of failures; auditing functions. These should no longer be considered as sufficient. In this way, even though SMEs require traditional activities from their professionals, SMPs could propose activities which fall beyond their traditional professional scope. SMPs should now also be familiar with corporate law, tax law, business management, finance and corporate sustainability. Such further skills require a good deal of effort and a continuous knowledge upgrading, but allow SMPs to offer a professional service differentiated from that of other accountants. In fact, the proposal of services and implementation assistance for CSR practices may improve the competitiveness and the profitability of SMPs. This would be related to their ability to provide practical assistance to those clients engaged in introducing such practices, to attracting new clients, to retaining staff as the SMP provides a greater variety of work, to enhancing specialized expertise. SMPs should, then, develop innovative, specialized and strategic competences necessitating the employment of dynamic professionals in order to differentiate their activity from that of the larger practices. Such innovation and specialization are also especially relevant in view of the growing penetration of the SMEs market by local offices of the 'Big Four' practices, making the audit market more competitive and depressing fee income from the 'traditional' audit market (Blackburn & Jarvis, 2010).

In order to confront this market penetration and increased competitiveness, SMPs may create networks to promote their expertise about CSR and integrated reporting, without losing their local dimensions. These specific projects for sustainability diffusion should help SMPs' resistance to change and upgrade the limited nature of traditional services provided to SMEs. Such a project ought to be sustained by public funding and by accounting bodies in order to support SMPs growth and competitiveness vis-à-vis larger practices. The survey results of an initiative promoted by an Italian accounting body (the *Associazione dei Dottori Commercialisti e degli Esperti Contabili delle Tre Venezie*) are presented in the following paragraph to empirically investigate the services offered by Italian SMPs and to verify how they ought to evolve over the next few years.

Analysis of SMP-SME Relationship in the Italian Context

The paragraph presents the results of a web survey about the SMPs in the Northeast of Italy. The survey was conducted in 2011. It focuses on the Northeast of Italy because it is an area with a very high presence of SMEs and SMPs. It investigates SMPs' actual and expected types of customers, services and work organization (Bagnoli & Biloslavo, 2012). Each of these aspects was investigated through a series of sub-questions. Six answers were expressed numerically, as a percentage for the actual situation and as a variation for prospective evolution to elicit whether either a reduction, increase or no-change was expected. The remaining answers were expressed through a five-item Likert scale where 1 stands for 'not important', 2 stands for 'of little importance', 3 stands for 'fairly important', 4 stands for 'very important', 5 stands for 'indispensable'). All 11267 SMPs in the Northeast of Italy were sent an e-mail invitation in 2011 by a local accounting body called the *Associazione dei Dottori Commercialisti e degli Esperti Contabili delle Tre Venezie*: 2.266 completed surveys were returned, of which 1.025 surveys were not considered because they had been only partially completed. Thus, 1241 completed surveys in total were processed. The results are analyzed hereunder under the following heads: customers, services and work organization.

Unlisted companies, individual professionals and businesses, and partnerships represent the most of SMPs' customers (Table 1). The only type of clientele that many SMPs expect to increase is that of unlisted companies. These results reflect the data collected at national level: Istat (2012) emphasized an increase in the Italian presence of unlisted companies by 3% over the previous year. The reason for this increase might lie in the legal, tax and financial benefits permitted to such companies.

The results of the survey emphasize the territorial rooting of SMPs' activity (Table 2). Customers, consistently with their typology, are almost entirely local. Moreover, also these data reflect those obtained at national level and most SMPs believe that the expected future situation will not be different from the actual one.

The SMPs relationship with customers (Table 3) is characterized by constructive collaboration and extreme frankness. This is considered necessary to raise awareness of real accounting and financial situations, since very often SMEs look for the advice of professional practices only when they are already in the midst of a financial problem. The intention is also to teach customers to spot the warning signals that precede such negative situations so that they can react promptly. This also helps to create a relationship of trust and constructive collaboration. The importance acknowledged to this behaviour is evident from the high percentage of SMPs expecting to maintain this type of relationship with customers into the future.

Interactions between current and potential customers (Table 4) is the most commonly used channel for acquiring new clientele, while technology is still little employed. These results seem slightly different

Table 1. Types of clients in both actual and expected perspectives

Typology of customers	Actual Perspective	Expected Perspective		
	%	*Decrease*	*The Same*	*Increase*
People without VAT registration number	6,73%	14,31%	71,46%	14,24%
Sole proprietorships and sole professionals (one-man businesses)	31,48%	16,07%	56,96%	26,97%
Partnerships	16,21%	22,17%	60,48%	17,35%
Unlisted companies	37,67%	18,60%	43,49%	37,90%
Listed companies	1,33%	15,89%	63,55%	20,56%
Associations and Foundations	1,92%	8,90%	75,92%	15,18%
Public enterprises	1,44%	16,28%	69,38%	14,34%
Others	3,22%	14,10%	67,62%	18,28%

Table 2. Customers' provenance in both actual and expected perspectives

Customers' Provenience	Actual Perspective	Expected Perspective		
	%	*Decrease*	*The Same*	*Increase*
Local	80,69%	10,51%	61,88%	27,61%
Regional	13,92%	9,05%	60,96%	29,99%
National	3,86%	8,06%	62,19%	29,75%
International	1,01%	7,83%	45,78%	46,39%
Others	0,52%	9,09%	60,61%	30,30%

Table 3. Types of relationship with customers in both actual and expected perspectives

Types of Relationship With Customers	Actual Perspective	Expected Perspective		
	%	*Decrease*	*The Same*	*Increase*
Extreme frankness	29,30%	5,24%	67,61%	27,15%
Objectivity, coolness, distance	2,27%	18,32%	62,87%	18,81%
Considerable tolerance	6,52%	41,10%	48,25%	10,65%
Constructive collaboration	31,17%	3,49%	60,94%	35,57%
Trusted relationship	28,62%	5,76%	67,11%	27,13%
Others	2,12%	9,82%	75,46%	14,72%

from the national average: as stated in the 2010 Census Report, about half of SMEs consider internet use a necessity for the business, and SMPs are a species of SMEs, as noted above. Advertising is also an unused resource, but this is largely due to specific ethical norms and professional boundaries. Even in this case, SMPs do not expect any change in the near future. Traditional channels are not considered obsolete or ineffective, while using the internet is thought to be an obstacle to direct communication with customers. The latter are accustomed to having a personal relationship with their accounting profes-

Table 4. Types of channels to acquire customers in both actual and expected perspectives

Types of Channel for Acquiring New Customers	Actual Perspective	Expected Perspective		
	%	*Decrease*	*The Same*	*Increase*
Interactions between customers	75,22%	6,39%	57,72%	35,89%
Direct presentation to customer	9,79%	7,23%	70,28%	22,49%
Presentation brochures, letters and / or emails	0,79%	11,52%	77,96%	10,52%
Advertising (paper or radio)	0,28%	12,11%	82,81%	5,08%
Websites and other computer technologies (Google, etc.)	1,14%	9,32%	72,67%	18,01%
Others	12,78%	9,47%	81,16%	9,37%

sionals and receiving personalized services, and might interpret different channels of communication as signals of diminished attention from SMPs.

Accounting activities represent the main type of service offered by SMPs at the time of the survey (Table 5). The second and third places on the list are 'tax consultancy and assistance' and 'auditing functions', and the provision of non-standard services is still marginal in the actual situation. There is, however, an evolution in the prospective situation: SMPs expect to expand the range of services offered to customers in order to guide them on the internationalisation path. This confirms what Ramirez (2009) also claims: what small businesses need, more than real accounting services, is business advice. In this perspective their role and expertise regarding integrated reporting is surely relevant.

Consistent with the size of SMPs, the main sources of competitive advantage (Table 6) are the following: the accuracy, fairness and reliability of the services offered to customers; the image and professional reputation of the SM; prompt response to customer requests and an established relationship. It is important for professionals to be figures imparting a sense of security to their existing customers, so that they will advise others to turn to their trusted SMP. In so far as personal interaction is the most often used way of procuring new customers, it is clear that building a good reputation is fundamental.

Dealing with mainly local clients, SMPs perform almost all of the services directly themselves (Table 7). International collaborations are approximately nil at the time of the survey, but are expected to increase.

Human resources (i.e. secretarial staff, employees and collaborators) and reputation resources (i.e. brand and professional reputation) are considered the most distinctive with the same average values (Table 8). Tangible resources associated with the office (such as regular office opening hours) and structural resources at the level of rapid communication systems follow these two. SMPs expect all four of the resources currently considered distinctive to undergo significant increases in the future. They also propose the growth of technological resources as a strength to optimize the service offered in the expected perspective.

Most of the SMPs' relationships are those with other chartered accountants (Table 9). Other collaborations are mainly with employment consultants, lawyers and notaries. The importance accorded to this cooperation is confirmed by the Memorandum of Understanding signed in February 2014 by the Italian Institute of Chartered Accountants and Accounting Experts, the Italian Notary's Foundation, the Italian High School of Law and the Italian Employment Consultants' Foundation. The purpose of this agreement is to carry out and organise professional activities of interest to professionals in the legal and economic area, with particular reference to ethics, professional culture and social roles. The interviewed SMPs expect a further increase of the above-mentioned collaborations. Even those with other types of

Table 5. Types of services proposed to customers in both actual and expected perspectives

Types of Services Proposed to Customers	Actual Perspective	Expected Perspective		
	%	*Decrease*	*The Same*	*Increase*
Real estate management	1,11%	6,43%	69,59%	23,98%
Administration and liquidation of companies' assets and individual assets	1,91%	6,31%	67,19%	26,50%
Arbitration	0,48%	1,65%	59,50%	38,84%
Insolvency proceedings	2,14%	6,49%	49,68%	43,83%
Tax consultancy and assistance	13,62%	4,82%	55,14%	40,04%
Payroll management	4,68%	9,48%	60,55%	29,97%
External and internal auditing	10,59%	14,67%	54,73%	30,61%
Accounting services (financial statements)	43,75%	8,33%	57,71%	33,97%
Appraisals and professional (technical) estimates	6,04%	6,64%	52,03%	41,33%
Average adjustments	0,07%	0,00%	80,95%	19,05%
Intestate and testate succession	0,75%	3,81%	64,29%	31,90%
Legal and commercial consultancy	3,85%	4,69%	59,91%	35,40%
Strategic consultancy	1,73%	3,95%	46,93%	49,12%
Marketing consultancy	0,10%	6,25%	50,00%	43,75%
Organization consultancy	2,00%	3,73%	52,24%	44,03%
Information technology consultancy	0,23%	2,63%	71,05%	26,32%
Financial consultancy	1,53%	3,97%	50,00%	46,03%
Internationalisation consultancy	0,67%	6,25%	39,58%	54,17%
Others	4,75%	6,77%	78,39%	14,84%

professionals are, however, expected to increase and this implies that they are likely to expand the type of service offered through the contribution of external professionals. This is necessary when the structure of the SMP does not allow the investment of large economic resources in hiring specialized personnel. In addition, specialising (with the help of external partners where necessary) in non-standard services can attract new and larger customers.

CONCLUSION

This chapter has focused on the support provided by SMPs in regard to SME's sustainability practices and reporting. The consolidated academic literature emphasizes the relevance of CSR (Ali *et al.*, 2017; Mio & Venturelli, 2013; Vázquez-Carrasco & López-Pérez, 2013; Venturelli *et al.*, 2017), but SMEs do not seem to be much involved in sustainability practices (Spence, 2016; Morsing & Perrini, 2009; Fassin, 2008) mainly because of cost barriers (Jenkins, 2009). Such involvement should be promoted in a variety of ways given SMEs' prominent economic role in both Europe and Italy (OECD, 2016). The accompanying initiatives to support SMEs' sustainability practices and reporting can be of different types and applied together. Some examples are the following: initial public funding (Schaltegger *et al.*, 2006);

Table 6. Sources of competitive advantage in both actual and expected perspectives

Sources of Competitive Advantage	Actual Perspective	Expected Perspective
	5-Item Likert Scale	*5-Item Likert Scale*
Price competitiveness	3,17	3,40
Ready and rapid response to customer requests/needs	3,98	4,11
Location (proximity to customers)	3,10	3,13
Control of customer acquisition channels	2,51	2,94
Accuracy, fairness and reliability in the services offered to customers	4,15	4,18
Wide range of services offered	3,35	3,67
Providing customised services for customers	3,61	3,81
Provision of complementary services (e.g. legal services)	3,21	3,58
Provision of innovative services	2,95	3,43
Relationships with customers	3,93	4,01
Image and professional reputation of the accountant	4,01	4,06
SMPs' size (number of professionals and / or employees)	2,81	3,20
Other	2,29	2,47

Table 7. Ways of providing services to customers in both actual and expected perspectives

Ways of Providing Services	Actual Perspective	Expected Perspective		
	%	*Decrease*	*The Same*	*Increase*
Services performed directly by the SMP	87,65%	6%	63%	31%
Services provided by collaborating with local, regional or national external professionals	6,51%	7%	68%	26%
Services provided through collaboration with international external professionals	0,78%	9%	81%	11%
Services provided through professional associations	3,06%	8%	79%	12%
Other	2,00%	7%	87%	7%

networks and shared projects with other more 'sustainability-conscious' and larger entities, which have already adopted sustainable practices legally or voluntarily; direct relationships with SMPs equipped with specific expertise about sustainability reporting and able to demonstrate the practical accounting returns deriving for SMEs from adopting sustainable approaches. This last can be especially relevant given the prevalent types of relationship between SMEs and SMPs. This has emerged also from the results of the web survey about SMPs in the Northeast of Italy. As described in paragraph 9, its results emphasize the territorial rooting of SMPs' activity, SMPs' frank relationship with customers who are used to enjoying personal contact and personalized services. Accuracy, fairness and reliability in the services offered to customers, the image and professional reputation of the SMP, and a prompt response to customer requests are identified as the main sources of competitive advantage for SMPs. The latter already constitute a species of business advisers, but looking forward they aim to increase external and also international collaborations and to specialize more in non-standard services while maintaining

Table 8. Distinctive resources in both actual and expected perspectives

Distinctive Resources	Actual Perspective	Expected Perspective
	5-Item Likert Scale	*5-Item Likert Scale*
Tangibles - related to the office: customer guarantee of a regular opening time of the office	3,48	3,50
Tangibles - related to the presence of multiple office locations: geographic proximity to customers	2,63	2,94
Tangibles - related to the archive: organization of paper resources, documents and archives	2,98	3,22
Financial Resources - extension of payment deferral for customers or anticipation of payments on behalf of customers	2,79	3,03
Relational Resources - with credit institution and other customers' stakeholders	3,13	3,41
Human Resources - secretarial staff, employees and collaborators	3,60	3,71
Human Resources – trainee accountants	2,85	3,17
Human Resources – employed chartered accountant	3,44	3,59
Human Resources – external SMPs	3,12	3,39
Technologies - for adoption and rapid use of technological tools such as electronic billing, certified e-mail system, etc.	3,29	3,56
Structural resources at the level of rapid communication systems with customers	3,57	3,74
Reputable brand and professional reputation	3,60	3,73
Other	2,49	2,59

Table 9. Partners in both actual and expected perspectives

Partners	Actual Perspective	Expected Perspective
	5-Item Likert Scale	5-Item Likert Scale
Chartered Accountants	3,24	3,50
Lawyers	3,07	3,44
Employment consultants	3,11	3,33
Notaries	2,85	3,03
Surveyors and architects	2,11	2,32
Financial consultants	2,23	2,58
Business consultants	2,21	2,55
Other	1,94	2,11

their local rooting. Such results and conclusions show the importance of the widespread dissemination of expertise in sustainable practices and reporting among SMPs as a fundamental tool in promoting a sustainability culture among SMEs.

The authors are aware of some limitations. Specifically, three main limitations can be suggested with a view to opening further avenues of research. First, more qualitative analysis (for instance through interviews) is needed in order to identify new and future areas of collaboration from both SMPs and SMEs' points of view. Second, further qualitative analysis may encourage a better understanding of CSR's meaning across different SMEs and an investigation of the proper role of SMPs in encouraging SMEs to see the opportunities arising from the adoption of CSR practices (Spence *et al.*, 2012). Third, the notion of SMPs could be expanded to include small sustainability advisors.

REFERENCES

Agostini, M., Cordazzo, M., & Saccon, C. (2018). Historical origins and evolution of Small and Medium Practices in the Northeast of the Italian peninsula. In The Origins of Accounting Culture: The Venetian Connection. London, UK: Routledge.

Agostini, M., & Costa, E. (2018). Financial and Sustainability Reporting: An Empirical Investigation of Their Relationship in the Italian Context. In Sustainability and Social Responsibility: Regulation and Reporting (pp. 411-441). Singapore: Springer Nature Singapore Pte Ltd. doi:10.1007/978-981-10-4502-8_17

Ali, W., Frynas, J. G., & Mahmood, Z. (2017). Determinants of Corporate Social Responsibility (CSR) Disclosure in Developed and Developing Countries: A Literature Review. *Corporate Social Responsibility and Environmental Management, 24*(4), 273–294. doi:10.1002/csr.1410

Bagnoli, C., & Biloslavo, R. (2012). L'innovazione strategica nei piccoli e medi studi commercialistici triveneti. *Rivista Dei Dottori Commercialisti, 63*(2), 247–273.

Baldwin, R. (2004). *Better Regulation: is it Better for Business? A report on behalf of The Federation of Small Businesses*. Retrieved August 10, 2017, from http://www.fsb.org.uk/LegacySitePath/policy/assets/0952%20Better%20Regulation.pdf

Bedeian, A. G., Mossholder, K. W., Touliatos, J., & Barkman, A. J. (1986). The accountant's stereotype: An update for vocational counsellors. *Career Development Quarterly, 35*(2), 113–122. doi:10.1002/j.2161-0045.1986.tb00771.x

Bennett, R. J., & Robson, P. J. A. (2004). The Role of Trust and Contract in Supply of Business Advice. *Cambridge Journal of Economics, 28*(4), 471–488. doi:10.1093/cje/28.4.471

Berry, A. J., Sweeting, R., & Goto, J. (2006). The effect of business advisors on the performance of SMEs. *Journal of Small Business and Enterprise Development, 13*(1), 33–47. doi:10.1108/14626000610645298

Blackburn, R., Carey, P., & Tanewski, G. A. (2011). *Business Advice to SMEs. Professional Competence, Trust and Ethics*. ACCA.

Blackburn, R., & Jarvis, R. (2010). *The Role of Small and Medium Practices in Providing Business Support to Small- and Medium-sized Enterprises*. New York: International Federation of Accountants.

Brown, J., & Fraser, M. (2006). Approaches and perspectives in social and environmental accounting: An overview of the conceptual landscape. *Business Strategy and the Environment*, *15*(2), 103–117. doi:10.1002/bse.452

Brown, R. B., Saunders, M., & Bresford, R. (2006). You owe it to yourself: The financially literate manager. *Accounting Forum*, *30*(2), 179–191. doi:10.1016/j.accfor.2006.03.001

Bürgi, J. (2010). A Comprehensive Model for SMEs: Measuring the Dynamic Interplay of Morality, Environment and Management Systems. Towards Continuous Improvement. In Ethics in Small and Medium Sized Enterprises (pp. 147-171). Dordrecht, The Netherlands: Springer.

Carnegie, G. D., & Napier, C. J. (2010). Traditional accountants and business professionals: Portraying the accounting profession after Enron. *Accounting, Organizations and Society*, *35*(3), 360–376. doi:10.1016/j.aos.2009.09.002

Chell, E., Spence, L., Perrini, F., & Harries, J. (2016). Social Entrepreneurship and Business Ethics: Does Social Equal Ethical? *Journal of Business Ethics*, *133*(4), 619–625. doi:10.100710551-014-2439-6

Ciliberti, F., Pontrandolfo, P., & Scozzi, B. (2008). Investigating corporate social responsibility in supply chains: A SME perspective. *Journal of Cleaner Production*, *16*(15), 1579–1588. doi:10.1016/j.jclepro.2008.04.016

Clarkson, M. B. (1995). A Stakeholder Framework for Analyzing and Evaluating Corporate Social Performance. *Academy of Management Review*, *20*(1), 92–117.

Collis, J., & Jarvis, R. (2002). Financial information and the management of small private companies. *Journal of Small Business and Enterprise Development*, *9*(2), 100–110. doi:10.1108/14626000210427357

Costa, E., & Agostini, M. (2016). Mandatory disclosure about environmental and employee matters in the reports of Italian listed corporate groups. *Social and Environmental Accountability Journal*, *36*(1), 1–23. doi:10.1080/0969160X.2016.1144519

Curran, J., & Blackburn, R. A. (1994). *Small firms and local economic networks: The death of the local economy?* London, UK: Paul Chapman/Sage.

DeCoster, D. T., & Rhode, J. G. (1971). The accountant's stereotype: Real or imagined, deserved or unwarranted. *The Accounting Review*, *46*, 651–664.

Deegan, C. (2002). The legitimising effect of social and environmental disclosures – a theoretical foundation. *Accounting, Auditing & Accountability Journal*, *15*(3), 282–311. doi:10.1108/09513570210435852

Deegan, C. (2007). Organizational legitimacy as a motive for sustainability reporting. In J. Unerman, J. Bebbington, & B. O'Dwyer (Eds.), *Sustainability Accounting and Accountability*. Abingdon, UK: Routledge. doi:10.4324/NOE0415384889.ch7

Doving, E., & Gooderham, P. N. (2008). Dynamic Capabilities as Antecedents of the Scope of Related Diversification: The Case of Small Firm Accountancy Practices. *Strategic Management Journal*, *29*(8), 841–857. doi:10.1002mj.683

European Commission. (2001). *Promoting a European Framework for Corporate Social Responsibility*. Green Paper, July. Author.

European Commission. (2011). *Communication from the Commission to the European Parliament, the Council, the European Economic and Social Committee and the Committee of the Regions*. A renewed EU strategy 2011-2014 for Corporate Social Responsibility. Brussels: EC.

European Commission. (2016). *Annual report on European SMEs 2015/2016*. .10.2873/886211

Eurostat. (2011). *Key figures on European business - with a special feature on SMEs*. Retrieved August 10, 2017, from http://ec.europa.eu/eurostat/documents/3930297/5967534/KS-ET-11-001-EN.PDF

Fassin, Y. (2008). SMEs and the fallacy of formalising CSR. *Business Ethics (Oxford, England)*, *17*(4), 364–378. doi:10.1111/j.1467-8608.2008.00540.x

Friedman, A. L., & Lyne, S. R. (2001). The beancounter stereotype: Towards a general model of stereotype generation. *Critical Perspectives on Accounting*, *12*(4), 423–451. doi:10.1006/cpac.2000.0451

Gooderham, P. N., Tobiassen, A., Doving, E., & Nordhaug, O. (2004). Accountants and Sources of Business Advice for Small Firms. *International Small Business Journal*, *22*(1), 5–22. doi:10.1177/0266242604039478

Granleese, J., & Barrett, T. F. (1990). The social and personality characteristics of the Irish Chartered Accountant. *Personality and Individual Differences*, *11*(9), 957–964. doi:10.1016/0191-8869(90)90278-Y

Grayson, D., & Hodges, A. (2004). *Corporate Social Opportunity! 7 Steps to Make CSR Work for Your Business. GreenLeaf*. Sheffield, UK: Google Scholar.

Greenwood, R., Suddaby, R., & Hinings, C. R. (2002). Theorizing change: The role of professional associations in the transformation of institutional fields. *Academy of Management Journal*, *45*(1), 58–80. doi:10.2307/3069285

IFAC. (2008). *The Crucial Roles of Professional Accountants in Business in Mid-Sized Enterprises*. Information Paper, International Federation of Accountants.

IFAC. (2010). *The Role of Small and Medium Practices in Providing Business Support to Small- and Medium-sized Enterprises*. Information Paper, International Federation of Accountants.

IFAC. (2016). *The Role of SMPs in Providing Business Support to SMEs: New Evidence*. Information Paper, International Federation of Accountants.

Jarvis, R., & Rigby, M. (2012). The provision of human resources and employment advice to small and medium-sized enterprises: The role of small and medium-sized practices of accountants. *International Small Business Journal*, *30*(8), 944–956. doi:10.1177/0266242612445403

Jarvis, R., & Thompson, P. (2014). *The Evolving Advisory Role of SMPs in Supporting the Internationalization of SMEs*. IFAC, International Federation of Accountants.

Jeacle, I. (2008). Beyond the boring grey: The construction of the colourful accountant. *Critical Perspectives on Accounting*, *19*(8), 1296–1320. doi:10.1016/j.cpa.2007.02.008

Jenkins, H. (2006). Small business champions for corporate social responsibility. *Journal of Business Ethics, 6*(3), 241–256. doi:10.100710551-006-9182-6

Jenkins, H. (2009). A 'business opportunity' model of corporate social responsibility for small- and medium-sized enterprises. *Business Ethics (Oxford, England), 18*(1), 21–36. doi:10.1111/j.1467-8608.2009.01546.x

Johnson, S., Webber, D. J., & Thomas, W. (2007). Which SMEs use external business advice? A multivariate sub-regional study. *Environment & Planning, 39*(8), 1981–1997. doi:10.1068/a38327

KMPG. (2015). *The KPMG Survey of Corporate Responsibility Reporting 2015.* Retrieved August 10, 2017, from https://home.kpmg.com/xx/en/home/insights/2015/11/kpmg-international-survey-of-corporate-responsibility-reporting-2015.html

Lamanna Di Salvo, D. (2004). Ragioniere e Dottore Commercialista: una storica diatriba tra differenziazione ed unificazione. *Rivista Scuola superiore dell'economia e delle finanze, 8/9*, 2.

Marriott, N., Marriott, P., Collis, J., & Son, D. D. (2008). *The Accountant and the Provision of Financial Advice to UK Smaller Companies.* British Accounting Association Annual Conference, Blackpool, UK.

Midttun, A. (2009). *Strategic CSR Innovation: Serving Societal and Individual Needs.* Oslo: BI Norwegian School of Management: Department of Innovation and Organizational Management.

Mio, C., & Venturelli, A. (2013). Non-financial Information About Sustainable Development and Environmental Policy in the Annual Reports of Listed Companies: Evidence from Italy and the UK. *Corporate Social Responsibility and Environmental Management, 20*(6), 340–358. doi:10.1002/csr.1296

Morsing, M., & Perrini, F. (2009). CSR in SMEs: Do SMEs matter for the CSR agenda? *Business Ethics (Oxford, England), 18*(1), 1–6. doi:10.1111/j.1467-8608.2009.01544.x

Murillo, D., & Lozano, J. (2009). Pushing forward SME CSR through a network: An account from the Catalan model. *Business Ethics (Oxford, England), 18*(1), 7–20. doi:10.1111/j.1467-8608.2009.01545.x

Murillo, D., & Lozano, J. F. (2006). SMEs and CSR: An approach to CSR in their own words. *Journal of Business Ethics, 67*(3), 227–240. doi:10.100710551-006-9181-7

OECD. (2016). *Financing SMEs and Entrepreneurs (2016): An OECD Scoreboard.* Retrieved August 10, 2017, from http://www.keepeek.com/Digital-Asset-Management/oecd/industry-and-services/financing-smes-and-entrepreneurs-2016_fin_sme_ent-2016-en#page306

Parker, L. (2001). Back to the future: The broadening accounting trajectory. *The British Accounting Review, 33*(4), 421–453. doi:10.1006/bare.2001.0173

Rawls, J. (1999). *A theory of justice* (Rev. Ed.). Oxford, UK: Oxford University Press.

Robson, P. J. A., & Bennett, R. J. (2000). SME growth: The relationship with business advice and external collaboration. *Small Business Economics, 15*(3), 193–208. doi:10.1023/A:1008129012953

Schaltegger, S., Bennett, M., & Burritt, R. (2006). *Sustainability accounting and reporting (21).* Springer Science and Business Media. doi:10.1007/978-1-4020-4974-3

Shaw, E. (2006). Small Firm Networking: An Insight into Contents and Motivating Factors. *International Small Business Journal*, *24*(1), 5–29. doi:10.1177/0266242606059777

Spence, L. J. (1999). Does size matter? The state of the art in small business ethics. *Business Ethics (Oxford, England)*, *8*(3), 163–174. doi:10.1111/1467-8608.00144

Spence, L. J. (2014a). Business ethics and social responsibility in small firms. In Handbook of research on small business and entrepreneurship. Northampton, MA: Edward Elgar. doi:10.4337/9781849809245.00031

Spence, L. J. (2014b). Small business social responsibility: Redrawing core CSR theory. *Business & Society*. doi:10.1177/ 0007650314523256

Spence, L. J. (2016). Small Business Social Responsibility: Expanding Core CSR Theory. *Business & Society*, *55*(1), 23–55. doi:10.1177/0007650314523256

Spence, L. J., Agyemang, G., & Rinaldi, L. (2012). *Environmental Aspects of Sustainability: SMEs and the Role of the Accountant*. London, UK: Certified Accountants Educational Trust.

Spence, L. J., & Rutherfoord, R. (2003). Small business and empirical perspectives in business ethics [editorial]. *Journal of Business Ethics*, *47*(1), 1–5. doi:10.1023/A:1026205109290

Stubbs, W., Higgins, C., & Milne, M. (2012). Why do companies not produce sustainability reports? *Business Strategy and the Environment*, *22*(7), 456–470. doi:10.1002/bse.1756

Teece, D. J., Pisano, G., & Shuen, A. (1997). Dynamic Capabilities and Strategic Management. *Strategic Management Journal*, *18*(7), 509–533. doi:

Unioncamere e Ufficio Studi di Mediobanca. (2016). *Le medie imprese industriali italiane*. Mediobanca Ufficio Studi.

Vázquez-Carrasco, R., & López-Pérez, M.E. (2013). Small & medium-sized enterprises and Corporate Social Responsibility: a systematic review of the literature. *Quality & Quantity, 47*(6), 3205-3218.

Venturelli, A., Caputo, F., Leopizzi, R., Mastroleo, G., & Mio, C. (2017). How can CSR identity be evaluated? A pilot study using a Fuzzy Expert System. *Journal of Cleaner Production*, *141*, 1000–1010. doi:10.1016/j.jclepro.2016.09.172

Vyakarnam, S., Bailey, A., Myers, A., & Burnett, D. (1997). Towards an understanding of ethical behaviour in small firms. *Journal of Business Ethics*, *16*(15), 1625–1636. doi:10.1023/A:1022452502299

Williamson, D., Lynch Wood, G., & Ramsay, J. (2006). Drivers of Environmental Behaviour in Manufacturing SMEs and the Implications for CSR. *Journal of Business Ethics*, *67*(3), 317–330. doi:10.100710551-006-9187-1

Wilson, C., Williams, I., & Kemp, S. (2012). An evaluation of the impact and effectiveness of environmental legislation in small and medium-sized enterprises: Experiences from the UK. *Business Strategy and the Environment*, *21*(3), 141–156. doi:10.1002/bse.720

Worthington, I., Ram, M., & Jones, T. (2006). Exploring corporate social responsibility in the UK Asian small business community. *Journal of Business Ethics*, *67*(2), 201–217. doi:10.100710551-006-9024-6

ENDNOTES

1 See Commission Recommendation, 2003/361/EC.

2 Commission Communication of 11 November 2005: "Implementing the Community Lisbon Programme - Modern SME Policy for Growth and Employment".

3 SMEs make up 99.8% of all enterprises (99.9% in Italy), 57.4% of value added, and 66.8% of employment. Start-ups (SMEs in most cases) are key contributors to the innovation and growth dynamics of the EU economy (European Commission, 2016).

4 The term 'chartered accountant' is often used as a synonym for 'book-keeper', even though they are two distinct qualifications from a legal point of view. This confusion has characterized the Italian situation for a very long time. Towards the mid-1920s, the C.P.A. (Certified Practising Accountants in Commercial Science) was locally set up the District Court of Appeal in Milan, which in 1921 proposed a new law for the official recognition of the accounting profession. This law proposal also listed the functions that the accounting practitioners wanted to be recognized. Italian Decree no. 103 (issued January 24, 1924) duly established that professional categories not yet regulated by the law would be established, with different 'public registries' that were called 'ordini' if they included university graduates or 'collegi' if they included only high school graduates (Lamanna Di Salvo, 2004). After this initial differentiation, the two professional categories sought to reach an agreement, but the differences were considered too deep. For years the struggle between the two professional accounting categories continued to rage, with proposals and counter-proposals to the Ministries, all rejected. Only in 1926 did the chartered accountants and bookkeepers come to an agreement: the C.P.A. (Certified Practising Accountants) was definitively established in 1953 and the rights of the bookkeepers already enrolled in the 'collegi' were safeguarded. Since the introduction of these regulations, the profession of chartered accountant has been recognized to have a specific technical competence concerning commercial, economic, financial, taxation and accounting matters and has been obliged to maintain professional secrecy.

5 He is typically a male because in the 1960s and 70s those who continued to study beyond secondary school were mostly males.

Chapter 2
Environmental Efficiency Analysis of Bus Transport in Italy:
SMEs vs. Large Companies

Simona Alfiero
University of Turin, Italy

Massimo Cane
University of Turin, Italy

Ruggiero Doronzo
University of Turin, Italy

Alfredo Esposito
University of Turin, Italy

ABSTRACT

Urban public transport seeks the mobility of citizens within the municipal area, and it is a service whose importance is on the increase as a consequence of the ever more dynamic changes in life and work. This chapter analyzes companies that provided services for Italian cities in 2010, estimating the environmental efficiency for the service, using DEA (data envelopment analysis) technique. In the Italian context, both large enterprises and SMEs operate, and this study compares whether the differences in efficiency levels can be explained in terms of the type of company.

DOI: 10.4018/978-1-5225-5267-3.ch002

INTRODUCTION

Urban transport provides residents with mobility in municipal areas and this increasingly important service is a consequence of far reaching changes in lifestyles and work patterns. As residential areas spread into the outskirts, businesses re-locate into industrial estates and university faculties create out-of-town campuses, there is greater need for access which public transport must provide.

There has often been a lot of focus on the economic outcomes of transport issues, but less consideration given to social and environmental aspects, like transport emissions.

Public transport is a means for people to move around a town efficiently with the least impact on the environment and help reduce, for instance, CO2 emissions.

During the last few decades, sustainability - and in particular the environmental issue - has become a variable that needs to be analysed and measured (Carpenter, 1993).

This chapter addresses two related themes concerning "good" and "green" urban transport with particular reference to the provision of urban bus services in Italy.

The first theme examines the way public urban transport providers can measure efficiency: in particular, the chapter considers the theoretical and practical issues that an urban transport provider could encounter when benchmarking the situation.

The results of empirical studies concerning the efficiency of public services indicate that private sector participation in public services has generally improved the efficiency of those services (as suggested by property rights and public choice theory). However, the effects are largely dependent on other governance arrangements (e.g. contracts) and the particular industry context (e.g. level of competition).

In Italy, externalisation of public services favoured different forms of governance: private corporations, outsourcing, public-private partnerships and privatisation (Doherty & Horne, 2002; Torres & Pina, 2002; Crediop, 2004; Reichard, 2008; Keune et al., 2008). The urban bus services sector was also subject to externalisation and today the sector is characterised by the presence of large companies (mostly public-private partnerships) and small-medium enterprises (SMEs), ie private companies.

The second theme considers the differences in behaviour of small-medium and large companies and how these differences can be a means of explaining the disparity in attitude by transport providers to the potential benefits of benchmarking.

This is important because understanding what is best quality performance and attempting to move towards an industry best is one of the most secure ways of ensuring the provision of quality services in a sustainability stable environment.

There is a plethora of management models and ideas which can be used in a business context to improve business performance. Benchmarking has been a key tool in the business improvement armoury for many years.

Benchmarking is a way of measuring how good the business is at what it does, making a quantitative statement as to whether its performance is as good as other businesses and using this information to improve its business process. Benchmarking, then, is a tool for finding an industry's best practices, leading to improvement in performance. Benchmarking can be applied widely and can cover all aspects of measurable activity: it could cover both inputs (internal efficiency) and outputs (revenue and passenger responses) in an urban bus context.

After having carried out some benchmarking, the organisation will have acquired an in-depth knowledge of itself. The benchmarking measurement process provides a baseline data set for improvement and for target setting which the whole organisation can understand. Areas for potential improvement are identified and target values (perhaps with intermediate milestones) can be set.

Benchmarking is a key step in a continuous improvement process although it will not add value in itself – it is the catalyst to change. Value is only added through achieving real improvements.

CHARACTERISTICS OF URBAN TRANSPORT IN ITALY

Legislation concerning public transport in Italy is the 1997 Law No. 59 and, in particular, the Decree No. 422 of the same year which triggered real reform in the sector in the late 90s. This law's main aim was to regionalise the sector so that regions and other local authorities (provinces, boroughs, rural communities, etc) would be assigned planning and delivering roles concerning public transport at regional and local levels. These are transportation services for both people and goods via land, water and air that are not part of the national network and that run continuously or periodically with set routes, times, frequencies and prices. These services are available to the public on a regional or inter-regional scale. So, the regions and other local authorities were assigned powers to legislate in order to carry out the principles established in the framework of the law. They could then give local authorities duties that did not require regional approval.

The state would maintain the following powers for:

- All those covering national public transport, for example:
  - Air transport, except exclusively regional connections and helicopter services.
  - Sea transport, except coastal navigation which is mostly done regionally.
  - International car transport, except cross border and inter-regional routes that connect more than two regions.
  - International railway services as well as medium-long, higher standard national railway services.
  - Sea connections between railway terminals.
  - Transport of dangerous, harmful and polluting goods.
- Some public transport services of regional and local interest, for example:
  - Agreements, conventions and international treaties concerning cross border services for transporting people and goods.
  - Safety measures.
  - Introduction of guide lines and framework principles in order to reduce pollution caused by the public transport system.

It is also important to mention the role carried out nationally by the *Transport Regulations Authority* which came into existence under Art. 37 of the Decree No. 201 in 2011 and which, together with certain amendments, became law under Law No. 214 of the same year. It operates within the public services regulations authority under the 1995 Law No. 481. This Authority is responsible for regulating the transport sector, access to relative infrastructure and accessory services. Its mandate includes defining the quality levels of both national and local transport services and minimum rights that users can exert over transport companies. According to Art. 14 (2) of Legislative Decree No. 422/1997, when undertaking their urban planning duties, the regions are responsible for the following: a) defining the routes when planning local transport and in particular local ways b) draw up regional transport plans and updates considering local authorities' planning and in particular local ways made available by the provinces and/or metropolitan areas. This is in connection with local planning and economic development plans and aims to guarantee a transport network that encourages integration between the different forms of transport and favours those with less environmental footprint.

The term "minimum services" indicates services which are qualitatively and quantitatively sufficient to satisfy people's demands for transport and costs are included in the regions' budget. In fact, under Art. 14 (3) of Legislative Decree No. 422/1997, the regions must approve three-year local public transport programmes with the aim of determining: a) the network and organisation of services; b) integration of different means of transport with prices; c) resources to assign to management and investments; d) ways of establishing prices; e) ways of implementing and revising public service contracts; f) system of monitoring the services; g) criteria for the reduction of congestion and pollution.

Additionally, Art. 16 (1 and 2) of Legislative Decree No. 422/1997 highlights important criteria for defining the "minimum services". For example: a) integration of transport networks; b) school and work commuter needs; c) use of services in order to access administrative, health and cultural facilities; d) need to reduce congestion and pollution; e) use of different means of transport most able to satisfy travellers' needs, with particular attention to those with reduced mobility; f) choice of solutions designed to guarantee sufficient transport services at as low a price as possible, including different means of transport; g) consideration of the impact of outside forces like traffic congestion and pollution, when determining the costs of road transport.

In order to appoint regional and local transport service providers, discourage monopolies and introduce rules of competitiveness, national and European laws (Legislative Decree No. 422 of 1997, Law No. 102 of 2002, Law No. 99 of 2009 and European Regulations No. 1370 of 2007) name three different application procedures: a) open tender; b) in house c) direct contracts within set thresholds.

Lastly, management of local and regional public transport by appointed transport operators – regardless of contract type – can only be regulated via service contracts that do not exceed nine years. These contracts must define: a) validity period; b) characteristics of the services offered and schedules; c) minimum standards of quality of service regarding age, maintenance, comfort and cleanliness of vehicles, regularity of services; d) price structure used; e) total sum local authority might have to pay the transport company for services rendered under contract and payment conditions, including possible adjustments following changes in fare structure; f) procedures for modifying contract following its conclusion; g) guarantees that transport company must give; h) fines following breach of contract; i) redefining commitment, with reference to staff and capital invested by the public transport company following drop in demand during the contract period; l) obligation of issuing recognised transport sector contracts for staff as required by the largest national trade unions and employers' associations.

The *National Report of Infrastructure and Transport* was set up by the Ministry of Infrastructure and Transport for bus transport services (which is of major interest in this paper). Its latest issue reports that there are 997 local public road transport companies in Italy operating regionally (in 2014) and 248 of these only transport passengers in and around the city (24.9%), 535 only out of town (53.7%) and 214 (21.5%) both (See Table 1).

Companies in the sector are extremely diverse in terms of size (number of employees). In fact, there are 592 operators (59.4%) in the 1-10 employees range (with 332 or 56.1% in south Italy and the islands), 179 with more than 50 employees (17.9%) and 126 (12.6%) large firms (over 100 employees) are mostly in north Italy. This distribution of companies over the country shows subtle differences. 29.5% (294) are

Table 1. Local public transport (bus sector): Companies shown by geographical area and type of services offered – Year 2014

Geographic Areas	Total Number of Companies	Only City Service	Only Out of Town Service	Mixed Service
North Italy	**294**	42	180	72
Central Italy	**163**	101	14	48
South Italy and islands	**540**	105	341	94
Total	**997**	**248**	**535**	**214**

Source: National Report of Infrastructure and Transport – Years 2014-2015, pag. 151

based in north Italy, 16.3% (163) in the centre and the remaining 54.2% (540) in the south and on the islands. 44.3% of the companies (239) with no more than 5 employees are in south Italy and the islands and just 9.1% (49) with over 100 (Table 2). Even observing the geographic distribution of the companies and number of means of transport used, a different structure can be seen. In fact, 243 companies of a total of 427 (56.9%) with a maximum of 5 buses operate in the south and on the islands, while 45.7% of firms with over 100 buses (53 out of 116) operate in the north (Table 3).

Table 4 highlights certain ratios between characteristics of local bus companies (total employees and total buses used) and the resident population in each of the three geographic areas. In particular, it

Table 2. Geographic areas of local public transport companies (bus services) by number of employees – Year 2014

Geographic Area	Total Number of Companies	Number of Employees (Classes)					
		1-5	**6-10**	**11-20**	**21-50**	**51-100**	**Over 100**
North Italy	**294**	124	51	21	21	20	57
Central Italy	**163**	59	26	24	25	9	20
South Italy and the islands	**540**	239	93	81	54	24	49
Total	**997**	**422**	**170**	**126**	**100**	**53**	**126**

Source: National Report of Infrastructure and Transport – Years 2014-2015, pag. 153

Table 3. Geographic areas of local public transport companies (bus services) by number of buses used – Year 2014

Geographic Area	Total Number of Companies	Number of Buses Used (Classes)					
		1-5	**6-10**	**11-20**	**21-50**	**51-100**	**Oltre 100**
North Italy	**294**	119	55	23	26	18	53
Central Italy	**163**	65	27	24	23	3	21
South Italy and the islands	**540**	243	112	72	57	14	42
Total	**997**	**427**	**194**	**119**	**106**	**35**	**116**

Source: National Report of Infrastructure and Transport – Year 2014-2015, pag. 154

Table 4. Geographic distribution of employees and buses used – local public transport companies (bus companies) – City and out of town services – Year 2014

Geographic Area	Total Employees	Buses Used	Pesident Population	Employees/Residents (x1,000)	Buses/Residents (x1,000)
North Italy	32,990	20,021	27,785,211	1.19	7.21
Central Italy	19,864	10,713	12,070,842	1.65	8.88
South Italy and the islands	31,626	15,210	20,926,615	1.51	7.27
	84,480	**45,944**	**60,782,668**	**1.39**	**7.56**

Source: National Report of Infrastructure and Transport – Years 2014-2015, pag. 156

comes to light that the ratio between employees per 1,000 residents and that between buses and every 1,000 residents have a higher value compared to the national average in central Italy (respectively, 1.65 v 1.39 and 8.88 v 7.56) while the minimums were recorded in north Italy.

Lastly, Table 5 shows some data concerning overall supply and demand of local public transport (buses).

FOCUS OF THE MAIN CHAPTER

The main objective of this chapter is to analyse efficiency in Italy's public urban transportation sector. In fact, CO2 emissions were also taken into account with the aim of highlighting the environmental impact.

We focused on CO2 emissions due to their major contribution to global climate change and consequential growing concerns.

Our analysis covers 156 Italian companies that provided urban bus services, in 2010.

As we saw earlier, both large and small-medium sized enterprises (SMEs) now operate this service following the outsourcing process of the sector.

The main methodology used to analyse this efficiency is Data Envelopment Analysis (DEA). DEA is a non-parametric technique that has enjoyed great popularity in measuring performance for benchmarking purposes by defining efficiency scores for each company.

We set the following objectives:

1. To estimate efficiency scores for public urban transportation service, using (among others) those resources to reduce e.g. Co2 emissions.
2. And to contrast whether differences in efficiency levels can be explained in terms of enterprise type (large companies versus smes). When analysing the resources used and outputs obtained, any excesses of input used or increases in output necessary to improve the performance come to light.

Therefore, this study attempts to contribute to the literature by presenting a non-radial and input-oriented DEA framework based on the slacks-based measure (SBM) to assess environmental efficiency in Italy's transportation sector.

Table 5. Some indicators of supply and demand of local public transport (bus companies) – Year 2014

Demand	
	2014
Total number of passengers (millions)	**3,746.0**
City service	2,822.9
Out of town service	923.1
Total passengers-km (billion)	**29.118**
City service	11.207
Out of town service	17.911
Supply	
	2014
City service	
Buses used	18,606
Bus-km (millions)	698.95
Places available (millions)	1.60
Places-km available (milioni)	62,810.24
Out of town service	
Buses used	27,338
Bus-km (millions)	1,047.69
Places available (millions)	1.84
Places-km available (millions)	70,884.89
Total	
Buses used	45,944
Bus-km (millions)	1,746.64
Places available (millions)	3.44
Places-km available (millions)	133,695.13

Source: Own data taken from National Report of Infrastructure and Transport – Years 2014-2015, pag. 156-158

CORPORATE EFFICIENCY STUDIES IN THE URBAN TRANSPORT SECTOR

Several studies have analysed urban transport service efficiency, with the use of non-parametric techniques. Here is a quick look at some of them.

Karlaftis et al. (2004) presented a review of papers analysing the performance of transport systems. Daraio et al. (2016) offered a critical discussion of the existing empirical studies, relating them to the main methodological approaches used. The comprehensive classification of selected relevant dimensions of the empirical literature, namely inputs, outputs, kinds of data analysed, methods adopted and policy relevant questions addressed, and the systematic investigation of their interrelationships are summarised.

Tomazinis (1977) analysed parameters in order to measure public transport systems and defined some simple concepts for evaluating them, like efficiency, productivity and service quality. Fielding et al. (1985 a,b) published many parameters that could be used to assess performance, and put them into three categories: efficiency, effectiveness and overall performance (which included the first two).

Viton (1997) studied the efficiency of the US bus system, applying DEA to 217 public and private companies and using these parameters: vehicles/distance in miles and passengers transported (outputs) and average speed, average age of fleet, miles travelled, fuel used, personnel employed in the transport service, maintenance personnel, administrative personnel, capital and costs (inputs).

Using a DEA model, Chu et al. (1992) and Viton (1998) created a unique measure of performance, determining that the US bus system saw an improvement in productivity between 1988 and 1992. They also noted that efficiency and effectiveness are generally negatively correlated.

Nolan (1996) analysed technical efficiency of 29 average sized US bus systems with a DEA model. They used bus numbers, total employee numbers and fuel consumed as input and vehicles per mile as output.

Levaggi (1994) used a DEA model to 55 urban transport companies in Italy. They selected the number of kilometres travelled, average speed, capital represented by proxy, vehicle numbers, and a capacity coefficient defined by the ratio between passengers by kilometre and available seats per kilometre and population densities as output. They used employee costs, fuel used, miles travelled, population density and vehicle numbers as input. They discovered that firms operated with excess capital, excess bus capacity and that salaries represented a high percentage of total costs.

Karlaftis and McCarthy (1997) found that systems that scored well on one aspect of performance (e.g. efficiency, effectiveness or overall performance) generally did well on the others although this contradicts Chu et al. (1992).

Karlaftis (2004) used a DEA model on 259 US systems and defined three different models matched to specific parameters. The models had different outputs: vehicles/distance in miles; passengers per mile or passengers transported; or both, together. They used total employee numbers, fuel used and vehicle numbers as inputs. They determined that efficiency was positively related to effectiveness and that the importance of economies of scale depended on the output selected.

Husain et al. (2000) also applied a DEA to evaluate Malaysian public transportation service efficiency, with 46 service units. They used employee numbers and total labour costs as inputs. They selected total services and companies' gross revenues as outputs. They determined that more efficient companies had higher revenues.

Pina and Torres (2001) compared the efficiency of public and private sectors in the provision of urban transportation services of Catalonia (Spain). The results conclude that exogenous factors are not relevant and that private management of urban transport service is not more efficient than public management.

As inputs they choose: gas/distance in kilometres; cost/km or cost/passenger; and subsidy/passenger. As output they selected: bus number per kilometre per employee (bus-km/employee) a variable that provides information on urban transport performance in respect to regarding total employees; number of buses per kilometre per year – a variable that shows average productivity and the bus use level; number of buses per kilometre per resident, representing public transport supply in each city; and as indicators of quality: accident rate and frequency and agility of service provided.

Garcia Sanchez (2009) undertook a comparative efficiency analysis of public bus transport in Spain using Data Envelopment Analysis. Efficiency levels are negative in relation to population density and peak-to-base ratio. Nevertheless, efficiency levels are not related to the form of public versus private ownership.

Roy and Yvrande-Billon (2007) investigated the impact of ownership structures and contractual choices on technical efficiency in the French urban public transport sector. They found that the technical efficiency of urban public transport operators depends on the ownership regime and type of contract governing their transactions.

De Gruyter et al. (2016) assessed the sustainability of urban public transport systems in cities by adopting a quantitative measurement framework containing 15 public transport sustainability indicators. It compares aggregate sustainability performance of urban public transport in international regions of cities, and then examines the relative sustainability of selected cities in the Asia and Middle East region.

Ying et al. (2014) improved a DEA model to evaluate eco-efficiency analysis using environmental pollution as an undesirable output in 30 Chinese provincial capital cities.

RESEARCH DESIGN

This section outlines the research design to assess urban transport efficiency. The research method is described first, followed by an overview of selected public transport variables (input and output) and the description of the sample identified to evaluate the level of efficiency.

Research Method

The study relies on efficiency measurement via Data Envelopment Analysis a non-parametric technique introduced by Charnes et al. (1978). The Constant Returns to Scale (CCR) DEA developed by Charnes, Cooper and Rhodes (1978) is grounded on Farrell's work (1957), "The measurement of productive efficiency" and the main advantages are the ability to accommodate multiple inputs and outputs, the no a priori weights assumption and the requirement of small numbers of observations (Sexton, 1986). The DEA has acquired huge popularity in measuring performances because of it providing a synthetic set of performance for similar units denominated Decision Making Units (DMUs). DMUs are defined as entities (firms) responsible for turning inputs into outputs and presenting its managers and decision- maker setting the goals and choosing how to achieve them.

The basic model was enhanced by Banker, Charnes and Cooper (1984) in order to account for the evaluation of Variable Returns to Scale and become the BCC model (VRS). The VRS model searches for pure technical efficiency (also called managerial efficiency) and includes the so-called convexity constraints by changing the specification of the problem and providing the measure of Managerial Efficiency θ VRS adding $e\lambda = 1$ to the programme (θ is a scalar and λ is a vector of constants). From its inception, the DEA has treated each DMU as a "black box" by only considering the inputs consumed and the final outputs produced by this "black box" (Färe & Grosskopf, 2000). However, the efficiency measure is associated to the use of a minimum number of inputs in order to produce a certain number of outputs or the maximum production of outputs using a certain number of inputs (Fethi & Pasiouras, 2010) from which the orientation issues descend.

As is widely known, there are two types of DEA models; the radial (CCR) and the non-radial.

Due to the neglect of slacks, by radial model, when reporting the efficiency score, it is important to remember how relevant slacks are when evaluating managerial efficiency. Therefore, the DEA frameworks of this study are based on the Slack-Based Model (SBM) a non-radial model developed by Tone (2001). The model deals with input excess and output shortfall of each DMU, called Slacks and projecting each DMU to the furthest point on the efficient frontier by minimising the objective function and finding the maximum slacks.

The following figure presents the SBM linear models. In the case of the SBM model the variables s^+ and s^- are the measurement of the distance of inputs $X\lambda$ and outputs $Y\lambda$ of a virtual unit from those of the unit that was evaluated.

Giving the purpose of the analysis, it is important to choose an appropriate model orientation (Charnes et al., 1978; Banker et al., 1984; Coelli, 1996; Coelli et al., 2005;). The SBM considers the input-oriented model efficiency under assumption of the constant and variable returns to scale in order to further account for the scale efficiency. The input orientation is, fundamentally, addressed by the question: "How much can input quantities be proportionally reduced without changing the output quantities produced?"

The input orientation is chosen because of its increasing efficiency by potential reduction in the level of inputs relative to the given level of outputs considered and because it satisfies the Pareto-Koopmans sense of technical efficiency quantified by non-radial DEA models and the assumption of the variable returns to scale as per (Tone, 2001).

The following table shows the linear formulation of the CRS SBM Model.

The variables s^+ and s^- measure the distance of inputs $X\lambda$ and outputs $Y\lambda$ of a virtual unit from those of the unit evaluated (X_o). The measurements of the average distance of inputs and outputs from the efficiency threshold is provided by the numerator and the denominator of the model. For the Variable Returns to Scale, the $e^T \lambda = 1$ condition needs to be added to the formula. Under the DEA framework an efficient DMU scores $\theta = 1$ (100% efficient), while the DMUs scoring less than 1 are inefficient. The SBM CRS efficiency rate is always lower or equal to that of the input-oriented VRS model.

Table 6. Linear formulation CRS SMB Model

SBM Model (Constant Return to Scale) *Input oriented*

$$\rho = \min_{\lambda, s^-, s^+} \frac{1 - \frac{1}{m}\sum_{i=1}^{m} \frac{s_i^-}{x_{io}}}{1 + \frac{1}{s}\sum_{r=1}^{s} \frac{s_r^+}{y_{ro}}}$$

$$s.t. \quad x_o - s^- = X\lambda$$

$$y_o + s^+ = Y\lambda$$

$$\lambda \geq 0, s^- \geq 0, s^+ \geq 0$$

Source: own elaboration

In order to account for scale dimension, the measure of the Scale Efficiency is evaluated by the ratio of SBM-CRS efficiency scores to SBM-VRS efficiency scores. The lower the scale efficiency, the higher the impact of scale size (Thanassoulis, 2001).

After having chosen the proper model and orientation, another relevant aspect refers to the variables selection. The variable must respect an initial condition regarding the number of inputs and outputs in relation to the number of DMUs. In this context, Golany and Roll (1989) postulate the "rule of thumb" for which the minimal number of DMUs for the selected model should be at least double the considered inputs number, while Bowlin (1998) mentioned the necessity of having a number of DMUs at least three times the sum of inputs and output. Ozbek et al. (2009) refer to this issue by considering the minimal number of DMUs (n) as: $n > 2ms$, where m is the number of inputs and s is the number of outputs.

Inputs and Outputs

Efficiency is the ratio of output (services or products) to input (resources) for a given production unit under given conditions. Outputs should be the key business drivers critical to business success and inputs should be the resources that lead to the key business drivers. The definitions of the set of inputs and outputs are of paramount importance in evaluating efficiency, yet the literature on efficiency analysis in urban public transport is relatively homogeneous regarding the definition of inputs and outputs. This study uses six inputs and three outputs.

Turning our attention first to input variables, these normally fall in two main categories: "physical" production factors with their own measurement units (number of employees, number of vehicles, etc.) on one side, and costs in monetary units on the other, that are further split into capital expenses and operating expenses. The average number of employees (workforce average), number of vehicles in the fleet (vehicles operated) and CO2 emissions in the first category are largely the most considered variables as they represent the main inputs in the production process. As regards the costs in monetary units we analogously find that the prices of labour (personnel costs), capital (investments) and the operational costs are the far more utilised.

On the output side, we put variables related to the effectiveness of the production process, such as number of passengers (passengers transported) and the financial counterpart of the second one, as it considers the service revenues (sales revenues) and production value.

Data Sample

The data on urban transportation was provided by the Italian Local Public Transport Association (ASSTRA) which welcomes companies both owned by local and private entities.

Urban and extra-urban transport companies, bus services, trams, metro, cableway installations, some railway stations and shipping companies adhere to ASSTRA.

The database produced by ASSTRA cover over 100 cities for 156 urban transportation companies and include a range of indicators spanning public transport supply and demand, user and operational costs, system productivity, and environmental impacts. The database is available for 2010 only. 31 small-medium companies and 125 large companies are included in the database. There are 114 public owned companies and 42 private.

Table 7 presents the definitions, units of measurement, and descriptive statistics (mean, standard deviation (SD), minimum (Min) and maximum (Max)) of the input and output variables.

Figure 1. Schematic diagram of inputs and outputs
Source: own elaboration

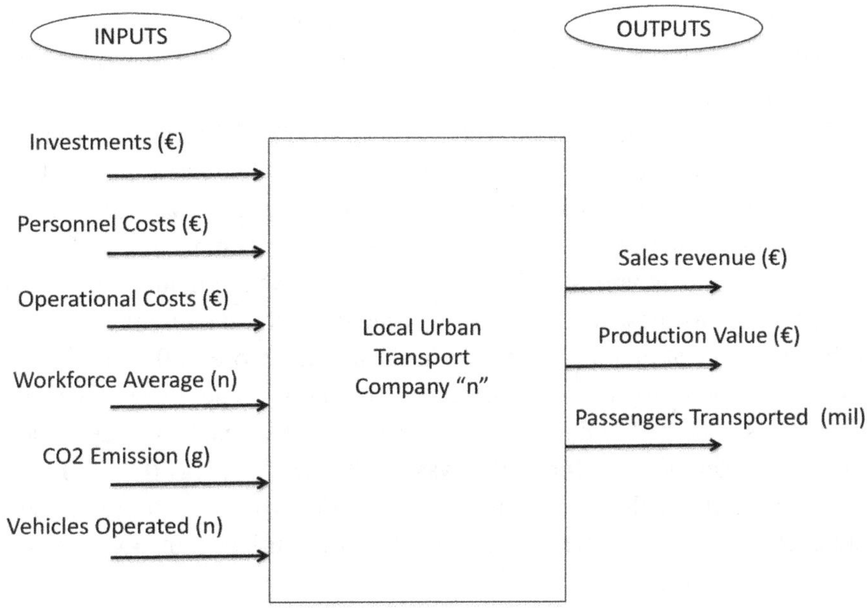

Table 7. Descriptive statistics

	Variables	Units	Min	Max	Mean	SD
Investments	Input	Euro	8.797	871.967.907	24.127.863	84.173.895
Personnel Costs	Input	Euro	63.218	566.150.343	24.953.493	55.042.888
Operational Costs	Input	Euro	361.837	1.356.703.558	52.216.798	126.663.469
Workforce Average	Input	Unit	2	12.693	575	1.231
CO2 Emission	Input	Gram	98,28	110.208	7.922	13.543
Vehicles Operated	Input	Unit	1	2.808	264	410
Sales Revenue	Input	Euro	144.759	853.704.878	33.603.361	83.618.396
Production Value	Input	Euro	278.490	1.049.186.481	49.873.208	106.595.673
Passengers Transported	Input	Million	0,02	670,27	26,86	69,29

Source: own elaboration

FINDINGS

Steps of the SBM DEA model were firstly *taken* with the assumption of constant returns to scale and then with variable returns to scale.

The data analysis showed that there were some significant differences between the urban transportation companies. After the efficiency performance analysis in SBM_CRS model, the final data showed that 30/156 (19.2%) urban transportation companies were technically efficient, with an efficiency score of 1.0, and seven of those were SMEs. The average technical efficiency score across all 156 urban transportation companies was 0.4586 and over 26% of the sample reached higher efficiency than the average i.e. the average efficiency score for SMEs is 0.4536 while it is 0.4598 for large companies (Table 8). Figure 2 shows the technical efficiency scores of the urban transportation companies, which are rank-ordered based on declining efficiency scores. The lowest scoring urban transportation companies had an efficiency score of 0.0857.

In the SBM_VRS model, the final data showed that 44/156 (28.2%) urban transportation companies were managerially efficient, with an efficiency score of 1.0, 10 of which were SMEs. The average managerial efficiency score across all the 156 urban transportation companies was 0.5628 and over 37% of the sample reached a higher efficiency than the average i.e. the average efficiency score for SMEs was 0.5812 while it was 0.5584 for large companies (Table 9). Figure 3 shows the managerial efficiency scores of the urban transportation companies, which are rank-ordered based on declining efficiency scores. The lowest scoring urban transportation companies had an efficiency score of 0.2028.

While analysing the scale of efficiency, it emerges that the average score across all the 156 urban transportation companies was 0.8415 and over 70% of the sample reached a higher level than the average i.e. the scale of efficiency score for SMEs was 0.7993 while it was 0.8520 for large companies (Table 10). Figure 4 shows the scale of efficiency scores of the urban transportation companies, which are rank-ordered based on declining scores. The lowest scoring urban transportation companies had a scale of efficiency score of 0.1231.

Figure 2. DEA SBM-CRS Technical Efficiency Score of the 156 urban transportation companies, rank-ordered in terms of declining scores. Large companies in blue, SMEs in red
Source: own elaboration

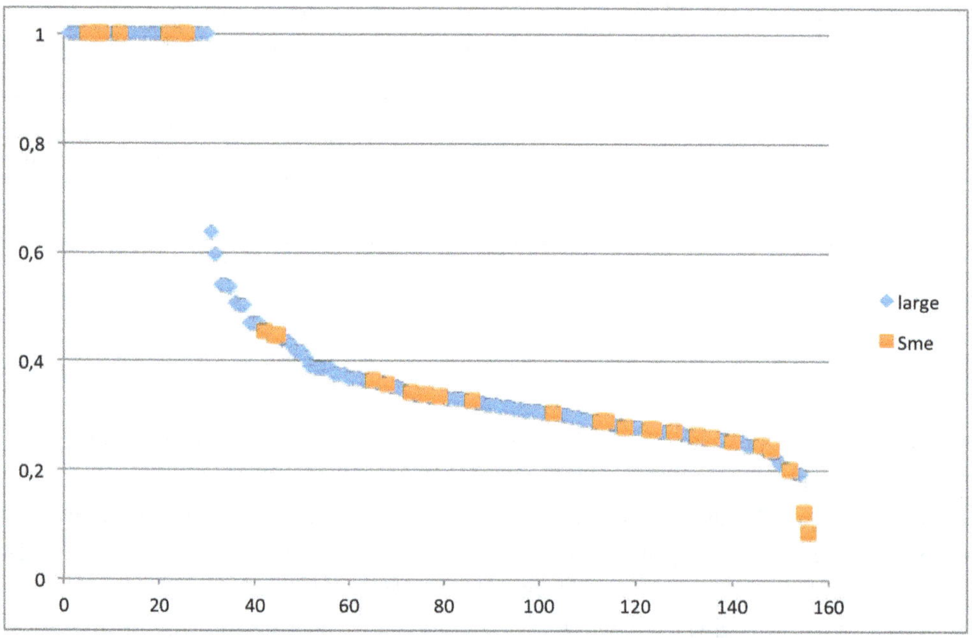

Table 8. DEA SBM-CRS technical efficiency score

	All	SMEs	Large
Mean	0.4586	0.4536	0.4598
Std. Dev.	0.2764	0.3098	0.2688
Min	0.0857	0.0857	0.1933
Max	1	1	1

Source: own elaboration

Figure 3.DEA SBM-VRS Managerial Efficiency score of the 156 urban transportation companies, rank-ordered in terms of declining score. Large companies in blue, SMEs in red
Source: own elaboration

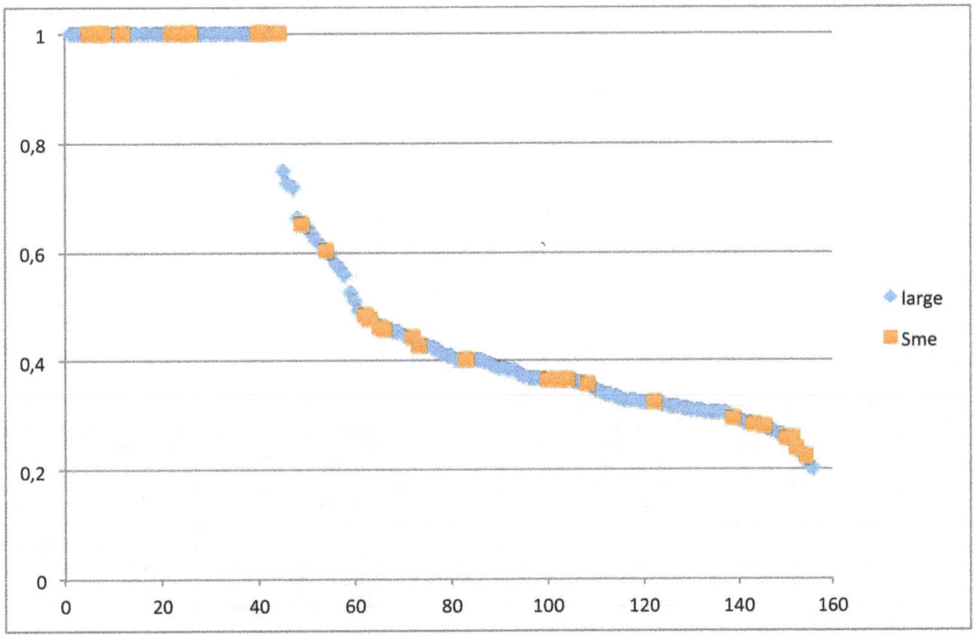

Table 9. DEA SBM-VRS managerial efficiency score

	All	SMEs	Large
Mean	0.5629	0.5812	0.5584
Std. Dev.	0.2916	0.3086	0.2883
Min	0.2028	0.2219	0.2028
Max	1	1	1

Source: own elaboration

Figure 4. DEA Scala Efficiency score of the 156 urban transportation companies, rank-ordered in terms of declining score. Large companies in blue, SMEs in red
Source: own elaboration

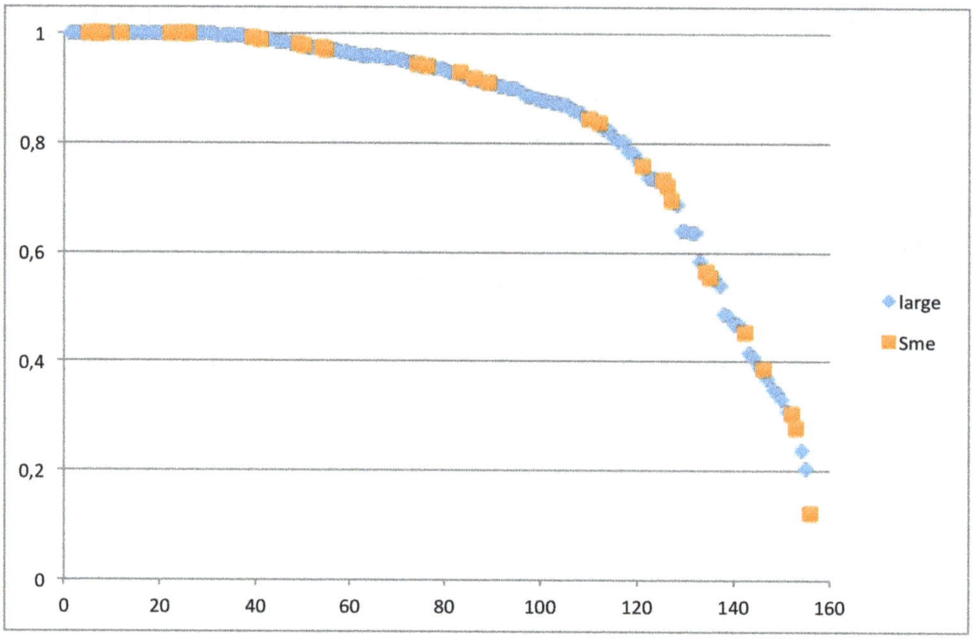

Table 10. DEA Scala Efficiency Score

	All	SMEs	Large
Mean	0.8415	0.7993	0.8520
Std. Dev.	0.2124	0.2560	0.1999
Min	0.1231	0.1231	0.2033
Max	1	1	1

Source: own elaboration

DISCUSSION

The previous Tables report the findings from CRS and VRS analysis of the urban transportation companies. Technical efficiency can be examined by breaking it down into pure technical efficiency and scale efficiency. The average index of pure technical efficiency was at 45.86% and of scale efficiency at 84.15%. However, the means show that most of the technical inefficiency is in the form of scale inefficiency.

Some limitations in the results of the analysis and discussion emerged, such as the number of selected variables and some uncontrolled external circumstances, even though the DEA method is an efficient system in the urban transportation sector. In order to go beyond these limitations and for a more in-depth analysis of the phenomenon, would be appropriate use a greater number of selected variables as well as the introduction of variables that took into account the different conditions of service delivery e.g. the number of hours of service, seating capacity, measured in total seats, the average number of stops per route, the frequency of the service, measured by means of the ratio Hours of service/Average time for route (Garcıa Sanchez, 2009).

It would also be a good idea to include some uncontrollable variables in the analysis that could influence the management of the urban transportation companies, e.g population density, numbers of private vehicles in circulation, the coefficient of intensity in rush hours.

However, the approach used to analyse the efficiency of the urban transportation sector is a valid tool and the results obtained provided useful indications as to the performance and management implications. The authors also calculated the potential for improvement for each inefficient unit in order to provide useful managerial tools.

This is presented as the percentage of change in each input or output variable necessary for the unit to become 100% efficient. It can have a positive or negative value, indicating whether the inputs or outputs are too large or too small to reach the optimal level. The potential improvement is calculated on the actual and target scores (the value of input or output that should be achievable by the sample and which would ensure a 100% efficiency) determined for each sample.

The analysis of slacks for large companies reveals a surplus of resources due to technical inefficiency of around 19 million for investments, 20 million for personnel costs, 3.8 million for operational costs and 1% for CO2 emissions and vehicles used. Production value should also be increased by at least 1%.

The analysis of slacks for SMEs reveals a surplus of resources due to technical inefficiency of around 11 million for investments, 8 million for personnel costs and 1% for CO2 emission and vehicles used. Sales revenues should also be increased by at least 1%.

The analysis of slacks for large companies reveals a surplus of resources due to managerial inefficiency of around 11 million for investments, 13 million for personnel costs, 300 units for workforce average, 1 million operational costs and 150 vehicles used. The number of passengers transported should also be increased by at least 2%.

The analysis of slacks for SMEs reveals a surplus of resources due to managerial inefficiency of around 11 million for investments, 7 million for personnel costs and 1% for CO2 emissions, 200 units for workforce average, and 180 vehicles used. The number of passengers transported should also be increased by at least 1%.

CONCLUSION

Growing interest in evaluating the efficiency of public services is especially important in the municipal area, because of its influence on residents' standards of living. Public bus transport is one of the councils' responsibilities and there is particular interest in introducing managerial improvements due to the characteristics surrounding its performance.

Regarding the results, analysis using the DEA technique reveals that:

- The average index of technical efficiency was 45.86%; managerial efficiency 56.29%, and scale efficiency 84.15%.
- 30 companies are technically efficient. In particular, seven smes – 22.58% - and twenty-three large companies – 18.4%.

Figure 5. Slacks DEA SBM-CRS for inputs and outputs
Source: own elaboration

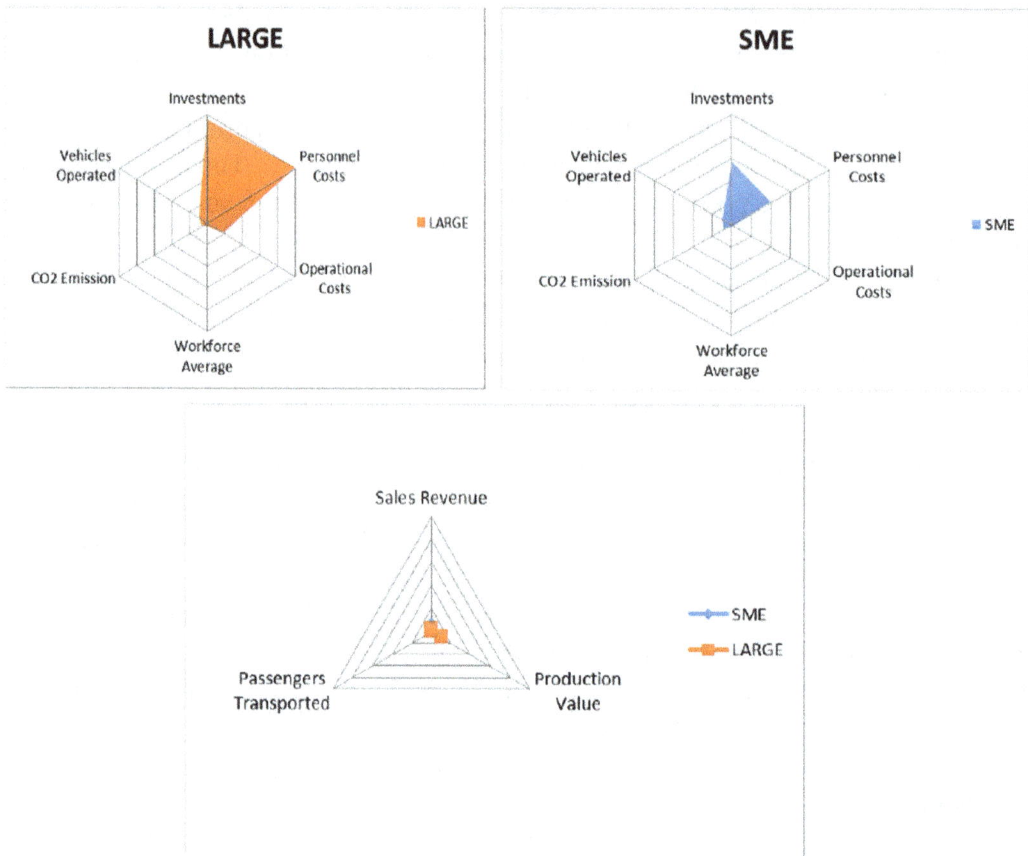

- 40 companies are managerially efficient. In particular, ten smes – 32.25% - and thirty-four large companies – 27.2%.
- The analysis of slacks reveals surplus resources for smes and large companies in order for them to improve technical and managerial efficiency, as well as a significant increase of sales revenues, production value and number of passengers transported.
- Regarding environmental impact, smes and large companies reached an acceptable level of co2 emissions.
- Efficiency performance of large companies is limited by ownership characteristics. Large companies are often public companies and limited by the "publicness effect" (Alfiero et al., 2017) that influences some managerial activity and attributes (for instance, the stock of investments, the number of employees, etc).

Our study also shows that the performance differentials between the various regulatory schemes are slight, although statistically significant. The efficiency scores of the operators, whether SMEs or large companies, are low. So, what our results demonstrate is about 81% of all operators operate far from their relative production frontier. Operators are under-producing or not meeting their goals._

Figure 6. Slacks DEA SBM-VRS for inputs and outputs
Source: own elaboration

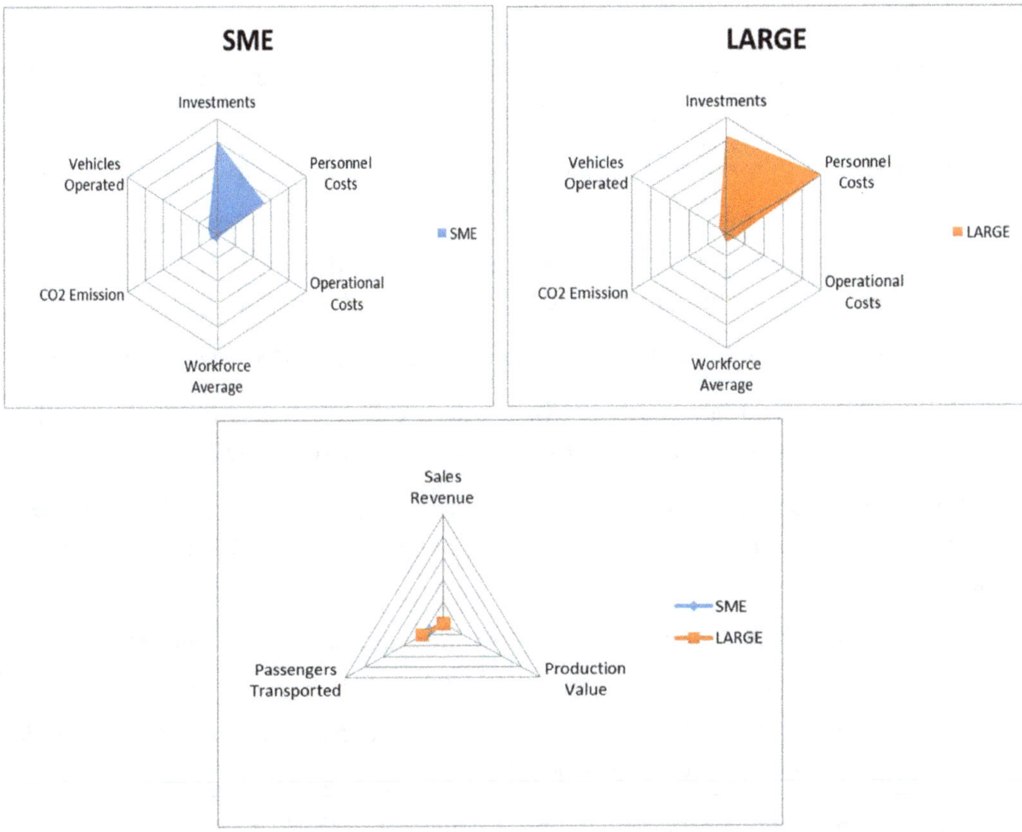

In terms of policy implications, what our study therefore suggests is that, given the current objectives imposed on operators by local authorities, only marginal positive results on technical efficiency are to be expected from regulatory changes that would consist of improvement of management and high-powered incentives.

This does not mean that the regulatory framework has no effect on technical efficiency, but rather that the main cause of the financial crisis endured by the sector is not technical inefficiency. Performance encompasses dimensions other than technical efficiency like service quality or commercial efficiency which will have to be considered in order to complete our research agenda.

REFERENCES

Alfiero, S., Elba, F., Esposito, A., & Resce, G. (2017). The Impact of Environmental Factors on the Measurement of Managerial Efficiency in the Italian Waste Management Sector: Framework and Empirical Evidence. *International Journal of Public Administration*, 1–13.

Autorità di Regolazione dei Trasporti. (2017, July). *Quarto Rapporto Annuale al Parlamento*. Camera dei Deputati.

Banker, R. D., Charnes, A., & Cooper, W. W. (1984). Some models for estimating technical and scale inefficiencies in data envelopment analysis. *Management Science*, *30*(9), 1078–1092. doi:10.1287/mnsc.30.9.1078

Bowlin, W. F. (1998). Measuring performance: An introduction to data envelopment analysis (DEA). *The Journal of Cost Analysis*, *15*(2), 3–27. doi:10.1080/08823871.1998.10462318

Caracciolo, F. F. (2012). *Il trasporto pubblico locale in Italia: stato, prospettive confronti internazionali*. Academic Press.

Carminucci, C., & Procopio, M. (2008). *La riforma del trasporto pubblico locale nelle regioni: lo stato di attuazione e le prospettive*. Istituto Superiore di Formazione e Ricerca per i Trasporti.

Carpenter, R. A. (1993). Can sustainability be measured. *Environmental Strategy*, *5*(February), 13–16.

Charnes, A., Cooper, W. W., & Rhodes, E. (1978). Measuring the efficiency of decision making units. *European Journal of Operational Research*, *2*(6), 429–444. doi:10.1016/0377-2217(78)90138-8

Chu, X., Fielding, G. J., & Lamar, B. W. (1992). Measuring transit performance using data envelopment analysis. *Transportation Research Part A, Policy and Practice*, *26*(3), 223–230. doi:10.1016/0965-8564(92)90033-4

Coelli, T. (1996). *A guide to DEAP version 2.1: a data envelopment analysis (computer) program*. Centre for Efficiency and Productivity Analysis, University of New England.

Coelli, T. J., Rao, D. S. P., O'Donnell, C. J., & Battese, G. E. (2005). *An introduction to efficiency and productivity analysis*. Springer Science & Business Media.

Crediop, D. (2004). *Local public companies in the 25 countries of the European Union*. Paris: Dexia.

Daraio, C., Diana, M., Di Costa, F., Leporelli, C., Matteucci, G., & Nastasi, A. (2016). Efficiency and effectiveness in the urban public transport sector: A critical review with directions for future research. *European Journal of Operational Research*, *248*(1), 1–20. doi:10.1016/j.ejor.2015.05.059

De Gruyter, C., Currie, G., & Rose, G. (2016). Sustainability Measures of Urban Public Transport in Cities: A World Review and Focus on the Asia/Middle East Region. *Sustainability*, *9*(1), 43. doi:10.3390u9010043

Doherty, T. L., & Horne, T. (2002). *Managing Public Services--implementing Changes: A Thoughtful Approach to the Practice of Management*. Psychology Press.

Färe, R., & Grosskopf, S. (2000). Network DEA. *Socio-Economic Planning Science, 34*, 35-49.

Farrell, M. J. (1957). The measurement of productive efficiency. *Journal of the Royal Statistical Society. Series A (General)*, *120*(3), 253–290. doi:10.2307/2343100

Fethi, M. D., & Pasiouras, F. (2010). Assessing bank efficiency and performance with operational research and artificial intelligence techniques: A survey. *European Journal of Operational Research*, *204*(2), 189–198. doi:10.1016/j.ejor.2009.08.003

Fielding, G. J., Babitsky, T. T., & Brenner, M. E. (1985). Performance evaluation for bus transit. *Transportation Research Part A, General*, *19*(1), 73–82. doi:10.1016/0191-2607(85)90009-3

Fielding, G. J., Brenner, M. E., & Faust, K. (1985). Typology for bus transit. *Transportation Research Part A, General*, *19*(3), 269–278. doi:10.1016/0191-2607(85)90015-9

Garcia Sanchez, I. M. (2009). Technical and scale efficiency in Spanish urban transport: Estimating with data envelopment analysis. *Advances in Operations Research.*

Giupponi, T. F. (2016, May). *Le frontiere del trasporto pubblico locale, tra competenze normative e situazioni giuridiche soggettive. Verso un "diritto alla mobilità"?* Università di Catania.

Golany, B., & Roll, Y. (1989). An application procedure for DEA. *Omega*, *17*(3), 237–250. doi:10.1016/0305-0483(89)90029-7

Husain, N., Abdullah, M., & Kuman, S. (2000). Evaluating public sector efficiency with data envelopment analysis (DEA): A case study in Road Transport Department, Selangor, Malaysia. *Total Quality Management*, *11*(4-6), 830–836. doi:10.1080/09544120050008282

ISFORT. (2017, April). *Quattordicesimo Rapporto sulla Mobilità in Italia*. Rome, Italy: Author.

Karlaftis, M., Kepaptsoglou, K., Stathopoulos, A., & Starra, A. (2004). Planning public transport networks for the 2004 Summer Olympics with decision support systems. *Transportation Research Record: Journal of the Transportation Research Board,* (1887), 71-82.

Karlaftis, M. G. (2004). A DEA approach for evaluating the efficiency and effectiveness of urban transit systems. *European Journal of Operational Research*, *152*(2), 354–364. doi:10.1016/S0377-2217(03)00029-8

Karlaftis, M. G., & McCarthy, P. S. (1997). Subsidy and public transit performance: A factor analytic approach. *Transportation*, *24*(3), 253–270. doi:10.1023/A:1004956532174

Keune, M., Leschke, J., & Watt, A. (Eds.). (2008). *Privatisation and liberalisation of public services in Europe. An analysis of economic and labour market impacts*. Brussels: ETUI.

Levaggi, R. (1994). *Parametric and non parametric approach to efficiency: the case of urban transport in Italy*. Studi Economici.

Ministero delle Infrastrutture e dei Trasporti. (2014). *Piano di Azione Nazionale sui Sistemi Intelligenti di Trasporto*. ITS.

Ministero delle Infrastrutture e dei Trasporti. (2015). *Conto Nazionale delle Infrastrutture e dei Trasporti.* Author.

Nolan, J. F. (1996). Determinants of productive efficiency in urban transit. *Logistics and Transportation Review*, *32*(3), 319.

Osservatorio Nazionale sulle Politiche del Trasporto Locale. (2014). *Relazione Annuale al Parlamento.* Author.

Osservatorio Nazionale sulle Politiche del Trasporto Locale. (2015). *Relazione Annuale al Parlamento.* Author.

Ozbek, M. E., de la Garza, J. M., & Triantis, K. (2009). Data envelopment analysis as a decision-making tool for transportation professionals. *Journal of Transportation Engineering, 135*(11), 822–831. doi:10.1061/(ASCE)TE.1943-5436.0000069

Pina, V., & Torres, L. (2001). Analysis of the efficiency of local government services delivery. An application to urban public transport. *Transportation Research Part A, Policy and Practice, 35*(10), 929–944. doi:10.1016/S0965-8564(00)00033-1

Reichard, C. (2008). Trend towards a more diversified institutional landscape. *Public Management Review, 10*(5), 569–571. doi:10.1080/14719030802264176

Roy, W., & Yvrande-Billon, A. (2007). Ownership, contractual practices and technical efficiency: The case of urban public transport in France. *Journal of Transport Economics and Policy, 41*(2), 257–282.

Sexton, T. R. (1986). The methodology of data envelopment analysis. *New Directions for Evaluation, 1986*(32), 7–29. doi:10.1002/ev.1438

Thanassoulis, E. (2001). *Introduction to the theory and application of data envelopment analysis.* Dordrecht: Kluwer Academic Publishers. doi:10.1007/978-1-4615-1407-7

Tomazinis, A. R. (1977). *Study of efficiency indicators of urban public transportation systems. Final report.* Philadelphia: Transportation Studies Center. doi:10.2172/5406787

Tone, K. (2001). A slacks-based measure of efficiency in data envelopment analysis. *European Journal of Operational Research, 130*(3), 498–509. doi:10.1016/S0377-2217(99)00407-5

Torres, L., & Pina, V. (2002). Delivering public services—mechanisms and consequences: Changes in public service delivery in the EU countries. *Public Money & Management, 22*(4), 41–48. doi:10.1111/1467-9302.00328

Viton, P. A. (1997). Technical efficiency in multi-mode bus transit: A production frontier analysis. *Transportation Research Part B: Methodological, 31*(1), 23–39. doi:10.1016/S0191-2615(96)00019-7

Viton, P. A. (1998). Changes in multi-mode bus transit efficiency, 1988–1992. *Transportation, 25*(1), 1–21. doi:10.1023/A:1004906024774

Yin, K., Wang, R., An, Q., Yao, L., & Liang, J. (2014). Using eco-efficiency as an indicator for sustainable urban development: A case study of Chinese provincial capital cities. *Ecological Indicators, 36*, 665–671. doi:10.1016/j.ecolind.2013.09.003

KEY TERMS AND DEFINITIONS

Data Envelopment Analysis (DEA): A nonparametric method in operations research and economics for the estimation of production frontiers. It is used to empirically measure productive efficiency of decision-making units (or DMUs).

Scale Efficiency: Success of a branch at operating in optimum scale. Scale efficient branch works at the most productive scale size.

Slacks-Based Model: A non-radial DEA model that deals with both input excesses and output shortfalls simultaneously and measures efficiency between 0 and 1. SBM is not translation invariant and it identifies more sources of inefficiency.

Chapter 3
Managing Small Business Social Responsibility (SBSR) in Formalized Network Using a Euclidean Perspective

Laura Corazza
University of Turin, Italy

Maurizio Cisi
University of Turin, Italy

ABSTRACT

This chapter deepens the knowledge of inter-firm collaborations to address sustainability issues between SMEs in adopting small business social responsibility (SBSR) approaches. The study investigates the role of formal network contracts (FNCs), where aspects of SBSR are formalized into legal agreements between the networkers. For this purpose, the authors identify three management implications declined as sub-variables: control, consensus, and consistency. Institutional theory and, specifically, isomorphism and normative theory of CSR are used as lenses through which to analyze the results. The methodology applied is a deductive qualitative content analysis, while results are shown using an Euclidean perspective. The study discovers the use of FNCs to clearly govern consistency and consensus, more than to control and audit sustainability herein the network. In addition, it demonstrates a relation between network size and use of the tool.

INTRODUCTION

The anthropocentric view of sustainable development considers the presence of the humans with their activities as an inseparable part and a menace of the future of our Planet (Griggs et al., 2013; Reid et al., 2010). Consequently, the sustainable development of our society cannot be reached without the sustainable development of corporations, as they are outputs of humans' activities (Wigginton, 2016). Despite the evident disparities between large corporations and small businesses in adopting socially and

DOI: 10.4018/978-1-5225-5267-3.ch003

environmentally responsible management practices, both are called to take a firm commitment towards the society and the environment without exception (Tilley, 2000). However, small and medium-sized enterprises (SMEs), micro-businesses and individual entrepreneurs can respond to such commitment with their limited resources, struggling with external forces, precarity, uncertainty, complexity and ambiguity (i.e. post 2008 crisis). Nonetheless, small businesses have considerable social and environmental impacts if considered in their totality (Perrini, 2006). In recent years, the academic interest towards the so-called Small Business Social Responsibility (SBSR) increased and scholars have just begun to analyse a fragmented phenomenon. The variety of the acronym SMEs includes: medium-sized companies that account for 1% of all European companies; micro businesses (92.8%) and small businesses (6%) that cover 98.8% of the entire European economy (according to the European definition of SME, in Eurobarometer, 2016) (European Commission, 2016). For this study we address sustainability, CSR and stakeholder management as related concepts, according to the Euclidean demonstration of closeness given by the study of Fassin et al. (2015) regarding the European as well as the Italian context.

Unfortunately, scholars continue to stress the lack or inconsistency of the existent tools to address sustainability issues at company level (Horisch, Johnson, & Schaltegger, 2015; Johnson, 2013, 2015; Johnson & Schaltegger, 2016). The lack of knowledge, resources (time, financial and human) and practical suitability of the such tools are limiting the development of theories on SBSR. Mainstream CSR theories are often developed having in mind large companies (Spence, 2014; Vázquez-Carrasco & López-Pérez, 2012). A solution to overcoming traditional limits of SBSR may rely on business model changes (Lai, Lionzo, Stacchezzini, & Rossignoli, 2015). Emerging studies are combining effective ways to overcome SBSR barriers through the adoption of collaboration strategies and strategic network alliances (Freeman, Edwards, & Schroder, 2006; Håkansson & Snehota, 2006; Kirkels & Duysters, 2010; Lee, Kelley, Lee, & Lee, 2012; Swoboda, Meierer, Foscht, & Morschett, 2011). The paper specific aim is to deepen the relation between network alliances and sustainability.

BACKGROUND

Despite the fact that the literature on inter-firm collaborations boasts many contributions, few studies directly address how and to what extent SMEs may use formal and informal collaboration to achieve social and environmental outcomes. Existing studies are mostly related to network performances, to interpersonal and organisational features and the distribution of power between network members (Keast, Brown, & Mandell, 2007; Keast, Mandell, Brown, & Woolcock, 2004; MacGregor, 2004; M. Mandell, Keast, & Chamberlain, 2016; M. P. Mandell & Keast, 2008; O'Donnell, 2004; Storey, 1994). The purpose of our study is to deepen the knowledge of inter-firm collaborations to address sustainability issues between SMEs. We locate our study in a national context of Italian SMEs that exploit the introduction of a juridical tool called Formalised Network Contract (FNC) to start-up network agreements (Baldo, 2011; Cantele, Vernizzi, & Ricciardi, 2016; Cardoni & Tiacci, 2013). In general, FNCs are devoted to boosting entrepreneurial internationalization (Haddoud, Jones, & Newbery, 2017; Kenny & Fahy, 2011; Lee et al., 2012) or to exchanging knowledge, research and development on new product and services (de Jesus Pacheco et al., 2016; Kirkels & Duysters, 2010; Konsti-Laakso, Pihkala, & Kraus, 2012; Mazzola & Perrone, 2013; Mazzola, Perrone, & Kamuriwo, 2016; van de Vrande, de Jong, Vanhaverbeke, & de Rochemont, 2009). FNCs are formed through interconnected bilateral or multilateral contracts, and they differ from other traditional forms of collaborations (such temporal agreement, consortia, joint ventures, etc.), as the contract itself manages outcomes related to specific business programs, compositions of the network and content. Turning back to our research question, our paper explores the management of sustainability inherent the network of SMEs through the use of two different theoretical lenses. The first is the contribution given by institutional theory to explain why SMEs must conform to the rules and belief systems prevailing in the environment (Di Maggio & Powell, 1991); in particular, we use isomorphism to explain the link between structural and procedural changes that lend the organisation legitimacy (Dowling & Pfeffer, 1975; Lindblom, 1994; Suchman, 1995). Secondly, we derive insights from reflexive regulation, the attempt to norm-making SBSR through the use of the networks. Crane (2010) called it governance, as the way that organizations go about managing partnerships through formal rules and procedures. In his research, he claimed the need of more studies on how cross sector partnerships should be organised and managed, how authority and decision-making powers should be allocated and how performance should be evaluated and reported.

The paper proceeds as follow: section 2 presents the literature review on the main barriers of SBSR and the opportunities given by formalised business networks in the institutional context; section 3 discusses the hypotheses development considering the theoretical lens above mentioned; section 4 is dedicated to the methodological discussion; section 5 presents the findings, while, at the end, section 6 provides discussions on the results of our analysis. Conclusions alongside managerial and social implications end the paper.

MAIN FOCUS OF THE CHAPTER

Issues, Controversies, Problems

A Discussion Over the Main Barriers of SBSR and the Potential Role of SMEs Networks

SMEs and their business networks can be considered relevant economic actors supporting the economic growth of territories (von Høivik & Shankar, 2011). Studies on SBSR confirms that SMEs face several issues in implementing a sustainable behaviour creating a situation of general unsustainability (Ahmad & Krishnan, 2017). The first issue regarding SBSR is due to the lack of resources to adopt social and environmental management practices or to comply environmental regulations (Avram & Kühne, 2008; Battaglia, Bianchi, Frey, & Iraldo, 2010; Williamson, Lynch-Wood, & Ramsay, 2006). The lack of time, finance, staff and expertise can limit the positive intention of entrepreneurs representing an insurmountable constraint to the adoption of SBSR business practices (Lepoutre & Heene, 2006; Russo & Perrini, 2010; Spence & Rutherfoord, 2001, 2003). The second issue is related to external pressure coming from suppliers and customers, especially when these customers are large corporations (Spence & Rinaldi, 2014; Vurro, Russo, & Perrini, 2009). As a consequence, SBSR should be consistent and strategically oriented to the business to become effective and produce factual results (Castka & Balzarova, 2008; Jenkins, 2006). Third, because most of the sustainability tools are developed having in mind large corporations, SBSR is perceived as distant from the core business, a business cost, or neglected (Horisch et al., 2015; Johnson, 2013, 2015; Johnson & Schaltegger, 2016). Definitely, size matters (Baumann-Pauly, Wickert, Spence, & Scherer, 2013; Fernandez & Camacho, 2016; Tomšič, Bojnec, & Simčič, 2015; Vázquez-

Carrasco & López-Pérez, 2012). One way to overcome the size problem can and should be represented by the so-called business networks.

A business network can represent a secure ecosystem to address sustainability issues safeguarding managerial organisation and governance and the internal value creation dynamics (Taurino, 2015). Sharing common social and environmental problems is typical of corporations operating in the same area or in the same business sector or supply chain (Battaglia *et al.*, 2010). As such, adopting collaborative networks give coordination and synergy among business partners in the process of addressing sustainability issues (D'Alessio, 2008; Noran, 2010). The network approach is suitable to coordinate the actions of networkers governing their synchronicity (time), localisation (space) and type of interactions (Floridi, 2009; Murillo & Lozano, 2009). The adoption of CSR in the network represents a managerial innovation denoted by its effect under structural, interactive and cognitive dimensions (Abdirahman, Sauvée, & Shiri, 2014; Santana, Vaccaro, & Wood, 2009). Network model becomes a mean to address the limitations faced by the SMEs when they try to implement CSR individually. Instead of maintaining CSR as a reactive-defensive strategy and as a pure support function to reduce risks and costs for shareholders, CSR must be taken to the next level as a fundamental value creation driver (von Høivik & Shankar, 2011). According to von Hoivik and Shankar (2011), the network is the pivot of a new value creation process that unlock organizations in achieving an increased ethical awareness. As part of a cluster of individual companies, those that are faced with resource challenges can improve their organisational capabilities, such as specialised staff, leadership, and management capabilities (suppliers-buyers' relations) (Vurro, Russo & Perrini, 2009). A feature of our study is the focus on formal network. Formal network can be defined as organizations that bring entrepreneurs together in order to share business information and experience for mutual advantage (Parker, 2008). While chambers of commerce, corporate roundtables and associations may play a key role for the advancement of CSR knowledge between small entrepreneurs, our study focuses only on networks that promote information sharing between SMEs entrepreneurs and where only SMEs entrepreneurs are involved. Small business owners appear to esteem formal business networks by and for small entrepreneurs more than any other form of formal network such joint agreements, business groups etc. (Chell & Baines, 2000). From a business ethic perspective, corporations are moved to adhere to a network considering four criteria (1) intention, shared goals and participative activities in the practice of networking; (2) exchange of resources and transmission of information and knowledge or/and learning these from other network actors; (3) the exercise of power of each actor toward other actors; and (4) the behavioural and ideological influence within a network (Melé, 2009).

Institutional Context of Formalized Business Networks

Introduced in Italy in early 2009, FNC is a juridical tool allowing two or more enterprises, on a purely contractual basis, to pursue the goal of individually and collectively increasing their capacity for innovation and their competitiveness in the market. The Italian formal network is as a specific contractual agreement aimed at bringing together firms to co-produce, co-market, co-purchase or co-operate in product or market development (Ferrari, 2010). Italian law defines the main guidelines for SMEs wishing to adopt a networked model, while companies are free to define the purpose, the management of the network, goals and sub-objectives within the network programme (Cerrato, 2016). According to Ricciardi et al. (2014), 75% of the total business entities within these network contracts are individual businesses, partnership and limited companies, i.e., the typical organisational structure of entrepreneurial and small-medium enterprises (SMEs) (Ricciardi, Cardoni & Tiacci, 2014).

The pool of FNCs are becoming popular between business and management scholars as they pose several organisational challenges to research and managerial implications (Aureli & Forlani, 2015; Baldo, 2011; Baldo & Aureli, 2012; Cardoni, Rossi, & Tiacci, 2011; Cardoni, Saetta, & Tiacci, 2010; Cardoni & Tiacci, 2013). Nowadays, the universe of FNCs available at September 2017 on the website of the Union of the Italian Chambers of Commerce account 3,985 contracts signed between 20,154 companies involved. The trend of FNC is of 10% every semester according to the in-time official data published by Unioncamere on their website[1] (18.079 companies involved and 3,588 FNCs signed accessed in April 2017). FNCs are private documents, while a summary of the content of each FNC is freely available on Unioncamere Excel database.

FNC, as a tool useful to the purpose of bringing SMEs on the right track of sustainability, is an under-explored topic, full of managerial implications. Only the study of Del Baldo (2016) considers FNC within the tourism sector as a vehicle of CSR and sustainable development.

Regarding formalisation, Guercini and Tunisini (2017) commented on the consequences of it in terms of internal [inside the network] and external. According to scholars, formalisation can act internally as an element to reduce ambiguity and building elements of "fragile trust," in the absence of basic elements of "resilient trust" and in the presence of changes in the competitive environment. Externally, FNC allows the policy maker to identify more clearly companies' aggregations in order to let them be destination of specific public investment initiatives. Our study will deepen the knowledge of the role of formalisation applied to sustainability issues in FNCs.

In this section, we have depicted the main limitations regarding the application of sustainability inherent in SMEs and we have presented the opportunities offered by the adoption of a networking business approach. In particular, we locate our study in the Italian context of formalised network contracts. We know there is no need for a contract to determine whether an entrepreneur is more or less ethical. For this purpose, we consider institutional theory, in its sub-declination of isomorphism, and reflexive regulation as a norm-making approach of a normative CSR.

THEORETICAL FRAMEWORK

The Contribution of Institutional Theory and Isomorphism to Frame FNC Between SMEs

Institutional theory suggests that companies must conform to the rules and belief systems prevailing in the environment (Di Maggio & Powell, 1991) particularly to obtain external legitimacy on their license to operate. Moreover, isomorphism explains the link between structural and procedural changes over this legitimacy (Dowling & Pfeffer, 1975; Lindblom, 1994; Suchman, 1995). Isomorphism describes a process whereby one organisation becomes similar to another organisation by adopting the same or similar characteristics of the other organisation (Rodrigues & Craig, 2007). In that sense, we can use the term isomorphism as substitute of homogeneity, convergence, conformity as companies tend to change their morphology towards structures and management practices which are considered legitimate and socially acceptable by other organizations in their field, according to predominant norms and social influences (Di Maggio and Powell, 1991).

Isomorphism assumes several declinations according to its nature of being: institutional, because other organizations are the major factors that organizations must take into account; mimetic when organizations emulate the actions of similar organizations; coercive when organizations are subject to external pressure, either from organizations they depend upon; and normative, when similar individuals promote a cognitive base, diffuse shared orientations and organisational practices, and legitimise their activities (Aldrich, 1979; Carruthers, 1995; Di Maggio & Powell, 1983).

Due to that different declination of isomorphism, and because the external business environment is pressing SMEs to conform their business behaviour towards the adoption of sustainable business practice, we assume that isomorphism can clarify the role of FNC in governing sustainability. We highlight a commonality between normative isomorphism and the use of reflexive regulation as FNCs.

FNCs as Reflexive Regulation in the Field of Normative CSR

Reflexive regulation is taking place in the field of CSR (Buhmann, 2009, 2011). In our study, the normative view of CSR is not in conflict with the understanding of CSR being 'voluntary', because FNCs are attempts to go beyond direct legal obligations (Buhmann, 2011). This patter to going beyond legal obligation generates the changes that companies prescribe and they would like to see about desirable/undesirable behaviour between their organizations (Mitnick, 1995). Applying this discourse to FNC, we can state that FNCs may play an important role in starting a dialogic role over the norm desirability and applicability, as the case of environmental compliance and SMEs (Ahmad & Krishnan, 2017; Fasterling, 2012). For instance, SMEs are not confident about the plethora of the existent CSR standards and often adopt those standards imposed by their market (Moratis, 2017). According to the study of Baden et al. (2011), when CSR is down-streamed along the supply chain between a large company and its SMEs suppliers, it is translated into a burden of imposed standards, with related increases in bureaucracy and costs, and it can create frustrations for such firms, resulting in a potential 'ceiling effect' and lower overall engagement with CSR (Baden, Harwood and Woodward, 2011).

FNCs can than stimulate a multi-company' decision about CSR standards to adopt. This is reflected by the translation of intents into formalisation of interests. Formalisation of SBSR aspects can reduce ambiguity and business costs about inefficient managerial choice, supporting the network awareness over a shared sustainability pattern to follow. For instance, each network might agree upon specific certifications, specific sustainability strategies, technologies, processes and actions. As such, the integration of sustainability aspect herein legal contract remembers instrumental and normative CSR. The work of del los Reyes et al. (2017) presents the norm-making approach as a suitable option for managers and entrepreneurs, when the compliance to mainstream legal options can produce business failures (de los Reyes, Scholz, & Smith, 2017). This is the case of sustainability tools, often criticised for their ineffectiveness in SMEs. On the opposite side, Spence (2014) imputes SBSR as an output of an entrepreneurial logic derived from the ethic of care and from the entrepreneurial proactive approach towards societal issues. In our study, the FNCs are di per se a voluntary norm-making approach to manage collaboration and to enhance business performance. In that sense, we support the work of Spence, formulating the hypothesis that FNCs are a factual translation of that entrepreneurial logic into a tool.

The Development of Our Research Question

As the purpose of our study is to deepen the knowledge of inter-firm collaborations to address sustainability issues between SMEs, we will focus on the deployment of FNC to serve the purpose of overcoming the barriers of SBSR (RQ). FNCs can be described as legal documents and guidelines for the management of the network. In order to overcome SBSR barriers, FNCs should mention three groups of sustainability multiple-variables ranging from intangible to more practical aspects. We define the management of sustainability in SMEs as functions of: control, consistency and consensus. Control is intended as practical instruments and procedures to exert the control of sustainability within the network for instance, ethical code, certifications, sustainability audit. This dimension has been supported by the evidence of the existent interplay among SMEs between morality, management systems and certification (Bürgi, 2010). Consistency means that sustainability issues must be connected to business initiatives to increase economic profitability, to increase profitability in dealing with large customers in the supply chain and to exploit business opportunities derived by public grants and/or tax exemption. This dimension has been already described in literature using the relation between customer power and customer interests (Lynch-Wood, Williamson, & Jenkins, 2009; Williamson et al., 2006). Third, consensus means the intricate bonds between behavioural and ethical commitment, shared goals and exchange of resources and transmission of information and knowledge or/and learning these from other network actors (Melé, 2009). Table 1 reports the sustainability managerial variables and the link with the relevant literature over SBSR.

Methodology

To answer our research question, we performed a qualitative deductive content analysis on the FNCs legal document. Content analysis is a research method widely applied in management sciences and it has been used in documentary analysis of sustainable public procurement by Testa et al. (2016). Alternative to direct interviews already applied in the field of SBSR (Battaglia, Testa, Bianchi, Iraldo, & Frey, 2014), the researcher examines the communication that a person/a company/ companies has produced to determine such behaviour/s (Kerlinger, 1964). Successively, the researchers replicate the study to enhance the validity and generalisability of the conclusions (Krippendorff, 1980). In particular, we performed a deductive content analysis. This deductive qualitative content analysis has been performed to enforce credibility, dependability, conformability, transferability, and authenticity to our methodology (Elo et

Table 1. Sustainability managerial variables in FNCs

Variable	Sub-Declination	Relevant Literature
CONTROL (CONT)	Ethical code	(Fernandez and Camacho, 2016)
	Sustainability management system (certification)	(Bürgi, 2010)
	External sustainability audit	(Albelda, 2013; Johnson and Schaltegger, 2016)
CONSISTENCY (CONST)	Increase profitability	(Tilley, 2000)
	Supply chain	(Avram and Kühne, 2008; Castka and Balzarova, 2008; Baden, Harwood and Woodward, 2011)
	Compliance with law and opportunities	(Ahmad and Krishnan, 2017)
CONSENSUS (CONSU)	Statement of ethical values or moral principles	(Melé, 2009)
	Knowledge exchange	
	Activism and shared commitment towards specific sustainability topics	

Source: authors' elaboration

al., 2014; Elo & Kyngäs, 2008). For the preparation phase, we collected the material starting from the original database of the Union of the Italian Chambers of Commerce that in April 2017 accounted 18.079 companies involved and 3.588 signed FNCs. We decided to sample a reasonable amount of FNCs in order to provide generalisable results safeguarding the amount of information to be analysed, as they are private legal documents, we had to have an authorised access and to pay the registration fees for each of these contracts[2]. We decided to collect at least 100 FNCs. We selected our sample basically on the presence of keywords in two relevant part of the FNC: the title and the network programme/objective of the contract. The research keys were: *sostenib *green *eco *social *responsab *verd *stakeholder *solid **CSR*. Researchers have doubly checked the sample selected in order to avoid any misunderstanding in the use of the word sustainability (abbreviated in Italian to *sostenib) as it can be used in several semantic contexts. Our sample includes only FNCs designed to reach sustainability purposes and aims; in that sense, we excluded all the FNCs that simply used the keywords as buzzwords or in an inconsistent way.

The unit of analysis is the single FNC composed by all its parts ranging in length from 2 to 48 pages. The interpretation and the categorisation occurred according to the model presented above. The variables used are dichotomous. In that sense, the maximum score of CONT, CONSU, CONST is 3 for each one. The number of organizations per FNC is 5.91, a result in line with the analysis of Unioncamere 2014 that shows as the majority of FNCs are signed between a range from 4 to 9 organizations.

In order to avoid misinterpretation of the meaning of "sustainability" and its practical translation into a business context, we used two different studies to support our categorisation of sustainability with reference to green economies and social innovation. The first is the Report of Green Italy (Symbola, 2010, 2016), while the second is the Third Report on social innovation edited by the research center CERIIS, International Research Center on Social Innovation, in 2017 (Caroli, 2017). QCAmap software has been used to code the parts of the FNCs collected under examination.

RESULTS

The management of sustainability (*MANSUS*) herein the FNCs has been expressed as a combination of control (*CONT*), consistency (*CONST*) and consensus (*CONSU*).

Where *MANSUS* (1) is obtained as:

$$MANSUS = \sum_{i=0}^{n} CONT + \sum_{i=0}^{n} CONST + \sum_{i=0}^{n} CONSU \qquad (1)$$

According to (1), we produced Table 2 in order to show the results of those three variables, grouped by number of companies in each FNC. Appendix 1 shows the 3D scatterplot of the FNCs by CONT, CONST and CONSU.

Table 2 shows that there is a linear relation between the number of organisations in the FNC and the use of FNC to give consistency to sustainability efforts and the use of FNC as a tool to build consensus over sustainability and social responsibility issues. In fact, the number of organisation per FNC is positively correlated to CONST and CONSU (Table 3). This means that the larger the network is, the more attention networkers pay to link sustainability to business results (CONST) and, to creating external awareness of and activism (CONSU) around the topic or the sustainability problem faced by the network.

Table 2. The management of sustainability within FNC expressed as variables and grouped by number of organisations in the FNC

Network Size	CONT	CONST	CONSU
From 2 to 5	1,15	1,35	2,17
From 6 to 9	1,03	1,38	2,72
From 10 to 19	1,8	1,6	2,8
20+	0,75	2	3

Source: authors' elaboration

Table 3. Correlation between the number of organisation in a FNC and the management variables

	CONT	CONST	CONSU
Number of organisation in FNC	-0,34216	0,98677	0,852653

Source: authors' elaboration

Looking at a graphical representation of sustainability management (Figure 1), it appears clear how SMEs can exploit FNCs to overcome SBSR barriers. In particular, larger FNCs rely on the formalisation to commit SMEs providing a statement of ethical values or moral principles, to foster the knowledge exchange and to create practical activism in order to explain and engage external stakeholders towards the specific sustainability topic faced by the FNC. The use of FNC to bring together business objectives and sustainability appears fundamental also in relation to network size, while the use of FNC to control sustainability issues with the use of certification and audit is not correlated to the dimension of the network. Of course, the higher number of SMEs are involved in the network the more complex is the management of sustainability. According to these results, the dimension of the network and the control of sustainability are not positively correlated because larger FNCs are composed of SMEs and single entrepreneurs that often belong to completely different business sectors, and the content of FNCs is related to the sustainability of their territory and their regional competitiveness. In that sense, the economic convenience of adopting sustainability management systems is not essential nor strategic to achieve the network objectives.

From this analysis, we can observe how the network dimension may influence the use of FNCs to govern sustainability in the network. Another perspective of analysis is that one of the simultaneous use of the FNCs to reach CONT, CONST and CONSU objectives. From the Euclidean geometry perspective, we can measure the area of the triangles and derive results on the proper exploitation of FNCs to manage sustainability. The areas of sub-triangles represent the Euclidean dimension of the use of the FNC to achieve pairs of variables. The area of each sub-triangles has been calculated as:

$$\text{AREA } MANSUS = A_1 + A_2 + A_3 = \frac{CONST * CONT \sin\alpha}{2} + \frac{CONST * CONSU \sin\beta}{2} + \frac{CONSU * CONT \sin\gamma}{2}$$

Figure 1. The graphical representation of the variables and network size

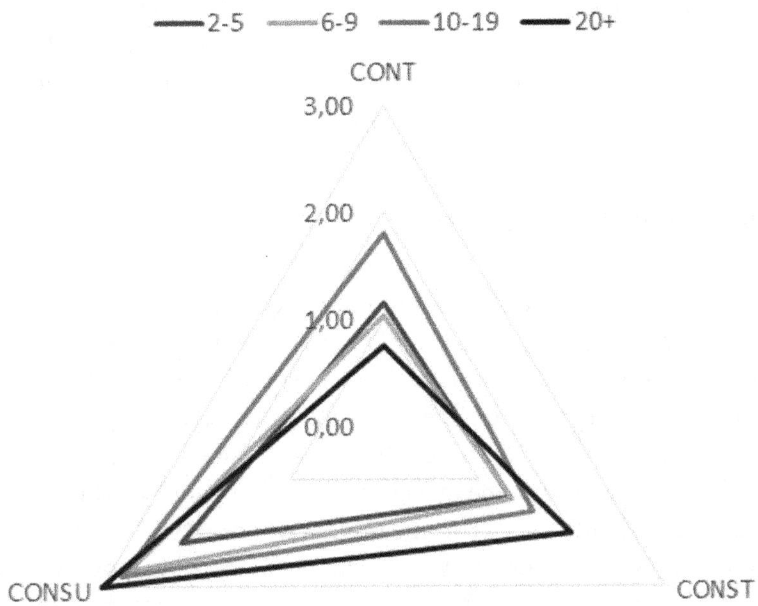

Figure 2. The areas of the triangles representing the variables

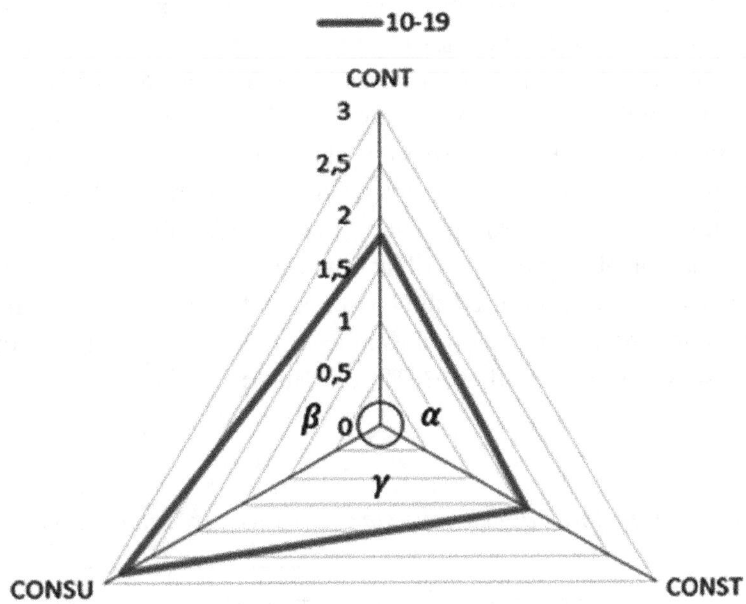

Where $\alpha = \beta = \gamma = 120°$ (see Figure 2 applied to a case of our sample)

As reported in Table 4, network size influences the use of FNC to govern control, consensus and consistency simultaneously. This finding suggests that FNCs are better exploited by larger networks than by smaller ones. Again, our results suggest that FNCs are driven by the aim to govern consistency and consensus, more than to control and audit sustainability.

SOLUTIONS AND RECOMMENDATIONS

FNCs are effective juridical and managerial tools to implement sustainability strategies in SMEs overcoming the traditional barriers. They might be useful to provide small entrepreneurs tangible benefits of SBSR, overcoming the perception of CSR as a business cost. Our study applies a model to explain the management of sustainability using three different variables. These are explained by the adoption of a range of actions, from more tangible tools to intangible ones. In our model, each variable is explained by a subset of three conditions that represents the managerial translation of SBSR in SMEs. All the variables have the same importance and significance. This means that when an FNC states that an ethical code will be mandatory for the networkers, for our study it counts the same as having explicitly prescribed that all the networkers are committed to sustainable development or the importance to achieve measurable increases in economic profitability ratios of the networkers.

To give the reader a complete overview of our analysis, we would like to report an extract of citations taken from these contracts included in our model (Table 5).

Our model is not influenced by the business turnover or by the business sector risks. Because most of the companies in our study are micro-businesses or single-entrepreneurs this has implied difficulties in systematically retrieving business results (which could be the focus for further studies).

From the sustainability perspective, we are aware that FNCs stipulated between companies of the same sector might be influenced by business sector sustainability issues, especially in terms of norms, codes and certifications. Conversely, FNCs are not strictly classifiable by business sector codes since they are composed of different companies operating in completely different sectors. For instance, the FNC#1013 for the defence of biodiversity in a local area puts together fishermen, sport shops, food producers and restaurants. We have not used the business sector as a driver in order to be neutral by specific sustainability problems. Precedents studies indeed, focus solely on FNCs in the tourism sector and its sustainability issues (Aureli & Forlani, 2015; Del Baldo, 2016).

Table 4. The management of the three dimensions simultaneously by Euclidean area

Network size	A_1 *CONST-CONT-0*	A_2 *CONST-CONSU-0*	A_3 *CONSU-CONT-0*	*MANSUS*
From 2 to 5	0,73	1,30	1,09	3,12
From 6 to 9	0,65	1,68	1,27	3,60
From 10 to 19	1,39	1,99	**2,34**	**5,72**
20+	0,97	**2,60**	0,97	**4,55**

Source: authors' elaboration

Table 5. Extracts from FNCs and the corresponding variable

Variable	Sub-Variables	Extracts From FNCs [Number of the FNC in the Brackets]
CONTROL	Ethical code	"The contract provides for the preparation of specific protocols and regulations for the production, processing and transport of products in accordance with the rules laid down in the Code of Ethics for Traceability" [#2195]
	Sustainability management system (certification)	"No later than three months from the end of each calendar year, each company must comply with the ISO14001 certification provided for in the network program" [#71]
	External sustainability audit	"For the purpose of designing, producing and disseminating the use of Sustainable Packaging, as defined by the principles of the Sustainable Packaging Coalition (SPC), the participants feel that they have to structure their own organizations, to provide them with a service that can be used to preserve the environment, social and economic sustainability audit" [#1682]
CONSISTENCY	Increase profitability	"Unify administrative and logistically the production process by improving vinification, especially with regard to environmental sustainability" [#2243]
	Supply chain	"[The aim of the FNC is to…] Improve the cultivation and distribution of cereals, harvest and other agricultural products used for the production of malt and successively agricultural and original beer of the Company XX produced with 100% Italian products, exclusively obtained on the Italian territory. With this network contract, the participant companies, thanks to a stabile fiduciary and synergic collaboration and to high professionalism in the various components of the production background, decided to start a project with the aim of increasing the level of our competitiveness, attending a sustainable agriculture and give value at the vocational products of the territory". [#2278]
	Compliance with law and opportunities	"The Affiliates intend to enter into a Network Agreement in compliance with the Call for Proposals issued by the Region 2007-2013 to lower environmental impacts in the production processes" [#797]
CONSENSUS	Statement of ethical values or moral principles	"To this end, companies undertake to implement common products / projects in accordance with the principles of environmental sustainability and CSR" [#200] "The parties agree and declare to pursue, through the present contract, the objective of increasing the penetration capacity of the participating companies on the national and international markets by a strong focus in terms of respect for ethical principles and intrinsic and organoleptic quality of products" [#1493]
	Knowledge exchange	"The added value of the network is that each company enjoys specific know-how, with its strong specialisation that if combined in synergy with that of other companies, it can create a very important degree of competitiveness in the market [of kenaf applications in the thermocouple insulation] compared to that reached individually" [#1045]
	Activism and shared commitment towards specific sustainability topics	"In order to stimulate the cultural, social and economic development of the Mediterranean and other regions of southern Italy, by increasing the competitive economy of the firms on international markets, networkers believe: […] to engage in joint activities of affirmation and dissemination of territorial cohesion in order to promote a sustainable, responsible, aware and balanced system, of which the territory and its traditions appear to be the most authentic and authoritative vehicle" [#1391]

Source: authors' elaboration

Applying Existent Theories to Our Results

According to normative isomorphism, similar individuals tend to promote a cognitive base, diffuse shared orientations and organisational practices to legitimise their activities (DiMaggio & Powell, 1983). SMEs in the sample are using the FNCs to promote a shared base of values, orientations and practices towards sustainability. In particular, using FNCs they legitimise themselves towards the sustainable choices they make in order to give credibility to their sustainability actions. For instance, they are favouring a particular sustainability strategy giving juridical importance to have chosen a particular certification instead of another. They also "contractualise" SBSR in the sense that they are normatively defining their own sustainable strategy among existent standards and rules. This formalisation happens to reduce ambiguity and business costs concerning inefficient management choice, as SBSR is often perceived as a business cost, more than a success factor (Tilley, 2000). According to del los Reyes et al. (2017), this norm-making approach is seen as suitable for small entrepreneurs (de los Reyes, Scholz & Smith, 2017) as they implement the vision of sustainability of their large customers, normally large multinational companies.

In addition, our study shed light on the management of SBSR using the FNC. In particular, our study has deepened the implications in terms of control, consistency and consensus. We demonstrated that consistency and consensus influence the management of sustainability especially in large networks of SMEs. The importance of consistency is in line with the literature and the implication of a managerial view of CSR linked to the business and source of competitive advantage (Porter & Kramer, 2011). The importance of consensus is in line with the conception of SBSR as a substantially proactive behaviour among small entrepreneurs explained by ethical motivation and not only by business objectives. In our sample, business motivations and ethical principles coexist as there are no written rules about the legal content of the FNC. Regarding control, our results demonstrate a negative correlation between the size of the network and the use of ethical code, certifications and sustainability audit. Since FNCs are developed having with a view to exploiting the network to increase the wellbeing of the networkers more than to control and evaluate their performance, control remains residual. As in our model, two main components of control are represented by certifications and audit. Our results are in line with the relevant studies of Johnson and Schaltegger (2016). Unfortunately, the mimetic isomorphism of the network doesn't seem to overcome the full cost of being certified and audited, and the "network effect" is translated into consistent actions and consensus claim. In fact, such certifications are applied at firm level and sometimes at site level, not at network level. Costs of audits and asseverations could not be divided by participants.

CONCLUSION

Several managerial impacts and practical output arise from our study. First, FNCs face directly some weakness of the SBSR providing practical solutions, as in the case of supply chain adaptation and knowledge sharing. The latter has been constantly reported in the related literature as one of the main barriers of SBSR. With FNCs public regulators can induce small companies and single entrepreneurs to become more aware of CSR and sustainability. Second, our study contributes to the growing literature on FNCs, providing a new perspective as invoked by several scholars (Tiacci & Cardoni, 2011; Cardoni & Tiacci, 2013; Aureli & Forlani, 2015; Del Baldo, 2016). Third, our study sheds light on the sustainable behaviour of SMEs and single entrepreneurs using a qualitative methodology and reporting results grounded in the territory.

Future development of our research regards/could include the implication of the network shape and structure for sustainability management. In addition, future development will consider the opportunity of interviewing directly a sample of networkers to compare the achievement of sustainability targets with the distribution of power in the network, and, moreover the implications arising from the diversity of business sectors involved in the achievement of such targets. Using the viewpoint of SBSR, further study will investigate more in depth the motivations that explained the decision of networkers to formalise ethical values and sustainability concepts with these contracts.

REFERENCES

Abdirahman, Z.-Z., Sauvée, L., & Shiri, G. (2014). Analyzing network effects of Corporate Social Responsibility implementation in food small and medium enterprises. *Journal on Chain and Network Science*, *14*(2), 103–115. doi:10.3920/JCNS2014.x005

Ahmad, J., & Krishnan, M. (2017). Environmental Related CSR Initiatives for Business Strategy: A Case Study on Small and Medium (SME) Industries in Malaysia. In The Dynamics of Corporate Social Responsibility (pp. 305–322). Springer.

Aldrich, H. E. (1979). *Organizations and environments*. Englewood Cliffs, NJ: Prentice-Hall.

Aureli, S., & Forlani, F. (2015). The effects of formal networks on territorial tourism offers. Current usage of network contracts in Italy. *European Journal of Tourism Research*, *10*(July), 76–94.

Avram, D. O., & Kühne, S. (2008). Implementing responsible business behavior from a strategic management perspective: Developing a framework for Austrian SMEs. *Journal of Business Ethics*, *82*(2), 463–475. doi:10.100710551-008-9897-7

Baden, D., Harwood, I. A., & Woodward, D. G. (2011). The effects of procurement policies on "downstream" corporate social responsibility activity. *International Small Business Journal*, *29*(3), 259–277. doi:10.1177/0266242610375770

Baldo, M. D. (2011, January). Il contratto di rete come strumento di sviluppo delle piccole e medie imprese. *Un'analisi delle prime esperienze*.

Baldo, M. D., & Aureli, S. (2012). Networks' contribution to small-sized firms' internationalization. *International Journal of Economic Behavior*, (2), 47–66.

Battaglia, M., Bianchi, L., Frey, M., & Iraldo, F. (2010). An innovative model to promote CSR among SMEs operating in industrial clusters: Evidence from an EU project. *Corporate Social Responsibility and Environmental Management*, *17*(3), 133–141. doi:10.1002/csr.224

Battaglia, M., Testa, F., Bianchi, L., Iraldo, F., & Frey, M. (2014). Corporate social responsibility and competitiveness within SMEs of the fashion industry: Evidence from Italy and France. *Sustainability*, *6*(2), 872–893. doi:10.3390u6020872

Baumann-Pauly, D., Wickert, C., Spence, L. J., & Scherer, A. G. (2013). Organizing Corporate Social Responsibility in Small and Large Firms: Size Matters. *Journal of Business Ethics*, 1–13. doi:10.100710551-012-1502-4

Buhmann, K. (2009). Regulating Corporate Social and Human Rights Responsibilities at the UN plane: Institutionalising new forms of law and law-making approaches? *Nordic Journal of International Law*, *78*(1), 1–52. doi:10.1163/157181009X397063

Buhmann, K. (2011). Danish CSR Reporting Requirement: Migration of CRS-Related International Norms into Companies' Self-Regulation through Company Law, The. *Eur. Company L.*, *8*, 65.

Bürgi, J. (2010). A comprehensive model for SMEs: Measuring the dynamic interplay of morality, environment and management systems–Towards continuous improvement. In *Ethics in Small and Medium Sized Enterprises* (pp. 147–171). Springer. doi:10.1007/978-90-481-9331-8_9

Cantele, S., Vernizzi, S., & Ricciardi, F. (2016). The emerging wave of agility-oriented business networks in Italy: A new strategy for facing global competition. *World Review of Entrepreneurship, Management and Sustainable Development, 12*(2/3), 270–284. doi:10.1504/WREMSD.2016.074967

Cardoni, A., Rossi, V., & Tiacci, L. (2011). Le reti d'impresa e la sfida per l'innovazione: un progetto di networking tra PMI nel settore della meccanica. *AUR&S Agenzia Umbria Ricerche*, 5–6.

Cardoni, A., Saetta, S., & Tiacci, L. (2010). Evaluating how potential pool of partners can join together in different types of long term collaborative networked organizations. *IFIP Advances in Information and Communication Technology, 336*, 312–321. 10.1007/978-3-642-15961-9_37

Cardoni, A., & Tiacci, L. (2013). The "Enterprises' Network Agreement": The Italian Way to Stimulate Reindustrialization for Entrepreneurial and Economic Development of SMEs. *The enterprises' Network Agreement,* 471–480. 10.1007/978-3-642-40543-3_50

Caroli, M. (2017). *L'innovazione delle imprese leader per creare valore sociale, Terzo rapporto CERIIS sull'innovazione sociale, Studi ed esperienze sull'innovazione sociale – CERIIS*. FrancoAngeli Editore.

Carruthers, B. G. (1995). Accounting, ambiguity, and the new institutionalism. *Accounting, Organizations and Society, 20*(4), 313–328. doi:10.1016/0361-3682(95)96795-6

Castka, P., & Balzarova, M. A. (2008). ISO 26000 and supply chains-On the diffusion of the social responsibility standard. *International Journal of Production Economics, 111*(2), 274–286. doi:10.1016/j.ijpe.2006.10.017

Cerrato, S. (2016). Appunti sul contratto di rete: un modello «à la carte» dal contratto all'istituzione... e ritorno. *Rivista Di Diritto dell'Impresa*, (3), 491.

Chell, E., & Baines, S. (2000). Networking, entrepreneurship and microbusiness behaviour. *Entrepreneurship and Regional Development, 12*(3), 195–215. doi:10.1080/089856200413464

Crane, A. (2010). From governance to Governance: On Blurring Boundaries. *Journal of Business Ethics, 94*(1), 17–19. doi:10.100710551-011-0788-y

D'Alessio, R. (2008). *Le coalizioni aziendali: caratteri del fenomeno e forme relazionali*. G. Giappichelli.

de Jesus Pacheco, D. A., ten Caten, C. S., Jung, C. F., Ribeiro, J. L. D., Navas, H. V. G., & Cruz-Machado, V. A. (2016). Eco-innovation determinants in manufacturing SMEs: Systematic review and research directions. *Journal of Cleaner Production, 142*. doi:10.1016/j.jclepro.2016.11.049

de los Reyes, G. Jr, Scholz, M., & Smith, N. C. (2017). Beyond the "Win-Win." *California Management Review, 59*(2), 142–167. doi:10.1177/0008125617695286

Del Baldo, M. (2016). Formal Cooperation for Developing Sustainability and Corporate Social Responsibility Among Tourism SMEs in Italy: Insights, Limits and Potentialities of the Network Contract BT - Key Initiatives in Corporate Social Responsibility: Global Dimension of CSR. Cham: Springer International Publishing; doi:10.1007/978-3-319-21641-6_5

Di Maggio, P. J., & Powell, W. (1991). *The New Istitutionalism in Organizational Fields*. Chicago: University of Chicago Press.

Di Maggio, P. J., & Powell, W. W. (1983). The iron cage revisited: Collective rationality and institutional isomorphism in organizational fields. *American Sociological Review*, *48*(2), 147–160. doi:10.2307/2095101

Dowling, J., & Pfeffer, J. (1975). Organizational legitimacy: Social values and organizational behavior. *Pacific Sociological Review*, *18*(1), 122–136. doi:10.2307/1388226

Elo, S., Kääriäinen, M., Kanste, O., Pölkki, T., Utriainen, K., & Kyngäs, H. (2014). Qualitative Content Analysis. *SAGE Open*, *4*(1), 2158244014522633. doi:10.1177/2158244014522633

Elo, S., & Kyngäs, H. (2008). The qualitative content analysis process. *Journal of Advanced Nursing*, *62*(1), 107–115. doi:10.1111/j.1365-2648.2007.04569.x PMID:18352969

European Commission. (2016). *Annual report on European SMEs 2015/2016*. 10.2873/886211

Fassin, Y., Werner, A., Van Rossem, A., Signori, S., Garriga, E., von Høivik, H. W., & Schlierer, H. J. (2015). CSR and Related Terms in SME Owner-Managers Mental Models in Six European Countries: National Context Matters. *Journal of Business Ethics*, *128*(2), 433–456. doi:10.100710551-014-2098-7

Fasterling, B. (2012). Development of Norms Through Compliance Disclosure. *Journal of Business Ethics*, *106*(1), 73–87. doi:10.100710551-011-1055-y

Fernandez, J. L., & Camacho, J. (2016). Effective Elements to Establish an Ethical Infrastructure: An Exploratory Study of SMEs in the Madrid Region. *Journal of Business Ethics*, *138*(1), 113–131. doi:10.100710551-015-2607-3

Ferrari, C. (2010). The Italian "Network Contract" A new tool for the growth of enterprises within the framework of the "SMALL BUSINESS ACT." *Colum. J. Eur. L. Online*, *16*, 77–89.

Floridi, L. (2009). Network Ethics: Information and Business Ethics in a Networked Society. *Journal of Business Ethics*, *90*(S4), 649–659. doi:10.100710551-010-0598-7

Freeman, S., Edwards, R., & Schroder, B. (2006). How Smaller Born-Global Firms Use Networks and Alliances to Overcome Constraints to Rapid Internationalization. *Journal of International Marketing*, *14*(3), 33–63. doi:10.1509/jimk.14.3.33

Griggs, D., Stafford-Smith, M., Gaffney, O., Rockström, J., Öhman, M. C., Shyamsundar, P., ... Noble, I. (2013). Policy: Sustainable development goals for people and planet. *Nature*, *495*(7441), 305–307. doi:10.1038/495305a PMID:23518546

Guercini, S., & Tunisini, A. (2017). Formalizing in business networks as a tool for industrial policy. *IMP Journal*, *11*(1), 91–108. doi:10.1108/IMP-07-2015-0040

Haddoud, M. Y., Jones, P., & Newbery, R. (2017). Export promotion programmes and SMEs' performance. *Journal of Small Business and Enterprise Development*, *24*(1), 68–87. doi:10.1108/JSBED-07-2016-0116

Håkansson, H., & Snehota, I. (2006). No business is an island: The network concept of business strategy. *Scandinavian Journal of Management*, *22*(3), 256–270. doi:10.1016/j.scaman.2006.10.005

Horisch, J., Johnson, M. P., & Schaltegger, S. (2015). Implementation of Sustainability Management and Company Size: A Knowledge-Based View. *Business Strategy and the Environment*, *24*(8), 765–779. doi:10.1002/bse.1844

Jenkins, H. (2006). Small business champions for corporate social responsibility. *Journal of Business Ethics*, *67*(3), 241–256. doi:10.100710551-006-9182-6

Johnson, M. P. (2013). Awareness and Application of Sustainability Management Tools in Small and Medium-Sized Enterprises. *Academy of Management Proceedings, 2013*(1), 1–18. 10.5465/AMBPP.2013.16036abstract

Johnson, M. P. (2015). Sustainability Management and Small and Medium-Sized Enterprises: Managers' Awareness and Implementation of Innovative Tools. *Corporate Social Responsibility and Environmental Management*, *22*(5), 271–285. doi:10.1002/csr.1343

Johnson, M. P., & Schaltegger, S. (2016). Two Decades of Sustainability Management Tools for SMEs: How Far Have We Come? *Journal of Small Business Management*, *54*(2), 481–505. doi:10.1111/jsbm.12154

Keast, R., Brown, K., & Mandell, M. (2007). Getting The Right Mix: Unpacking Integration Meanings and Strategies. *International Public Management Journal*, *10*(1), 9–33. doi:10.1080/10967490601185716

Keast, R., Mandell, M. P., Brown, K., & Woolcock, G. (2004). Network structures: Working differently and changing expectations. *Public Administration Review*, *64*(3), 363–371. doi:10.1111/j.1540-6210.2004.00380.x

Kenny, B., & Fahy, J. (2011). Network resources and international performance of high tech SMEs. *Journal of Small Business and Enterprise Development*, *18*(3), 529–555. doi:10.1108/14626001111155691

Kerlinger, F. N. (1964). Foundations of Behavioral Research. New York: Holt, Reinhart, and Winston.

Kirkels, Y., & Duysters, G. (2010). Brokerage in SME networks. *Research Policy*, *39*(3), 375–385. doi:10.1016/j.respol.2010.01.005

Konsti-Laakso, S., Pihkala, T., & Kraus, S. (2012). Facilitating SME Innovation Capability through Business Networking. *Creativity and Innovation Management*, *21*(1), 93–105. doi:10.1111/j.1467-8691.2011.00623.x

Krippendorff, K. (1980). Validity in Content Analysis. *Computerstrategien Für Die Kommunikationsanalyse*, 69–112. Retrieved from http://repository.upenn.edu/asc_papers/291

Lai, A., Lionzo, A., Stacchezzini, R., & Rossignoli, F. (2015). *Dall'impresa al network. Profili di governance e modelli di business: Profili di governance e modelli di business*. FrancoAngeli.

Lee, H., Kelley, D., Lee, J., & Lee, S. (2012). SME survival: The impact of internationalization, technology resources, and alliances. *Journal of Small Business Management*, *50*(1), 1–19. doi:10.1111/j.1540-627X.2011.00341.x

Lepoutre, J., & Heene, A. (2006). Investigating the impact of firm size on small business social responsibility: A critical review. *Journal of Business Ethics*, *67*(3), 257–273. doi:10.100710551-006-9183-5

Lindblom, C. K. (1994). The implications of organizational legitimacy for corporate social performance and disclosure. In Critical perspectives on accounting conference (Vol. 120). New York: Academic Press.

Lynch-Wood, G., Williamson, D., & Jenkins, W. (2009). The over-reliance on self-regulation in CSR policy. *Business Ethics (Oxford, England)*, *18*(1), 52–65. doi:10.1111/j.1467-8608.2009.01548.x

MacGregor, R. C. (2004). Factors associated with formal networking in regional small business: Some findings from a study of Swedish SMEs. *Journal of Small Business and Enterprise Development*, *11*(1), 60–74. doi:10.1108/14626000410519100

Mandell, M., Keast, R., & Chamberlain, D. (2016). Collaborative networks and the need for a new management language. *Public Management Review*, *9037*(August), 1–16. doi:10.1080/14719037.2016.1209232

Mandell, M. P., & Keast, R. (2008). Evaluating the effectiveness of interorganizational relations through networks. *Public Management Review*, *10*(6), 715–731. doi:10.1080/14719030802423079

Mazzola, E., & Perrone, G. (2013). A strategic needs perspective on operations outsourcing and other inter-firm relationships. *International Journal of Production Economics*, *144*(1), 256–267. doi:10.1016/j.ijpe.2013.02.012

Mazzola, E., Perrone, G., & Kamuriwo, D. S. (2016). The interaction between inter-firm and interlocking directorate networks on firm's new product development outcomes. *Journal of Business Research*, *69*(2), 672–682. doi:10.1016/j.jbusres.2015.08.033

Melé, D. (2009). The Practice of Networking: An Ethical Approach. *Journal of Business Ethics*, *90*(S4), 487–503. doi:10.100710551-010-0602-2

Mitnick, B. M. (1995). Systematics and CSR. *Business & Society*, *34*(1), 5–33. doi:10.1177/000765039503400102

Moratis, L. (2017). The (In) credible Bulk: The Role of CSR Standards in Enhancing the Credibility of Corporate CSR Claims. In *The Dynamics of Corporate Social Responsibility* (pp. 239–263). Springer. doi:10.1007/978-3-319-39089-5_13

Murillo, D., & Lozano, J. M. (2009). Pushing forward SME CSR through a network: An account from the Catalan model. *Business Ethics-a European Review*, *18*(1), 7–20. doi:10.1111/j.1467-8608.2009.01545.x

Noran, O. (2010). Towards an Environmental Management Approach for Collaborative Networks. *Collaborative Networks for a Sustainable World*, *336*, 17–24. doi:10.1007/978-3-642-15961-9_2

O'Donnell, A. (2004). The nature of networking in small firms. *Qualitative Market Research*, *7*(3), 206–217. doi:10.1108/13522750410540218

Parker, S. C. (2008). The economics of formal business networks. *Journal of Business Venturing*, *23*(6), 627–640. doi:10.1016/j.jbusvent.2008.01.003

Perrini, F. (2006). SMEs and CSR theory: Evidence and implications from an Italian perspective. *Journal of Business Ethics*, *67*(3), 305–316. doi:10.100710551-006-9186-2

Porter, M. E., & Kramer, M. R. (2011). The Big Idea: Creating Shared Value. *Harvard Business Review*, *89*(1), 1–2. doi:10.2469/dig.v41.n1.28

Reid, W. V., Chen, D., Goldfarb, L., Hackmann, H., Lee, Y. T., Mokhele, K., ... Schellnhuber, H. J. (2010). Earth system science for global sustainability: Grand challenges. *Science*, *330*(6006), 916–917. doi:10.1126cience.1196263 PMID:21071651

Ricciardi, A., Cardoni, A., & Tiacci, L. (2014). Strategic Context, Organizational Features and Network Performances: A Survey on Collaborative Networked Organizations of Italian SMEs. In *Working Conference on Virtual Enterprises* (pp. 534–545). Springer. 10.1007/978-3-662-44745-1_53

Russo, A., & Perrini, F. (2010). Investigating stakeholder theory and social capital: CSR in large firms and SMEs. *Journal of Business Ethics*, *91*(2), 207–221. doi:10.100710551-009-0079-z

Santana, A., Vaccaro, A., & Wood, D. J. (2009). Ethics and the Networked Business. *Journal of Business Ethics*, *90*(S4), 661–681. doi:10.100710551-010-0599-6

Spence, L. J. (2014). Small Business Social Responsibility: Expanding Core CSR Theory. *Business & Society*. 10.1177/0007650314523256

Spence, L. J., & Rinaldi, L. (2014). Governmentality in accounting and accountability: A case study of embedding sustainability in a supply chain. *Accounting, Organizations and Society*, *39*(6), 433–452. doi:10.1016/j.aos.2012.03.003

Spence, L. J., & Rutherfoord, R. (2001). Social responsibility, profit maximisation and the small firm owner-manager. *Journal of Small Business and Enterprise Development*, *8*(2), 126–139. doi:10.1108/EUM0000000006818

Spence, L. J., & Rutherfoord, R. (2003). Small business and empirical perspectives in business ethics. *Journal of Business Ethics*, *47*(1), 1–5. doi:10.1023/A:1026205109290

Storey, D. J. (1994). *Understanding the Small Business Sector*. Thomson Learning Emea; doi:10.1016/0024-6301(95)90953-2

Suchman, M. C. (1995). Managing Legitimacy: Strategic and Institutional Approaches. *Academy of Management Review*, *20*(3), 571–610. doi:10.5465/AMR.1995.9508080331

Swoboda, B., Meierer, M., Foscht, T., & Morschett, D. (2011). International SME Alliances: The Impact of Alliance Building and Configurational Fit on Success. *Long Range Planning*, *44*(4), 271–288. doi:10.1016/j.lrp.2011.04.002

Symbola, U. (2010). *GreenItaly Rapporto 2010*. Academic Press.

Symbola, U. (2016). *GreenItaly Rapporto 2016*. Academic Press.

Taurino, T. (2015). A Cluster Reference Framework for Analyzing Sustainability of SME Clusters. *Procedia CIRP*, *30*, 132–137. doi:10.1016/j.procir.2015.02.138

Testa, F., Grappio, P., Gusmerotti, N. M., Iraldo, F., & Frey, M. (2016). Examining green public procurement using content analysis: Existing difficulties for procurers and useful recommendations. *Environment, Development and Sustainability*, *18*(1), 197–219. doi:10.100710668-015-9634-1

Tilley, F. (2000). Small firm environmental ethics: How deep do they go? *Business Ethics (Oxford, England)*, *9*(1), 31–41. doi:10.1111/1467-8608.00167

Tomšič, N., Bojnec, Š., & Simčič, B. (2015). Corporate sustainability and economic performance in small and medium sized enterprises. *Journal of Cleaner Production*, *108*, 603–612. doi:10.1016/j.jclepro.2015.08.106

van de Vrande, V., de Jong, J. P. J., Vanhaverbeke, W., & de Rochemont, M. (2009). Open innovation in SMEs: Trends, motives and management challenges. *Technovation*, *29*(6–7), 423–437. doi:10.1016/j.technovation.2008.10.001

Vázquez-Carrasco, R., & López-Pérez, M. E. (2012). Small & medium-sized enterprises and Corporate Social Responsibility: A systematic review of the literature. *Quality & Quantity*. doi:10.100711135-012-9713-4

von Høivik, H. W., & Shankar, D. (2011). How Can SMEs in a Cluster Respond to Global Demands for Corporate Responsibility? *Journal of Business Ethics*, *101*(2), 175–195. doi:10.100710551-010-0708-6

Vurro, C., Russo, A., & Perrini, F. (2009). Shaping Sustainable Value Chains: Network Determinants of Supply Chain Governance Models. *Journal of Business Ethics*, *90*(S4), 607–621. doi:10.100710551-010-0595-x

Wigginton, N. S. (2016). Evidence of an Anthropocene epoch. *Science*, *351*(6269), 134–136. doi:10.1126cience.351.6269.134-j

Williamson, D., Lynch-Wood, G., & Ramsay, J. (2006). Drivers of environmental behaviour in manufacturing SMEs and the implications for CSR. *Journal of Business Ethics*, *67*(3), 317–330. doi:10.100710551-006-9187-1

KEY TERMS AND DEFINITIONS

Corporate Social Responsibility (CSR): The responsibility of organizations for their impacts over the societies and environment.

Euclidean Geometry: Geometry based upon the postulates of Euclid, especially on the postulate that only one line may be drawn through a given point parallel to a given line.

Formalized Network Contract: Italian juridical tool introduced by regulators as a formal network agreement.

ENDNOTES

1 For further information: http://contrattidirete.registroimprese.it/reti/

2 As the research has been conducted within a research agreement with the local Chamber of Commerce, these contracts have been provided just for research purposes by them.

APPENDIX

Figure 3. The 3d scatter plot of the FNCs analyzed

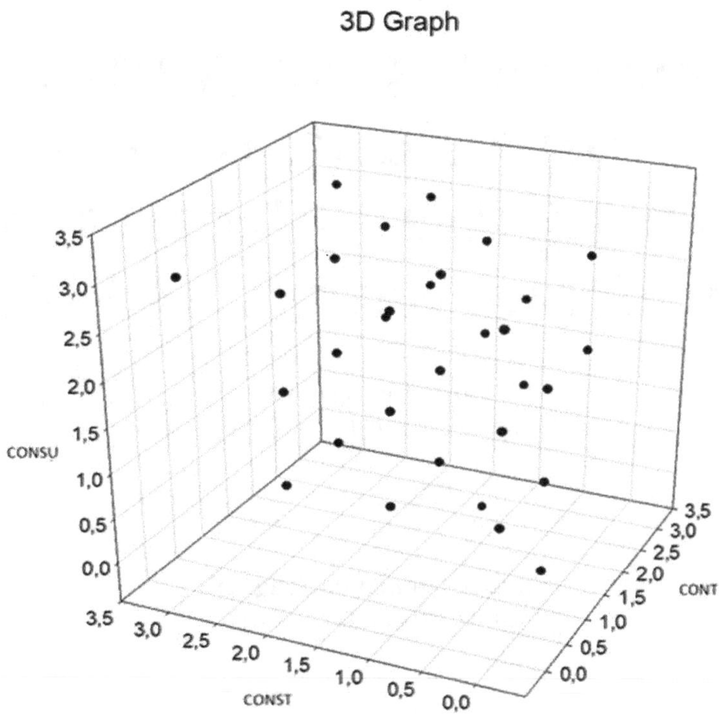

Chapter 4
Fostering Organic Farming Sustainability Throughout Alternative Food Networks (AFNs)

Paola De Bernardi
University of Turin, Italy

Lia Tirabeni
University of Turin, Italy

Simone Domenico Scagnelli
University of Turin, Italy

ABSTRACT

This chapter presents the preliminary results of an ongoing research that empirically investigates the role of alternative food networks (AFNs) in supporting the development of the organic farming sector; moreover, it contributes in fostering sustainability approaches by small farmers. Specifically, the authors focus on how AFNs can boost sustainability in food consumption models and create an integrated way to support long-term competitiveness of organic farmers and, at the same time, satisfy consumers' expectations. By adopting a mixed case-based methodology, the authors propose an analysis of the sustainability dimensions of organic farming and the sustainability characteristics of AFNs as agro-food systems alternatives to the conventional supply chains of modern distribution. Moreover, the authors identify customers' perceptions on organic products and sustainability as well as their purchasing rationale and motivation into a wide range of innovative AFN, such as "food assembly."

DOI: 10.4018/978-1-5225-5267-3.ch004

INTRODUCTION AND BACKGROUND INFORMATION

Sustainability in food production chains and systems is becoming an increasing key practice, in response to biodiversity, climate change, water, soil and air quality and producers' and consumers' well-being issues (Rockström et al., 2009; FAO, 2013; Schader et al., 2014; Forssell and Lankoski, 2015). Despite the modern globalized and conventional food system has contributed to enhance productivity and increase food security and safety, it has also created negative environmental and social impacts as well as economic uncertainties (Godfray et al., 2010; Freibauer et al., 2011; Spaargaren et al., 2012; Doernberg et al., 2016).

The need for more sustainable practices in the global food supply-chain, particularly in the small farming system, is becoming paramount. It has been argued (Alrøe et al., 2017) that a "sustainability revolution" is underway in the form of a broad, long-term shift in governance paradigms, however, this transformation is still fragmented and localised. While Europe is facing major systemic risks in term of security, supply and quality of the food, there is already an urgent need to develop more resilient food systems and value chains (Beck et al., 2014). In fact, although the European food law regulations and politics are more and more strict, Europe continues to be hit from a wide range of food safety scandals, such as the recent one that caused millions of potentially contaminated eggs. These scandals are the ultimate consequence of intensive food production based on industrial paradigms focusing on quantity rather than quality, treating food as a commodity and not as an integral and important element for human health or the environment, with serious impacts for whole ecosystems and for the dignity of small farmers.

Given this scenario, environment-friendly production methods, such as organic farming, are considered more sustainable than conventional ones (Lampkin et al., 2011; Padel et al., 2013; Torquati et al., 2016) and represent a way to meet society's needs for low-impact agriculture as well as consumers' specific preferences.

According to the EU Council Regulation 834/2007 organic farming system

[. . .] is an overall system of farm management and food production that combines best environmental practices, a high level of biodiversity, the preservation of natural resources, the application of high animal welfare standards and a production method in line with the preference of certain consumers for products produced using natural substances and processes. The organic production method thus plays a dual societal role, where it on the one hand provides for a specific market responding to a consumer demand for organic products, and on the other hand delivers public goods contributing to the protection of the environment and animal welfare, as well as to rural development (European Commission, 2007).

Although organic farming represents only 1% of worldwide agriculture, it is one of the fastest growing sectors in agro-food systems. The largest organic shares of the total available farming lands are in Oceania (5.4%) and in Europe (2.5%). Organic food is the most successful product category within the growing ethical and sustainable products market (Gruère, 2015), with a global market share for organic food and drinks that expanded by almost four-fold between 2000 and 2015 (Figure 1), with more than 90% of consumers' demand concentrated in Europe and North America. Looking forward, positive growth is expected to continue in the coming years (Willer and Lernoud, 2017). According to the SINAB (Italian Information System on Organic Agriculture) study, the farms adopting organic methods in Italy increased by 20% in 2016 with more than 300.000 hectares converted to organic farming and raise of related operators by 20.3%. The Italian agro-food model is regarded as one of the most sustainable in

Europe, confirming that sustainability is a strategic key to increase competitiveness of small organic farming system (Mercati, 2016).

Although there is evidence of positive impacts of farming systems and markets based on organic principles, including consumer health, animal welfare, biodiversity and the improved livelihoods of producers, in many cases, the standards carried on by State governments and private organizations define only minimum requirements for organic production and processing, not enough for a real sustainable farming system (Padel et al., 2009; Arbernz et al., 2016; Rahmann et al., 2016). Despite many authors and practitioners discuss the potential contribution of organic farming to more sustainable food systems (Padel et al., 2013 Schader et al., 2014) there is a lack of comprehensive as well as empirical evidence for the manifold related benefits. Specifically, how farming sustainability is perceived by the consumers, who are getting more and more attentive not only to organic products, but even to the origin of the products, preferring local ones when possible, or even the opportunity of knowing directly the farmer and the production method adopted.

Some scholars have analysed the positive role of the short food chain in achieving sustainability goals with relevant effects on the reinterpretation of market food performing principles and on rural development, with a dynamic role played by small organic farms (Barbera et al., 2014; Canfora, 2016; Matacena, 2016). A consumer's approach to organic food system is also described in the IFOAM Best Practice Guidelines (SOAAN-IFOAM, 2013), as it emphasizes that changing to sustainable agro-food systems implies stakeholder-oriented initiatives tailored to local priorities as well as deep changes in the behaviours of all the actors of the value chain, including the final consumer. This means that producers and consumers, that are two of the key players in the organic agro-food chain, need to experience a better awareness in consumption and production practices.

Given this context, shorter organic supply-chains provide environmental, social and economic benefits that can be better supported by giving a greater emphasis on Alternative Food Networks (AFNs) whose role is to ensure, in an innovative and collaborative way, that the value chain is strongly linked to

Figure 1. Organic farmland and market in Italy
Source: The global Market for organic Food and Drink (Organic Monitor) and The World of Organic Agriculture (FiBL). (2017)

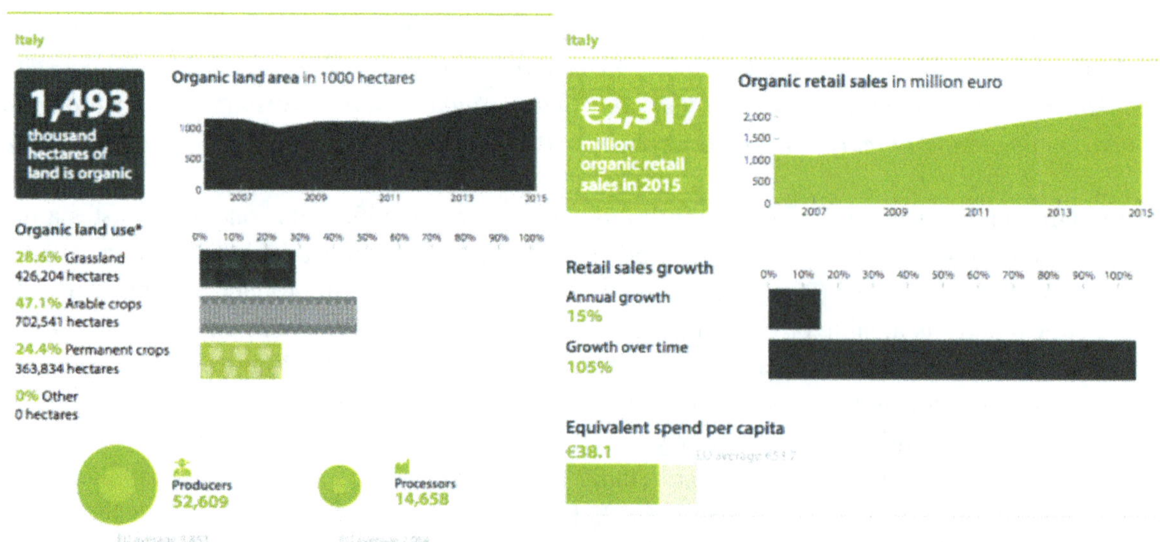

the organic principle of fairness; meaning cooperation amongst all chain actors, from farmers, workers, and processors to consumers. Such developments will ensure a balanced approach to local and regional sustainable development, rather than simply conforming or adjusting to existing agro-food systems. The Food Assembly Networks, throughout the promotion of a cutting-edge chain, wants to recover and reinvent a new, ethical, ecological, fair and socially sustainable way of producing and consuming food within a real network that acts locally with the goal of achieving a healthy, critical and conscious economy.

In the literature, the concept of AFN is linked to the issue of farmers' attention to the quality and sustainability of food production and, on the other side, on the symbolic value of food products for consumers (local, traditional, etc.) as well as their relationship characterised by mutual trust, direct relations and ongoing information concerning purchases and sales (Whatmore et al., 2003). The reasons for the focus on sustainability of organic small farming and the role played from the short supply chain named "Food Assembly", is the rapid development both of the organic sector and the AFNs phenomenon.

The remainder of this chapter is structured as follows. The first section discusses the sustainability dimensions of the organic food system from a FAO viewpoint and with the analysis of SAFA guidelines (Sustainability Assessment of Food and Agriculture Systems), in order to identify multiple determinants of sustainability of agro-food system. At the same time, the key characteristics of the AFNs sustainability are analysed. The second section, presents the research design, methodology and data collection. The third section presents the case study, an organisation operating within a short supply chain system, named "Food Assembly" (FA), especially underscoring the perception and rationales behind the decision to purchase organic products of a wide range of AFNs' consumers. The last section provides further discussion and conclusions, by addressing implications, limitations and future research directions.

THE DIFFERENT DIMENSIONS OF THE ORGANIC AGRO-FOOD SUSTAINABILITY

This first section provides an overview of the sustainability dimensions of organic food systems, from a producer as well as a consumer's point of view. We start by presenting the SAFA guidelines, then focus on the consumers perception, and discuss previous research on Alternative Food Networks.

Organic Farming Sustainability and the SAFA Guidelines

Despite previous studies have clearly shown that sustainability is a key factor of the organic food system, sustainability is still a multifaceted concept that relies on many different areas of scientific and practitioners' knowledge (Noe & Alrøe, 2015). Arbenz et al. (2016) stated that organic farming is a lighthouse for truly sustainable farming systems and agricultural products, positioning organic as a modern and innovative food system that integrates holistic ecology, economy, society, culture and responsibility in the local and regional context. Consistently, the concepts that guide the construction of a new organic culture and foster social development are: resource regeneration, responsibility for production, consumption adequacy and the ethical and spiritual development of human values, practices and habits, (FiBL & IFOAM, 2016; Barbanova et al., 2015). Annunziata and Vecchio (2015) observed that organic farming relies on ecological processes, biodiversity and cycles adapted to local conditions, rather than the use of inputs with adverse effects. Furthermore, they acknowledge that it is a production system that sustains the health of soils, ecosystems and people, combining tradition, innovation and science to benefit the shared environment and promote equitable relationships and a good quality of life for all involved. Moreover, organic food system not only preserves the environment but it also improves public health, bringing significant benefits to the economy as well as to the social cohesion of rural areas (Thorsøe et al., 2016). An interesting research (Alrøe et al., 2017), investigated two ideal approaches to sustainability transformation of food systems by employing Max Weber's distinction between instrumental rationality and value-rationality in social action. It compared, on the one hand, performance-based approaches that measure performance by setting up sustainability indicator targets and benchmarks to motivate the agents in the food system to change, and on the other hand, values-based approaches that aim at communicating and mediating sustainability values to enable coordinated and cooperative action in transforming the food system. Performance-based approaches can be retrieved in the growing emphasis of literature on the need to make assessments of food system sustainability with trusted and accountable methods, based on integrated, holistic and multicriteria tools (Alrøe et al., 2016; Peano et al., 2014; Schader et al., 2016). However, many of them produced different results, depending on the complexity of farming systems, supply-chains, networks and actors, often with conflicting goals. Specifically, a great majority of studies paid attention to the tools that enhance, with multiple perspectives, sustainability comparison at farm level, in different agro-food systems, like organic and conventional ones and along the food value chain (Blockeel et al., 2016; Capone et al., 2016; Schader et al., 2016), as well as the relationship with consumers perspectives on purchase decision-making (Abitabile et al., 2015; Annunziata & Vecchio, 2015; Basha et al., 2015; Hughner et al., 2007). The value-based approaches are based on a set of institutionalized values, for example, a set of agreed values that direct the decisions and actions of the daily farming practices and development initiatives (Alrøe et al., 2017). Many organic agro-food system approaches to sustainability transformation are values-based, as directed by overall values and ethical principles (Bond et al., 2008; Annunziata & Vecchio, 2015; Agovino et al., 2017).

The propensity to be sustainable, in this industry, is also influenced by a series of variables which are effectively represented by the framework for Sustainability Assessment of Food and Agriculture (SAFA), published by the Food and Agriculture Organization of the United Nations (FAO). Acknowledging that there are many definitions of sustainability, depending on values, power relationships, time and space considered, SAFA represents a holistic global framework for the assessment of sustainability along food and agriculture value chains. Its guiding vision is that food and agriculture systems are characterized by four dimensions of sustainability: good governance, environmental integrity, economic resilience and social well-being. It is universally recognized that these dimensions are broad and encompass many aspects, and they can be implemented at any level: national, supply chain or operational unit, providing a common understanding of what "sustainability" means in a practical context. The inclusion of the new dimension of governance in addition to the financial, social and environmental dimensions answers the need to assess the ability of an operator (i.e., a farm, a processor, a retailer) in delivering adequate sustainability performance (Blockeel et al., 2016; Schader et al., 2016). Each of these four dimensions of sustainability are outlined into a hierarchical structure of 21 themes and 58 sub-themes for each of the sustainability pillars (Figure 2). Goals are established for the themes while objectives are defined for the sub-themes, with the selection of measurable and verifiable indicators applicable to food and agriculture supply chains.

Figure 2. Overview of SAFA sustainability dimensions, themes and sub-themes
Source: Food and Agriculture Organization of the United Nations, 2013, SAFA Guidelines, (http://www.fao.org/fileadmin/templates/nr/sustainability_pathways/docs/SAFA_Guidelines_Final_122013.pdf). Reproduced with permission.

GOOD GOVERNANCE

CORPORATE ETHICS	Mission Statement	Due Diligence		
ACCOUNTABILITY	Holistic Audits	Responsibility	Transparency	
PARTICIPATION	Stakeholder Dialogue	Grievance Procedures	Conflict Resolution	
RULE OF LAW	Legitimacy	Remedy, Restoration & Prevention	Civic Responsibility	Resource Appropriation
HOLISTIC MANAGEMENT	Sustainability Management Plan	Full-Cost Accounting		

ENVIRONMENTAL INTEGRITY

ATMOSPHERE	Greenhouse Gases	Air Quality	
WATER	Water Withdrawal	Water Quality	
LAND	Soil Quality	Land Degradation	
BIODIVERSITY	Ecosystem Diversity	Species Diversity	Genetic Diversity
MATERIALS AND ENERGY	Material Use	Energy Use	Waste Reduction & Disposal
ANIMAL WELFARE	AnimalHealth	Freedom from Stress	

ECONOMIC RESILIENCE

INVESTMENT	Internal Investment	Community Investment	Long-Ranging Investment	Profitability	
VULNERABILITY	Stability of Production	Stability of Supply	Stability of Market	Liquidity	Risk Management
PRODUCT QUALITY & INFORMATION	Food Safety	Food Quality	Product Information		
LOCAL ECONOMY	Value Creation	Local Procurement			

SOCIAL WELL-BEING

DECENT LIVELIHOOD	Quality of Life	Capacity Development	Fair Access to Means of Production	
FAIR TRADING PRACTICES	Responsible Buyers	Rights of Suppliers		
LABOUR RIGHTS	Employment Relations	Forced Labour	Child Labour	Freedom of Association and Right to Bargaining
EQUITY	Non Discrimination	Gender Equality	Support to Vulnerable People	
HUMAN SAFETY & HEALTH	Workplace Safety and Health Provisions	Public Health		
CULTURAL DIVERSITY	Indigenous Knowledge	Food Sovereignty		

The Alternative Food Networks: A Sustainable Food System

The Alternative Food Networks (AFN) are new patterns of food chain, based on "re-localization" and "re-socialization" of food production, distribution and consumption practices (Dansero & Putilli, 2014; Marsden et al., 2000; Matacena, 2016), founded on environmental, social and economical sustainable food system at a local level (Forssell & Lankoski, 2015; Torquati et al., 2016; Barbera & Dagnes, 2016). Renting et al. (2003) defined AFNs as a way to "cover new emerging networks of producers, consumers, and other actors that embody alternatives to the more standardized industrial mode of food supply". Within the designation of AFNs, it is possible to identify a comprehensive body of practices related to food provisioning like farm shops, farmers markets, box schemes, community-supported agriculture (CSA), consumer cooperatives, bio-districts, solidarity purchasing groups, etc., which are, in a general sense, different from mainstream food systems (Murdoch et al., 2000; Goodman et al., 2012). In this heterogeneous and complex situation, AFNs assume very different configurations and meanings, depending on their territorial, cultural, and economic contexts. Despite these differences, they all rely on different forms of proximity between producers and consumers among which new relationships are created, based on mutual trust and interpersonal connections. The proximity is intended not only in a geographical sense, in relation to how consumers and producers are physically close to one another, but also about the attention given to the economic support of local communities and the development of fair and trustworthy relationships between actors (Barbera & Dagnes, 2016).

According to the Alternative Food Networks and Interdisciplinary Assessment research (AFNIA) conducted by the University of Turin, Italy between 2013 and 2016, the characteristics of AFNs in the Piedmont region, North Italy, are linked and integrated within four perspectives of sustainability (Corsi et al., 2014), namely economic, social, geographical, and environmental. The perspectives are focused, firstly, on the impact of consumer perception of the quality of production and distribution practices, then on the environmental impact of the entire supply-chain of alternative networks, from production to end-consumers, as well as the role of AFNs towards re-territorialization of the food system and, finally, on the new proximity relationships between urban and rural productive areas. The same research, at regional scale, has also shown that the choice of farmers to directly deliver their products is linked to several factors, including: a) characteristics of companies, normally of small size and with one type of production, mainly dedicated to horticulture, viticulture or mixed crops productions; b) the personal characteristics of the company's owner, that normally is young and with a university degree, and c) the geographical position of the company, generally located in rural areas, like hills and mountains.

Dansero & Puttilli (2014) adopted a Raffestin-style territorial approach (Raffestin & Butler, 2012) to carry out the relationship between AFNs and sustainability. As underlined from the authors, AFNs sustainability can be empirically defined according to three dimensions: (i) the spatial organisation (i.e. food miles and emissions related to different models of food production and distribution), (ii) the link to resources (i.e. local values, tradition and cultures reinterpreted and reshaped by food networks) and (iii) the social relations (i.e. fair and equal relationships for different categories of people).

Several studies demonstrate the concept of embeddedness, as the social character of alternative networks (Sonnino & Mardsen, 2006), but also as an ecological and cultural characteristic, connecting the concept to the valorisation of the territory and of local productions so to contribute to revitalize rural areas and support the value-enhancement of the territory (Bazzani & Canavari, 2013).

Other authors argued that the organic agro-food has lost some of its distinctiveness as a result of the growing global standardization and industrialization, causing a shift in consumers' preferences from organic to local food products (Adams and Salois, 2010; Campbell et al., 2013). In response, food chain innovations have been gaining more attention, building upon more sustainability issues, with an increasing relevance of ecological and social values, as well as technological and behavioural changes (Seyfang, 2006; Maye & Kirwan 2010; Naspetti et al., 2011; Doernberg et al., 2016). In AFNs, quality emerges as a multi-dimensional social product resulting from a negotiation between producers and consumers, and referring to the origin of the product (Goodman, 2003), as well as to its traceability, identity and cultural traits (Sonnino & Marsden, 2006; Jouzi et al., 2017).

In Italy, Piedmont is one of the country regions most affected by the increase in AFNs during the last decade, as a result of a local context which is favourable for food quality productions and for the onset of initiatives to enhance "food culture".

Organic Farming and Its Sustainability Perception: The Consumer's Perspective

There is quite confusion around the term "organic" (Chryssochoidis, 2000) and the word actually owns many meanings for consumers of organic food. Such consumers are an important trend in sustainable food consumption (Colucci et al., 2012). They represent a population not homogeneous in demographics or in beliefs (Hughner et al., 2007), often aware of the organic central features – namely, that the food is chemical-free – but usually not familiar with organic farming standards and practices (Harper & Makatouni, 2002; Hill & Lynchehaun, 2002). Thus, many scholars have investigated how consumers perceive organic products, analysing issues related to the demand of organic production, and consumers' attitudes and profiles (see i.e. Zanoli & Naspetti, 2001; Magnusson et al., 2001; Fotopoulos et al., 2003; Hughner et al., 2007; Hamzaoui-Essoussi & Zahaf, 2012).

With respect to the organic consumers' perception, the literature can be grouped according to some specific topics, such as safety, health, and environmental issues; food origins and organic certifications; cost-related issues; and intangible attributes. These issues deeply influence the perception of consumers concerning the organic food sustainability, and encourage or, on the contrary, restrain the organic consumption and purchase. Concerning safety and health, studies on the consumer perceptions underline that consumers believe that organic food is safer compared to the conventional one (Rimal et al., 2005). Furthermore, the perceived healthiness of organic food is seen as a parameter of quality for many consumers (Wander & Bugge, 1997; Magnusson et al., 2001), and also the use of nutritional labels affects the purchasing behaviour, by influencing valuations and perceptions of the product (Drichoutis et al., 2006). Consumers generally associate organic food with natural process, care for the environment and animal welfare and the non-use of pesticides and fertilisers (Shafie & Rennie, 2012). Many authors (Hughner et al., 2007; Basha et al., 2015) as the main purchase motives influencing consumer preferences of organic foods, identify health, safety and lifestyle aspects, better taste and quality of products; environmental and animal welfare concerns, and support of the local economy. For example, in a Norwegian study it has been found that the primary reasons for buying organic food are health and environmental concerns, while animal welfare is of little importance (Hughner et al., 2007). Consumers purchase organic food not just because they perceive it is healthier or more environmentally friendly, but also because they feel it is more supportive of the local economy (Zepeda & Deal, 2009), and probably this is because they believe that organic food is locally grown, perhaps by smaller, family-owned farms (Hughner et al., 2007). Generally, consumers with a local orientation in the food market seem to have preference in buying organic food (Torjusen et al., 2001). Many authors suggest a consumer preference for production in relation to its origin and focus on the importance of geographical proximity and direct interaction as a mechanism for re-embedding consumers and securing credible local food systems (Renting et al., 2003; Sage, 2003; Kirwan, 2006; Jarosz, 2008). Furthermore, the local origin seems to be positively related to quality aspects, and generally better valued (Fotopoulus et al., 2003; Scarpa and Del Guidice, 2004). This is in line with other studies suggesting that local food is associated with higher perceived food quality (e.g., Carpio & Isengildina-Massa, 2009) as well as a perceived freshness increase of the products (Roininen et al., 2006). Accordingly, as underlined by Annunziata and Vecchio (2016), consumers may therefore believe that they support the local community when purchasing locally produced food, and local food production may also imply environmental benefits due to reduced "food miles". This finally means that consumers tend to perceive local food as more sustainable than conventional one both from a social (supporting local community) and an environmental (reducing food miles) perspectives. However, while consumer preferences and attitudes towards organic food products have been extensively studied, there is relatively less empirical work on consumer preferences for organic products locally produced (Gracia et al., 2014; Annunziata and Vecchio, 2016). Concerning the local dimension, also the personal interaction seems to be particularly relevant (Thorsøe, 2015). As suggested by Sage (2003) it is important for consumers to develop trust in the producers, indeed spatial proximity enables face-to-face interaction between the food actors, and shared values are important features for sustaining regard between them (Milestad et al., 2010).

Another relevant dimension relates to the trust concerning organic labelling. Organic labelling schemes are an important foundation for consumers' trust in organics, since they ensure that the food systems are controlled (Daugbjerg et al., 2014; Smed et al., 2013). Since consumers are not able to clearly assess the organic quality of food simply by looking at it, organic quality must be assured by the application of reliable and trustworthy industry standards, including strict organic labelling. However, by exploring consumer trust in organics and investigating the relationship between reliability, trust, and knowledge, Thorsøe et al. (2015) find that knowledge does not lead to trust. Although from the consumers' point of view such certification must be of crucial importance to their organic food perception, studies underline that consumers distrust certification bodies (Canavari et al., 2002; Aarset et al., 2004). In the Romanian territory, Petrescu et al. (2017) even found that uncertified organic food (from farmers' market or self-production) is considered to be more "organic" than certified organic food.

Some studies investigated the premium price consumers are willing to pay for organic products and the factors explaining this premium (Schleenbecker & Hamm, 2013). In fact, although consumers can be strongly oriented toward organic food, driven by health concerns and taste, they are primarily deterred by price and lack of availability (Petrescu et al., 2017), and generally premium price continues to limit organic food consumption (Shafie & Rennie, 2012). Several studies showed that the high price of organic food has been found to be the main obstacle in its purchase (Roddy et al., 1996; Magnusson et al., 2001; Zanoli and Naspetti, 2002).

Last but not least, organic food has been said to exist in both the rational and emotional spheres, and it is in this latter context that we find the most intangible aspects of quality perception in relation to consumer preferences (Midmore et al., 2005). In fact, its quality attributes incorporate a wide range of symbolic, imagined and other less tangible characteristics, as organic food convey in the consumers mind an image along with a perception of sustainable agriculture and healthy lifestyle.

RESEARCH QUESTION, DESIGN, AND METHODOLOGY

We have applied a mixed case methodology, incorporating both qualitative and quantitative elements, aiming at exploring the role of Food Assemblies to boost organic farming sustainability. The inquiry has begun (P0) with a local survey administered directly during interviews to consumers of two different Food Assemblies located in the city of Turin, Italy. It was designed in order to understand what consumers currently know about organics, the relationship between their organic food decision-making, the sustainability knowledge and trust in local farmers and in the Food Assembly governance model. In a first phase (P1), a sample of 16 consumers and 4 organic producers has been recruited for a total of 4 collective meetings (three for consumers and one for organic producers). This phase was finalized at exploring and deepening interpretations of the survey results and adding insights into the configuration of customers' and producers' sustainability rationales. In a second phase (P2), the CEO of the Italian Food Assemblies (FA) and the Piedmont coordinator have been interviewed in order to describe and explain the origins and evolution of the case under study, namely the Italian Food Assembly, a particular form of AFN which has emerged in Italy since 2014, and then exponentially grown. The interviews have been conducted with the two managers in order to understand the business model of this innovative AFN and investigate if the food network governance and the whole emerging community can enhance the sustainability of organic small farmers, thus becoming a tool able to boost their competitiveness. In addition, the consumers' motivations to join the FA have been investigated, and consequently the possibility to define the ideal-type of FA customers, understanding their perception on sustainability. This analysis is justified by the fact that, previous studies reported that consumers' profiles are a relevant aspect in the determination of consumers' valuation both for local and organic food (Campbell et al., 2013; Costanigro et al., 2014; Gracia et al., 2014).

Consequently, the topic of our research lies at the intersection of these two developments, precisely (i) the aim of exploring the AFN role in shaping organic small farmers attitude toward sustainability, and (ii) to identify determinants and drivers of consumers' preferences for organic food system. Therefore our research question (RQ) is:

RQ: What are the main drivers leading Food Assembly (FA) in enhancing both small farmers sustainability, and customers' awareness of their sustainable purchasing choices, and how?

In order to answer the RQ, a case study has been developed (P3), as it is a particularly suitable method when the research question is in the form of a 'how' question (Brinkmann & Kvale, 2008) and enables to present situational explanations of the problematic under investigation, vivid illustrations from the reality of organizations, by providing insights into cause-effect relationships beyond what can be achieved from a quantitative analysis (Denzin & Lincoln, 2017). Figure 3 shows our research phases and their underlying rationales.

According to Yin (2014), case study methodology follows an approach of design and execution involving a criterion sampling strategy, data collection through multiple sources of evidence, an analysis strategy that aims at the greatest possible completeness of the targeted information throughout a sequential and cumulative analysis; a detailed and standardized research protocol, including an interview guide reflecting the areas of investigation. Particularly, a single-case design has been adopted (Eisenhardt, 1989; Eisenhardt et al., 2007). The rationales underlying this methodological choice relate to the exploratory nature of our study: the platform Food Assembly (FA) is employed as a revelatory case, particularly ap-

Figure 3. Phases (P. 0 – 3) of research and rationales
Source: authors' analysis

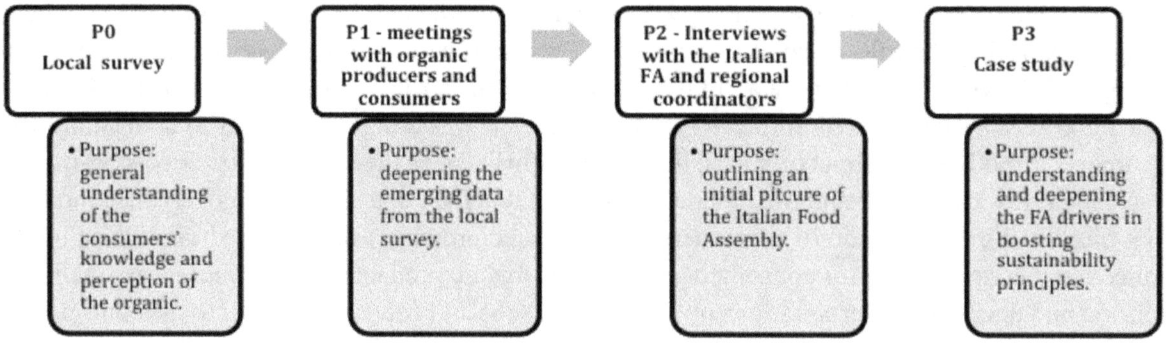

propriate in single-case design: as part of the European Network, Food Assembly is born in Italy very recently, but in less than two years gained the first positions in terms performance parameters, such as the number of active 'Assemblies' and their earnings. Despite its limits, the single-case design has the ability to richly describe the existence of a particular phenomenon (Siggelkow, 2007); and particularly this research sheds light on the Food Assembly Network and its ability in unlocking the organic small farmers sustainability.

Data have been collected between January 2017 and July 2017 from interviews, questionnaires, field observations, meetings, documentary analysis and review of internal and external information sources such as organization documentation, Internet sources and publicly available studies and reports. It is worth to notice that this research benefits also from the first author's active participation as a regular customer and member of the platform under study, that leads to an internal perspective consequently enriching data collection. Data analysis was carried out by using open and axial coding techniques (Strauss & Corbin, 1998) for identifying and linking the qualitative data collected to the research question. Particular attention has been paid to coding separately the categories of objective descriptive data on the one hand, and of interpretative data based on perceptions on the other. The analysis was inductively oriented. The first and the second authors read all the transcripts several times, in order to understand and better "own" the data. They separately made initial notes about their observations, then these notes were transformed into emerging codes, highlighting common patterns. Finally, the two researchers compared and reviewed the results to assess consistency. All inconsistencies were discussed and resolved. More in details, during the open coding, data have been first broken down by taking apart an observation, a sentence, a paragraph and giving each separate idea or event a conceptual label. Ideas and events have been then grouped in categories, pulling together around them groups of ideas and events as sub categories. Finally, archival data have been analysed to complement and triangulate the primary data in search of further precision but also to identify incoherencies or conflicting information. During the axial coding, concepts have been structured in sub-categories and then grouped in coherent and integrated conceptual categories. Finally, sub categories have been linked within and between categories to each other, and then the conceptual categories linked in a coherent explanatory scheme, facilitating the formulation of theoretical propositions.

The consumers' questionnaire survey consisted primarily of closed-ended questions which allowed quantification, while the qualitative follow-up was semi-structured and consisted mainly of open-ended questions that enabled the interviewees to express their opinion and reflections on the subject. The combination of quantitative and qualitative methods resulting in a mixed-method approach provides different types of information. This approach, by validating and strengthening our knowledge on social phenomena (Tashakkori & Teddlie, 2010) offers a detailed picture of the consumer perspectives and the connection between sustainability of organic farming system and the role played from the Italian Food Assembly platform for their organic consumption choices.

ANALYSIS AND RESULTS

This section presents the case study, namely the Italian Food Assembly, and analysis and results from the consumers' groups interviewed.

The Food Assembly Case

Food Assembly (FA) is an alternative food network (AFN) originated in France in 2010 with the name of "La Ruche Qui Dit Oui!" (meaning "the hive that says yes"), as a hybrid form of farmer's market and online buying group, which had rapidly growth across many European countries. The project landed in Italy in 2014, in Turin, throughout a start-up of the Polytechnic of Turin's incubator.

Specifically, Food Assembly is an online platform aiming at strengthening the relationship between local producers and consumers through organized pop-up markets, called 'Food Assemblies'. It is an innovative pop-up and pre-order food shopping system that bypasses the large distribution supply chains, bringing together the modern side of retail: the online ordering side, plus all the benefits of face-to-face retail. FA is a revolutionary AFN that combines a web technological platform with the short supply chain by creating a community 2.0, made by consumers with the desire to change the way they do their shopping. The sales platform enables direct exchanges between local farmers and the consumer community, once a week, creating small temporary markets, called "Hives" (in the Italian language, "Alveari").

In Italy, the first Assembly was born in Turin in November 2014. In 2017, the total FAs in Turin and province are 34, while in the other provinces of Piedmont there are 11 FAs, for a total of 44 FAs, of which 26 are developing, ready to open. Active FAs involve on average two small organic farmers, with a greater concentration in the urban area of the city of Turin, where in some FAs, particularly sensitive to organic food philosophy, there are also 5 or 6 organic producers with an average of 12 total producers, so almost half of the total supply offer. The network is mostly feminine, as 80% of Assembly leaders are women as well as about 67% of the members enrolled. The age of Piedmont FA producers is on average 35 years old, confirming that it is a business model that meets the favour of new generations, increasingly dedicated to small businesses linked to field and to agro-food production. This Italian network currently has more than 34.800 members between Assemblies Host/leader, Farmers/Producers and Consumers. See Table 1 for a summary.

The CEO of the Italian FA platform confirms that 2016 was the first full year of activity, with 121 assemblies registered on the site and with growing requests coming to the rhythm of one per day, especially from women host. The global turnover for 2016 was 500.000 euros and the trend is positive, in fact the objective is to reach by the end of the 2017, a turnover of two million euros.

At present, in Europe the network is composed by more than 1.400 assemblies, managed from FA leaders/host coming from all backgrounds, a variety of regions and all with different professional experiences and more than 100 employees who are constantly working to improve the platform and the

Table 1. The Food Assembly network

	Food Assemblies	Farmers/Producers	Consumers
2015	4	23	748
2016	121	419	25.000
2017 (May)	165	847	34.800

Source: authors' analysis on FA data

interaction between producers and consumers. In Italy the 165 assemblies are concentrated in the North (75%), particularly in Lombardy with 58 FAs and in Piedmont with 39 FAs, but the global coordinator says that the aim is to bring the FA network reality to the South.

Food Assemblies are a sort of new social enterprise model where solidarity and strong social relations impact on consumers' food consumption habits. The Italian coordinator says that the network aims at a more efficient distribution of local, fresh, genuine and zero-kilometre food products, combining the technological innovation of an e-commerce site with a direct market experience. It's a way to enable healthy local economies by encouraging a more environmentally friendly shopping experience. In the purchasing process, the FA is not an intermediary, but rather a simple service provider, in fact trade is done through direct channel (consumer and farmer/food maker), while the platform is used as a marketplace for meeting demand and supply.

The most innovative aspect with respect to other similar AFNs models is the union between social network technologies and territory, by combining their spatial organisation, their link to resources and their social relations (Dansero and Putilli, 2014; Doernberg et al., 2016). This business model is based on the community of consumers and local producers, emphasizing the genuineness of products, their quality, the traceability along the short chain, and the fairness of price for all the involved actors. Producers can communicate directly with the FA members both online by chat, forum or by email and off-line at the distribution day.

Each FA is managed by a leader/host (an individual or a group) who signs up to be an "assembly leader", deciding to bring a FA to his neighbourhood and give his community access to local products in a convenient and affordable way. His role is to find a place for the delivery of products (can be a café, a restaurant, an oratory, a neighbourhood house, etc.), contacting farmers and producers within 250 kilometres to join the initiative. He manages the FA local website, connected to the FA main website. All the producers are visited by the assembly leader, who controls, on the customer behalf, some key value factors related to sustainability dimensions, like soil quality, animal welfare, employment practices, production and products quality, the requirements for organic production, etc., ensuring the inclusion in the assembly only of truly sustainable realities.

In the Piedmont Food Assemblies, there are, overall, 41 producers, selling their products to the FA members; among them, 21 are organic small farmers that have a number of common features: the average number of employees is 4, of whom, approximately 75%, are a family member. Farmer owners is, on average, 35 years old and the 42% of them are women. The Utilized Agricultural Area (UAA) of the organic small farms, doesn't exceed, on average, 5 hectares (excluding the two largest organic farms each with, approximately, 60 hectares). Farmers net income tends to be at the level of the same size conventional farms in the FA, because, despite the high certification costs declared by organic producers, as well as the low productivity yields during the conversion period, the premium price fixed by the market, is able to remunerate all the factors of production and to ensure an adequate profit for the farmer. Another consideration arising from meetings with organic producers is their ability to take advantage of relationships within other FA producers, to plan joint production and distribution strategies, often through the provision of specific network contracts that favor the achievement, first of a critical mass production and in a second way, common distribution activities that both increase local development. In general, the economic feasibility of the organic production method, compared with the conventional one, depends, in particular, on a number of elements, such as: yields, production costs, premium prices, public funding support for agro-environmental and market policies, the management ability of agricultural entrepreneurs not only on the agronomic techniques adopted on the farm, but also and above all, by advanced commercial and communication strategies towards the consumer.A selection of locally sourced products are published on the page each week alongside prices, set by the producers who personally take care for the disclosure of any information about their company in general and the periodic availability of products to sell.

The consumers have to pre-browse and pre-order within a six-day period and paying the local products online, then go to the weekly Food Assembly collection point to meet farmers and producers and collect their purchases. Everyone in the FA –farmers, assembly leader and consumers - attend this weekly event

For the farmers and food producers interviewed, the advantage is that the food is pre-sold and the actual assembly event is a two-hour time slot necessary for people to collect their food. This is a way for farmers to use technology to sell their products while also having the social engagement with the community. As mentioned by Barabanova et al. 2015, the development of ICT can have an important impact on the farm practices and structure as well as on the ways the whole food chain operates.

This model also offers great flexibility: sellers have to attend events only if they have sold a minimum level of products online to make it worth their journey. Moreover, the FA service provider offers online tools to help them set up a personalized shop (on the e-commerce site), define fair prices and payment methods and keep track of accounting and customer analytics.

Products can be organic or conventional, in any case there is a strong emphasis on small farming system which share the philosophy of sustainability interpreted in all its dimensions (good governance, economic resilience, environmental friendly and social well-being). Indeed, among the members of the FA is shared an ethical report with the values driving their actions: transparency, cooperation, transition, entrepreneurship and creativity.

In the Piedmont Food Assemblies, there are, overall, 41 producers, selling their products to the FA members, among which 21 are organic small farmers that have a number of common features: the average number of employees is 4, of whom, approximately 75%, are family members. Farmer owners are, on average, 35 years old and the 42% of them are women. The Utilized Agricultural Area (UAA) of the organic small farms, doesn't exceed, on average, 5 hectares (excluding the two largest organic farms each with, approximately, 60 hectares). Farmers net income tends to be at the level of the same size conventional farms in the FA, because, despite the high certification costs declared by organic producers, as well as the low productivity yields during the conversion period, the premium price fixed by the market, is able to remunerate all the factors of production and to ensure an adequate profit for the farmer. Another consideration arising from meetings with organic producers is their ability to take advantage of relationships within other FA producers, to plan joint production and distribution strategies, often through the provision of specific network contracts that favor the achievement, first of a critical mass production and in a second way, common distribution activities that both increase local development. In general, the economic feasibility of the organic production method, compared with the conventional one, depends, in particular, on a number of elements, such as: yields, production costs, premium prices, public funding support for agro-environmental and market policies, the management ability of agricultural entrepreneurs not only on the agronomic techniques adopted on the farm, but also and above all, by advanced commercial and communication strategies towards the consumer. The producers are putting their heart in such model, they set their own prices, so that they are remunerated in a fair way. The farmer/food maker, when subscribing (free) to the network, determines the price of the products he would sell and the quantities available. On the total pre-tax turnover realized on each delivery, a commission on sales of 20% is deducted, which is fairly subdivided between the assembly leader and the platform, for service fees and for the use of the central IT support and the online platform. The "80-10-10" model allows a fair remuneration of the farmer/producer and at the same time maintain affordable prices for consumers; exactly the opposite of what it gets by selling to large organized distribution.

In conclusion, the FA brings thousands of producers and citizens together to the transition of finding new ways of producing and consuming food, fostering the global sustainability as an economic, environmental, and social asset in the communities, connecting people together and helping them achieve more than they could do alone. The FA network is an innovative project that combines sustainability and technology in a simple and intuitive way. By referencing the short and direct channel, consumers have the guarantee on the products they are going to buy and at the time of withdrawal they will be able to receive more information for an even more conscious purchasing act.

The Consumers' Perception

Among the consumers interviewed, there is the awareness that the FA and its community can enhance sustainability and resilience of food systems by connecting local initiatives into a global network where global challenges and successful solutions continue to build global solidarity. As underlined by some scholars (Blay-Palmer et al., 2016), consumers believe that organic food is safer compared to the conventional one. Indeed, throughout what appears to be a quasi-distracted act, often fast like spending money, it is possible by acting locally to contribute to the fight against exploitation, climate change, intensive farming, pollution of entire territories and ecosystems too far from us.

The interviewed consumers say that the main distinctive element of the FA is that it stimulates and revives urban areas, creating a strong sense of community, since the time of the expenditure retreat becomes social time for festive gatherings, allowing people of the neighbourhood to get together once a week. Consequently, this fosters individual relationships and increases social capital.

From our explorative analysis is possible to investigate the emerging consumers' profile. Regarding the socio-economic profile, our sample is composed of women (58,3%), aged between 35 to 49 year old (43,3%), mainly married (48,4%) and living in city residential suburbs, in families with an average of 3 individuals. Among them, 49,2% have child (on average 10 years old), 68,9% are employees, 14,8% self-employed, 1,3% students, 24% housewives and 8% retired. With reference to the education level, 51,7% holds a bachelor degree, while 38,3% a secondary school diploma; both education and household income is remarkably high.

The sample is widely represented by strong organic consumers (42%) who allocate, on average, 50% of food expenditure to buy organic products, both at the FA and other points of sale (such as large-scale distribution channels and specialized organic shops). More than 65% of the interviewed consumers express their motivation to take full advantage of the opportunity to meet the producers, in order to satisfy the curiosity about the products they have bought, as well as to share comments, ideas and recipes with other consumers. Only 20% of the consumers is represented by those who do not have time to spend on the market and buy online, simply coming to pick up the expense after work, before coming back home. The 93% of consumers are strongly satisfied with the relationship established with the community members (host, producers and other consumers) as well as the on-line and on-site organization of the network. In contrast, the most critical aspect of the consumers experience is the limited product diversification due to seasonal production with limited references. Therefore, the 45% of them ask for the introduction of new products.

During the interviews, organic consumers have been questioned on confidence and trust in organic farming methods, and they have assigned a particular value to social and environmental dimensions of sustainability. On the contrary, they have not given particular value to the good governance dimension, while the economic dimension of sustainability has been recognized as of average importance. Finally, regarding opinions and requests, 82% of the consumers agree with the prices paid for their purchase.

DISCUSSION AND CONCLUSION

The FA network's goal is to develop a regional food system able to provide locally-grown food at a price that "is fair" for both consumers and producers. Beside this declared goal, as an unexpected result, the FA has the ability to foster individual social relations between consumers, producers, and other kinds of stakeholders, thus increasing the social capital at both the community and the individual level. This is strongly confirmed by the interviewed consumers that affirm they are greatly satisfied with the relationship established with all the community members as well as with the on-line and on-site organization of the FA network. Specifically, in all collettive interviews, there is the idea that organic farmers are more engaged with values like preserving natural resources, using ecological processes with care to biodiversity and cycles adapted to local conditions. Additionally, it seems that the FA role of organic farmers' is to transmit these values to promote sustainable production and consumption practices, fostering knowledge and trust in the organic sector; certainly, a more complex role than the simple delivery of agri-food products. Therefore, FA provides an alternative to long organized distribution, but also a support for local producers by giving them an additional window to propose their products, using the innovative technology of a platform that enable relationship among FA members. Farmers and customers can easily track all products, contributing to the spread of a direct farmer-to-consumer relationship. Indeed, cloud technology is already making data sharing easier and leads to the development of the platform for the exchange of information between all parts of the FA community in a standardised format, as highlighted by Barbanova et al., 2015. Moreover, FA tries to give the best value and the right price for the food that must be produced according to the economic sustainability dimension, and last but not least, to trigger trust and good relationship between consumers and producers.

As many authors discussed in their studies (Marsden et al., 2000; Doernberg et al., 2016), FA farmers face high operating costs because of their disaggregated distribution system, having to deliver small quantities in so many assemblies, however, the interviewed producers have pointed out that inefficiency in distribution is offsetted by the fair price recognized in direct sales, without the interposition of an intermediary that normally takes 30-40% of the final price. Consumers increasingly perceive the sustainability added-values of organics products (e.g., environmentally friendly, healthy, safe and of high quality) so that in the community it rises the desire to buy organic food. At the same time, the fair price of organic food, good profits and attractiveness of organic farming to other FA farmers also encourages the increase and the conversion to organic farming.

Throughout the case study and the analysis of consumers' perception, it was possible to answer the research question and finally identify the FA drivers for fostering the organic agri-food sustainability. Table 2 represents a summary of the identified drivers, their impact, and implications for boosting the sustainability.

The main drivers are the combination between an e-commerce platform with the short supply chain that deeply impacts on the logic of doing shopping, because it enables direct exchanges between local farmers and the consumer community throughout small temporary markets. This has important implications for the enhancement of organic sustainability, because it can enable the communication of organic production throughout different and unusual channels. A second driver is the link between social network technologies and the territory. This driver impacts mainly on the local community – both producers and consumers – enabling a deeper and direct knowledge of the purchased products. This driver can consequently increase also the general awareness of organic food at a local level, thanks to a direct and face to face sharing between all the stakeholders. This prompt us to the third driver, namely strong social relations and solidarity. This driver can deeply change food consumption habits, involving cultural level, and obviously it can lead to a promotion of organic food culture too.

Table 2. FA drivers for the enhancement of small farmers sustainability and consumers awareness

Driver	Impact	Implications for Boosting Organic Sustainability
Web technology combined with short supply chains	On the logic of doing shopping: the sales platform enables direct exchanges between local farmers and the consumer community.	Enabling the promotion and knowledge of the organic food through unusual channels.
Social network technologies linked to the territory	• On the local community of consumers and producers. • On the genuineness of products, their quality, the traceability along the short chain, and the fairness of price for all the involved actors.	Increasing the awareness of organic food sustainability at a local level.
Solidarity and strong social relations	• On consumers' food consumption habits. • On the local healthy economies. • On a more environmentally friendly shopping experience.	Promoting the organic food culture thanks to a change in the food consumption habits at a deeper cultural level.
Direct communication	On transparency at all levels.	Directly communicating the logic behind the organic food production.
Great flexibility	On the ways producers can sell their products: sellers have to attend events only if they have sold a minimum level of produce online to make it worth their while; the FA service provider offers online tools to help them set up a personalized shop (on the e-commerce site), define fair prices and payment methods and keep track of accounting and customer analytics.	Possibility for the organic producers to personalize their sale, and promote in novel ways their products.
Ethical values	• On small farming systems which share the philosophy of sustainability interpreted in all its dimensions (good governance, economic resilience, environmental friendly and social well-being). • On transparency and cooperation.	Spreading of the values behind the organic food consumption and production.

The last three drivers are direct communication, great flexibility and ethical values. The direct communication impacts on the transparency at all the levels, while the great flexibility means an opportunity for producers to sell differently their products (i.e. with a personalized shop, define fair prices and payment methods as well as keep track of accounting and customer analytics). The last driver, the ethical values of FA, represents the philosophy of sustainability interpreted in all its dimensions, and has an important impact on stakeholders cooperation. These last drivers can enable a better and direct communication of the organic food sustainability and related values, together with the opportunity for organic producers to promote their products in innovative ways. In conclusion, our empirical analysis confirms that short supply chains can contribute to effectively enhance the sustainability of regional organic small farmers, along with future upscaling and diffusion perspectives.

LIMITATIONS AND FUTURE RESEARCH DIRECTIONS

This research is a first attempt to depict an emergent phenomenon, namely the Italian Food Assembly, and its potentialities in fostering the organic food sustainability. It is not free from limitations, because case studies approach faces criticism in terms of lack of generalizability. However, the objective of a case study is to pinpoint singular examples, stories and phenomena that although not generally perceived, are significant enough, both from a theoretical and applied perspective, to have an impact on the subject of study, and on the conclusions and recommendations that can be made upon completion of that study. This is exactly what we have attempted to do with this research: the Italian FA represents a revelatory example of how the Food Assembly Network can further foster the organic farmers sustainability, starting from singular countries' experiences. However, this research suffers an evident limit, namely the absence of a deeper investigation of how the European Food Assembly Network developed in other European countries, different from Italy from both a cultural and a socio-economical point of view. Instead, investigating other European cases, along with the Italian one, would enable a great comparison and a deeper knowledge about the phenomenon under study. Thus, this represents the next step in the authors' research agenda in order to fill the gap.

REFERENCES

Aarset, B., Beckmann, S., Bigne, E., Beveridge, M., Bjorndal, T., Bunting, J., ... Young, J. (2004). The European consumers' understanding and perceptions of the "organic" food regime: The case of aquaculture. *British Food Journal*, *106*(2), 93–105. doi:10.1108/00070700410516784

Abitabile, C., Giuca, S., Madau, F., & Sardone, R. (2015). Le politiche per il consumo sostenibile e il caso dei prodotti biologici. *Agriregionieuropa (Ancona)*, *11*(41), 28–32.

Adams, D., & Salois, M. (2010). Local versus organic: A turn in consumer preferences and willingness to pay. *Renewable Agriculture and Food Systems*, *25*(4), 331–341. doi:10.1017/S1742170510000219

Agovino, M., Crociata, A., Quaglione, D., Sacco, P., & Sarra, A. (2017). Good Taste Tastes Good. Cultural Capital as a Determinant of Organic Food Purchase by Italian Consumers: Evidence and Policy Implications. *Ecological Economics*, *141*, 66–75. doi:10.1016/j.ecolecon.2017.05.029

Alrøe, H., Moller, H., Læssøe, J., & Noe, E. (2016). Opportunities and challenges for multicriteria assessment of food system sustainability. *Ecology and Society*, *21*(1), art38. doi:10.5751/ES-08394-210138

Alrøe, H. F., & Noe, E. (2016). Sustainability assessment and complementarity. *Ecology and Society*, *21*(1), 30. doi:10.5751/ES-08220-210130

Alrøe, H. F., Sautier, M., Legun, K., Whitehead, J., Noe, E., Moller, H., & Manhire, J. (2017). Performance versus Values in Sustainability Transformation of Food Systems. *Sustainability*, *9*(3), 332. doi:10.3390u9030332

Annunziata, A., & Vecchio, R. (2015). Organic farming and sustainability in food choices: An analysis of consumer preference in Southern Italy. *Agriculture and Agricultural Science Procedia*, *8*, 193–200. doi:10.1016/j.aaspro.2016.02.093

Arbenz, M., Gould, D., & Stopes, C. (2016). *ORGANIC 3.0 – for truly sustainable farming and consumption. 2nd updated edition*. Bonn: IFOAM Organics International, Bonn and SOAAN.

Arbenz, M., Gould, D., & Stopes, C. (2017). ORGANIC 3.0 - the vision of the global organic movement and the need for scientific support. *Organic Agriculture*, 1–9.

Barabanova, Y., Zanoli, R., Schlüter, M., & Stopes, C. (2015). *Transforming Food and Farming: An Organic Vision for Europe in 2030*. Brussels: IFOAM EU.

Barbera, F., Corsi, A., Dansero, E., Giaccaria, P., Peano, C., & Puttilli, M. (2014). Cosa c'è di alternativo negli Alternative Food Networks? Un'agenda di ricerca per un approccio interdisciplinare. *Scienze del territorio,* (2), 35 - 44.

Barbera, F., & Dagnes, J. (2016). Building Alternatives from the Bottom-up: The Case of Alternative Food Networks. *Agriculture and Agricultural Science Procedia,* (8), 324 – 331.

Basha, M. B., Mason, C., Shamsudin, M. F., Hussain, H. I., & Salem, M. A. (2015). Consumers attitude towards organic food. *Procedia Economics and Finance*, *31*, 444–452. doi:10.1016/S2212-5671(15)01219-8

Bazzani, C., & Canavari, M. (2013). Alternative agri-food networks and short food supply chains: A review of the literature. *Economia Agro-Alimentare*, *15*(2), 11–34. doi:10.3280/ECAG2013-002002

Bazzani, C., & Canavari, M. (2017). Is local a matter of food miles or food traditions? *Italian Journal of Food Science*, *29*(3), 505–517.

Beck, A., Cuoco, E., Häring, A. M., Kahl, J., Koopmans, C., Micheloni, C., & Rasmussen, I. A. (2014). *Strategic Research and Innovation Agenda for Organic Food and Farming*. Brussels: Tp Organics.

Blay-Palmer, A., Custot, J., & Sonnino, R. (2016). A food politics of the possible? Growing sustainable food systems through networks of knowledge. *Agriculture and Human Values*, *33*(1), 27–43. doi:10.100710460-015-9592-0

Blockeel, J., Baumgart, L., Landert, J., & Schrader, C. (2016). Sustainability performance of organic and conventional farms in Ticino: How well does the SMART-Farm Tool capture the differences? *Proceedings of the 20th Conference of the Environmental and Sustainability Management Accounting Network (EMAN).*

Bond, C. A., Thilmany, D., & Bond, J. K. (2008). What to choose? The value of label claims to fresh produce consumers. *Journal of Agricultural and Resource Economics*, *33*, 402–427.

Brinkmann, S., & Kvale, S. (2008). Ethics in qualitative psychological research. In C. Willig & W. Stainton-Rogers (Eds.), *The SAGE Handbook of Qualitative Research in Psychology* (pp. 263–279). New Delhi: Sage. doi:10.4135/9781848607927.n15

Brunori, G., Galli, F., Barjolle, D., Van Broekhuizen, R., Colombo, L., Giampietro, M., ... de Roest, K. (2016). Are local food chains more sustainable than global food chains? considerations for assessment. *Sustainability*, *8*(5), 449. doi:10.3390u8050449

Campbell, A., Fischel, S., Bowman, N., Duffy, S., Sedler, M., & Thornton, S. (2013). Retrospective analysis of outcomes after IVF using an aneuploidy risk model derived from time-lapse imaging without PGS. *Reproductive Biomedicine Online*, *27*(2), 140–146. doi:10.1016/j.rbmo.2013.04.013 PMID:23683847

Canavari, M., Bazzani, G.M., Spadoni, R., & Regazzi, D. (2002). Food safety and organic fruit demand in Italy: a survey. *British Food Journal*, *104*(3/4/5), 220–232.

Canfora, I. (2016). Is the short food supply chain an efficient solution for sustainability in food market? *Agriculture and Agricultural Science Procedia,* (8), 402-407.

Capone, R., El Bilali, H., & Bottalico, F. (2016). Assessing the sustainability of typical agro-food products: Insights from Apulia region, Italy. *New Medit*, *15*(1), 28–36.

Carpio, C. E., & Isengildina-Massa, O. (2009). Consumer willingness to pay for locally grown products: The case of South Carolina. *Agribusiness*, *25*(3), 412–426. doi:10.1002/agr.20210

Chryssochoidis, G. (2000). Repercussions of consumer confusion for late introduced differentiated products. *European Journal of Marketing*, *34*(5/6), 705–722. doi:10.1108/03090560010321992

Colucci, F., Menegoni, P., Nocenzi, M., & Presenti, O. (2012). L'evoluzione dei modelli di consumo e degli stili alimentari tra sostenibilità e benessere. *Rivista di studi sulla sostenibilità*, *2*, 47-67.

Corsi, A., Novelli, S., & Pettenati, G. (2014). *Alternative Food Networks in Piedmont: determinants of on-farm and off-farm direct sales by farmers*. Paper presented at the Third Congress of Italian Association of Agricultural and Applied Economics (AIEAA), Alghero, Italy.

Costanigro, M., Kroll, S., Thilmany, D., & Bunning, M. (2014). Is it love for local/organic or hate for conventional? Asymmetric effects of information and taste on label preferences in an experimental auction. *Food Quality and Preference*, *31*, 91–105. doi:10.1016/j.foodqual.2013.08.008

Dansero, E., & Puttilli, M. (2014). Multiple territorialities of alternative food networks: Six cases from Piedmont, Italy. Local Environment. *The International Journal of Justice and Sustainability*, *19*(6), 626–643.

Daugbjerg, C., Smed, S., Andersen, L. M., & Schvartzman, Y. (2014). Improving eco-labelling as an environmental policy instrument: Knowledge, trust and organic consumption. *Journal of Environmental Policy and Planning*, *16*(4), 559–575. doi:10.1080/1523908X.2013.879038

Denzin, N. K., & Lincoln, Y. S. (2017). *The Sage Handbook of qualitative research* (5th ed.). Thousand Oaks, CA: Sage Publications.

Doernberg, A., Zasada, I., Bruszewska, K., Skoczowski, B., & Piorr, A. (2016). Potentials and Limitations of Regional Organic Food Supply: A Qualitative Analysis of Two Food Chain Types in the Berlin Metropolitan Region. *Sustainability*, *8*(11), 1125. doi:10.3390u8111125

Drichoutis, A. C., Lazaridis, P., & Nayga, R. M. Jr. (2006). Consumers' use of nutritional labels: A review of research studies and issues. *Academy of Marketing Science Review*, *2006*, 1.

Eisenhardt, K. M. (1989). Building theories from case study research. *Academy of Management Review*, *14*(4), 532–550.

Eisenhardt, K. M., & Graebner, M. E. (2007). Theory Building from Cases: Opportunities and Challenges. *Academy of Management Journal*, *50*(1), 25–32. doi:10.5465/AMJ.2007.24160888

European Commission. (2013). *Facts and figures on organic agriculture in the European Union*. Retrieved January 10, 2017, from http://ec.europa.eu/agriculture/markets-and-prices/more-reports/pdf/organic-2013_en.pdf

FiBL & IFOAM. (2016). *The world of organic agriculture. Statistics and emerging trends 2016*. Bonn, Germany: FiBL and IFOAM. Retrieved January 10, 2017, from https://shop.fibl.org/CHen/mwdownloads/download/link/id/785/?ref=1)

Food and Agriculture Organisation of the United Nations (FAO). (2013). *Sustainability Assessment of Food and Agriculture Systems (SAFA)*. FAO. Retrieved January 10, 2017, from http://www.fao.org/nr/sustainability/sustainability-assessments-safa/en/

Forssell, S., & Lankoski, L. (2015). The sustainability promise of alternative food networks: An examination through "alternative" characteristics. *Agriculture and Human Values*, *32*(1), 63–75. doi:10.100710460-014-9516-4

Fotopoulos, C., Krystallis, A., & Ness, M. (2003). Wine produced by organic grapes in Greece: Using means-end chains analysis to reveal organic buyers' purchasing motives in comparison to the non-buyers. *Food Quality and Preference*, *14*(7), 549–566. doi:10.1016/S0950-3293(02)00130-1

Godfray, H. C. J., Beddington, J. R., Crute, I. R., Haddad, L., Lawrence, D., Muir, J. F., ... Toulmin, C. (2010). Food Security: The Challenge of Feeding 9 Billion People. *Science*, *327*(5967), 812–818. doi:10.1126cience.1185383 PMID:20110467

Goodman, D. (2003). The quality 'turn' and alternative food practices: Reflections and agenda. *Journal of Rural Studies*, *19*(1), 1–7. doi:10.1016/S0743-0167(02)00043-8

Goodman, D., DuPuis, E. M., & Goodman, M. K. (2012). *Alternative food networks: Knowledge, practice, and politics*. London: Routledge.

Gracia, A., Barreiro-Hurlé, J., & Galán, B. L. (2014). Are local and organic claims complements or substitutes? A consumer preferences study for eggs. *Journal of Agricultural Economics*, *65*(1), 49–67. doi:10.1111/1477-9552.12036

Gruère Guillaume, P. (2015). An Analysis of the Growth in Environmental Labelling and Information Schemes. *Journal of Consumer Policy*, *38*(1), 1–18. doi:10.100710603-014-9275-z

Hamzaoui-Essoussi, L., & Zahaf, M. (2012). Canadian organic food consumers' profile and their willingness to pay premium prices. *Journal of International Food & Agribusiness Marketing*, *24*(1), 1–21. doi:10.1080/08974438.2011.621834

Harper, G. C., & Makatouni, A. (2002). Consumer perception of organic food production and farm animal welfare. *British Food Journal*, *104*(3/4/5), 287-299.

Hill, H., & Lynchehaun, F. (2002). Organic milk: Attitudes and consumption patterns. *British Food Journal*, *104*(7), 526–542. doi:10.1108/00070700210434570

Hughner, R. S., McDonagh, P., Prothero, A., Shultz, C. J., & Stanton, J. (2007). Who are organic food consumers? A compilation and review of why people purchase organic food. *Journal of Consumer Behaviour*, *6*(1), 1–17.

Jarosz, L. (2008). The city in the country: Growing alternative food networks in Metropolitan areas. *Journal of Rural Studies*, *24*(3), 231–244. doi:10.1016/j.jrurstud.2007.10.002

Jouzi, Z., Azadi, H., Taheri, F., Zarafshani, K., Gebrehiwot, K., Van Passel, S., & Lebailly, P. (2017). Organic farming and small-scale farmers: Main opportunities and challenges. *Ecological Economics*, *132*, 144–154. doi:10.1016/j.ecolecon.2016.10.016

Kirwan, J. (2006). The interpersonal world of direct marketing: Examining conventions of quality at UK farmers' markets. *Journal of Rural Studies*, *22*(3), 301–312. doi:10.1016/j.jrurstud.2005.09.001

Magnusson, M. K., Arvola, A., Koivisto Hursti, U. K., Aberg, L., & Sjoden, P. O. (2001). Attitudes towards organic foods among Swedish consumers. *British Food Journal*, *103*(3), 209–227. doi:10.1108/00070700110386755

Makatouni, A. (2002). What motivates consumers to buy organic food in the UK? Results from a qualitative study. *British Food Journal*, *104*(3/4/5), 345-352.

Marsden, T., Banks, J., & Bristow, G. (2000). Food Supply Chain Approaches: Exploring their Role in Rural Development. *Sociologia Ruralis*, *40*(4), 424–438. doi:10.1111/1467-9523.00158

Marsden, T., & Smith, E. (2005). Ecological entrepreneurship: Sustainable development in local communities through quality food production and local branding. *Geoforum*, *36*(4), 440–451. doi:10.1016/j.geoforum.2004.07.008

Matacena, R. (2016). Linking alternative food networks and urban food policy: A step forward in the transition towards a sustainable and equitable food system? *International Review of Social Research*, *6*(1), 49–58. doi:10.1515/irsr-2016-0007

Maye, D., & Kirwan, J. (2010). Alternative Food Networks. *International Journal of Agricultural & Food*, *20*(3), 383–389.

Mercati, V. (2016). Organic Agriculture as a Paradigm of Sustainability: Italian Food and its Progression in the Global Market. *Agriculture and Agricultural Science Procedia*, *8*, 798–802. doi:10.1016/j.aaspro.2016.02.071

Midmore, P., Naspetti, S., Sherwood, A. M., Vairo, D., Wier, M., & Zanoli, R. (2005). *Consumer attitudes to quality and safety of organic and low input foods; a review. Report of EU-funded project "Improving Quality and Safety and Reduction of Cost in the European Organic and 'Low Input' Food Supply Chains."*. Aberystwyth, UK: University of Wales.

Migliore, G., Forno, F., Guccione, G. D., & Schifani, G. (2014). Food Community Networks as sustainable self-organized collective action: A case study of a solidarity purchasing group. *New Medit*, *13*(4), 54–62.

Milestad, R., Bartel-Kratochvil, R., Leitner, H., & Axmann, P. (2010). Being close: The quality of social relationships in a local organic cereal and bread network in Lower Austria. *Journal of Rural Studies*, *26*(3), 228–240. doi:10.1016/j.jrurstud.2010.01.004

Murdoch, J., Marsden, T., & Banks, J. (2000). Quality, nature, and embeddedness: Some theoretical considerations in the context of the food sector. *Economic Geography*, *76*(2), 107–125. doi:10.2307/144549

Naspetti, S., Lampkin, N., Nicholas, P., Stolze, M., & Zanoli, R. (2011). Organic supply chain collaboration: A case study in eight EU countries. *Journal of Food Products Marketing*, *14*(2), 141–162. doi:10.1080/10454446.2011.548733

Noe, E., & Alrøe, H. F. (2015). Sustainable agriculture issues explained by differentiation and structural coupling using social systems analysis. *Agronomy for Sustainable Development*, *35*(1), 133–144. doi:10.100713593-014-0243-4

Padel, S., & Foster, C. (2005). Exploring the gap between attitudes and behaviour: Understanding why consumers buy or do not buy organic food. *British Food Journal*, *107*(8), 606–625. doi:10.1108/00070700510611002

Padel, S., Röcklinsberg, H., & Schmid, O. (2009). The implementation of organic principles and values in the European Regulation for organic food. *Food Policy*, *34*(3), 245–251. doi:10.1016/j.foodpol.2009.03.008

Padel, S., Vaarst, M., & Zaralis, K. (2015). Supporting Innovation in Organic Agriculture: A European Perspective Using Experience from the SOLID Project. *Sustainable Agriculture Research*, *4*(3), 32–41. doi:10.5539ar.v4n3p32

Peano, C., Migliorini, P., & Sottile, F. (2014). A methodology for the sustainability assessment of agri-food systems: An application to the Slow Food Presidia project. *Ecology and Society*, *19*(4), art24. doi:10.5751/ES-06972-190424

Petrescu, D. C., & Petrescu-Mag, R. M. (2015). Organic food perception: Fad, or healthy and environmentally friendly? A case on Romanian consumers. *Sustainability*, *7*(9), 12017–12031. doi:10.3390u70912017

Petrescu, D. C., Petrescu-Mag, R. M., Burny, P., & Azadi, H. (2017). A new wave in Romania: Organic food. Consumers' motivations, perceptions, and habits. *Agroecology and Sustainable Food Systems*, *41*(1), 46–75. doi:10.1080/21683565.2016.1243602

Raffestin, C., & Butler, S. A. (2012). Space, territory and territoriality. *Environment and Planning. D, Society & Space*, *30*(1), 121–141. doi:10.1068/d21311

Rahmann, G., Ardakani, M. R., Bàrberi, P., Boehm, H., Canalis, S., Chander, M., ... Hamm, U. (2016). Organic Agriculture 3.0 is innovation with research. *Organic Agriculture*, 1–29.

Renting, H., Marsden, T. K., & Banks, J. (2003). Understanding Alternative Food Networks: Exploring the role of short food supply chains in rural development. *Environment and planning. Part. A*, *35*(3), 393–411.

Rimal, A. P., Moon, W., & Balasubramanian, S. (2005). Agro-biotechnology and organic food purchase in the United Kingdom. *British Food Journal*, *107*(2), 84–97. doi:10.1108/00070700510579162

Rockström, J., Steffen, W., Noone, K., Persson, Å., Chapin, F. S. I. I. I., Lambin, E., ... Foley, J. (2009). Planetary boundaries: Exploring the safe operating space for humanity. *Ecology and Society*, *14*(2), art32. doi:10.5751/ES-03180-140232

Roddy, G., Cowan, C. A., & Hutchinson, G. (1996). Consumer attitudes and behaviour to organic foods in Ireland. *Journal of International Consumer Marketing*, *9*(2), 41–63. doi:10.1300/J046v09n02_03

Roininen, K., Arvola, A., & Lähteenmäki, L. (2006). Exploring consumers' perceptions of local food with two different qualitative techniques: Laddering and word association. *Food Quality and Preference*, *17*(1), 20–30. doi:10.1016/j.foodqual.2005.04.012

Sage, C. (2003). Social embeddedness and relations of regard: Alternative 'good food' networks in south-west Ireland. *Journal of Rural Studies*, *19*(1), 47–60. doi:10.1016/S0743-0167(02)00044-X

Scarpa, R., & Del Giudice, T. (2004). Market segmentation via mixed logit: Extra-virgin olive oil in urban Italy. *Journal of Agricultural & Food Industrial Organization*, *2*(1). doi:10.2202/1542-0485.1080

Schader, C., Baumgart, L., Landert, J., Muller, A., Ssebunya, B., Blockeel, J., ... Gerrard, C. (2016). Using the sustainability monitoring and assessment routine (smart) for the systematic analysis of trade-offs and synergies between sustainability dimensions and themes at farm level. *Sustainability*, *8*(3), 274. doi:10.3390u8030274

Schader, C., Grenz, J., Meier, M., & Stolze, M. (2014). Scope and precision of sustainability assessment approaches to food systems. *Ecology and Society*, *19*(3), 42. doi:10.5751/ES-06866-190342

Schleenbecker, R., & Hamm, U. (2013). Consumers' Perception of Organic Product Characteristics. A Review. *Appetite*, *71*, 420–429. doi:10.1016/j.appet.2013.08.020 PMID:24012637

Seyfang, G. (2006). Ecological citizenship and sustainable consumption: Examining local organic food networks. *Journal of Rural Studies*, *22*(4), 383–395. doi:10.1016/j.jrurstud.2006.01.003

Shafie, F. A., & Rennie, D. (2012). Consumer perceptions towards organic food. *Procedia: Social and Behavioral Sciences*, *49*, 360–367. doi:10.1016/j.sbspro.2012.07.034

Siggelkow, N. (2007). Persuasion with case studies. *Academy of Management Journal*, *50*(1), 20–24. doi:10.5465/AMJ.2007.24160882

Smed, S., Andersen, L. M., Kærgård, N., & Daugbjerg, C. (2013). A Matter of Trust: How Trust Influence Organic Consumption. *The Journal of Agricultural Science*, *5*(7), 91.

SOAAN-IFOAM. (2013). *Best practice guidelines for agriculture and value chains*. Retrieved November 15, 2016, from www.ifoam.bio/sites/default/files/best_practice_guideline_v1.0_ratified.pdf

Sonnino, R., & Marsden, T. K. (2006). Beyond the divide: Rethinking relations between alternative and conventional food networks in Europe. *Journal of Economic Geography*, *6*(2), 181–199. doi:10.1093/jeg/lbi006

Spaargaren, G., Oosterveer, P., & Loeber, A. (2011). *Sustainability Transitions in Food Consumption, Retail and Production. Food practices in transition: changing food consumption, retail and production in the age of reflexive modernity*. New York, NY: Routeledge.

Strauss, A., & Corbin, J. (1998). *Basics of qualitative research: Techniques and procedures for developing grounded theory*. Thousand Oaks, CA: Sage Publications.

Tashakkori, A., & Teddlie, C. (2010). *Sage Handbook of Mixed Methods in Social & Behavioral Research*. Thousand Oaks, CA: Sage Publications. doi:10.4135/9781506335193

Thorsøe, M. H. (2015). Maintaining trust and credibility in a Continuously Evolving Organic Food System. *Journal of Agricultural & Environmental Ethics*, *28*(4), 767–787. doi:10.100710806-015-9559-6

Thorsøe, M. H., Christensen, T., & Povlsen, K. K. (2016). Organics' are good, but we don't know exactly what the term means! Trust and Knowledge in Organic Consumption. *Food, Culture, & Society*, *19*(4), 681–704. doi:10.1080/15528014.2016.1243767

Thorsøe, M. H., Kjeldsen, C., & Noe, E. (2017). It's never too late to join the revolution!–Enabling new modes of production in the contemporary Danish food system. *European Planning Studies*, *25*(7), 1166–1183. doi:10.1080/09654313.2016.1267112

Torjusen, H., Lieblein, G., Wandel, M., & Francis, C. A. (2001). Food system orientation and quality perception among consumers and producers of organic food in Hedmark County, Norway. *Food Quality and Preference*, *12*(3), 207–216. doi:10.1016/S0950-3293(00)00047-1

Torquati, B., Viganò, E., & Taglioni, C. (2016). Construction of Alternative Food Networks for organic products: A case study of "Organized Groups of Supply and Demand". *New Medit*, *15*(4), 53–63.

Tregear, A. (2011). Progressing knowledge in alternative and local food networks: Critical reflections and a research agenda. *Journal of Rural Studies*, *27*(4), 419–430. doi:10.1016/j.jrurstud.2011.06.003

Wander, M., & Bugge, A. (1997). Environmental concern in consumer evaluation of food quality. *Food Quality and Preference*, *8*(1), 19–26. doi:10.1016/S0950-3293(96)00004-3

Whatmore, S., Stassart, P., & Renting, H. (2003). What's alternative about food networks? *Environment & Planning*, *35*(3), 389–391. doi:10.1068/a3621

Willer, H., & Lernoud, J. (Eds.). (2017). *The World of Organic Agriculture. Statistics and Emerging Trends 2017. Research Institute of Organic Agriculture (FiBL)*. Frick & IFOAM – Organics International Bonn.

Yin, R. K. (2014). *Case study research: Design and methods* (5th ed.). Thousand Oaks, CA: Sage Publications.

Zanoli, R., & Naspetti, S. (2001). *Values and Ethics in Organic Food Consumption.* Paper presented at the third EurSafe Congress on: "Food Quality and Food Ethics," Florence, Italy.

Zanoli, R., & Naspetti, S. (2002). Consumer motivations in the purchase of organic food: A means-end approach. *British Food Journal, 104*(8), 643–653. doi:10.1108/00070700210425930

Zepeda, L., & Deal, D. (2009). Organic and local food consumer behaviour: Alphabet Theory. *International Journal of Consumer Studies, 33*(6), 697–705. doi:10.1111/j.1470-6431.2009.00814.x

KEY TERMS AND DEFINITIONS

Alternative Food Network: Emerging networks of producers, consumers, and other actors that embody alternatives to the more standardised industrial mode of food supply. They are environmentally benign, based on artisanal, natural, and organic production methods, territorially embedded, and usually characterized by small scale.

Organic Farming: A production system that sustains the health of soils, ecosystems, and people. It relies on ecological processes, biodiversity, and cycles adapted to local conditions, with forms of cultivation and breeding that tend to enhance and preserve the biological production systems, without the use of synthetic chemicals.

Sustainability: The combination of environmental, social, economic, and good governance aspects in business processes, products, and services.

Chapter 5
Determinants of Sustainability Reporting in Medium Enterprises

Inna Sousa Paiva
Lisbon University Institute, Portugal

Irina Filipa Gavancha
Lusófona University of Humanities and Technology, Portugal

ABSTRACT

The importance of the relationship between sustainability and accountability in the business world has increased in the last few years. This chapter examines the determinants of sustainability reporting in 100 medium enterprises operating in Portugal with an excellent financial performance over the past three years. The main results demonstrate that firm characteristics, such as size, ownership structure, and sales growth, contribute significantly to explaining sustainability in these firms. The authors also find that medium firms exhibit a lack of interest in changing their business conduct to improve sustainability. Sustainability accounting is in a relatively early phase of development and the authors hope that this study will further the understanding of the firm characteristics that explain sustainability in medium enterprises.

INTRODUCTION

In recent years, the importance of Corporate Social Responsibility (CSR) for the economy in general and for firms in particular has attracted growing interest due to the competitive success and advantages it generates (Weber, 2008; Gallardo-Vázquez & Sánchez-Hernández, 2014). The business world is encouraged to work actively towards CSR because, in addition to providing a business opportunity in today's world, it frequently reflects the expectations of firms' customers, human resources, society, and stakeholders (Mark-Herbert & Von Schantz, 2007).

DOI: 10.4018/978-1-5225-5267-3.ch005

Nowadays, firms are being encouraged to change their business conduct so as to address sustainability issues and, as a result, the accounting community has been discussing the relationship between accounting and sustainability and trying to understand how accounting can face this challenge (Passetti, Cinquini, Marelli, Tenucci, 2014; Burritt, 2012).

Empirical studies have demonstrated that there is no universal and cohesive method to measure sustainability and drawn attention to the problem of multiple and contrasting goals (Gallardo-Vázquez & Sanchez-Hernandez, 2014; Montiel, 2008; Saeidi, Sofian, Saeidi, Saeidi, & Saaeidi, 2015), the influence of internal and external factors (Christ & Burritt, 2013), and specifically industrial contexts (Azapagic, 2004; Nordheim & Barrasso, 2007). While the environmental and economic dimensions have been the focus of many of these studies (Saeidi et al., 2015; Bouwens & Abernethy, 2000; Castilla-Polo, Sánchez-Hernández, & Gallardo-Vázquez, 2017; Clarkson, Li, Richardson, & Vasvari, 2008), the accounting dimensions of sustainability have been neglected due to the difficulty of assessing some of these issues from an accounting perspective (Cooper, Coulson, & Taylor, 2011; Gallhofer, Haslam, & van der Walt, 2011).

In the last few years, a discussion has evolved on sustainability accounting in small and medium businesses in an attempt to understand how accounting can respond to the challenges of sustainable development. In light of this, this chapter analyzes the determinants of corporate social responsibility in medium sized firms that stand out for their excellent financial performance. In order to rule out effects due to differences in the regulatory environment, we focus on Portuguese private firms. There is a large predominance of small and medium-sized companies (SMEs) in the Portuguese economy as compared to listed companies. Although CSR is mainly discussed in the context of larger companies, it also is a strategic tool to enhance the competitiveness of SMEs. This makes it an ideal environment to study sustainability in private firms. The data set is formed by 100 medium enterprises operating in Portugal in 2016. .

The main results provide evidence of large firms investing in sustainability management and external reporting to increase visibility and to inform stakeholders. They also demonstrate that the control of power in medium firms could lead to less interest in adopting business conduct that addresses sustainability. More specifically, our study reveals that firms with higher ownership concentration and sales growth characteristics have great difficulty in accepting changes leading to greater sustainability.

Sustainability accounting is in a relatively early phase of development and our study makes several contributions to the literature addressing medium-sized enterprises. Our aim is to foster a more balanced relationship between business and environmental and social issues.

This chapter is structured as follows: Section 2 reviews the concept and measurement of corporate social responsibility, and relationship with accounting. Section 3 develops the hypotheses of the determinants of sustainability. Section 4 describes the data collection process, variables, measurement and methodology. Section 5 presents the findings and section 6 concludes and suggests avenues for further research.

CORPORATE SOCIAL RESPONSIBILITY

Concept, Measurement, and Relationship With Accounting

The term corporate social responsibility is used universally to describe the practice of good corporate citizenship. CSR comprises a number of corporate activities that focus on the welfare of stakeholder groups other than investors, such as customers, employees, suppliers, and society.

There is no common definition of CSR. Davis (1973, 312) defines CSR as "the firm's considerations of, and response to, issues beyond the narrowly economic, technical, and legal requirements of the firm to accomplish social benefits along with the traditional economic gains which the firm seeks". The European Commission (2011, 4) defines CSR as "a concept whereby companies integrate social and environmental concerns in their business operations and in their interaction with their stakeholders on voluntary basis".

Corporate sustainability is a common term used in association with CSR. The activities of corporate sustainability are very similar to those of CSR but somewhat broader in scope. Corporate sustainability focuses on long-term shareholder value by incorporating the best practices in the following areas: ethics, governance, transparency, business relationship, financial return, product value, employment practice and environmental protection (Epstein, 2008). According to previous literature (e.g. Galbreath & Shum, 2012; Montiel, 2008; Saeidi et al., 2015), there is no universal and cohesive method to measure CSR. Previous empirical studies developed indicator-based methods for this purpose. The CSR conceptualization presented by Carroll (1979) consists of four main dimensions of CSR (legal, economic, discretionary and ethical) in order to determine the firm's CSR orientation. This is considered the first attempt to capture the multidimensional nature of CSR and was subsequently developed by Maignan and Ferrell (2000, 2001) by ranking the instruments used to assess CSR. Quazi and O'Brien (2000) designed a scale with a two-dimensional model to measure attitudes to CSR and the results of implementing socially responsible actions.

Previous literature have demonstrated that there is no universal and cohesive method to measure sustainability. Recent studies have used accounting and reporting tools to measure the CSR orientation of firms. Schaltegger, Kleiber, and Muller (2002) identified and analyzed 46 different tools and divided them into three dimensions: environmental, social and integrative. This method has been extensively used to measure sustainability in empirical studies (Schaltegger et al., 2002; Passetti et al., 2014). It develops and optimizes product characteristics and operational activities in the relationship between the economic value added, use of natural resources and the firm's objectives.

Some studies developed models to measure CSR in specific contexts. Veleva and Ellenbecker (2001) presented a tool to foster business sustainability based on indicators of sustainable production for the industry sector. In the same line, Azapagic (2004) developed sustainability indicators as a tool for performance assessment and improvements in the metallic, construction and industrial minerals sectors. Nordheim and Barrasso (2007) developed indicators for the aluminum industry and Acosta-Alba, López-Ridaura, van der Werf, Leterme, and Corson, (2012) analyzed sustainability by exploring new indicator configurations for agricultural land.

Other methods for measuring CSR, use content analysis of financial and accounting documents, case studies, surveys, databases or indices. For example, Ullman (1985) examined the extent of social disclosure by analyzing annual reports, and Clarkson et al. (2008) developed a content analysis index to evaluate the level of environmental disclosure in sustainability reporting. Keeble, Topiol, and Berkeley, (2003) employed case studies to explore the use of proxies for business sustainability. Passetti et al. (2014) used combined data, namely database and survey, to capture the environmental, social and integrative tools of sustainability accounting. In another study, regarding the disclosure of corporate social responsibility and value of cash holdings, Lu, Shailer and Yu (2016) use the binary variable to define the firm issued a standalone CSR report during the year, for measure the corporate social responsibility.

Recently, Gallardo-Vázquez & Sanchez-Hernandez (2014) have developed an overall scale to cover social, economic and environmental dimensions by analyzing the cause-effect relationship with performance and competitive success. The aim of this model was to develop a fairly complete scale by defining CSR as a variable that incorporates the economic, social, and environmental blocks. The authors applied structural equation methodology based on partial least squares path modeling. This measure of indicators that define CSR was used in various empirical studies to analyze responsible actions taken to upgrade the success and performance of firms (Gallardo-Vázquez & Sánchez-Hernández, 2014; Castilla-Polo et al., 2016; Junior et al., 2017; Sánchez-Hernández, Bnegil-Palacios, & Sanguino-Galván, 2017; Sánchez-Hernández, 2015).

Previous studies on the relationship between accounting and sustainability argue that the concept of sustainability and the associated use of accounting have been deliberately simplified and oriented towards supporting the business interests of firms. Firms only adopt a sustainability approach if it can generate economic returns. In this regard, Milne, Tregidga, and Walton (2009) defend that sustainability issues are managed exclusively for the purposes of maintaining control over natural resources and technologies, and boosting economic efficiency.

The Importance of Sustainability Reporting for Medium Enterprises

Small and medium enterprises (SMEs) play a very important role in Europe, as they provide employment opportunities and key players for the well-being of local and regional communities. Small entrepreneurs and entrepreneurs are pillars of society and it is necessary to support and motivate SMEs to develop in a sustainable way.

SMEs need to successfully address the forces that prevail for change if they are to survive and growth, meet expectations in creating investment, and also respond to the development of sustainable corporate responsibility. Although CSR is mainly discussed in the context of larger companies, it also is a strategic tool to enhance the competitiveness of SMEs. According to previous studies, SMEs normally has the following characteristics: they are owner-managed, with concentration of ownership control, and they have successive generations of family owner-managers (Poutziouris & Chittenden, 1996). These characteristics are different from those of large companies. SMEs are interested in the long-term viability of your business and in preserving your entrepreneurship business. The specific impact of corporate social responsibility actions often cannot be expressed in hard facts and figures and it may take some time until they become manifest.

Generally, CSR can positively influence SMEs' competitiveness in a way of improved products and production processes, resulting in a better customer satisfaction and loyalty. These activities target, on the one hand, at the customers and, on the other hand, as business partners and suppliers. Additionally,

CSR can positively influence SMEs' competitiveness in the way of higher motivation and loyalty of employees, resulting in a creativity and innovation. A focus on employees includes the improvement of working conditions and job satisfaction work, equal opportunities and diversity, and training and staff development.

Moreover, CSR can influence SME's competitiveness by offering the better position in the labor market and better networking with business partners and authorities, including better access to public funds due to a better company image. CSR activities targeted at the society may refer to social and labor market integration at community level, improvement of the regional infrastructure, and donations to local community institutions.

Farther, market-oriented CSR activities target, on the one hand, at the customers and, on the other hand, as business partners and suppliers. Respective initiatives include activities to improve the quality or safety of products provision of voluntary services to the clients, fair pricing, ethical advertising, and contracting local partners.

Finally, CSR activities in the field of the protection of the environment focus on designing environmentally friendly products or production processes, an efficient use of resources, the reduction of waste and pollution, applying an ecologic assessment on the suppliers concerning their environmental standards. All workforce, society, market and environment activities have a positive impact on cost savings and increased profitability and increased sales, consequently, improve a competitive advantage of the SME's.

Portuguese Medium Enterprises

There is a large predominance of small and medium companies in the Portuguese economy as compared to listed companies. SMEs are nowadays of great importance in various topics of the present day, namely the area of economics, more precisely in the Portuguese business structure.

SMEs represents about 99.9% of the Portugal business structure, and representing approximately 71 million euros of the total revenue or quid pro quo of 39.7% of the Portuguese Gross Development Product (GDP) or 0.48% of the UE's GDP in that year (composed by 28 member states), as shown in the following Table 1:

Santos (2017) argue that one of the most relevant management trends in the last decade is the increasing incorporation of social concerns in the activity of entrepreneurs and companies, because it is mandatory

Table 1. Portuguese enterprises and the GDP of Portugal and UE

<table>
<tr><td colspan="8">Currency: EUR</td></tr>
<tr><th colspan="4">Companies</th><th colspan="4">GDP</th></tr>
<tr><th>Size</th><th>Number</th><th>%</th><th>Volume of Business</th><th>Portuguese</th><th>%</th><th>UE 28</th><th>%</th></tr>
<tr><td>Micro</td><td>1,136,865</td><td>96.2</td><td>64,329</td><td rowspan="4">179.504</td><td>35.84</td><td rowspan="4">14,715,117</td><td>0.44</td></tr>
<tr><td>Small</td><td>37,515</td><td>3.2</td><td>66,215</td><td>36.89</td><td>0.45</td></tr>
<tr><td>Medium</td><td>5,951</td><td>0.5</td><td>71,218</td><td>39.67</td><td>0.48</td></tr>
<tr><td>Large</td><td>1,075</td><td>0.1</td><td>157,742</td><td>87.88</td><td>1.07</td></tr>
<tr><td>Total</td><td>1.181.406</td><td>100</td><td>359.504</td><td>-</td><td>200.28</td><td>-</td><td>2.44</td></tr>
<tr><td>Average</td><td>295.372</td><td>-</td><td>89.876</td><td>-</td><td>59.63</td><td>-</td><td>0.73</td></tr>
</table>

Source: PorData and Portuguese National Institute of Statistics, 2015

for companies to act responsibly in their day-to-day management because they place the long-term concerns of society as a source of inspiration in the definition of their business and their business conduct.

Medium and small enterprises are extremely important for the development of the country, namely through the creation of wealth by means of the contracting of several indispensable elements to the good functioning of the companies. In this perspective, if SMEs increase their concerns on socially responsible grounds, they may be to some extent, creating new jobs either through existing companies in the market or through the potential of new markets that may emerge in geographic decertified areas and outside large urban centers.

Portugal counts several examples of "green companies", either through the recycling of paper itself through Renova, SA or Portucel Recicla, SA, as well as innovation with the introduction of products such as 100% natural and biodegradable Jackson Reece wipes or biodegradable plastics distributed by the company based in Benavente, the well-known Silvex. In addition to proving themselves as a decoy of potential investors in the country, the economy through the creation of wealth or through the increase of jobs, are integrating and moving the foundations for current and future companies that are seen in the implementation of socially responsible practices and of widespread concern in the communities: health, safety, protection of the environment and others.

DETERMINANTS OF SUSTAINABILITY

Ownership

The few empirical studies on sustainability have analyzed its relationship with ownership concentration. Existing empirical research based on agency theory states that ownership concentration leads to closer monitoring by the owners and this improves the quality of managerial decisions and, consequently, firm value. On the other hand, greater ownership concentration may also result in more management entrenchment (Morck, Shleifer, & Vishny, 1988), which may not contribute to a greater alignment of shareholder and manager interests and thus increase agency problems. In small and medium firms, it is easier to obtain and maintain a diversified and concentrated equity position, which gives them power to seek private benefits at the expense of other shareholders. In addition, Brammer and Pavelin (2006) indicate that when a company's ownership is dispersed, its stockholders have less ability to directly exercise their authority over managers and therefore only monitor them. Hence, the control of power of ownership concentration in medium firms could reduce interest in business conduct that addresses' sustainability. Accordingly, we expect sustainability to be negatively and significantly related to ownership concentration.

Size

Large firms have strong management and are concerned about the reputation and visibility. Environmental performance indicators are used for waste management, natural resources, air emission and cost reduction in gas and water use. The study of Perrini, Russo, and Tencati (2007) has demonstrated that large firms invest in sustainability management and external reporting to increase visibility and to inform stakeholders. Additionally, Deegan (2003) concluded that the benefits of implementing environmental management accounting in Australian firms depend on firm size. Moreover, Hyršlová (2014) indicate that the content of a sustainability report is extraordinarily influenced by the size of the company, because the larger the company, the greater its responsibility towards the elements that surround it (employees, society, suppliers, among others). Large firms attract more attention from stakeholders, analysts and society and will therefore be more sustainable. Empirical studies found that CSR disclosure is positively associated with firm size (Rahman, Zain, & Al-Haj, 2011; Reverte, 2009; Thanasanborrisude & Phadoongsitthi, 2015).

Hence, we expect sustainability to be positively and significantly related to firm size.

Growth

Firms with high growth opportunities have greater investment opportunities, but financing future investment implies a higher cost of capital. Therefore, growth firms may reduce their sustainability to avoid raising the cost of capital or to maintain access to capital. While extant empirical studies found a positive relationship between growth and sustainability (Maigan, Ferrell, & Ferrell, 2005; Maron, 2006; Wu, Tsai, Cheng, & Lai, 2006), others found a negative or neutral relationship (Teoh, Welch, & Wazzan, 1999).

Based on previous findings, we expect sustainability to be positively and significantly related to sales growth.

Experience

Firms with a longer life expectation have countless reasons to foster socially responsible actions. They have high ethical standards, positive commercial values, their actual name may be the bearer of both reputation and a sense of responsibility and therefore help maintain their business sustainability. Hence, the number of years since the founding of the firm or the oldest of its predecessor firms is an important characteristic that represents the experience of the firms (Villalonga & Amit, 2006). Roberts (1992) added that when a corporation matures, its reputation and history of involvement in social responsibility become entrenched. Empirical studies found that CSR disclosure is positively associated with firm age (Roberts, 1992).

We expect sustainability to be positively and significantly related to experience of firms.

Governance

Legal compliance and proactive management of any environmental issues influence the use of environmental performance indicators. Specifically, the size of the board of directors can play a significant role in developing the sustainability policy. Adams and McNicholas (2007) found that the elaboration and presentation of a sustainability report increase the analysis of environmental and social issues and, consequently, firms give greater value to environmental performance and strive to improve their business actions. Dittmar and Mahrt-Smith (2007) found that good corporate governance increases the value of cash holdings in corporate responsibility firms. In another study, Wiengarten, Lo and Lam (2017) explore how certain characteristics of the newly appointed chief executive of CSR impact on a firm's financial performance in the US corporations. The authors suggest that appointing a chief executive of CSR does under certain conditions and characteristics result in financial performance benefits. Additional results demonstrated that the greatest financial performance benefits can be achieved if the appointee is female.

We expect sustainability to be positively and significantly related to the number of directors on the board.

Performance

There is much empirical evidence about the relationship between sustainability and firms' performance. However, the results are not conclusive. While some positive relationships were found, namely in attracting investment (Smith, 2005), improving financial performance (Barnett & Salomon, 2006), financial returns (Barnett, 2007), the decision to disclose (Dhaliwal et al., 2011), others were negative or neutral (Galbreath & Shum, 2012; Lys et al., 2015). Additionally, Deng et al. (2013) suggest a positive relationship between corporate social responsibility performance and a firm´s future performance. The impact of CSR on firm performance among Taiwanese firms was also examined and a positive association between CSR and monetary performance was identified (Lin et al., 2009). Moreover, Galbreath (2008) found strong positive links between CSR and organizational benefits among Australian firms. Despite the heterogeneity of results and conclusions to be found in the literature, they all indicate that firms which are carrying out actions of CSR clearly perform better.

According to the findings, better financial performance is a result of firms' increased sustainability and, therefore, we expect sustainability to be positive and significantly related to financial performance.

RESEARCH DESIGN

Sample Selection and Data Sources

The empirical study investigates determinants of corporate sustainability in Portuguese medium enterprises operating in Portugal that stand out for their excellent financial performance over the past three years (Exame, 2017). We use the data of the Portuguese medium and small-sized companies published in the Portuguese Journal Exame, together with additional information from the Amadeus database and from each company's website to obtain specific corporate governance and firm characteristics. Firms in the banking and insurance industries were not selected (Bouwens & Abernethy, 2000). Our sample is composed of 100 observations in 2016 of fifty-six public limited firms and forty-four private limited firms.

Table 2 displays the distribution of the legal form of the companies in the sample based on the SIC one-digit code. The trade and wholesale code have the largest percentage (52%) of private limited firms, followed by mining and manufacturing (33%). The services group is less significant (8%) and the utilities group is the smallest (7%). Overall, Table 2 shows that public and private firms in our sample operate in a wide range of industries, which should to some extent help alleviate concerns about the generalizability of our findings to medium firms.

Dependent Variable

The objective of this study is to analyze the determinants of corporate social responsibility in medium-sized firms. Sustainability reporting communicates a firm's environmental, social and economic results to external stakeholders in order to demonstrate its commitment to sustainability determinants and therefore increases the level of transparency.

Table 2. Sample composition

Industry		Public Limited Firms		Private Firms		All Firms	
Designation	**SIC**	**N**	**%**	**N**	**%**	**N**	**%**
Mining and manufacturing	1, 2 and 3	23	41%	10	23%	33	33%
Utilities	4	6	11%	1	2%	7	7%
Trade and wholesale	5	24	43%	28	64%	52	52%
Services	7 and 8	3	5%	5	11%	8	8%
Total		**56**	**100%**	**44**	**100%**	**100**	**100%**

Sustainability is the dependent variable of our study. In the literature, there are not generalized model to measure of sustainability. Some studies used measure of sustainability for developing Global Reporting Initiative (GRI) model, the other used the use content analysis of financial and accounting documents, case studies, surveys, databases, indices (Keeble, et al., 2003; Passetti et al., 2014) or used binary variable to define the firm issued a standalone CSR report during the year (Lu et al., 2016). Accordingly, Lu et al. (2016), we use a binary variable which assumes the value of 1 if a company publishes a sustainability report or makes it available in any management or accounting documents, and 0 otherwise.

Independent Variables

Firm characteristics may also affect their sustainability. Consistent with the literature, we include a set of firm characteristics that can determine sustainability, namely ownership concentration, firm size, sales growth, experience, governance, and net income. We include an industry dummy variable to control for the possible industry effect. Detailed descriptions of all variables used in this study are provided in Table 3.

Table 3. Variables used in the study

Variable Label	Variable Name	Variable Measurement
Sustainability	Sustainability report	The dummy variable, which takes the value 1 if the company publishes a sustainability report and 0 otherwise (Available in the company website)
Ownership	Ownership concentration	The percentage of shares held by the group of owners (Amadeus)
Size	Ln Assets	The natural logarithm of a firm's total assets at the end of year (Amadeus)
Growth	Sales Increase	Change in a firm's total sales at the end of year between 2015 and 2016 (Exame, 2017)
Years of Activity	Experience	The number of years since the founding of firm or the oldest of its predecessor firms (Amadeus)
Governance	Governance	The number of directors on the board of the firm at the end of year (Amadeus)
Net Income	Performance	Net income divided by total assets (Amadeus)
SIC	SIC Industry	Industry dummy variable (SIC_1 takes the value 1 for SIC 1000 to SIC 3999 and 0 otherwise; SIC_2 takes the value 1 for SIC 4000 to SIC 4999 and 0 otherwise; SIC_3 takes the value 1 for SIC 5000 to SIC 5999 and 0 otherwise; SIC_4 takes the value 1 for SIC 7000 to SIC 7999 and 0 otherwise) (Amadeus)

Research Model

The aim of this study is to analyze whether companies are concerned about sustainability and its impact on accounting. A regression analysis studies how dependent and independent variables relate to each other, more specifically how a dependent variable is influenced by the independent variable. The model for the study is:

$$Sustainability_{(1,0)} = Ownership + Size + Growth + Experience + Governance + Net\ Income + SIC_n + \varepsilon \quad (1)$$

See Table 3:

RESULTS

Descriptive Statistics

Table 4 presents descriptive statistics of all variables used in this study for the entire sample and for public and private firms separately. The results in Panel B and C of Table 4 demonstrate that the characteristics of public and private firms are very similar. Table 4 shows that the mean size of public and private firms is 10.493 and 10.520 respectively. Sustainability reporting is available in 14% of all firms. These findings are consistent with previous literature and show that medium firms are not interested in changing their business conduct to improve sustainability (Cooper et al., 2011). They underline firms' reluctance to adopt the sustainability principle.

The high level of ownership concentration in Portugal in comparison to other countries is reflected in the average value of 99%, which is also higher than the values reported in studies such as Morck et al. (1988). The average firm size is 10.5. Firms have an average of 2 directors; public firms have fewer directors than private firms, 1.7 and 2.6 respectively. The overall experience of the firms is 29 years, 27 years for public firms and 31 years for private firms. Overall, the descriptive statistics demonstrate that firms' characteristics such as ownership concentration, firm size, growth and net income are similar in

Table 3.

SUSTAINABILITY	The dummy variable, which takes the value 1 if the company publishes a sustainability report and 0 otherwise.
OWNERSHIP	The percentage of shares held by the group of owners.
SIZE	The natural logarithm of a firm's total assets at the end of year.
GROWTH	Change in a firm's total sales at the end of year between 2015 and 2016.
EXPERIENCE	The number of years since the founding of firm or the oldest of its predecessor firms.
GOVERNANCE	The number of directors on the board of the firm at the end of year.
NET INCOME	Net income divided by total assets.
SIC	Industry dummy variables.
ε	Residual term.

Table 4. Descriptive statistics

Variable	Mean	Standard Deviation	5%	Median	95%
Panel A: All firms					
Sustainability	0.140	0.349	0.000	0.000	1.000
Ownership	99.105	6.337	100.000	100.000	100.000
Size	10.505	0.148	10.314	10.471	10.794
Growth	10.041	19.898	-17.090	6.600	42.300
Experience	29.490	20.382	5.000	25.000	77.950
Governance	1.760	1.415	1.000	1.000	4.950
Net Income	4.144	6.147	-3.230	-33.535	14.362
Panel B: Public Limited Firms					
Ownership	98.431	8.365	96.055	100.000	100.000
Size	10.493	0.143	10.320	10.457	10.788
Growth	12.328	23.097	-18.520	7.300	53.900
Experience	27.719	19.348	4.000	23.000	78.200
Governance	1.070	0.320	1.000	1.000	2.000
Net Income	3.440	7.069	-6.871	3.532	15.824
Panel C: Private Limited Firms					
Ownership	99.998	0.015	100.000	100.000	100.000
Size	10.520	0.154	10.312	10.500	10.809
Growth	7.009	14.333	-17.340	6.600	31.440
Experience	31.837	21.685	10.000	28.000	84.400
Governance	2.674	1.756	1.000	2.000	6.800
Net Income	5.077	4.568	0.418	4.041	13.143

public and private firms. In contrast, some differences are found in corporate governance characteristics such as experience and board size.

Table 5 presents pairwise Pearson correlation among all variables. The variables show low correlation; no pairwise correlation coefficients exceed 0.80, which indicates that the threat of multicollinearity is limited. We followed Belsley-Kuh-Welsch to diagnose collinearity; the non-tabulated results reveal no collinearity problems in our sample.

Regression Results

Table 6 reports the Ordinary Least Squares (OLS) regression for sustainability determinants, estimated for the total sample under analysis. Two logit estimations are presented: column C1 includes all variables and industry dummies of the regression of the research model, and column C2 includes all variables. The main findings are similar in the two estimated regression models.

In estimations C1 and C2, the coefficient of determination assesses how the independent variables influence the variation of the dependent variable. In the study of our model and for the analyzed sample (N = 100), the eight independent variables explain roughly 14.9% of the dependent variable in ques-

Table 5. Correlation matrix based on Pearson's coefficients

	Ownership	Size	Growth	Experience	Governance	Net Income
Ownership	1.000					
Size	-0.193	1.000				
Growth	0.020	0.157	1.000			
Experience	-0.201	0.051	-0.058	1.000		
Governance	0.077	-0.004	0.049	0.218	1.000	
Net Income	0.021	0.009	0.005	-0.076	-0.055	1.000

Table 6. Regression estimates of sustainability

Variable	C1 (t-stat)	C2 (t-stat)
Ownership	-0.000*** (-3.752)	-0.000*** (-3.378)
Size	0.112** (2.117)	0.0005** (0.015)
Growth	-0.005*** (-2.709)	-0.006*** (-2.572)
Experience	-0.000 (-0.137)	0.000 (0.141)
Governance	-0.141 (-0.552)	-0.0762 (-0.517)
Net Income	0.000 (-0.137)	0.000 (0.049)
Industry dummies	Yes	No
Adj. R^2	0.149	0.103
F-Stat (p-value)	0.002	0.002

*, ** &*** indicates significance at the 1%, 5% and 10% levels, respectively

tion. Since the p-value of the F-Stat is approximately 0 and is below the level of significance, we can say that the model is significant and presents a good overall fit. In accordance with our expectation, sustainability is negatively and significantly related to ownership concentration and sales growth. This demonstrates that the control of power in medium firms could lead to less interest in business conduct addressing sustainability (Passetti et al., 2014).

Additionally, our results demonstrate that growth firms support more costs, and this reduces their commitment to sustainability. In line with our expectation, sustainability is positively and significantly related to firm size. This is consistent with previous literature and confirms that large firms invest in sustainability accounting and external reporting to increase visibility and to inform stakeholders (Perrini et al. 2007).

Surprisingly, the net income variable is not statistically significant in our study. Moreover, the corporate governance determinants of sustainability, such as the number of directors and experience, are not statistically significant in our study. This may demonstrate that corporate governance characteristics in medium firms are not determinant for business conduct addressing sustainability issues.

CONCLUSION

This chapter analyzes the determinants of sustainability in medium-sized firms operating in Portugal in 2016 and with excellent financial performance over the last three years. The results indicate that ownership structure, firm size and sales growth are determinants of sustainability and contribute significantly to explaining the sustainability of medium firms. This can also be explained as follows: first, few medium firms published sustainability reports for external users. This is consistent with previous literature (Cooper et al., 2011) and indicates that medium firms show little interest in changing their business conduct to improve sustainability. It suggests accounting departments are not sufficiently involved in analyzing sustainability and have a limited role in its development. Second, from the set of characteristics examined in this study, the only firm size provides a positive incentive for sustainability reporting. More specifically, large firms invest in sustainability management and external reporting to increase visibility and to inform stakeholders. Thirdly, from the set of characteristics analyzed herein, ownership concentration and sales growth determine a negative incentive for sustainability reporting. This reveals that firms with these characteristics find it very difficult to accept changes leading to greater sustainability.

Additionally, our study argues that sustainability and the associated use of accounting have been deliberately simplified and oriented towards supporting the business interests of firms.

The results of our study contribute to the ongoing debates in the accounting literature addressing the relationship between accounting and sustainability and suggest directions for further research. Future studies can use quantitative and qualitative data to analyze the external and internal characteristics of firms as determinants for sustainability reporting. It would also be useful to identify other tools or more complete measures of sustainability that are not included in this study and influence the contingency factors in sustainability accounting. Moreover, the relationship between sustainability accounting and environmental and social dimensions is another future research area of interest.

REFERENCES

Acosta-Alba, I., López-Ridaura, S., van der Werf, H. M. G., Leterme, P., & Corson, M. S. (2012). Exploring sustainable farming scenarios at a regional scale: An application to dairy farms in Brittany. *Journal of Cleaner Production*, *28*, 160–167. doi:10.1016/j.jclepro.2011.11.061

Adams, C. A., & McNicholas, P. (2007). Making a difference: Sustainability reporting, accountability and organisational change. *Accounting, Auditing & Accountability Journal*, *20*(3), 382–402. doi:10.1108/09513570710748553

Azapagic, A. (2004). Developing a framework for sustainable development indicators for the mining and minerals industry. *Journal of Cleaner Production*, *12*(6), 639–662. doi:10.1016/S0959-6526(03)00075-1

Barnett, M. L. (2007). Stakeholder influence capacity and the variability of financial returns to corporate social responsibility. *Academy of Management Review*, *32*(3), 794–816. doi:10.5465/AMR.2007.25275520

Barnett, M. L., & Salomon, R. M. (2006). Beyond dichotomy: The curvilinear relationship between social responsibility and financial performance. *Strategic Management Journal*, *27*(11), 1101–1156. doi:10.1002mj.557

Bouwens, J., & Abernethy, M. (2000). The consequences of customization on management accounting system design. *Accounting, Organizations and Society*, *25*(3), 221–241. doi:10.1016/S0361-3682(99)00043-4

Brammer, S., & Pavelin, S. (2006). Voluntary environmental disclosures by large UK companies. *Journal of Business Finance & Accounting*, *33*(7-8), 1168–1188. doi:10.1111/j.1468-5957.2006.00598.x

Burritt, R. (2012). Environmental performance accountability: Planet, people, profits. *Accounting, Auditing & Accountability Journal*, *25*(2), 370–405. doi:10.1108/09513571211198791

Carroll, A. B. (1979). A three-dimensional conseptual model of corporate performance. *Academy of Management Review*, *4*, 4497–4530.

Castilla-Polo, F., Sánchez-Hernández, M. I., & Gallardo-Vázquez, D. (2017). Assessing the Influence of Social Responsibility on Reputation: An Empirical Case-Study in Agricultural Cooperatives in Spain. *Journal of Agricultural & Environmental Ethics*, *30*(1), 99–120. doi:10.100710806-017-9656-9

Christ, K., & Burritt, R. (2013). Environmental management accounting: The significance of contingent variables for adoption. *Journal of Cleaner Production*, *41*(2), 163–173. doi:10.1016/j.jclepro.2012.10.007

Clarkson, P. M., Li, Y., Richardson, G. D., & Vasvari, F. P. (2008). Revisiting the relation between environmental performance and environmental disclosure: An empirical analysis. *Accounting, Organizations and Society*, *33*(4-5), 303–327. doi:10.1016/j.aos.2007.05.003

Commission of the European Communities. (2011). *Renewed European Union Strategy for 2011-2014 on Social Responsibility.* Available at: http://eur-lex.europa.eu

Cooper, C., Coulson, A., & Taylor, P. (2011). Accounting for human rights: Toxic health and safety practices the accounting lesson from ICL. *Critical Perspectives on Accounting*, *22*(8), 738–758. doi:10.1016/j.cpa.2011.07.001

Davis, K. (1973). The case for and against business assumption of social responsibilities. *Academy of Management Journal*, *16*(2), 312–323. doi:10.2307/255331

Deegan, C. (2003). *Environmental management accounting: An introduction and case studies for Australia (EMAP).* Sydney: Institute of Chartered Accountants in Australia.

Deng, X., Kang, J., & Low, S. (2013). Corporate social responsibility and stakeholder value maximization: Evidence from mergers. *Journal of Financial Economics*, *110*(1), 87–109. doi:10.1016/j.jfineco.2013.04.014

Dhaliwal, D., Li, Z., Tsang, A., & Yang, Y. (2011). Voluntary nonfinancial disclosure and the cost of equity capital: The initiation of corporate social responsibility reporting. *The Accounting Review*, *86*(1), 59–100. doi:10.2308/accr.00000005

Dittmar, A., & Mahrt-Smith, J. (2007). Corporate governance and the value of cash holdings. *Journal of Financial Economics*, *83*(3), 599–634. doi:10.1016/j.jfineco.2005.12.006

Epstein, M. J. (2008). *Making sustainability work: Best practices in managing and measuring corporate, social, environmental, and economic impacts*. San Francisco: Berret-Koehler Publishers, Inc.

Exame. (2017). Conheça as 1000 melhores PME do país. *Edição Expresso*, 207.

Galbreath, J., & Galvin, P. (2008). Firm factors, industry structure and performance variation: New empirical evidence to a classic debate. *Journal of Business Research*, *61*(2), 109–117. doi:10.1016/j.jbusres.2007.06.009

Galbreath, J., & Shum, P. (2012). Do customer satisfaction and reputation mediate the CSR-FR Link? Evidence from Australia. *Australian Journal of Management*, *37*(2), 211–229. doi:10.1177/0312896211432941

Gallardo-Vâzquez, D., & Sanchez-Hernandez, M. I. (2014). Measuring Corporate Social Responsibility for competitive success at a regional level. *Journal of Cleaner Production*, *72*, 14–22. doi:10.1016/j.jclepro.2014.02.051

Gallhofer, S., Haslam, J., & van der Walt, S. (2011). Accountability and transparency in relation to human rights: A critical perspective reflecting upon accounting, corporate responsibility and ways forward in the context of globalization. *Critical Perspectives on Accounting*, *22*(8), 765–780. doi:10.1016/j.cpa.2011.07.002

Hyršlová, J. (2014). Sustainability reporting – a review of trends and situation in CR. *The 8th International Days of Statistics and Economics.*

Junior, F. H., Galleli, B., Gallardo-Vâzquez, D., & Sánchez-Hernåndez, M. I. (2017). Strategic aspects in sustainability reporting in oil & gas industry: The comparative case-study of brazilian Petrobras and Spanish Repsol. *Ecological Indicators*, *72*, 203–214. doi:10.1016/j.ecolind.2016.08.007

Keeble, J. J., Topiol, S., & Berkeley, S. (2003). Using indicators to measure sustainability performance at a corporate and project level. *Journal of Business Ethics*, *44*(2), 149–158. doi:10.1023/A:1023343614973

Lin, C. H., Yang, H. L., & Liou, D. Y. (2009). The impact of corporate social responsibility on financial performance: Evidence from business in Taiwan. *Technology in Society*, *31*(1), 56–63. doi:10.1016/j.techsoc.2008.10.004

Maignan, I., & Ferrell, O. C. (2000). Measuring corporate citizenship in two countries: The case of the United States and France. *Journal of Business Ethics*, *23*(3), 283–297. doi:10.1023/A:1006262325211

Maignan, I., Ferrell, O. C., & Ferrell, L. (2005). A stakeholder model for implementing social responsibility in marketing. *European Journal of Marketing*, *39*(9/10), 956–977. doi:10.1108/03090560510610662

Mark-Herbert, C., & Von Schantz, C. (2007). Communicating corporate social responsibility and brand management. *Electronic Journal of Business Ethics and Organization Studies*, *12*(2), 4–11.

Maron, I. Y. (2006). Toward a unified theory of the CSP–CFP link. *Journal of Business Ethics*, *67*(2), 191–200. doi:10.100710551-006-9023-7

Milne, M. J., Tregidga, H. M., & Walton, S. (2009). Words not actions! The ideological role of sustainable development reporting. *Accounting, Auditing & Accountability Journal*, *22*(8), 1211–1257. doi:10.1108/09513570910999292

Montiel, I. (2008). Corporate social responsibility and corporate sustainability. *Organization & Environment*, *21*(3), 245–269. doi:10.1177/1086026608321329

Morck, R., Shleifer, A., & Vishny, R. (1988). Management ownership and firm value: An empirical analysis. *Journal of Financial Economics*, *20*(1), 293–315. doi:10.1016/0304-405X(88)90048-7

Nordheim, E., & Barrasso, G. (2007). Sustainable development indicators of the European aluminium industry. *Journal of Cleaner Production*, *15*(3), 275–279. doi:10.1016/j.jclepro.2006.02.004

Passetti, E., Cinquini, L., Marelli, A., & Tenucci, A. (2014). Sustainability accounting in action: Lights and shadows in the Italian context. *The British Accounting Review*, *46*(3), 295–308. doi:10.1016/j.bar.2014.05.002

Perrini, F., Russo, A., & Tencati, A. (2007). CSR strategies of SMEs and large firms. Evidence from Italy. *Journal of Business Ethics*, *74*(3), 285–300. doi:10.100710551-006-9235-x

Quazi, A. M., & O'Brien, D. (2000). An empirical test of a cross-national model of corporate social responsibility. *Journal of Business Ethics*, *25*(1), 33–51. doi:10.1023/A:1006305111122

Rahman, N. H. W. A., Zain, M. M., & Al-Haj, N. H. Y. Y. (2011). CSR disclosures and its determinants: Evidence from Malaysian government link companies. *Social Responsibility Journal*, *7*(2), 181–201. doi:10.1108/17471111111141486

Reverte, C. (2009). Determinants of corporate social responsibility disclosure ratings by Spanish listed firms. *Journal of Business Ethics*, *88*(2), 351–366. doi:10.100710551-008-9968-9

Saeidi, S. P., Sofian, S., Saeidi, P., Saeidi, S. P., & Saaeidi, S. A. (2015). How does corporate social responsibility contribute to firm financial performance? The mediating role of competitive advantage, reputation, and customer satisfaction. *Journal of Business Research*, *68*(2), 341–350. doi:10.1016/j.jbusres.2014.06.024

Sánchez-Hernández, M. I. (2015). Clusters as entrepreneurial ecosystems for Corporate Social Resposibility in SMEs. In L. Carvalho (Ed.), *Handbook of Research on Entrepreneurial Success and its Impact on Regional Development* (pp. 72–87). Hershey, PA: IGI Global.

Sánchez-Hernández, M. I., Bnegil-Palacios, T., & Sanguino-Galván, R. (2017). Competitive success in responsible regional ecosystems: An empirical approach in Spain focused on the firms'relationship with stakeholders. *Sustainability*, *9*(3), 449. doi:10.3390u9030449

Schaltegger, S., Herzing, C., Kleiber, O., & Müller, J. (2002). *Sustainability management in business enterprises. Concepts and instruments for sustainable organisation development* (2nd ed.). Bonn, Germany: The Federal Ministry for the Environment, Nature Conservation and Nuclear Safety.

Smith, T. (2005). Institutional and social investors find common ground. *Journal of Investing, 14*(3), 57–65. doi:10.3905/joi.2005.580550

Teoh, S. H., Welch, I., & Wazzan, C. P. (1999). The effect of socially activist investment policies on the financial markets: Evidence from the South African boycott. *Journal of Business Ethics, 72*(1), 35–89.

Thanasanborrisude, J., & Phadoongsitthi, M. (2015). Firm characteristics and CSR disclosures: Case study in MAI firms. *Journal of Accounting Profession, 11*(30), 23-40. (in Thai)

Ullman, A. (1985). Data in search of a theory: A critical examination of the relationship among social performance, social disclosure and economic performance of US firms. *Academical Management Review, 10*, 540–557.

Veleva, V., & Ellenbecker, M. (2001). Indicators of sustainable production: Framework and methodology. *Journal of Cleaner Production, 9*(6), 519–549. doi:10.1016/S0959-6526(01)00010-5

Villalonga, B., & Amit, R. (2006). How do family ownership, control and management affect firms value? *Journal of Financial Economics, 80*(2), 385–417. doi:10.1016/j.jfineco.2004.12.005

Wagner, M. (2010). Corporate Social Performance and Innovation with High Social Benefits: A Quantitative Analysis. *Journal of Business Ethics, 94*(4), 581–594. doi:10.100710551-009-0339-y

Weber, M. (2008). The business case for corporate social responsibility: A company level measurement approach for CSR. *European Management Journal, 26*(4), 247–261. doi:10.1016/j.emj.2008.01.006

Wiengarten, F., Lo, C., & Lam, J. (2017). "How does Sustainability Leadership Affect Firm Performance? The Choices Associated with Appointing a Chief Officer of Corporate Social Responsibility". *Journal of Business Ethics, 140*(3), 477–493. doi:10.100710551-015-2666-5

Wu, J. (2009). Environmental compliance: The good, the bad, and the super green. *Journal of Environmental Management, 90*(11), 3363–3381. doi:10.1016/j.jenvman.2009.05.017 PMID:19573979

ADDITIONAL READING

Ballou, B., Casey, R., Grenier, J., & Heitger, D. (2012). Exploring the strategic integration of sustainability initiatives: Opportunities for accounting research. *Accounting Horizons, 26*(2), 265–288. doi:10.2308/acch-50088

Burritt, R., Schaltegger, S., & Zvezdov, D. (2011). Carbon management accounting: Explaining practice in leading German companies. *Australian Accounting Review, 21*(1), 80–98. doi:10.1111/j.1835-2561.2010.00121.x

Burritt, R., & Tingey-Holioyak, J. (2012). Forging cleaner production: The importance of academic-practitioner links for successful sustainability embedded carbon accounting. *Journal of Cleaner Production, 36*(1), 39–47. doi:10.1016/j.jclepro.2012.02.001

Commission of the European Communities. (2001). *Green Paper. Promoting a European Framework for Corporate Social Responsibility*, 366 e end, Available at: http://eur-lex.europa.eu

Ferreira, A., Moulang, C., & Hendro, B. (2010). Environmental management accounting and innovation: An exploratory analysis. *Accounting, Auditing & Accountability Journal, 23*(7), 920–948. doi:10.1108/09513571011080180

Garriga, E., & Mele, D. (2004). Corporate social responsibility theories: Mapping the territory. *Journal of Business Ethics, 53*(1/2), 51–71. doi:10.1023/B:BUSI.0000039399.90587.34

Jones, M. (2010). Accounting for the environment: Towards a theoretical perspective for environmental accounting and reporting. *Accounting Forum, 34*(2), 123–138. doi:10.1016/j.accfor.2010.03.001

Maignan, I., & Ferrell, O. C. (2001). Antecedents and benefits of corporate citizenship: As investigation of French businesses. *Journal of Business Research, 51*(1), 37–51. doi:10.1016/S0148-2963(99)00042-9

Miles, M. P., Munilla, L. S., & Covin, J. G. (2004). Innovation, Ethics, and Entrepreneurship. *Journal of Business Ethics, 54*(1), 97–101. doi:10.1023/B:BUSI.0000043501.13922.00

Porter, M. (1991). America's Green Strategy. *Scientific American, 264*(4), 96.

Spence, C., Husillos, J., & Correa-Ruiz, C. (2010). Cargo cult science and the death of politics: A critical review of social and environmental accounting research. *Critical Perspectives on Accounting, 21*(1), 76–89. doi:10.1016/j.cpa.2008.09.008

KEY TERMS AND DEFINITIONS

Corporate Social Responsibility: A number of corporate activities that focus on the welfare of stakeholder groups other than investors, such as customers, employees, suppliers, and society.

Corporate Sustainability: Corporate sustainability focuses on long-term shareholder value by incorporating the best practices in the following areas: ethics, governance, transparency, business relationship, financial return, product value, employment practice, and environmental protection.

Chapter 6
SME and Sustainability:
A Managerial Model to Enhance Relationships and Interactions Between Different Local Actors of the Territory

Cecilia Casalegno
University of Turin, Italy

Christian Rainero
University of Turin, Italy

Giacomo Büchi
University of Turin, Italy

Fabrizio Mosca
University of Turin, Italy

ABSTRACT

The analysis and the consideration of the sustainability development throughout the SMEs has been less considered by the academic literature than the one developed by large firms so far, although small and medium enterprises represent the majority of the local businesses in many geographical areas of the world. Since small and medium entrepreneurs usually do not know how to tackle the challenges concerning internationalization and sustainability, a managerial model for underling which kind of relationships and interactions must be built is the real aim of the present chapter. In order to do that the chapter is focused of a limited area, the Piedmont Region (Italy), to deep analyse the relationship SMEs can create and improve with the local institutions, associations, and business partners.

DOI: 10.4018/978-1-5225-5267-3.ch006

INTRODUCTION

The analysis and the consideration of sustainability development have been given less consideration by academic literature when related to SMEs than they have for large firms, despite the fact that small and medium enterprises represent the majority of local businesses in many geographical areas of the world. According to the Organization for Economic Co-operation and Development (OECD), 99.9% of Italy's profitable organizations are SMEs and this means that they employ less than 250 people (Coppa & Sriramesh, 2012). It is clear that the study of SME sustainability drivers is becoming fundamental at a time when every stakeholder is asking firms for more information about their sustainable processes and policies, whatever their size.

Many authors consider the challenges in terms of innovation that the application of the concept of sustainability represents for firms in general (Bos-Brouwers, 2010) and, if we consider SMEs, we have to underline their natural tendency to approach innovation cautiously, preferring traditional practices and policies (Donckels & Frohlich 1991; Morck & Yeung 2003). As stated by Bos-Brouwers (2010), SMEs usually have behavioural advantages and resource-related disadvantages when it comes to innovation. For example, a critical factor for innovation is represented by a horizontal management style, which can make the management of change and innovation leaner, thanks to better decision-making skills at the bottom line (Rothwell, 1992). Nevertheless, sustainability, together with internationalization, represents the most interesting challenge for SMEs for several reasons:

- Many of the characteristics of SMEs are in open contrast with sustainable innovation. SMEs are mostly poor not only in terms of capital but also in terms of knowledge, core skills and international relationships;
- SMEs are, by definition, more involved in everyday matters and problems than in planning a strategy that considers new threats and opportunities from the outside;
- SME innovations can be seen as incremental innovations (Bhasrakan, 2006), while sustainable innovations are usually radical or closely linked to the daily analysis of nature, society and the environment in general.

Moreover, as regards interaction between SMEs and the local organizations that could help them, it should be emphasized that SMEs find it harder to span their own knowledge than their interaction with universities or local incubators and accelerators (Tether, 2002; Klewitz, 2015).

Furthermore, as stated by Redmond et al. (2016), SMEs appear to be more vulnerable to global problems such as climate change, the rise in insurance and running costs, damage from macro environmental factors in general, and forces represented by the other players in the supply and production chains.

Looking at the second big challenge, internationalization, problems are related to process innovation (Davenport, 1993), product innovation (Dougherty, 1992), innovation in relationships with foreign markets which are, obviously, influenced by the local culture (Usunier et al., 2005), and strategic innovation, which must take into account how virtuous it can be to forge partnerships with other organizations (Tikkanen, 1998).

It is clear that, in such a context, small and medium organizations need to interact with the Institutions, as well as local associations and the other players in their value system, in order to maintain transparent communication and gather all the necessary information to build a useful background of knowledge and profitable skills.

As small and medium entrepreneurs usually don't know how to tackle the above-mentioned challenges, a managerial model indicating which kind of relationships and interactions must be built is the real aim of this chapter. In order to achieve this, the chapter focuses on a limited area, the Piedmont region (Italy), to deeply analyse the relationship that SMEs can create and improve with the local Institutions, associations and business partners.

A first analysis of the composition of SMEs in the Piedmont region will be carried out. The second step involves a benchmarking (McNair & Leibfried, 1992) throughout all the Italian regions, to trace the state of the art, with the particular aim of understanding how the problems analysed have been solved by other Italian Universities, and whether other Institutions have already planned how to help the local business structure. Lastly, semi-structured formal interviews (Bernard, 1988) will be conducted face to face, not only involving local managers and entrepreneurs, but also association members and boards, together with the directors of incubators and local accelerators.

By crossing the elements from the research, we will be able to present a managerial model in which we can highlight the crossing points among the various above-mentioned local players in a specific area. The case of Piedmont will be used to develop a model suitable for use everywhere, presenting a large number of SMEs.

The chapter doesn't look at things from the SME viewpoint alone. It closely analyses each of the above-mentioned local players, the main aim being to show which kind of interactions among the various players (both public and private) need to be put in place to help local small and medium enterprises create value for themselves by creating a common value made up of relationships, a deep and ongoing communication, and exchanges (of goods, services and ideas).

SMALL AND MEDIUM ENTERPRISES: LATEST DAILY TRENDS, CHALLENGES, AND OPPORTUNITIES

From a study of SMEs in Piedmont carried out by Cerved (2017), in 2015 "Piedmont – with ten thousand companies falling within the European definition of SME (enterprises with 10-250 employees and a turnover of between two and 50 million euro), 286 thousand employees, a turnover of 62 billion euro and an added value of 15 billion – is the fifth Italian region in terms of size of the fabric of small and medium enterprises.

The system of Piedmontese SMEs differs slightly from that at national level in that it is characterised by more operation in manufacturing (34.4% of Piedmont's SMEs operate in industry, compared to a national figure of 29.7%) and is larger (29 employees per business compared to 27 in SMEs at Italian level), with a weight of the average company exceeding the national weight (19% of Piedmontese SMEs, against 17% at Italian level)". Moreover, if we extend the analysis to the Italian context, which could be interesting after the start-up phase, it is a good idea to highlight that, in the last financial statements available, 136,114 companies can be classified as SMEs, with 112,378 of these falling within the definition of "small enterprise" and 23,736 within that of "medium" enterprise. These companies, which represent over a fifth (22%) of the companies that deposit valid financial statements, employed 3.8 million people, over two million of which in small enterprises.

In 2015, SMEs generated revenues of 852 billion euro and an added value of 196 billion euro (12% of GDP), accounting for 240 billion euro in financial debt. Compared to non-financial companies in general, they account for 37% in terms of sales turnover, 41% in terms of added value and 29% in terms of financial debt.

Considering the characteristics that influence the action of small and medium enterprises, Piedmont's SMEs are more sensitive to the economic cycle: they suffered more during the first phase of the financial crisis but were also quicker to react when the marketplace began to invert the trend, showing much more positive signs than their Italian counterparts. This stems partly from a greater presence of sectors linked to the cycle of investments (instrumental mechanics or "mechatronics") and of the automotive chain. The automotive sector, in particular, was one of those worst hit by the crisis, but is now one of the leaders of the recovery.

Another challenge concerns Italian companies in general and those of Piedmont in particular: global competition. Companies which weren't interested in globalisation until just a short while ago have learned that they either open up to the international market and try offering their products north of the Alps or they will be unable to maintain their competitive edge.

We also find ourselves facing a real global competition. While, until a few decades ago, companies were able to ignore what was being accomplished by companies operating in different countries and sectors, this is no longer possible today. Obviously, in today's marketplace, companies of all sizes are forced to rethink their business model, with small enterprises being naturally more sustainable and responsible than bigger companies. The challenge regarding internationalisation poses the problem of the sustainability of business from every point of view and the need to be more open to global or at least international challenges also poses matters linked to trust and reputation, as well as the need to implement company. Markets are becoming bigger and more open, and it is essential to increment the competitive edge, mitigate the effects of economic fluctuations, defend the market share and seek the best sources of raw materials, labour and services. All of this has to take into account the influences of structures and competition in the sector of pertinence.

For years it has been said that the step towards an internationalised and global approach is a complex problem, the solutions of which have a radical impact on enterprise and the territory where it resides. The transition towards a global approach is complex, in that it has a considerable impact on consolidated balances and rooted habits, imposing extensive processes of innovation, especial in terms of business and management culture, and structural and functional modernisation, which are often hard to plan and manage. As sustained by Cedrola and Battaglia (2011), the main complexities and problems refer to the concept of innovation and are undoubtedly attributable to the orientations necessary to the survival and growth of a company, as follows:

- Process innovation (Davenport, 1993);
- Product innovation (Dougherty, 1992);
- The innovation of the approach to the market, deeply influenced by the cultural distances between countries (Usunier, 2005);
- Strategic innovation, which must increasingly consider the virtuosity of collaborations between companies (Tikkanen, 1998).

It is also necessary to consider that the opening towards international markets implicates the interfacing with different reference targets, which leads to more complexity in decisions relating to the codes of communication to be adopted. This obviously represents an even bigger problem when communication refers to contents linked to sustainability and responsibility. Secondly, opening up towards international markets involves companies in relationships with new customers, suppliers and, above all, with new interlocutors (government organisations) which increasingly expect companies to adopt sustainable and ethical behaviours.

The importance of collaboration between companies and universities is quite rightly recognised by the universities and by the organisations involved. The different trade associations have recently promoted collaboration through seminars, meetings, analyses and training courses. What they are trying to create is a bridge which can easily put managers, entrepreneurs, consultants, new talents and new areas of knowledge applicable to strategic management in touch with one another.

The attention of universities is focusing increasingly on higher education. For example, Turin University currently places at least 50 level one and 50 level two courses at the disposal of its graduates. These courses are run by the single Departments, jointly by two or more Departments from the same University in Turin or jointly by two or more Departments of different Universities.

Regardless of training, advisories or observatories that can be created by the Departments, at the moment there is no real answer to the demand to create professional figures that are young, well trained and adequately prepared to tackle a professional activity. What is missing is an enterprise workshop that acts as a bridge between university and organisations, capable of identifying on-the-job training of young graduates and undergrad students as the main aim, putting them in a position to interface with the working world within a short space of time.

In terms of the response from Italian universities, over the past 20 years, certain organisations with the aim of promoting the transferral of knowledge have emerged; incubators (of ideas or enterprise) focus their attention on the development of innovation throughout the territory, whether this is linked to the sciences of life, social sciences, the study of agri-food applications, mechatronics or the iron and steel industry.

Incubators are created to favour the growth and success of firms through a network of resources and support services for business activities; they provide sites, basic logistical services and networks of personal contacts, formed as a result of carrying out business activities in a single structure. The most well-equipped incubators also provide managerial services and advice on technical, legal and tax issues.

However, incubators are merely a temporary solution, as the authorization to carry out business activities in an incubator is usually year-to-year and, at most, three to five years. After the start-up phase, the firm, if successful, is transferred outside the incubator into an independent structure, thereby completing a process for the creation of new business, employment, and regional and national economic stimulus.

Many incubators were formed in Europe when, in 1984, the European Commission decided to favour measures aimed at developing business enterprises in member countries. These incubators were all of the BIC (Business Innovation Centre) type, with public capital, and aimed at providing local enterprises a set of basic services: spaces in which to operate, logistical infrastructures, communication channels, and opportunities for outside financing.

Subsequently, the private capital and for-profit incubators began to spread. Often incubators are in scientific and technological parks. These are geographic poles that enhance the benefits of the joint localization of firms and institutions such as universities, venture capitalist associations, etc., operating in high-tech and knowledge-based sectors.

The growth of start-ups is the result of the entrepreneurial spirit of one or more individuals with innovative ideas.

SUSTAINABILITY: A DRIVER TO SUCCEED

One of the main challenges faced by SMEs when they find themselves before the difficult choice of internationalisation is linked to the alteration of their business model, which shifts from being focused on a specific territory, to a combination of strategies that have a bigger social and environmental impact, naturally dictated by a broader range of actions. Considering the importance of sustainability as a strategic corporate function, but also as the basis of the competitive advantage, how can SMEs accept the challenge of change while keeping the promise of sustainability?

Before understanding how an SME experiences the concept of sustainability, we ought to take a brief look at the concept itself and the need to pay attention to issues related to sustainability, business responsibility, ethics and the choice of the best communication tools to spread the word, considering that the choice of how, with which tools and how often to communicate the commitment of responsibility in terms of social enterprise and of business sustainability and ethics, is now a matter of "managerial embarrassment". Very often, problems arise from an inability to properly balance the two business functions: Communication and Sustainability. First of all, we have to point out that business communication, seen as a transversal and integrated strategic corporate function, has the main task of sustaining and protecting the company's reputation, maintaining communication with stakeholders in the long term. Business sustainability, as an integrated strategic business function (Casalegno and Civera, 2016, chapter 3), on the other hand, has numerous aims in the environmental, social, ethical and economic sphere, which originate in communication and in the multi-stakeholder value relationship.

The logic of contemporary sustainability is the output of theories and debates which represent influences and theoretic foundations for the construction of a model characterised by dimensions, activities and methods of innovative implementation. Consider also that, in actual fact, all the terminology linked to the concept of sustainability and responsible business has been and continues to subject to change.

In the logic of the theoretic model developed, the concept of sustainability refers to everything that includes the sphere of attention to the interests of stakeholders, environmental, economic and social sustainability, and ethics with a view to big (corporate) business. The concepts of responsibility and sustainability run parallel, so much so that examples of new definitions come from literature, like Corporate Sustainability and Responsibility (CSR) by Visser (2014).

Despite the various definitions considered by different scholars and academics for years, one of the main concepts that companies seem to consider is the attention to relations with their stakeholders. The multi-stakeholder approach, theorised by Edward Freeman many years ago, is the main concept for building the vision of Company Stakeholder Responsibility (2006) or of integrated CSR (Freeman et al., 2010) or, as it is called in this chapter, Sustainability. Firstly, it becomes an integral part of the concept, core processes and decision-making processes for companies and imposes the redefinition of the management of relationships with stakeholders. If we want to follow this point of view, then it is easy to understand that the logic doesn't intend to further regulate business, the aim being too redefine the policy of the organisation, and of the foundations and priorities of management. It isn't a matter of imposing new rules upon business, but of highlighting the need to redefine the business policy and the aims of managerial responsibilities. In this way, the concept of sustainability combines perfectly with the innovative contribution supplied by Wayne Visser in 2012. The author starts with the assumption that the responsibility and sustainability of organisations, like the business, governance and ethics system, has failed, at least in terms of social, environmental and ethical indicators, which sometimes present declining values. By identifying the evolutions of the concept of sustainability with respect to different stages of economic development, Visser defines the basis of the contemporary concept of sustainability. According to the author, the current stage of development of what he calls responsibility and sustainability is "systemic" and stems from an awareness that the current context is characterised by a failure of responsibility on several levels (from individual responsibility to the business context and the capitalistic system), especially following the financial crisis. The aim of systemic sustainability is the innovation of the corporate business model and the change in strategy, rethinking and revolutionising processes, products and services, and going beyond the boundaries of the company itself. The aim of sustainability is to understand the interconnections established between society, communities, the economy and ecosystems (Casalegno & Civera, 2016).

The first step towards implementing a business strategy linked to the concepts of sustainability and responsibility as described above, systemic and integrated, definitely lies in the governance system adopted. In this sense, sustainability has to occupy an independent strategic position within the organisation, on a level with all the other functions, (such as marketing, human resources, logistics, operations, etc..) and should integrate perfectly with all of these (Mosca et al., 2016).

Obviously, this goes for bigger and better organised companies, while for SMEs it is logical to consider that the activities of responsibility and sustainability are decisions that come from the different functional areas. However, the important thing is still the ability to connect these actions together, strategically and coherently. The communication of management with regard to sustainability should take place transversally to all functions because, while it is true that the contemporary logic of responsibility and sustainability imposes the redefinition of business models, its aim should be to change and improve the work of other business functions.

After explaining the principles on which contemporary sustainability is founded and the basis on which it evolves, it is possible to draw up an integrated model to supply a theoretic picture of it, highlighting the dimensions in which the strategic actions and activities of social, environmental, ethical and philanthropic sustainability are implemented (Casalegno & Civera, 2016).

In short, sustainability is a strategic function which is integrated with all the other business functions to help them in the definition and development of new strategies and policies; it takes a multi-stakeholder approach, in which actions integrate with the communication function to activate a two-way proactive dialogue and collect the feedback and needs of stakeholders in order to strengthen internal and external communication; this involves multiple areas of intervention: "environment, quality, ethics, human resources, community, consumers, economic development, causes of social interest, sport and culture: it isn't a proclamation of values but envisages tangible and measurable actions to define performance; it pursues projects that respond to a real and tangible need by society, in the environment or in the area/ community of reference; it includes the definition, creation and development of goods and services, processes and policies, and their continuous improvement thanks to innovation and technology; it pursues aims in line with the company's core business; it includes activities and actions that are integrated with the business itself and are carried out on an ongoing basis, pursued in the long term to increase the positive impact on society, the environment and the company; it takes a systemic and circular approach to rethinking the business model, revolutionizing products, services and processes along the whole chain of value; it follows the rational of reducing waste and making resources more efficient, to increase savings with a view to maximizing reinvestment in society and in the company itself; its aim is to increase competitiveness and reduce social costs" (Casalegno & Civera, 2016, p.64).

The company builds its integrated sustainability strategy within three dimensions: requirements, strategic philanthropy and integrated outputs. Within each dimension there are a variety of activities, from the adhesion to standards and codes that are universally recognised, to the partnership with a non-profit organisation to help support a social cause, or the redefinition of an entire production process to reduce the waste of water.

In particular, the first dimension of sustainability, "requirements", encompasses all the codes and standards (both national and international) that the company intends to observe in the pursuit of its activities in relation to the environment, quality, ethics, employees and the preparation of economic and business reports. Clearly, compliance with these standards and codes imposes on the company the respect of determined standards and the observance of a certain number of regulations, along with adaptation of conduct and processes to them.

The dimension of "strategic philanthropy" on the other hand, represents an evolution compared to any obligatory implementation relating to the previous dimension. This is the area in which the organisation chooses to expand its aims, supporting non-profit organisations and various institutions, from non-governmental to sporting associations, to sustain causes of social interest (ranging from support of developing countries to intervention in the case of humanitarian crises or environmental disasters), sorting and cultural events, with a view to improving the wellbeing of the communities in which it operates.

The activities of strategic philanthropy are the following:

- Donations to ngos or other institutions that support causes of social interest, which can take the form of disbursement of cash or material donations (for which the company makes infrastructures, food or technology available, depending on the sector in which it operates);
- Partnership and sponsorship, usually implemented over the long term, in which the company supports ngos or other institutions for causes of social interest, within the spheres of sport or culture;
- Cause Related Marketing, a more commercial than philanthropic technique, through which the company supports a social or environmental cause by linking its brand to that of the cause to be supported (typically a specific project pursued by a non-profit organisation), with reciprocal benefits for the company and the organisation itself (BITC, 2004);
- The formation of social enterprises which connected with the business and the creation of foundations to pursue determined strategic philanthropic activities;
- The involvement of employees in voluntary work (more typical in English-speaking countries than in Italy, as we will see), in which employees devote set days to tangibly supporting a cause of social interest supported by an NGO with which the company has activated a partnership.

Lastly, the dimension of "integrated outputs" (Mosca, Casalegno, Civera, 2016) is that which, more than others, aims to redefine the company's business model. This dimension requires the elaboration and development of goods and services, processes and policies which are sustainable socially and are ethic and responsible in relation to the environment. This is a dimension that invests not only in business but goes further, along the whole value chain, transforming resources into opportunities for the enterprise and for the partners involved.

This terminology indicates, for example, the development of compostable and eco-compatible products, the production of goods from production waste, the offering of micro-credit services to disadvantaged people, the implementation of an energy saving process that affects the whole organisation (from production to all the infrastructures at headquarters and in the company's secondary offices), policies, elaborated as integrated outputs, comprise the training of employees and supplies in CSR practices, the exclusion of certain commercial and other partners considered to be unethical, strategic welfare, including services for employees to improve their level of involvement and attachment to the company, the assessment of the steps along the whole value chain to identify waste and other areas that can be improved.

The dimension of integrated outputs offers evidence of how sustainability heavily influences the company's business and the actions of its partners, with the aid of innovation and technology, which represent key factors. Big business, in particular, can have access to new markets with new products (e.g.: those deriving from waste) or favour the creation of new small and medium enterprises. It can also increase consumer markets: just think of responsible projects aimed at developing and improving the conditions of local suppliers and distributors which not only creates a more efficient supply and distribution chain, but also a consumer base with more income to spend on the company's goods and services.

HOW TO COMMUNICATE SUSTAINABILITY

Through the integrated implementation of sustainability, the company not only gains access to new markets and niches, rationalising resources and reducing social costs, it can also improve the relationship with its stakeholders, strengthen the positive word of mouth and exploit the faith of financial players. The enhancement of the reputation of its brand will have an impact on the perception by consumers and their level of trust, on the sense of belonging felt by employees and on the increase in their level of satisfaction (McWilliams & Siegel, 2001; Bevan & Wilmott, 2002; Dawkins & Lewis, 2003; Casalegno & Pellicelli, 2008; Haanaes et al., 2011). Researches carried out in recent years highlight the aims of sustainability strategies and all converge in the theory that sustainability is the lever for activating valuable communication with all stakeholders (Vallaster at al., 2012; Candelo et al., 2014) as well as with the company's target market. The communication of sustainability is an essential requirement for the creation of awareness of company initiatives and towards determined social, ethical and environmental issues, and for strengthening the commitment of groups with an interest in the company as a whole. Meeting these needs means finding a code that allows the company to facilitate relationships, making the foundations uniform at the same time. Freeman et al. (2010) suggest how this aim can be more easily achieved when the company has a strong purpose and when this purpose is transformed into tangible actions with measurable impacts and is communicated consistently and in a standardised way. Increasingly, the purposes of businesses refer to aims of a social, environmental and ethical nature and the strategies connected to it, linked with business responsibility.

Just like the implementation of sustainability can provide the joint answer to opposing interests, in the same way, integrated communication of actions and initiatives can be considered the strategy to use to set up the aforementioned dialogue. To be more precise, the integrated communication of the actions and initiatives of sustainability can contribute to the increase and improvement of certain key concepts that various authors consider to be the basis of corporate communication: corporate personality, identity, corporate image and reputation (Siano et al., 2015).

Considering this, it is possible to build a model which analyses the different types of communication suited to each dimension of sustainability, i.e.: "requirements", which refer to the reporting activity of the company, in compliance with the law or general convention; "strategic philanthropy", which identifies the sum of the activities pursued to meet the numerous demands for sustainability of the community and support for projects and initiatives linked to local development which are of social interest; and, last but not least, "integrated outputs", which refer to products, services, processes and policies, linked intrinsically to the concept of sustainability (Casalegno & Civera, 2016).

Literature and business researches, for example, show that customer experiences define the reputation of the brand (Sen and Bhattacharya, 2001; Pomering and Dolnicar, 2009; Candelo et al., 2014; Hur et al., 2014). Consequently, the attitudes of the reference target, along with intents to purchase, can be influenced by responsible and sustainable initiatives. In other words, the communication of responsibility, when well developed within an articulate, organic and constantly evolving plan, has a positive impact on the reference target and on its perception of the company's reputation (Sen & Bhattacharya, 2001; Pomering & Dolnicar, 2009; Matute-Vallejo et al., 2011). In particular, a good reputation can be a quicker way to develop the brand within the reference markets (Werther & Chandler, 2005; Wheeler, 2009; Aaker, 2010; Candelo et al., 2014; Hur et al., 2014).

Socially responsible communication messages are increasingly frequent and extend to every dimension of responsibility, regardless of the typical reporting system. Reference is no longer made to the use of the sustainability report alone for the dissemination of messages relating to the actions and promises of responsibility, going beyond standards reporting activities, which are now taken for granted in that they are produced by all the big players. At this point, we can build an "Integrated sustainability communication framework" in which the different types of message are used in a way calibrated to suit the reference target and its area of action. It is here that the communication of sustainability proves that it is oriented towards the dissemination of strategies, results and tangible actions.

To disseminate and obtain a sense of legitimisation of the actions in this sense, a general communication towards stakeholders is necessary; this is a communication which aims to inform, using a common code, all stakeholders of a certain enterprise of the actions (and results) of responsibility and sustainability. This type of communication is based on reporting and sustainability tools (Financial Statements, Sustainability Report), on codes of conduct, ethical codes, press communications (the main PR tool), territorial events, company web pages, and the internal mail system (because those who work within a company are strategic stakeholders). It is possible to think, in this case, more of an institutional communication, where the corporate brand has most weight and where the subjects to be disclosed are related to the environment, management of diversity, inclusion of protected categories of subjects within the business structure, respect of quality standards, ethics and human rights. In short, communication, in this case, is the vehicle via which all stakeholders are informed of the management policies that the public expects the company to pursue, along with the publication of the values that guide its business.

The second type of communication refers to maintaining relationships with the communities which are, in some way, influenced by the company's actions. The relationships that the company wants to maintain here aim to enhance the corporate image, so that it is perceived in a good light in the area(s) where it is present. This type of communication is pursued through local events, sponsorship and partnership, information relating to voluntary work carried out by employees (and the results achieved), web pages and social network profiles, the financial statements (because this document provides not only the information that the company has to or should consider by law or by convention), press releases (common to all types of communication of responsibility, and internal mailing systems.

Communication towards partners (i.e.: employees, suppliers, retailers, customers/consumers/users), on the other hand, concerns all the actions that the organisation undertakes in terms of product (goods or service), process and policies implemented. The inclusion of a reduced-impact process in the production of the social purpose, the use of compostable or biodegradable materials (the two are very different), the assumption of sustainable internal policies and policies in relation to the target market. The tools used

Figure 1. The Sustainability communication framework
Source: adapted Casalegno, Civera, 2016

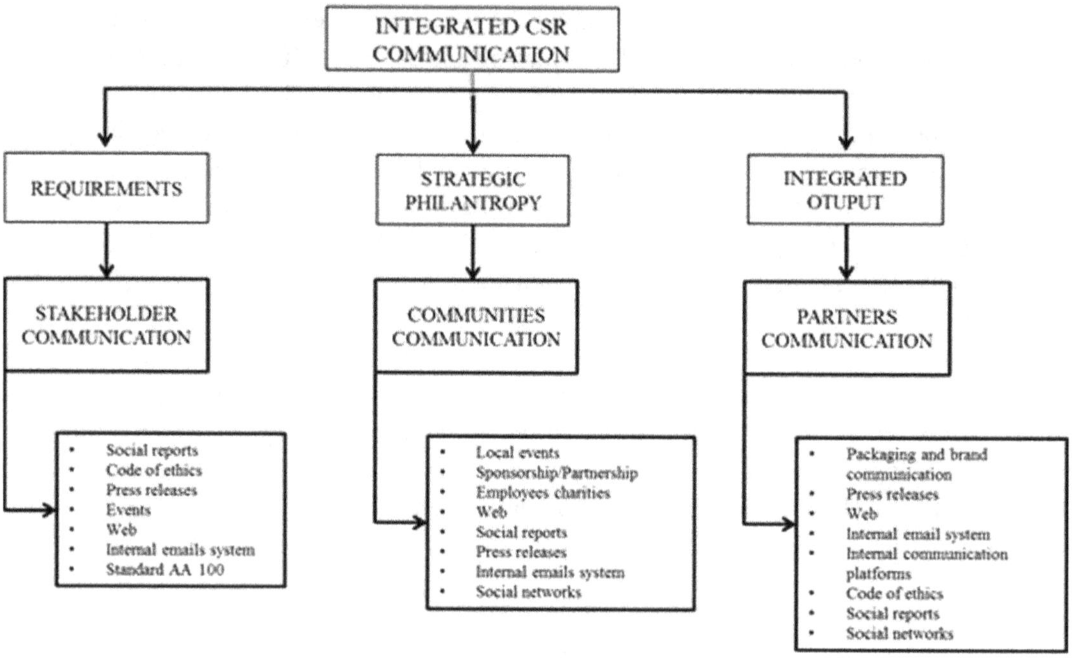

to communicate these actions of responsibility and sustainability regard the aforementioned websites, along with social network profiles, reporting on sustainability, the code of ethics, the financial statements, and internal communication platforms. The communication of sustainability through the packaging of a product is another example of integrated output communication towards partners. This type of communication also contains the information related to actions in favour of employees not already contained in the company welfare declaration – which is standard, having to comply with specific dictates – but refers to works of "internal philanthropy", so as to speak, by the company.

Every aspect and dimension of the communication of sustainability, in this sense, should be standard and transparent. This concept matches that of integrated communication, expressed to the full. Seen from this point of view, sustainability is linked to the communication strategy, considering that this "should be accompanied by transparent communication which proves the sustainability of the conduct of a company at economic, environmental and social level" (Perrini, 2005).

SME, INTERNATIONALIZATION AND SUSTAINABILITY: HOW TO ACT? A TERRITORIAL ANALYSIS

Considering the above mentioned literature and problems higlited by previous researches, SMEs seem to have serious problems in adapting their business model for international markets: on one hand, they need to keep the promise of sustainability, which is implicit in the majority of SME business models (containing emissions, being linked to the local community, augmenting social values, employing local people). On the other hand, they have to cope with a different kind of competition, which is normally based on row material massive consuptions, delocalised workforce and a higher impacting distribution.

Their job is to customize a new and strategic business model, which will answer the key search questions concerning the process innovation (Davenport, 1993) and the product one (Dougherty, 1992), the different approaches required by different countries (Usunier, 2005), the collaboration between firms anc territorial actors (Tikkanen, 1998), the systemic sustainability (Visser, 2012) and its degree of innovation (Bhasrakan, 2006). This business model is to be applied to the players who strive towards shifting from operating at local level to adopting a logic of international sustainable entrepreneurship, without losing their particular features. This "hybrid" business model needs to be tailored to the specificities of the chosen industries/value chains. The main goal is to facilitate the knowledge transfer, the assets and competitive business strategy methods implementation, sustainability and its communication, quality, entrepreneurship and internationalization strategies. Due to their dimensions and scarce resources, SMEs are often unable to develop the above and they need to be helped. At this point, the territory itself should be able to give them the support they need but, at least so far, it is not possible to enumerate public infrastructures capable of doing so. In order to undertsnd the existing state of the art, a benchmark analysis has carried on, considering that public infractructures are fundamentals for the SMEs' livelihood, expecially when they represent a fundamental part for the local economy development. Incubators have been not included, since their daily mission is more focused on developing start-ups than assisting SMEs. To sum up the research methodology, the literarure review helped to find which benchmark to investage and what SMEs problems and their required knowledge were. The scheme below (Figure 2) helps to understand the research flow.

As it is easy to see, the Italian territory has made several attempts to support SMEs' ideas and actions, as well as the technological transfer. The best benchmark that it is possible to talk about is represented by the Start-up Lab (University of Naples), which plays an incubator role. Thanks to the application of the knowledge of researchers and professors, it helps existing innovative SMEs to develop their businesses.

Figure 2. The research flow

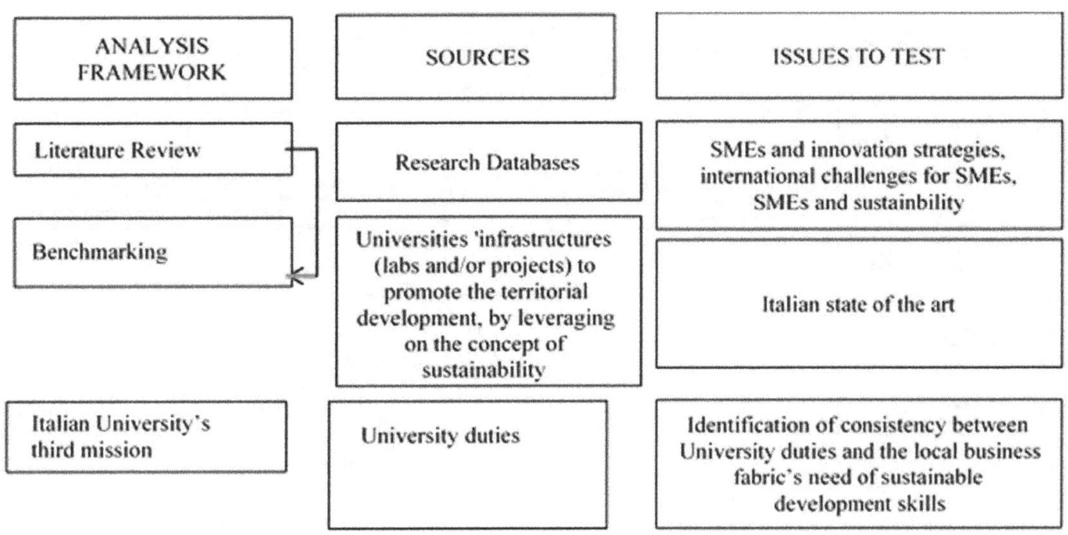

The Start-up Lab model acts as follows: tailor-made services, considering the specific needs of start-ups and other firms, activities to implement the interaction between firms and investors or the best consultants available. Moreover, Start-up Lab offers 360-degree support with the aim of helping firms to get bigger, to perform better on the markets and to represent a value-added element for the territory. All the Labs analysed come from the efforts of University Departments and are funded by private partners, associations and, in two cases (Contamination Lab Catania and Contamination Lab Cà Foscari), they have received government funds from the national research programme 2015-2020. It is important to highlight that every lab is a project output and is never a profitable organization.

In the light of what has been said, a lack of communication appears to be the cause of the scarce knowledge about these projects; except for the Start-up Lab, it was very difficult to gather enough information about the other cases and, above all, evidence of their action on their territory.

Moreover, these labs don't represent a strong link between the different players on a same territory; in this case too, information on these kinds of link were hard to find.

THINKING ABOUT A DIFFERENT WAYOUT

In the light of the above, the need for SMEs to develop long-terms relationships with the local institutions emerges. Universities have always forged talent, knowledge and technology, being able to enhance the value of the know-how and skills of individuals, on one hand, and entrepreneurial ideas linked to the

Table 1. The benchmark analysis

	Start up Lab University of Naples	Clab contamination lab Catania University	Clab contamination lab Politecnica University Marche	Clab Contamination Lab Reggio Calabria University	Cà Foscari Contamination Lab Venice University
Who	University infrastructure which has the aim of creating a bridge between the local entrepreneurs and the Academy	The project aims to provide innovative training courses for students of Master Degree courses aimed at fostering the spread of entrepreneurship culture, combining it with the vision of territorial development of Horizon 2020 and the regional strategies of Smart Specialization.	Promote the culture of engaging and stimulating the contamination among students of the various disciplinary areas and between the academic world and the socio-economic system. It is an initiative inspired by what was promoted in 2013 by MIUR	Place of promotion of culture aimed at entrepreneurship	Within the framework of the professional development for the Cafoscarini, the Contamination Lab, a contamination project created by the initiative of Ca 'Foscari University and H-Farm Ventures, is included.
Mission	It firmly believes that the birth and development of innovative startups are strategic leverage to foster socio-economic development of the territories and improve people's quality of life.	It promote the ideas contamination	The c Lab aims to promote the culture of entrepreneurship, innovation and making, foster interdisciplinarity and new learning models, expose students to a stimulating environment for the development of innovative projects, in close contact with managers And entrepreneurs	The Contamination Lab is a place where ideas and opportunities meet with creativity and entrepreneurial projects	The promotion of new businesses
Services	Business Entrepreneurship Assessment - Business Plan Drafting - Support for Academic Spin-offs - Entrepreneurship Growth in Large Enterprises - Entrepreneurship and Spin-off in Research Centers - Support for Creating Business Incubators - Pitch and executive summary development - Networking - Mentoring and Management Consulting - Start Up Lab School - Open Innovation Development - Assistance - Choice of Business Plan Competitions and Acceleration / Incubation Programs - Intellectual Property Management.	The model will favor contamination between different disciplines, between different visions, to guide training to integrated paths that develop the culture of working together, creativity, sharing new learning paths	The model will favor contamination between different disciplines, between different visions, to guide training to integrated paths that develop the culture of working together, creativity, sharing new learning paths	The CLab Reggio Calabria will promote the participation of groups in national and international competitions and will facilitate access to sources of finance for the most promising business ideas.	To enrich the offer available to students who will find "home" in the Contamination Lab it will also be the collaboration of VeNetWork, a network of Venetian entrepreneurs who, with the story of their experiences and strong presence in the market, will help address the ideas of Young students so that they can quickly become a business or enter a company.
Main goals	Traditional (food, agribusiness, fashion) but with innovative projects - biotech and life science - aerospace - Web and digital - cleantech - automotive - logistics and transportation - electronics.			Innovative ideas promotion.	Product and process innovation
To whom?	Start-up and spin off promoters, large corporations, universities and public and private research centers, start-up companies, aspiring entrepreneurial students.	students	Students	The recipients of the notice are mainly students and students of the Mediterranean University of Reggio Calabria, students of the University for Foreigners "Dante Alighieri" of Reggio Calabria and students of the Academy of Fine Arts in Reggio Calabria but also students of foreign universities and other Italian universities. 40 available places.	The Contamination Lab is open to all students enrolled at Ca 'Foscari University, any faculty and year of study.

Source: authors' processing

Table 2.

SBM Model (Constant Return to Scale) ***Input oriented***

$$\rho = \min_{\lambda, s^-, s^+} \frac{1 - \frac{1}{m}\sum_{i=1}^{m}\frac{s_i^-}{x_{io}}}{1 + \frac{1}{s}\sum_{r=1}^{s}\frac{s_r^+}{y_{ro}}}$$

$$\begin{aligned} s.t. \quad & x_o - s^- = X\lambda \\ & y_o + s^+ = Y\lambda \\ & \lambda \geq 0, s^- \geq 0, s^+ \geq 0 \end{aligned}$$

concept of sustainability (profit or non-profit) of small, medium and big organisations (initially local and then decentralised) on the other. In this case, university professors, researchers, fellows, undergraduate and gradutate students, PhD students can assume the role of knowledge suppliers, helping small and medium territorial entreprises in projects planning and development, since those firms usually do not have adequate resources to engage big players to advise them.

Considering the theme of the third mission, alongside the two essential aims of training and research, the University pursues a third and important aim: enhancing the knowledge transfer to favour the territorial economics growth. This goal can be pursued through research contracts and consulting agreements with independent players, patents, the creation of spin-off, participation in incubators and consortia aimed at technological and knowledge transfers.

This context includes the opportunity to think of the creation of an infrastructure, which performs the abovementioned supporting activities, maintaining a particular focus on the concept of sustainability and its communication, considering the concept of multi-stakeholder value relatioships. The idea of creating this infrastructure stems from a dual need, more keenly felt today than in the past. First of all, small and medium enterprises in the area are showing increasing interest in pursuing relations with Universities, which continue to retain their excellent reputation for producing talent, as well as catalysing relationships which would be hard to manage otherwise. A second requirement is manifested by those trained in university courses, because while university education continues to represent a plus on one hand, on the other, those who obtain a university qualification at the end of their studies are well-prepared in theoretic terms but lack the practical skills to take on an increasingly difficult working world, considering that the offer tends to exceed demand in many cases. Both students and firms in the same area have to be able to rely on an infrastructure that provides answers to needs which – at the moment – are taken on individually by researchers and professor, who are unable to provide a long-term solution, with the consequent lack of establishment of long-term relationships with the area's business fabric. This causes a lot of lost opportunities for the public administration, which can lose the opportunity to tackle the real problems of local firms, and for local firms, which find themselves forced to outsource research, engaging the expensive aid of consultants who are often unable to provide long-term assistance.

Under the attentive supervision of university professors and researchers, undergraduates, PhD students and graduates ones can work on real problems, current projects and future plans handed to them voluntarily by companies and organisations in general, always considering the theme of sustainability and its communication. Making reference to the abovementioned infrastructure (which we call InSu, as Infrastructure for the Sustainability), they will see a pool of people work, for a period of time agreed to and considered, to accomplish the project or find a solution to the problem linked to enterprise sustainability.

The action of InSu doesn't intend to replace an important infrastructure already consolidated in the area, i.e.: the incubator, but wants to work as an organisation capable of cooperating with it, creating a partnership for the provision of useful services. Looking at the specific case considered, Piedmont, the Incubator of Turin University (2i3t) currently places a series of services at the disposal of those with a business idea:

- Scouting for ideas;
- Definition of the business model;
- Definition of the industrial plan;
- Accompaniment of the business in the first three years of its life;
- Services linked to industrial property;
- Tutoring services;
- Incubation of start-ups.

At this point, InSu would also have the aim of creating partnerships in the following areas, with the Incubator UNITO (2I3T) and the others present in the same territory. In particular, it can work on the following:

1. Managerial infrastructure in SMEs:
    a. Marketing and Communication over sustainable development;
    b. Administration;
    c. Finance;
    d. Auditing concenrning the sustainability;
    e. Specific skills linked to the above mentioned functions (psychological, sociological, security, technology, etc).
2. Synergy and network between SMEs in order to face the international challenge in the light of their sustainability;
3. Synergy and network between SMEs and big players, considering the concepts of cooperation and partnerships;

In the light of the above, the intention is not to replace the infrastructures of Turin University (UNITO) that are already present, but to create a reality which adds services in a coordinated and systemic way and which increases the relational capacities of UNITO with the following actions:

- Training on the job;
- Cooperation and integration with Incubator (2I3T), SAA and UNITO (Departments);
- Collaboration with: Local Public Authorities (Region, Metropolitan City, Municipalities), Local Health Department, Industrial Union, Chamber of Commerce, CEIP, Trade Association, etc.

Figure 3. The infrastructure for sustainability: a multi-stakeholder framework attempt
Source: authors' processing

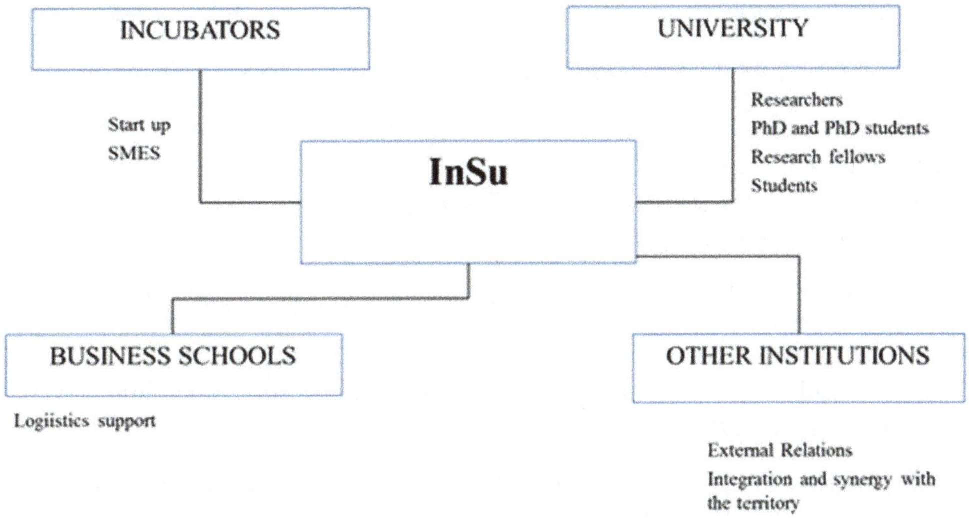

As regards the specific needs and skills required by the single project in which the concept of sustainability is considered essential (be it social, economic, environmental), this database will be used to cope with the needs for knowledge. The choice of the single supplier of knowledge for every project will be pondered: specific abilities and skills of every member of the database will be considered, in relation to the type of problem that spinlab has to tackle. Moreover, considering the same knowledge, the individual resource will be chosen by the Board of Directors. The members of the database, who hold various roles within the university (structured or otherwise) having accepted the task of working to a project, will take operational responsibility for the project, interfacing with each other, choosing a project manager and relating to the organisation with the problem to be solved.

In conclusion, InSu intends to provide a bridge between university research and its application, local businesses and those who intend to refine their skills and knowledge, working on projects and entrepreneurial and business problems, or issues linked to the growth and development of the territory, in a multi-stakeholder perspective.

Basically, the services that the lab intends to provide are:

- Training on the job for undergraduate students and new graduates;
- Research possibilities, via the study of business cases, for PhD students, fellows, researchers and all those who, having a role within the university, intend to face the problems linked to the territory and, at the same time, want to have the chance to pursue researches which also have academic/scientific value;
- Activities as a catalyser for the creation of interdepartmental relations, capable of increasing the value of actions linked to the university's third mission.

REFERENCES

Aaker, D. A. (2010). *Brand Relevance: Making Competitors Irrelevant*. John Wiley & Sons.

Bevan, S., & Wilmott, M. (2002). *The Ethical Employee*. London: The Work Future Foundation.

Candelo, E., Casalegno, C., & Civera, C. (2014). Meanings and Implications of Corporate Social Responsibility and Branding in Grocer Retailers: A Comparative Study over Italy and the UK. In F. Musso & E. Druica (Eds.), *Handbook of Research on Retailer-Consumer Relationship Development* (pp. 351–370). IGI Global. doi:10.4018/978-1-4666-6074-8.ch019

Casalegno, C., & Civera, C. (2016). *Impresa e CSR: la non comunicazione di successo*. Milan, Italy: Franco Angeli.

Casalegno, C., & Pellicelli, M. (2008). The Human Capital Impact on the Shareholder Value Creation. *Economia Aziendale On Line 2000 Web, 1*(2/3).

Cedrola, E., & Battaglia, L. (2011). Piccole e medie imprese e internazionalità: Strategie di business, relazioni, innovazione. *Sinergie, 85*(11), 71–92.

Dawkins, J., & Lewis, S. (2003). CSR in stakeholder expectations: And their implication for company strategy. *Journal of Business Ethics, 44*(2/3), 185–193. doi:10.1023/A:1023399732720

Dougherty, D. (1992). Interpretive barriers to successful product innovation in large firms. *Organization Science, 3*(2), 179–202. doi:10.1287/orsc.3.2.179

Freeman, E. D., & Driver, J. (2006). Subjective appearance of ambiguous structure-from-motion can be driven by objective switches of a separate less ambiguous context. *Vision Research, 46*(23), 4007–4023. doi:10.1016/j.visres.2006.07.008 PMID:16996558

Freeman, R. E., Wicks, A., Harrison, J., Parmar, B., & de Colle, S. (2010). *Stakeholder Theory: The State of The Art*. Cambridge, UK: Cambridge University Press. doi:10.1017/CBO9780511815768

Haanaes, K., Balagopal, B., Arthur, D., Kong, M. T., Velken, I., Kruschwitz, N., & Hopkins, M. S. (2011). First Look: The Second Annual Sustainability & Innovation Survey. *MIT Sloan Management Review, 52*(2), 77–83.

Hur, W. M., Kim, H., & Woo, J. (2014). How CSR Leads to Corporate Brand Equity: Mediating Mechanisms of Corporate Brand Credibility and Reputation. *Journal of Business Ethics, 125*(1), 75–86. doi:10.100710551-013-1910-0

Matute-Vallejo, J., Bravo, R., & Pina, J. M. (2011). The influence of Corporate Social Responsibility and Price Fairness on Customer Behaviour: Evidence from the Financial Sector. *Corporate Social Responsibility and Environmental Management, 18*(6), 317–331. doi:10.1002/csr.247

McWilliams, A., & Siegel, A. D. (2001). Corporate Social Responsibility: A Theory of the Firm Perspective. *Academy of Management Review, 26*(1), 117–127.

Mosca, F., Casalegno, C., & Civera, C. (2016, September). *Opportunities and Peculiarities of the Online for Communicating Corporate Social Responsibility. A cross investigation on luxury players and consumers' perceptions*. Paper presented at the meeting of the British Academy of Management (BAM), Newcastle, UK.

Perrini, F. (2005). Building a European Portait of Corporate Social Responsibility Reporting. *European Management Journal*, *23*(6), 611–627. doi:10.1016/j.emj.2005.10.008

Pomering, A., & Dolnicar, S. (2009). Assessing the Prerequisite of Successful CSR Implementation: Are Consumers Aware of CSR Initiatives? *Journal of Business Ethics*, *85*(2), 285–301. doi:10.100710551-008-9729-9

Porter, M., & Kramer, R. (2002). The Competitive Advantage of Corporate Philanthropy. *Harvard Business Review*, *80*(12), 57–68. PMID:12510538

Rainero, C., Puddu, L., & Migliavacca, A. (2016). Aziende, Amministrazione Razionale e Impatto Sociale. In *Aziende non-profit etica e responsabilità sociale* (pp. 7–26). Milan, Italy: Franco Angeli.

Rainero, C., & Brescia, V. (2016). Corporate Social Responsibility» and «Social Reporting»: The Model of Innovation «Piedmont Method. *International Journal Series in Multidisciplinary Research*, *2*(3), 18-40.

Sen, S., & Bhattacharya, C. B. (2001). Does Doing Good Always Lead to Doing Better? Consumer Reactions to Corporate Social Responsibility. *JMR, Journal of Marketing Research*, *38*(2), 225–243. doi:10.1509/jmkr.38.2.225.18838

Siano, A., Vollero, A., & Siglioccolo, M. (2015). *Corporate Communication Management*. Torino, Italy: Giappichelli.

Small, L. (2011). *Corporate Responsibility, Marketing and Economic Development in Emerging Markets*. Retrieved from http://www.accountability.org/about-us/news/accountability-1/accountability.html

Strand, R., Freeman, R. E., & Hockerts, K. (2015). Corporate social responsibility and sustainability in Scandinavia: An overview. *Journal of Business Ethics*, *127*(1), 1–15. doi:10.100710551-014-2224-6

Tikkanen, H. (1998). The network approach in analyzing international marketing and purchasing operations: A case study of a European SME's focal net 1992-95. *Journal of Business and Industrial Marketing*, *13*(2), 109–131. doi:10.1108/08858629810213333

Usunier, J. C., Lee, J. A., & Lee, J. (2005). *Marketing across cultures*. Pearson Education.

Vallaster, C., Lindgreen, A., & Maon, F. (2012). Strategically Leveraging Corporate Social Responsibility: A Corporate Brand Perspective. *California Management Review*, *54*(3), 34–60. doi:10.1525/cmr.2012.54.3.34

Visser, W. (2012). The Future of CSR: Towards Transformative CSR, or CSR 2.0. *Kaleidoscope Futures Paper Series*, *1*, 1–17.

Visser, W. (2014). *CSR 2.0: Transforming corporate sustainability and responsibility*. Berlin: Springer. doi:10.1007/978-3-642-40874-8

Werther, W. B. Jr, & Chandler, B. (2005). Strategic Corporate Social Responsibility as Global Brand Insurance. *Business Horizons*, *48*(4), 317–324. doi:10.1016/j.bushor.2004.11.009

Wheeler, A. (2009). *Designing Brand Identity: An Essential Guide for the Whole Branding Team*. New York: Wiley.

KEY TERMS AND DEFINITIONS

Infrastructure: A system that allows the organizations to work better with major results in terms of incomes and good relationships with the territory.

Integrated Communication: The sum of organized and planned effords in building strong and long-lasting relatioships with the stakeholders.

Internationalization: The effort of becoming international.

Network: A large system consisting of many parts that are connected together to allow movement or communication between or along the parts.

Relationship: The way through which the organization can be connected with its stakeholders or other territorial actors.

SME: Small and medium entreprises; a small enterprise is defined as an enterprise which employs fewer than 50 persons and whose annual turnover and/or annual balance sheet total does not exceed EUR 10 million.

Sustainability: The combination of environmental, societal, and ethical concerns in processes, goods/products, and services development.

Chapter 7
An Innovative Company in a Smart City:
A Sustainable Business Model

Francesca Culasso
University of Turin, Italy

Sara Giovanna Mauro
University of Turin, Italy

ABSTRACT

The aim of this chapter is to analyze the business model of an innovative company in the context of a smart city. Specifically, this research investigates key components and challenges concerning the operationalization of a business model originally conceived to be sustainable. This chapter relies on the analysis of the empirical evidence collected at the organizational level by combining different data sources, including official and internal documents, face-to-face interviews, and questionnaires. It is thus designed to contribute to the lively debate on sustainability by providing empirical evidence and shedding light on the operationalization of the concept of sustainable business model. Further, in light of the smart context where the company operates, this research paves the way for further investigation into the potential win-win collaboration between innovative companies and smart cities to foster sustainability consistent with a systems approach to the topic.

INTRODUCTION

In recent years, it has been argued that sustainability is a key challenge for both private and public-sector organizations, calling for the integration of environmental, societal, and economic issues to support sustainable development. The changes needed to pursue a sustainable economy call for significantly revising the purpose of business and how it is conducted (Bocken et al., 2014). In this context, scholars and practitioners have become aware of the need to innovate traditional business models by incorporating the pursuit of sustainable development in the management of business, thus implementing what has

DOI: 10.4018/978-1-5225-5267-3.ch007

been defined a "sustainable business model" (SBM) (Stubbs & Cocklin, 2008). However, whether and how that can happen are difficult-to-answer questions (Birkin et al., 2009).

While a proliferation of definitions and descriptions of business models has characterized the last few decades (Morris et al., 2005; Osterwalder & Pigneur, 2010; Zott & Amit, 2013), the literature on practical applications of SBMs is still limited (Bocken et al., 2014) even though the theory of business models for sustainability is somewhat more extensive (Stubbs & Cocklin, 2008). Indeed, on the one hand, a growing body of literature has investigated key issues regarding definitions and developments of SBMs (Birkin et al 2009; Laukkanen & Patala, 2014; Lee & Casalegno, 2010; Schaltegger et al., 2012); on the other hand, there is still a need to unravel how a theoretical model of sustainable business can be translated into practice and how and whether it can contribute to the context in which it is adopted.

Since the concept of sustainability calls for a "systems concept" going beyond organizational boundaries and embracing different actors present in a specific context (Milne, 2007), organizations are expected to collaborate (Kerret & Menahem, 2016) to achieve the shared goal of sustainable development. Accordingly, an SBM should be a construct involving a focal firm and other interested organizations (Zott et al., 2011). Indeed, the most recent approaches have stressed the relevance of the role played by a focal firm that produces value for a network of organizations involved in its business model (Zott et al., 2011). Accordingly, the present chapter describes and explains the SBM of an innovative company while exploring the relationship between the focal firm and other actors operating in the same context. Specifically, this context is characterized by an orientation to smartness, which is determined by, among the other factors, a commitment to the realization of sustainable development (Caragliu et al., 2011).

To this end, this research has purposefully selected a firm operating in what has been considered a smart context, namely the city of Turin in northern Italy (EY, 2016). By analyzing the company's official documents and internal reports, collecting and studying information available on official websites and in newspapers, and interviewing the actors operating in and with the company, this research describes their SBM and explains how it works. In particular, it sheds light on the key components of the SBM and discusses which components have been, and still are, the primary challenges and obstacles.

By adopting this approach, the research aims to contribute to the body of knowledge on SBMs by providing empirical evidence regarding a company conceived to make sustainability the object of its core business and by shedding new light on the key elements and issues of SBM development in the context of a smart city. To achieve this goal, the next section provides a brief overview of previous studies of SBM and then introduces the framework adopted for the empirical analysis. Then, it describes the research setting and method and provides empirical evidence regarding the design and implementation of the business model. Finally, relying on the interpretation of the findings, implications for future research are discussed followed by some concluding remarks.

BACKGROUND

Sustainability and Business Models

Numerous challenges, ranging from climate changes and pollution to financial crises, have altered the business scenario worldwide, putting growing pressure on individual actors and institutions to respond quickly. Consequently, sustainability and sustainable development have become key priorities to be managed carefully by both public and private organizations; nowadays, "there is no alternative to sustainable development" (Nidumolu et al., 2009, p. 57).

Thus, the idea of sustainability and sustainable development have attracted increasing attention from both scholars and practitioners, and an academic debate has grown around the definition of these concepts and their challenging operationalization. Special attention is being paid to the integration of the idea of sustainability with management accounting, investigating the design and application of sustainability management control systems, which are intended essential for supporting sustainable development (e.g., Bebbington & Thomson, 2013; Contraffatto & Burns, 2013; Lueg & Radlach, 2016). A starting point for finding solutions to the realization of sustainable development could be identified in the generation of innovation, the preferred way to address numerous current challenges (OECD, 2011). Consequently, this need to do things differently has often been connected with the need to create innovative business models and has been positively connected with sustainability challenges (Porter & Kramer, 2011). Indeed, since the late 1990s, sustainability and sustainable development have been related to the concept of the business model (Boons et al., 2013), a perspective that takes into account the several elements a company should integrate and balance to be successful in realizing sustainable development, broadening the debate regarding the integration of business models with the philosophy of sustainability.

The general debate on business models is extensive and lively, but it has not resulted in a unique definition of the concept. Indeed, as a comprehensive review of the literature has shown (Zott et al., 2011), a wide range of articles have been published on business models, but its conceptualization is not unique even as a consequence of the different streams of literature contributing to the topic (e.g., e-commerce, strategy, and technology and innovation management).

The business model can be a "heuristic logic" linking technical potential and economic value (Chesbrough & Rosenbloom, 2002) or a template depicting the content, structure, and governance of the value obtained through the collaboration between a focal firm and its partners (Amit & Zott, 2001; Zott & Amit, 2008). Further, it can be broadly intended as a strategic management tool designed to improve a company's value chain (Boons & Ludeke-Freund, 2013). Focusing on the latest goal of the business model as identified by scholars, it is possible to interpret it as a construct whereby a company creates, delivers, and captures value for itself, its partners, and its customers (Osterwalder et al., 2005; Osterwalder & Pigneur, 2010). Following this reasoning, the business model assumes relevance as a new proper unit of analysis (Zott et al., 2011) calling for integration with sustainability thinking in order to provide an appropriate answer to current challenges. Indeed, a growing awareness of the need to find alternative ways to produce value in terms of sustainability has emphasized the need to change existing business models. In this regard, since the concept of sustainability calls for being a "systems concept" that goes beyond organizational boundaries and embraces different actors present in a specific context (Milne, 2007), it becomes even more crucial for an SBM to be a construct involving a focal firm and other interested organizations (Zott et al., 2011), the collaboration among which can contribute to achieving the shared goal of sustainable development.

Thus, sustainability becomes a driver of innovation leading to the development of new business models (Nidumolu et al., 2009). Consequently, the business model approach to sustainability has attracted growing attention over the last years (Lee & Casalegno, 2010), since sustainability as a goal can strongly contribute to achieving a competitive advantage (Nidumolu et al., 2009). A growing body of research combining sustainability and existing business models has thus attempted to elaborate principles and tools suitable for supporting sustainability development (Birkin et al., 2009; Bocken et al., 2014; Boons & Lüdeke-Freund, 2013; Schaltegger et al., 2012), but the link between SBM and sustainable innovations needs to be explored further. SBM, business cases for sustainability, business model for sustainability have emerged as key terms. Specifically, an SBM can be an innovation of the business model, representing an approach whereby firms re-conceptualize their logic to encompass sustainability (Bocken et al., 2014). The innovation of business models has received increasing attention in the literature (Chesbrough, 2010; Lüdeke-Freund, 2010; Zott et al., 2011) as a key to success using a variety of approaches: defensive, accommodative, and proactive (Schaltegger et al., 2012). Defensive strategies consist of incremental adjustments made to the existing business model to protect it. Accommodative strategies are designed to improve the current business model through experimentation, and proactive strategies concern the redesign of the core business logic of the firm in order to encompass sustainability. However, the proactive innovation approach represents a more effective strategy for achieving sustainability. Further, the innovations of the business model can be of different types including the discovery of a new product or service or new ways to create and deliver existing services. Thus, the business model can act as a tool whereby innovations spread, implying that the same technology can produce different results according to the innovation capabilities (Chesbrough & Rosenbloom, 2002; Chesbrough, 2010). Alternatively, the business model can be modified to bring innovation (Calia et al., 2007) including innovations in technology, product, or process, but they can go beyond these changes bringing new values to the market (Zott et al., 2011). Indeed, the research on this kind of innovation is particularly concerned with the sustainability of the whole system, emphasizing the need for structural and cultural changes (Boons et al., 2013; Stubbs & Cocklin, 2008).

In addition, other conceptualizations of the concept of SBM exist. They can encompass "a narrative of sustainability practices; a description of features, attributes, and/or characteristics; a list of necessary and sufficient conditions; a representation of business processes; a firm-level description; a systems-level description; or some combinations of these" (Stubbs & Cocklin, 2008, p. 104). According to Lüdeke-Freund (2009, p. 56), a business model for sustainability "is the activity system of a firm which allocates resources and coordinates activities in a value creation process which overcomes the public/private benefit discrepancy. That is, a business model for sustainability is the structural template of a business logic which creates the business case for sustainability." This implies that customers are key partners in the value creation process, which realizes a value proposition that integrates public and private benefits. Indeed, in a follow-up study, Lüdeke-Freund (2010) reflected on SBM by referring to the "superior customer value" created by such a business model and the consequent contribution to the sustainable development of the company and society, elaborating on several concepts such as eco-innovation and extended customer value. Further, Stubbs and Cocklin (2008) defined what an SBM can look like starting from the analysis of two cases and showing that the model should be based on both structural and cultural capabilities to achieve firm-level sustainability and, at the same time, collaborate with key stakeholders to achieve sustainability for the system of which that organization is a part. Thus, firm and system perspectives should be combined.

These considerations demonstrate the existence of a lively debate aimed at conceptualizing the SBM. Nevertheless, there is not yet a standard definition of the concept, used in a fuzzy way (Lüdeke-Freund, 2010; Schaltegger et al., 2012), and the body of knowledge on its practical application is even less developed. Previous research has reviewed the empirical studies on business models (Lambert & Davidson, 2013) and pointed out that research on business model innovation was increasing but still in its infancy. Carayannis et al. (2014) studied how an organization can achieve sustainability through business model innovation and the role of different factors in this process, while Laukkanen and Patala (2014) analyzed the barriers to SBMs. However, the investigation of SBM is relatively new (Boons et al., 2013) and the literature on this topic calls for further investigation, especially concerning the practical attempts of the firms to combine and integrate the different dimensions of the business model (Bocken et al., 2014) and to analyze the interactions occurring with the other stakeholders and, more generally, with the surrounding context. The smartness of the context under investigation, and especially its orientation to sustainability, are expected to influence the development of collaborations between local governments and private organizations. In this regard, while an increasing body of knowledge has recognized the relevance of collaborations and partnerships in the context of smart city (e.g., Caragliu et al., 2011; Meijer & Bolivar, 2016), the impact of this context on the sustainability of the business models of private organizations, and thus, on the development of SBMs in the context of smart city, appears under-investigated.

MAIN FOCUS OF THE CHAPTER

Issues

As previously pointed out, despite the relevant attention paid to sustainability issues, more studies on the application of theoretical systems are needed (Berry et al., 2009; Nixon & Burns, 2012). In this specific context, the ambiguity of the meaning of the concept of sustainability (Gray, 2010; Milne et al., 2009) influences the attempts to translate this multi-faceted concept into practice. Hence, the application of a sustainability orientation to traditional tools is a key challenge. As Lueg and Radlach (2016) pointed out, tensions exist, for instance, between traditional understanding of control tools and systems with their focus on profitability and growth, and the main interest in protecting and preserving national resources in accordance with the philosophy of sustainability. Thus, reviewing and innovating business models represents an even more complex challenge. Although business model innovations are considered suitable mechanisms for paving the way to new opportunities, their implementation is not without difficulties (Chesbrough, 2010) and there are several barriers to SBMs (Laukkanen & Patala, 2014).

In this regard, a great part of the literature has focused on the analysis of existing businesses that have changed their models to cope with sustainability challenges. Indeed, many companies have started to record, manage, and report the environmental and social aspects of business performance in addition to the economic dimension in accordance with the triple bottom line concept of sustainability, which includes these three pillars in defining sustainability despite the difficulties and limitations (Birkin et al., 2009). However, fewer attempts have been made to explore what companies are doing in practice to contribute to a sustainability development from a comprehensive perspective (Bocken et al., 2014) and what firms have to cope with when including sustainability in the business model from the outset (Porter & Kramer, 2011; Stubbs & Cocklin, 2008). For this reason, the current chapter contributes to the debate through its empirical analysis of an innovative company pursuing sustainability goals from its formation and by focusing on the company's business model. The next sub-section introduces the framework used for interpreting the empirical findings. Then, the chapter proceeds with a description of the research setting and the illustration of the research method adopted.

Framework of Analysis

According to the existing literature on the topic, key elements of a business model have been identified in key activities, partner network, key resources, cost structure, revenue flow, value proposition, client segments, and client relationships (Osterwalder, 2004). Bocken et al. (2014) have gathered these elements and, revising the frameworks of Osterwalder et al. (2005) and Richardson (2008), they have identified three main components of a business model: value proposition, value creation and delivery, and value capture.

The value proposition points out the relevant role played by the exchange of values through the production of specific products or the delivery of particular services to customers. Traditionally, the focus has been on products and services designed to offer an economic return. In the case of a sustainable business, the focus is on the value produced in line with a comprehensive approach that balances economic, environmental, and social interests. For sustainability purposes, balancing these interests assumes importance in determining the value to propose. In this way, the strategy of the company builds a connection with the related market and customers based on the value created.

The value creation and delivery represents the following logical step as it operationalizes the value proposition. It includes all the activities needed to produce the product or deliver the service. In order to fulfil these goals, the company must identify and obtain the resources needed to carry out the key activities, building sound collaborations with the partners, and relying on the most suitable technology infrastructure. Particularly, since the company is part of a broader system, the operationalization of the value proposition requires the establishment and management of a set of relationships involving multiple actors who share its sustainability orientation.

Finally, the value is captured by the company through the design of a specific cost and revenue structure (value capture). Value should be produced and captured by the company through a suitable system whereby revenues are earned and costs are covered allowing a long-term equilibrium.

In line with this framework, the present research investigated how an innovative and young company, born to be sustainable and foster sustainable development, has built its business model. Indeed, a case-study methodology was used to focus on a start-up that has adopted an innovative business model for a last-mile sustainable urban logistics service, which has received increasing recognition in Italy and beyond. In line with a proactive strategy (Schalteger et al., 2012), sustainability objects are a key part of the core business of the firm. Indeed, this start-up implements an innovative business designed to reduce CO2 emissions and improve quality of life, and it operates in Turin.

Research Setting

Although Turin has been intended as a smart city, the definition of what smart city means has been the object of a lively debate among both scholars and practitioners over the last several years (Caragliu et al., 2011; Chourabi et al., 2012). Different interpretations of the "smart" dimension have been developed, as can be seen by the wide variety of labels used; intelligent city, knowledge city, ubiquitous city, sustainable city are only a few examples (Cocchia, 2014). From a comprehensive perspective, a city can be considered smart when it is able to invest in both human and social capital and information-technology infrastructure in order to fuel sustainable development through an efficient and effective use of resources and by employing participatory mechanisms of governance (Caragliu et al., 2011). The sustainability orientation is thus a key purpose of smart city initiatives. Indeed, since the beginning, the smart city concept has reflected the need for supporting urban environments by making their development sustainable (Alawadhi et al., 2012). Hence, the concept reflects the importance of sustainable development by performing well in different fields, among which are mobility, environment, and living (Giffinger et al., 2007).

Turin has been recognized as a smart city (EY, 2016), and the local government has expressed its intention to realize smart initiatives as shown, for instance, by the master plan developed in 2011 to design several initiatives in the fields of smart mobility, inclusion, life and health, and energy. The logic beyond this initiative was to foster the realization of sustainability-oriented activities in the local context involving the actors operating in that environment. The city elaborated a vision to become smart by producing high technology while respecting the environment, reducing CO2 emissions, and improving quality of life. In this context, environmental concerns were predominant. To address such challenges, the city of Turin has put increasing efforts into adopting ad-hoc policies and plans, as shown by the "Turin Action Plan for Energy" aimed at reducing C02 emissions, which was signed in 2010. Further, the city of Turin has tried to support the formation of firms able to address emerging problems and translate innovative ideas in products and services suitable for generating environmental, economic, and social value. These initiatives include the business and financial support given to innovative ideas proposed by young people, among which is the company under investigation.

In 2011, two friends decided to work as bike messengers in a last-mile urban logistics service delivery in Turin, and their winning ideas were transformed into a limited company in 2013. On its website, the company, called Ponyzero, describes itself as a company "disrupting the last mile delivery sector through its proprietary dispatching platform, using optimization algorithms and automatic delivery assignment." Indeed, the company operates in the last-mile delivery sector and distinguishes itself from its competitors because of its sustainability orientation and technological innovations. Specifically, the company aims to support sustainable development, improving the quality of the environment and consequently, quality of life, with the support of technological innovations. The company delivers different types of services, such as fresh food delivery, last-mile delivery, and pony express delivery, by using only ecological means of transport—a bike fleet (traditional and cargo bikes, tricycles, and big tricycles) and an e-fleet (electric scooters, electric cars, and electric vans). The fresh food delivery (up to 10 kg) uses cargo bikes designed to maintain the necessary temperature to guarantee the preservation of the food quality. The last-mile delivery includes the delivery of goods in the last mile in an "ecological, fast and safe" manner, as stated on the official website of the organization. The pony express service is express delivery done on the same day of the request with the possibility of selecting an express delivery in one hour for packages weighing less than 5 kg. The company delivers orders received by international couriers and e-commerce operators who are their primary clients.

The origins of Ponyzero can be traced back to the need to address three key challenges, which can be identified from the following perspectives:

- **Environmental and Societal Perspective:** Pollution problems are recognized by civil society, governments and international institutions, and private organizations. The increasing awareness of the existence of these problems should go hand-in-hand with the increasing attention paid to handling them by reducing CO2 emissions and air pollution and improving general well-being. Further, societal problems, such as unemployment and changing working conditions, pose numerous pressures on firms nowadays to create new and more jobs through innovation.
- **Customer Perspective:** Nowadays, users increasingly call for immediate delivery of goods and rely on online orders and the use of technology platforms.
- **Financial Perspective:** Gasoline costs, for instance, challenge traditional business activities, which calls for more efficient and sustainable initiatives.

In order to realize these services, the company relies on an innovative technological infrastructure that allows the business to deliver services by managing an ecological fleet in an efficient and effective way. Indeed, according to the archetypes of business model innovations identified by Bocken et al. (2014), it is possible to categorize Ponyzero as a technological-oriented innovator. In particular, their technological innovation is represented by their software and a mobile app that allows them to manage deliveries in a flexible and expedient manner. By creating this integrated technological infrastructure with specialized fleet tracking, the company has tried to integrate civil society's perspective and needs with the needs of the business.

The company has thus become one of the first Italian companies to adopt an innovative business model for last-mile delivery in the sustainable urban logistic sector and has experienced significant growth over the last years. Indeed, its innovative approach to traditional services has been widely recognized and rewarded. The company has received several prizes issued by widely-recognized non-profit associations with the mission of making the environmental culture the center of a new kind of development (e.g., Legambiente) and by international summits (e.g., Web summit) for technological innovations.

The increasing relevance of the business and its development in other cities has led the company to break even in 2016, three years after its establishment, thanks to a significant increase in its revenues. To make this possible, in addition to the 20 employees working in the administration of the company, they rely on a fleet of bikers and drivers to make the deliveries. However, despite the growing relevance of the company, it is still a small business whose development is influenced by the collaborations, built or to be built, with local providers and public administrations. Indeed, the external context influences its business model and can be influenced by the business itself. Specifically, in relation with the sustainability purpose, organizations can be sustainable only when the whole system is sustainable from a systemic point of view (Boons et al., 2013).

In light of these considerations, the smartness orientation of the city can be expected to contribute to strengthening and facilitating the sustainability orientation of the organizations operating in the same context. At the same time, the sustainability orientation of private organizations, such as Ponyzero, can be expected to contribute to the sustainability of the system and to the smartness of the city.

Research Method

As emerged from the previous considerations, the selected case-study company is interesting and suitable for achieving the research purpose since it provides empirical evidence on an SBM and sheds light on its key elements and challenges. Specifically, this explanatory single-case study (Ryan, et al., 2002) aims to provide a sound explanation of the specific case under investigation through the lens of the framework adopted, which is thus used as input for the research. Indeed, the business model developed by Bocken et al. (2014) provides the key elements to be investigated in order to determine how Ponyzero has designed its sustainable business from its conception.

This study was carried out through the integration of multiple sources of evidence used to enable a comprehensive understanding of the case and reinforce the reliability of the findings. The first source of evidence consisted of official documents and information publicly available from the company website and from the website of workshops where the company took part as invited speakers and the authors as auditors. The second source of evidence consisted of internal documents and reports used to plan and manage activities and internal meetings, set objectives, and define individual and organizational key performance indicators. The third source of evidence consisted of two face-to-face semi-structured interviews conducted with key informants, one representative of the company (specifically, one of the founders), and one representative of the main local actor playing the role of funder, supporter, and potential partner (local government). These interviews have been registered, transcribed, and analyzed. The fourth source of evidence consisted of 15 questionnaires that depicted the points of view of company's founders, top and middle managers, and technical and administrative staff. Overall, the questionnaires covered the various actors involved at different levels in the creation, development, and management of the business. Appendix 1 details the outline of the questionnaire, and Appendix 2 reports the list of people contacted.

The data coming from all sources were categorized according to the three pillars of the business model identified by the reference model (Bocken et al., 2014). For each pillar, the main issues in terms of challenges and strengths were identified and categorized according to the actor's position and function in the organization (Dent, 1991; Granlund, 2003).

Although the focus on one company in a specific context can be seen as a limitation in terms of the generalizability of results, the purpose of this single-case study is to pave the way to further investigation of the complex set of relationships needed to realize systemic sustainable development by analyzing the development of a sustainable business in an innovative context, namely that of a smart city.

EMPIRICAL EVIDENCE AND RECOMMENDATIONS

Value Proposition

The value proposition is conceived as the enabling mechanism for conceptualizing and implementing a business model (Carayannis et al., 2014). The construction of the value proposition of Ponyzero has relied, first, on the commitment of the young entrepreneurs who started the business with the aim of exploiting an under-known field. Then, they received growing recognition from the market and the business took the form of a limited liability company in 2013. The intention was to create a new ecological manner of delivery that respected the environment, which was realized by introducing a relevant change in the value proposition: delivery services performed on bikes supported by technological innovations, that is, software that optimized the delivery services. Thus, the company has become specialized in the delivery of goods, distinguishing itself from the other companies for its technological features. Indeed, as confirmed by interviews and questionnaires, the main values of the company are reflected in its *innovation and eco-friendly approach* (CIO).

Consequently, the company has a single value proposition that relies on its core capability of delivering products through ecological means of transport, which has been operationalized into different kinds of offerings, added over the years following market trends and customers' needs, and influencing the organizational structure. Currently, there are two main divisions, one for last-mile delivery and one for express delivery. This decision has responded to the need of managing the services according to their logistics. Indeed, for the last-mile delivery services it is possible to know in advance the number of deliveries, which are then assigned and distributed to the fleet automatically by the software. Express delivery is on demand and thus the time from the request to the delivery is shorter, and the service is managed on an order-by-order basis. A new division dedicated to the food delivery has become a spin-off entirely controlled by the organization. Thus, although the sustainability orientation has remained unchanged over time, the value proposition has been modified in order to broaden the offerings guaranteeing responsiveness to customer needs. According to the chief information officer, over the years the main idea of the company has not changed, but the way it translates into practice has. As the marketing manager says:

We have passed from a 'handmade' phase to an industrial phase.

However, the analysis of the interviews and questionnaires reveals that different perceptions can be seen as responses to different perceived challenges. For instance, according to one of the founders, the company has to change the typology of its main customers in the future to work directly with the final client and stop being an intermediary. Indeed, nowadays, the main clients of the organization are represented by international couriers, e-commerce operators, and e-commerce food providers. The clients of the organization are leaders in their sectors, and this issue points out the increasing recognition of the relevance of such business nowadays. However, the organization aims at changing its business model by establishing direct contacts with the final customer to increase the number of orders.

The sales and marketing manager focuses on the need to broaden the services offered through the elaboration of ad-hoc solutions and technological innovations. Accordingly, the company's vision is to realize *a gradual increase in the services offered through a continuous technological upgrade, by designing new transportation models suitable for the last-mile delivery, by improving the capacity to think and build ad-hoc solutions and guarantee a more and wider coverage at both national and international levels* (MKT MGR). The brand manager underlines the ambition to realize a shift in the interpretation of the delivery step in order to make it a value-adding component instead of a cost. Further, the coordinator of fleet managers states that the aspiration of the company should be to change the habits of the whole supply chain in order to foster a green orientation. These considerations show that, from a comprehensive point of view, the system is still not completely committed to this sustainability philosophy and the organization has to convince its partners and clients of the goodness of this kind of delivery.

These empirical considerations reveal that opinions about the future differ among the actors, but they share the need to enlarge the business while maintaining its green orientation. Indeed, the sustainability orientation remains undebated. The intention is to invest in enlarging the services provided for environmental and societal issues, reducing the CO2 emissions and the air pollution, improving the well-being of people, and facing employment problems; as for economic issues, the goal is to increase productivity by increasing the number of orders.

This strong commitment toward the key values of the company has emerged as one of the main reasons of the company's success. The marketing manager puts it this way:

The certainty about the goodness of our project is the factor driving the business growth in the market. Inside the company, this generates a constant search for innovative solutions, means and technologies adequate to the development, and above all, a strong attention to the market evolution and to the new trends in Italy and in the other countries (MKT MGR).

The strong commitment toward sustainability demonstrated in the interviews and questionnaires shows that when a business model includes sustainability from its outset, organizational barriers to sustainable development in terms of employees' attitudes and values, awareness, and understanding are less frequent (Laukkanen & Patala, 2014). However, the sustainability orientation is motivated not only by ethical issues, but also by for-profit interests. According to the fleet manager, The Company mission acts as an incentive for the group to act in a proper way and facilitates the attainment of financial resources and benefits useful for achieving the stated goals.

In this regard, there emerges a lack of sufficient support by the local actors and the existence of structural barriers (e.g., lack of recharging stations) as challenges to the development of the business, especially in order to scale up. From this perspective, indeed, on the one hand, the value proposition of the company fits well with the smartness of the city where the company started. As the accountant said, there is a synergy within the smart context of the city (ACC). On the other hand, operative difficulties were pointed out in the interviews with regard to the context, as will be discussed in the next sub-section.

To sum up, the sustainability orientation does not change but its operationalization can. Consequently, the business model should not be taken as fixed; on the contrary, it can and should be innovated. To make innovation and growth possible, the relationship between focal firm and surrounding context has to be improved.

Value Creation and Delivery

Key activities in the organizational model of Ponyzero concern the key dimensions and objectives of the business and involve leading by strategy definition and research and development, improving by human resource management, connecting by ICT, managing by financial administration and purchasing activities, protecting by risk management and legal control, attracting by investing in marketing and improving sales, telling through reports, relations and public affairs, and operating with the identification of specific professional figures (operations manager and city manager). Each of these activities is guided by a specific professional figure who, in a matrix organizational structure, concern all the divisions of the company according to its offerings, all the geographical areas covered, and the projects realized.

To deliver its services, the company relies on a set of key technological, human, and financial resources. First, technology represents a key success factor and is the enabling tool for carrying out the key activities of the company. Therefore, the company makes constant and significant investments in research and development and has an ad-hoc unit inside the company working to continuously improve its software. Indeed, one of the company's distinctive traits is the innovative infrastructure used to manage and control its deliveries through different and specialized systems that guarantee the respect of the specific features of each type of delivery and that has been built with the support of the local university and research institutes. The company's software, based on ad-hoc algorithms, calculates the best path to make the delivery as fast as possible and manage the different deliveries in a flexible manner. In addition, the app developed for the smartphone guarantees the tracking of each delivery and registers it with the final client through both audio and digital signatures. Further, the software calculates the amount of CO_2 emissions saved per delivery and thus provides managers with useful information for the social report.

Despite the functionality of the software, one of the main current challenges concerns the optimization of resources in order to increase the productivity. Further, the company is aware of the need to rely on an updated transportation fleet to satisfy growing and changing demands. Thus, it has also made relevant investments in outsourcing research to specialized third parties to design transport technologies so that deliveries can become made more efficiently and effectively. Indeed, the research is always designed to strengthen the core business of the company, the ecological delivery services, but it also aims to strengthen safety, as demonstrated by a special box designed and manufactured exclusively by and for the company to deliver goods.

Another significant component of the company's infrastructure is its human resources. The company has 20 employees working across the different functions of the organization (e.g., human resources, sales and marketing, quality manager, and so on) and a fleet of 100 bikers and drivers, which is the most significant category of "partners," as declared by one of the founders (CD), but they have become employees of the company. Indeed, the delivery services strongly depend on this fleet, which can pose significant challenges for the company because of its high turnover. This is one of the main problems with which managers currently cope. Consequently, they are trying to set a stable team on which the company can rely in addition to external providers of services and collaborators. In this regard, strong support is expected to be provided by the policy makers. The following quotes provide interesting insights:

The precariousness is a constant factor in the job market in Italy. It is at the base of many problems concerning the management of human resources (FLEET COORD).

In the field of human resources, it is absolutely necessary to be ready to adapt to quick changes. This is designed to improve conditions for everybody, but it is often not easily accepted and understood (HRM).

Further, in terms of working environment, the company has a team of young people who are motivated to put increasing effort into improving sustainability. However, the company has known significant growth in a short period of time, and that has resulted in numerous changes that have required additional efforts in guaranteeing a positive working environment where everyone feels they have a stake in the company.

Finally, the financial means that have made the company possible come mostly coming from private sources, as demonstrated by the investments made by investment funds. The company has obtained only an initial public funding from the local government in the context of a smart initiative lunched by the city.

In addition to the key resources, the company has built a network of collaborations with several different actors and has ongoing relationships with the providers of utilities, the providers of the e-fleet and bike fleet, and the providers of the cargo. Further, the potential positive role of public-private partnerships and network configuration to improve efficiency and reduce pollution has been recognized, and in the last year, the firm has reached dimensions suitable for being considered an interlocutor and establishing a relationship with local government. However, this collaboration is multi-faceted and challenging for several reasons. On the one hand, such collaboration is considered necessary for the future of the company, as the following quote by one of the founders points out:

The issue concerning the collaboration with the local government is crucial for the scalability of the business . . . Nowadays, after so many talks, if we do not integrate the mobility of people with good transportation, we will not succeed. If everybody builds their own circuit, it is not possible to realize scale economies. Let's share a common infrastructure . . . so that we can optimize the situation. . . . A public-private partnership on the recharging infrastructure would be very important (CD).

In particular, the contribution of the local government is expected to be significant since a smart city is more inclined to changes and innovations, which is a perfect match with what is offered by our company (SD). The fit between the company and the city appears perfect on paper, but in practice, the support given by the city to the company's growth has been marginally recognized. Although several different initiatives have been suggested by the company to address its primary problems (e.g., the lack of recharging spaces), a cultural backwardness (CD) exists that is difficult to overcome, an opinion borne out in the interviews. The fleet coordinator said:

It is important to make the city understand that the bikers are not just strangers in the urban context and increase its awareness that the locomotion methods and working activities are evolving in order to support the environment. Bikers are not doing pleasure activities; they are providing services to the city (FLEET COORD).

In this regard, the lack of shared and widespread efforts to translate into practice normative expectations challenge the sustainability development of the company and of the city and thus, of the whole system. A sort of disappointment has emerged and led the company to direct its attention toward private actors rather than public organizations and institutions. An example is provided by the elimination of the ad-hoc team dedicated to the elaboration of projects and plans for obtaining public funds. The most important relationships still link the company with the main couriers for which it works.

To support the growth of this sustainable development, two issues appear to play key roles and, thus, call for further improvement: technological and infrastructure development, as a necessary enabling tool, and a widespread cultural awareness about the relevance of sustainable businesses.

Value Capture

Finally, the value capture encompasses structure whereby the company can control and manage its costs and revenues. Indeed, the value capture can be analyzed in terms of financial impacts beyond the environmental and social effects. From a financial perspective, the company captures value thanks to its innovativeness, which is recognized and appreciated by users, and by its ability to provide personalized services. Indeed, according to the interviewees, users are most willing to pay more to receive fast and flexible deliveries and to support the company's sustainability orientation. Ponyzero has succeeded in building loyal relationships with its partners and clients, with positive financial returns. As anticipated in the previous sections, the main clients and partners of the organization are companies acting as leaders in their fields, demonstrating that the position and work of the company have been increasingly recognized.

As far as the costs incurred, despite the reduction in the economic costs regarding fuel, tariffs and prices have represented key challenges, especially in a sector strongly influenced by economic and financial crises. According to the marketing manager, All these issues are made more complicated by the fact that green transportation is considered less expensive and complex than traditional transportation, but that is not true (MKT MGR). Indeed, costs are still high compared to traditional delivery services. Thus, the innovativeness of this sustainable business and the challenges still faced to build a value network suitable for lowering costs contribute to challenge cost and revenue structure of the company, which requires time to be efficient and effective. Further, the supportive economic incentives needed to encourage a sustainable economy (Laukkanen & Pattala, 2014), have not been recognized by interviewees.

With regard to the environmental and societal impacts in terms of value captured, since the image of the company is strongly connected to environmental protection and its core goal is to reduce CO_2 emissions, the key component of the value captured is represented by the positive environmental impact. As the official documents of the company reveal, 69000 kg of CO_2 emissions are saved each day by ecologically delivering 1500 packages. Further, the impact of the company's mission on society can be conceived not only in terms of pollution reduction, but also by taking into explicit account the potential to diffuse a culture of sustainable mobility and general well-being (QLT MGR).

Thus, social benefits can be identified since each activity produces a positive environmental impact, directly or indirectly, on society. By relying more on sustainable means of delivery, the traffic in the city center can be reduced, along with acoustic and air pollution, which thus improves quality of life.

Finally, the creation and delivery of value is guided by a comprehensive "management by results" system as can be seen in the documents provided by the company: The only way to not lose control of the organization in a period of growth is to make management responsible on the basis of clear and shared key performance indicators.

By planning and controlling continuously, management guides its business toward the achievement of its stated goals. In particular, key performance indicators (KPI) and objectives are defined by the CEO, then discussed and shared with the different managers and assessed monthly. In the company, the KPI regard constant aspects that the company should always guarantee, while the objectives represent strategic objectives defined from time to time. The CEO and the division managers hold weekly meetings to set objectives and update operative strategies; on a monthly basis, the CEO, the division manager, and the various other managers meet to evaluate the manager's objectives and KPI. The assessment of the KPI and objectives has been recently combined with the assignment of bonuses linked to results. In this regard, in order to motivate the team, the performance rewards at the individual level are also determined by the results achieved at the unit level. Then, the results achieved in terms of individual and unit performance, ranging from number of deliveries and on-time deliveries to the number of new clients, are combined with the organizational positive impact in terms of environmental and societal issues, with a specific focus on the impact of the reduction of CO2 emissions. This system is supported by the use of traditional and innovative tools such as collaboration apps and project management apps.

FUTURE RESEARCH DIRECTIONS

This chapter has analyzed an empirical case of an innovative organization that has adopted a strong sustainability orientation by building its business on environment protection and technological innovations. The research has shed light on the practical application of an SBM, by analyzing its main elements and challenges. A particularly interesting issue is represented by the potential fit between the company and the context where it operates, which has proved challenging and complex. Specifically, the context is represented by a smart city oriented to support sustainable initiatives. Thus, according to a systems approach and the fact that sustainability goals can be achieved only by making sustainable the society as a whole, the smartness orientation of a context would be expected to support and facilitate the development of SBMs. In this regard, however, the empirical evidence analyzed in this chapter has provided initial insights and underlined key obstacles. Further research can and should investigate the challenging relationships between a focal company and its context, providing, for instance, empirical evidence by studying and comparing multiple cases studies to determine under what conditions a win-win relationship can be built.

CONCLUSION

The present chapter has contributed to the body of knowledge on SBMs by providing empirical evidence regarding a company founded on the core belief of sustainability and by shedding new light on the key elements and issues of an SBM developed in the context of a smart city. Thus, this research provides original evidence on a company that included sustainability from the outset rather than incorporating it into an existing business.

The company is characterized by a strong commitment towards sustainability. This issue has demonstrated that when a business model includes sustainability issues from its outset, organizational barriers to sustainable development in terms of employees' attitudes and values, awareness, and understanding are less frequent (Laukkanen & Patala, 2014). Thus, an informal and embedded cultural control system seems to be at play at Ponyzero. In addition, the organization adopts formal mechanisms of control such as a performance measurement system connected with a reward system aimed at motivating the employees to achieve the stated goals.

Sustainability has thus been the success factor of the company and has never been called into question. The environmental impacts are measured through the software developed by the company and are the most appreciated dimension of the organization. Societal impacts exist but appear to be more difficult to measure explicitly and less considered by managers. Finally, the eco-friendly and technological approach of the company have been recognized as key revenue drivers as appreciated by the clients. However, in the case under investigation, a significant challenge is to find the proper way to balance the sustainability aspect of the company with the need to build a sound revenue and cost structure. To this end, the organization has undertaken continuous changes to improve the software to increase efficiency and effectiveness and to update its offerings according to market needs.

The innovative orientation of the business and its technological peculiarities have helped the company find the necessary funding and attract big players, but the company has yet to convince the surrounding environment about the reliability and quality of its business. Despite the normative recognition of the relevance of such deliveries, several obstacles challenge the establishment of an extensive value network. Organizations can be sustainable only when the whole system is sustainable from a systemic perspective (Boons et al., 2013), and this issue appears to be the most challenging. The empirical results emphasize the need for networks and collaborations around key sustainability issues that can thus work as enabling mechanisms for new innovations (Laukkanen & Pattala, 2014). This broad perspective of the system is assuming growing relevance, but it is still far from being translated into practice. Therefore, the research shows that sustainability can be a success factor, but it requires cooperation and collaboration in its operationalization to be feasible in the long term.

ACKNOWLEDGMENT

This research received no specific grant from any funding agency in the public, commercial, or not-for-profit sectors.

REFERENCES

Alawadhi, S., Aldama-Nalda, A., Chourabi, H., Gil-Garcia, J. R., Leung, S., Mellouli, S., . . . Walker, S. (2012). Building understanding of smart city initiatives. Electronic Government, 40-53.

Amit, R., & Zott, C. (2001). Value creation in e-business. *Strategic Management Journal, 22*(6-7), 493–520. doi:10.1002mj.187

Bebbington, J., & Thomson, I. (2013). Sustainable development, management and accounting: Boundary crossing. *Management Accounting Research, 4*(24), 277–283. doi:10.1016/j.mar.2013.09.002

Berry, A. J., Coad, A. F., Harris, E. P., Otley, D. T., & Stringer, C. (2009). Emerging themes in management control: A review of recent literature. *The British Accounting Review, 41*(1), 2–20. doi:10.1016/j.bar.2008.09.001

Birkin, F., Polesie, T., & Lewis, L. (2009). A new business model for sustainable development: An exploratory study using the theory of constraints in Nordic organizations. *Business Strategy and the Environment, 18*(5), 277–290. doi:10.1002/bse.581

Bocken, N. M. P., Short, S. W., Rana, P., & Evans, S. (2014). A literature and practice review to develop sustainable business model archetypes. *Journal of Cleaner Production, 65*, 42–56. doi:10.1016/j.jclepro.2013.11.039

Boons, F., & Lüdeke-Freund, F. (2013). Business models for sustainable innovation: State-of-the-art and steps towards a research agenda. *Journal of Cleaner Production, 45*, 9–19. doi:10.1016/j.jclepro.2012.07.007

Boons, F., Montalvo, C., Quist, J., & Wagner, M. (2013). Sustainable innovation, business models and economic performance: An overview. *Journal of Cleaner Production, 45*, 1–8. doi:10.1016/j.jclepro.2012.08.013

Calia, R. C., Guerrini, F. M., & Moura, G. L. (2007). Innovation networks: From technological development to business model reconfiguration. *Technovation, 27*(8), 426–432. doi:10.1016/j.technovation.2006.08.003

Caragliu, A., Del Bo, C., & Nijkamp, P. (2011). Smart cities in Europe. *Journal of Urban Technology, 18*(2), 65–82. doi:10.1080/10630732.2011.601117

Carayannis, E. G., Grigoroudis, E., Sindakis, S., & Walter, C. (2014). Business model innovation as antecedent of sustainable enterprise excellence and resilience. *Journal of the Knowledge Economy, 5*(3), 440–463. doi:10.100713132-014-0206-7

Chesbrough, H. (2010). Business model innovation: Opportunities and barriers. *Long Range Planning, 43*(2), 354–363. doi:10.1016/j.lrp.2009.07.010

Chesbrough, H., & Rosenbloom, R. S. (2002). The role of the business model in capturing value from innovation: Evidence from Xerox Corporation's technology spin-off companies. *Industrial and Corporate Change, 11*(3), 529–555. doi:10.1093/icc/11.3.529

Chourabi, H., Nam, T., Walker, S., Gil-Garcia, J. R., Mellouli, S., Nahon, K., & Scholl, H. J. (2012). Understanding smart cities: An integrative framework. In *System Science (HICSS), 2012 45th Hawaii International Conference on* (pp. 2289-2297). IEEE.

Cocchia, A. (2014). Smart and digital city: A systematic literature review. In R. Dameri & C. Rosenthal-Sabroux (Eds.), *Smart city* (pp. 13–43). Cham, Switzerland: Springer International Publishing. doi:10.1007/978-3-319-06160-3_2

Contrafatto, M., & Burns, J. (2013). Social and environmental accounting, organisational change and management accounting: A processual view. *Management Accounting Research*, *24*(4), 349–365. doi:10.1016/j.mar.2013.10.004

Dent, J. F. (1991). Accounting and organizational cultures: A field study of the emergence of a new organizational reality. *Accounting, Organizations and Society*, *16*(8), 705–732. doi:10.1016/0361-3682(91)90021-6

EY. (2016). *Italia Smart*. Rapport Smart City Index.

Giffinger, R., Fertner, C., Kramar, H., & Meijers, E. (2007). *City-ranking of European medium-sized cities*. Vienna: Cent. Reg. Sci.

Granlund, M. (2003). Management accounting system integration in corporate mergers: A case study. *Accounting, Auditing & Accountability Journal*, *16*(2), 208–243. doi:10.1108/09513570310472822

Gray, R. (2010). Is accounting for sustainability actually accounting for sustainability… and how would we know? An exploration of narratives of organisations and the planet. *Accounting, Organizations and Society*, *35*(1), 47–62. doi:10.1016/j.aos.2009.04.006

Kerret, D., & Menahem, G. (2016). Many Hands Make Light Work: The Role of Collaborative Management in Improving Environmental Information Management by Local Authorities. *International Public Management Journal*, *19*(4), 427–452. doi:10.1080/10967494.2015.1062066

Lambert, S. C., & Davidson, R. A. (2013). Applications of the business model in studies of enterprise success, innovation and classification: An analysis of empirical research from 1996 to 2010. *European Management Journal*, *31*(6), 668–681. doi:10.1016/j.emj.2012.07.007

Laukkanen, M., & Patala, S. (2014). Analysing barriers to sustainable business model innovations: Innovation systems approach. *International Journal of Innovation Management*, *18*(06), 1440010. doi:10.1142/S1363919614400106

Lee, K. J., & Casalegno, F. (2010). An Explorative Study for Business Models for Sustainability. *PACIS*, 423-432.

Lüdeke-Freund, F. (2009). *Business model concepts in corporate sustainability contexts: From rhetoric to a generic template for 'business models for sustainability*. Leuphana University of Lueneburg: Centre for Sustainability Management.

Lüdeke-Freund, F. (2010). Towards a Conceptual Framework of 'Business Models for Sustainability'. In R. Wever, J. Quist, A. Tukker, J. Woudstra, F. Boons, & N. Beute (Eds.), Knowledge collaboration & learning for sustainable innovation. Delft, The Netherlands: Academic Press.

Lueg, R., & Radlach, R. (2016). Managing sustainable development with management control systems: A literature review. *European Management Journal, 34*(2), 158–171. doi:10.1016/j.emj.2015.11.005

Meijer, A., & Bolívar, M. P. R. (2016). Governing the smart city: A review of the literature on smart urban governance. *International Review of Administrative Sciences, 82*(2), 392–408. doi:10.1177/0020852314564308

Milne, M. J. (2007). Downsizing Reg (me and you)! Addressing the 'real' sustainability agenda at work and home. In B. Gray & J. Guthrie (Eds.), *Social Accounting, Mega Accounting and Beyond: A Festschrift in Honour of MR Mathews* (pp. 49–66). St. Andrews, UK: The Centre for Social and Environmental Accounting Research Publishing.

Milne, M. J., Tregidga, H., & Walton, S. (2009). Words not actions! The ideological role of sustainable development reporting. *Accounting, Auditing & Accountability Journal, 22*(8), 1211–1257. doi:10.1108/09513570910999292

Morris, M., Schindehutte, M., & Allen, J. (2005). The entrepreneur's business model: Toward a unified perspective. *Journal of Business Research, 58*(6), 726–735. doi:10.1016/j.jbusres.2003.11.001

Nidumolu, R., Prahalad, C. K., & Rangaswami, M. R. (2009). Why sustainability is now the key driver of innovation. *Harvard Business Review, 87*(9), 56–64.

Nixon, B., & Burns, J. (2012). The paradox of strategic management accounting. *Management Accounting Research, 23*(4), 229–244. doi:10.1016/j.mar.2012.09.004

OECD. (2011). *Better policies to support eco-innovation*. Paris, France: OECD Publishing.

Osterwalder, A. (2004). *The Business Model Ontology-a proposition in a design science approach* (Doctoral Dissertation). Universite de Lausanne.

Osterwalder, A., & Pigneur, Y. (2010). *Business model generation: a handbook for visionaries, game changers, and challengers*. Hoboken, NJ: John Wiley & Sons.

Osterwalder, A., Pigneur, Y., & Tucci, C. L. (2005). Clarifying business models: Origins, present, and future of the concept. *Communications of the Association for Information Systems, 16*(1).

Porter, M. E., & Kramer, M. R. (2011). The big idea: Creating shared value. *Harvard Business Review, 89*(1).

Richardson, J. (2008). The business model: An integrative framework for strategy execution. *Strategic Change, 17*(5-6), 133–144. doi:10.1002/jsc.821

Ryan, B., Scapens, R. W., & Theobald, M. (2002). *Research method and methodology in finance and accounting*. London, UK: Thompson Learning.

Schaltegger, S., Lüdeke-Freund, F., & Hansen, E. G. (2012). Business cases for sustainability: The role of business model innovation for corporate sustainability. *International Journal of Innovation and Sustainable Development, 6*(2), 95–119. doi:10.1504/IJISD.2012.046944

Stubbs, W., & Cocklin, C. (2008). Conceptualizing a "sustainability business model". *Organization & Environment*, *21*(2), 103–127. doi:10.1177/1086026608318042

Zott, C., & Amit, R. (2008). The fit between product market strategy and business model: Implications for firm performance. *Strategic Management Journal*, *29*(1), 1–26. doi:10.1002mj.642

Zott, C., & Amit, R. (2013). The business model: A theoretically anchored robust construct for strategic analysis. *Strategic Organization*, *11*(4), 403–411. doi:10.1177/1476127013510466

Zott, C., Amit, R., & Massa, L. (2011). The business model: Recent developments and future research. *Journal of Management*, *37*(4), 1019–1042. doi:10.1177/0149206311406265

KEY TERMS AND DEFINITIONS

Business Model: A plan whereby an organization defines what to do and how to do in order to create, deliver, and capture value successfully.

Smart City: A city able to invest in order to support a sustainable development, an efficient and effective use of resources, participative mechanisms of governance, in order to improve the quality of life and the responsiveness to citizens' needs also through the use of information and communication technologies.

Sustainable Business Model: A model that drives an organization towards the achievement of firm-level sustainability and supports the sustainability for the system of which that organization is a part, through the collaboration with other stakeholders.

APPENDIX 1

- **Expert Background**
    - Previous experience
    - Main activities and responsibilities
- **Business Model – Value Proposition**
    - Ideation of the company: reasons
    - Mission and vision
    - Key values
    - Impact of values on activities
    - Services delivered
    - Market segment and client relationships
- **Business Model – Value Creation & Delivery**
    - Key activities and objectives
    - Definition and assessment of performance
    - Tools and techniques used
    - Reports/documents produced and used
    - Collaborations, internal and external
    - Partner
- **Business Model – Value Capture**
    - Human, financial and technological resources at disposal
    - Cost and revenues structure
- **Challenges and Criticalities**
    - Problems faced by the company/interviewee
    - Solutions proposed
    - Actual challenges
- **Context**
    - Company's contributions to the context smartness
    - Smart context's contributions to the company
- **Additional Information**

APPENDIX 2

Table 1. List of people contacted

Interviewee	Organizational role	Contact type
BP	Founder & Business Partner	Questionnaire
MGR 1	Manager	Questionnaire
MGR 2	Manager	Questionnaire
BRAND MGR	Brand Manager	Questionnaire
MKT MGR	Sales and Marketing Manager	Questionnaire
QLT MGR	Quality Manager and Process Engineer	Questionnaire
FLEET COORD	Coordinator Fleet Managers	Questionnaire
FLEET MGR	Fleet Manager	Questionnaire
CIO	Chief Information Officer	Questionnaire
HRM	Human Resource Manager	Questionnaire
JHRG	Junior Human Resource Generalist	Questionnaire
AM	Administrative Manager	Questionnaire
ACC	Accountant	Questionnaire
SD	Software developer	Questionnaire
CD	Founder & Head of Corporate Development	Visit
LG	Local Government - Politician	Visit

Chapter 8
Energy Management and Auditing in Indian MSMEs: A Business Ecosystem Perspective

Shounak Basak
Indian Institute of Management Calcutta, India

Kushal Saha
Indian Institute of Management Calcutta, India

Sudhanshu Shekhar
Indian Institute of Management Calcutta, India

ABSTRACT

Energy management has emerged as a comprehensive framework for implementing sustainable accounting initiatives. This chapter elaborates and explains the energy management and auditing practices in the context of Indian micro, small, and medium enterprises (MSMEs). MSMEs form a neglected but a large part of the Indian economy. The chapter delves upon the importance of implementing energy management in MSMEs. Moreover, MSMEs are generally inefficient in their energy usage due to lack of technological upgradation. Therefore, energy management initiatives are of greater relevance for this sector. Energy management requires the coordination among a network of organizations including the focal organization, the government bodies, NGOs, and trained energy consultants. For energy management practices to take root, a business ecosystem perspective is required. The chapter highlights the theoretical dimensions of energy management and emerging ecosystem of energy management through case studies of the Firozabad glass industry and the Morbi ceramic tiles industry.

INTRODUCTION

Sustainability means meeting the needs of the present generation without compromising the ability of the future generations to meet their own needs (UN Documents, n.d.). It is a multi-dimensional concept that aims to balance the economic, social and environmental objectives of the society. The business sector

DOI: 10.4018/978-1-5225-5267-3.ch008

has an important role to play in achieving sustainability related objectives as the activities undertaken by them have significant economic, environmental, and social implications. Therefore corporate sustainability constitutes an important prerequisite for creating a sustainable economy and society (Schaltegger, Bennett, & Burritt, 2006). However, shareholders' expectations of value creation – often solely concerned with economic profit– makes it challenging for the concerned management to remain committed towards all the three aspects of the sustainability triangle - economic, environmental, and social (Schaltegger, Burritt, & Petersen, 2003; Van Marrewijk, 2003). To balance these often-conflicting set of sustainability objectives, managers need accurate and timely information about implementation costs and impacts of various sustainable interventions. This has led to the emergence of field of sustainable accounting in the recent times. Sustainable accounting is concerned with reporting of social and environmental costs incurred by the current business practices and associated economic benefits of adopting sustainable business operations (Schaltegger & Müller, 1997). Sustainable accounting and reporting – through the collection, analysis, and communication of such information – is thus crucial in facilitating an organization's journey towards sustainability (Schaltegger, Bennett, & Buritt, 2006). International conventions like the Kyoto Protocol, the United Nations Framework Convention on Climate Change (UNFCC) (UN, n.d.) and the recently concluded Paris Agreement on Climate Change (C2ES, n.d.) too have highlighted sustainable accounting as an important aspect of sustainability.

Implementation of the sustainable practices with the help of accounting framework contributes to ingrain the benefits of the energy management systems into the operating profits of the company. Though there has not been sufficient number of studies on the use of accounting in sustainability (Hopwood, 2009), sustainable accounting practices have been in use for quite some time now and include examples such as sustainable balanced scorecard (Figge, Hahn, Schaltegger, & Wagner, 2002) and full cost accounting (Bebbington, Gray, Hibbitt, & Kirk, 2001). Another increasingly popular and comprehensive form of sustainable accounting relates to energy management and auditing (Environmental Protection Agency, 2008). Energy management and auditing forms an important aspect of sustainable accounting and can guide a business entity to manage the conflicting set of sustainability objectives. Energy management and auditing involves calculating, reporting and optimizing the energy costs incurred by businesses.

Sustainable accounting and energy management has been adopted by large enterprises to some extent (Kannan & Boie, 2003). However, the same cannot be said about micro, small, and medium scale enterprises (MSMEs). Further it has been noticed that many MSMEs contribute significantly to environmental pollution due to unsustainable business practices. The pollution footprint of these enterprises can be considerably lowered by introduction of sustainable practices such energy management and auditing (Jain, 2011). However, it has remained a concern in policy circles that energy management and auditing has not yet witnessed widespread adoption among the MSMEs. It is only recently that a specialized group of private organizations has emerged with an objective to help MSMEs to implement energy management and auditing practices and seamlessly transition towards sustainable operations.

In this chapter, we investigate this pertinent issue of adoption of energy management by MSMEs. In the Indian context, MSMEs account for 30 percent of exports in and contribute about 40 percent of the gross industrial value (Ministry of Micro Small and Medium Enterprises, 2011). Constituting 80 percent of the total number of industrial enterprises active in India, MSMEs form the main backbone of employment generation in the Indian economy. They employ nearly 80 percent of the industrial workforce of the nation. These small enterprises are spread in the rural as well as the urban areas - mostly in clusters. Thus the question of adoption of energy management assumes greater significance in the Indian context. The specific questions that motivate our study are: How do MSMEs transition towards sustainable operations through adoption of energy management initiatives? What are the challenges faced by MSMEs in adopting energy management initiatives? How can these challenges be overcome? We investigate these questions in the context of two Indian MSME clusters – (1) Firozabad glass industry and (2) Rajkot ceramic industry.

The first finding of this chapter suggests that the most important challenge faced by Indian MSMEs in adoption of energy management practices relates to financial constraints. The other important challenge faced by MSMEs relates to technological change and associated change in the organizational practices. In identifying these challenges, our study supports the finding of earlier studies (Ghosh & Roy, 2011; Kannan & Boie, 2003) which have identified similar challenges in adoption of energy management practices by MSMEs. The second important finding from these two case studies relates to the role of inter-organizational linkages in fostering of energy management practices. Often, energy management is conceptualized at the level of a single organization. However, our study reveals that energy management requires the development of inter-relationships between a network of organizations which includes the focal business enterprises, government organizations, non-government organizations (NGOs) and energy consultants. This finding suggests that a network or business ecosystem (Gossain & Kandiah, 1998; Moore, 1993) perspective is required to foster implementation of energy management initiatives in MSMEs. The authors further draw upon the business ecosystem literature to analyze and suggest further avenues for development of energy management ecosystem in MSMEs.

THEORETICAL BACKGROUND

Energy Management

As early as in 1975, the company 3M pioneered a program 'pollution prevention pays (3P)' aimed at reducing the wastage created in the production process (Hart & Ahuja, 1996). The program involved the production line workers as well as specialized personnel from the pollution control staff. This practice led to the identification of waste reduction opportunities and framing of appropriate strategies. Implementation of these strategies resulted in lower raw material cost, higher compliance, and lower liability cost. The strategy was emulated by many other companies in the years to come. Also, this has been taken as a win-win outcome for both the environment and the business as it leads to higher competitiveness for the concerned companies by having higher innovation capabilities and energy efficiency. Energy management now forms a part of this "efficiency" building strategy.

To address the environmental concerns without diluting the economic value creation potential, it is essential to devise an appropriate metric which can fit into the accounting framework of a company and help reap monetary benefits from adopting environment-friendly strategies. Rather than resorting to an abstract level of environment friendliness derived by some multi-criteria decision making, the extent of energy use can be employed as an important metric to measure the commitment of a firm towards environment as well as evaluate the monetary value of energy with lesser effort, which in turn can be helpful in assessing the exact amount of economic gains to the company. Comparative performance assessments of different processes or alternatives are made possible using composite sustainable development scores. Energy, to be more specific energy consumption, is considered to be one of the common determinants in evaluating the 'sustainable development' performance of an initiative/process. Our heavy dependence on polluting forms of energy makes energy impact assessment a critical aspect in assessing sustainability along an environmental dimension (Bebbington, 2007). Energy intensity of a process/unit is often taken as a substitute for its environmental performance (ibid). Augmenting the energy efficiency for harvesting higher profits has been identified as a critical segment in the business practices, and this also helps to address the societal concerns on the environment (Zhu, Geng, & Lai, 2011). Energy management is the primary way for achieving energy efficient production processes. Energy management has been defined as the appropriate and judicious use of energy sources available to an organization with the aim of maximizing profits, minimizing costs, and improving its market position (Capehart, Turner, & Kennedy, 2006). It calls for a comprehensive approach towards managing the energy resources. Only a carefully designed energy management system focused on eco-efficiency will be able to usher in sustainable economic success for the company. Energy management consists of five elements - strategy/planning, implementation/operation, controlling, organization, and culture (Schulze, Nehler, Ottosson, & Thollander, 2016). It involves energy audit, implementation of energy efficient processes, and continuous monitoring. The figure below shows different components of an energy management program (Figure 1).

Figure 1. Energy management program

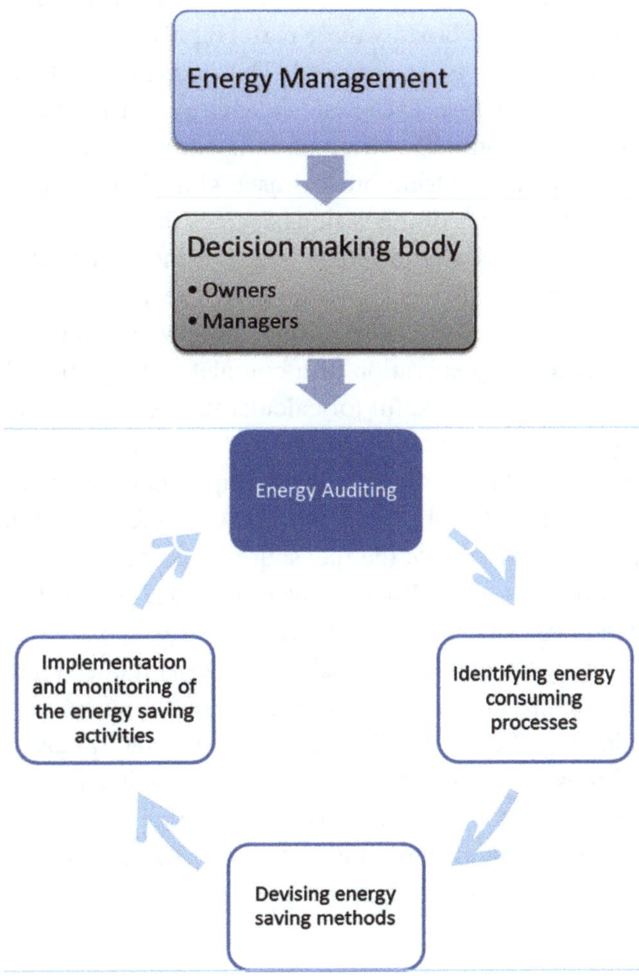

As seen in the figure above, the energy audit is an important part of energy management. An energy audit is a specialized task and can be undertaken only by a trained energy auditor. Research conducted to evaluate the effectiveness of energy audit practices shows that it plays a major role in setting up an efficient energy management system (Fleiter, Gruber, Eichhammer, & Worrell, 2012; Shen, Price, & Lu, 2012). Energy auditing involves preparing energy balance sheets to identify the amount of energy being consumed by different processes in the production. It has a tabular form similar to the financial balance sheet which shows the income and expenditure of a particular company. A sample representation of the energy balance sheet is presented in the case studies presented later in this paper.

The energy balance sheet represents a set of quantitative metrics that tabulates the record of energy availabilities, and the energy uses. This is similar to an accounting problem that relates to the manufacturing of a product in terms of economic value; only the difference lies with the economic value being substituted by the energy equivalent value. The energy balance sheet essentially captures the energy flow from production to consumption. The energy flow, however, is not transformed in the same state throughout the process of production. The initial state of the energy is different from the state when it is consumed - it is not consumed in the same form as it is produced. Thus, energy goes through a transformation in the production line. Consequently, one part of the energy flow is to represent the input of energy that goes into the production and the other is to represent the amount of energy that is obtained from consumption. The difference between these is the loss of energy in the manufacturing process.

The energy balance sheet consists of broadly three parts. Firstly, an account of the amount of energy supplied by the primary sources needs to be prepared. This account is calculated based on individual production activities in the production line. The amount of energy consumed by each production activity is aggregated and, thus, the total account of consumption is prepared. Secondly, the amount of energy that is actually required for the manufacturing process as a whole is measured. This amount primarily takes care of the operational efficiencies of the various devices that use the energy for the manufacturing process. The transformational losses at different stages of the energy flow are highlighted in this part. Lastly, the amount of raw materials required to produce the amount of energy is calculated. This takes into account the energy efficiency of energy producing devices and raw materials. An combination of these three parts leads to the preparation of a complete energy balance sheet of a production line. The last part of the balance sheet is useful for calculating the exact economic impact of different energy management strategies. Otherwise, the first two parts are sufficient to calculate the aggregate energy requirement of a production line. Further, when multiple fuel sources are in use, the aggregation of the energy requirement cannot be done based on the amount of fuel required but is calculated based on the amount of energy produced by each of the fuel sources (as shown by the sample balance sheet in Figure 5). The production processes carried out all over the world primarily use coal-based products, oil-based products, gas-based products, or electricity as the energy source. Coal related energy sources include hard coal, coke, lignite, peat, and brown coal. All the coal related energy sources are measured by the units of mass. Oil related products include crude oil, motor spirit, paraffin oil, naphtha, diesel oil, etc. and are measured in "liter." Gas related products include natural gas, ethane, LPG, etc. Lastly, electricity is measured in "kilowatt-hours" which is a unit of energy itself. Therefore, though the energy equivalent from coal based energy sources are measured in "kilogram" and that of natural gas based energy sources are measured in "cubic meter", it is less cumbersome to measure the energy equivalent in "kilowatt-hours" to have a smooth conversion between the various energy sources when multiple sources of energy are used.

Once the tabulation of energy consumption by different processes is complete, a decision can be made regarding the least energy efficient processes and steps can be undertaken to improve their energy efficiencies. To mark the energy-inefficient processes, it is important to initially create a set of parameters which can be used to identify improvements in energy efficiencies. The need for a key parameter to carefully benchmark the improvements due to the adoption of the energy management practices is critical to support the case for these practices. Usually, these parameters have to be defined as the relationship between the energy input/output and a particular activity (Bunse, Vodicka, Schönsleben, Brülhart, & Ernst, 2011). For example, in identifying the energy efficiency of the process, it is the specific energy consumption that needs to be taken into account and not the total energy consumption. Specific energy consumption is an important unit of comparison which denotes the amount of energy consumed for a production process/line for producing a fixed amount of finished product. Thus, specific energy consumption helps in a 'like for like' comparison of the production processes given the same produced item. Nevertheless, Virtanen, Tuomaala, & Pentti (2013) concluded that specific energy efficiency calculated by the ratio of total energy used and the useful energy required for the process did not allow proper energy management due to further technical complexities. Thus, none of these parameters can be considered as a one stop solution for the measurement of the energy management process, but a collection of these parameters will lead to a better assessment. The improvement in the production process by adopting relevant technological advancement or changing raw materials can bring in monetary benefits by making the energy flow more efficient. The extent of improvement is dependent on the energy efficiency gap (energy efficiency gap is defined as the actual level of energy efficiency and theoretically achievable energy efficiency level while adopting feasible technologies) (Hirst & Brown, 1990) that is calculated for the production process. This gap is dependent on the energy management practices to be adopted by the companies. Adoption of better energy management practices would lead to higher energy efficiency gap and thus provide a bigger opportunity for lowering the operating costs of the company. The figure below shows a diagrammatic representation of the importance of energy management system (Figure 2).

An energy management system is a control system similar to other management control systems but provides a framework that helps define the energy specific targets that need to be put in place and influence the operations of the company to achieve the goals.

Business Ecosystem

Business ecosystem perspective, draws upon the biological ecosystem metaphor, and emphasizes the fact that organizations are part of a network (Moore, 1993). A business ecosystem includes a network of firms whose futures are closely intertwined and dependent on each other (Iansiti & Levien, 2004). The biological ecosystem provides the valuable insight regarding the interdependence of different living beings. Similarly, a business ecosystem conceptualizes organizations as interdependent entities. Normally a firm is conceptualized as belonging to a single industry. However, the business ecosystem emphasizes that a company is conceptualized as an ecosystem, which may be spread across several industries. Similar to the evolution of biological ecosystem, firms also evolve their capabilities around innovations as they work cooperatively with their partners to support the emerging consumer needs and products. Thus business ecosystem provides a dynamic view of firms where their capabilities are the function of emerging market conditions. Therefore firms need to focus not just on their internal capabilities but also contribute to the development of their business ecosystem.

Figure 2. Diagrammatic representation of the importance of energy management system

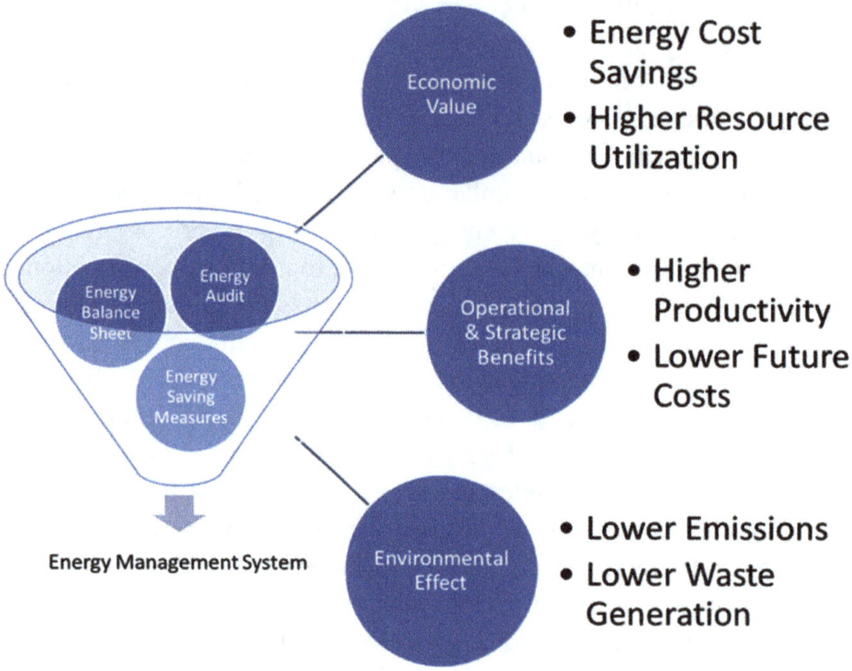

Li (2009) studied the emergence of technological business ecosystem Cisco. They showed that Cisco adopted a mergers and acquisition strategy for the development of its ecosystem. They relied on external partners who provided the necessary capabilities for the health of its ecosystem. Similarly Isckia (2009) studied the evolution of Amazon's ecosystem from a cyber-bookstore to an application service provider. Over the years Amazon has been transformed from an e-retailer to an e-retailing platform. For this it had to work closely with a network of third party firms, such as physical retailers, manufacturers, logistics provider, etc., and also ensure the health of the ecosystem. It did this by continuously investing in the development of its innovative web service platforms such as Amazon E-Commerce Service (ECS) and Amazon Simple Storage Service (Amazon S3). There are other studies which have applied the business ecosystem perspective to study the emergence of new industries and challenges to their growth. For example, Fransman (2010) studied the European information and communication technology (ICT) ecosystem and identified challenges to its future growth. He identified four layers of the ICT ecosystem which he termed as networked elements, distribution networks, platforms/contents and final consumers and growth challenges for these layers. Similarly Shang and Shi (2013) adopted a business ecosystem perspective to study the emergence of elective vehicle industry in the Chinese province of Shandong. Basole (2009) adopted the business ecosystem perspective to study the global mobile industry. He identified the important players, such as mobile network operators, system integrators, internet service providers, etc., in the ecosystem and recommended that relationship development among these players would play an important role in the evolution of this ecosystem.

As is evident from the latter examples, the business ecosystem perspective has special relevance for studying the emergence of new industries and business practices. The emergence of innovative business practices is dependent on collaboration among a network of firms. New business practices must draw resources from a variety of supporters such as customers, suppliers, capital providers, and technologists. Therefore, business ecosystem perspective is essential for developing effective strategies and business models in an emerging industry (Basole, 2009). This is the case with the energy management practices in India where the focal firms in the industry must collaborate with the government bodies, NGOs, funding agencies and trained energy consultant to ensure its effective implementation. Therefore the development of the fledgling energy management practices in India requires that the stakeholders adopt a business ecosystem perspective in its implementation.

NEED OF ENERGY MANAGEMENT IN MSMES

The salience of energy management arises from the fact that reduction of environmental pollution has become a top priority at international forums such as the United Nations. Years of industrial development has degraded the environment and given rise to problems such as global warming and ozone depletion. Historically, energy costs were comparatively low with respect to other raw materials. Thus, the concern with the energy cost was non-existent and, consequently, companies across the globe did not feel the requirement for any energy management practices to have efficient energy usage. However, growing concerns about rising energy costs along with the global awareness on environmental protectionism have made energy management increasingly relevant in today's context.

The need for energy management studies was felt as early as in 1979 as evident in a study by Lambert and Stock (1979). They emphasized the importance of an energy policy given the strategic planning of a company. However, only one-third of the companies surveyed by the authors had a written energy policy. Subsequent studies investigating energy policies followed by business enterprises indicated a lack of

Figure 3. Energy management business ecosystem

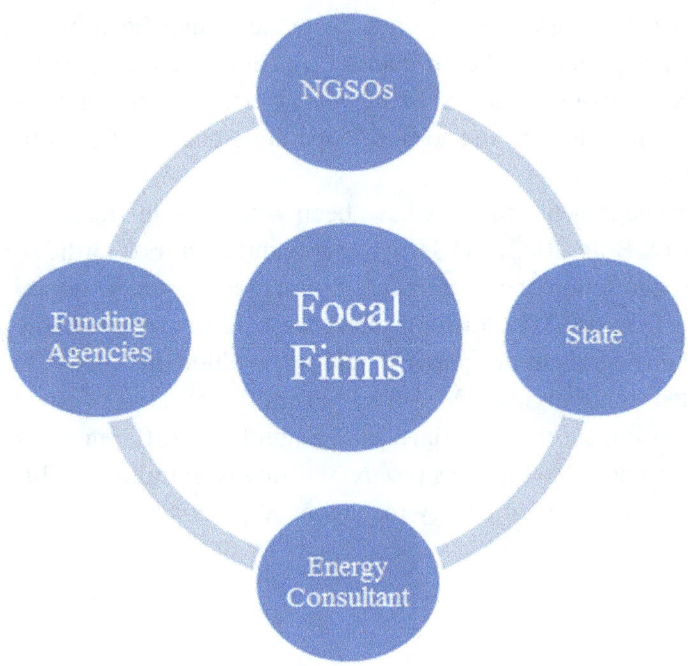

such policies as part of their long term strategic plans (Thollander & Ottosson, 2010). Most companies either did not have an energy policy in their scheme of plans or mentioned it in the short term plans. The insertion of energy policy in the strategic framework of a company is dependent on the external factors as environmental regulations and internal factors as energy saving initiatives (Rudberg, Waldemarsson, & Lidestam, 2013). Recent increase in energy cost has enhanced the importance of energy conservation initiatives and associated risks. Energy risk is particularly a significant factor in energy intensive industries. This risk is related to the volatility of the energy prices which is accentuated by increased energy usage (Vasudevan & Higgins, 2004). Thus, bottom lines of the companies would be improved by the adoption of energy management strategies as these will moderate the effect of energy prices on the financial gains of the firms.

Additionally, environmental issues affect the cash inflows and outflows of a company and, therefore, directly impact the economic value of a company (Hamilton, 1995). The company and its shareholders should be rightly concerned about the environmental regulations because legal implications might arise out of a violation of environmental norms leading to financial liabilities. Also, not to forget the loss of goodwill endured due to such an ordeal which affects its future business propositions. Operational profits of a company are based on the sales and the costs incurred by it. Energy management practices can influence both the factors in a positive way and provide impetus to the operating profits. The incorporation of environmental considerations improves the long term competitive position of the company and thus leads to growth in sales (Porter, 1980; Porter & Linde, 1995). The other aspect of higher operating profits is lowering costs by the implementation of appropriate cost-cutting measures. The economic goal of cost reduction is in sync with the societal goal of curtailing environmental costs. Typically, energy costs fall within the ambit of environmental cost that society has to bear. Reducing the energy costs can lessen the operating costs of the company as well as lower the environmental burden on the society. Controlling these energy operating costs of the company can be accomplished by using efficient energy management practices. This will lead to internalizing the external environmental costs into the financial accounts of the firm leading to prioritization of energy related costs while devising the operational strategies of the company (Spitzer, 1992). Operating costs can be reduced significantly by minimization of waste associated with different segments of the production process. The waste reduction also considers the energy waste that can be combated by undertaking energy efficient strategies. The reduction of energy usage can lead to improvement in current and future operating costs while contributing to the reduction of environmental costs.

Benefits of energy management practices have been witnessed in small and medium enterprise of German Bakery (Kannan & Boie, 2003) and Serbian car manufacturers (Gordić et al., 2010). This makes a strong case for the need of adoption of energy management practices in the organization to improve upon the cost advantage of the firm. MSMEs forming such a large part of the economy, it becomes imperative that adoption of energy management programs should not exclude this sector. Furthermore, it has been found that use of outdated technologies in MSMEs is a significant cause of environmental pollution and energy management practices have the potential to create significant differences. Notwithstanding this, the adoption energy management in MSMEs has progressed slowly in India and abroad. In the next section, challenges associated with adoption of energy management practices by MSMEs have been discussed.

CHALLENGES OF ENERGY MANAGEMENT IN MSMES

MSMEs in India constitute a significant chunk of the industries and are starting to take concrete steps to follow sustainable operations. However, in doing so, they face a number of challenges. Financial constraints and wide ranging technological and organizational change requirements have been identified as the main reasons leading to the lower-than-expected level of adoption of energy management practices among the MSMEs (Ghosh & Roy, 2011; Kannan & Boie, 2003).

Financial Constraints

Small industries work with little working capitals and focus on their core business functions. One of the important reasons behind their lack of interest in energy management is the associated cost of technological upgradation and long payback periods. Additionally, banks and insurance companies have not seriously considered the effects of the environmental regulations on the operating profits of a company (Leggett, 1996). This has led to lower support on the part of the banks to extend financial help to the firms combating environmental regulations. However, the banks have increasingly started recognizing the importance of environmental regulations and their effect on the internal profits of the companies. Additionally, government support helps the companies to financially sustain themselves by adhering to policies leading to reduced environmental costs. Government sponsored banks in India provide loans to the MSMEs for procuring energy saving equipment to reduce carbon footprint and also improve their productivity (Small Industries Development Bank of India, n.d.). The financial assistance achieves the dual aim of reducing the green house gas (GHG) emissions as well as demonstration and commercialization of the innovative and advanced technology in the micro, small, and medium enterprises. Further, proper credit lines specially designed for financing the energy efficient measures to be adopted by a company would make the proposition lucrative. Most importantly, MSMEs should be made aware of these financing platforms or credit lines. Tax based incentives provided to the MSMEs can also act as an impetus in alluring the firms to adopt advanced technologies to combat environmental concerns. For example, installing a fuel heater to increase the efficiency of the furnaces would require capital investment along with future repair and maintenance costs. The tax burden on the capital equipment would further increase the liability of the company making it undesirable. A tax incentive can provide a significant relief to lessen the associated financial burden and make it financially attractive and viable.

Apart from this, the most significant challenge is the identification of the financial benefits of the energy management measures in the accounting books of the company. It has been found that many a times energy costs are not allocated properly under the cost heads of (Rohdin & Thollander, 2006). This creates an impediment to improving the perception among the management with respect to the benefits energy management practices deliver leading to hampering decision making related to enforcement of such practices. Indian MSMEs, due to their not so proper book keeping styles, have been left vulnerable in realizing the true benefits of energy management strategies. Proper assistance from the government or industry associations will help in improving their book keeping styles and, thus, improve their accounting standards. Consequently, the impact of the energy saving measures can be distinctly reflected on the accounting books making a strong case for their implementation.

Technological Changes

The adoption of energy efficient technologies comes with its own set of challenges. The implementation of energy efficient systems is compounded by the difficulty in the compatibility with the legacy industrial energy systems. The production systems vary with different industrial sites and compatibility of the energy efficient systems with these systems is a technological challenge that needs to be addressed on a case by case basis. This can also involve a consequent change in adopted technologies suiting the changed requirements. MSMEs face a problem in making this transition as off-the-shelf technologies are costly and not suited to their needs. Research has established that lack of implementation of energy efficient production processes is due to various barriers which lead to delayed or non-adoption of associated technologies (Brunke, Johansson, & Thollander, 2014). Further, as in most cases, they do not have in-house research and development facilities, they face difficulties in designing new technologies on their own. The technological change thus requires working with the ecosystem partners such as energy consultants to design new and innovative interventions. The task for the management and other stakeholders is to ensure that initiatives with minimum expenditure but maximum environmental impacts should be prioritized. The activities which aptly can be dubbed as low hanging fruits should be employed in use for the MSMEs. Many of these technologies or practices may already be in practice in larger firms. Nevertheless, making them attractive to the small and medium sector is the daunting task. Also, specific understanding of energy efficiency systems can increase the incidence of their adoption (Fleiter et al., 2012). This understanding includes the likely impacts of the energy efficiency practices on various aspects of the production process such as higher productivity, lower raw material costs, lower operational costs, and lower labor costs. This distinction of the effects helps a faster and credible adoption of the energy efficiency practices. For example, an important aspect of improving energy efficiency in MSMEs is the transition to cleaner fuel such as natural gas, which can be attributed to higher productivity and lower labor costs.

Organizational Practice Change

Changes in organizational structure due to energy management practices depend on the size of the company, number of employees, type of industry, and type of fuel sources used (Turner & Doty, 2007). The changes also include the appointment of an energy manager on roles of the company or an energy consultant, who has access to the top management and can bring about the changes from a strategic point of view. This also requires commitment from the highest level of management to support the practices and support the venture, should it face difficulties.

The change in technologies also requires investment in terms of training staff to operate the new technologies. This also requires a change in organizational practices which entails a cost in terms of both time and money. Moreover, change is a destabilizing process and has its inherent challenges which is evident from the organizational change literature (By, 2005). The classic organizational change model of Kurt Lewin suggests the initial unfreezing of existing organizational practices, changing these practices and then freezing the new practices (Cummings, Bridgman, & Brown, 2016). Similarly, changing the existing organizational practices to incorporate the energy efficient strategies requires the initial unfreezing of the current practices. The unfreezing part is a long-drawn process and might involve retaliation from existing staff who might feel threatened by it. This requires negotiation between the energy consultants and organizational staff. After unfreezing of the existing practices, the next stage is the introduction of state of the art energy management practices in the MSMEs. The challenge at this stage is the introduction of external energy consultants who can do the pilot and introduce the energy management practices in the organization. The refreezing would involve training organizational staff to continue with the new set of energy management practices which have been introduced by the energy consultants.

ENERGY MANAGEMENT IN INDIAN MSMES

The MSMEs contribute a major chunk to the GDP of India along with the creation of employment opportunities for a considerable section of Indian population. The improvement in the productivity of the MSMEs is an essential part of the rigorous drive to ramp up the productivity of the overall Indian industrial sector. Energy management can play a major role in this productivity improvement. As mentioned earlier, energy management can contribute in various ways to improve the bottom line of the companies that adopt them. Following case studies have been used to exemplify the preparation of an energy balance sheet and conduct an energy audit in two Indian industrial contexts.

ENERGY MANAGEMENT IN FIROZABAD GLASS INDUSTRY

The glass making units in Firozabad, an industrial town located near Agra (India), accounts for more than 70% of the glass production in India (International Seminar on Inclusive Development of Firozabad Glass Art Ware Industry, 2011). The Firozabad glass industry cluster is more than two hundred years old. It manufactures traditional glass bangles and glass wares for the domestic market and also exports to international market. Most the units in Firozabad are labor intensive and employ traditional modes of the production. Due to its use of antiquated technology and coal as a fuel source, the industry, for long, has been a source of air pollution. This has been a point of concern to policy makers and has led to judicial and regulatory sanctions against the industry in the recent times. The Tajmahal of Agra, one of the world heritage sites, was threatened by the polluting smoke emanating from these units. The Supreme Court of India took cognizance of this issue and ordered these units to adopt pollution control measures during the late 1990s. This forced the glass making units to introduce a series of steps to improve upon their pollution footprint. An important part of this exercise was improving their energy efficiency by adoption and implementation of comprehensive energy management programs. The first step in this direction involved a detailed study of the production process of glass making to identify the opportunities for energy management.

Manufacturing Process of Glass Products

The initial step in the manufacture of glass involves the batch preparation of raw materials in definite proportions. The raw materials mainly consist of soda ash, lime, and silica. The raw materials are mixed and separated into batches to be *charged* into the furnace for melting. The raw materials are melted at a high temperature of 1400-1500 °C. The furnace used for *melting* the raw material can be of different kinds like pot furnace or tank furnace. Also, the energy source of the furnace can be coal, oil or natural gas. The energy efficiency of the furnace is dependent on the type of furnace and the kind of fuel used for burning. The melting process is the most energy intensive process in glass manufacturing. Ideally,

645 KWh of energy is required to melt one ton of glass. The efficiency of the furnace determines the actual heat needed to melt the glass. The raw materials used for the production of glass also include crushed scrap glass known as cullet. Cullet help in lowering the energy required for melting the raw material and provides better consistency to the molten mixture. The amount of cullet added can range up to 50%. A raw material mixture with 30% cullet might require 27 kg of raw material to produce 25 kg of finished glass. Other raw materials used for batch preparation include feldspar, potash, magnesia, dolomite saltcake, carbocite, iron pyrite, iron chromite, cobalt oxide, selenium, lead, etc. These materials are used to impart specific characteristics to glass. For example, lead is used to make the glass tougher. Melting is carried in pot furnaces, where the hot draft of air, generated by the burning of coal, is used to melt the raw material in the pots. An iron rod is used to take out a lump of molten glass through a working hole to *form a gob*. This is followed by forming the lump into the initial shape of the product which is called *parison preparation*. The parison is a basic model of the finished product. Therefore, this step also involves joining of various parisons. This is followed by the *press and blow formation* when the parisons are mouth blown and repeatedly pressed with the help of appropriate dies to transform it into the required shape. The pressing operation leads to cooling the glass, which might result in unnecessary cracking of glass. This is avoided by reheating the parison at regular intervals to maintain the tractability. After the required shape is obtained, the glass product is reheated to 500°C for 30 to 90 minutes to reduce the stress in the product. This step is called *annealing*. This is followed by *finishing* process where the product is rubbed with a cloth to make it shine. *Sorting* the products for quality is followed by packing it for shipping. Following is a diagrammatic representation of the glass manufacturing process (Figure 4).

Opportunities and Challenges of Energy Management

The micro, small, and medium enterprises (MSME) from the glass making industry, mostly run as family enterprises, faced an uphill task to survive the imposition of the pollution control regulations. The pollution caused by the units was due to the use of antiquated equipment which had highly inefficient energy usage. Though they were made aware of the available pollution control technologies, low business turnover and low productivity did not allow the units to purchase expensive pollution control equipments. The problem was compounded by the fact that the industry employed a large number of people and thus the closure of these industries was also not a viable option for the policy makers. Therefore, alternative technologies had to be developed in collaboration with the government to improve the energy efficiency and productivity of these units. The first step in the process was conducting a detailed energy audit to identify areas of improvement. This audit was undertaken by The Energy Research Institute (TERI), a private energy consultant.

The first step in an energy audit is the preparation of an energy balance sheet. The individual stages of the production process are studied in detail. An energy flow chart is prepared to show the energy inputs and energy sources for each of the individual steps. The amount of energy used for each step is calculated based on the ideal requirement of the energy and the efficiency of the energy source. A detailed itemized list of energy required for each production process is prepared. This is populated in the energy balance sheet such that the production processes with their corresponding energy usage are listed. The energy balance sheet gives a holistic and metrics based picture of the energy usage scenario for the concerned production unit. The figure below presents an illustrative energy balance sheet for glass production (Figure 5).

Figure 4. Production process of glass products manufacture

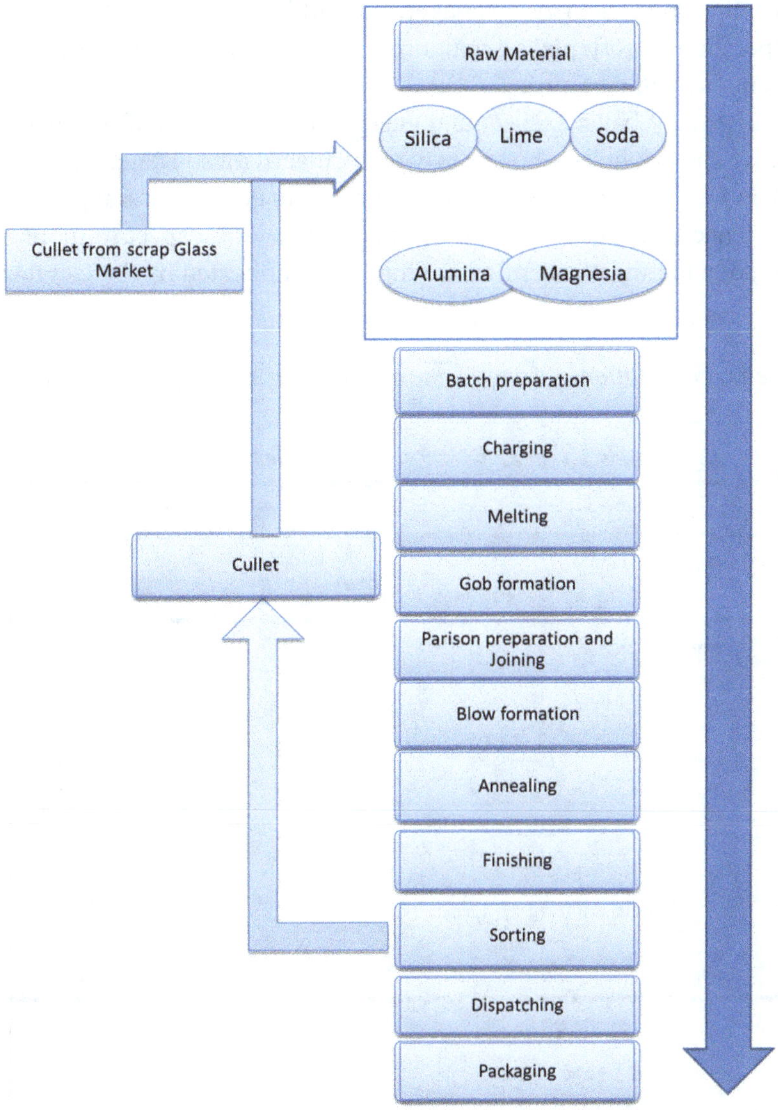

The energy intensive processes can be easily identified with the help of the energy balance sheet. The ratio of the energy consumed in the particular sub-process and the amount of glass produced is a key parameter for comparing the energy efficiency of different sub-processes. This ratio is referred to as specific energy consumption. The energy balance sheet also comprises a section on the polluting effects of the production processes. Thus, while making an economic case for the adoption of energy management practices, it addresses the environmental concerns as well.

As energy balance sheet shows, melting is the most energy intensive process in glass production. Identification of energy intensive processes is followed by the implementation of various techniques or adoption of technologies to reduce the energy usage in the particular sub-process. Techniques, like having even batch sizes of raw materials and minimizing the excess air in the furnace, can provide with significant savings in energy usage. The expected energy saving will provide monetary value as less energy usage means less fuel which means lower cost of production. The investment in the new technologies and the monetary savings through energy management will have a net effect on the operational profits. This effect on the operational profit plays a major role in persuading the management of the production unit to adopt the energy saving measures.

The preparation of energy balance sheet and energy audits are specialized activities. This poses a challenge for the glass making units who are new to such activities. The energy saving measures may further include fuel and furnace changes such as shifting from coal to natural gas. This may be difficult for the units as the cleaner fuel such as natural gas is costly with respect to more polluting coal. The financial constraints for adopting cleaner fuel are further complicated by the fact that new fuel requires

Figure 5. Illustrative representation of sample energy balance sheet of glass manufacturing unit

Sample Energy Balance sheet	*Glass Unit in Firozabad*
Description	Data as of 2005
Production (in MT)	
Quantity of Molten Glass	1500
Energy Consumption (in GWH)	
Coal Usage	
Melting	10.5
Forming	2.4
Annealing	1.3
Refining	1.1
Others	0.8
Electricity usage	
Forming	0.018
Overhead	0.006
Total Energy Cost ($)	34846
Coal Usage	33538
Electricity usage	1307
Emissions (in MT)	
Suspended particulate Matter (SPM)	97.5
Carbon Dioxide	4743
Sulphur Dioxide	43
Nitrogen Oxides	16
Summary (per MT of Glass manufactured)	
Specific Energy Consumption (Mwh)	10.7
Specific Energy Cost Consumption (INR)	23.2
Specific SPM Consumption (kg)	65
Specific Carbon Dioxide Consumption (kg)	3162
Specific Sulphur Dioxide Consumption (kg)	28.7
Specific Nitrogen Oxides Consumption (kg)	10.7

new technologies. These technologies need to be manned by trained personnel. Thus it would involve an additional cost in terms of training the existing workers or recruiting new ones.

Implementing Energy Management Program

The energy management program in the Firozabad glass industry has been guided by The Energy Research Institute (TERI) (Sethi & Ghosh, 2008). TERI is a non-government research organization engaged in consultancy and technology development in the energy conservation domain. It collaborates with like-minded non-government organizations (NGOs) and government agencies to implement energy saving measures in different industries. Over the years it has developed expertise in energy auditing and energy consultancy. The energy audit conducted by TERI revealed significant opportunities for improving energy efficiency in Firozabad glass industry. The audit identified scopes of changes in technology and operational practices of the firms to improve energy efficiency. TERI collaborated with the Swiss Development Corporation (SDC) and the local consultants to design appropriate technologies, such as the open pot furnace, to implement the energy management program. Thus, the success of energy management initiative in Firozabad could be attributed to the collaboration between multiple stakeholders and assimilation of complementary skillsets.

ENERGY MANAGEMENT IN MORBI CERAMIC INDUSTRY

The Morbi ceramic cluster of is located in the Indian state of Gujarat and accounts for 70% of India's ceramic tiles production. There are more than 450 micro, small, and medium enterprises (MSMEs) in this cluster engaged in the work of manufacturing a variety of tiles and sanitary wares. The ceramic units in Morbi at the present import most of their equipments from Italy and China. The main raw materials used for the ceramic production are feldspar and silica. Both these are sourced from nearby mines in the Gujarat and Rajasthan state. The main energy sources used in the manufacturing process in the cluster are electricity, natural gas, and lignite. The inefficient use of these fuels leads to environmental pollution and increases the cost of production of ceramic tiles. A detailed analysis of the manufacturing process of ceramic tiles suggests several opportunities for energy management in this industry.

Production Process of Ceramic Tiles

The first step in the manufacturing process of ceramic manufacture is *grinding*. This stage involves the mixing of raw materials, such as clay, feldspar, etc., in proper proportion and grinding it to prepare a homogenous mixture. The grinding can be done either through the wet or dry process and can follow batch or continuous processing. The units in Morbi use the wet grinding process with batch processing. As the name suggests, in wet grinding, water is added to the raw material mixture, and they are ground in blungers and ball mill. As batch processing is prevalent in Morbi, after completion of one batch of ball mill, the slurry is taken out and stored in underground tanks containing agitator motors. The agitations in these tanks maintain the uniformity of the slurry. The second step in the production process is spray drying. In this process, the moisture that gets added in the grinding process is removed from the slurry. For this, the slurry is pumped through hydraulic mechanism onto a spray dryer. The drying process is energy intensive and requires the reduction of the moisture content of the slurry from around 40% to

5%. The necessary heat for reducing the moisture content is provided by heating the slurry in a spray dryer at temperatures of 550-600°C. Flue gases provide the heat used in this process. These are generated through direct combustion or gasification of fuels such as natural gas, charcoal, Indonesian coal, briquette, and saw dust. The third step in the production process is pressing. It involves the pressing of spray dried mixture through the hydraulic press which converts the mixture into biscuit sized tiles. The main energy source for running the hydraulic press is electricity. The fourth step in the production process is drying. In this step, the hydraulically pressed tiles are sent to the dryer through conveyor belts. The drying process further reduces the moisture content of the tiles. The fifth step in the process is glazing. During this process, the tiles are sent to glaze line. Glazing is required for engraving the different designs on the tiles. The sixth step in the production process is firing and baking. As the name suggests, in this process, the tiles are fired in the baking kilns at temperatures of about 1100-1150°C. The required temperature is generated through the burning of natural gas and producer gas from the gasifier. The last step in the production process is sizing and polishing. Sizing involves precision cutting the tiles so that all the tiles have the same dimension. In case of some of the tiles, such as vitrified tiles, after sizing the tiles are further polished. Polishing is also energy intensive and utilizes 40%-50% of overall electricity consumption in case of vitrified tiles. After sizing and polishing, the tiles are sent for dispatch. The diagram below is a diagrammatic representation of the production process (Figure 6).

Opportunities and Challenges of Energy Management

It was in 2010 that Bureau of Energy Efficiency (BEE) (Bureau of Energy Efficiency (BEE), 2010), the government agency to implement energy management programs, started its intervention in the cluster. BEE is the governmental organization which is at the forefront of devising policies and programs for energy efficiency. It also specializes in providing advisory and consultation services to industries on energy management. It also provides training to energy auditor and energy consultants. BEE aimed at identifying the energy saving opportunities in the cluster and suggesting the appropriate measures for the implementation of the same. BEE in the energy audit in the Morbi cluster identified the areas for improving energy efficiency. The first step in the identification of the areas of improving energy efficiency was preparation of an energy balance sheet for the ceramic production process. The figure below shows an illustrative energy balance sheet for the ceramic tile manufacturing process (Figure 7).

BEE then recommended several technological improvements in the cluster to improve the energy efficiency of the production process. The first technological improvement was the installation of variable frequency drive (VFD) in the ball mill. This would lead to saving of electricity consumption in the grinding process. Moreover, ensuring smaller size pebbles of raw materials such as feldspar would ensure efficient use of energy in the grinding process. In addition to these, energy efficient agitator motors employed in underground tanks would also contribute to improved energy efficiency of grinding process. Improvement of energy efficiency in spray drying can be achieved by improvement of insulation in the kiln to avoid leakage of energy. Ensuring energy efficiency in baking and firing process can be accomplished by avoiding loss of heat and ensuring optimum air to fuel ratio. The heat loss could be prevented by installing kiln curtains. Also preheating of combustion air by solar heating can lead to energy efficiency and also reduce pollution. Furthermore, significant energy savings can be achieved in this context by adopting the cogeneration technology. Cogeneration involves the use of gas turbines for generating both electricity and heat for spray dryer.

Figure 6. Production process of ceramic tiles manufacture

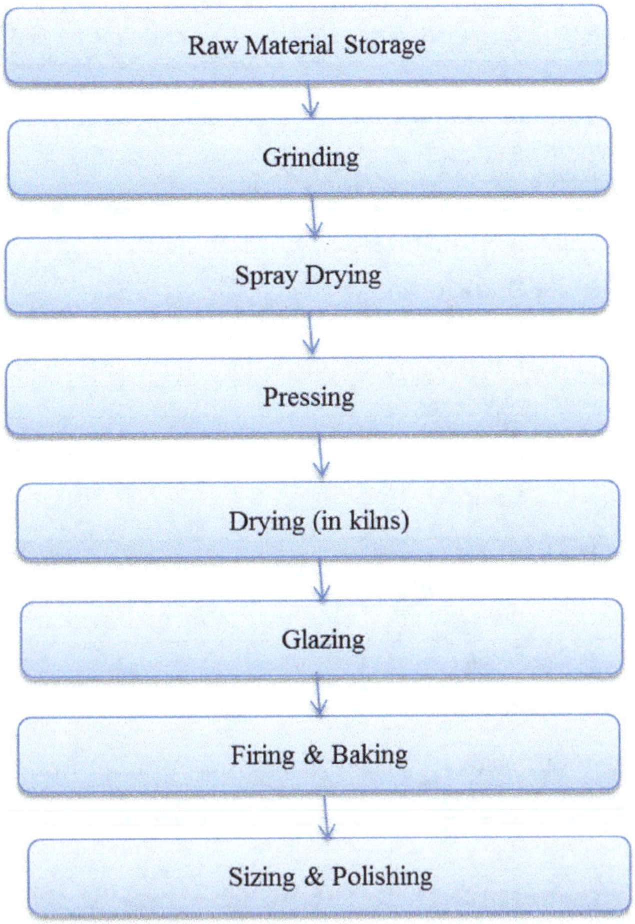

The implementation of energy management programs in Morbi was filled with several challenges. Although the owners of ceramic units were convinced that significant energy savings could be achieved by adopting energy management program, they were hesitant to be the first one to adopt the technology. They wanted that success of these measures to be demonstrated at some of the units so that they can be convinced of its benefits. Further, the adoption of new technologies such as gas turbines would require them to train their existing staff and may require hiring new staff. They further pointed out that adoption of the new technologies would involve additional financial commitments.

Implementing Energy Management Program

BEE has spearheaded the energy efficiency program in the Morbi ceramic industry. The energy audit by BEE revealed several opportunities for improving energy efficiency in Morbi ceramic cluster. The audit revealed several gaps in technology and operational practices of the firms to improve energy efficiency. These gaps, if successfully addressed, have the potential to tremendously benefit the bottom line of the

Figure 7. Illustrative representation of sample energy balance sheet of ceramic tiles manufacturing unit

Sample Energy Balance sheet	*Ceramic Unit in Morbi*
Description	Data as of 2010
Production (in Sq m)	
Quantity of ceramic floor tile production	900000
Energy Consumption (in GWH)	
Electricity Usage (Gwh)	0.9
Grinding	0.29
Pressing	0.22
Drying	0.06
Glazing	0.05
Firing	0.07
Sizing	0.21
Natural Gas Usage (SCM)	900000
Spray Drying	130000
Drying	28000
Firing	742000
Total Energy Cost ($)	276923
Electricity Usage	69230
Natural Gas Usage	207692
Emissions (in MT)	
Suspended particulate Matter (SPM)	0.01
Carbon Dioxide	1993
Sulphur Dioxide	0.12
Nitrogen Oxides	1.57
Summary (per sq m of tile manufactured)	
Specific Electrical Energy Consumtion (kwh)	1
Specific Electrical Energy Consumtion (SCM)	1
Specific Energy Cost Consumtion ($)	0.31
Specific SPM Consumtion (g)	0.02
Specific Carbon Dioxide Consumtion (kg)	2.21
Specific Sulphur Dioxide Consumtion (g)	0.13
Specific Nitrogen Oxides Consumtion (g)	1.74

concerned firms. As it happens in case of most of the MSME contexts in the developing economies, it was also witnessed in the case of Morbi Ceramic Cluster that the capabilities to address the gaps are not readily available with a firm. Different entities with different competencies have to come together. In this particular case, BEE conducted the audits and Small Industries Development Bank of India (SIDBI) helped with loans to procure required technological equipments to make the initiative successful.

DISCUSSION

As mentioned earlier, the business ecosystem perspective (Moore, 1993) stipulates that an organization is viewd not as a stand alone entity, but rather needs to be conceptualised as an ecosystem, spanning across the organizational boundary, encompassing partner firms from same/different industries. According to this perspective, capabilities internal to the focal firm are not sufficient. The concerned firm has to make sure that the combined skillsets of the network cooperatively evolve to respond to the challenges posed by changing business scenarios. This dynamic view of firm capabilities becomes even more significant when faced with adoption of new business practices as the whole ecosystem has to make an collaborative attempt to idenify and aquire newer competiencies to ensure success for any such initiative. In case of MSMEs, the involvement of partnering firms become all the more important because often times the focal firms lack the resources necessary to successfully see them through such major change initiatives. To provide supporting evidences, two cases have been showcased in this paper - Firozabad Glass Industry and Morbi Ceramic Industry.

Apart from the focal firms, adoption of energy management practices in Firozabad involved participation from other stakeholders from within their partnering networks. TERI, SDC, and local consultants proved to be critical actors of this ecosystem. However, continuous effort needs to be invested in maintaining the health of the ecosystem (Isckia, 2009). In the absence of such efforts, the ecosystem might collapse. In the case of Firozabad glass industry, one such instance was witnessed when some of the units decided to revert to polluting fuels like coal in the face of rising prices of natural gas. Such situations which threaten the health of ecosystem require timely government interventions. Appropriate financial inducements and support mechanisms need to be devised to ensure the sustainability of such energy management ecosystems.

Overcoming challenges posing threats to successful implementation of energy management programs in case of Morbi Ceramic Cluster also involved adoption of a business ecosystem perspective. The involvement of BEE in conducting energy audits and subsequently identifying areas for improving the energy efficiency validates the point that collaboration among the ceramic units and a host of other network partners is needed for successful implementation of such initiatives. Industrial banks, such as Small Industries Development Bank of India (SIDBI), etc., also played critical roles by extending credit lines to the firm owners for upgrading the firm-machinery and incorporating necessary changes in the business processes followed by them. At present, there is a shortage of technically skilled resources for providing repair and maintenance services for existing technologies used by these units. As the focal firms adopt the new energy saving technologies, necessary interventions are to be put in place so that a network of local repair and service provider firms can provide the required technical services.

According to the business ecosystem perspective, identification of capabilities needed by a firm is a dynamic process as firm requirements change with emerging market conditions (Iansiti & Levien, 2004). As evidensed in the cases of Firozpur and Morbi, emergence of new business practices in response to adoption of new energy management programs is dependent on successful collaboration of networked stakeholders. Without supports from policy-makers, lenders, suppliers, consultants, technologists, and other service providers, such an initiative cannot succeed. Adoption of business ecosystem perspective is necessary not only for the initial stages, but also to ensure sustainability of such energy management programs. The extant literature on energy management (e.g. Schulze, Nehler, Ottosson, & Thollander, 2016) has highlighted the significance of internal firm capabilities in adopting these practices. The theoretical relevance of business ecosystem perspective is that it highlights the importance of external linkages in fostering energy management practices.

CONCLUSION AND FUTURE RESEARCH DIRECTION

Using the case studies of Firozabad glass industry and the Morbi ceramic industry, we investigate the evolution of sustainable accounting practices in Indian MSMEs. Energy management and auditing constituting an integral part of sustainable accounting, our focus has been specifically on the adoption of energy management and auditing practices by the organizations in these two clusters. These case studies demonstrate both the challenges and opportunities involved in adopting the energy management practices. Particularly the hurdles of financial constraints, technological modernization, and organizational changes render it difficult for MSMEs to adopt these practices (Ghosh & Roy, 2011; Kannan & Boie, 2003). However, our findings further suggest that it is possible for MSMEs to embark on the path of sustainable accounting with the appropriate support from government bodies, energy consultants, and funding agencies. Therefore the focus in implementation of energy management and auditing should be on development of linkages between these organizations. In other words, a business ecosystem perspective (Moore, 1993) needs to be adopted for implementation of sustainable accounting practices. Moreover, continuous effort is needed on the part of stakeholders as well as the policy makers to maintain the health of such ecosystems. Business ecosystem perspective has shed important light on the development of information and technology industries (Basole, 2009; Fransman, 2010; Isckia, 2009). The present study shows that the business ecosystem has important relevance for the recent development of sustainable accounting in MSMEs too.

Although our findings suggest important aspects of sustainable accounting, it has important limitations. First, our study is focused specifically on the MSME sector. Some of the challenges that we have identified in the case of MSMEs such as that of financial constraints may not be applicable in the case of large scale manufacturing enterprises. Though, at a theoretical level we know that large scale enterprises have the financial capability to design and adopt firm level sustainable accounting initiatives, it requires to be investigated whether large firms are doing so in practice. The large scale manufacturing units have their own research and development departments. Thus energy consultants may need to play a different role in that context. Additional studies would be required to investigate the role of energy consultants in implementing sustainable accounting initiatives in large scale manufacturing clusters. Our findings suggest the relevance of adopting a business ecosystem perspective for studying the evolution of sustainable accounting in MSME clusters. Future studies would need to validate whether it is true in the case of large scale manufacturing clusters. Second, our study is concerned with the manufacturing sector where the relevance of sustainable accounting is somewhat more apparent. However, the relevance of sustainable accounting for service based firms is not so much apparent. Further studies can be taken up to understand the implications of sustainable accounting in service based firms.

REFERENCES

Basole, R. C. (2009). Visualization of interfirm relations in a converging mobile ecosystem. *Journal of Information Technology*, *24*(2), 1–16. doi:10.1057/jit.2008.34

Bebbington, J. (2007). *Accounting for Sustainable Development Performance* (1st ed.). Burlington: CIMA Publishing.

Bebbington, J., Gray, R., Hibbitt, C., & Kirk, E. (2001). *Full cost accounting: An agenda for action.* Certified Accountants Educational Trust London.

Brunke, J.-C., Johansson, M., & Thollander, P. (2014). Empirical investigation of barriers and drivers to the adoption of energy conservation measures, energy management practices and energy services in the Swedish iron and steel industry. *Journal of Cleaner Production*, *84*, 509–525. doi:10.1016/j.jclepro.2014.04.078

Bunse, K., Vodicka, M., Schönsleben, P., Brülhart, M., & Ernst, F. O. (2011). Integrating energy efficiency performance in production management--gap analysis between industrial needs and scientific literature. *Journal of Cleaner Production*, *19*(6), 667–679. doi:10.1016/j.jclepro.2010.11.011

Bureau of Energy Efficiency (BEE). (2010). Manual on Energy Conservation Measures in *Ceramic Industry*. Author.

By, R. T. (2005). Organizational Change Management : A Critical Review. *Journal of Change Management*, *5*(4), 369–380. doi:10.1080/14697010500359250

Capehart, B. L., Turner, W. C., & Kennedy, W. J. (2006). *Guide to Energy Management* (5th ed.). Lilburn, GA: The Fairmont Press.

Cummings, S., Bridgman, T., & Brown, K. G. (2016). Unfreezing change as three steps : Rethinking Kurt Lewin ' s legacy for change management. *Human Relations*, *69*(1), 33–60. doi:10.1177/0018726715577707

Environmental Protection Agency. (2008). *Ensuring a Sustainable Future: An Energy Management Guidebook for Wasterwater and Water Utilities*. Washington, DC: Energy Protection Agency.

Figge, F., Hahn, T., Schaltegger, S., & Wagner, M. (2002). The sustainability balanced scorecard - Linking sustainability management to business strategy. *Business Strategy and the Environment*, *11*(5), 269–284. doi:10.1002/bse.339

Financing Schemes for Sustainable Development including Energy Efficiency and Cleaner Production in MSMEs. (n.d.). *Small Industries Development Bank of India.*

Fleiter, T., Gruber, E., Eichhammer, W., & Worrell, E. (2012). The German energy audit program for firms-a cost-effective way to improve energy efficiency? *Energy Efficiency*, *5*(4), 447–469. doi:10.100712053-012-9157-7

Fransman, M. (2010). The new ICT ecosystem: Implications for policy and regulation. Cambridge, UK: Academic Press. doi:10.1017/CBO9780511676130

Ghosh, D., & Roy, J. (2011). Approach to energy efficiency among micro, small and medium enterprises in India: Results of a field survey (No. 8). Vienna: Academic Press.

Gordić, D., Babić, M., Jovičić, N., Šušteršič, V., Končalović, D., & Jelić, D. (2010). Development of energy management system - Case study of Serbian car manufacturer. *Energy Conversion and Management*, *51*(12), 2783–2790. doi:10.1016/j.enconman.2010.06.014

Gossain, S., & Kandiah, G. (1998). Reinventing value: The new business ecosystem. *Strategy and Leadership*, *26*(5), 28–33. doi:10.1108/eb054622

Hamilton, J. T. (1995). Pollution as news: Media and stock market reactions to the toxics release inventory data. *Journal of Environmental Economics and Management*.

Hart, S. L., & Ahuja, G. (1996). Does it pay to be green? An empirical examination of the relationship between emission reduction and firm performance. *Business Strategy and the Environment*, *5*(1), 30–37. doi:

Hirst, E., & Brown, M. (1990). Closing the efficiency gap: Barriers to the efficient use of energy. *Resources, Conservation and Recycling*, *3*(4), 267–281. doi:10.1016/0921-3449(90)90023-W

Hopwood, A. G. (2009). Accounting and the environment. *Accounting, Organizations and Society*, *34*(3–4), 433–439. doi:10.1016/j.aos.2009.03.002

Iansiti, M., & Levien, R. (2004). Strategy as Ecology. *Harvard Business Review*, 1–11. PMID:15029791

International Energy Agency. (2016). *CO2 Emissions from Fuel Combustion*. Paris: International Energy Agency.

Isckia, T. (2009). Amazon's Evolving Ecosystem : A Cyber-bookstore and Application Service Provider. *Canadian Journal of Administrative Sciences*, *26*(4), 332–343. doi:10.1002/cjas.119

Jain, A. (2011). *Unlocking Energy Efficiency Market in India's SME Sector: Cluster Approach and Role of ESCOs & Fiscal Incentives*. University of Southern California.

Järvi, K., & Kortelainen, S. (2017). Taking stock of empirical research on business ecosystems : A literature review Samuli Kortelainen. *International Journal of Business and Systems Research*, *11*(3), 8–11. doi:10.1504/IJBSR.2017.085469

Kannan, R., & Boie, W. (2003). Energy management practices in SME - case study of a bakery in Germany. *Energy Conversion and Management*, *44*(6), 945–959. doi:10.1016/S0196-8904(02)00079-1

Lambert, D., & Stock, J. (1979). The corporate energy policy: A management planning perspective. *Long Range Planning*, *12*(2), 45–51. doi:10.1016/0024-6301(79)90072-4

Leggett, J. K. (1996). *Climate change and the financial sector*. Gerling Akademie.

Li, Y.-R. (2009). The technological roadmap of Cisco's business ecosystem. *Technovation*, *29*(5), 379–386. doi:10.1016/j.technovation.2009.01.007

Ministry of Micro Small and Medium Enterprises. (2011). Annual report 2010-11. New Delhi: Author.

Moore, J. F. (1993). Predators and Prey: A New Ecology of Competition. *Harvard Business Review*, 75–84. PMID:10126156

Porter, M. E. (1980). *Competitive Strategy: Techniques for Analyzing Industries and Competitors*. New York, NY: The Free Press.

Porter, M. E., & van der Linde, C. (1995). Green and Competitive. *Harvard Business Review*, *73*(5), 120–134. doi:10.1207/S15374424JCCP3203_02

Rohdin, P., & Thollander, P. (2006). Barreirs to and driving forces for energy efficiency in the non-energy intensive manufacturing industries in Sweden. *Energy*, *31*(12), 1836–1844. doi:10.1016/j.energy.2005.10.010

Rudberg, M., Waldemarsson, M., & Lidestam, H. (2013). Strategic perspectives on energy management: A case study in the process industry. *Applied Energy*, *104*, 487–496. doi:10.1016/j.apenergy.2012.11.027

Schaltegger, S., Bennett, M., & Buritt, R. (2006). *Sustainability Accounting and Reporting*. Dordrecht: Springer. doi:10.1007/978-1-4020-4974-3

Schaltegger, S., Bennett, M., & Burritt, R. (2006). Sustainability Accounting and Reporting: Development, Linkages and Reflection. In R. B. S. Schaltegger & M. Bennett (Eds.), *Sustainability Accounting and Reporting* (pp. 1–33). Dordrecht: Springer. doi:10.1007/978-1-4020-4974-3_1

Schaltegger, S., Burritt, R., & Petersen, H. (2003). *An Introduction to Corporate Environmental Management: Striving for Sustainability*. Sheffield, UK: Emerald Group Publishing Limited; doi:10.1108/meq.2003.14.4.541.4

Schaltegger, S., & Müller, K. (1997). Calculating the true profitability of pollution prevention. *Greener Management International*, 53–68.

Schulze, M., Nehler, H., Ottosson, M., & Thollander, P. (2016). Energy management in industry – a systematic review of previous findings and an integrative conceptual framework. *Journal of Cleaner Production*, *112*, 3692–3708. doi:10.1016/j.jclepro.2015.06.060

Sethi, G., & Ghosh, A. M. (Eds.). (2008). *Towards Cleaner Technologies A process story in the Firozabad glass industry cluster*. New Delhi: The Energy and Resources Institute.

Shang, T., & Shi, Y. (2013). The emergence of the electric vehicle industry in Chinese Shandong Province: A research design for understanding business ecosystem capabilities. *Journal of Chinese Entreprenuership*, *5*(1), 61–75. doi:10.1108/17561391311297888

Shen, B., Price, L., & Lu, H. (2012). Energy audit practices in China: National and local experiences and issues. *Energy Policy*, *46*, 346–358. doi:10.1016/j.enpol.2012.03.069

Spitzer, M. A. (1992). Calculating the benefits of pollution prevention. *Pollution Engineering*, *24*(15), 33–42.

Thollander, P., & Ottosson, M. (2010). Energy management practices in Swedish energy-intensive industries. *Journal of Cleaner Production*, *18*(12), 1125–1133. doi:10.1016/j.jclepro.2010.04.011

Thomson, I. (2014). Accounting and Sustainability: Mapping the terrain. In J. Bebbington, J. Unerman, & B. O'Dwyer (Eds.), *Sustainability accounting and accountability*. Routledge.

Turner, W. C., & Doty, S. (2007). *Energy Management Handbook*. Fairmont Press.

Van Marrewijk, M. (2003). Concepts and Definitions of CSR and Corporate Sustainability: Between Agency and Communion. *Journal of Business Ethics*, *44*(2), 95–105. doi:10.1023/A:1023331212247

Vasudevan, S., & Higgins, B. (2004). Strategic Energy Risk Management for End Users. *Journal of Structured and Project Finance*, *10*(1), 74–78. doi:10.3905/jsf.2004.74

Virtanen, T., Tuomaala, M., & Pentti, E. (2013). Energy efficiency complexities: A technical and managerial investigation. *Management Accounting Research*, *24*(4), 401–416. doi:10.1016/j.mar.2013.06.002

Walley, N., & Whitehead, B. (1994). It's not easy being green. *Harvard Business Review*, *72*(3), 46–51. doi:10.2345/0899-8205(2007)41[336:INEBG]2.0.CO;2

Zhu, Q., Geng, Y., & Lai, K. (2011). Environmental supply chain cooperation and its effect on the circular economy practice-performance relationship among Chinese manufacturers. *Journal of Industrial Ecology*, *15*(3), 405–419. doi:10.1111/j.1530-9290.2011.00329.x

ADDITIONAL READING

C2ES (n.d.) Outcomes of the U.N. climate change conference in Paris. Center for Climate and Energy Solutions. Retrieved from: https://www.c2es.org/international/negotiations/cop21-paris/summary

Autio, E., & Thomas, L. D. W. (2014). Innovation Ecosystems : Implications for Innovation Management. In M. Dodgson, D. Gann, & N. Phillips (Eds.), *The Oxford Handbook of Innovation Management* (pp. 204–228). Oxford, UK: Oxford University Press.

Chaudhry, V. P., Gangwar, B., Pandey, D. K., & Gangwar, K. S. (2009). Energy auditing of diversified rice–wheat cropping systems in Indo-gangetic plains. *Energy*, *34*(9), 1091–1096. doi:10.1016/j.energy.2009.04.017

Documents, U. N. (n.d.) Our common future, chapter 2: Towards sustainable development. United Nations. Retrieved from: http://www.un-documents.net/ocf-02.htm#I

Doty, S. (2011). *Commercial Energy Auditing Reference Handbook* (2nd ed.). Lilburn, GA: The Fairmont Press.

Ericsson, K., Nilsson, L. J., & Nilsson, M. (2011). New energy strategies in the Swedish pulp and paper industry — The role of national and EU climate and energy policies. *Energy Policy*, *39*(3), 1439–1449. doi:10.1016/j.enpol.2010.12.016

Galateanu, E., & Avasilcai, S. (2016). Framing the Competitive Behaviors of Niche Players : The Electric Vehicle Business Ecosystem Perspective. *Procedia: Social and Behavioral Sciences*, *221*, 342–351. doi:10.1016/j.sbspro.2016.05.124

International Seminar on Inclusive Development of Firozabad Glass Art Ware Industry. (2011) Adoption of advanced technology & design innovations. International Seminar on Inclusive Development of Firozabad Glass Art Ware Industry. Retrieved from: http://www.aigmf.com/International-Seminar-Firozabad.pdf

Järvi, K., & Kortelainen, S. (2017). Taking stock of empirical research on business ecosystems : A literature review Samuli Kortelainen. *International Journal of Business and Systems Research*, *11*(3), 8–11. doi:10.1504/IJBSR.2017.085469

Mendes, J., & Santos, I. (2014). Energy Management in Four and Five Star Hotels in Algarve (Portugal). *Turizam*, *18*(3), 95–112. doi:10.5937/Turizam1403095M

Nachira, F., Nicolai, A., Dini, P., Le Louran, M., & Leon, L. R. (2007). *Digital Business Ecosystems*. European Commission.

Suh, Y., & Kim, M. (2015). Dynamic change of manufacturing and service industries network in mobile ecosystems: The case of Korea. *Telematics and Informatics*, *32*(4), 613–628. doi:10.1016/j.tele.2015.02.004

Tripathy, S. C., Roy, M., & Balasubramanian, R. (1992). Energy Auditing Kit for Cement Industries. *Energy Conversion and Management*, *33*(12), 1073–1078. doi:10.1016/0196-8904(92)90004-G

UN. (n.d.) Kyoto Protocal to the United Nations framework convention on climate change. United Nations. Retrieved from: https://unfccc.int/resource/docs/convkp/kpeng.html

KEY TERMS AND DEFINITIONS

BEE: The Bureau of Energy Efficiency (BEE) is an agency under the Ministry of Power, Government of India and was created 2002 with an objective to promote and support the conservation and efficient use of energy in India.

Energy Audit: Energy audit refers to the process of verification and analysis of energy usage in a plant or a building with an objective of identifying opportunities to reduce the amount of energy input without compromising with the amount or quality of the output.

Energy Balance Sheet: An energy balance sheet contains detailed data energy usage in a process/plant and considers energy transformation/consumption from different types of input sources.

Energy Efficiency: Energy efficiency is a measure of how efficiently energy is used in a particular plant, building, or process to provide required products or services.

Energy Management: Energy management refers to the strategy of planning, adjusting, and optimizing processes so as to reduce energy consumption per unit of output.

GHG: A greenhouse gas (GHG) is a gas that absorbs infrared radiation (IR) from the sun and radiates heat in all directions leading to heating up of the earth's atmosphere.

MSME: Micro, small, and medium enterprises (MSMEs) are defined based on the investment in plant or machinery for enterprises engaged in manufacturing of goods and equipment for enterprises engaged in provisioning of services. For the first category investment cutoffs are 2.5, 50, and 100 million INR are the respective cutoffs to be considered as micro, small, and medium enterprises. For service firms, the corresponding cut-offs are 1, 20, and 50 INR.

SIDBI: Small Industries Development Bank of India (SIDBI) was set up in 1990 through an act of parliament with an objective to promote, finance, and aid of micro, small, and medium-scale enterprises (MSME) in India.

Sustainable Accounting: Sustainable accounting aims to improve upon the transparency and accountability of financial reporting process of organizations by reporting on triple P's—social (people), ecological (planet), or economic (profit)—with an objective to ensure that sustainability is embedded into organizational culture.

TERI: The Energy and Resources Institute (TERI) is a research institute based in New Delhi dedicated to conducting research in the field of sustainable development (primarily of India and the Global South).

UNFCCC: The United Nations Framework Convention on Climate Change (UNFCCC) is an international environmental treaty adopted in 1992 with an objective to keep in check the increasing greenhouse gas (GHG) concentrations by imposing non-binding limits on GHG emissions for individual countries.

Chapter 9

Innovation, Sustainability, and Organizational Change in a Social Portuguese Organization: A Strategic Management Perspective

Fernando Barbosa
University of Minho, Portugal

Fernando Romero
University of Minho, Portugal

Jorge Cunha
University of Minho, Portugal

ABSTRACT

Social economy has been a prominent topic among scholars, politicians, and practitioners. Social economy organizations are mission-driven with the purpose of creating social value, overcoming a social problem, and contributing to attain sustainable social development. In this chapter, a particular weakness underlying those organizations is addressed: lack of managerial skills and the importance of a well-structured process of strategic management and organizational innovation. Based on the analysis of a Portuguese case study, the goal is to increase the knowledge on the facilitating factors and barriers to the improvement of the quality of service and the efficiency of the management of a social economy organization, in order to understand how it creates and delivers social value and ensures its future sustainability. The findings highlight a number of best practices in the design of a structured innovation process which were supported by the Portuguese program Q3-qualifying the third sector, which may help similar organizations to improve their innovation and organizational processes.

DOI: 10.4018/978-1-5225-5267-3.ch009

INTRODUCTION

The concept of social economy has been a highly prominent topic among scholars, politicians and practitioners (Spear, 2013). However, there is no widely agreed definition of that concept (Noya & Clarence, 2007). As a working definition, social economy is understood in this chapter as integrating the set of activities with social and economic expression, managed by non-profit entities and aimed at satisfying needs not met by market mechanisms (Borzaga & Tortia, 2007). Within this context, organizations belonging to the social economy are mission driven organizations with a social purpose, since they try to meet a social need or tackle a social problem (Millar & Hall, 2013). Social economy organizations do not belong either to the public or the private sectors, they develop their activities within the economy as a whole, forming a third sector, whose role is to provide services that address social needs that are not served by the state or the market. Social economy organizations are characterized by democratic and participative decision-making processes, and profits are employed to expand the organization and improve its services to its members and to society (Bastida, Marimon & Tanganelli, 2017). In this way, they differ from the organizations of the business (or market) sector, which are profit-maximization oriented. Social economy organizations have grown in number and relevance, contributing to employment, social inclusion, democratic participation and community building (Noya & Clarence, 2007) and they have focused, particularly, on improving social cohesion, on achieving sustainable development, on protecting the environment and consumers, and enhancing/complementing social security policies (Monzon & Chaves, 2008). Examples of social economy organizations are (Pérez & Perdomo, 2017): cooperatives; mutual associations; foundations; philanthropies; social enterprises; holy house of mercy; and private social solidarity institutions.

The importance of the social economy in the overall economic context of a country is increasingly recognized (Bastida, Marimon & Tanganelli, 2017). For example, the European Commission highlights that a "significant proportion of Europe's economy is intended to make profits for people other than investors or owners." (European Commission, https://ec.europa.eu/growth/sectors/social-economy_en). In Europe, there are 2 million social economy organizations, contributing to about 10% of the output of the European business sector, with a share of about 6% in total employment (about 11 million people), revealing an industry that will be called to give a greater contribution to the current problems of unemployment and social cohesion due to the social and economic transformation under way. In the particular case of Portugal, this sector has a dimension as large as or more important than other traditional sectors of the economy, not only for the universe of 55,000 organizations that constitute it, for the 227,000 people it employs, but also for being responsible for 5.5% of national paid employment and 2.8% of gross value added (Decree-Law no. 172-A / 2014).

The main sources of funding for social economy organizations are (Dragan & Popa, 2017): public funds; private sources; revenues from the sale of goods and services and user contributions. However, it should be noted that, especially, for those organizations that are primarily aimed at responding more directly to the satisfaction of social needs, public funding is the major source of funds (López-Arceiz, Bellostas & Rivera-Torres, 2017). It is, however, imperative that these organizations move towards ensuring the conditions for greater financial autonomy.

In spite of the growing importance of the social economy, research on the phenomena of the Social Economy still lacks in many respects, concerning, for example, its role in the development of local, regional and national competitiveness (López-Arceiz, Bellostas & Rivera-Torres, 2017). There is a lack of methodologies, tools and indicators appropriate to the social economy, which allow the reconciliation of the satisfaction of basic needs with the optimization of economic and social value (Granados, Mohamed & Hlupic, 2017). This could be caused by the complexity and diversity of the organizations, on one hand, which is a barrier to their comparability, and on the other hand, to their late and recent recognition on the production/provision of public services. Changes on public policies, the economic and financial crisis, the spread of unemployment and poverty, brings to the light the importance of these organizations (López-Arceiz, Bellostas & Rivera-Torres, 2017), which are ceasing to be residual in economic terms, and are becoming, alongside the State and the Market, a mainstay of the economy (Veltmeyer, 2017).

In this chapter, we focus on a particular weakness found in several social economy organizations (Cardoso, Meireles & Peralta, 2012): lack of entrepreneurial skills and the fact that social organizations managers and/or starting social entrepreneurs must be aware of the importance of a well-structured process of strategic management and innovation, in order to understand how the organization creates and delivers social value. This is an important research topic since it is in the social economy organizations that the greatest capacity to respond to new social and societal challenges can be found (Chaves & Sajardo-Moreno, 2004), by innovating, advancing, and pooling resources and wills, particularly in areas where addressing increasing inequalities, social exclusion and poverty require solidarity solutions and mobilization of the community (Kerlin, 2006).

The aim of this chapter is to contribute to the empirical literature on the organizational sustainability of social economy organizations, based on the analysis of a Portuguese case study. Specifically, in this case study we look at the process of organizational change and innovation in a non-profit institution (the Luis Bernardo de Almeida Foundation, LBAF). Departing from a review of concepts related to social economy and to strategic management and innovation in social mission organizations, an analytic framework to be used in the analysis and interpretation of the case study was designed.

The remainder of the chapter is organized as follows. Next section comprises a brief description of the conceptual framework supporting the study undertaken, where the concepts of social economy and social economy organizations are presented, a brief explanation of the Portuguese social economy sector is provided, and the resource-based perspective is described. Section 3 presents the research methodology undertaken in this study – the case study approach. Section 4 presents the case study, describing the profile of the social economy organization analyzed. Section 5 describes the process of organizational change followed by this organization, emphasizing the main findings. Section 6 discusses the main findings. Finally, section 7 draws the main conclusions of the chapter and presents avenues for future work.

CONCEPTUAL FRAMEWORK

Social Economy and Social Economy Organizations

Usually, the term social economy is understood as a broad concept (Araújo, Rodrigues, Telles, Vaz & Bittencourt, 2017). As underlined by Noya and Clarence (2007), several terms can be found in the literature to name the same phenomenon “without any strong delineation of the distinctions” (p. 10). Some examples of those terms are: social economy, solidarity economy, third sector, non-profit sector, and third system. The reason for this maybe be the fact that authors are trying “to capture both the social element as well as the economic element, inherent in those organizations which inhabit the space between the market and the state” (Noya & Clarence, 2007, p. 10) and the fact that the concept of social economy has evolved in a way that reflected "the historical dimensions and developments of a range of different organizational types which have come to be identified with it" (Noya & Clarence, 2007, p. 10)[1].

Social economy is at the center-stage of the European Union action regarding active social policies (Fekete, Hubai, Kiss & Mihály, 2017) addressed to overcome problems of poverty and social exclusion of persons in a vulnerable position, and as a way to achieve the Sustainable Development Goals, contributing for a sustainable and inclusive growth (Moore, 2015). The social economy symbolizes the driving force to achieve a more stable and decent process of job creation, social cohesion, local sustainable development and social innovation (Laurentiis, Klaer & Martignetti, 2017). In fact, the social economy can be understood as an agency of social transformation, a space for social cooperation and grassroots solidarity action within a broader macroeconomic system, allowing the creation of spaces within the system for poverty reduction based on local sustainable self-development, the social capital of the poor and the empowerment and agency of the poor (Veltmeyer, 2017). Thus, as emphasized by Salustri and Vigano (2017), the social economy can constitute a powerful driver of territorial cohesion and community development, since it can be seen as the missing link between the market economy and local development, and, many times, it is backed by participative social movements. In this sense, the broader societal anchorage of the social economy can easily serve as a way to raise awareness of social change needs (Hudon & Huybrechts, 2017).

The core element of the social economy are social economy organizations, which have been growing in number and relevance whether in developed countries or in emerging or transition countries, and their relevance for balanced social and economic development is now widely recognized (Borzaga & Tortia, 2007). Those organizations put the pursuit of social aims at the heart of their economic activity, therefore embracing a holistic approach to social change (Hudon & Huybrechts, 2017), with an aspiration to transform social relationships based on self-help, mutual support and social solidarity (Vézina, Malo & Selma, 2017), and having a multi-bottom line (with both social and economic goals) and a multi-stakeholder dimension with a focus on finding sustainable solutions and empowering stakeholders (Granados, Mohamed & Hlupic, 2017). Underlying social economy organizations action (or practice) is the adoption of a bottom-up approach to solve societal challenges, because they often experiment with grassroots innovations responding to local social problems, and taking into account the needs and expectations of local communities (Hudon & Huybrechts, 2017). In fact, social economy organizations are able to compensate the lack of private and public provision of social services and to narrow spatial inequalities by fostering the connection between market and non-market economic activities and by exerting a productive and distributive function (Salustri & Vigano, 2017).

In the context of what can be called the social economy, a great diversity of organizations can be included in that sector of an economy. Taking into account that diversity and different schools of thought, Young, Searing and Brewer (2016) proposed the idea of a "Social Enterprise Zoo" to analyze the conceptual developments and practical experiences of this type of organizations. As stated by those authors "the zoo serves as a metaphor to signal that designation of social enterprise is an intentional construct, reflecting the limits within which we are willing to call something a social enterprise versus a conventional business, nonprofit, cooperative, association, or governmental entity" (p. 10) and "is particularly well suited for appreciating the complexity and diversity of social enterprise and the likelihood that no one simple model will suffice to understand social enterprise as a phenomenon or to advance it as a social strategy" (p. 10).

According to Dragan and Popa (2017), from a legal and institutional point of view, social economy organizations can be grouped in three categories of organizations: non-governmental organizations (associations and foundations, the non-market sub-sector of the social economy), cooperatives and mutual societies (the market or business sub-sector of the social economy). In this context, there are some common characteristics that allow one to classify an organizations as belonging to the social economy, as for example: independence of action, self-government and autonomy from government authorities; freedom of involvement, implying voluntary and open membership; democratic control by members; the person and the social objective taking precedence over capital, reconciling the interests of the members and the general interest; provision of services aimed at members and communities; and the protection and enforcement of the principles of solidarity and responsibility.

In a nutshell, the main motivation of social economy organizations is to overcome deficiencies of social policy and their ability to recognize both long-standing and new social needs (Laurentiis, Klaer & Martignetti, 2017), and to address them through original solutions emerging from new collaborations established among and within a variety of sectors (private sector, public sector or third sector) and scales (international, national, regional or local levels). As emphasized by Terziev (2017, p. 12), there are two main characteristics through which social economy organizations demonstrate their potential: "First, they act locally networked with multiple stakeholders and knowing well the local problems and they can offer solutions proven to work in a place like reach those groups at risk of poverty or social exclusion to which active social policies reach very rarely in comparison to purely passive assistance. Second, social economy organizations have the potential to mobilize and activate people that are themselves at risk of poverty and social exclusion and thus enable them to engage in improving their living situation".

A Brief Description of the Portuguese Social Economy Sector

According to CASES (2010), the term social economy is ambiguous because it accommodates a wide range of concepts, such as the "third sector", "non-profit sector", "social economy", and "alternative economy", among others. It is very difficult to establish a single concept and define the frontiers of social economy. As emphasized by Parente, Marcos, Costa and Amador (2013), the themes of social economy and social economy organizations in Portugal raise in the discourse a series of concepts that are more or less associated with them, which are influenced by theoretical and ideological points of view. The Portuguese national statistics office (INE) and the non-profit institution CASES (Antonio Sergio Cooperative for Social Economy) use the definition proposed by CIRIEC (2012) on the pilot project Satellite Account of Social Economy for Portugal (SASE)-2010:

Set of private firms, formally organized, with autonomy of decision and freedom of membership, created to meet the needs of its members through the market, producing goods and services, ensuring financing, where the process of decision making and benefit or surpluses sharing is not directly linked to capital or contributions of each member, but corresponding to each member one vote. The Social Economy includes also private entities formally organized, with autonomy of decision and freedom of membership that produce non-market services for households and whose surpluses, if any, may not be appropriated by the economic agents that create, control or finance them.

In Europe, social economy activities contribute to about 10% of the output of the European business sector, with a share of about 6% in total employment (about 11 million people), revealing an industry that will be called to give a greater contribution to the current problems of unemployment and social cohesion due to the social and economic transformation under way (Dragan & Popa, 2017). According to the CIRIEC (2016) report, in spite of this important role of the social economy in Europe, its impact and weight differs among EU countries. As stated in that report, "while employment in the social economy accounts for between 9% and 10% of the working population in countries such as Belgium, Italy, Luxembourg, France and the Netherlands, in the new EU Member States such as Slovenia, Romania, Malta, Lithuania, Croatia, Cyprus and Slovakia the social economy remains a smaller, emergent sector, employing under 2% of the working population" (CIRIEC, 2016, p. 67). However, it can also be seen that regarding the evolution of paid employment in the social economy, Austria, Croatia, Cyprus, Hungary, Luxembourg, Malta and Slovenia have an important increase in this values whereas countries such as Bulgaria, Denmark, Lithuania, Poland and Sweden experienced a sharp decrease in paid employment. In terms of the types of organizations of the social economy, according to the same report, "measured in terms of employment, associations, foundations and other similar forms remain the main social economy 'family', comprising most of the social entities / enterprises and about 66% of the employment in this social sector" (CIRIEC, 2016, p. 67). As would be expected, social economy organizations (e.g. cooperatives, mutual societies, associations, foundations and similar entities) are in higher number on those countries with a larger population, such as United Kingdom (about 876,941 entities), Italy (350,356), France (195,584), Spain (189,538), and Germany (113,963), and are less numerous on those countries with less population (e.g. Malta, 749; Luxembourg, 845; Cyprus, 5,196; Denmark, 13,766; or Latvia, 19,611) (CIRIEC, 2016). However, if the indicator social economy organization's density (meaning that one organization covers a given number of inhabitants) is taken into account the ordering of countries changes. Countries like Germany, Belgium, Luxembourg, Malta, Denmark, Romania, Poland, France and Austria show a higher density (ranging from 725 to 306) whereas Hungary, Sweden, Lithuania, Slovakia, Latvia, Croatia, Czech Republic, United Kingdom, and Finland show a much lower density (ranging from 151 to 38).

Regarding the Portuguese case, and following the zoo metaphor of Young et al. (2016), the panorama concerning social economy organizations is not much different from what has happened in other countries. In fact, an increasing complexity and diversity of the social economy organizations should be recognized because the ways in which these organizations can potentially address societal problems and needs are manifold. Those social economy organizations can be differentiated by their legal nature, by the way they are internally organized, by their primary area of intervention (e.g. social service, health, education, culture), by how social organizations interrelate and behave, among others. In Portugal, this sector, according to INE and Cases (2013), comprises Cooperatives (2,260 units); the Mutual Societies (119 units); a network of charities known as Santa Casa da Misericórdia (Holy House of Mercy) (381 units); Foundations (537 units) and Associations and other organizations in the Social Economy (52,086 units), involving 55.383 organizations, with a share of 5.5% of the total paid employment, representing a proportion of 2.8% of the gross value added.

According to Soares et al (2012) two thirds of the expenses of these organizations are related to the cost of goods sold and materials consumed (including the cost of food), staff costs, services and utilities costs. On the other hand, they indicate on their budget a great proportion of State contribution. The Social Economy Sector is facing a huge set of challenges and weaknesses, which include, among others, the following: (1) the high dependence on financial support from the state; (2) the requirement to fulfill a set of criteria and rules imposed by the State, in order to maintain public support, particularly in terms of professionalism, quality and accreditation; (3) sustainability in a context of economic crisis, with a probable reduction in support and growth of social problems; (4) the need to reinvent their business models in order to avoid chronic shortages; (5) professionalization of top management; (6) economies of scale; (7) the qualifications of employees; (8) leadership; (9) equipment and facilities; (10) ICT integration; (11) demographic change; (12) asymmetries in population distribution.

To face these challenges and weaknesses it is imperative to improve the quality of the services and the effectiveness of management, thus contributing to competitiveness and sustainability. The following areas are particularly important: (1) forms of organization and management; (2 value chain of services; (3) integration of ICT; (4) improvement of procedures for quality certification; (5) development of internal skills: training and development for leaders and training for employees; (6) models of inter-institutional cooperation.

Parente (2016) undertook a study attempting to operationalize the notion of social entrepreneurship within the context of social economy organizations in Portugal, and concluded that these organizations show a fragile form of social entrepreneurship, reflected on state dependency both in terms of models of financial management and the definition and regulation of activities, recipients and social intervention. Also, Pais and Parente (2015) focused on the issue of how work-teams are represented and work in social economy organizations. Resorting to a case study methodology, they concluded that no significant differences between the way teams work in these organizations and in profit-making organizations were found.

Social economy organizations need to rethink their operating logic, without, however, neglecting the purposes for which they were established, so it seems particularly relevant the establishment of structured practices on strategic management and innovation. These weaknesses can be addressed through a program to support the development and qualification of individuals and organizations, integrating actions of training and consultancy.

Thus, one can argue that these organizations can apply principles, methodologies and practices of strategic and innovation management that for-profit organizations also regularly apply. The use of these principles and practices is not incompatible with their not-for-profit nature and, on the contrary, can provide a basis on which their activities and their purposes can be pursued and achieved on a more consistent, sustainable and effective way. In the following paragraphs elaborations are made on the concepts of strategy and innovation management and their articulation with the activities and purposes of social economy organizations. Specifically, the arguments are based on a resource-based perspective of the organization, where specific competencies provide the means by which organizations can leverage their resources and fulfil their purposes.

Strategic Management and the Resource-Based Perspective

To Rumelt, Schendel and Teece (1994, 1991) strategic management (also called "policy" or "strategy") is related to the course of an organization, including the issues that are at the heart of top management preoccupations and those who are associated with the reasons why a business succeeds or fails. Hitt, Ireland and Hoskinsson (2011) state that "the strategic management process is the full set of commitments, decisions, and actions required for a firm to achieve strategic competitiveness and earn above-average returns", or in other words, it is the successful formulation and implementation of a strategy that creates value. These statements are perfectly applicable to social economy organizations, if terms such as "competitiveness" are replaced by "effectiveness", and terms such as "returns" or "value" are understood in the context of non-profit objectives.

The basic elements constituting the cycle of strategic management are the analysis of the environment, the formulation and implementation of strategy, assessment and monitoring. The analysis of the environment includes analysis of: the general environment, the industry/sector, competition, organizational structure, organizational culture and the resources that the organization has at its disposal. The process of formulation of strategy is closely linked to the progress of long-term plans in order that an organization deals effectively with the opportunities and threats that it faces in its environment, in light of its strengths and weaknesses. Strategy formulation is then made by the mission, objectives, strategies, (comprehensive description of how the organization will achieve its mission and objectives) and policies (which are lines of action that will support decision making). Strategy Implementation is related to the execution/implementation of strategies through the explanation of programs (activities necessary for the completion of a plan), budgets (programs in financial terms) and procedures (sequential steps that describe in detail how to perform a specific task or function). Assessment and control are processes that allow the tracking of activities and results of the organization in order to be able to compare the actual to the desired performance, allowing the introduction of measures to mitigate the observed deviations.

Hrebiniak (2006) argued that there is a gap between strategy formulation and strategy implementation. A possible reason for that is the fact that managers are not trained to implement strategy as well as they are to plan and formulate strategic intentions (Barbosa & Romero, 2014). Another problem is related to the general conviction that strategy implementation plays a minor role in terms of the hierarchy of strategic actions, being more adequate for lower levels of management, forgetting that management commitment is essential to a successful implementation. The author also argues that the top six obstacles that managers face are: (1) inability to manage change; (2) poor or vague strategy; (3) not having guidelines or a model to guide implementation efforts; (4) poor or inadequate information sharing; (5) unclear responsibility and accountability; (6) working against the organizational power structure. The case study addressed in this article shows the importance of such items, and the role that competencies related to strategy formulation and implementation can play in the performance of the organization.

The gap between strategy formulation and strategy implementation can be analyzed through the lens of the resource-based view theory of the firm (Hadjimanolis, 2000), which, we argue, can be applicable to social economy organizations taking due account of their different motives, management preoccupations and priorities and objectives in terms of the services that are provided and to whom they are provided. In any case, whether it is a for profit firm or a nor for-profit organization, both types of organizations need to acquire, integrate, develop and deploy competencies and skills that are needed to the provision of goods and services to their customers or to the recipients of their services, in a way that it is effective and sustainable (Vézina, Malo, & Selma, 2017). The resource-based view theory of the firm tries to explain the source of sustained competitive advantage of a firm by asserting that such a sustained and competitive position is dependent on the acquisition and leverage by the organization of valuable, rare, inimitable and non-substitutable (VRIN) resources and capabilities (Kraaijenbrink, Spender and Groen, 2010). Among the many resources and capabilities that an organization can master, there are specific types that seem particularly important to achieve that aim, which are the so-called "dynamic capabilities". According to Teece (2007) "...dynamic capabilities can be disaggregated into the capacity (1) to sense and shape opportunities and threats, (2) to seize opportunities, and (3) to maintain competitiveness through enhancing, combining, protecting, and, when necessary, reconfiguring the business enterprise's intangible and tangible assets..." (Teece, 2007, pp. 1319).

These capabilities are intimately linked to the obstacles faced by managers and referred to above. Social economy organizations face particular challenges regarding these issues, due to a somewhat differential approach to the style and practice of management, which is not exclusively based on hierarchal systems, typical of for profit firms, but are instead based on a more cooperative and collaborative stance, where employee loyalty and common value sharing may condition the management approach of the organization (Sanzo-Perez, Álvarez-González, & Rey-Garcia, 2015).

Strategy and innovation are distinct concepts both in terms of definition and function, being innovation a source of competitive advantage which grows out of specific (dynamic) competencies that are developed inside the organization. In the context of non-profit organizations, the "competitive" advantage of the organization is translated into its capacity to deliver the goods and services in a sustainable and effective way, under certain identified resource restrictions. Thus, innovation and strategy are complementary and feed on each other (Dobni, 2010). According to the Oslo Manual (2005), which establishes the guidelines for the collection and interpretation of data on innovation, developed by the OECD: "An innovation is the implementation of a new or significantly improved product (good or service), or process, a new marketing method, or a new organizational method in business practices, workplace organization or external relations". Social economy organizations provide and develop essentially services, which have a set of characteristics that distinguish them from goods: (1) Intangibility; (2) Heterogeneity; (3) Simultaneity; and (4) Perishability. According to Dantas and Moreira (2011), and Booz, Allen and Hamilton, cited by Edvarsson et al (2000), innovation in services can be classified into categories that range from "Worldwide new services" to "Cost reductions". Social economy organizations output could also be eventually classified into those categories, although the purpose of this chapter is to look at the internal organizational innovation, and so at the innovations classified by the Oslo Manual (2005) as "process innovations", but also, and primordially, at innovations classified as "organizational innovations".

Organizational change is the process of converting an organization from its current state to a desired future state (O'Sullivan & Dooley, 2009). All innovation results in change, but not all change is innovation. The core techniques referred in the management literature for managing organizational change include: (a) Strategic planning: The changing areas are called objectives or strategies and are intended to guide the teams in the development of ideas or projects to achieve objectives; (b) Performance Evaluation: Assign measures or indicators to critical aspects of organizational performance; (c) Management of Creativity: Generating ideas or problem solving; (d) Project Management: Need to effectively manage multiple tasks and initiatives; (e) Knowledge management: How to effectively manage change for managing the information associated with the change.

All these techniques are potentially applicable within the environment of social economy organizations, with due adjustments that reflect their nature, their management ethos and practices, and their "costumers" (Rodriguez & Guzman, 2013). To define and implement a structured process of strategic management and innovation, it is important that the organization defines how it creates, delivers and gets value (business model). The business model is like a plan for a strategy to be implemented through organizational processes and systems structures. The application of this concept is new in the area of social economy (Picciotti, 2017). In the remainder of this chapter, through the presentation of a case study, it will be shown how these concepts and elements were applied in this area, namely how an organization acquired management competencies and dynamic capabilities related to strategy and innovation.

RESEARCH METHOD

The research strategy used in this work was the case study. This methodology is used as a valid way of exploring existing theory and as an exploratory way to provide an integral vision and a general understanding of a phenomena (Yin, 2009). The research qualitatively describes and analyses the phenomena of organizational change operated on a Social Portuguese Organization. It was an intentional and thought out process that the organization implemented within a defined time period and in collaboration with an external consultancy organization. The case study is focused on this specific event that changed the whole organizational structure of the Foundation and, as such, it disregards intentionally other events and phenomena, for which information was collected, but that do not have meaningful implications on the specific phenomena of organizational change. The decision to include or exclude events from the description and the analysis of the case is based on the subjective perception of the researchers. The research process was made in two distinct phases. The first phase consisted of a literature review. The two main themes addressed in this review were strategic management and the social economy. Other subthemes addressed consisted of the resource-based view and social innovation. The main, but not exclusive, query on the literature review was the search for studies that integrated the main themes and subthemes on specific situations. The second phase consisted on the collection of data from the object of study. Secondary data was extracted from reports and other documents of the Foundation. Primary data was obtained from in-depth interviews conducted with eleven managers in Luiz Bernardo de Almeida Foundation. The fact that the primary data was obtained from several managers of the organization, which occupied different hierarchical positions and had different responsibilities, made it possible to compile a much more complete perspective of the change phenomena, than it was otherwise possible if the interviews were restricted to just one or a few top managers. This primary data constitutes the main empirical evidence on which the case is based. The integration of the different sources of the primary data into a coherent perspective, and using conceptual frameworks provided by the literature review, was made by the authors.

The methodology is not prone to generalizing the results, which is a characteristic of the case study strategy, and due to the specificity of the context, but it highlights a set of practices concerning the key factors for the establishment of an effective innovation and sustainability strategy for social economy organizations, based on established conceptual frameworks from the management literature.

CASE STUDY DESCRIPTION

The Luiz Bernardo de Almeida Foundation (hereafter LBAF) is located in the municipality of Vale de Cambra, district of Aveiro, Portugal, and was established in 1957 in order to fulfil the testamentary disposition of Commander (by honorable distinction) Luis Bernardo de Almeida. Its heritage consists on the assets of its founder and the other values acquired throughout its existence. The institution provides a diverse set of services aimed at the elderly and the children. The institution started functioning with a nursing home in 1972, and in 1985 implemented a Home Support Service, directed at the elderly. This service was one of the first to be created at the District level. The institution also manages a Day Centre, where the beneficiaries are also elderly people that are independent in terms of mobility. In 1999 an Office of Family and Community Support was created. In October 2004, a nursery school was built. The Family Support Service is directed at kindergarten level children.

In fact, social economy organizations with their links to local communities and their ability to harness resources from those communities, play an important role on the provision of social services, particularly for those more vulnerable groups of the society (such as the elderly and the young), and in that way fostering social inclusion (Noya & Clearence, 2007). However, due to the increasing concern with long-term financial sustainability, social economy organizations (such is the case of LBAF) need to develop new organizational structures and adopt new business models to allow them to achieve both their social and economic goals and to ensure their future sustainability (Hudon & Huybrechts, 2017). Furthermore, for those social economy organizations that rely heavily on public funding (such is the case of LBAF) that dependence may become problematic if a decline in public support is experienced. In the last six years, the Portuguese state budget was faced with severe financial constraints which prevented public funding from growing at an appropriate rate to support organizations of the social economy. In this context, revenue diversification is crucial to ensure longer-term financial sustainability.

A broader forward-looking long-term perspective is needed if the socio-economic success of the social economy organizations is to be achieved. One possibility to explore is to call for a strategic management perspective and a focus on the adequate process of organizational change and innovation. As pointed out by Kinyuira (2017), social value creation and economic performance management should be seen as a strategic process capable of making wealth creation more effective and fair, implying the adoption of a systematic management and reporting framework integrating both social and economic dimensions. In the particular case of the LBAF organization some of the most important weakness found (as will be described and explained in more detail in the following section) were: slow level of organizational response compared to environmental changes; difficulties on inter-departmental communication; narrow vision of the organizational objectives; lack of unity of command and difficulty in determining the extent of the authority and competence of managers and inadequate control range. To overcome these problems and to the accomplishment of their social and economic mission, management ability and skills need to be improved, enabling the LBAF to adapt to the new environment in which it operates.

THE PROCESS OF ORGANIZATIONAL CHANGE

The Initiation of the Process

The process of organizational change begun when the board of LBAF took certain decisions that proved to be crucial for the survival of the institution. These decisions were followed by an application to the so-called Q3 Program (Qualifying the 3rd Sector), a national program that aims at developing skills and organizations of the 3rd sector, improving the quality of their services, the effectiveness of management and contributing to their competitiveness and sustainability through participated and sustained processes of consultancy and training. The aim of the board was to ensure the sustainability of LBAF, and the improvement of the quality of services. There was a strong belief that the organization had a poor organizational performance, which was translated into weak economic and financial results and on poor service provision, so it would be extremely important to know the causes of this poor performance in order to mitigate or even eliminate them.

Besides providing financial support, the Q3 Program would provide access to an integrated, impartial and experienced vision by an external and recognized entity, that would identify the main problems that the institution was facing and provide a framework to manage the actions to mitigate or extinguish those problematic situations, through actions of training and consulting made to fit the organization profile, its size, the problems identified and the defined objectives. The Q3 Program involves a strong partnership between some important organizations in Portugal: AEP (Chamber of Commerce and Industry), Fenacerci (National Association of Social Solidarity Cooperatives), Minha Terra Federation (Portuguese Federation of Local Development Associations), CPCCRD (Portuguese Confederation of Culture, Recreation and Sport communities), UTAD (University of Trás-os-Montes and Alto Douro), among others. The intervention follows a model, which involves several phases: recruitment and selection, conducting a diagnosis, preparation of a development plan, implementation measures, review plan and recommendations. All activities are evaluated externally and internally validated, and all actors (consultants and trainers) have certified skills in order to act in accordance with the procedures to ensure the quality and effectiveness of the intervention. The intervention on the organization had a duration of about one year and followed the steps described below.

In analytic terms, and under the resource-based perspective, this phase corresponds to the efforts of organizations in sensing and trying to learn, acquire and integrate the required resources and capabilities that would benefit the organization. The following phases, described in the following sections, corresponds to the efforts of integration and leverage of resources and new capabilities, which involved the reconfiguration of tangible and intangible assets of the organization.

Organizational Diagnosis

This phase began with the signing of the Development Contract - the document which defines the commitments between the organization and the organization that manages the intervention in order to promote the desired organizational development of the beneficiary of the intervention.

The organizational diagnosis is essential because at this stage all the problems are identified and the goals that are the target of the intervention are defined. It is, therefore, necessary to resort to the holders of the knowledge of the organizational reality, elements that experience the daily life of the organization and make the exploration of problematic situations. The idea is to maximize the participation of the whole organization in gathering problems, where the consultant only assumes the role of a listener/agent/moderator.

In the realization of the organizational diagnosis, the main reference activities that sustain it are: (1) Listening to people; (2) Documentation review, (3) Sectoral framework and context; (4) Problem tree; (5) Current Situation/Desired Situation; (6) Objectives Tree.

In addition to listening to people, there are also, at this stage, activities that promote their participation in all stages of the process: (1) Meetings with Top Management; (2) Meetings/contacts with an internal facilitator; (3) General Sessions held for the entire organization. On the analysis of the tree problem, a key tool of the diagnosis, it was found that the general problem of LBAF was a poor organizational performance. Seven intermediate problems were identified as causes of this general problem: poor organizational structure; poor planning of activities; poor management practices in human resources; scarcity of financial resources; poor implementation of quality and a lack of employee skills, having been detected 85 terminal problems as causes of these intermediate problems.

To analyze the organizational structure, five basic components of it were considered (Mintzberg, 1999), where some terminals problems of LBAF were fit:

- **Strategic Level:** The strategic level comprises the organizational decision makers, here materialized in the board function. The problems identified relating to this component were, among others: poor strategic management and reduced operational presence of the board.
- **The Techno-Structure:** Comprising the rules and procedures for managing the behaviors of employees. In this component were identified, among others, issues of horizontal and vertical differentiation, which were manifested in a poor communication between hierarchical levels and lack of team spirit; problems of formalization as a poor definition of roles and tasks and also problems located at the level of centralization, such as an excessive number of tasks and responsibilities centralized in the Technical Director.
- **The Support Staff:** Includes employees that are not directly involved in producing goods or services. However, they have the responsibility to support the primary activities, such as, for example, cleaning and feeding. In this field, several problems were detected, including deficient HACCP (a quality norm related to food processing) and cleaning practices.
- **Intermediate Level:** Includes managers who make the connection between the strategic level and the operational level. The services and technical direction, as well as the sector supervisors, are included in this level. In this component, problems such as poor management of teams (inadequate control range), lack of sectoral meetings, lack of performance evaluation, and a poor distribution of tasks were identified.
- **Operational Level:** Includes all employees of the institution running the production of goods or services. Here problems were also detected, among others, difficulties in interpersonal relationship, resistance to change and lack of a training plan.

Although the weaknesses of each component of the structure were identified above, the weak points in this structure, in general terms, were due to a slow level of organizational response compared to environmental changes, to inter-departmental communication difficulties, to a restricted vision of the organizational objectives, to a lack of unity of command, to a difficulty in determining the extent of the authority and competence of managers and to inadequate control range.

The Process of Implementation

The Development Plan

In this section the development plan established to bring change to the organizational structure is presented, showing the main results of the actions made. A summary of the evaluation of these actions is made in the next section.

On this phase, it was crucial to develop two enabling dimensions: (1) an active participation of all members of the organization in order to promote an open debate, generating and sharing ideas to jointly achieve the targeted objectives and (2) an approach based on management by objectives (MBO) in order to establish appropriate objectively verifiable indicators, using the SMART (Specific, Measurable, Assignable, Realistic and Time-related) philosophy to monitor and evaluate the implementation and to decrease the resistance to change.

The Development Plan establishes the training actions which allows the transition from the current situation to the desired situation. The plan is based on the following tools: (1) Actions tableau; (2) Actions tableau by activities; (3) Project Planning by Objectives Matrix; (4) Implementation Schedule. In the development plan we look for appropriate and feasible solutions to solve the problems of the current situation and achieve the goals of the desired situation. The technical expertise of the consulting team and of the elements of the organization was instrumental, seeking to expand the use of the knowledge hold by these elements, and using creativity to find the most appropriate, diversified and financially encompassed solutions.

Under the Q3, all the predicted actions are of a training nature, and may fit into the following types:

- **Employees Qualification:** Within this typology the following training activities directly related to the problems of organizational structure identified above were established: (1) Operations Management; (2) Interpersonal and conflict management; (3) Quality Management - Food Area and (4) Customer Service.
- **Implementation of Improvement Projects:** Within this typology, the following training activities aimed at solving problems related to organizational structure were established: (1) Strategic Management Practices; (2) Quality Management System; (3) Cooking Techniques; (4) Geriatrics; (5) Team management and (6) Human Resources Management.
- **Thematic Workshops**.

The development plan was pre-validated by the management and was discussed with everyone in the organization before the final version, benefiting, therefore, of the participation of all in the definition/specification of the actions to implement. The presented development plan solely corresponded to the set of eligible actions under the Q3 Program, although the board itself draw up a set of own actions in order to simultaneously eliminate or mitigate problem situations not eligible by the Q3 Program.

Implementation Schedule

The capacity to monitor and control the development plan was essential to the success of the implementation. There were some mandatory mechanisms and requirements which were necessary to achieve that: (1) an external team of consultants that provided a detached and an independent view of the work; (2) a high degree of commitment and skills of the liaison consultant in charge of the process, namely his capacity to monitor and control the process and his capacity to articulate the functioning of a team, in particular regarding the specialists consultants in charge of the implementation of the specific measures and actions, through a clear and fluid communication channel; (3) knowledge of the development plan and active participation of the members of the organization in its execution which established a commitment of the entire organization with the external team in order to achieve the goals without deviations from the original plan.

A timeline was stipulated for the implementation of training activities leading to the resolution of identified problems, which had a duration of five months. The entire project had a one-year duration, and it was composed of approximately one hundred hours of consultancy and two hundred and forty hours of training activities.

In the initial diagnosis eighty-five terminal problems were detected that resulted in eighty-five goals. Thirty of these were not achievable by conducting training activities, so the eligible objectives supported by Q3 funds were fifty-five. These resulted in twenty-three results to be achieved. In addition to the actions recommended in the Q3 Program, eight actions were established in conjunction with the board of the organization, in order to achieve the objectives not covered by the Q3 Program. An activity tableau of ten actions/activities was prepared, but it was possible to perform one more action in addition to the initial proposal (Management Control).

Results of the Actions

Results Achieved

All twenty-three expected results were achieved. In addition to these, the intervention allowed for several changes, which affected several areas of management and operation of the organization, particularly with regard to its organizational structure. From the results achieved, it is particularly important to stress those that are most directly related to the organizational structure. A new organizational structure was defined whose main goal was to move from a mechanistic bureaucratic structure to a horizontal structure. The main motives which motivated the development of this type of structure were related to greater customer proximity based on speed, efficiency and quality of services, a greater flattening of the organizational structure, the search for competitive advantage in a turbulent external environment, the creation of real teams and the facilitation of collaboration, a greater emphasis on operational processes as a creator of value, a delegation of work to the lowest level.

In order that the implementation of the new organizational chart was successful, the chart was redesigned, adding activities and services actually rendered by the organization and which were not reflected in the older chart, having as a direct result the ability to clearly define the roles, tasks and responsibilities of each member in the organization.

It was also implemented a methodology for evaluating the individual and team performance and development, identifying the training needs of each element in order to maximize their performance at the individual level or at the level of working groups. In order to simplify procedures and minimize the resistance of employees in its implementation, two training actions were undertaken in quality management systems, and the organization decided to move forward in the implementation of the ISO 9001: 2008 standard in its five dimensions.

A final observation is due related to the conduction of training activities directed to all managers, in order to develop skills in implementing effective leadership, and two training activities designed to improve the skills of employees in teamwork and conflict resolution.

Summary of Actions Assessment

In order to know if the problems were solved and what improvements the organization experienced, the opinion of the organization leaders and the facilitator were sought considering the Actions or Activities implemented and the most important results, either in the immediate or short term. There was a strong commitment in the implementation of the Actions and in achieving the expected results, which led to a successful result. All the implemented measures were considered very important by the leaders and the facilitator. The measures that were believed to have a greater impact in the organization, and that fitted the problems related to the Organizational Structure of LBAF identified above, were the following:

- Quality Management System.
- Quality Management-Food Area.
- Strategic Management Practices.
- Human Resources Management.

Regarding the results achieved which had the greater impact, they were those derived inherently from the above actions:

- Implementation of Quality Management System in Social Responses.
- Implementation of HACCP System.
- Strategic objectives definition.
- Organizational Structure Restructuring materialized in the design of a new organizational chart, with a consequent redefinition of roles, tasks and responsibilities.

In general terms, it can be said that the following constituted good practices in the implementation of the organizational process of change:

- The involvement of Top Management.
- The involvement of the operational teams.
- The existence of a structured, tested and friendly methodology.
- Independence, experience, openness and involvement of the external consultant.
- Tailor made to the problems of the organization.

DISCUSSION OF FINDINGS

Social economy organizations are being promoted as a responsive and innovative way for the provision of public services (Millar & Hall, 2013), based on the idea that such social organizations have the potential to deliver greater responsiveness, efficiency and cost effectiveness. But at the same time, those organizations are increasingly requested to demonstrate the social and economic value they create. In this context, such organizations need to have (or implement) formal standards and administrative procedures that allow to measure their performance. However, it is often argued that emphasis on outcomes and evidence-based performance misses out important features of the social economy organizations functioning (Millar & Hall, 2013).

From the findings presented in the previous section, one can have an idea of the perception of the Board of LBAF about the strengths and weaknesses of the Q3 model intervention, and the results of the external evaluation, conducted by UTAD (University of Trás-os-Montes), regarding the implementation of the program. The board of LBAF recognized that the positive aspects or strengths far outweigh some of the negative aspects or existing weaknesses. The managers interviewed even had some difficulty in identifying negative aspects or weaknesses of the intervention. The concentration of the implementation of the various steps/activities within a relatively short period of time, five to six months, was the weak point mentioned by the interviewees. This resulted, for example, in the reduction of the availability of time by managers and employees in the implementation of the actions, which in some periods was very demanding. In general, the strengths of the intervention were highly valued by the leaders of the organization.

The Q3 project increased motivation and the degree of participation of the people in the organization; it identified in a clear way the existing needs; it improved internal operations (e.g., by redefining organizational structure, new processes and services); it forced members of the organization to look inward and to look for solutions; it allowed new learning through training focused on very specific needs; it allowed to have an enlarged, both external and internal, vision. Essentially, the project's strong point was the creation of favorable conditions for change in the organization which, as mentioned above, involved large parts and several dimensions of the organization, and which is a fundamental dynamic capability that fosters innovation and sustainability of the organization.

The methodology of participatory action training, implemented by external elements with facilitation skills and processes in the field of management, as well as sensitivity and experience in the context of non-profit organizations, is an efficient and effective tool for organizational change, adaptable to various circumstances. However, their success depends largely on its appropriation by the organizations, through the commitment and participation of managers, technicians and employees. In addition, the state of necessity and awareness of the urgency of change in organizations is also a factor of great importance (Baptista, 2011).

The final evaluation report of the implementation of the Q3 Program, conducted by UTAD in partnership with CETRAD praised the implementation of the Q3 program in LBAF, considering it an example of best practice in implementing change that crossed several fields of management and operation of the organization. It highlighted the participation of the leaders, including the Board, its commitment and permanent participation (it followed daily activities, being present in the training sessions), the degree of employee involvement, which was marked by adherence to the process and the interest and potential that they saw on it. These results corroborate the idea of Granados, Mohamed and Hlupic (2017) that social economy organizations may rely on external sources of knowledge to support their operations and strategies. This knowledge transfer is essential to accurately tackle and assess their social impact. Furthermore, Bastida, Marimon and Tanganelli (2017) stressed that alliances with other stakeholders are important for social economy organizations, because they are mainly of relatively small and medium size and need to collaborate to improve their access to resources and knowledge, so that they can improve their performance and enhance their creation of social and economic value.

This case study showed how the process of change in a social economy organization was sustained by an approach based on the acquisition of competencies related to strategy formulation and implementation, and to practices of innovation management, leading to the development and consolidation of dynamic capabilities, which, according to the resource-based view of the organization, are important factors that provide competiveness and sustainability to organizations, and in particular, to social economy organizations, that can benefit from this management perspectives to improve their service providing potential. Dynamic capabilities that were acquired during this process included capabilities related to developing and integrating learning processes, capabilities to strategically manage processes and procedures and capabilities related to establishing and maintaining a network of external relations. Resources developed by these processes included the new organizational layouts, the improved processes for interdepartmental communication and the revised roles for managers and employees, among many others. The acquisition of competencies was made possible through the financial support of a government program and by the intervention of a set of external actors that acted as vehicles of knowledge transfer. As stated above, it is difficult to generalize the perceptions of this case study, but it seems that some factors may be very important points to have in consideration: a structured approach to strategy formulation and implementation, a systematic consideration of innovation practices, an interface between external knowledge providers and the organization to enable effective knowledge transfer ad a capacity and willingness to acquire and absorb knowledge.

Social economy organizations play an extremely important role not only in attaining economic growth but also achieving sustainable social development (Juliani, Silva, Cunha & Benneworth, 2017). Taking into account that those organizations cannot grow or develop without a forward-looking long-term perspective, adequate processes of strategic management and of organizational change assume a preponderant role also in these organizations of the social economy. Some of these organizations succeed, while others fail, so the strategy adopted by their top decision-makers is important (e.g. in terms of social value creation, meeting the needs of their target public/community, and the motivation of their employees). The definition of this strategy is based on the identification of the actions that the managers intend to put into practice, in order to achieve a higher level of performance and a competitive advantage.

A difficulty that social economy organizations face is related to the fact that their main source of revenue is, essentially, government funding (López-Arceiz, Bellostas & Rivera-Torres, 2017). Given the financial constraints on which the Portuguese economy, in general, and the public administration, in particular, went through in recent years, these state-sponsored support is becoming increasingly scarce, causing an important negative impact on those organizations. Confronted with this situation, the challenge that social economy organizations face is to find other sources of revenue and forms of funding, in order to ensure their future sustainability. In this context, it is understood that the implementation of a strategic action that takes into account an adequate process of organizational change coupled with a clear focus on social entrepreneurship initiatives is essential to contribute to the creation of social value while ensuring its economic-financial viability. However, as pointed out by Noya and Clarence (2007, p. 20), it is necessary to recognize that "there is no simple solution to how social economy organizations can achieve financial sustainability, although it is evident that social economy organizations need the opportunity to exploit the full range of potential resources". In this context, sharing knowledge, experiences and good practices across social economy organizations might play an important role if these organizations intend to have a major impact upon the lives of individuals and communities.

The practice of social economy organizations points to a successful and sustainable experience due to the multiple interactions and social relations established with all the stakeholders. Thus, their impact is felt not only on the social and economic dimensions but also on the cultural and territorial ones. They contribute to community development, through job creation, increased income and poverty eradication, and to overcome problems of social exclusion, especially those affecting more vulnerable and disenfranchised groups of the society. As highlighted by Hudon and Huybrechts (2017), in the practice of social economy organizations, democracy, a participatory mode of governance and collective action are implemented to empower stakeholders that are not traditionally given a voice in the shaping of organizations, promoting social justice and social change and helping to increase the well-being and social capital of people as well as to respond to the emergence of new societal needs.

CONCLUSION

Due to their characteristics, social economy organizations have been responsible for the existence of a different approach to socio-economic activity, which is to privilege people instead of capital. Until recently, the frontiers of the social economy were seen as a blurred concept between the market and the state (Defourny & Nyssens, 2013). However, nowadays social economy represents an important part of the economy and social economy organizations face significant challenges in terms of management ability and knowledge, resource allocation, social entrepreneurship, and social accountability (Besana, 2017), while, at the same time, they thrive through the effort of dedicated individuals and organizations committed to ethical entrepreneurship (Amin, 2009). Those organizations can be seen not only as organizations producing goods and/or services, but also as enablers of social connections and collaborative action, a fundamental aspect for the creation of social value and social capital. Actually, these kind of organizations are well-placed to address the grand challenges of the 21st century, namely ageing of population, high rates of unemployment, inequality in income distribution, and social exclusion problems, as well as, to foster active citizenship, solidarity, and democratic participation (Cunha, Benneworth & Oliveira, 2015).

The current empirical study offers a significant contribution to the literature on the use of the strategic management approach and the process of organizational change in the context of a social economy organization, providing an important contribution to assessment of the validity and appropriateness of those tools in that kind of organization. However, it should be bear in mind that the empirical study was focused on only one case study, within the specific context of a social care provision institution, and conducted at a particular point in time. Thus, one should be careful when trying to generalize the findings to other contexts. From the actions and/or activities implemented the following main results were achieved. Firstly, a new organizational structure was defined, whose main goal was to move from a mechanistic bureaucratic structure to a horizontal structure. Secondly, the organizational chart was redesigned, adding activities and services actually rendered by the organization and which were not reflected in the older chart, having as a direct result the ability to clearly define the roles, tasks and responsibilities of each member in the organization. Thirdly, a methodology for evaluating the individual and team performance and development was implemented, identifying the training needs of each element in order to maximize their performance at the individual level or at the level of working groups. Finally, it should be stressed that a strong commitment in the implementation of the actions and in achieving the expected results, which led to a successful result, was observed. As underlined by López-Arceiz, Bellostas and Rivera-Torres (2017), it is most likely that the success of social economy organizations is due to their capacity to seek new opportunities, diversify their activities, innovate, and develop new strategies and management models.

The social economy can be seen as an important incubator for the support of social innovation initiatives (Hubrich, Bund, Schmitz & Mildenberger, 2012). Social economy organizations might be a fruitful ground for social and organizational innovation contributing to solve social needs and to achieve social change (Juliani, Silva, Cunha & Benneworth, 2017), which means that start-ups and innovation in the social economy need to be encouraged. In fact, the development process of social economy organizations shares some characteristics with the social innovation process, namely in terms of being a localized, bottom-up process, with multiple actors, democratic governance, a social inclusion and cohesion perspective (Benneworth & Cunha, 2015), and with an objective of transforming the policy framework in order to advance new agendas (Vézina, Malo & Selma, 2017).

REFERENCES

Amin, A. (2009). Extraordinarily ordinary: Working in the social economy. *Social Enterprise Journal*, *5*(1), 30–49. doi:10.1108/17508610910956390

Araújo, A. L., Rodrigues, B. A., Telles, L. B., Vaz, M. C., & Bittencourt, J. V. (2017). A bibliometric analysis of the Scielo database: A Brazilian portfolio of the solidarity economy. *Scientometrics*, *112*(1), 1–20. doi:10.100711192-017-2382-2

Baptista, C. (2011). *Relatório de Avaliação Final-Implementação do Projecto Q3 Norte*. Porto: Federação Minha Terra.

Barbosa, F., & Romero, F. (2014). Strategy, Innovation and Internationalization in SMEs: The Implementation Issue. *Proceedings of the 9th European Conference on Entrepreneurship and Innovation.*

Bastida, R., Marimon, F., & Tanganelli, D. (2017). Alliance success factors and performance in social economy enterprises. *Management Decision*, *55*(5), 1065–1080. doi:10.1108/MD-12-2016-0881

Benneworth, P., & Cunha, J. (2015). Universities' contributions to social innovation: Reflections in theory & practice. *European Journal of Innovation Management*, *18*(4), 508–527. doi:10.1108/EJIM-10-2013-0099

Besana, A. (2017). Animal Spirits or Engaging Spirits?: The Importance of the Not-for-Profit Economy – Coopetitiveness and Grant-Making Foundations. In A. Vlachvei, O. Notta, K. Karantininis, & N. Tsounis (Eds.), *Factors Affecting Firm Competitiveness and Performance in the Modern Business World* (pp. 223–250). Hershey, PA: IGI Global. doi:10.4018/978-1-5225-0843-4.ch008

Borzaga, C., & Tortia, E. (2007). Social Economy Organisations in the Theory of the Firm. In *The Social Economy: Building Inclusive Economies*. Paris: OECD Publishing. doi:10.1787/9789264039889-3-en

Cardoso, L., Meireles, A., & Peralta, C. (2012). Knowledge management and its critical factors in social economy organizations. *Journal of Knowledge Management*, *16*(2), 267–284. doi:10.1108/13673271211218861

CASES-INE. (2012). *Conta satélite da Economia Social: 2010 Resultados preliminares*. Retrieved February 6, 2017, from http://www.animar-dl.pt/index/documentacao/documentos/economia_social/ine

Chaves, R., & Sajardo-Moreno, A. (2004). Social Economy Managers: Between Values and Entrenchment. *Annals of Public and Cooperative Economics*, *75*(1), 139–161. doi:10.1111/j.1467-8292.2004.00246.x

CIRIEC. (2012). *The Social Economy in the European Union*. Brussels: European Economic and Social Committee.

CIRIEC. (2016). *Recent evolutions of the Social Economy in the European Union*. Brussels: European Economic and Social Committee.

Cunha, J., Benneworth, P., & Oliveira, P. (2015). Social entrepreneurship and social innovation: A conceptual distinction. In L. Farinha, J. Ferreira, H. L. Smith, & S. Bagchi-Sen (Eds.), *Handbook of Research on Global Competitive Advantage through Innovation and Entrepreneurship* (pp. 616–639). Hershey, PA: IGI Global. doi:10.4018/978-1-4666-8348-8.ch033

Dantas, J., & Moreira, A. C. (2011). *O Processo de Inovação*. Lisboa: Edições Lidel.

Defourny, J., & Nyssens, M. (2013). Social innovation, social economy and social enterprise: What can the European debate tell us? In F. Moulaert, D. MacCallum, A. Mehmood, & A. Hamdouch (Eds.), *International Handbook on Social Innovation. Social Innovation, Collective Action and Transdisciplinary Research* (pp. 40–52). Cheltenham, UK: Edward Elgar. doi:10.4337/9781849809993.00013

Dobni, C. B. (2010). Achieving Synergy between Strategy and Innovation: The Key to Value Creation. *International Journal of Business Science and Applied Management*, *5*(1), 48–58.

Dragan, A., & Popa, N. (2017). Social Economy in Post-communist Romania: What Kind of Volunteering for What Type of NGOs? *Journal of Balkan & Near Eastern Studies*, *19*(3), 330–350. doi:10.1080/19448953.2017.1277088

Edvardsson, B., Gustafsson, A., Johnson, M., & Sandém, B. (2000). *New service Development and Innovation in the New Economy*. Lund: Studentliteratur, European Commission, Retrieved December 12, 2016, from: https://ec.europa.eu/growth/sectors/social-economy_en

Fekete, G., Hubai, L., Kiss, J., & Mihály, M. (2017). *Social Enterprise in Hungary.* ICSEM Working Papers, No. 47. Liege: The International Comparative Social Enterprise Models (ICSEM) Project.

Granados, M. L., Mohamed, S., & Hlupic, V. (2017). Knowledge management activities in social enterprises: Lessons for small and non-profit firms. *Journal of Knowledge Management*, *21*(2), 376–396. doi:10.1108/JKM-01-2016-0026

Hadjimanolis, A. (2000). A resource-based view of innovativeness in small firms. *Technology Analysis and Strategic Management*, *12*(2), 263–281. doi:10.1080/713698465

Hitt, M. A., Ireland, R. D., & Hoskinsson, R. E. (2011). *Strategic Management: Competitiveness and Globalization*. South Western Cengage Learning, Mason.

Hrebiniak, G. L. (2006). Obstacles to Effective Strategy Implementation. *Organizational Dynamics*, *35*(1), 12–31. doi:10.1016/j.orgdyn.2005.12.001

Hubrich, D.-K., Bund, E., Schmitz, B., & Mildenberger, G. (2012). *Comparative Case Study Report on the State of the Social Economy. A deliverable of the project: "The theoretical, empirical and policy foundations for building social innovation in Europe" (TEPSIE), European Commission – 7th Framework Programme*. Brussels: European Commission, DG Research.

Hudon, M., & Huybrechts, B. (2017). From Distant Neighbours to Bedmates: Exploring the Synergies between the Social Economy and Sustainable Development. *Annals of Public and Cooperative Economics*, *88*(2), 141–154. doi:10.1111/apce.12170

Juliani, D., Silva, A., Cunha, J., & Benneworth, P. (2017). Universities' contributions to sustainable development's social challenge: A case study of a social innovation practice. *International Journal of Social Ecology and Sustainable Development*, *8*(3), 1–18. doi:10.4018/IJSESD.2017070101

Kerlin, J. (2006). Social Enterprise in the United States and Europe: Understanding and Learning from the Differences. *Voluntas*, *17*(3), 247–263. doi:10.100711266-006-9016-2

Kinyuira, D. K. (2017). Pursuing social mission as part of a deliberate and managed strategy: Social performance management in Co-operatives. *Journal of Strategy and Performance Management*, *5*(2), 23–41.

Kraaijenbrink, J., Spender, J.-C., & Groen, A. J. (2010). The resource-based view: A review and assessment of its critiques. *Journal of Management*, *36*(1), 349–372. doi:10.1177/0149206309350775

Laurentiis, I., Klaer, E., & Martignetti, L. (2017). Social Economy. In D. Domanski & C. Kaletka (Eds.), *Exploring the Research Landscape of Social Innovation – A deliverable of the project Social Innovation Community (SIC)*. Dortmund: Sozialforschungsstelle.

López-Arceiz, F. J., Bellostas, A. J., & Rivera-Torres, M. P. (2017). The Slaughtered and the Survivors: Collaboration between Social Economy Organizations as a Key to Success in Times of Financial Crisis. *Voluntas*, 1–26.

Millar, R., & Hall, K. (2013). Social Return on Investment (SROI) and Performance Measurement. *Public Management Review*, *15*(6), 923–941. doi:10.1080/14719037.2012.698857

Mintzberg, H. (1999). *Structure et Dynamique des Organisations*. Paris: Les Éditions d'Organisation.

Monzon, J. L., & Chaves, R. (2008). The European Social Economy: Concept and Dimensions of the Third Sector. *Annals of Public and Cooperative Economics*, *79*(3/4), 549–577. doi:10.1111/j.1467-8292.2008.00370.x

Moore, H. (2015). Global Prosperity and Sustainable Development Goals. *Journal of International Development*, *27*(6), 801–815. doi:10.1002/jid.3114

Noya, A., & Clarence, E. (2007). The Social Economy. Building Inclusive Economies. Paris: OECD, Local Economic and Employment Development (LEED).

O'Sullivan, D., & Dooley, L. (2009). *Applying Innovation*. London: Sage Publications.

OECD. (2005). *Oslo Manual: Guidelines for Collecting and Interpreting Innovation Data*. Organization for Economic Co-operation and Development, European Commission.

Pais, C. A., & Parente, C. (2015). Representations of team work among organizations with a social entrepreneurship profile: A multiple case-study. *Team Performance Management*, *21*(1/2), 65–84. doi:10.1108/TPM-07-2014-0042

Parente, C. (2016). Social entrepreneurship in Portugal: Intervention and management models in third sector. *The International Journal of Sociology and Social Policy*, *36*(7-8), 531–546. doi:10.1108/IJSSP-01-2016-0002

Parente, C., Marcos, V., Costa, D., & Amador, C. (2013). Representações sobre empreendedorismo social. *Cooperativismo e Economía Social*, *35*, 37–65.

Pérez, C., & Perdomo, J. (2017). An Alternative Financial Reporting Model: Social Economy Organizations. *Lex Social*, *7*(2), 229–249.

Picciotti, A. (2017). Towards sustainability: The innovation paths of social enterprise. *Annals of Public and Cooperative Economics*, *88*(2), 233–256. doi:10.1111/apce.12168

Rodriguez, M. J., & Guzman, C. (2013). Innovation in social economy firms. *Management Decision*, *51*(5), 986–998. doi:10.1108/MD-08-2012-0538

Rumelt, R. P., Schendel, D. E., & Teece, D. J. (1991). Strategic Management and Economics. *Strategic Management Journal*, *12*(S2), 5–29. doi:10.1002mj.4250121003

Rumelt, R. P., Schendel, D. E., & Teece, D. J. (1994). *Fundamental Issues in Strategy: A Research Agenda*. Boston: Harvard Business School Press.

Salustri, A. & Vigano, F. (2017). *The non-profit sector as a foundation for the interaction among the social economy, the public sector and the market*. MPRA Paper No. 78113, p. 27.

Sanzo-Perez, M. J., Álvarez-González, L. I., & Rey-García, M. (2015). How to encourage social innovations: A resource-based approach. *Service Industries Journal*, *35*(7/8), 430–447. doi:10.1080/02642069.2015.1015517

Soares, C., Fialho, J. A. S., Chau, F., Gageiro, J., & Pestana, H. (2012). *A Economia Social e a sua Sustentabilidade como Fator de Inclusão Social*. Lisboa: Serga.

Spear, R. (2013). *Social economy - laying the groundwork for innovative solutions to today's challenges. European Commission*. Luxembourg: Publications Office of the European Union.

Teece, D. J. (2007). Explicating dynamic capabilities: The nature and microfoundations of (sustainable) enterprise performance. *Strategic Management Journal*, *28*(13), 1319–1350. doi:10.1002mj.640

Terziev, V. (2017). *Social entrepreneurship as an opportunity to model an active social program. In Topical issues of contemporary science: Collection of scientific articles* (pp. 6–12). Valencia, Venezuela: C.E.I.M.

Veltmeyer, H. (2017). The social economy in Latin America as alternative development. *Canadian Journal of Development Studies*, 1–17. doi:10.1080/02255189.2017.1294052

Vézina, M., Malo, M.-C., & Ben Selma, M. (2017). Mature social economy enterprise and social innovation: The case of the Desjardins environment fund. *Annals of Public and Cooperative Economics*, *88*(2), 257–278. doi:10.1111/apce.12169

Yin, R. (2009). *Case study research: Design and methods*. Sage Publications.

Young, D. R., Searing, E. A. M., & Brewer, C. V. (2016). *The Social Enterprise Zoo. A Guide for Perplexed Scholars, Entrepreneurs, Philanthropists, Leaders, Investors, and Policymakers*. Cheltenham, UK: Edward Elgar Publishing.

KEY TERMS AND DEFINITIONS

Organizational Change: Occurs as a response to the drivers of change, leading organizations to implement new strategies and management models that can ensure success in the process of adaptation to the environment in which they operate.

Organizational Innovation: Relates to changes in an organization's organizational methods and structures in order to gain a competitive advantage over its competitors. This type of innovation has a more intangible nature than product or process innovation.

Social Economy: Includes those organizations with their own management and positioned between the market and the state. Such organizations view the possibility of profit as a mere instrument rather than an end in itself, since they are more focused on accomplishing social goals. The main objective is to serve the population, always based on the private sphere of the society.

Social Economy Organization: An organization that delivers a service and is social mission oriented in order to create social value.

Social Entrepreneurship: A field of action involving different kinds of actors, in which sociocultural and historical contexts emerge as key features, where individuals, the social entrepreneurs, construct outcomes, using entrepreneurial alertness and motivation to solve societal problems.

Social Innovation: A true social innovation is systems-changing by developing novel solutions in border spanning learning communities to create social value and promote community development, challenging existing social institutions through collaborative action developing wider networks.

Social Mission: The willingness of an individual or organization to pursue social goals focused on helping social excluded citizens, improving the quality of social services, and contributing to increase social responsibility.

Social Value: The value that accrue to society from social entrepreneurship/social innovation initiatives and that allow to solve social problems and create social capital.

Strategic Management: Relates to the definition by the top management of an organization of its main objectives and action plans to achieve those objectives, taking into account the resources available in the organization and an assessment of the internal and external environments in which the organization operates.

ENDNOTE

1 A review of the literature about the concept of social economy is beyond the scope of this chapter. The working definition presented in the introductory section is assumed to fit the needs of the current chapter.

Chapter 10
Integration of Sustainability and Management Control Systems:
A Challenge for Family SMEs

Paola Vola
University of Eastern Piedmont, Italy

ABSTRACT

In order to support family SMEs in developing more responsible, innovative, and competitive business models, this chapter proposes to study the role and interaction between sustainability control systems (SCSs) and management control systems (MCSs). The chapter will examine management control and family business literature with the purpose of discussing the following research issues: What are the interactions between different forms of social responsibility in family SMESs? How can we transfer the family firms' attitude to social responsibility in a sustainable business model? What are main elements of a sustainable business model that can leverage on family firms business model? The conceptual framework will be defined through literature review: the main aim is to convey the meaning of sustainability and investigating the integration between SCSs and MCSs in family SMEs.

INTRODUCTION

The current economic scenario, because of the financial crisis, shows a decrease of wealth creation and weak business confidence. Many European countries have to face social problems like unemployment, underemployment, while poverty is increasing. In this context, the need to promote economic development consistent with social and environmental concerns has drastically emerged.

There is an increasing opportunity to assess value creation from a sustainability standpoint and with a social responsibility approach.

Since Small and Medium businesses (SMEs) contribute significantly to the European GDP and employment, the discussion of sustainability in all of its features (economical, ecological and societal) has revealed already important issue for SMEs that want to be in business for years to come.

DOI: 10.4018/978-1-5225-5267-3.ch010

Companies are expected, more than before, to account for many aspects of their performance – not just financial or economic results – but also social and environmental performance (Farneti et alii, 2017; Cramer, 2002). Schaltegger et alii (2006) define this paradigm as "Sustainability Performance Management".

In the new context, also the concept of value creation has to be changed from value creation for shareholders to value creation for all stakeholders. Value creation also embed sustainable value (based on a triple bottom line approach), and social responsibility.

According to Karatzolglou (2006), the pursuit of sustainability in business practises has necessitated the integrated management and assessment of corporate economic, environmental and social performances.

Although sustainability has been discussed in management control literature to highlight the need of Sustainability Control Systems (SCSs), little is known about the mode of integration between sustainability and traditional Management Control Systems (MCSs).

Since Small and Medium businesses (SMEs) contribute significantly to the European GDP and employment, the discussion of sustainability in all of its features (economical, ecological and societal) has revealed already important issue for SMEs that want to be in business for years to come.

Sustainability has long been recognized as central issuesby EU institutions and a way for fundamental shifts in business practice and models, that can drive progress, strive for innovation and unleash business value. Since 2001, the EU institutions have highlighted firms' responsibility in managing the impacts of their actions on society.

In this situation, a new role of both EU institutions and European firms has drastically emerged that asks for promoting economic development consistent with social and environmental concerns.

In the EU environment, SMEs (especially family ones) are recognized to adopt business models more sensitive to societal and ecological issues and stakeholder needs. However, they are characterized also by weaknesses, which come to light especially during growth processes.

Although many organizations are devoted to sustainability in their external reporting, there is a scarce attention to the role management control systems can play in supporting sustainability within organizations (Durden, 2008; Herzig et alii, 2012).

Even if scholars (Burgelman, 1991) argue that Sustainability Control Systems (SCSs) can contribute to an effective integration of sustainability within strategy, little is known about the relationship between Managerial Control Systems (MCSs) and SCSs.

In order to support family SMEs in developing more responsible, innovative and competitive business models, this chapter proposes to study the relationship between SCSs and MCSs. More specifically, the chapter will analyze how systems together can faciliate the emergence of sustainability at a strategic level and ultimately the integration of sustainability and strategy.

BACKGROUND

The end of 20th century has seen an important increase in scientific research on sustainable thinking: the term "sustainable" has become a buzzword which as been interpreted in very different ways (like "green", "eco-efficient", "ethical" and "socially responsible") (Carrol, 1999; Bieker, 2002).

For many years, the contribution of firms towards sustainability has been called Corporate Social Responsibility (CSR) (European Commission, 2002).

According to Carroll (1979), CSR is made by the subset of corporate responsibilities that addresses a firm's voluntary or discretionary relationship with its stakeholders.

Therefore, CSR practises encompass all the initiatives to improve an important aspect for society or the relationship with communities, with non-governmental entities or with non-profit organizations.

Schaltegger and Wagner (2006) argue that this definition of CSR led to the operationalization of CSR in terms of community relations, philanthropic activities, multi-sector collaborations, or volunteer activities, which cover only very limited aspects of the broader definition.

As authors underline, this approach do not integrate core business issues with social and environmental activities and do not consider the general economic relevance of corporate engagement; in this way, CSR activities are confined in a parallel organization of the company, such as CSR department, dealing with non-economic issues, measuring non-economic aspects of performance (Schaltegger et alii, 2017; Schaltegger & Wagner, 2006; Porter, 2011).

Schaltegger and Wagner (2006) discuss the implications of this approach, underlying three main problems.

Firstly, establishing a parallel organization for social or environmental issues contrast with the basic vision of sustainability that integrate social, environmental and economic issues.

Secondly, sustainable development requires participation and involvement of stakeholders but also of business managers: sustainable business strategy, communication and reporting should be linked with sustainability performance management.

Thirdly, as parallel organizational structures, CSR practises become discretionary activities and could be cut back in period of economic difficulties.

Epstein (2008) exposes that management is continuously looking for tools to identify, manage and measure the drivers of sustainability, as well as systems and structure to improve performance measurement.

Thus scholars (Epstein, 2008; Schaltegger & Wenteges, 2006; Johnson, 2007) propose that sustainability performance measurement has to encompass factors regarding economic, ecological, and social issues.

While management science has widely investigated performance, there is still no generally accepted definition of the concept.

Scholars have indeed proposed numerous definitions.

In this study, we propose to refer to the one by Bourguignon (2000): performance is about the achievement of the organizational goals, whatever their nature and their variety.

The traditional vision of performance, focused on short term and financial vision of the company, has progressively been replaced by a more global and inclusive one.

In this study, we define sustainable performance, accordlying to Schaltergger and Wenteges (2006), as the performance in all dimensions and for all drivers of corporate sustainability.

Elkington (1997) introduces the concept of the "Triple-P Bottom Line", which includes profit (economic side), planet (environmental side), and people (social side); according to the scholars, companies need to refer to these all three areas if they want to label their business as sustainable.

Even if nowadays there is no consensus, many researches have shown a positive relationship between societal (social and environmental) performance and financial results (Moskowitz, 1972; Chrisman, 2000; Konar & Cohen, 2001; Dentchev, 2004).

In this win-win paradigm, economic, environmental and social aspect of corporate sustainability are, at least partly, in harmony with each other; consequently, management should seek to identify opportunities in which economic, environmental and social corporate objectives can be achieved simultaneously.

Bourguignon (2000) adds that a firm will be performing well if it reaches its objectives.

This consideration lead to a reflection about the importance of strategic performance management. So, once strategy has been formulated and implemented, it is necessary to monitor if the fixed objectives have been met, thus leading firm to a good performance.

Sustainability performance management represents a managerial framework, which, on one hand, links environmental and social management with the business strategy, and, on the other hand, integrates environmental and social information with economic business information and reporting.

IMPLEMENTING SUSTAINABILITY PERFORMANCE MANAGEMENT IN FAMILY SMES

Literature recognizes two categories of motivation for implementing performance management, as internal and external reasons.

Among others, Herzig and Schaltegger (2006) indicate that the main external reason is connected to legitimation: the adoption of sustainability performance management allows to legitimate corporate activities, products, and services with environmental and social impact towards stakeholders.

Moreover, it may contribute to increasing corporate reputation and value.

As sustainability reporting activities can be considered a proxy of overall performance, it can be used to indicate a superior prospective performance compared to competitors.

In addition, it allows to anticipate national and international legislative requirements since many countries are imposing mandatory information and reporting on sustainability. In case of compelled information this issue, performance management permits institutional compliance (Schaltegger & Burrit, 2006).

The internal reasons that led to performance management regard internal legitimation of sustainability activities: it increase transaparency and accountability within the company.

Moreover, it can contribute to support employees' motivation and control of internal processes.

Sustainability performance management, as a system to determine if the company is performing well or not, allows to better understand the determinants of success or failure in achieving objectives (Morse et alii, 2003).

Finally, the introduction of sustainability performance management allows to identify and realize the economic potential of social and environmental activities in terms of cost reduction or revenues increase. This aspect is critical for the corporate engagement into sustainable strategy.

Over the past recent years, many researchers and practitioners have proposed new tools (and adapted those already available) to enable the strategic performance management of sustainability by companies.

This great number of contributions has led to different categories of tools, but nowadays there is no consensus on the definition and classification of tools useful to manage and measure corporate sustainability performance.

Schaltegger at alii (2006) and Gond et alii (2012) present an overview of major tools.

The Challenge of Integrating Sustainability Into Control Mechanisms

Fiksel at alii (1999) argues that sustainability performance management must be approached as a systematic business process in order to be integrated effectively into company strategic planning and control.

Lasting attempts to integrate sustainability within strategy should be reflected into formal control mechanisms.

Table 1. Sustainability tools based on Schaltegger alii (2006) and Gond et alii (2012)

Sustainability tools	Main Features
Green or social accounts in conventional accounting (Christophe, 1995; Schaltegger and Burrit, 2006)	Integrating the cost and revenues related to the firm's activities in favour of environment or society in conventional accounting
Green or social appendices in conventional accounting (Christophe, 1995; Schaltegger and Burrit, 2006)	Explanation of the nature of the cost and revenues related to the firm's activities in favour of environment or society in specific document within conventional accounting
Green, social or sustainability budgets (Ito et alii, 2006; Henri and Journeault; 2009; Roth, 2008; Burrit and Schaltegger, 2001)	A plan specifying goals to be achieved in the next year referred also to environmental and social objectives
Environmental, social or sustainability cost accounting (Antheaume, 2004; Gluch and Baunmann, 2004; Herbohn, 2005)	Generating information for management planning and control and decision making encompassing also sustainability issues
Sustainability planning (Bonacchi and Rinaldi, 2007)	Long range planning covering a five-ten years period, based on forecast of competitive environment
Balanced Scorecard (Kaplan and Norton, 1992, 1996, 2001; Hockerts, 2001; Bieker, 2002; Fiegge et alii, 2001; Hahn and Wagner, 2002; Schaltegger, 2004; Schaltegger and Dyllick, 2002; Hubbard, 2009)	A set of financial and non-financial indicators to assess the achievement of strategic objectives, including economic, social and environmental dimension
Scandia Navigator (Edvinsson and Malone, 1997)	Performance measurement system focused on intellectual capital; set of measures based on human resources as key element in business value creation
Reward system based on multidimensional performance system (Dutta and Lawson, 2009)	Reward system including sustainability dimension

Source: personal elaboration.

Source: personal elaboration.

Making sustainability an integral part of company's business strategy is the critical key to obtain the bottom-line benefits.

Some scholars (Sebhatu, 2009; Schaltegger, 2006) name them Sustainability Performance Measurement (SPM) while other scholars, such as Gond et alii (2012) and Henri and Journault (2009; 2010) refer to Sustainability Control Systems (SCSs).

Hereafter we will make reference to SCSs as mechanism to encompasse the performance of a company in all dimensions of corporate sustainability.

Even if scholars (Burgelman, 1991) argue that SCSs can contribute to an effective integration of sustainability within strategy only when they inform MCSs and are not used as autonomous strategic tools, little is known about the mode of integration between SCSs and traditional MCSs.

Since MCSs shape actor's practises (Ahrens and Chapman, 2007) they can be used to push organization towards sustainability.

Gond et alii (2012) underlines the importance of the neglected relationship between MCSs and SCSs and propose to clarify how the two kind of systems are related; at the same time, they analyse how systems together can facilitate the emergence of sustainability at a strategic level and ultimately the integration of sustainability and strategy.

They propose eight type of organizational configuration, according to the level of integration between MCSs and SCSs.

Results show that companies usually are moving towards sustainability through long paths of integration.

In this chapter, we want to discuss if the characteristics of family firms can led them to a natural integration of sustainability.

What About Sustainability in Family Firms?

Literature on family business, discussing sustainability issue, has identified family firms as organization that encourage long term, socially responsible orientation in dealing with all stakeholders (Le Breton-Miller, Miller, 2015).

Scholars have investigated the relationship between family business and sustainability practises making reference to agency, behavioural agency, stewardship, reputational, institutional, stakeholder and conflict theory.

If, on the one hand, family firms seem to be likely to adopt sustainability practises, on the other hand, some family firms' features seem to interfere to their path towards sustainability.

Features Enhancing Sustainability Practices

Long-Term Orientation

Family firms are unanimously recognized as log-term oriented; the roots of long-term orientation can be traced in the desire to pass to next generation a healthy business.

In this way firms resist the opportunistic treatment of stakeholders and tend to adopt practises to extend the enduring viability of the business (Berrone, Cruz, Gomez-Mejia & Larraza-Kintana, 2010).

Although authors pointed out that business strategy varied in the extent to which each of sustainability practises was required, they underlined that all of the successful long-lived firms ensured an adequate level of initiatives.

Stewardship

Arrangle et alii (2007) defined family firms as stewards that invest in longer term associations with their stakeholders with the intent of building a strong social capital.

Families, who own businesses are usually well-anchored in their communities, are likely to value, nurture and exploit social capital they have built with customers, suppliers, employees, and community in general.

These kinds of necessity tend to play against the opportunistic and short-term orientation that damage sustainability.

Family Values

The personal long-term commitment is also a vehicle of family values, connected to, above all, firm's continuity, responsibility towards stakeholders, quality of products and strong links with the territory: these values really distinguish family firms from other enterprises (Aronoff, 2004).

Literature suggests that family businesses, given their intergenerational aspirations, are attached especially closely to community stakeholders (Berrone et alii, 2010); so honouring family values and reputation represents a top priority in family firms.

Agency Costs

Agency costs occur when family firms have to manage the risk of opportunism and short-term orientation by non-family managers (Fama & Jensen, 1983; Andreson & Reeb, 2003).

Non-family managers could be tempted to obtain private benefits, exploiting firms' resources that otherwise could be contribute to sustainability.

Scholars notice that public family firms are able to reduce these risks through family involvement and more effective control capacities (Anderson & Reeb, 2003).

In private family firms, family managers are usually aligned with their commitment and are interested into business durability.

Features Against Sustainability Practices

Conflict

In family firms, conflicts occur when family members fail to get along.

The grater the distance between family members in terms of family ties, the greeter the probability of arising conflicts.

In these situations, owners are focused on their own advantage that becomes the priority, neglecting stakeholders and community responsibilities.

Conflicts tend to push the company far from sustainability practises.

Socioemotional Wealth (SEW)

According to SEW theory (Gomez-Mejia, Haynes, Nunez-Nickel, Jacobson and Moyano-Fuentes, 2007), family firm owners view their firm as a way to contribute to the social and emotional well-being of the family; this conservative approach can erode the service to stakeholders (Block, 2012).

Some SEW scholars argue that family, in order to satisfy family's needs, could use firm resources for private benefits; this risk is represented by some negative behaviours such as nepotism and cronyism.

It is plain that this interpretation of SEW is far away from sustainability perspective.

Owner-Owner Agency-Costs

In addition, also family owners could be subject to a specific agency costs: these kind of costs occur to monitor that the more influent and powerful owners do not appropriate firm's resources at the expenses of smaller and less powerful owners.

This conduct represents an inequity for smaller owners and compromise resources that can serve other stakeholders or fulfil social purpose.

To summarize discussion, Figure 1 presents a research framework useful to investigate sustainability in family firms.

Figure 1. Features influencing sustainability in family firms
Source: personal elaboration.

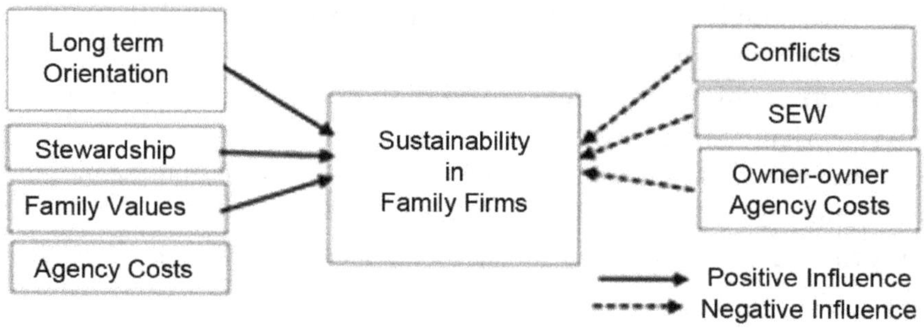

FUTURE RESEARCH DIRECTIONS

The design of the framework needs to be refined and tested through case studies; a panel of selected family SMEs will be selected by author in order to test features influencing sustainibility.

More specifically, through case studies author will investigate the intensity of influence of each feature on sustainability and, at the same time, the implementation of sustainibility practises within MCSs.

SOLUTIONS AND RECOMMENDATIONS

As far as concern MCSs, many studies highlighted that family firms are characterized by a lower diffusion of MCSs, because of a widespread entrepreneurship, and strong linkages between the family and the enterprise, at the ownership, governance and management levels, which cause lower agency costs (Schulze et al. 2001).

In family firms, social and individual control systems fit more than the bureaucratic-administrative ones (Moores and Mula, 2000). At the earlier stage of the life cycle of a family firm (the founder or entrepreneurial experience) informal MCSs are used, little planning and coordination activities are run and decision-making processes are centralized by the entrepreneur.

However, successful growth leads to a critical stage, named professionalization, which requires the owner-manager to change his/her entrepreneurial approach and take a more professional one. In this stage of development, the enterprise adopts managerial mechanisms in order to cope with the increased complexity of the environment and the firm (Moores, and Yuen 2001).

The faster the growth and the greater the complexity, the more important the role of such mechanisms. Thus, we can say that the way SP and MCSs are implemented and used by companies may have a great impact on the performance and survival of the family firm in the long term (Dyer, 1996).

CONCLUSION

As shown below, it is not easy to describe the relationship between family firm's characteristics and their tendency to engage in suitability practises.

On one side, long-term orientation, stewardship, family values and agency costs have a positive influence. However, the dark side of family firms emerges in terms of conflicts, private socio-emotional wealth and owner-owner agency costs.

A deeper analysis on moderating factors is required to explain the extent family firms will purse sustainability. In other word, it is important to identify under which conditions family firms are expected to embrace sustainability practices. Such factors regard, for instance, education, ownership structure, managers' (non-family and family) characteristics, board of directors and competitive environment.

As far as concern the MCSs, the path towards professionalization will be critical to their diffusion among family firms.

REFERENCES

Ahrens, T., & Chapman, C. S. (2007). Management accounting as practise. *Accounting, Organizations and Society*, *32*(1-2), 1–27. doi:10.1016/j.aos.2006.09.013

Anderson, R. C., & Reeb, D. M. (2003). Founding-Family Ownership and Firm Performance: Evidence from the S&P 500. *The Journal of Finance*, *58*(3), 1301–1328. doi:10.1111/1540-6261.00567

Aronoff, C. (2004). Self-Perpetuation Family Organization Built on Values: Necessary condition for long-term family business survival. *Family Business Review*, *17*(1), 55–59. doi:10.1111/j.1741-6248.2004.00003.x

Arrangle, J., Hitt, M., Sirmon, D., & Very, D. (2007). The development of organizational social capital: Attributes of family firms. *Journal of Management Studies*, *44*(1), 73–95. doi:10.1111/j.1467-6486.2007.00665.x

Berrone, P., Cruz, C., Gomez-Mejia, L., & Larraza-Kintana, M. (2010). Socioemotional wealth and corporate response to institutional pressures: Do family-controlled firms pollute less? *Administrative Science Quarterly*, *55*(1), 82–113. doi:10.2189/asqu.2010.55.1.82

Bieker, T. (2002). *Managing corporate sustainability with the Balanced Scorecard: developing a Balanced Scorecard for Integrity Management*. Oikos PhD Summer Academy.

Block, J. H. (2012). R&D investments in family and founder firms: An agency perspective. *Journal of Business Venturing*, *27*(2), 248–265. doi:10.1016/j.jbusvent.2010.09.003

Bourguignon, A. (2000). *Performance et control de gestion. In Encyclopedie de Comptabilitè, Control de gestion et Audit* (pp. 931–941). Ed. Economica.

Carroll, A., & Buchholtz, A. (2014). *Business and society: Ethics, Sustainability, and stakeholder management*. Cengage Learning.

Carroll, A. B. (1979). A Tridimensional Conceptual Model of Corporate Social Performance. *Academy of Management Review*, *4*, 497–505.

Carroll, A. B. (1999). Corporate social responsibility: Evolution of a definitional construct. *Business & Society*, *38*(3), 268–295. doi:10.1177/000765039903800303

Christman, P. (2000). Effects of Best Practises of Environmental Management on Cost Advantage: The role of Complementary Assets. *Academy of Management Journal*, *43*(4), 663–680. doi:10.2307/1556360

Cramer, J. (2002). From Financial to Sustainable Profit. *Corporate Social Responsibility and Environmental Management*, *9*(2), 99–106. doi:10.1002/csr.12

Dentchev, N. A. (2004). Corporate social performance as a business strategy. *Journal of Business Ethics*, *55*(4), 397–412. doi:10.100710551-004-1348-5

Durden, C. (2008). Towards a socially responsible management control system. *Accounting, Auditing & Accountability Journal*, *21*(5), 671–694. doi:10.1108/09513570810872969

Epstein, M. J. (2008). *Making Sustainability Work: Best practises in managing and measuring social and environmental impacts*. Sheffield, UK: Greenleaf.

European Commission (2002). *Communication: Corporate Social Responsibility: A Business Contribution to Sustainable Development.* Author.

Fama, E., & Jensen, M. (1983). Separation of Ownership and Control. *The Journal of Law & Economics*, *26*(2), 301–325. doi:10.1086/467037

Farneti, F., Siboni, B., & Del Sordo, C. (2017). La misurazione della performance sociale nell'esperienza dell'Università di Bologna [The social and environmental performance measurement at the University of Bologna]. *Management Control*, *1*(1), 135–164. doi:10.3280/MACO2017-001007

Fiksel, J., McDaniel, J., & Mendenhall, C. (1999). Measuring progress towards sustainability: principles, process, and best practices. In Greening of industry network conference: best practise proceedings. Battelle Memorial Institute.

Gomez-Mejia, L. R., Haynes, K. T., Nunez-Nickel, M., Jacobson, K. L., & Moyano-Fuentes, J. (2007). Socioemotional Wealth and business risks in family controlled firms. *Administrative Science Quarterly*, *52*(1), 106–137. doi:10.2189/asqu.52.1.106

Gond, J. P., Grubnic, S., Herzig, C., & Moon, J. (2012). Configuring management control systems: Theorizing the integration of strategy and sustainability. *Management Accounting Research*, *23*(3), 205–223. doi:10.1016/j.mar.2012.06.003

Gond, J. P., & Herrbach, O. (2006). Corporate social reporting as a learning tool? A theoretical framework. *Journal of Business Ethics*, *65*(4), 359–371. doi:10.100710551-006-6405-9

Henri, J. F. (2006). Management control systems and strategy: A resource based view. *Accounting, Organizations and Society*, *31*(6), 529–558. doi:10.1016/j.aos.2005.07.001

Henry, J. F., & Journault, M. (2009). *Revisiting the link between management control systems and strategy in contingency-based research.* Paper of the Annual Conference of the Canadian Accounting Academic Association.

Henry, J. F., & Journault, M. (2010). Eco-control: The influence of management control systems on environmental and economic performance. *Accounting, Organizations and Society*, *35*(1), 63–80. doi:10.1016/j.aos.2009.02.001

Herzig, C., & Schaltegger, S. (2006). Corporate Sustainability Reporting. In Sustainability Accounting and Reporting. Springer.

Herzig, C., Viere, T., Schaltegger, S., & Burrit, R. (2012). *Environmental Management Accounting. Case Studies of South East-Asian Companies*. London: Routledge.

Johnson, M. (2007). *Stakeholders dialogue for sustainable service* (Doctoral Dissertation). Karlstad University Studies.

Konar, S., & Cohen, M. (1997). Information as Regulation: The effect of community right to know laws on toxic emissions. *Journal of Enronvmental Economic and Management*, *32*(1), 109–124. doi:10.1006/jeem.1996.0955

Le Breton-Miller, D., & Miller, D. (2015). Family firms and practises of sustainability: a contingency view. *Journal of Family Business Strategy*, (7), 26-33.

Moores, K., & Mula, J. (2000). The salience of market, bureaucratic, and clan controls in the management of family firm transitions: Some tentative Australian evidence. *Family Business Review*, *13*(2), 91–106. doi:10.1111/j.1741-6248.2000.00091.x

Moores, K., & Yuen, S. (2001). Management Accounting Systems and Organizational Configuration: A Life Cycle Perspective. *Accounting, Organizations and Society*, *26*(4-5), 351–389. doi:10.1016/S0361-3682(00)00040-4

Morse, W., Davis, J., & Hartgraves, A. (2003). *Management accounting: a strategic approach*. Moscove, Thomspon/South-Western.

Moskovitz, M. (1972). Choosing Socially Respnsible stocks. *Business and Society Review*, (1): 72–75.

Moskovitz, M. (1972). Choosing Socially Responsible stocks. *Business and Society Review*, (1): 72–75.

Otley, D. T. (1999). Performance management; a framework for management control system research. *Management Accounting Research*, *10*(10), 363–382. doi:10.1006/mare.1999.0115

Porter, M. E., & Kramer, M. R. (2011). The Big Idea. Creating Shared Value. *Harvard Business Review*, *89*(1-2), 62-77.

Schaltegger, S., Bennet, M., & Burrit, R. (2006). Sustainability Accounting and Reporting: Development, Linkages and Reflection: An Introduction. In S. Schaltegger, M. Bennet, & R. Burrit (Eds.), *Sustainability Accounting and Reporting*. Springer. doi:10.1007/978-1-4020-4974-3_1

Schaltegger, S., & Burrit, R. (2006). Corporate Sustainability Accounting: A Catchphrase for Compliant Corporations or a Business Decision Support for Sustainability Leaders? In Sustainability Accounting and Reporting. Springer.

Schaltegger, S., Etxeberria, I. Á., & Ortas, E. (2017). Innovating Corporate Accounting and Reporting for Sustainability – Attributes and Challenges. *Sustainable Development*, *25*(2), 113–122. doi:10.1002d.1666

Schaltegger, S., & Wegner, M. (2006). Integrative Management of Sustainability Performance Measurement and Reporting. *International Journal of Accounting and Performance Evaluation*, (3), 1-19.

Schulze, W. S., Lubatkin, M. H., Dino, R. M., & Bucholtz, A. K. (2001). Agency Relationships in Family Firms: Theory and Evidence. *Organization Science*, *12*(2), 99–116. doi:10.1287/orsc.12.2.99.10114

Sebhatu, S. P. (2009). *Sustainability performance measurement for sustainable organizations: beyond compliance and reporting*. Karlstad: Service Research Centre Karlstad University.

Simons, R. (2000). *Performance Measurement and Control Systems for Implementing Strategy: text and cases*. Englewood Cliff, NJ: Prentice Hall.

KEY TERMS AND DEFINITIONS

Family Firm: A commercial organization in which decision making is influenced by multiple generations of a family—related by blood or marriage or adoption—who has both the ability to influence the vision of the business and the willingness to use this ability to pursue distinctive goals.

Management Control System: A system that gathers and uses information to evaluate the performance of different organizational resources like human, physical, financial, and also the organization as a whole in light of the organizational strategies pursued.

SMEs: Small and medium-sized enterprises, also small and medium enterprises; this kind of organizations are businesses whose personnel numbers fall below certain limits.

Sustainability: Meeting the needs of the present without compromising the ability of future generations to meet their needs. The concept of sustainability is comprised of three pillars: economic, environmental, and social—also known informally as profits, planet, and people.

Chapter 11
Entrepreneurial Orientation and Family Influence Factors for Sustainable Small Business:
First Insights From the Leading Italian Craft Beer Producer

Chiara Civera
University of Torino, Italy

Damiano Cortese
University of Torino, Italy

Simona Fiandrino
University of Torino, Italy

ABSTRACT

This chapter addresses the issue of sustainability in small family firms, considering the relation between entrepreneurial orientation and family influence factors. The literature describes positive links between small firms and sustainability outlining their power in spreading good practices. Furthermore, the role of family is crucial to strengthen such intrinsic links. The aim of this study is to first demonstrate the influence that family factors play on entrepreneurial orientation and, second, highlight how factors and orientations shape small family firms' sustainable approach. The study employs a case-based method, illustrating a peculiar case: the leading Italian small family-owned craft beer producer Baladin. It provides fertile ground for the development of functioning as a learning process and being replicable in smaller firms. It also highlights the relevance of family culture even when an entrepreneur engages in a countertrend against his usual family path, by undermining the traditional family business but maintaining a local commitment to sustainable outcomes.

DOI: 10.4018/978-1-5225-5267-3.ch011

INTRODUCTION

Small and medium enterprises (SMEs) can play a crucial role in the current social, environmental and economic scenario as responsible and socially engaged actors and can contribute to reshaping the course of events in a sustainable way (Jamali, Zanhour, & Keshishian, 2009; Jenkins, 2009). Given that the majority of small businesses are family owned and do not respond to stockholder logics (Panwar, Paul, Nybakk, Hansen, & Thompson, 2014) their social and environmental concerns might appear more genuine. This is because they are deeply rooted in the context—both geographical and societal—within which small family enterprises were born, grew and established relationships with their stakeholders based on the owners' and family's personal values (Fitzgerald, Haynes, Schrank, & Danes, 2010; Russo & Tencati, 2009; Spence & Rutherfoord, 2003). SMEs play a fundamental role in society and contribute significantly to its business economy. As the EU Commission (2016) underlines, they represent the heart of Europe's economy, as 99% of all businesses in the EU are small and medium sized (EU Commission, 2016). In Italy, SMEs generate 68% of the total value added, which is more than 10.6% the percentage in other EU countries. In addition, SMEs are responsible for almost 80% of employment (EU Commission, 2016). Over the last few years, the connection between economic growth and social matters has become more and more evident. Clearly, the sustainable impact that SMEs can achieve it is still circumscribed to their local territories and measured on their sizes; therefore, cooperation and sharing of best sustainable practices are needed between larger companies (that still contribute the most to both positive and negative impacts on the environment, for instance) and smaller enterprises (that are more flexible and peculiar in embarking sustainable matters).

The impact that small and medium family businesses can have on regional development and local growth through sustainability is relevant; these businesses have certain intrinsic characterizations that require further investigation (Basco, 2015). Firstly, the sustainable advantages resulting from the proximity within which small family businesses operate ensure stakeholder engagement and the quality of relationships (Besser, 2012; Jenkins, 2006, 2009). Secondly, the stronger links that these businesses have with the community and its values represent a catalyst for small family business owners to act ethically because they are directly accountable for their actions (Vives, 2006; Spence & Rutherfoord, 2003). Thirdly, the combination of the family's and owner's values can tilt the decision-making process in favor of sustainability and the engagement of competitors and other groups of stakeholders in carrying out sustainable activities for the benefit of the community (Perrini, 2006). There are many challenges associated with increasing sustainability in these businesses; however, most of the academic literature on sustainability and corporate social responsibility (CSR) is focused on larger companies, and therefore, there is a strong need for research on small family enterprises (Williams & Schaefer, 2013; Jamali et al., 2009). Studies in the literature debate about how bigger companies implement CSR and what the expected outcomes are, and in this way, they have contributed to the development of more innovative and integrated approaches to CSR. Similarly, arguing about how sustainability and CSR are forged and designed in small family businesses in a more informal way can provide fertile ground for the development of common frameworks that can be replicated in smaller family contexts.

To shed light on the approach to sustainability of small family firms, some researchers have studied the factors and the orientations forming their values and strategic decisions. In this regard, the literature has extensively debated the family influence factors (Frank, Lueger, Nosé, & Suchy, 2010), family involvement, and the impact of entrepreneurial orientations on business growth (Casillas, Moreno, & Barbero, 2010). Although the current management literature on entrepreneurial orientations is growing and addresses multiple dimensions of the phenomenon (Wales, Gupta, & Mousa, 2011), academic studies call for investigation into how such attitudes can ensure the long-term sustainability of small family business.

Accordingly, this chapter aims at exploring the interlinks between and impact of family influence factors (Frank et al., 2010) and entrepreneurial orientations (Wales et al., 2011; Baker & Sinkula, 2009; Lumpkin & Dess, 1996) through the first research question: How do family influence factors affect the entrepreneurial orientation of small family firms?

Accomplishing the first aim of the research can allow for a better understanding of how factors and/or orientations affect a firm's sustainability approach and strategy the most, and help answer the second research question: How do factors and orientations shape sustainability patterns in small family firms?

In order to respond to the aforementioned questions, the research employs a case-based approach developed around the leading Italian small family-owned craft beer producer Baladin. The choice of the industry and the case study are relevant to the investigation. The "craft beer revolution" (Hindy, 2014) finds its roots in cultural changes that shift from mass and "fast" to "slow food" consumption based on sustainable approaches. Baladin is the pioneer of such a revolution in Italy and has achieved a leading positioning in the market despite being small in size. The case study will outline the firm's strong link with sustainability and the unique and well-recognized characteristics of the entrepreneur that represent a sort of turnaround compared with typical family business behaviors and will work as a theoretical illustration of how family influence factors and entrepreneurial orientations can help form a winning sustainable approach.

The chapter is structured as follows: Section 2 outlines the concepts of entrepreneurial orientations and family influence factors within small family firms. Section 3 reviews the literature and new conceptualizations of CSR and sustainability in smaller firms. Section 4 explains the methodology of the study. Section 5 describes the food and beer industries as the context of the research. Section 6 illustrates the interlinks among family factors, entrepreneurial orientations and approach to sustainability through the Baladin case study. Section 7 moves to the conclusions of the study and discusses its limitations.

BACKGROUND

Small Family Firms: Entrepreneurial Orientation and Family Influence Factors

The managerial and organizational aspects of family firm entrepreneurship are unique and might depend upon the contingency factors of the surrounding environment such as the community culture, industry, family life-stage as well as the family influence on strategic decision-making (Zellweger & Sieger, 2012). In other words, the organizational attitude in approaching the business, also known as entrepreneurial orientation (Miller, 1983) relies on both historical local roots, in terms of where the firm was founded, and emotional patterns, in the form of the beliefs and values of the family. In this section, after a review of the concepts of entrepreneurial orientation and family influence factors, the nexus between those two catalysts in the context of entrepreneurship in small family firms is addressed.

A stream of scholars (Wales et al., 2011; Baker & Sinkula, 2009; Lumpkin & Dess, 1996) define entrepreneurial orientation as the strategic mindset and organizational attitude based on which entrepreneurs take business actions and make decisions. Entrepreneurial orientation was first investigated by Miller (1983) who characterized it based on three essential dimensions: innovativeness, proactiveness and risk-taking. Innovativeness is defined as the capability to develop new products and create different business opportunities and to enhance existing business processes and systems by discovering alternative solutions through experimentation and a problem-solving attitude (Lumpkin & Dess, 1996). Proactiveness is the capacity to acknowledge potential opportunities concerning the core business, stakeholder relationships and supply chain management. In other words, this attitude serves to prevent and anticipate strategic decisions in order to achieve results in the short-term period, but also to envision a forward-thinking view. Innovativeness and proactiveness can help to strategically identify opportunities in the market and develop new sustainable business ventures (Jansson, Nilsson, Modig, & Hed Vall, 2017; Menguc & Ozanne, 2005). The risk-taking orientation can be defined as the entrepreneurial attitude that contradistinguishes entrepreneurs from hired employees because of the uncertainty of self-employment (Lumpkin & Dess, 1996). Several researchers (Morck & Yeung, 2003) agree that, generally, family firms are less prompt in taking risks, and consequently, they make more prudential choices due to their higher risk aversion (Schulze, Lubatkin, & Dino, 2002) and the context of increasing asymmetry of information.

Lumpkin and Dess (1996) extend the entrepreneurial orientation framework as conceptualized by Miller (1983) by including two additional features: competitive aggressiveness and autonomy. Competitive aggressiveness is a firm's capacity to "directly and intensely challenge its competitors to achieve entrepreneurship or improve positions, to outperform industry rivals in the marketplace" (Lumpkin & Dess, 1996; p. 148). Autonomy is the independence to take entrepreneurial decisions that lead to development. Literature has previously classified these entrepreneurial orientation attributes according to the impact on business affairs in terms of business performance and economic sustainability and the effect on business continuity as well as managerial organization. In particular, entrepreneurial orientation affects performance in terms of sales growth, market share, profitability and stakeholder satisfaction (Lumpkin & Dess, 1996). With respect to the effect on business continuity, Lumpkin et al. (2010) have found that innovativeness, proactiveness and autonomy are strictly related to long-term objectives, whereas competitive aggressiveness and autonomy mainly affect short-term business decisions. Furthermore, entrepreneurial orientation has been also studied in relation to family involvement in the business in order to clarify the extent to which family involvement leads to competitive advantage and strategic synergies.

Family involvement is generally known as the presence of family in the business context, and it has been assessed based on the family influence factors: power, experience and culture (i.e., F-PEC) (Frank et al., 2010). The F-PEC framework integrates the components of the involvement approach with the essence of the family influence approach. F-PEC combines the components of family involvement (i.e., power) and more attitudinal and intrinsic elements (i.e., experience and culture). Power depends on family ownership, governance, and management involvement. Experience is typically influenced by a family's previous generations and their activity in terms of both management and governance. Finally, culture is connected to family values and business values, which typically converge to form family business commitment (Astrachan, Klein, & Smyrnios, 2002).

Authors have studied how power, experience and culture interact with family business activity (Astrachan, & Smyrnios, Klein, 2005; Astrachan et al., 2002;). They have analyzed the family influence on business success, failure, strategy, and operations, as well as family impact on the long-term survival of the business through different generations (Lumpkin et al., 2010). Similarly, (Holt, Rutherford, & Kuratko, 2010) have investigated the impact of family influence factors on long-term commitment, by defining the F-PEC framework as follows: power influences governance and management mechanisms; experience bridges the nexus between one generation and the upcoming ones; culture serves a moderating role in the alignment between the family's and firms' goals (Klein et al., 2005). These three dimensions are considered as a measure of familiness (Frank et al., 2010). Habbershon and Williams (1999) define familiness "as the unique bundle of resources a particular firm has because of the systems of interactions between the family, its individual members, and the business" (p. 11). The familiness characteristics are a range of specific resources and capabilities that family businesses possess and develop due to the interaction between values and core-business actions. As a matter of fact, families are crucial in "guiding both the family and the firm's decision-making" (Zellweger & Sieger, 2012).

Thus, family influence factors represent the key elements and distinguishing features by which familiness influences the direction of the business and the decision-making process. The family influence factors can affect entrepreneurial orientation at various levels, and family involvement in management is expected to be positive with regard to reducing the risk of business failure (Revilla, Pérez-Luño, & Nieto, 2016) and influencing business performance (Sciascia, Mazzola, Astrachan, & Pieper, 2012).

The first aim of the research is to investigate how family influence factors form the entrepreneurial attitudes or orientations of small family firms, and how factors and orientations affect the decision-making process with regard to sustainability. In this section, we report the set of factors and orientations (Fig. 1) that we aim to demonstrate interlinks between, by responding to the first research question

(RQ1): How do family influence factors affect the entrepreneurial orientation of small family firms?

Sustainability: Definitions and Implications for Small Family Business

The word sustainability is used in a plurality of contexts with wide meanings—from the protection of biodiversity to the guaranty of world development without compromising on the wellbeing of the present generations and the capacity of future ones "to meet their own needs" (Bruntland, 1987; p. 8). In management literature, this concept is defined as the ability to sustain social, environmental and economic objectives through fair and ethical business behaviors and actions that involve commitment to stakeholders at the core of any activity (Harrison & Freeman, 1999; Freeman, 1984).

Figure 1. Family influence factors and entrepreneurial orientation
Source: Authors' elaboration based on various literature sources

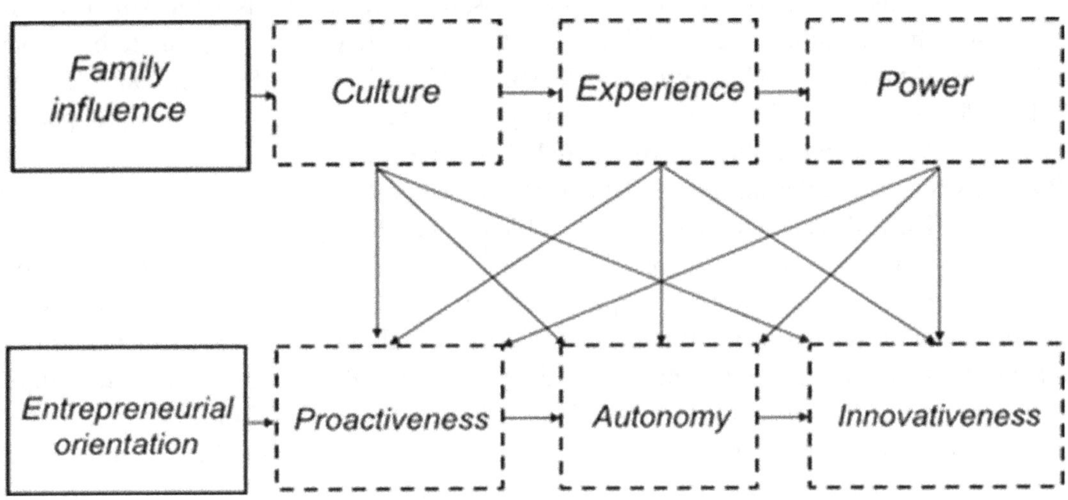

Within a business context, the institutionalization of all implemented practices and attitudes to achieve sustainable outcomes typically refers to the CSR approach. The World Business Council for Sustainable Development (WBCSD) defines CSR as ''the commitment of business to contribute to sustainable economic development, working with employees, their families and the local communities'' (WBCSD, 2001). CSR is therefore viewed as a compelling strategy for dealing with the shrinkage of resources and environmental and social concerns that companies implement to different extents and with various implications, based on the features of specific industries and the size of the business (de Colle, Henriques, & Sarasvathy, 2014; Freeman, Harrison, Wicks, Parmar, & de Colle, 2010; Jamali et al., 2009; Campbell, 2007). However, some characteristic traits of CSR can be identified in the following activities: implementation of standards and norms in order to meet fair criteria for ethics, environment, quality and human resources; development of strategic philanthropy programs (Porter & Kramer, 2002) that vary from cash donations to the creation of social enterprises, in order to increase a firm's engagement with their reference communities; and the development of sustainable products and processes that make use of recyclable materials, or are based on systematic waste management programs and an overall redesign of business models (Visser, 2012). According to Freeman et al. (2010) the more CSR programs are coherent to the companies' core business and are designed to integrate economic, social and environmental outcomes—overcoming a residual and rhetoric approach—the more integrated value they create for their stakeholders (Visser & Kymal, 2015). Integrating the triple bottom line principles (Elkington, 1994) in a comprehensive strategy for responsibility means that companies interiorize a cooperative approach with their stakeholders based on continuous dialogue and partnership creation with them (Strand & Freeman, 2015). The transition from residual approaches to integrated logics of CSR has led to a proliferation of CSR literature on successful practices that has possibly improved the impact on society and the company's performance (Harrison & Wicks, 2013) and reiterated some of the old skeptical debates around companies' natures and the dualism between wealth creation and social responsibility (Clement-Jones, 2005).

While a stream of scholars attributes such debate to and argue over the meanings and implications of CSR within large companies—typically multinational corporations subjected to a higher level of scrutiny (Brammer & Pavelin, 2006)—there is now growing academic interest in CSR implementation within SMEs (Williams & Schaefer, 2013) as they are now the engine of many economies (such as the EU) (Vallejo, 2008; Jenkins, 2006). At the same time, there is now increasing interest in family businesses and CSR, because of their peculiar system of relationships, which tightly binds them to their stakeholders and their communities in an informal, flexible and yet more stable way that appears to be intrinsically responsible and sustainable (Niehm, Swinney, & Miller, 2008; Déniz & Suárez, 2005; Uhlaner, van Goor-Balk, & Masurel, 2004). Therefore, small family businesses clearly present a heap of peculiarities with regard to the way sustainability is pursued and CSR is designed.

CSR as such does not fit the attitudes and the implemented practices of small family businesses. One of the reasons is that CSR is not completely applicable to small family firms: this is an issue related to both terminology and the interpretation of CSR in the context of business size. As explained by Freeman and Velamuri (2006), why would companies of any size be excluded from the process of joint value creation with all stakeholders? It is a fact that small family businesses are more entangled with their stakeholders and participate in community value creation with them through relationships based on trust (Spence, 2007; Jenkins, 2006; Perrini, 2006). Therefore, the stakeholder approach—which is the root for developing CSR in larger companies—applies even more in smaller family contexts, and this justifies the inclusion of Company instead of Corporate in Freeman and Velamuri's CSR definition.

The second reason why CSR as such needs new interpretations is related to the use of the word social: in the authors' view, the use of this word implies a separation from and a trade-off with the economic aspect of responsibility. However, if we consider sustainability as the integration of economic, social and environmental objectives, CSR should not mark any separation between these objectives, but instead, should integrate them. This makes even more sense for smaller businesses, which, by intrinsically acknowledging ethics and values in their relationships with stakeholders, confirm the idea that the concept of CSR is "superfluous" (Freeman & Velamuri, 2006; p. 5). If the responsibility of creating value for stakeholders replaces mere social responsibility, CSR becomes an acronym for company stakeholder responsibility (Freeman & Velamuri, 2006).

Remarking on the criticisms of residual and traditional CSR logics, which do not consider a wider range of companies and responsibilities at multiple levels, Visser (2012) suggests further approaches to CSR and describes them as Corporate Sustainability and Responsibility and systemic CSR or CSR 2.0. According to the author, these new conceptualizations of CSR allow to take into account current urgent social and environmental matters through an inclusive logic. Stakeholder involvement and innovative partnerships represent the solutions for achieving sustainable outcomes in the form of reconfigured business models and products/services. Visser's understanding of CSR reflects the shift from "few and big" to "many and small" (2012; p. 9) and is therefore applicable to small family businesses, as they possess a DNA founded on joint individual and business interests and an interlinked network of stronger relationships with stakeholders (Besser, 2012; Spence, Habisch, & Schmidpeter, 2004).

The peculiar nature of small family businesses constitutes fertile ground for sustainability and responsibility to be included in the firm's core business in a much more transparent and integrated way than in larger corporations, even though the implementation would be much less formalized and standardized (Jamali et al., 2009). This statement has several justifications. The first justification is the relevance of proximity for small family firms. The physical proximity of managers, owners and family members to the reference groups of stakeholders favors continuous dialogue and collaborations, even in a more informal way (Besser, 2012; Russo & Tencati, 2009). This can lead to the creation of a sort of morally implicit contract according to which owners become personally accountable for the social performance of their activity, and therefore, integrity becomes the key to foster commitment, trust, personal engagement and the maintenance of good relationships and positive stakeholder perception (Spence, 2007; Jenkins, 2006; Vives, 2006). Proximity can also result in sustainable advantages such as a shorter supply chain, which family owners can better control for implementing sustainable sourcing, processes and products and spreading their culture more effectively. Secondly, the way small family businesses deal with internal stakeholders, such as employees and management, who do not belong to the family is based on a larger extent to the attention they pay toward their needs; these businesses tend to place importance on good health conditions and balanced relationships between work and family, which gives internal stakeholders higher motivation to be part of the "family" (Jenkins, 2006; Vives, 2006). According to this logic, strategic philanthropy has more chances of being tailored on the actual community's and firm's needs as family, owners, employees and management are all part of that community. Thirdly, the fact that the territory where the small firm was originally founded is, in the majority of cases, the place where family members and business owners still live and conduct their business, personal choices and business choices converge to safeguard the wellbeing of that particular territory and foster its development for the benefit of all (Basco, 2015). Eventually, in many cases, small family firms capitalize on their uniqueness and flexibility to formally and informally partner together with other firms in the same reference territory to strengthen their competitiveness through integrated products and services that are delivered to an enlarged concept of community. This increases the impact of social, environmental and economically sustainable outcomes. Traditional conceptualizations of competition à la Porter shift towards collaboration among small family businesses to facilitate innovative forms of entrepreneurship and create more social and intellectual capital (Perrini, 2006), which can lead to the establishment of common patterns of sustainability due to a higher power of advocacy. It is not surprising that groups of small businesses can foster local sustainability by implementing waste management practices, providing access to alternative energy sources, creating greater impact through shared recycling policies, and exchanging materials and best practices for reuse of materials.

For better clarity and coherency in the context of the business size hereby considered, sustainability will be referred to as a concept that groups together: new conceptualizations of CSR including the integration of environmental responsibility, social concerns and economic sustainability.

This chapter aims at examining how factors influence the sustainability approach in family SMEs and its patterns, in order to shape future research around small family business motivations and antecedents to sustainability and responsibility that can contribute to make such an approach—if and when it is effective—replicable in firms with similar characteristics in terms of size and contextual conditions. Therefore, this research seeks, as a second step, to answer the following research question.

(RQ2): How do factors and orientations shape sustainability patterns in small family firms?

MAIN FOCUS OF THE CHAPTER

The Context: Evolutions in the Food and Beer Industry

In the last few years, there have been some growing trends in the food and beer industry that are transforming firms' business models and necessitating a redefinition of priorities and stakeholder relationships. Among these trends, the main ones are linked to a shift in consumers' mentality towards more responsible and sustainable contents. None of the current approaches to food consider it as satisfying a nutritional purpose: it is, in most cases, a way of living, a state of mind, a "political act" (Petrini, 2012), an "agricultural act" (Berry, Dernini, Burlingame, Meybeck, & Conforti, 2015), a social activity or a contribution to society—in other words, a potential way to enhance sustainability. Culturally, such a revolution takes place in a new consciousness that aims at achieving multiple goals: conserving the natural and nutritional characteristics of food and incrementing its access to all (Shiva, 2016); reconstructing the link between enterprises and local economies, local economies being all the communities within which a firm interacts with stakeholders through supply chain activities; and keeping the food culture alive in order to recover and communicate traditional values and beliefs (Cacciolatti, Garcia, & Kalantzakis, 2015). In this context, food is not considered a mere source of profit; instead, it needs to be interpreted as a crucial element for reaching an "Earth Democracy" (Shiva, 2010) and for fostering a sustainable way of sourcing and living through the achievement of "Food Independence" (Petrini, 2016). One of the main challenges for food independency is certainly to be found in the supply chain and its autonomy. This is why many players in the food industry are working toward tracing back each activity to obtain a zero-waste supply chain, along with a guaranty of quality at any level and, therefore, sustainability.

Another trend is the growing market expectation for food companies to act in the interest of social, health and environmental issues (Zepeda & Reznickova, 2017). Accordingly, the commodity-oriented approach to food has evolved into a strategy-oriented approach. That is, when the commercial response to consumers' needs is accompanied by all the intangible, cultural and social characterizations of food products, sustainability shifts from being an intrinsic approach to a common strategy within the enterprise.

Following the changes within food culture, the beer sector has also transformed dramatically, and an economic and consumption revolution has occurred. The "craft beer revolution" that started in the United States underlines a cultural and commercial approach that has extended to countries that are not typically beer producers, such as Italy for instance (Fastigi, Esposti, & Viganò, 2015; Hindy, 2014). In the American case, a cultural "neolocalism," was born out of home brewing (Schnell & Reese, 2014) due to regional distribution of microbreweries (Cabras, Higgins, & Preece, 2016) "that are meaningful in reference to the history of the field" (Lamertz, Foster, Coraiola, & Kroezen, 2016; p. 819). In Italy, consumers' new orientations toward "quality, choice and variety" (Thurnell-Read, 2016; p. 68) have a history of twenty years and are associated with the growing popularity of craft beer, which was started by the owner of Baladin, Teo Musso (Musso & Drago, 2013). In fact, Lorenzo Kuaska Dabove, the most well-known Italian beer critic, defines the national phenomenon as a "new Made in Italy", which conventionally started in 1996, with the opening of the first craft breweries, such as Baladin (Musso & Drago, 2013). According to Biancolillo et al. (2014), the Italian "Beer Renaissance" or "craft beer revolution" (Hindy, 2014) is motivated by the same cultural change that marks food transformation—the shift from a mass and "fast" to a "slow food" consumption model (Garavaglia, 2015). Consumers become better tasters, because they start understanding the importance of sharing passion and experience associated with the food and beer flavors (Donadini & Porretta, 2017; Fastigi et al., 2015; Garavaglia, 2015; Schnell & Reese, 2014). Clearly, as evident in the food industry, beer consumers forge their identity based on new experiences in beer consumption, which are strongly connected with the territory, its biodiversity, and local peculiarities and needs (Garavaglia, 2015).

The context within which the sustainable approach of Baladin and its link with family influence and entrepreneurial orientation is investigated is peculiar in nature. In fact, the craft beer phenomenon is already an expression of some of the characteristics of sustainability, social responsibility and stakeholder engagement. According to contemporary definitions, craft is considered as an active and relational concept that is "oppositional to the anonymity of disembodied mass-production" (Thurnell-Read, 2014; p.2). Craft represents a mix of skills, passion and good relationships and the use of traditional ingredients without adjuncts (Toro-González, McCluskey, & Mittelhammer, 2014). In this sense, beer is considered an element of protection and enhancement of a territory, to foster locally-based economies (Schnell & Reese, 2014).

The food and beer evolution is a very strategic challenge and opportunity that has affected multiple spheres of interest—from economics and marketing, to society and relations. The echoed attention to food and beer products represents a big opportunity for job creation, attention to stakeholders, an orientation toward biodiversity protection and waste reduction, intensified use of local ingredients, and adoption of sustainable and quality-oriented food and beer production processes (Nicholls & Murdock, 2012).

Methodology

In order to address the aforementioned research questions, a single case study methodology (Yin, 2013) has been employed. According to the literature, a single case study is used when researchers need to understand the meanings of a particular event, the activities and the actions undertaken by the firm or the contexts within which the firm operates (Maxwell, 2008). Case studies are "empirical descriptions of particular instances of a phenomenon that are typically based on a variety of data sources" (Eisenhardt, 2007; p. 25); they might serve as a theoretical illustration or description and be useful for theory testing and theory refinement (Voss, Tsikriktsis, & Frohlich, 2002; Handfield & Melnyk, 1998). The uniqueness of the case study compared to the prior literature makes it suitable for illustrating whether existing literature addresses the phenomenon under investigation or whether new areas of research can emerge and new theories can be generated (Eisenhardt & Graebner, 2007; Eisenhardt, 1989). One of the most remarkable strengths of a case-based methodology is its potential to identify insights that a large survey would have not have identified (Chetty, 1996).

This study has been developed around an Italian small-family craft beer producer, which is a peculiar object of investigation, because of its leading position in the market despite its small size, its strong link with sustainability and the unique and well-recognized entrepreneur characteristics that mark a sort of turnaround compared with typical family business behaviors.

In order to more effectively illustrate how family factors, entrepreneurial orientations and approach to sustainability are interlinked, inter-affected and forged in this case, the authors use the method of data triangulation (Yin, 2013). To this end, three methods were employed—systematic review of the literature, semi-structured interviews, and observations. The systematic review included the literature on family influence factors, entrepreneurial orientation, sustainable approaches within small family businesses, and food and beer industry characteristics. The semi-structured interviews (Russel Bernard, 1988) were conducted with primary sources of information such as the firm's owner, marketing manager and public relation manager. Finally, extra information was obtained through secondary sources by directly observing phenomena within the firm (by conducting several site visits) and by analyzing the company's reports, books and stakeholders' opinions gathered through news and blogs. Eventually, for contextualization and conceptual interpretation of information (Borgerson, Schroeder, Escudero Magnusson, & Magnusson, 2009), quotes from the respondents were adopted, which allowed the illustration of themes that emerged from the literature and favored the understanding of how these themes are interlinked (Arnold & Fischer, 1994).

The case study was carried out over a period of 12 months, starting in June 2016, and involved two main steps. The first was to gain a general understanding of the company's history, main strategies and current and future approach to sustainability through analysis of reports and documents and a questionnaire sent to the marketing and PR managers and the owner. The questionnaire aimed at gathering general information about strategic orientation with regard to a variety of matters (including sustainable production, link with the territory, and activities to engage stakeholders). The objective of the second phase was to deepen the analysis by discussing the gathered responses through semi-structured interviews conducted on multiple occasions in order to cross-check collected information. It also expanded the investigation to the influence of the family and the emergence of entrepreneurial orientations that affect sustainability through several meetings with the business owner and company visits.

The analysis of data and information involved three steps. First, the interviews were transcribed, reviewed and summarized. Second, the interviews were matched with models and frameworks reported in the literature. Third, a schematic view (Lau & Woodman, 1995; Ranson, Hinings, & Greenwood, 1980) was adopted to illustrate theories and highlight the interlinks among family influence factors, entrepreneurial orientations and approach to sustainability emerging from the case study.

Baladin: The Leading Small Italian Craft Beer Firm

In 1986, Teo Musso, the founder of the Baladin brewery, opened the first Le Baladin pub in his hometown, Piozzo, a small village located in the province of Cuneo, Piedmont, an area famous for hosting Italy's most well-known wine cultivations, such as Barolo and Dolcetto. In 1996, ten years later, the pub was converted into a brewpub, which produced Baladin's first craft beer: Super Baladin. In 1997, Musso began to produce a series of beers dedicated to his family: Isaac (the name of his son), Wayan (his daughter), and Nora (the mother of his children). In 2003, as the demand for beer grew, he decided to move production to a family-owned former henhouse and created the Baladin distribution department. In 2005, Michael Jackson, "The Beer Hunter," included Isaac in the Italian edition of his guide to the 500 best world beers. In the same year, Musso, the first Italian to receive an award from the large Danish beer producer Carslberg, received the Semper Ardens Award for Beer Culture, a prize commemorating Musso's contribution to the development and promotion of beer culture. In 2006, Baladin launched a cooperation with the local Institute for Agricultural Studies, taking its first step towards becoming a "farm brewery" through cereals farming and the development of a 100% Italian supply chain. With Lorenzo Kuaska Dabove – the most famous beer critic – Musso developed a new beer tasting glass called the TEKU, drawing the name from the union of TEo and KUaska. In 2007, he extended his business by opening Casa Baladin: a restaurant offering special beer-based menus in various rooms and relaxation areas. The year 2008 marked Riad Baladin's Morocco opening and the launch of the Open project, the first experimental initiative to share an open source beer recipe replicable by homebrewers. In the same year, Baladin extended the Bottega Baladin challenge, adding more classic food and beer products and a selection of clothes and fabrics. In 2009, further steps toward the creation of a 100% Italian beer were taken with Baladin's first hops planting. The same year witnessed the launch of Open Baladin Roma (Italy): a large pub with no fewer than 40 taps and more than 100 Italian craft beer labels. In 2010, Musso pioneered an innovative distribution formula for selling draught craft beer in reusable glass bottles. In 2011, Baladin landed in New York (US) through the US brand Eataly (Oscar Farinetti), and Musso presented his first 100% Italian craft beer, an achievement he celebrated by naming the beer Nazionale. Musso also honored his commitment to his territory and family, both characterized by a history of wine, through the Terre and Lune project, which focuses on producing barley wine from malt. In 2012, Baladin officially became a farm brewery and changed its legal status and name to Birrificio Baladin Società Agricola (Agricultural Firm). In 2014, the Open project was expanded to Turin (Italy), and the project launched an engagement strategy to involve homebrewers by distributing malt extract kits that allowed them to produce their own Baladin-style beers. The year 2015 marked a breakthrough in the beer packaging and distribution sector with the production of the first craft beer in can: an option with less environmental impact in terms of waste and recycling. In 2016, the new Baladin brewery plant in Piozzo was opened as an expression of a new structure for increasing local stakeholders' consciousness and engagement. The plant is surrounded by the Baladin Garden, which attracts visitors who wish to experience Baladin's world.

SOLUTIONS AND RECOMMENDATIONS

Connections and Interconnections Between Family Influence Factors and Entrepreneurial Orientation

Family factors had a very interesting impact on Musso's entrepreneurial orientation and sustainability approach, since they affected his personal and business choices in a way that nearly directly opposed the traditional rules of family business. Musso's family held economic power through traditional agricultural activities and wine production, and the main lesson the family transferred to young Musso was financial stability. Musso described his family's orientation by recalling the words of his father, who said: "We have always done so; therefore, we must do so." This conservative orientation appears to oppose innovation and risk-taking. However, according to Musso, on one hand, this orientation gave him remarkable autonomy and the assurance that "things done in the same way will lead me to more sustainable economic outcomes." On the other hand, the personal experiences and interests Musso had during his youth helped him develop a strong sense of proactiveness. To describe his own entrepreneurial orientation, Musso refers to the image of a funambulist (i.e. tightrope walker) in a circus—one of his greatest passions. Specifically, he describes his entrepreneurial ability as one of constantly maintaining equilibrium, even in adverse conditions and limited space. This illustrates an approach built on the advantages of both the security and power offered by Musso's family culture and Musso's own risk-taking attitude, which stems from personal choices and charisma.

A trade-off with respect to the influence of family factors in forming Musso's entrepreneurial orientation emerges in Musso's approach to innovation. Musso's family's involvement in agriculture and the wine sector was a natural consequence of their being based in Langhe, which is known for these businesses. In Musso's words: "Imagine an area where wine dominates and it's the only product that sells, in Italy and in foreign countries [...], the only secure activity that sons are expected to preserve, continue and, when possible, expand [...]. Imagine me sitting in a table with my family and refusing to drink wine, because 'I only like beer' [...]." Clearly, the family expected successors to continue the family's traditions. However, Musso's choices marked a breakthrough in both the continuation of his family's business and the tradition of Langhe. Specifically, his decision to produce beer in what was—at least at the time—a culturally hostile territory was a strong sign of Musso's innovativeness and personal orientations. He took on extreme economic risk, since his family did not support him in his beer production and would have refused to invest more than a nominal amount in innovation focused on testing beer products. Moreover, in order to develop an innovation orientation opposite the path of his family's experience, Musso required training and new experiences in other territories: in other words, a sort of "on-site training" for budding entrepreneurs. Therefore, during his youth, and with the support of his uncle, Musso began a series of study and work trips to a hotel where his uncle led the confectionery department. These trips supported Musso's emancipation and strengthened his freedom of choice. He recalls, "It was during that summer I approached for the first time something that would have modified not only my taste but also my choices: the Blue Chimay." Such personal experiences have always been crucial for Musso's business transformation. In 1996, he took his first trip to Belgium to work for the large beer producer Brasserie d'Achouffe and learn the technical aspects of the business. He later expanded his experience into the philosophical realm by sharing his knowledge and visions with Jean-Luis Dits, a brewer at the Brasserie à Vapeur.

A remarkable aspect of Musso's entrepreneurial approach that created significant local tension is his choice of his family's home village as Baladin's production site, headquarters, and main cultural hub, where Musso has developed incredibly strong commitments. Innovativeness is a new family power that Musso developed by formally and informally involving his own family members (partners and children) in his business. As noted previously, two of his most well-known beers are named after his daughter and son. By making these choices, Musso has combined a proactive orientation (as the first craft beer producer in Langhe and, more broadly, in Italy) with the influence of his family's culture and the choice to establish all of his activities in Piozzo as way to rebuild his relationship with his father following initial tensions. Thus, in Musso's words, even though "Beer is the result of a teenage conflict between father and son, Beer is Earth" (where "Earth" refers to Piozzo as the origin and expression of Musso's family's culture).

Factors and Orientations Forming Baladin's Sustainable Approach

Baladin's sustainable approach will be described in relation to the peculiarities that make small businesses more interested in sustainability, which are underlined in the third section of this chapter. Particular focus will be paid to: the key role of proximity in shaping the sustainable approach; the advantages of closer relationships with external and internal stakeholders facilitated by commitments to local territory; and greater chances for partnering formally and informally with stakeholders.

The way that Musso set up Baladin's supply chain leverages the advantages of proximity and Musso's choice to establish all of his business activities in Piozzo. One of his most ambitious goals since the beginning of his business activity has been the creation of an autonomous and independent local supply chain. In 2006, the brewery planted its first experimental field of cereals for beer production in the Piedmont region, which it later expanded to the Basilicata region. Thus, through a cooperation with the local Institute for Agricultural Studies, the first national cultivation of hops. The aim was to demonstrate that "Beer is Earth" and to establish a stronger connection between farming and production. Though this connection is clear in winemaking, brewing is still considered a "chemical alchemy." These experiments led to the production of Nazionale, the first 100% Italian beer, which the operation manager describes as a "one-of-a-kind production, made from only Italian raw ingredients, local processing and higher local sustainable impacts." In Musso's view: "this is achievable only through continuous and trustworthy collaborations among all local stakeholders." This is why the role played by local agriculture-oriented institutions and strong commitments from suppliers were crucial to the achievement. To reflect its desire to reconcile farming and production, in 2012, Baladin became a farm brewery and changed its legal name to Birrificio Baladin Società Agricola (Agricultural Firm).

Musso's vision has always been oriented toward the maintenance of local agricultural activities. He uses innovation as a trigger strategy to develop products and processes that are sustainable to their core, from material to distribution. The first tangible example of this orientation is the innovative distribution formula of draught craft beer sold through reusable glass bottles, an experiment that Musso began in 2010 and strengthened in later years. In 2012, Musso's other innovations included sealing classic beers with corks and protecting them with a layer of shellac made of all natural and recyclable materials. The year 2015 marks a breakthrough in the beer packaging sector as craft beer was produced and distributed for the first time in a can: a much more environmentally friendly option than plastic in terms of the amount of waste and lean recycling processes.

The attention to energy use, water, recycling and reuse are all central to Baladin's priorities. "We have embarked on a path towards becoming completely independent in covering our energy needs," Musso states, explaining that, "both the brewery and the Baladin pubs and restaurants are powered exclusively with electricity from renewable sources. Part of it is produced directly through its photovoltaic system." Currently, solar cells cover approximately 80% of the electric and mechanical energy needs of the production plant and the brewery. The remaining 20% of energy is 100% renewable. "We want to invest to make sure that the environmental impact of our production processes is kept to a minimum, and this is the basis for becoming independent from external sources," says Baladin's operation manager. Furthermore, Baladin purifies its wastewater and reintroduces it into the environment and uses a heat recovery system coming from the fermentation cellar in the beer re-fermentation room, thereby avoiding the use of fuels. Baladin also provides animal feed and fertilizers for local farms via the processing of brewers' grains. To strengthen the circularity of waste and materials, Baladin's research and development department is currently studying a new process that will permit the brewers' grains to serve as the heat source for the entire plant (including the production area, warehouse, reception area, and offices).

Clearly, family culture has played a crucial role in Musso's choice of production land and his attachment and respect for such territory. By contrast, Musso's orientation toward innovation for sustainability is something that his has learned over the course of his personal life experiences by meeting unique brewers and developing the capacity to understand the complex beer market. Neither Musso nor his collaborators consider Baladin's sustainable innovation a strategy for sustainability; instead, "it is simply the way to be on the market and to be a craft producer," says Musso. Similarly, the marketing manager at Baladin explains: "the sustainable approach is in our DNA, in our core; it is not formalized because it does not need to be; it is just how we do things. That is why we do not communicate much about it."

Baladin's commitment to the local community has allowed the company to create stronger relationships with external and internal stakeholders. Musso considers Baladin's human resources to be an extension of a new and diverse concept family. Hence, he has created a working climate that focuses on cooperation and dialogue to find and discuss new ideas and solutions. The concept of family is most evident in the ideation of a place to meet and discuss, which is directly related to a typical home picture: the dining table (i.e. the corporate restaurant) as a pleasant place for assembling members and continuing work in a convivial and more relaxed atmosphere. The enlargement of the family to employees also extends outside the firm to local stakeholders and communities where Baladin has expanded its activities and distribution. Over time, Baladin has created numerous cultural events and sponsored several local initiatives in Piozzo area, including the musical festival organized in 2017 for its 29th edition. Music is a great passion of Musso's, who says that: "one of the pillars of the pub, in addition to beer, of course, was music in its many expressions." Because of this passion, Baladin has supported the creation of La Scala del Re, a music school "for everyone," "a 'clean' place for children, where people can meet after work or after school to communicate through the wonderful language of music." This school not only exemplifies Musso's personal philanthropic involvement, typical of a small family business, but also connects and links the core business of Baladin to social causes of interest. Therefore, it makes the philanthropic approach more strategic, to the point that the brewery named one famous beer after a music genre: Rock'n'Roll.

The approach described above demonstrates an evolution of the concept of family in which the village itself is a kind of "extended family," with grander relationships, values, opportunities, and responsibilities. The most important confirmation of this perception, according to Musso, has been the recent opening of the Baladin Open Garden: the park of Italian craft beer. This is "a space devoted to agriculture and the revitalization of a place […] a meeting place for the community […] open and available to anyone" tells the Marketing Manager. The Garden hosts several cooperation experiences with the University of Gastronomic Sciences located in Pollenzo, where students can both learn how to make craft beer and contribute with their knowledge to the improvement of different business aspects and beer recipes at Baladin. As Teo Musso states: "I hope that each visitor can rediscover a part of themselves in the garden, and join in the spirit of a project that aims at creating culture and a community around the values of the earth and craft beer". The Garden emphasizes Baladin's conception of beer as "culture and sharing" by solidifying the firm's availability and orientation toward cooperation with consumers and competitors. This mental "opening" originated in 2008 with the Open project, which sought to create "the first 'open source' beer in Italy" by publishing a recipe replicable by homebrewers. This is a new communication strategy for beer culture dissemination. The project was later extended to Open pubs (in Rome, Turin, and Cuneo), which sell, in addition to Baladin products, beers from other selected Italian craft breweries. Musso describes the Open project as "an important window to producers." The same can be said of the Open Baladin Fest, a festival of Italian craft brewers where visitors can taste an average of 160 draught beers. For both initiatives, the goal is the same: "using an innovative communication tool to target a mass audience, because innovating also means being able to cooperate" (marketing manager). The important feedback from this "open culture" and, in particular, from the physical opening of the Garden is, according to Musso, the constant and intense presence—even without strong communication actions—of Piozzo elders and local senior citizens. This is an exciting proof and demonstration that even tradition can be simultaneously undermined and restructured to reach an engagement, as long as the audience comprehends the social and cultural value of the initiative and trusts the company organizing it. As Musso states, "This is what I mean about 'territory:' the strongest conquest in making myself understood and sharing my idea." Through networking and partnerships, Baladin strives to educate each stakeholder in the supply chain and a wider audience about the beer culture and ways to achieve and maintain sustainable social, environmental, and economic outcomes. That is why, when Musso describes sustainability, he states that it is "a duty of small enterprises to move and 'sow' culture to the advantage of those—the medium and large firms—who must make choices in the direction of a sustainable growth."

FUTURE RESEARCH DIRECTIONS

Baladin case is relevant for explaining how sustainability can be replicated in other similar contexts and similarly sized businesses that leverage the role of family culture. Given that both the sector and the business size represent peculiarities in the approach to sustainability, interesting avenues for future research are addressed to compare and identify best practices of CSR and sustainable policies among a wider sample of food and beer small family firms. Furthermore, by identifying how CSR and sustainability are carried out in such a peculiar way, the debate around how integrated CSR is concretely implemented and achieved can be strengthened.

CONCLUSION

This research illustrates how sustainability is shaped in small family businesses by family factors and entrepreneurs' own orientations. It furthers the discussion surrounding the sustainable role that family businesses and small enterprises can play in activating a sort of learning process for larger companies to really contribute to sustainable growth.

The study describes the peculiarities that characterize sustainability and responsibility in small businesses (such as proximity and commitment to local territory) and also considers the role of families within such businesses. It shows that family influence factors moderate entrepreneurial orientations toward sustainability and constitute the basis for the formation of a sustainable approach. Through the analysis, we demonstrate that, in the specific case under investigation, family influence acts as a catalyst for sustainability via the culture, which affected the business owner's choice to develop the business on the same land the family had cultivated for generations. However, the issues that push a business to respond sustainably and responsibly are shaped by the challenges of the current economic and social scenario, which are inherently new and unimagined by past generations. Our analysis shows that family culture strongly shapes the choice of production land and continuity in local stakeholder relationships, but also suggests that more innovative sustainable outcomes, such as products and processes, depend on entrepreneurs' proactive and innovative approaches. Such orientations are a matter of competitive advantages that all small businesses potentially possess against sustainability. In the studied case, these advantages, combined with a family culture reinterpreted by the entrepreneur, produced a winning sustainable approach. Most interestingly, Baladin does not even describe this approach as sustainable, since Musso considers sustainable innovations to be the only way to be a craft brewer.

While the Baladin case is relevant for explaining how sustainability can be replicated in other similar contexts and similarly sized businesses that leverage the role of family culture, it also suffers some limitations regarding generalization. In particular, one must consider the intrinsic peculiarities of the business owner, who engaged in a countertrend against his usual family path, ultimately undermining the traditional family business but maintaining a local commitment in order to achieve success.

REFERENCES

Arnold, S. J., & Fischer, E. (1994). Hermeneutics and consumer research. *The Journal of Consumer Research*, *21*(1), 55–70. doi:10.1086/209382

Astrachan, J. H., Klein, S. B., & Smyrnios, K. X. (2002). The F-PEC scale of family influence: A proposal for solving the family business definition problem1. *Family Business Review*, *15*(1), 45–58. doi:10.1111/j.1741-6248.2002.00045.x

Baker, W. E., & Sinkula, J. M. (2009). The complementary effects of market orientation and entrepreneurial orientation on profitability in small businesses. *Journal of Small Business Management*, *47*(4), 443–464. doi:10.1111/j.1540-627X.2009.00278.x

Basco, R. (2015). Family business and regional development-A theoretical model of regional familiness. *Journal of Family Business Strategy*, *6*(4), 259–271. doi:10.1016/j.jfbs.2015.04.004

Berry, E. M., Dernini, S., Burlingame, B., Meybeck, A., & Conforti, P. (2015). Food security and sustainability: Can one exist without the other? *Public Health Nutrition*, *18*(13), 2293–2302. doi:10.1017/S136898001500021X PMID:25684016

Besser, T. L. (2012). The consequences of social responsibility for small business owners in small towns. *Business Ethics (Oxford, England)*, *21*(2), 129–139. doi:10.1111/j.1467-8608.2011.01649.x

Biancolillo, A., Bucci, R., Magrì, A. L., Magrì, A. D., & Marini, F. (2014). Data-fusion for multiplatform characterization of an Italian craft beer aimed at its authentication. *Analytica Chimica Acta*, *820*, 23–31. doi:10.1016/j.aca.2014.02.024 PMID:24745734

Borgerson, J. L., Schroeder, J. E., Escudero Magnusson, M., & Magnusson, F. (2009). Corporate communication, ethics, and operational identity: A case study of Benetton. *Business Ethics (Oxford, England)*, *18*(3), 209–223. doi:10.1111/j.1467-8608.2009.01558.x

Brammer, S., & Pavelin, S. (2006). *Voluntary Environmental Disclosures by Large UK Companies*. Academic Press. doi:10.1111/j.1468-5957.2006.00598.x

Cabras, I., Higgins, D., & Preece, D. (2016). *Brewing, Beer and Pubs: A global perspective*. Springer. doi:10.1057/9781137466181

Cacciolatti, L. A., Garcia, C. C., & Kalantzakis, M. (2015). Traditional Food Products: The Effect of Consumers' Characteristics, Product Knowledge, and Perceived Value on Actual Purchase. *Journal of International Food & Agribusiness Marketing*, *27*(3), 155–176. doi:10.1080/08974438.2013.807416

Campbell, J. L. (2007). Why would corporations behave in socially responsible ways? An institutional theory of corporate social responsibility. *Academy of Management Review*, *32*(3), 946–967. doi:10.5465/AMR.2007.25275684

Casillas, J. C., Moreno, M., & Barbero, J. L. (2010). A Configurational Approach of the Relationship Between Entrepreneurial Orientation and Growth of Family Firms. *Family Business Review*, *23*(1), 27–44. doi:10.1177/0894486509345159

Chetty, S. (1996). The case study method for research in small-and medium-sized firms. *International Small Business Journal*, *15*(1), 73–85. doi:10.1177/0266242696151005

Clement-Jones, T. (2005). *Bottom line issue or public relations exercise. In Investing in Corporate Social Responsibility: A Guide to Best Practice, Business Planning and the UK's Leading Companies* (pp. 5–13). London: Kogan Page.

de Colle, S., Henriques, A., & Sarasvathy, S. (2014). The paradox of corporate social responsibility standards. *Journal of Business Ethics*, *125*(2), 177–191. doi:10.100710551-013-1912-y

Déniz, M. de la C. D., & Suárez, M. K. C. (2005). Corporate social responsibility and family business in Spain. *Journal of Business Ethics*, *56*(1), 27–41. doi:10.100710551-004-3237-3

Donadini, G., & Porretta, S. (2017). Uncovering patterns of consumers' interest for beer: A case study with craft beers. *Food Research International*, *91*, 183–198. doi:10.1016/j.foodres.2016.11.043 PMID:28290323

Eisenhardt, K. M. (1989). Building Theories From Case Study Research. *Academy of Management Review*, *14*(4), 532–550.

Eisenhardt, K. M., & Graebner, M. E. (2007). Theory Building from cases: Opportunities and challenges. *Academy of Management Journal*, *50*(1), 25–32. doi:10.5465/AMJ.2007.24160888

Elkington, J. (1994). Towards the sustainable corporation: Win-win-win business strategies for sustainable development. *California Management Review*, *36*(2), 90–100. doi:10.2307/41165746

EU Commission. (2016). *2016 SBA Fact Sheet — Italy*. Retrieved from https://ec.europa.eu/docsroom/documents

Fastigi, M., Esposti, R., & Viganò, E. (2015). La craft beer revolution in Italia ei birrifici agricoli: traiettorie evolutive e principali criticità. *Argomenti*, (2), 67–92.

Fitzgerald, M. A., Haynes, G. W., Schrank, H. L., & Danes, S. M. (2010). Socially responsible processes of small family business owners: Exploratory evidence from the national family business survey. *Journal of Small Business Management*, *48*(4), 524–551. doi:10.1111/j.1540-627X.2010.00307.x

Frank, H., Lueger, M., Nosé, L., & Suchy, D. (2010). The concept of "Familiness". Literature review and systems theory-based reflections. *Journal of Family Business Strategy*, *1*(3), 119–130. doi:10.1016/j.jfbs.2010.08.001

Freeman, R. E., Harrison, J. S., Wicks, A. C., Parmar, B., & de Colle, S. (2010). *Stakeholder Theory. The state of the art*. Academic Press.

Freeman, R. E., & Velamuri, S. R. (2006). A new approach to CSR: Company stakeholder responsibility. In *Corporate social responsibility* (pp. 9–23). Springer. doi:10.1057/9780230599574_2

Garavaglia, C. (2015). *Entrepreneurship and entry of small firms into a mature industry: the case of microbreweries in Italy*. AAWE Working Paper No. 179–Economics, American Association of Wine Economists.

Habbershon, T. G., & Williams, M. L. (1999). A resource-based framework for assessing the strategic advantages of family firms. *Family Business Review*, *12*(1), 1–25. doi:10.1111/j.1741-6248.1999.00001.x

Handfield, R. B., & Melnyk, S. A. (1998). The scientific theory-building process: A primer using the case of TQM. *Journal of Operations Management*, *16*(4), 321–339. doi:10.1016/S0272-6963(98)00017-5

Harrison, J. S., & Wicks, A. C. (2013). Stakeholder Theory, Value, and Firm Performance. *Business Ethics Quarterly*, *23*(1), 97–124. doi:10.5840/beq20132314

Hindy, S. (2014). *The craft beer revolution: How a band of microbrewers is transforming the world's favorite drink*. Macmillan.

Holt, D. T., Rutherford, M. W., & Kuratko, D. F. (2010). Advancing the field of family business research: Further testing the measurement properties of the F-PEC. *Family Business Review*, *23*(1), 76–88. doi:10.1177/0894486509349943

Jamali, D., Zanhour, M., & Keshishian, T. (2009). Peculiar strengths and relational attributes of SMEs in the context of CSR. *Journal of Business Ethics*, *87*(3), 355–377. doi:10.100710551-008-9925-7

Jansson, J., Nilsson, J., Modig, F., & Hed Vall, G. (2017). Commitment to Sustainability in Small and Medium-Sized Enterprises: The Influence of Strategic Orientations and Management Values. *Business Strategy and the Environment*, *26*(1), 69–83. doi:10.1002/bse.1901

Jenkins, H. (2006). Small business champions for corporate social responsibility. *Journal of Business Ethics*, *67*(3), 241–256. doi:10.100710551-006-9182-6

Jenkins, H. (2009). A "business opportunity"model of corporate social responsibility for small-and medium-sized enterprises. *Business Ethics (Oxford, England)*, *18*(1), 21–36. doi:10.1111/j.1467-8608.2009.01546.x

Klein, S. B., Astrachan, J. H., & Smyrnios, K. X. (2005). The F-PEC scale of family influence: Construction, validation, and further implication for theory. *Entrepreneurship Theory and Practice*, *29*(3), 321–339. doi:10.1111/j.1540-6520.2005.00086.x

Lamertz, K., Foster, W. M., Coraiola, D. M., & Kroezen, J. (2016). New identities from remnants of the past: An examination of the history of beer brewing in Ontario and the recent emergence of craft breweries. *Business History*, *58*(5), 796–828. doi:10.1080/00076791.2015.1065819

Lau, C.-M., & Woodman, R. W. (1995). Understanding organizational change: A schematic perspective. *Academy of Management Journal*, *38*(2), 537–554. doi:10.2307/256692

Lumpkin, G. T., Brigham, K. H., & Moss, T. W. (2010). Long-term orientation: Implications for the entrepreneurial orientation and performance of family businesses. *Entrepreneurship and Regional Development*, *22*(3–4), 241–264. doi:10.1080/08985621003726218

Lumpkin, G. T., & Dess, G. G. (1996). Clarifying the entrepreneurial orientation construct and linking it to performance. *Academy of Management Review*, *21*(1), 135–172.

Maxwell, J. A. (2008). Designing a qualitative study. The SAGE Handbook of Applied Social Research Methods, 2, 214–253.

Menguc, B., & Ozanne, L. K. (2005). Challenges of the "green imperative": A natural resource-based approach to the environmental orientation–business performance relationship. *Journal of Business Research*, *58*(4), 430–438. doi:10.1016/j.jbusres.2003.09.002

Miller, D. (1983). The correlates of entrepreneurship in three types of firms. *Management Science*, *29*(7), 770–791. doi:10.1287/mnsc.29.7.770

Morck, R., & Yeung, B. (2003). Agency problems in large family business groups. *Entrepreneurship Theory and Practice*, *27*(4), 367–382. doi:10.1111/1540-8520.t01-1-00015

Musso, T., & Drago, M. (2013). *Baladin: La birra artigianale è tutta colpa di Teo*. Feltrinelli Editore.

Nicholls, A., & Murdock, A. (2012). The nature of social innovation. In *Social innovation* (pp. 1–30). Springer. doi:10.1057/9780230367098_1

Niehm, L. S., Swinney, J., & Miller, N. J. (2008). Community social responsibility and its consequences for family business performance. *Journal of Small Business Management*, *46*(3), 331–350. doi:10.1111/j.1540-627X.2008.00247.x

Panwar, R., Paul, K., Nybakk, E., Hansen, E., & Thompson, D. (2014). The legitimacy of CSR actions of publicly traded companies versus family-owned companies. *Journal of Business Ethics*, *125*(3), 481–496. doi:10.100710551-013-1933-6

Perrini, F. (2006). SMEs and CSR theory: Evidence and implications from an Italian perspective. *Journal of Business Ethics*, *67*(3), 305–316. doi:10.100710551-006-9186-2

Petrini, C. (2012). *Slow food: le ragioni del gusto*. Gius. Laterza & Figli Spa.

Petrini, C. (2016). *Buono, pulito e giusto*. Giunti Editore.

Porter, M. E., & Kramer, M. R. (2002). The competitive advantage of corporate philanthropy. *Harvard Business Review*, *80*(12), 56–68. PMID:12510538

Ranson, S., Hinings, B., & Greenwood, R. (1980). The structuring of organizational structures. *Administrative Science Quarterly*, *25*(1), 1–17. doi:10.2307/2392223

Revilla, A. J., Pérez-Luño, A., & Nieto, M. J. (2016). Does family involvement in management reduce the risk of business failure? The moderating role of entrepreneurial orientation. *Family Business Review*, *29*(4), 365–379. doi:10.1177/0894486516671075

Russel Bernard, H. (1988). *Research methods in cultural anthropology*. Qualitative and.

Russo, A., & Tencati, A. (2009). Formal vs. informal CSR strategies: Evidence from Italian micro, small, medium-sized, and large firms. *Journal of Business Ethics*, *85*(S2), 339–353. doi:10.100710551-008-9736-x

Schnell, S. M., & Reese, J. F. (2014). Microbreweries, place, and identity in the United States. In *The geography of beer* (pp. 167–187). Springer. doi:10.1007/978-94-007-7787-3_15

Schulze, W. S., Lubatkin, M. H., & Dino, R. N. (2002). Altruism, agency, and the competitiveness of family firms. *Managerial and Decision Economics*, *23*(4-5), 247–259. doi:10.1002/mde.1064

Sciascia, S., Mazzola, P., Astrachan, J. H., & Pieper, T. M. (2012). The role of family ownership in international entrepreneurship: Exploring nonlinear effects. *Small Business Economics*, *38*(1), 15–31. doi:10.100711187-010-9264-9

Shiva, V. (2010). Earth Democracy: Beyond Dead Democracy and Killing Economies. *Capitalism, Nature, Socialism*, *21*(1), 83–95. doi:10.1080/10455751003655922

Shiva, V. (2016). *Who Really Feeds the World? The Failures of Agribusiness and the Promise of Agroecology*. North Atlantic Books.

Spence, L. J. (2007). CSR and small business in a European policy context: The five “C” s of CSR and small business research agenda 2007. *Business and Society Review*, *112*(4), 533–552. doi:10.1111/j.1467-8594.2007.00308.x

Spence, L. J., Habisch, A., & Schmidpeter, R. (2004). *Responsibility and social capital: The world of small and medium sized enterprises*. Palgrave Macmillan. doi:10.1007/978-1-349-72886-2

Spence, L. J., & Rutherfoord, R. (2003). Small business and empirical perspectives in business ethics. *Journal of Business Ethics*, *47*(1), 1–5. doi:10.1023/A:1026205109290

Strand, R., & Freeman, R. E. (2015). Scandinavian cooperative advantage: The theory and practice of stakeholder engagement in Scandinavia. *Journal of Business Ethics*, *127*(1), 65–85. doi:10.100710551-013-1792-1

Thurnell-Read, T. (2014). Craft, tangibility and affect at work in the microbrewery. *Emotion, Space and Society*, *13*, 46–54. doi:10.1016/j.emospa.2014.03.001

Toro-González, D., McCluskey, J. J., & Mittelhammer, R. C. (2014). Beer snobs do exist: Estimation of beer demand by type. *Journal of Agricultural and Resource Economics*, *39*(2), 174–187.

Uhlaner, L. M., van Goor-Balk, H. J. M., & Masurel, E. (2004). Family business and corporate social responsibility in a sample of Dutch firms. *Journal of Small Business and Enterprise Development*, *11*(2), 186–194. doi:10.1108/14626000410537128

Vallejo, M. C. (2008). Is the culture of family firms really different? A value-based model for its survival through generations. *Journal of Business Ethics*, *81*(2), 261–279. doi:10.100710551-007-9493-2

Visser, W. (2012). *The future of CSR: Towards transformative CSR, or CSR 2.0*. Browser Download This Paper.

Visser, W., & Kymal, C. (2015). Integrated value creation (IVC): Beyond corporate social responsibility (CSR) and creating shared value (CSV). *Journal of International Business Ethics*, *8*(1), 29.

Vives, A. (2006). Social and environmental responsibility in small and medium enterprises in Latin America. *Journal of Corporate Citizenship*, 21.

Voss, C., Tsikriktsis, N., & Frohlich, M. (2002). Case research in operations management. *International Journal of Operations & Management Production Management*, *22*. 10.1108/01443570210414329

Wales, W. J., Gupta, V. K., & Mousa, F.-T. (2011). Empirical research on entrepreneurial orientation: An assessment and suggestions for future research. *International Small Business Journal*, *31*(4), 357–383. doi:10.1177/0266242611418261

Williams, S., & Schaefer, A. (2013). Small and medium-sized enterprises and sustainability: Managers' values and engagement with environmental and climate change issues. *Business Strategy and the Environment*, *22*(3), 173–186. doi:10.1002/bse.1740

World Business Council for Sustainable Development. (2001). *The Business Case for Sustainable Development: Making a Difference Towards the Johannesburg Summit 2002 and Beyond*. Available: http://www. wbcsd. org

Yin, R. K. (2013). *Case study research: Design and methods*. Sage Publications.

Zellweger, T., & Sieger, P. (2012). Entrepreneurial orientation in long-lived family firms. *Small Business Economics*, *38*(1), 67–84. doi:10.100711187-010-9267-6

Zepeda, L., & Reznickova, A. (2017). Innovative millennial snails: The story of Slow Food University of Wisconsin. *Agriculture and Human Values*, *34*(1), 167–178. doi:10.100710460-016-9701-8

KEY TERMS AND DEFINITIONS

Corporate Social Responsibility: CSR is therefore viewed as a compelling strategy for dealing with the shrinkage of resources and environmental and social concerns that companies implement to different extents and with various implications, based on the features of specific industries and the size of the business.

Entrepreneurial Orientation: The strategic mindset and organizational attitude based on which entrepreneurs take business actions and make decisions.

Family Influence Factors: These are the factors (such as power, experience, and culture, also known as F-PEC) interacting with family business activity and the family involvement in the business. The F-PEC framework integrates the components of the involvement approach with the essence of the family influence approach. F-PEC combines the components of family involvement (i.e., power) and more attitudinal and intrinsic elements (i.e., experience and culture).

Sustainability: This concept is defined as the ability to sustain social, environmental and economic objectives through fair and ethical business behaviors and actions that involve commitment to stakeholders at the core of any activity.

Chapter 12
The Family Company in Spain:
Its Principal Activity, Its Human Capital, Its Challenge, Its Sustainability

Ma Asunción López-Arranz
Universidad de a Coruña, Spain

ABSTRACT

The objective and justification of the chapter focuses on the importance that family businesses in Spain have in the current business environment, which is characterized by great instability. Also in the center of focus is how these family businesses integrate family values with a sustainable business. Innovation, technological advances, market internationalization, quality requirements, and the differentiation of products and/or services, among others, have led to important reflections on how to organize companies, especially family businesses. Nowadays and as a result of the economic crisis, it has been possible to observe a growing creation of family businesses in Spain, which reflects a driving role of business activity in its capacity to undertake and contribute to innovation. Thus, the figures provided by the Institute of Family Business in 2016 show that 90% of Spanish companies are family businesses and contribute about 60% of Spanish GDP and represent 70% of jobs in the private sector as a whole.

INTRODUCTION

This work strives to analyse the family business by considering its human capital (that is, the people who work in the business) and combining that with the current need for developing sustainable companies (Stafford, Duncan, Danes, & Winter, 1999). The economic and social importance of family businesses cannot be denied. Currently between 50% and 80% of companies have a family nature and among the 500 largest companies, 40% are family-based (1). In Europe, it is estimated that 60% of companies, both small and large, employ between 40% and 50% of workers (EC, 2009). In most economies, a very high percentage of companies are micro-enterprises or SMEs, which explains why most of the family-owned enterprises also belong to this sector.

DOI: 10.4018/978-1-5225-5267-3.ch012

Family businesses as a substantial part of the Spanish productive fabric, cannot be removed from the current tendency towards sustainability, through the implementation of ethical or social values, in achieving their economic objective, everything cannot be win-win (Antequera, González, 2005).

The first studies on the family business from an economic and psychological point of view begin in the decade of the 60s to differentiate it from the rest of the companies. It is in the 70's that analyses of their weaknesses and strengths began (Levison, 1971). Later, in the 1980s, practical studies on family enterprises were started, taking into account the experience gained up to that time (Lansberg, 1983). In Spain studies on family businesses have been developed in the last thirty years. The doctrine has concentrated above all on analysis and research, which has led to a greater knowledge of these enterprises themselves. The importance it has acquired in Spain is determined by the existence of the Family Business Section, within the Scientific Association of Economics and Business Management (ACEDE), which demonstrates the development of family business theme in Spain. The reality shows us the multidisciplinary nature of the literature on family business. It has dealt with different disciplines that analyse issues related to organization, management and human resources, corporate governance, finance or accounting, marketing, or any other aspect of a legal nature. Also, the Network of Chairs of Family Business was created, promoted and coordinated by the Institute of Family Business. In addition, specialized publications have emerged, such as The Family Business Review.

In family businesses, sociological concepts such as domestic family and business family are intermingled. The domestic and business phases are not the same but routes between them are difficult to conceptualize.

However, if we view the domestic family in a more anthropological sense, it would not be an exaggeration to say that the business family moves in the opposite direction, since its proposition is to continue emotionally and economically united beyond the founding generation. But in addition to the differentiating factor of intergenerational continuity, business families are characterized by the fact that this intergenerational continuity soon turns business families into a conglomerate of multiple families (Nogales, 2007).

For the European Union (EU) the family business was the subject of an important analysis by means of a Decree of the European Economic and Social Committee drawn up on 22 January 2015 in accordance with Article 29 (2) of its Rules of Procedure entitled "The family business in Europe as a source of renewed growth and better jobs" (2016/ C013/03), (OJEU of 15/01/2016). It states that "Family businesses form the backbone of many economies around the world and are developing very dynamically. They are a source of economic growth and employment and pay particular attention to conditions at the regional and local levels. The reasons for creating a family business are varied, although all have as common denominator a system of values that comes naturally, a willingness to dedicate and sacrifice and a sense of responsibility facing both the creators of the company and those who take the relay. Family businesses are more capable of going through difficult periods of recession and stagnation, and one of the main reasons for their longevity is the sense of personal responsibility for the company's image" (1.1). The European Economic and Social Committee (EESC) recognizes the unique value of family businesses and states that "the EU and the Member States must establish a framework within which entrepreneurs and family businesses can prosper and within which entrepreneurship can be rewarded". At the same time it calls on the European Commission to implement a strategy to promote best practices in the field of family businesses in the Member States (1.2).

Thus, for the European Union the main characteristics of family businesses are:

1. A long-term perspective that involves the creation of long-lasting relationships with stakeholders (workers, clients, suppliers and local communities).
2. A desire to pass the baton to the next generation as well as the commitment and responsibility towards their workers. These aspects reinforce even more the sense of responsibility within the family business, where relationships are based on trust.
3. A dedication of the greatest possible percentage of its profits to the construction of a solid, independent, innovative and capital-supported business with the primary intention of minimizing risks, so that the company can pass from generation to generation. Family businesses are developed more evenly in order to achieve their long-term (multigenerational) goals.

For the EU, family businesses face a series of challenges that must be overcome and can be divided into two categories: those valid for all companies and those specific to family businesses.

The first category includes all factors affecting a country's economy, such as domestic demand, demography and socio-economic status. In its Decree, the EESC focuses on the second category, namely the specific challenges faced by family businesses that are decisive for their development and growth, as follows:

1. Property that does not consist of liquid assets but everything that the family has been building and developing through the generations and which includes specific values, traditions and technical know-how. For this reason, the transfer of ownership of the company to the next generation is the biggest challenge this type of company faces (COM, 2012).
2. It is therefore obvious that the complex elaboration of a succession plan is an important step for family businesses since the intention of the owners is to leave the company in a good position for the next generation.
3. Each year, some 450,000 companies, which employ approximately two million people, face this challenge. About 150,000 are closed each year due to a failed succession, which means a loss of 600,000 jobs (EU, 2011).
4. The challenge of planning for succession and supporting measures to facilitate the transfer of undertakings, for example in the context of inheritance law or through tax incentives to support such transfers.
5. The attempt to create long-term employment, which contributes to establishing a family business culture. For this reason, family businesses can be an attractive place of work for mothers, for example. This family business environment should be supported, which can be a competitive advantage.
6. Innovation in family businesses should not only focus on traditional markets and products, but also on new innovative solutions.
7. The support of innovation in the family business through an innovative system of public procurement in which prices are not the only criterion for the selection of an offer. Family businesses are characterized by competing on the basis of a high quality service centred on the customer, which is guaranteed, among other things, by the family brand (often the name of the owner or the family of the founder). For this reason, family firms generally do not participate in public tenders whose sole criterion is prices. It has been suggested that the values of the Most Economically Advantageous Tender (MEAT) should be used as evaluation criteria and that this information be disclosed to family businesses.

8. The challenge of globalization, which obliges companies to open themselves to new markets, technologies and skills. Family businesses should take these aspects into account when designing their development strategies. This may mean that they have to be open to new workers, also at the management level.
9. At the national level States should recognize the role of family businesses in the economy and then create favourable conditions for them in the areas of taxation and company law (including laws on family business) and support training for this type of company.
10. Among the countries with specific training for family business owners are Cyprus (Institute of Family Business of the International Institute of Management of Cyprus), France (Master 2 professional: Governance des enterprise familial et patrimonial - M2 GEFP, organized by the University of Bordeaux) and Finland (Omistajuusjahallitustyöskentely -valmennusohjelmajatkajille- Structure of ownership and management of enterprise: training program for successors).There are also family business support organizations that offer courses to family entrepreneurs, for example the Swedish branch of the Family Business Network (FBN) with its Family Business Academy, or the Spanish Family Business Institute, which organizes training.
11. Recognizing the role of family enterprises in the economies of the Member States and supporting them could contribute to the recovery of the family craft tradition.

In order to overcome these risks confronted by family businesses, the European Commission's Decree proposes that when defining patient capital, it is worth considering the possibility of using tax breaks for reinvested earnings. Consideration should also be given to bonuses for family businesses (and not only these) that reinvest their profits and prefer to contribute their own capital rather than resorting to the capital of others.

The development of the work is based on an analytical method consisting of the legal economic analysis of the situation of family businesses in Spain taking into account the European guidelines, from a social sustainability point of view. The methodology used is therefore the framework within the legal social areas, through the study of legislation, collective agreements and jurisprudence and doctrine.

CONCEPT OF A FAMILY BUSINESS

Providing a definition of a family business is an arduous task. It is necessary to start with the three characteristic aspects of these companies: the family, the company and the property structure (Tagiuri, 1982). The incidence of the family aspect affects the other two in determining if a company can be considered a family business. This factor implies that family businesses are more complex than non-family businesses, and therefore require appropriate treatment. Thus, in Spain and Finland, family businesses are defined at the ministerial level, the Ministry of Economy and the Ministry of Commerce, respectively. Spain has defined a family business as one in which "an essential part of its property is in the hands of one or several families whose members intervene decisively in the administration and direction of the business. There is, therefore, a close relationship between ownership and management or, in other words, between the life of the company and the life of the family" (MITC, 2008).

Italy (Civil Code) and Romania also have a definition of family businesses. Hungary has adopted a definition of the agricultural family business. Danish legislation refers to the hiring of young people in family businesses. In Austria, federal legislation provides that establishments in the hands of a family can apply flexible opening hours, and regional legislation on agriculture includes a definition of business. The Lithuanian Supreme Court has issued an opinion according to which a company created on the occasion of a new marriage is to be considered as a family business. In Bulgaria and Slovakia, family co-ownership is taken into account in relation to self-employment activities. The first law in the world dedicated to family business is being prepared in Malta. In the European case, the EU has recommended that a definition of family business be: "the majority of the voting rights is in the possession of the natural person or persons who created the company, or who has acquired its share capital, or is in the possession of their spouses, parents, children or direct heirs"(CESE, 2016, 3.4). This is too broad a definition. The adoption of a common definition in European countries would enable the collection of quantitative data, which in turn would allow the creation of statistics on these companies, once the data were aggregated. These data would make it possible, in particular, to analyse the family business in new Member States, where they play a crucial role.

The doctrine has striven to provide a definition of family business and thus we find authors like Gallo (1993) who distinguishes four types of family businesses: family work company, family management company, family investment company and short-term family company.

- **Family Work Company:** One in which the owners are willing to remain united in the property and in which many of the family members are encouraged to work in it.
- **Family Management Company:** One in which the owners are willing to remain united in the property. This is different than that of the previous paragraph in that only some members of the family, the most qualified for the business activity, are sought out to work in the family business. These would soon be holding positions of responsibility, such as members of the board of directors of the company or the senior management team.
- **Family Investment Company:** One in which the family members are united to make investments in business activities. This consists mainly of their work in the family business, in the adoption of these investment decisions and in the control of investments. Their work would not be so much in the management of the companies in which they have invested, precisely in order to have greater freedom in the formulation and implementation of the strategy.
- **Short-Term Family Business:** One in which the family members are united as owners, more by historical circumstances of inheritance than by a positive manifestation of their will to be united. In this case if a change of circumstances developed and the members of the family had the opportunity to sell their shares, associate with third parties, etc. under appropriate economic conditions, they would do so without worrying about the lack of continuity of the link between their company and their family.

Daily and Thompson (1994) propose a typology of companies using as classification criteria the relationship between the ownership of the company's capital and the person or persons who manage them. Thus, the following types of companies are designated:

- **Family Businesses Proper:** Companies that are directed by the descendants of the founder.
- **Enterprise Companies:** Companies that are led by its founder who is also its current owner.
- **Sole Proprietorships:** Companies that have a single owner but are not run by either the founder or his descendants.
- **Professional Companies:** Companies that are not run by its founder, neither by a single manager, nor by the descendants of the founder.

Ward and Dolan (1998) use a criterion very similar to that used by the previous authors, given that they are based on the ownership structure of family companies, specifically on the distribution of voting power, to classify them as follows:

- Jointly owned and managed family businesses: these companies are characterized by their emphasis on autocracy and being run by one or two of their founders, so that the success and continuity of the company depends on them. Within this category several subtypes are distinguished:
    - Solely owned: a person, usually the founder, holds 100% of the voting power.
    - Matrimonial property: one person, usually the founder and spouse each have 50% of the voting power.
    - Solely owned or matrimonial property with the participation of successors: either a person, almost always the founder, or the latter and spouse jointly control the ownership of capital even though one or some of the members of the next generation participate in the ownership of the property.
    - Owned by successors with parental involvement: The majority of voting power belongs to one person of the next generation but one or both parents still have a stake in the capital.
- Family businesses, Associations of siblings: Despite the fact that in the name of this type of family business the word “sibling” appears, the authors consider that there may be companies whose capital is in the hands of siblings but do not correspond to the characteristics that this type of company has. Similarly, family businesses not controlled by siblings but by cousins or other descendants can be treated, for all purposes, as an association of siblings. Thus, they typify an association of siblings as being comprised of eight or fewer siblings, or four or fewer cousins. Within this consideration can be found evidence of effective ownership control and the possibility of working together. Possible variants of this type of family business include:
    - Jointly owned or equidistributed: when the voting power is more or less evenly distributed.
    - Controlling partner: when one of the owners has the effective control of the company agglutinating the greater voting power and leaving the remaining voting power in the hands of the other partners.
    - Family company consortium of cousins: based on the same observation that we made in the case of sibling society, the authors consider that this type of family business is one whose voting power is divided between nine or more siblings, or between five or more cousins.

In this context, in 2009, the European Group of Family Enterprises agreed on a definition of family business. The proposed definition combines the two traditional ideas of the concept of family business, the participation of members of the same family in ownership and in management. Thus, regardless of size and legal form, if a company is run by its owners, and these belong to a family, it can be considered family. But this definition does not capture a third notion that is also considered important in this type of business. That notion is continuity, that is to say the concept of including future generations and therefore the intention that the business will last over time (Kraus, Pohjola & Koponen, 2012). Thus, a family business can be defined as one in which the members of one or more families participate in an important way in capital of the business, assume responsibilities in its direction and intend to transmit the business to future generations (Lopez-Cozar, 2014).

Two legal terms on the subject can demonstrate two different realities, family business on the one hand and family entrepreneur on the other. The first would be a capitalist association in which two or more families unite as entrepreneurs holding power of management in addition to ownership in the company. The second could be defined as any individual or corporate employer who hires a family member for any type of work (Ron, 2011).

Considering international labour standards such as the International Labour Organization (ILO) Conventions, Convention No. 138 of 26 June 1973 talks about the minimum age. This article refers to "plantations and other farms which are produced mainly for the purpose of trade, to the exclusion of small family businesses which produce for the local market and which do not regularly employ workers" (Article5.3).

We can therefore conclude that attempts have been made to define the concept of family business both by economic doctrine and by legal doctrine. We can also state that at present the concept (although in an ambiguous way) has been defined in the case of Spain by the Spanish Labour Ministry after the transposition of the recommendations of the EU, although it is a pending subject for labour law (Martínez, Arufe, Carril, 2006, 2012).

FORM OF ORGANIZATION OF SUSTAINABLE BUSINESS MANAGEMENT

In family businesses, it is integrating the principle of responsible government through the implementation of CSR measures.In the social sphere, the measures relate to the creation of quality employment and the continuous training of its management bodies and its workers.Also, the search for equality of opportunities, through policies of family reconciliation.On the other hand and in the environmental field, it is showing a commitment to responsible consumption and reuse of its products through a commitment to the environment and the use of renewable energy (Rodriguez 2011).

The implementation of all sustainable policies in small and medium-sized enterprises has been promoted through government policies since until now SMEs have been reluctant to combine sustainability with profits.In Spain as a member of the EU, the greatest logistical and economic contribution is being made to the development of the Europe 2020 strategy related to economic policies and employment. The aim is to establish the design of a new Community cohesion policy. To this end, both the Spanish State and the Galician Autonomous Government have developed an ERDF 2014-2020 operational program. The main measures for this type of family-owned enterprises in the field of sustainable development have been focused on promoting SMEs in renewable energy (focused on the development of biomass) and energy efficiency (public housing, public buildings and efficiency promotion energy in SMEs by the administration).In contrast to the main axes in which the AGE operates (investments in savings of the Spanish electricity system, investments in rationalization of the distribution system and electric transport, and direct versions in energy efficiency, Galicia has an energy intensity that almost doubles the average value of average EU (295 ktoe per € 1,000, in 2011, compared to 157.8 ktoe per € 1,000).Although the trend is downward, it remains at excessively high levels.In addition, greenhouse gas emissions are currently 18 points above the 2020 target.The objective is to reduce the energy intensity of the business fabric, saving and energy efficiency in companies, as well as consolidating the culture of energy audits and the search for efficiency through energy saving in the business field (Fabra, 2011).To achieve this, priority will be given to measures aimed at the development of energy audits in SMEs in the industrial and services sectors. To this end, management systems and energy saving and efficiency measures will be implemented. These actions are part of the Galicia Energy Strategy 2015-2020.

On the other hand, and taking into account the principle laid down in Article 7 of Regulation (EU) No 1303/2013, an attempt has been made to actively promote equal opportunities between women and men and gender mainstreaming co-financing.The integration of the principle of equality in the selection criteria of operations will be effective by considering the following aspects:

1. The selection criteria for operations will be designed in accordance with the gender gaps identified in the diagnosis, as well as the equality objectives of the program. They will therefore encourage co-financed actions to seek, in a specific or cross-cutting way, to reduce disparities between men and women.
2. In this line, the selection criteria will be able to establish measures to promote the incorporation of the gender perspective in the design and execution of operations, to contemplate specific operations for women, to incorporate the use of gender clauses in subsidies and contracts, and any other proportional criteria.

The next line of action in Spain concerning the sustainable performance of small and medium-sized enterprises, including family members, focuses on the implementation of Implementing Regulation (EU) 215/2014 of 7 March 2014, around axis 5 which develops promotion and adaptation to climate change and risk prevention and management.This operational program is carried out in the case of Galicia from 2014 to 2020. The public policies in progress and the knowledge of the reality on which it intends to intervene have been key in this process.The indicators have been established on the basis of a list of common and specific indicators presented by the General Directorate of Community Funds of the Ministry of Finance and Public Administration in order to maintain a common logic between all the ERDF Operational Programs in Spain.

Having identified the indicators was established for its implementation began the year 2018 and the target for the year 2023. Those that best meet the objective of the performance framework have been selected:

1. Indicator to measure the degree of implementation and compliance of the program. In this part of the process, managing entities have also played a key role in identifying which actions and indicators are most adequate to ensure that the performance framework adequately reflects the objectives and results to be achieved by each priority or objective axis thematic. Two productivity indicators have been selected:
   a. C020, population benefiting from flood prevention measures;
   b. E023, population benefited by planning measures for the prevention of disasters and restoration of damaged areas. The financial concentration of the selected actions linked to these two indicators represents 50.7% of the total ERDF aid so that it exceeds the 50% concentration required by Regulation.
2. Regarding the measurement of financial performance (in terms of total cost), the financial indicator F02 was selected, establishing a total of € 20,619,761 for the implementation milestone in 2018; and the total financing (49,422,659 €) of the axis support through financial instruments: interest subsidies, guarantee commission subsidies, technical support or equivalent.

The actions that are programmed in this axis respond clearly to the importance that the environment, nature, landscape and its relation with economic and social activity present, for a sustainable economic and social development. The planned interventions in this area are part of an overall strategy based on the transversal principle of sustainable growth, in accordance with the European 2020 strategy, which will seek to achieve sustainable growth and employment, achieving the following results:

1. Reduction of waste generation, and progress in prevention and reuse, encouraging separation, and promoting selective collection, separation, recycling and waste treatment.
2. To complete the water cycle, with the completion of the sanitation network in order to achieve the environmental objectives of the Water Framework Directive, reform and optimization of the sanitation systems of the Galician estuaries and actions to achieve good condition ecological of the rest of masses of water and get the decrease of the discharges in rainy weather.
3. To value the natural, cultural and patrimonial resources of the region and to preserve the material and immaterial heritage of Galicia.
4. Ensure the conservation of biodiversity in the region.

On the other hand, measures have also been developed to support the implementation of ICT in SMEs and digital entrepreneurship. Projects to develop R & D & I, projects in the ICT business sector. Development of digital education measures In addition to the coordination mechanisms already being used between the Autonomous Communities and the General State Administration such as the Telecommunications and Information Society Sectoral Conference or the signing of Collaboration Agreements where the objectives, distribution of responsibilities, execution and follow-up of the actions. Thus, under thematic objective 2, the Commission's guidelines on synergies and interoperability with the digital service platforms of the Connecting Europe mechanism included in the guide will be taken into account "Enabling synergies between European Structural and Investment Funds, Horizon 2020 and other research, innovation and competitiveness.It will be possible to create a specific coordination mechanism to integrate all these actions.

The management of the family business starts from three important challenges that have to be managed and that in many cases are a source of serious problems: the emotional aspect, the successor question and finally the situation in which lives of the family members are intertwined.

Emotional problems are the basis of most of the problems that family businesses face. Here we are talking about jointly managing family and business relationships. The dividing line between home and work is completely diluted. The generational conflicts between parents and children and disputes between siblings can generate an important conflict that has serious repercussions in the company. Concepts alien to the world of business and labour relations converge in this type of business since the world of emotions and feelings that act in family matters have nothing to do with work and undertakings that governs business matters. Unresolved conflicts can affect the management of the company and thus can paralyze the organization.

Regarding the subject of succession there are two issues that must be raised, the transmission of management and the transmission of ownership of the company. This theme requires great planning given its difficulty. The work of the company must be organized with a view to training future leaders of the company, which is not an easy task. In addition, the company can be harmed by an important family fragmentation that leads to a lack of control. That is why the involvement of its members is so important in these companies. Transmission is not always easy, rather it is often complex.

Finally, regarding the circumstantial issue in how business activity is developed, the family business does not differ from that of other companies. The difference is found that many times in family businesses the labour relations are carried out by members of the family who are not trained for said activity. Secondly, the influences of third-parties related to the family making business decisions can be a source of conflict that does not exist in other companies. All this can cause the company to become stagnant and less competitive (Veláz, 2005).

This relates to the multidisciplinary dimension that family businesses have, in which civil matters such as family succession are related to market place questions: those regarding the configuration of the company and its management, financial questions and human resource matters.

In the case of the human resources is important to know how they are managed in these companies. For this we will investigate the mechanisms and peculiarities employed in the selection and promotion of personnel, training, incentives to directors and, finally, the process of succession of the leader in the company. As we already have indicated, the family implication in these companies is very significant and thus the management has important peculiarities. We can find ourselves with two important situations. The first concerns the manner in which management has an important inclination towards the family aspect, much in matter of selection, promotion, training and reward, to the detriment of the rest of the employees. The second situation speaks to more egalitarian principles, in function of merits and capacity, independently of whether the employee was a family member or not. Quality operation of these companies will depend in most cases on how these two situations are managed. Thus, the degree of success and efficiency of the company can be explained by the resources available in the organization, either by the characteristics of these resources or by the capacity of the company to combine and use them in different organizational activities. Not all business resources are capable of achieving such sustainability; only those of a rare group of an intangible nature have been shown to be the most valuable (Barney, 1991, Grant, 1996), as well as durable in time.

Relationships in family businesses blend property, family and business. This mix produces a peculiar form of business management. To make it sustainable requires a combination of a common bond and a group of mutual expectations supported in psychological aspects that are different from contractual aspects. These are based on emotions, feelings and values (equity, trust, altruism, loyalty ...) and affect the operation and management of the company. In the case of access to employment in family businesses, we find that the search and selection of the best person for the position to be covered can be affected by family relationships. If the person selected is a worse choice among the applicants, the interests of the company will not be covered and they will clearly be harmed. After an unfavourable selection is made, a conflict of interests between the parties involved appears and leads to a loss of efficiency of the company. This can lead to negative external effects and create a bad external image, affecting possible future recruitment and selection processes, as potential external candidates may perceive that the company is not the best alternative to work.

Another important factor in the management of family businesses is training as one of the fundamental practices necessary to maintain the company in the long term. This will allow a competitive development of their human resources in knowledge, skills and competencies. As a consequence, we could say that, in general, training in family businesses must be more intensive and more oriented in the long term than in the non-family business. In the case of family businesses, a mistake often made is prioritizing the desire to continue the family business into the future with family members managing it (Pérez et al. Al., 2007) over the career development of family members. This can be detrimental to the efficiency of the training and can lead to the consequent loss of motivation and involvement of non-family employees.

Similarly, in terms of remuneration, one of the most important risks in family businesses is that, in order to strengthen the emotional and family ties, the management of the company attempts to create special remuneration packages for employed members of the family. To do this, they use indirect remuneration (that is, rewarding family members with benefits such as company car, cell phone, travel, etc.). This has a devastating effect on the perception of equity of other employees and is a reason for high dissatisfaction and labour unrest that undermines the efficiency of the company.

Promotion and succession are closely linked with each other and with training since those employees who show the ability to acquire skills, attitudes and concrete knowledge for their current and future work are the employees in which the company has to prepare so that they can occupy positions of greater responsibility. The development of the professional career and the succession of work activities and positions carried out by a person throughout the life in the company are of great relevance for their promotion and for the management of the company (Dolan et al., 2007). This situation produces negative externalities in the market, since current or potential current employees who can contribute more cannot attain such positions. In order to avoid these problems, the family business must establish succession criteria that, in due course, must apply in search of the ideal candidate, family or non-family (Perez-Gisbert-2012).

Good family business management will depend on the balance between family and business and on how human resources policies are oriented to a greater or lesser extent to the application of principles of equity and professionalism. This will keep human capital motivated and efficient, which will add value to the company (Carrasco-Sánchez, 2014).

Within human resources a factor of great relevance is to be a woman and to carry out an activity outside the home and to combine that activity with family matters. If, in addition, this activity is carried out in a family business, it is even more complex. Being able to reconcile the responsibilities demanded in the home and at work is a problem that employers and employees experience with greater intensity each and every day. (Rodríguez, Rodríguez-2011).

The participation of women in the management bodies of family businesses is 27.8%, reaching 72.3% of companies that have at least one woman on their teams. Although most Ibex-35 companies include women among their members, in none of them do women represent more than 50%.In Spanish family

Figure 1. Percentage of incidences in the management of family businesses
Source: Generated by the author

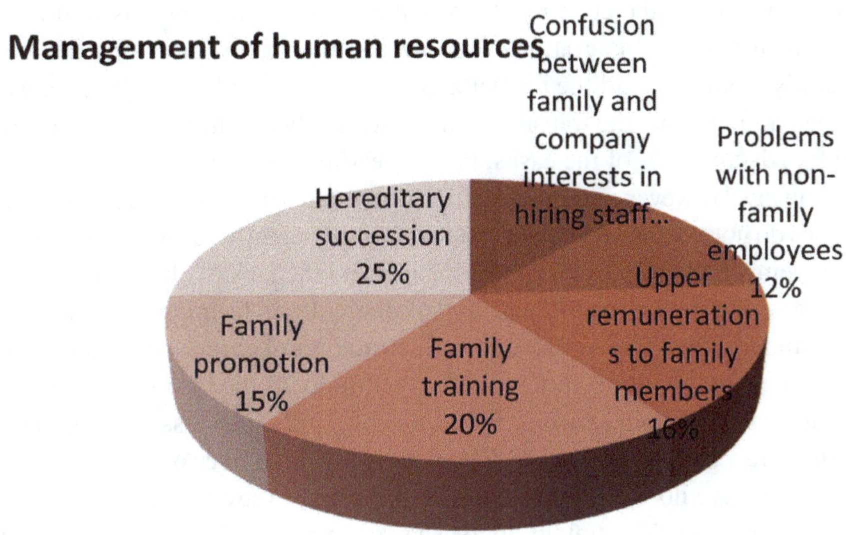

businesses, on the contrary, 28.9% of management councils have a majority of women. The Report of the Women's Institute (2015) analyses compliance with the Equality Act of 2007, and recommends that women's participation on boards of directors reach a minimum of 40%.This study concludes that this percentage is only reached in 26.3% of the companies in general, whereas in the family business, however, it rises to 34.7%.With regard to the General Shareholders' Meeting, the body par excellence of ownership representation, the presence of women is at the same percentages. Finally, regarding the participation of women in family management bodies, although their presence is slightly higher than the previous two cases, it is still below one third. This is especially striking in some management bodies in which it is supposed that the presence of women would have to be at least at parity with male participation since, traditionally, women play significant roles as managers of family emotions.

As for the current situation in family businesses, in the past year future prospects have been more optimistic, supported by the good results achieved this year in terms of turnover, employment and internationalization. 75% of the family businesses have declared increased net sales in 2016 (compared to the 70% expressed in 2015), while only 11% have declared reduced sales. Among those who have seen their sales grow, seven out of ten have done so above 5% (EFB-KPMG European Barometer of Family Business 2016).

The greater worries of this year concern political surroundings, competition and profitability. The political uncertainty continues to represent, for the second consecutive year, the major problem that family businesses face in the present.55%express insecurity facing recent events like the Brexit or the stage of indecisiveness and political division in Spain. Competition constitutes the second most notable worry for Spanish family businesses. Decrease of profitability also continues being one of the main worries of family businesses. Nevertheless, it has diminished its importance with regard to previous cases: three years ago 58% signalled it as their main problem; in 2015 it was 44% and in 2016 it descended to 35%. On the contrary, the war for talent **is** gaining positions. It has risen in the list of worries compared to previous years. Finally, in spite of the financial crisis, the worry about access to finance goes down to occupy the lowest places in the ranking. (EFB-KPMG, 2016).

The principal and most innovative measures family businesses have included first in their strategic business plans are investing in innovation and talent. This is related to innovation and diversification in new products and services as a measure of being more competitive. The attraction of new talent also has gained importance compared to the 2015 results, when only 9% identified it as significant compared to 17% today. Next in the list are the integration of following generations, professionalization with managers who are not family members, and the formalization of governing bodies. In the case of the integration of following generations, that the transmission of the family business is of great importance can be confirmed by the fact that, in 58% of the cases, the succeeding generation already occupies managerial positions in the company. However, integration difficulties can arise if the older members of the family and the younger ones do not communicate with each other sufficiently. Each generation has its own worries. The youngest members usually fear family conflicts and the lack of clarity in career perspectives in the company. The older generation instead usually has difficulty in keeping up to date with the constant changes of the surroundings. In this sense, having good structures of corporate management and processes is essential to ensure healthy family relations and the continuity of the business throughout generations.

With respect ton on-family management, the owners of family businesses sometimes have to decide whether they should hire a general director (CEO) who is not a member of the family. Examples would include times when there are no heirs or the heirs do not want, or are not prepared, to take the reins of the business. The defenders of this strategy increase every year. In 2016 96% of the owners indicated that having external directors would result as being beneficial for the business and 87% already have them working managerial positions in their companies. Nevertheless, in spite of recognizing the need to have them, the owners still show reluctance to yield control to them. Formalizing management structure and having good management structures are essential to ensure correct implantation. Conscious of this, 89% of Spanish family businesses have formal management mechanisms in place. The majority have established a Board of Directors and a Family Protocol or Code of Behaviour. Also common is the establishment of a Family Council. On the contrary, processes of welcoming, training and introduction to the company for family members are the less frequently applied and, thus, form an important area in which to focus upon to attain a suitable integration of all the personnel of the company.

Other measures that family businesses consider necessary to improve the business are: 37% indicate the lowering of taxes, 36% indicate lower contributions to Social Security and 29% are inclined towards simpler and more flexible labour agreements. The European companies situate this last item as the one with the greatest impact and think that the reduction of bureaucracy would help them even more that a tax cut.

Finally, all that is intended is to provide the company with a tool to successfully face the current challenges in CSR by guaranteeing the health and well-being of workers, efficient management of energy resources and the search for an inclusive society that integrates diverse profiles.

INCIDENCE OF FAMILY BUSINESS IN SPAIN

According to data of Institute of Family Business, in Spain family businesses represent 90 percent of Corporations or Limited Liability Companies. These are responsible for 60 percent of the Gross Value Added, as well as 70 percent of the employment generated by the private sector group. Spain has 1.1 million family businesses (of the total of 1.25 million mercantile societies that exist) that, in a direct way, contribute annually to the economy an added value equivalent to 262,000 million Euros and around 7 million job positions (of the 460,000 million Euros and the 10 million employments generated by the mercantile societies of the private sector).In terms of employment, family businesses contribute to the economy roughly double the job positions that non-family businesses do. We could say that the family businesses are, therefore, the backbone of the Spanish economy.

The Institute of Family Business determined that in Spain in the year 2016, 90% of the companies were family businesses with the following distribution by Autonomous Communities (Figure 2).

Spain's territorial system is divided into Autonomous Communities. It can be seen that some of them have a higher creation of family businesses and not all will have the same percentage. It is possible to identify three large groups of autonomous communities, depending on whether the intensity of the contribution of these companies to the main aggregates of the regional economy is superior, inferior or similar to the Spanish average.

Thus, through Table 1 we can see the important differences between the various Autonomous Communities in terms of the number of family businesses.

The main characteristic of family businesses in Spain, apart from being a type of company, is their heterogeneity, since there is no single model as revealed by the Institute of Family Business. To define the types of family businesses, were contemplating two professionalization dimensions: the business and the family. In this manner, the business perspective contemplates the strategic and innovative attitude of the company. The companies with the highest scores in this dimension are the most dynamic in ac-

Figure 2. Distribution by autonomous communities in Spain
Source: Institute of Family Business

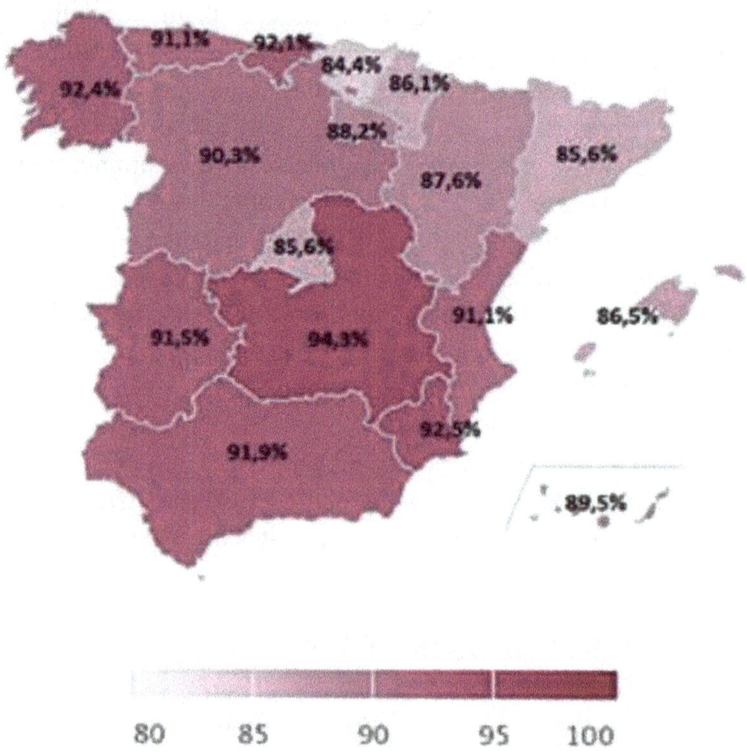

cess to new markets, sectors and the most innovative. The professionalization of the family perspective translates into the concern for managing family questions with tools like protocols, family training, the assessment of actions and the knowledge of existing fiscal benefits. In this case, the higher scores are for the companies that plan for succession in greater detail in both managerial terms and ownership terms. These defining characteristics of a typical family business in Spain can be seen in Figure 3, which shows a main characteristic of having an average size of 29 employees, which would be considered in the category of small companies, and of having an average life span of 33 years.

The form of management organization of family businesses reveals an inclination towards either a more family-oriented management style or a more professional management style. See Figure 4.

In this type of company, the matter of succession is source of conflict and the principal objective can be seen in Figure 5.

Another important characteristic of these companies is the family dimension as can be seen in Figure 6.

According to what the preference might be, we can find ourselves with the following classifications:

1. *Family Businesses whose dimensions is predominately Family (PF).* Only 1 of every 10 family businesses is in this category. These are the companies that show greater concern for planning family matters.
2. *Family Businesses whose dimension is predominately Business (PB).* This category is distributed at 30%, as is the case for the other two remaining categories (DF and DB). The companies of this

Table 1. Distribution of family businesses by autonomous regions in Spain

DISTRIBUTION OF FAMILY AND NON-FAMILY ENTERPRISES BY REGION				
	Family	**Non-Family**	**All**	**Percentage Family Business**
Andalucía	154.936	13.719	168.655	91,9%
Aragón	28.091	3.970	32.061	87,6%
Asturias	17.654	1.732	19.386	91,1%
Baleares	29.946	4.682	34.628	86,5%
C. Valenciana	132.032	12.873	144.905	91,1%
Canarias	48.344	5.677	54.021	89,5%
Cantabria	5.322	455	5.777	92,1%
Castilla-La Mancha	43.477	2.612	46.089	94,3%
Castilla y León	27.279	2.941	30.220	90,3%
Cataluña	207.793	34.888	242.681	85,6%
Extremadura	16.069	1.500	17.569	91,5%
Galicia	62.900	5.178	68.078	92,4%
La Rioja	6.443	860	7.303	88,2%
Madrid	215.146	36.138	251.284	85,6%
Murcia	30.907	2.511	33.418	92,5%
Navarra	13.047	2.104	15.151	86,1%
País Vasco	42.557	7.858	50.415	84,4%
SPAIN	**1.084.617**	**137.024**	**1.221.641**	**88,8%**

Source: Institute Family Business

Figure 3. Family business model in Spain
Source: Generated by the author

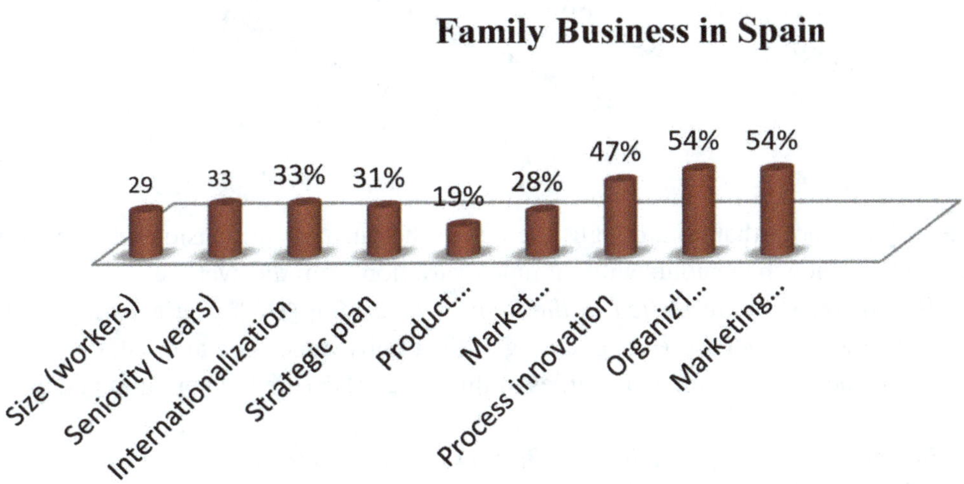

Figure 4. Family business management in Spain
Source: Generated by the author

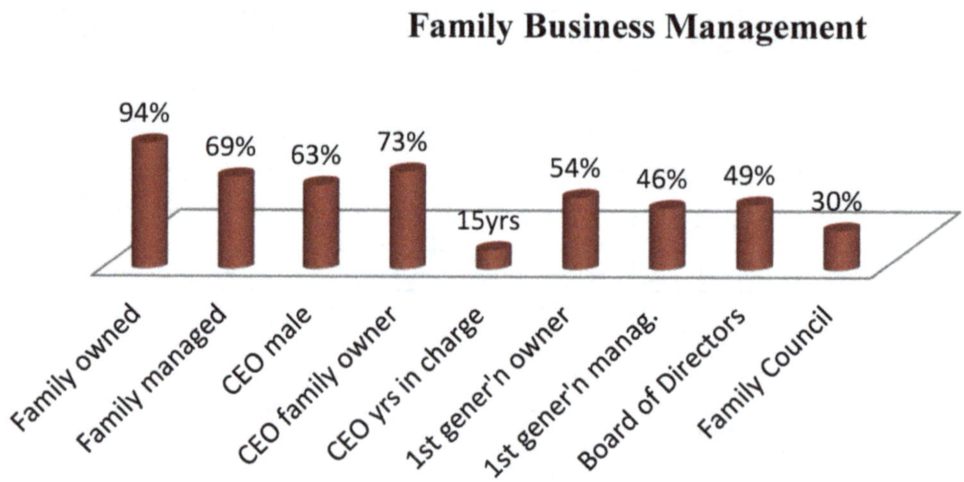

Figure 5. Succession of the family business Spain
Source: Generated by the author

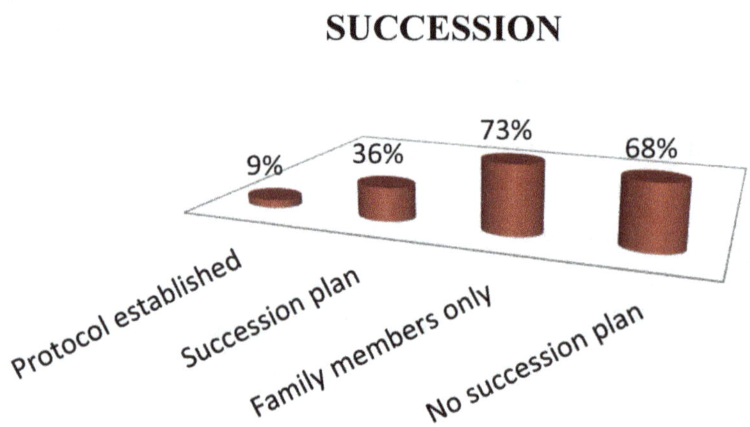

PB category are those that obtain higher scores in the business dimension whereas in the family dimension they show behaviours without much variation from the average.

3. *Family Businesses showing Deficit in the Family dimension (DF).* These family businesses are companies showing lower scores in planning of the family dimension and without a clear-cut pattern in the business dimension. Companies of this group (DF) are the youngest and have a smaller size.
4. *Family Businesses showing Deficit in the Business dimension (DB).* This type of company is characterised fundamentally by behaviour below average in the business dimension.

Figure 6. Dimension of the family business Spain
Source: Generated by the author

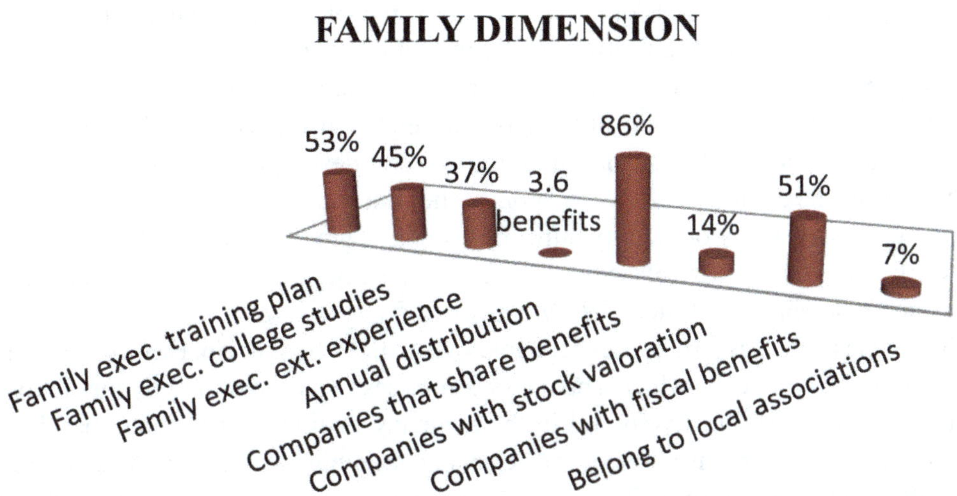

The companies of the Predominantly Business (PB) group, as a whole, are those oriented towards business matters, in fact have a lower presence of family members as directors, and have the greater levels of internationalisation and distribution of profits. The companies of the group Predominantly Family (PF) obtain the greater scores in the family dimension because they are more tightly consolidated and show more concern about the transmission of the company on to heirs; they are companies of a larger size and are more multigenerational, and also are those with a greater index of belonging to associations of family businesses.

The DF companies are companies in evolution which have not yet made decisions on the family position in the company. They could move to any of the other three types. If they attend properly to the family matters they would convert into PF companies. If they focus mainly on business matters they would become PB companies. However, if they concentrate on family matters at the expense of business matters they would end up as DB companies. Precisely this last type would contain companies that could have greater problems. The PB companies are business projects with more potential. In this case, it would be necessary to analyse the role that family ownership could play. Finally, the PF companies are the most consolidated companies and possess a culture and tools for the continuity of the family venture. It would be necessary to put greater attention on the business questions to avoid any type of risk.

In this manner of studying family businesses, it will be necessary to analyse the work relations among the family members that work in the company. The Workers Statute of 2015 indicates that, "Family labour is excluded from the scope of this law, except when it can be demonstrated that family members who carry out the work are paid a salary. Individuals will be considered family members for this purpose, provided that they live together with the employer, the spouse, the descendants, ancestors and other relatives by consanguinity or affinity, until the second degree inclusive and in the case of adoption" (Art.1.3. e). The family concept here stated would therefore not create any labour link. Outside of these suppositions therefore, we would be considering family members that do have labour links and therefore we would be speaking of the obligation of the family member employer to place them within the General Regime of Social Security (RGSS in Spanish). The Royal Legislative Decree 8/2015, of 30

October, which approves the text of the General Law of the Social Security (LGSS) (BOE 31 October 2015), establishes that the following will be included in the Social Security system, to the effect of making contributory payments, regardless of sex, civil state and profession: Spaniards that reside in Spain and foreigners that reside or find themselves legally in Spain, whenever, in both suppositions, exercise their activity in national territory and are included in any of the following sections: "…self-employed workers, whether or not they are owners of the business, eighteen years old or older, that fall under the requirements that are determined in this law and in its rule of development"(7.1.b), with the exception (except with proof to the contrary) of"… the spouse, the descendants, ancestors and other relatives of the employer, by consanguinity or affinity until the second degree included and the case of adoption, performing work in the family workplace, when they live together in the self-employed worker's home and are under his or her charge"(Article 7.2)(Montoya, 2000).

The family business, such as it is, is a concept unknown to the labour norm. However, it can be defined similar to all capitalist societies in which a business comprises two or more family members, having (in addition to the property) the directive power in the company. Similarly, it is mentioned in agreements of the International Labour Organisation, or even certain community legislation. And, for example, ILO Convention 138, of June 26, on the minimum age for admission to employment, provides in Art. 5.3, that its wording applies at a minimum to "plantations and other farms producing mainly for trade, to the exclusion of small-scale or family-owned enterprises producing for the local market and not regularly employing wage-earners". Directive 1994/33/EC of 22 June 1994 on the protection of young people at work allows Member States to exclude from their scope "work which is not considered to be harmful or dangerous for the young in the family business".

The presence of family members as employees of the company can have some importance from the perspective of the succession of company. In this sense, the labour elements of the Family Protocol are very important, first, to determine the legal procedure of the people in charge of the transmission, management and administration of the company. Secondly, they are important for regulating the future incorporation of family members as employees, as well as their conditions of work. Thirdly, they are important for anticipating the conditions of retirement and egress of the managers from the company (Garrido-Villalba, 1999).

The general norm established in the LGSS (General Law of Social Security) obligates all family members that provide services in a family business to enter the RGSS (General Regime of Social Security), except for possible special cases of exclusion. This is established inArticle 7.2 LGSS (Martinez, Varela, Lane 2013). The apparent clarity of the conclusion blurs, however, when two new rules are examined. The first is the obligation for the so-called *autonomous dependent* to enter the RETA (Special Regime for Self-Employed Workers). The second concerns cases where family members work for the family business in certain work categories that will allow them to transfer from the RGSS to the RTSS, when they are not actually working for an employer outside the family. (Lujan, 2006).

The cancellation of a work contract in family businesses also has its peculiarities. The Superior Court of Justice of Galicia (TSJG), inSentence number 560/2014 of 21 January 2014, regarding the matter of cancellation of a work contract for economic causes, addressed the peculiarities of family businesses and their essential characteristics with respect to labour and market aspects of family business groups.

CONCLUSION

First: Family businesses have family character as a main underpinning of its nature. This family character is a source of both their weaknesses and their strengths. Finding a sustainable balance in their operation and organisation can ensure its continuation or its disappearance if family conflicts are not resolved.

Second: In pursuing their objectives, family businesses have their focus concentrated on the family as well as the business. It is important to see how coordinating economic and family interests in different manners can result in determining the success or failure of the family business.

Third: The family business has a very clear idea as to which are the factors of success and sustainability of the company: a good corporate management, a clear plan of succession and an excellent control of the business. Despite the advances which have been produced up until now, the reality shows us that the prevision for the future is not something that always occupies the highest place in the agenda of family businesses. Family businesses are accustomed to address these issues from a more informal perspective, without being provided, in many occasions, systems for good management.

Fourth: Within the environment of Labour Rights and Social Security we often find judicial resolutions that evidence some distrust towards labour and insurance relations regarding the work in a family business, especially when it deals with the realisation of managerial functions.

REFERENCES

Lujan Alcaraz, J. (2006). *La empresa familiar ante el Derecho del Trabajo y de la Seguridad Revista Doctrinal Aranzadi Social num.10/2006 parte Tribuna Social*. Editorial Aranzadi, S.A.U.

Barney, J. (1991). Firm resources and sustained competitive advantage. *Journal of Management, 17*(1), 99–120. doi:10.1177/014920639101700108

Barómetro Europeo de la Empresa Familiar (EFB-KPMG). (2016). *Exitosa y Resilente*. Author.

COM. (2012). *795 final, "Plan de Acción sobre Emprendimiento 2020, Relanzar el espíritu emprendedor en Europa"*. COM.

Daily, C. M., & Thompson, S. S. (1994). Ownership structure, strategic posture, and firm growth: An empirical examination. *Family Business Review, 7*(3), 237–249. doi:10.1111/j.1741-6248.1994.00237.x

Dolan, C., & John, W. (1998). Defining and Describing Family Business Ownership Configurations. *Family Business Review, 1*, 301–3101.

Dolan, S. V., Ramón, J., Susan, E., & Schuler, R. (2007). La gestión de los recursos humanos. Madrid: McGraw-Hill.

European Commission. (2009). *Final Report of the Group of Experts: Overview of family-business-relevant issues: research, networks, policy measures and existing studies*. Author.

European Union. (2011). *Business Dynamics: Start-ups Business transfers and Bankruptcy.* Retrieved from http://ec.europa.eu/enterprise/policies/sme/business-environment/files/ busines_dynamics-report_en.pdf

FabraUtray, J. (2011). Sostenibilidad económica y sostenibilidad medioambiental: ¿son compatibilidad en el sector eléctrico? *Economistas, 29*, 299-301.

Gallo, M. Á. (1993). *La cultura en empresa familiar*. Publicaciones de la Cátedra de Empresa Familiar.

Garrido Palacios, J., & Villalba Salvador, B. (1999). La empresa familiar: aspectos laborales y de Seguridad Social. *Boletín del Ilustre Colegio de Abogados de Madrid*, (12), 195-198.

Martínez Girón, J., & Arufe Varela, A. (2006). *Derecho del Trabajo*. Netbiblo SL.

Martínez Girón, J., & Arufe Varela, A. (2012). *Derecho Crítico del Trabajo*. Netbiblosl.

Girón, M. (2013). *Derecho de la Seguridad Social*. A Coruña: Netbiblo.

Grant, R. (1996). Prospering in dynamically-competitive environments: Organizational capability as knowledge integration. *Organization Science*, *7*(4), 374–380. doi:10.1287/orsc.7.4.375

Levison, H. (1971). Conflicts that plage family businesses. *Harvard Business Review*, 91-92.

Instituto de Empresa Familiar. (2015). La Empresa Familiar en España. Madrid: Instituto de Empresa Familiar.

Instituto de la Mujer para la Igualdad de Oportunidades. (2015). *Informe Periódico*. Ministerio de Sanidad, Sevicios Sociales e Igualdad.

Josep & Ernesto. (2005) ¿Medir la sostenibilidad? una aproximación al tema de los indicadores de sostenibilidad. *Cátedra UNESCO a la UPC de Sostenibilidad, 5*, 140-144.

Kraus, S., Pohjola, M., & Koponen, A. (2012). Innovation in family firms: An empirical analysis linking organizational and managerial innovation to corporate success. *Review of Managerial Science*, *6*(3), 261–270. doi:10.100711846-011-0065-6

Lansberg, I. (1983). Managin Human resources in family firms: The problem of institutional overlan. *Organizational Dynamics*, *12*(1), 40–42. doi:10.1016/0090-2616(83)90025-6

Ron Latas, R. (2011). La *empresa familiar en el Derecho del Trabajo*. netbiblo.

López-Cózar Navarro, C. (2014). Peculiaridades de la pequeña empresa familiar ante la responsabilidad social empresarial. *Un análisis exploratorio enla Comunidad de Madrid*, (18), 42.

Nogales Lozano, F. (2007). Las culturas familiares: gestión clave para la cohesión y continuidad de las familias empresarias, en La Empresa Familiar y los nuevos retos de gestión, Coordi. Nogales Lozano, Colección EOI Empresas, págs. 241-242.

Montoya Melgar, A. (Ed.). (2000). *Curso de Seguridad Social*. Servicio de Publicaciones de la Facultad de Derecho. Universidad Complutense, 2ª edición, Madrid, 2000, Capítulo XIII, págs. 299 y ss.

Pérez Molina, Ana Isabel, Gisbert Soler, Victor (2012), La continuidad en la empresa familiar: estudio de casos, 3 Ciencias, Editada por Área de Innovación y Desarrollo, S.L., págs. 7-8.

Negueruela, V., & Luis, J. (2005). Especial Problemática de la Empresa Familiar. Actualidad Jurídica Aranzadi num.678/2005(opinión), ed. Aranzadi, page 3-4.

Pérez, M. J., Basco, R., García-Tenorio, J., Giménez, J., & Sánchez, I. (2007). *Fundamentos en la dirección de la empresa familiar*. Madrid: Thomson.

Report of de EY y Kennesaw State University. (2014). *Staying power: How do familybusinesses create lasting success*? Author.

Rodríguez Muñoz José Manuel. (2011). la políticas públicas de fomento de la responsabilidad social empresarial. *Aranzadi, 7*, 7.

Rodríguez Zapatero, Maribel, Rodríguez Jiménez Magdalena, la mujer en la empresa familiar, revista de empresa familiar, Volumen 1, nº 2., págs. 20-25.

Stafford, K., Duncan, K. A., Danes, S. M., & Winter, M. (1999). A research model of sustainable family businesses. *Family Business Review, 12*(3), 197–208. doi:10.1111/j.1741-6248.1999.00197.x

Tagiuri, R., & Davis, J. A. (1982). *Bivalent Attributes of the Family Firm*. Working paper. Harvard Business School.

Vallejo Martos, M. C. (2005). Cuando definir es una necesidad. Una propuesta integradora y operativa del concepto de empresa familiar. *Investigaciones Europeas de Dirección y Economía de la Empresa, 11*(3), 151–171.

KEY TERMS AND DEFINITIONS

Family Business: The family business is one in which the members of one or more families participate in an important way in their capital, assume responsibilities in the management, and intend to transmit the business to future generations.

Human Capital: Human capital is the most precious asset of companies. This will depend on the production of the same, being more productive the greater the formation of the same.

Sustainable Business: The company is sustainable because it creates economic, environmental and social value in the short and long term, thus contributing to the welfare of society and its workers.

Values: The values are the measures of progress and social welfare that companies collect in their CSR measures.

ENDNOTE

1 Report of EY and Kennesaw State University, designated *Staying power: how do familybusinesses create lasting success*? Survey conducted in 2014 on the 2,400 largest family businesses in the world from the following countries: Australia, Belgium, Brazil, Canada, China, France, Germany, Persian Gulf Countries (Bahrain, Kuwait, Oman, Qatar, Saudi Arabia and the United Arab Emirates), India, Indonesia, Italy, Japan, Mexico, Holland, Russia, South Korea, Spain, Switzerland, Turkey, the United Kingdom and the USA, P. 1.

Chapter 13
Matching Sustainability Strategy and Results:
A Successful Family Firm Case Study

Laura Broccardo
University of Turin, Italy

Elisa Truant
University of Turin, Italy

ABSTRACT

The aim of the research is to analyze the strategy and the value creation system from a sustainable point of view adopted in an Italian family firm, with a particular focus strategic intensions and strategic projects under implementation. This work has been conducted through the qualitative method of case study, where theory and empirical research are intertwined. In particular, semi-structured interviews and internal document analysis have been conducted. The research shows how the company has implemented the strategy, focusing on sustainability critical success factors and key projects in order to lay the foundation for innovation and growth. The chapter has some theoretical and practical implications as it contributes to integrate the existing literature on family firms, strategic planning, and sustainability, and allows managers better understand how a sustainability strategy can be translated into operational terms.

INTRODUCTION

Over the last years, increasing attention was given to the topic of family business and to management systems.

The importance of family business for the worldwide economy has been largely demonstrated in literature and it derives from the significant presence of family firms in many countries, as continental Europe, Asia, and Latin America, (Claessens *et al.*; 2000; Faccio & Lang, 2002; IFERA 2003; La Porta *et al.*, 1999; Neubauer and Lank 1998).

DOI: 10.4018/978-1-5225-5267-3.ch013

At the same time, literature has widely recognized the importance of managerial tools for companies' management and performances, as they allow to drive the organization towards the established goals (Brusa, 2007; Kaplan & Norton, 1996, 2001, 2004, 2006, 2008; Shank, 1989, 1996). Among the management accounting systems, an important role is played by the tools that allow to facilitate the strategy implementation by explicating a wide range of strategic variables on a long-time horizon and integrating economic and financial dimensions with the non-financial ones through cause-and-effect links. Indeed, a strategy, whatever it is, cannot be effective if it is not supported by managerial system able to translate the conceptual roles of the strategy's tangible and intangible elements into operational terms (Culasso et al., 2016). In addition, it should also be noticed that a part of the literature focused on sustainability within management accounting systems in order to create an organizational sustainability-oriented culture (Epstein & Buhovac, 2014; Epstein & Roy, 2001; Schaltegger et al., 2012). Figge et al. (2002) argued that the business performance model can help to account for all relevant aspects of sustainability issues in a balanced way.

Despite the relevance of such tools, researches on management accounting systems in family firms are fragmented (Salvato & Moores, 2010; Songini et al. 2013; Prencipe et al., 2014) and require a greater attention by scholars (Songini et al., 2013)

Consequently, this study tries to fill this gap understanding the features of strategic planning systems, as a means that aid managers in strategic decision-making process and address the behavior of managers and employees towards company's goals (Horngren et al. 2010), with a particular focus on the sustainability strategy and on implementation projects. In particular, Hansen and Schaltegger (2016) suggest to study performance management systems with regard to their design, implementation, use and evolution (de Geuser et al. 2009; Searcy 2012). This research tries to follow this recommendation, analysing the design and implementation of sustainability strategic goals in an Italian family firm operating in the beverage sector that was able to integrate the profit needs with a sustainability orientation. In particular, the research aims at investigating in the selected case how the economic, social and environmental goals are related to each other in order to guarantee high quality products, respectful of the environment and the local community's needs.

This research is also justified also by the scarce number of research about economic and financial features of firms that operate in beverage sector (Capasso et al., 2015).

The next section of this paper focuses on the literature review on management accounting systems in family firms, sustainability strategy and management accounting tools. Then, the research goals, the method chosen and the findings are provided. Finally, the last section focuses on discussion, conclusions and future developments.

BACKGROUND

Management Accounting Systems in Family Firms

Over recent decades, interest in the study of family businesses has significantly increased in the business and management literature (Bird et al., 2002; Gedajlovic et al., 2012).

It is not easy to find a definition for the expression "family firm" and ambiguities persist in the literature. When researchers try to give a precise definition, it emerges that the phenomenon is very complex (Hoy & Verser, 1994). The doubt exists because different criteria have been used to classify FFs.

Referring to family businesses, usually researchers investigate the performances of these companies and found that publicly traded firms that are family owned/controlled perform better than NFFs (Anderson & Reeb, 2003; Lee, 2004; 2006; McConaughy, 1998; Villalonga & Amit, 2006). These researches were mainly conducted in Europe and Asia (Claessens et al., 2002; Maury, 2006).

The family business phenomenon, especially in Italy, has been strongly analyzed in terms of relationship between FFs and governance. In particular, there are studies that focused on FFs by taking into account the organisational structures and the decision making process (Gubitta & Giannecchini, 2002; Songini, 2007), the corporate governance (Corbetta et al., 2002; Montemerlo, 2000), the second and third generation succession (Corbetta et al., 2002; Montemerlo, 2010; Zocchi, 2004a; 2004b), the international development (Stampacchia et al., 2008) and performance (Culasso et al., 2012; Faccio et al., 2001). The family business characteristics, following explained, have potential influence on management accounting systems: (i) family businesses' long-term orientation may influence the choice of strategic MA instruments; (ii) family businesses' emphasis on non-financial goals may be reflected in their performance measurement and management systems, placing more weight on non-financial goals; and (iii) MA systems may generally be organised more informally due to management positions being held by family members and the resulting trust among management team members.

Analyzing the literature, it was observed a lack of researches about the use of managerial systems in FFs. Indeed, the researches on MA in family firms are fragmented (Salvato & Moores, 2010; Songini et al. 2013; Prencipe et al., 2014), focusing on single papers and not addressing the extant literature on MA in family businesses.

A study, in particular, underlines that managerial accounting represents an area in family business that requires increasing attention from accounting scholars and it studies in deep "why has accounting, representing one of the eldest business disciplines, only recently started to consider family business, representing the majority of business organizations around the world, as a relevant research context?" (Songini et al., 2013). This study identifies three main reasons: i) theoretical frameworks used in the accounting discipline are in part different from those used by family business scholars, because accounting scholars are more interested in accounting generalizations, principles and mechanisms, than in specific empirical contexts; ii) different developmental stages of the two disciplines. Family business is a relatively young field and may not have yet attracted the interest of a great number of accounting scholars; iii) contingency approach, they mainly focus on publicly listed companies, where agency conflicts prevail.

Consequently, this study tries to fill this gap, understanding the management accounting systems, defined by Horngren et al. (2010) "as a means of gathering and using information to aid and coordinate the process of making planning and control decisions through- out the organisation and to guide the behaviour of its managers and employees. The goal of MA system is to improve the collective decisions within an organisation in an economically feasible way" with a particular focus on the sustainability strategy and on the balanced scorecard as management accounting system.

The Sustainability Issues and Strategy Implementation

There are several sustainability definitions that evolved over time. In general, the sustainability highlights the interdependence of three spheres: the economic, the social and the environmental one (Elkington, 1997). The sustainability orientation aims at achieving both ecological, social and economic goals (Figgie et al., 2001, Schaltegger & Burrit, 2000, O' Connor, 2006).

Different types of sustainability strategy (Dyllick, 2002; Baumgartner & Ebner, 2010) can be formulated by companies to deal with the challenge of sustainability:

- **Risk Mitigation Strategy:** Focus on legal and other external standards concerning environmental and social aspects in order to avoid risks for the company;
- **Legitimating Strategy:** Focus on external relationships, license to operate;
- **Efficiency Strategy:** Focus on eco-efficiency and cleaner production;
- **Holistic Sustainability Strategy:** Focus on sustainability issues within all business activities; competitive advantages are derived from differentiation and innovation, offering customers and stakeholders' unique advantages.

In order to develop sustainability strategies, it is necessary to be aware of the range of sustainability issues that have to be managed through environmental and social management accounting systems in order to implement, manage and control sustainability-related issues (Bieker, 2002).

Companies with a sustainability orientation, often adopt operational tools to monitor environmental or social performances. However, these tools, such as the ISO 14000, usually are not linked with the strategy formulated. Indeed, it becomes very important to consider the issue of sustainability not only at the operational level but also at the strategic level.

It literature it has been underlined the importance of including the theme of sustainability within the strategic intentions and the related critical success factors, also in order to create an organizational sustainability-oriented culture (Epstein & Buhovac, 2014; Epstein and Roy, 2001; Schaltegger et al., 2012). Some researchers have also emphasized the importance to include, within business performance models, the sustainability indicators (Epstein & Buhovac, 2014; Schaltegger & Wagner, 2006; Figge et al., 2002; Dias-Sardinha & Reijnders, 2001).

Strategic planning systems are therefore relevant because they are able to push the whole organizational structure towards the sustainability strategy and goals.

Scholars have emphasised the potential of the sustainability business models for integrating conventional strategic management with corporate sustainability management (Figge et al., 2002) as it allows management to address goals in all three dimensions of sustainability by integrating economic, environmental and social issues

Epstein and Wisner (2001) suggest a list of social and environmental indicators.

In conclusion, the strategic planning tools, whatever structure is chosen, can offer a valid support in implementing the sustainability-oriented strategy and driving operational actions towards sustainability goals. However, in a sustainability-oriented company, these tools should also explicit the social and environmental key factors within a system of determinants and indicators.

MAIN FOCUS OF THE CHAPTER

The aim of the research is to analyze the sustainability strategy and its implementation in a family firm, with a particular focus on the implementation of sustainability strategic goals and projects. In particular, the research investigates the features of company' business model, particularly referring on the presence of the three pillars - environmental, social and economic - of sustainability among key success factors and expected outcomes. Indeed, if the company declared to formulate sustainability-oriented strategy, it is necessary that the implementation and monitoring processes underline the environmental and social factors.

The case study analyzed is constituted by an Italian family firm of excellence, small-medium sized, with a strong sustainability orientation: this company operates in the beverage industry, both in Italy and in foreign markets. To define a family firm, a mixed criterion (Broccardo 2011; Culasso et al., 2012) has been chosen, which includes: both a controlled participation in the capital by the family/ies and the presence on the Board of at least one family member. The case study following described can be considered relevant as it is pioneer in its sector in offering quality products with a strong sustainability orientation. In addition, it is very difficult to find formalized sustainability business performance models in small-medium sized family firms as they are usually characterized by a low adoption of strategic and managerial tools, may be due to a lack of human resources which are always involved in the operating activities (Garengo et al., 2005; Hudson et al., 2000).

The case study, called 'Piedmont Excellence', operates in the beer sector, through the production and sale of hand crafted beer for Italian and foreign markets.

Piedmont Excellence brewery was originally created in 1996 as a brewpub (production and bar) in a small city of Piedmont in the Langhe area. In 2000, thanks to the products success, there was the first transformation of the activity. Soon after, the founder is forced to come up with the idea of the "beerduct": an underground duct to transfer the beer to the pub in the surroundings. Since 2000s the company started to create new tastes of beers and it also created a new distribution company to better supply the products on the national territory. Piedmont Excellence has also been directly involved in the production of most of the ingredients used for its beers, and in January 2012 it officially became a farmer brewery company, introducing, from the wine sector, a widespread concept based on the binomial 'beer – territory', verifying the quality of the raw materials, selecting suppliers and introducing traceability logics of ingredients.

The company, from the very beginning, sought to achieve operational excellence, particularly focusing on sustainability performances, through investments in research and development and a re-engineering of the most critical processes. In particular, the beer production processes and techniques are constantly rethought in order to drastically reduce the environmental impact deriving from company activities, and so to preserve the local environment. Piedmont Excellence is characterized by a remarkable sustainability orientation: indeed, the company's philosophy is to produce a high-quality craft beer through sustainable production processes.

This work has been conducted through the method of case study, a qualitative research where theory and empirical research are intertwined. Although this method is partially affected by subjectivity and it is often criticized for lack of statistical reliability and validity, it excels especially when it is necessary to understand a complex issue (Yin, 2013); it can develop expertise and it strengthen what is already known through previous researches. Case studies emphasize detailed contextual analysis of a limited number of events or conditions and their relationships.

In this study it was appropriate to use a qualitative method because, as also affirmed by Yin, it is complex to understand the strategy and its implementation with a special focus on sustainability, and it is not possible to recognize internal dynamics with a quantitative method. Also Scapens (1990) reiterates the importance of case studies to understand the reality. For these reasons it becomes fundamental the choice of an appropriate survey tool: for the research goals, it is not adequate the use of a questionnaire because it doesn't allow to verify if the respondents know the strategy and structure dynamics. So, this study is conducted through interviews to ensure that the interlocutors were prepared on strategy and structure features. In fact, the interviewed were exclusively addressed to the CEO, the CFO and the Directors of key functional areas. The interviews started in September 2014 and ended in December 2016 in order to well understand the strategic planning process, tool and dynamics. Each interview lasted between 32 and 66 minutes.

The interview, as a survey tool, has advantages such as flexibility, nonverbal behavior, environmental control, the order of questions, the completeness, the response from the interested interviewed, but it has also disadvantages such as the costs, the time, the interviewer's influence and a less standardization of the questions formulation. Consequently, the interviews were semi-structured to be kept within the main question area but still open the possibility to get the interviewees own ideas and feelings. The interviews included also some questions to test and verify the good quality of answers.

In addition to interviews, relevant information was also obtained from the Annual Reports and internal documents such as the business model, the strategy map, the balanced scorecard, the budgets and the reporting documents. Information achieved with interviews have been compared with those of the documents in order to increase the amount and the quality of data.

Concluding, for the purposes of this research, a qualitative investigation was necessary to deeply understand how the sustainability goals are integrated and measured within the strategic planning documents.

SOLUTIONS AND RECOMMENDATIONS

This section discusses the features of the business performance models implemented by the selected company.

The Strategy of Piedmont Excellence

The Piedmont Excellence (PE) business strategy started in 1996 when the craft beer was still unknown for most of the consumers. Since the beginning, the strategy was focused in the segment of craft beer, trying to strongly differentiate the quality of offered products.

Over the years, significant investments in research, development and facilities have been done by the brewery PE in order to constantly improve the taste and flavor of the beers offered and - at the same time - environmental performances, through rigorous controls of emissions and wastes.

The differentiation strategy was also realized through the increasing of products range. In fact, in order to extend the range of potential consumers the brewery decided to produce and sells, in addition to crafted beers, the following products:

- Soft drinks (ginger and cola);
- Cider;
- Distillates.

The strategy was also focused on the bond of the territory and the local communities, stressing the attention on the strong relationship between the territory and the ingredients used in the beer.

In addition, the company is the only Italian microbrewery that created partnerships with other companies as those of water industry, in order to wider the range of products offered. Seven beer brands are crafted in partnership with a company that distributes an Italian high quality water.

As far as the marketing distribution strategy is concerned, Piedmont Excellence sells its products through:

- 15 mono-brand owned stores;
- High quality markets (such as eataly)
- High quality brewery pubs
- On-line, on its web site.

Thanks to the successful realized strategy, PE became one of the renowned craft beer producers in Italy. Demand of PE beer has drastically increased in recent years and, consequently, production. The 25% of this production is now already exported. For this reason, the company needs to expand production in a new plant, in particular a green brewery plant.

The current strategy of PE is oriented to invest in research and development activities in order to improve the quality and characteristics of its products and differentiate them to those already on the market. In particular, the strategy aims at expanding the company's presence in the domestic and international markets through an enrichment of existing products both in terms of characteristics, improving the products quality and sustainability, and in terms of volumes.

The differentiation strategy is based on a revamp of the entire beer brewing plant, focusing on:

- Products quality and safety as, in order to constantly increase the taste, the benefits and organoleptic characteristics of beers, as well as reducing unwanted micro-organisms in the final product, the company will study new techniques and methods of fermentation and storage;
- Environment, through a rethought of beer production processes and techniques, in order to drastically reduce the environmental impact deriving from company activities.

This latter aspect - the environment- is the main pillar of PE philosophy and mission; however, at the same time, it is considered an element of differentiation and a source of competitive advantage because more and more customers orient their purchasing choices towards 'green products' and companies that demonstrate to be proactive in improving environmental performances.

The company is also studying an 'open' project, based on an open-didactic system, which should lead to a general growth of the unpasteurized beer market and to generate relevant environmental and social benefits as well as an improvement of the company's image. This project is based on the development of an IT platform where Piedmont Excellence and other companies, operating in the same field, can share innovation outcomes, knowledge, techniques and ingredients.

The Business Model of Piedmont Excellence

The strategic intentions and the related key success factors formulated by Piedmont Excellence, coherently with the strategy, are intended to enhance and enrich the portfolio of crafted beers through:

- Increase the company's image and knowledge:
    - Increase the presence on the italian and foreign market;
    - Investment in social network and events;
    - Partnership;

- Research and development of strategic investments to increase the quality of products and significantly reducing the environmental impact:
  - Research and develop a method to generate thermal and electrical energy from spent grains;
  - Develop technologies and techniques to ensure better detection performance and rapidity leading to a better control of the fermentation cycle and consequently an improvement in quality and safety of the final product;
- Re-engineering of the main strategic processes and activities:
  - Design and develop, in its own plant, a line for the self-production of pet containers;
  - Create an automated warehouse process;
  - Selection of strategically relevant suppliers based on quality and Italianism of raw materials.

In order to achieve the strategic intentions formulated, PE formalized different strategic projects under implementation:

- **Metagenomics of Fermentation Monitoring Plant:** The activities are finalized to the implementation of a pilot plant and a metagenomics laboratory to study the genetic transcription, the physiology and the metabolism of the yeast during fermentation, identifying the correlation between fermentation biodiversity (fermentation diagrams) and the presence of desirable or undesirable species on the final product, improving safety and quality of the final product. Focusing on food safety and product quality, the project is aimed at introducing, at industrial level, a system to foresee fermentation process in order to: i) identify the correlation between fermentation biodiversity and the presence of desirable or undesirable species on the end product; ii) reduce any unwanted micro-organisms in the final product; iii) improve the use of raw materials.
- **Valorisation of By-Products (Brewers' Grains):** Waste prevention is the over-riding priority of the food and drink Industry and full by-product utilization is an outstanding contributor to waste prevention. Due to their renewable nature, by-products and waste can reduce dependence on fossil fuels and achieve lower levels of greenhouse gas emissions. Spent grains are the most abundant brewing by-product and represent an unstable material that deteriorates rapidly due to microbial activity. So, in the project, brewery's spent grain will be totally reused with wood chips in a co-generator in order to produce thermal and electrical energy. For the waste prevention, there is going to be assembled a pilot plant: waste as spent grains (brewing process by-products) will be totally reused in a co-generator in order to produce thermal and electric energy. In particular, due to their renewable nature, by-products and waste can reduce dependence on fossil fuels and achieve lower levels of greenhouse gas emissions.
- **Sustainable Production of PET Kegs:** Packaging is a critical component of the beer production process and brewers are conscious of its impact on the environment. Many small brewing companies cannot afford the self-production of the kegs, therefore they are forced to purchase it. This implies costs and a heavy impact on the environment (i.e. transportation of the empty kegs). With this project, the company plans a line for self- production of recyclable PET kegs that will imply the utilization of less plastic and the elimination of sanitization process. The application of this system will save natural resources and energy in the production process and transportation (more lightweight) minimising the impact on the environment.
- **Automated Warehouse for Beer Re-Fermentation:** Production of bottled beer is characterised by substantial loss of the product due to problems in the refermentation process. The project aims

at improving the processes of storage, distribution and fermentation, designing and building a new, high-technologized warehouse where the natural stratification of the heat will be used for the second fermentation (that usually is in air conditioned cellars). In this innovative and 100% automated storehouse there will be used the natural stratification of the heat for the second fermentation (that usually is in the bottle in air conditioned cellars). This process will lead to save energy consumption removing the conditioned room generally utilized for the secondary fermentation and eliminating the need to condition the air temperature at different layers.

The activities necessaries to achieve the planned results of the strategic processes are briefly described below:

- **Metagenomics of Fermentation Monitoring Plant:** Firstly, a working group that involves also University experts will be created. This group will study if different fermentation conditions can lead to changes of expression of genes involved in the brewery process, bringing consequently to variations on beer specific metabolites. Therefore, it will be implemented a DNA methodology for quality control and identification of beneficial and negative yeast strains in order to more effectively manage them during the fermentation process. The activities implemented are finalized to the implementation of a pilot plant and a metagenomics laboratory to study the genetic transcription, the physiology and the metabolism of the yeast during fermentation. In particular, in order to comprehend if different fermenting conditions can induce changes in the expression of genes involved in the brewery process and therefore can modify the metabolites production in beer, the project will require, as key-actions, the creation of testing brewery and metagenomics lab and the analysis of the related impact.
- **Valorisation of By-Products (Brewers' Grains):** With the goal of minimizing the by-products production and reusing them for the heat and electricity production as energetic inputs to be used in the brewery process, a system to totally reuse spent grains (brewing process by-products) will be implemented, in order to produce thermal and electric energy. In particular, the spent brewer's grains will be separated from the mash in a plant designed to automatically collect, dry and reuse them by co-generation (combining electricity and heat production). Waste heat from the plant is harnessed to produce steam which is used in the brewing process.
- **Sustainable Production of PET Kegs:** In regards to emissions in atmosphere, carbon dioxide is a critical by-product of beer brewing and packaging process. In order to contribute to minimize gas emissions the project will focus also on the improvement of the packaging operations. The proposed solution is the implementation of a prototype blowing system for the production and 100% reuse on-site of the barrels. In particular, PE will design and develop a line for the self-production of PET containers (kegs), compatible with any beer filling and dispensing system. The plant will be studied in order to ensure the possibility to regulate some parameters, according to the final utilization of the keg, such as the thickness, the diameter and the height of the barrel.
- **Automated Warehouse for Beer Re-Fermentation:** The improvement of the processes of storage, distribution and fermentation will be achieved designing and building a new, high-technologized warehouse 100% automated in which there will be used the natural stratification of the heat for the secondary fermentation (that usually is in the bottle in air conditioned rooms). In fact, some PE's beers require a second fermentation in bottle. The project idea is to store the beer in the warehouse where an automatic system driven by a software will move the bottles through the

shelves according to specific fermentation diagrams and the logistics needs until the achievement of the product stability and the consequent placement in the right storage shelves. This process will lead to save energy consumption removing the conditioned room generally utilized for the secondary fermentation and eliminating the need to condition the air temperature at different layers. In particular, at this stage, the key actions will be oriented to design and build an automated warehouse, to design of an ad-hoc software and to design and realize the cold/heat water production- ground-source heat pump.

Summary of Expected Outcomes and Expected Financial Results

In particular, there are some expected benefits related to final products, hereunder described:

- Social benefits deriving from an increase in the shared knowledge on tools, techniques and materials that can be used in craft beer production processes and logistic system, thanks to the technology and process studied;
- Environmental benefits deriving from the reduction of wastes, energy rationalization, reduction of gas emissions. The brewers' grains, once considered mere waste, nowadays represent in fact, the most important sources of secondary products and are usually used as animal feed or to produce biogas in biomass plants. The solution proposed in the project will utilize the spent grains with a consequent reduction of waste going to landfill. The energy rationalization thanks to the technologies that will enable to generate energy from spent grains, allowing recovering the energy embedded in biodegradable residues in a combustion process and reuse it in the production process. Furthermore, the direct production of PET kegs contributes to energy saving, reducing needs in term of steam production (normally needed for kegs sterilization). Finally, the automated warehouse for beer re-fermentation has been planned to exploit the natural air thermal stratification in a closed space. This process will lead to save energy removing the conditioned room generally employed for re-fermentation and eliminating the need of conditioning the temperature air at different levels; this will be achieved with the natural air stratification. The projects also allow to reduce the gas emission from transport: the closed-loop waste (spent grain) management causes a pollution reduction as there will be a minimization of transport for waste disposal. Furthermore, the implementation of the PET keg line directly in the production plan will imply a considerable reduction in terms of gas emissions as no more transport for empty kegs will be necessary.
- Economic benefits thanks to an improvement in competitiveness. The process innovation developed through the projects it is expected to cut the production costs down, being therefore able to position PE's beer in the market at a lower price than usual, without decreasing the quality and the notable taste. Thanks to a lower price for the 33 cl bottle, PE will be finally able to sell also to the large scale retailers. Furthermore, a capital saving will be possible by the elimination of transport and cleaning costs and the final cost of a PET self-produced keg is lower than 50% comparing the purchased container.

Figure 1 shows the main expected indicators.

Figure 1. PE main expected indicators

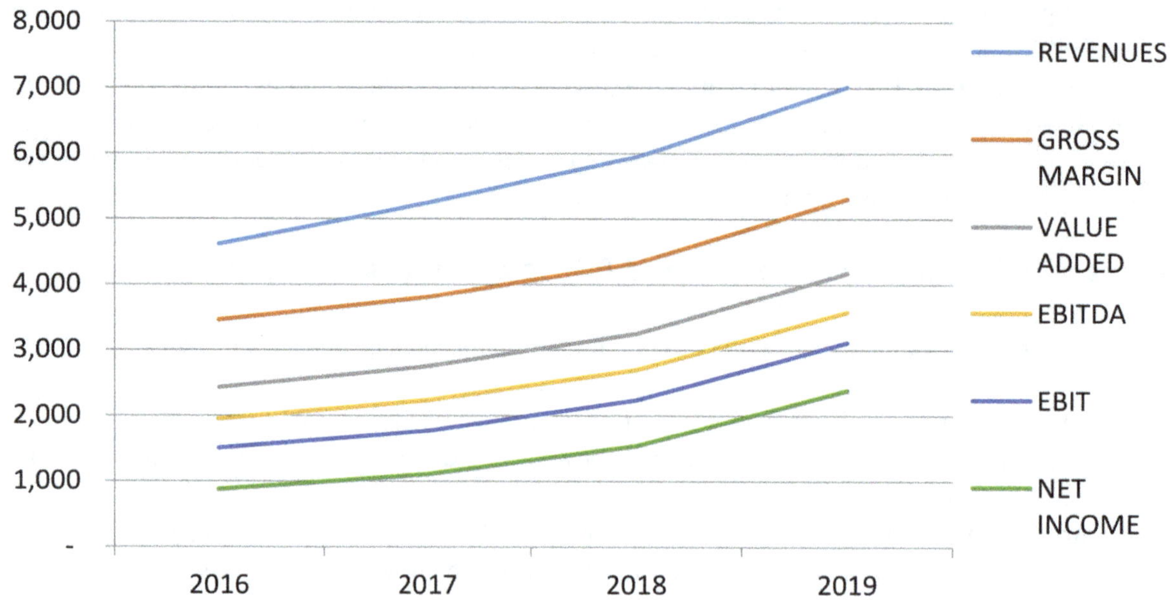

**For a more accurate representation see the electronic version.*

FUTURE RESEARCH DIRECTIONS

The paper has some interesting theoretical and practical implications as it contributes to integrate the existing literature on family firms, strategic planning and sustainability and allows managers better understand how a sustainability strategy can be translated into operational terms. However, to make effective the business model and consequently monitor the correct implementation of the strategy, the company should identify and link the key performance indicators to the key success factors. In this way it is able to monitor the goals achievement.

The main limit of this work is represented by the method chosen. Starting from this limitation, future researches could involve additional case studies, also in order to validate or confute the current results. Another future development can be focused in investigating if investments in sustainability lead to adequate economic benefits, as suggested by many authors (Schaltegger and Wagner, 2011; Nidumolo et al., 2009). Indeed, the sustainability management requires economic and financial efforts, but, at the same time, can generate significant benefits: for example, the 'green philosophy' can improve the company's image and can impact on economic performances. The technologies introduced to minimize the environmental impacts, can contribute to reduce the consumption and improve efficiency.

CONCLUSION

In the analyzed case study, the strategy has been explicated, implemented and then communicated to the various organizational levels through strategic planning tools.

Despite the main literature on strategic and management control tools in small and medium sized family firms has underlined a poor adoption of advanced strategic and management tools (Gareco, Biazzo, Bititci, 2005), the company analyzed has shown a good strategic orientation, identifying a sustainable strategy further explicated into strategic intentions and key success factors. At this stage, the three pillars of sustainability are visible in the will to expand the company's profitability (economic), to rethought techniques and processes in order to improve the safety of products (social) and reduce the environmental impact (environmental), as recommended in literature (Epstein & Buhovac, 2014; Schaltegger & Wagner, 2006; Figge et al., 2002; Dias-Sardinha & Reijnders, 2001).

According to Hansen and Schaltegger (2016) and Van Marrewijk (2004) a sustainable business model resembles a profit-driven value system where organizations maintain an active hierarchy, seek for progress and success and benchmark themselves against competition, while success is primarily measured in financial and monetary terms; the sustainability is a key factor to generate not only profit but also a global wealth. In addition, as it also emerged from the case study analyzed, sustainability is considered an opportunity to achieve success, reduce risks and enhance reputation or image. At the same time, profit-driven concept doesn't signify that the respective value system is the only one linked to for-profit companies, as also declared by PE.

In conclusion, the analysis of the PE shows that the sustainability management could be considered a basis for innovation and growth. The company is aware that it needs considerable investments to achieve the planned goals and consequently to implement the "green philosophy".

REFERENCES

Anderson, R. C., & Reeb, D. M. (2003). Founding-family ownership and firm performance: Evidence from the S&P 500. *The Journal of Finance*, *58*(3), 1301–1328. doi:10.1111/1540-6261.00567

Bieker, T. (2002). *Sustainability management with the Balanced Scorecard*. Paper of Institute for Economy and the Environment at the University.

Bird, B., Welsch, H., Astrachan, J. H., & Pistrui, D. (2002). Family business research: The evolution of an academic field. *Family Business Review*, *15*(4), 337–350. doi:10.1111/j.1741-6248.2002.00337.x

Broccardo, L. (2011). Family Versus Non Family Firms in the Luxury Yachts Sector: Strategy – Structure Combination to Manage the Performance. *Electronic Journal of Family Business Studies*, *5*(1-2), 96–125.

Brusa, L. (2007). *Attuare e controllare la strategia aziendale – Mappa strategica e Balanced Scorecard*. Giuffrè Editore.

Capasso, A., Gallucci, C., & Rossi, M. (2015). Standing the test of time. Does firm performance improve with age? An analysis of the wine industry. *Business History*, *57*(7), 1037–1053. doi:10.1080/00076791.2014.993614

Claessens, S., Diankov, S., & Lang, L. H. P. (2000). The Separation of Ownership and Control in East Asian Corporations. *Journal of Financial Economics*, *58*(1-2), 81–112. doi:10.1016/S0304-405X(00)00067-2

Claessens, S., Djankov, S., Fan, J. P., & Lang, L. H. (2002). Disentangling the incentive and entrenchment effects of large shareholdings. *The Journal of Finance*, *57*(6), 2741–2771. doi:10.1111/1540-6261.00511

Corbetta, M., & Shulman, G. L. (2002). Control of goal-directed and stimulus-driven attention in the brain. *Nature Reviews. Neuroscience*, *3*(3), 201–215. doi:10.1038/nrn755 PMID:11994752

Culasso, F., Broccardo, L., Manzi, L. M., & Truant, E. (2016). Management Accounting and Enterprise Risk Management. A potential integration as a new change in managerial systems. *Global Business and Economics Review*, *18*(3-4), 344–370. doi:10.1504/GBER.2016.076238

Culasso, F., Broccardo, L., Mazzoleni, A., & Giacosa, E. (2012). Corporate Governance in Listed Italian Family Firms: Impact on Performance and Comparison with Non-Family Firms. *Journal of Management & Change*, *29*(1).

De Geuser, F., Mooraj, S., & Oyon, D. (2009). Does the balanced scorecard add value? Empirical evidence on its effect on performance. *European Accounting Review*, *18*(1), 93–122. doi:10.1080/09638180802481698

Dias-Sardinha I, Reijnders L., (2001). Environmental performance evaluations and sustainability performance evaluation of organizations: an evolutionary framework. *The Journal of Corporate Environmental Management*, *8*(2), 71-79.

Dyllick, T., & Hockerts, K. (2002). Beyond the business case for corporate sustainability. *Business Strategy and the Environment*, *11*(2), 130–141. doi:10.1002/bse.323

Elkington, J. (1997). *Cannibals with forks: the triple bottom line of 21st century business*. Oxford, UK: Capstone.

Epstein, M. J., & Buhovac, A. R. (2014). *Making sustainability work: Best practices in managing and measuring corporate social, environmental, and economic impacts*. Berrett-Koehler Publishers.

Epstein, M. J., & Roy, M. J. (2001). Sustainability in action: Identifying and measuring the Key performance drivers. *Long Range Planning*, *34*(5), 585–604. doi:10.1016/S0024-6301(01)00084-X

Epstein, M. J., & Wisner, P. S. (2001). Using a Balanced Scorecard to implement sustainability. *Environmental Quality Management*, *11*(2), 1–10. doi:10.1002/tqem.1300

Faccio, M., Lang, L., & Young, L. (2001). Dividends and expropriation. *The American Economic Review*, *91*(1), 54–78. doi:10.1257/aer.91.1.54

Faccio, M., & Lang, L. H. P. (2002). The Ultimate Ownership of Western EuropeanCorporations. *Journal of Financial Economics*, *65*(1), 365–395. doi:10.1016/S0304-405X(02)00146-0

Figge, F., Hahn, T., Schaltegger, S., & Wagner, M. (2002). The Sustainability Balanced Scorecard – linking sustainability management to business strategy. *Business Strategy and the Environment*, *11*(5), 269–284. doi:10.1002/bse.339

Figgie, F., Hahn, T., Schaltegger, S., & Wagner, M. (2001). The Sustainability Balanced Scorecard – a tool for value oriented sustainability management in strategy-focused organizations. *Conference Proceedings of the 2001 eco-management and auditing conference*, 83-90.

Garengo, P., Biazzo, S., & Bititci, U. S. (2005). Performance measurement systems in SMEs: A review for a research agenda. *International Journal of Management Reviews*, *7*(1), 25–47. doi:10.1111/j.1468-2370.2005.00105.x

Gedajlovic, E., Carney, M., Chrisman, J. J., & Kellermanns, F. W. (2012). The adolescence of family firm research taking stock and planning for the future. *Journal of Management*, *38*(4), 1010–1037. doi:10.1177/0149206311429990

Gubitta, P., & Gianecchini, M. (2002). Governance and Flexibility in family-owned SMEs. *Family Business Review*, *15*(4), 277–297. doi:10.1111/j.1741-6248.2002.00277.x

Horngren, C. T., Foster, G., Datar, S. M., Rajan, M., Ittner, C., & Baldwin, A. A. (2010). Cost accounting: A managerial emphasis. *Issues in Accounting Education*, *25*(4), 789–790. doi:10.2308/iace.2010.25.4.789

Hoy, F., & Verser, T. G. (1994). Emerging business, emerging field: Entrepreneurship and the family firm, *Entrepreneurship. Theory into Practice*, *19*(1), 9–24.

Hudson, M., Bourne, M., Lean, J., & Smart, P. A. (2000). Only just managing – no time to measure. In *Proceedings Performance Measurement – Past, Present and Future*. Craneld University.

Kaplan, R., & Norton, D. (2004). *Strategy Maps: Converting Intangible Assets into Tangible Outcomes*. Boston: Harvard Business School Press.

Kaplan, R., & Norton, D. (2006). *Alignment: Using the Balanced Scorecard to Create Corporate Synergies*. Boston: Harvard Business School Press.

Kaplan, R., & Norton, D. (2008). *Execution Premium: Linking Strategy to Operations for Competitive Advantage*. Boston: Harvard Business School Press.

Kaplan, R. S., & Norton, D. P. (1996). *The Balanced Scorecard*. Boston: Harvard Business School Press.

Kaplan, R. S., & Norton, D. P. (2001). *The Strategy-Focused Organization*. Boston: Harvard Business School Press.

La Porta, R., Lopez-De-Silanes, F., Shleifer, A., & Vishny, R. (1998). Law and Finance. *Journal of Political Economy*, *106*(6), 1113–1155. doi:10.1086/250042

Lee, J. (2004). The effects of family ownership and management on firm performance. *S.A.M. Advanced Management Journal*, *69*(4), 46.

Maury, B. (2006). Family ownership and firm performance: Empirical evidence from Western European corporations. *Journal of Corporate Finance*, *12*(2), 321–341. doi:10.1016/j.jcorpfin.2005.02.002

Montemerlo, D. (2000). *Il governo delle imprese familiari: modelli e strumenti per gestire i rapporti tra proprietà e impresa*. Milano: Egea.

Neubauer, F., & Lank, A. G. (1998). *The Family Business: Its Governance for Sustainability*. London: Macmillan Business. doi:10.1007/978-1-349-14465-5

Nidumolo, R., Prahalad, C. K., & Rangaswami, M. R. (2009). Why sustainability is now the key driver of innovation. *Harvard Business Review*, *87*(9), 56–64.

O' Connor, M. (2006). The four spheres framework for sustainability. *Ecological Complexity*, *3*(44), 285–292. doi:10.1016/j.ecocom.2007.02.002

Prencipe, A., Bar-Yosef, S., & Dekker, H. C. (2014). Accounting research in family firms: Theoretical and empirical challenges. *European Accounting Review, 23*(3), 361–385. doi:10.1080/09638180.2014.895621

Salvato, C., & Moores, K. (2010). Research on accounting in family firms: Past accomplishments and future challenges. *Family Business Review, 23*(3), 193–215. doi:10.1177/0894486510375069

Schaltegger, S., & Burrit, R. (2000). *Contemporary environmental accounting: issues, concepts and practice*. Sheffield, UK: Greenleaf.

Schaltegger, S., Lüdeke-Freund, F., & Hansen, E. G. (2012). Business cases for sustainability: The role of business model innovation for corporate sustainability. *International Journal of Innovation and Sustainable Development, 6*(2), 95–119. doi:10.1504/IJISD.2012.046944

Schaltegger, S., & Wagner, M. (2006). Integrative management of sustainability performance, measurement and reporting. *International Journal of Accounting, Auditing and Performance Evaluation, 3*(1), 1–19. doi:10.1504/IJAAPE.2006.010098

Schaltegger, S., & Wagner, M. (2011). Sustainable entrepreneurship and sustainability innovation: Categories and interactions. *Business Strategy and the Environment, 20*(4), 222–237. doi:10.1002/bse.682

Searcy, C. (2012). Corporate sustainability performance measurement systems: A review and research agenda. *Journal of Business Ethics, 107*(3), 239–253. doi:10.100710551-011-1038-z

Shank, J. (1989). Strategic cost management: New wine or just new bottles? *Journal of Management Accounting Research, 1*, 47–65.

Shank, J. (1996). Analysing technology investments from NPV to strategic cost management. *Management Accounting Research, 7*(2), 185–197. doi:10.1006/mare.1996.0011

Songini, L. (2007). The professionalization of family firms: theory and practice. In *Handbook of Research on Family Business*. Cheltenham, UK: Edward Elgar.

Songini, L., Gnan, L., & Malmi, T. (2013). The role and impact of accounting in family business. *Journal of Family Business Strategy, 4*(2), 71–83. doi:10.1016/j.jfbs.2013.04.002

Stampacchia, P., Mele, C., & Russo Spena, T. (2008). Processi di governo e crescita internazionale nelle PMI familiari. Il caso Harmont&Blaine. In C. Devecchi & G. Fraquelli (Eds.), *Dinamiche di sviluppo e internazionalizzazione del family business* (pp. 501–518). Bologna: Edizione Il Mulino.

Villalonga, B., & Amit, R. (2006). How do family ownership, control and management affect firm value? *Journal of Financial Economics, 80*(2), 385–417. doi:10.1016/j.jfineco.2004.12.005

Yin, R. K. (2013). *Case study research: Design and methods*. Sage publications.

Zocchi, W. (2004a) Discontinuità e sinergie generazionali nell'azienda di famiglia. Un'indagine empirica nel Lazio. Luiss University Press – Pola Srl, Roma.

Zocchi, W. (2004b) Il family business. Famiglia, azienda di famiglia e il patrimonio dell'imprenditore. Il Sole 24 Ore, Milano.

KEY TERMS AND DEFINITIONS

Family Firm: Family firm is a company where: 1) at least 50% of shares are owned by the family and the family is responsible for the management of the company; 2) or at least 50% of shares are owned by the family, the company is not family-run, but the CEO perceives it as a family firm; 3) or family ownership is less than 50%, the company is family-run, the CEO perceives it as a family firm and a venture capital or investment company owns at least 50% of the shares.

Key Success Factors: Limited number of key variables that have a strong impact on how successfully and effectively an organization meets its strategic goals.

Sustainability: Focuses on meeting the needs of the present without compromising the ability of future generations to meet their needs. The concept of sustainability is comprised of three pillars: economic, environmental, and social.

Chapter 14
"Glocal" Small Business for Sustainability: What Reporting?

Guido Migliaccio
University of Sannio, Italy

ABSTRACT

In socioeconomic areas, the "glocal" model, which mediates the characteristics of globalization with those of the more entrenched localization, seems to flourish. Glocalization is a social and economic phenomenon, and has intuitive implications also on the environment. Therefore, it causes sustainability issues. As it is governed by its own principles, it modifies traditional business management systems. When can a business be defined glocal? What are the characteristics of its management? What are the features of his promotional communication? How does its social, environmental, and financial reporting change? Must the many stakeholders always be spectators of a communication imposed by property and regulations, or can they become "prosumers" in the financial statement? These initial reflections will require subsequent empirical verifications.

INTRODUCTION

Faced with the vast and complex phenomenon of globalization, the economic think-tank is located between two virtual extremes: On the one hand, the hypothesis of standardization of lifestyles and, thus, productive assets, investments, and consumption; on the other hand, the ability to accentuate and exalt the differences of customs, and therefore logical processes and procedures for value creation.

The reality has shown a model of production and consumption that seems to fall between the above-mentioned extremes, in which the innovative aspects of globalization are simultaneously combined with local traditions, as a recurrent key factor in successful competitive strategy. This is glocalization.

The causes that lead to this condition are many and complex. Glocalization seems to mediate the characteristics of globalization with those of the more entrenched localization. Certainly glocalization raises questions resulting in new socioeconomic areas, and then specific issues related to business

DOI: 10.4018/978-1-5225-5267-3.ch014

communications and public administration. Governed by its own principles, radical mutation leads to a logical management of business and its reports.

This chapter aims to answer the following questions:

RQ1: When can a business be defined "glocal"?
RQ2: What are the characteristics of management, which is certainly complicated by the simultaneous presence of global, local, and glocal functions?
RQ3: How to change the need for effective communication for a business that is simultaneously present in different areas?
RQ4: May economic and financial communications be limited to a single financial statement?
RQ5: Must the many stakeholders always be spectators of a communication imposed by property and regulations, or can they become "prosumers" in the financial statement?
RQ6: Do the principles of glocalism favor the logic of sustainability? And, is glocal small business a typical example of sustainable entrepreneurship?

BACKGROUND

The most recent contributions to literature can be distinguished through analysis: Sociological, highlighting group changes in different nations; economic, which instead focuses on the effects of the new social fabric on the global economy; managerial, which is particularly relevant to this study and which emphasizes the effects on the management of the companies of the new actors of the international economic stage (Mourdoukoutas & Ioannidis, 2007).

Glocalization and glocal are neologisms that were coined in the eighties in Japan, then imported into the English language by the British sociologist Roland Robertson (1992, 1994, 1995), and then extensively developed by Zygmunt Bauman (2005) to mediate the demands of globalization with those of local realities.

Among the many sociological studies that followed the first definitions of the phenomenon, surely de Burgh-Woodman's (2014) research has many interdisciplinary elements between sociology, psychology, and economic implications. This chapter aims to expand current theories of globalisation with a consideration of its impact on the individual. The finding that the Self/Other divide is altered in the current era of globalisation has impact for cultural and marketing theory, since it refocuses attention on the shifting nature of identity and how individuals encounter the Other in their daily existence.

Such a psychological and social approach characterizes Yama's (2016) contribution. Starting from an analysis of Japan's typical situation, Yama proposes a comparison between Oriental and Western mentalities as they evolve in relation to globalized and, above all, "glocalized" economic trends: the notions of global and glocal mindset are important for international business.

Different social links and interdependencies between economies also pose serious problems of political representativeness and, thus, question the classical canons of the democracies that characterized the previous century. Chan (2016) firmly states that diplomacy is in trouble. International policy-making suffers from "democratic deficits". Surprisingly, scholars of international relations have largely neglected the role of cities in global governance. This chapter argues for city diplomacy and glocal governance to fill the theoretical gap.

The sociological and political sciences also discuss the equilibrium that the new economic systems are making. Unfortunately, the problem of inequalities is certainly not overcome by the establishment of a glocal model. Lenger and Schumacher (2015) address this theme more in particular. Indeed, these authors, building up on of Ronald Robertson's (1992, 1994, 1995) famous distinction, treat inequality as a culturally glocalized phenomenon, i.e. integrating both the global and the local effects of inequality into the analysis of global inequality. In a nutshell, they argue that globalization has two structural effects on social stratification. On the one hand, it creates glocal inequalities on a local level. On the other hand, it shapes the social structure on the global level.

In any case, the new glocal landscape is the result of many factors, including specific events that favor its affirmation. This is Marques's (2013) view, which analyzes in particular the glocal project of 's-Hertogenbosch.

New glocal arrangements also contribute to the development of education at various school and university levels. Indeed, glocalism is not only a subject of study at major research centers, but directly affects young people's education and training paths. This is the case, for example, in art schools as Hartman (2016) described. However, also, and above all, universities need to respond to glocal challenges adequately (Grau, 2016). The vision of a university as a 'social force for good' makes engagement compatible with the immediate needs of local societies and the global challenges of the world.

These changed social contexts derive and generate a new globalized global economic equilibrium which is described in its key features in numerous contributions of macroeconomics and economic policy that cannot be cited in this essay.

International bibliographic contributions on relationships between glocalism and management can be distinguished in two groups: Studies related to impacts on key management functions (e.g., strategies, marketing, organization, and finance) and those related to specific sectors (e.g., finance, tourism, and transport). The "think global, act local" (Champy, 1997; Onkvisit & Shaw, 2002) relationship that synthesizes the principles of glocalism must necessarily inform business strategies, especially market approaches. This emerges, in particular, in Japutra, Nguyen, and Melewar's (2015) study, although it refers exclusively to Indonesia. In order to successfully develop a brand in a culturally diverse market, three important factors need attention: Glocalization, consumer-brand relationships, and societal marketing.

Referring to Chinese reality, Rowley and Warner (2013) hypothesize adaptation of business management strategies to all realities, local, glocal, or global. Also, with reference to China, see Matusitz and Leanza (2009).

Wherever any problems occur related to the need for the corporate organization to assimilate the new glocal strategies using special diffusion and fertilization techniques for various employees and collaborators (Søderberg, 2015). The recent tendencies of the glocal strategies that characterize the marketing mix are, however, already subject to some authors' critical reflection, especially when the question is: "Is glocal the most effective strategy?" (Anonymous, 2013).

As it turns out, marketing strategies are the focus of being a glocal-type adaptation (Arnold, 2007). Thus, it is in specialized marketing writings that the most frequent references to glocalism are found (Tai & Wong, 1998; Thompson & Arsel, 2004; Young, 2003). They point out the role of cultural capital in creating glocal brand relationships (Kjeldgaard, Askegaard & Eckhardt, 2015) and how local habits affect consumption as well as goods considered as needed, such as drugs (Smith, 2013). Marketing papers, however, apart from extremely specific contributions, also include studies that try to define the glocal problem according to broader parameters. Bjerrisgaard and Kjeldgaard (2013), for example, focus on how various ideological representations of the market produce certain effects on the way in which the market spaces materialize and simultaneously draw the contours of ideal organizational and consumer subjectivities. Authors employ a governmentality perspective to address the global myth of market creation and hence the emergence of glocal market spaces.

The focus of major marketing scholars, however, is on cultural differences that find local origins and the opposite tendency to respond to common global logic criteria. This obviously affects market demand and therefore marketing strategies, especially those related to the brand. This emerges, for example, in Kipnis, Broderick, and Demangeot's (2014) contribution.

The theme of the cultural characterization of a market is also outlined in Strizhakova and Coulter's (2013) work, which the authors subsequently resumed, considering its interesting reflections on sustainability.

Orienting management strategies according to glocal logics that are inspired by glocal marketing also has significant effects on the organization of production units (Beukema, 2004; Beukema & Carrillo, 2004; Gonzalez, 2006; Shi, 2007) which are necessarily based on intercultural competences. Nava (2017) examined in depth this interesting topic in the era of postbureaucratic organizations acting within a global/glocal scenario and facing new challenges related to cultural and intercultural issues. Intercultural competences must be acquired already in the university classrooms, considering the glocal student's physiognomy (Ramanau, 2016).

In the context of the international bibliographic panorama, glocal problems characterize studies in specific fields, above all finance and tourism (Granelli, 2002; Peghin, 2008).

Global strategies in banking and finance explore the concept of a glocal industry through case studies, emerging research, and interdisciplinary perspectives applicable to a variety of fields in banking and finance (Dinçer & Hacioğlu, 2013; Lo Turco & Maggioni, 2017).

The glocal dimension of tourism is, however, described in numerous essays (Bookin Blog, 2008[1], 2008[2]; Jolliffe, Cave & Baum, 2013; Papathanassis, 2014; Salazar, 2005). It can affect all the protagonists, such as entire cities (Hudak, 2017) and even nongovernmental associations of fauna development (Van Wijk, Van der Duim, Lamers & Sumba, 2015).

Other economic sectors that are particularly affected by the glocal phenomenon are: Agri-food (Nascente, 2015), energy (Müller, 2017), transport (Angelidou et al., 2015), and fashion (Sobh, Belk & Gressel, 2014).

The threefold declination of the concept of sustainability in the environmental, economic, and social spheres has also generated a fruitful bibliography of authors of different cultural extraction. Consequently, relations between sustainability and the glocal dimension of societies and the economy have had some interesting insights in the latest international bibliographic panorama.

Certainly, the writings that relate the concept of sustainability to its ecological dimension are more widespread. Svensson, Padin, and Eriksson (2016), for example, describe and debate business sustainability beyond zero emissions that is necessary to achieve glocal business sustainability.

Further interesting considerations come from cultural identity theory, global consumer culture theory, and sustainability research. Strizhakova and Coulter (2013), for example, examine the "green" side of materialism in emerging BRIC (Brazil, Russia, India and China) markets and in developed (U.S. and Australian) markets. For individuals with a glocal cultural identity, they observe a significant positive relationship between materialism and the measures of environmentally friendly tendencies.

Within the framework of these analyzes, UNESCO's educational role is fundamental, because, in approving its Earth Charter, explicitly refers to relations between sustainability and glocal reality. (Ángeles Murga-Menoyo, 2009).

Many landscaping assets are considered as patrimony of mankind and society even in its local development. Mountains, for example, are considered glocal heritage (Debarbieux & Price, 2008).

Studies of the economy of the companies belonging to the primary sector can always be considered in the field of ecological sustainability. In particular, they point out that (Spillare, 2016) the agro-ecological consumerism can be interpreted as an expression of a "glocal reflexivity" phenomenon, in which action is focused on community as participation for common good. The glocal dimension of ecological sustainability in the aquaculture industry is defined in Barton and Fløysand's (2010) work.

Leaving aside specific aspects of a particular sector, Loorbach and Lijnis Huffenreuter (2013) provide a convincing interpretation of the recent economic crisis, which seems to have also been the result of the abandonment of sustainable economic policies. Transition management research and practice should focus on identifying and providing the necessary generic-'glocal governance'-conditions under which the unsustainable regimes are discouraged and emerging sustainability transitions are accelerated. Nevertheless, the transition to sustainable economic systems must be facilitated by the guidelines of the main businesses, as in the interesting study by Barkemeyer and Figge (2014). Anyhow, the relationships between sustainability principles and the glocal setting of human life transcend considerations that are only ecological or limited to the economic aspects of societies. In fact, they characterize new relationships of greater scope to affect the life of people in urban agglomerations. In particular, politics and economic policy must assimilate the already well-known needs of sustainability, given the glocal dimension of countries and cities. The multifaceted reflection of international literature ranges from studies of glocal resistance to the new world neoliberal order (Stahler-Sholk, 2010), to proposals for new sustainable glocal structures that can be identified over the next decades (Smida, Hrdinova, Sakal & Syc, 2011).

The urgent need for a glocal strategy that governs the complex systems that have now shown significant resistance to globalization emerges (Laszlo, 2013). Much more concretely, the new demands for sustainability are felt especially in the big cities that have assumed the glocal dimension for years. The importance of this theme is evidenced by numerous specialized sociourban studies (Asprone & Manfredi, 2015; Rivera, 2017; Zhao & Li, 2017).

These first bibliographic records highlight that there are no contributions that outline in general a unified but synthetic concept of glocal enterprise that characterizes its main managerial traits and consequently adapts communication, including economic and financial, to the various global and local stages, to which it is simultaneously addressed.

MAIN FOCUS OF THE CHAPTER

This chapter presents some considerations about the new small glocal business that characterizes a large part of the Western economy. It begins by defining the phenomenon of glocalization: It has numerous economic and social implications and involves individuals, families, business, and the whole society (Shamsuddoha, 2008).

In a glocal world, the role of small businesses is central to the fact that they are better able to blend the characteristics of globalization with the widespread desire to maintain local traditions of production and consumption. Small glocal businesses can be protagonists of a sustainable economy. However, it is necessary to try to define the glocal business, trying to identify their peculiar characteristics. It is also necessary to identify the best forms of economic and social communication they could use to foster better relations with local and international stakeholders.

The objectives of this chapter will be achieved with some theoretical considerations based on a qualitative approach (Maylor & Blackmon, 2005; Yin, 1994, 2003), including an updated conceptualisation of the literature review and references to some case studies.

The decision to propose conceptualisations based on qualitative research proposals from the international literature is derived from the social and economic characteristics of the analysed subject.

Qualitative research proposals are designed to help researchers understand the social and cultural contexts within which people live.

One of the key benefits of qualitative research is that it allows an understanding of the context in which all decisions and actions take place (Myers, 2013). Often human decisions and actions can only be understood in context, because the context helps to 'explain' why someone acted as they did. This context (or multiple contexts) is best understood by observing the evolution of technology, economy, and culture, which greatly influence people's behaviour.

This chapter, therefore, does not offer results from a specific type of quantitative or qualitative research, but instead proposes a number of critical considerations taking into account the latest developments, as described by the best international bibliography. This work offers interdisciplinary value because it originates from the combination of technical, general economic, managerial, ethical, and other fields.

THE "PRINCIPLES" OF GLOCALISM

Faced with the vast and complex phenomenon of globalization, the economic think-tank is located between two virtual extremes: On the one hand, the hypothesis of standardization of lifestyles, and thus productive assets, investments, and consumption (Levitt, 1983, 2006); on the other hand, the ability to accentuate and exalt the differences of customs and therefore logical processes and procedures for value creation.

The reality has shown a model of production and consumption that seems to fall between the above-mentioned extremes, in which the innovative aspects of globalization are simultaneously combined with local traditions, as a recurrent key factor in successful competitive strategy (Shamsuddoha, 2008).

The causes that lead to this condition are many and complex. Glocalization seems to mediate the characteristics of globalization with those of the more entrenched localization.

Probably, the main reason for the diffusion of the glocal model is the resistance of local communities to automatically and uncritically acquire the logic of globalization rather than their tradition. In this regard, a clear example is regional values that have strengthened over the centuries and that are sometimes in clear contradiction with globalizing believes. It is also worth considering the justified fears that global actors can plunder local resources only to the benefit of major economic powers. In other words, it is feared that a globalized market can significantly increase the imbalances in resource distribution, accentuating inequalities.

Nonetheless, far beyond the economic aspects, it is also important to consider the social and cultural perspectives that have always characterized, typifying, entire areas of the globe. Noticeably, the dynamics of tourist flows is just the effect of the desire to know and appreciate different human situations profoundly. In a mutual comparison, those flows would like to remain so, to better meet individuals' psychological needs.

Economic globalization, in fact, does not only affect consumption, but it also aims to massify ethical choices and, therefore, to homologate every person's behaviors to a few standardized scripts, in order to place globalized companies' goods and services. However, it is understood that the globalization process is necessarily unstoppable, also considering its benefits. Indeed, it promotes the spread of culture and scientific progress and thus frees millions of people from ignorance and misery, which, instead, reduce the quality and hope of their life.

These short reflections show that the analysis of the causes of glocalization is complex and requires an interdisciplinary interpretative effort that will necessarily develop further in the future. Certainly glocalization raises questions resulting in new socio economic areas and then specific issues related to corporate communications and public administration.

Firstly, definitional problems arise for the phenomenon of glocal, in general, and of the actors of economic competition, in particular.

The first look, which is founded on principles and ethical values, is an easy and informal way to get to the complex. It believes the person and his/her group, the local material and immaterial heritage, the local community, the interaction of individuals in the community, and the subsystems of an organization complex are central. This particular view of the new social reality has led to the creation of a series of principles (Table 1), in Italy. Indeed, technology has a major influence on the evaluation of what time and space are. In addition, it is crucial to unify a world in which innovation feeds new knowledge, innovative customs, and alternative values to traditional ones. These considerations lead to the conclusion that mobility must prevail over placidity. The mobility is certainly a source of opportunities, but also of threats, mainly arising from new relationships without the protection of the traditional boundaries.

Yet, glocalism is the real alternative to apolid uniformity. Nevertheless, glocalism requires new policies and new institutions, especially with the emergence of new powers that are called upon to manage the new cultural, ethnic, and territorial identities in which social movements will acquire an absolute value. In glocalism, the central institution is (and will be) the global regulated enterprise in which the networks of economic and social actors will become the first protagonists. However, it will still need to have global public institutions capable of linking global businesses and the many local businesses, mediating between the needs of the global economy and local cohabitation, thus reconciling efficiency and democracy.

Glocal politics will have to solve a central problem: Equal coexistence between individuals, ethnicities, and different nations that require a new concept of multinational citizenship to be able to operate freely in the rich and dynamic structure of functional and territorial networks that the glocal world is generating.

The economic implications of this view are based primarily on the production of goods and services which are designed for a global market, but are adapted to local laws and demand, hence the famous motto: Think global, act local (Champy, 1997; Onkvisit & Shaw, 2002).

The necessary global free market is therefore instrumental to the needs of the protagonist of the micro group, but it grows, develops, interacts with the other increasingly complex groups, until it reaches the global realities.

As a result, the global and the local may well coexist, considering the first which evolution of the second, complex system that preserves however the original local structures.

In this articulated context, businesses must accrue logical managerial significantly different from those only local or in the typical international (Amato Mangiameli, 2006; D'Agostino, 2002; Preti, 2006; Sedda, 2004;Tardia, 2002; Vaciago, 2003).

Meanwhile, the government and local authorities are called upon to perform functions in new areas, beyond their traditional social competence, and also in support of productive activities. Accordingly, these changes encourage innovative methods of communication from businesses and local authorities to usual and new categories of stakeholders.

Table 1. The "principles" of glocalism

Introduction
• Technology changes the ideas of time and space, and has unified the world; • Innovation facilitates the encounter between knowledge and power to build values; • Innovation means new opportunities but also threats; • Mobility dominates the permanence, so it develops independent reports from the territories; • Endless relations change the meaning of place and open new relationships be-tween the global and local levels: the global penetrates all loci and each locus is part of the global dimension; • The new world will be the glocal world and the destiny of peoples; • Glocalism must not mean uniformity stateless, imbalances, eco-drama; • New policies, new institutions, new powers are needed; • To qualify for the global people and defend the premises do not need borders, nationality, sovereignty; • The end of nationalism does not mean the end of ethnic and regional cultural identities; • Mobility management and call for new political relations of territory; • In mediating between cohabitation and economy, the central institution is the company regulated by the global markets where it operates in networks of logic functions intertwined with global scale; • These functions determine the mobility of goods, people and relationships are often dropped from the territory and therefore they are difficult to adjust from the traditional institutions; • New glocal institutions able to link global corporations and people from local businesses can mediate global economy and local partnerships.
Claiming
• A new statehood in which individuals, ethnicities, different nations can live together in equality; • Territorial communities without local or national influences; • A new citizenship based on multi-membership: the possibility, that is, to feel all cosmopolitan, Italian, European, Mediterranean, Catholics, Muslims, liberals, socialists, etc. without losing the sense of political identity; • The ability to operate freely in the rich and dynamic structure of functional and territorial networks • A new cosmopolitan governance is essential to ensure, in a glocal world, environment, peace, rights, justice
Aims
• Building new thoughts, subjects, institutions and political practices that will assume the role of guiding and actors of the new glocal era; • Building new relationships between permanence and mobility of things, people, ideas; • Building rules of coexistence that reconcile efficiency and democracy in the new communities of functional and global and local practices • Reorganize the city, also in relation to glocal cities that are springing up, where new complexes of functional networks meet with the pre-existing civic groupings; • Establish new institutions and new powers, and especially new levels of meta national statehood. • Glocalized institutions such as Chambers of commerce, banking foundations, Provinces, Regions, which should better coordinated with the multinationals, major banks, groups of small and medium businesses already immersed in the glocalists challenge; • Interconnect the thousands of partnership structures and local services with the dense web of networks that cross a functional glocal scale; • Forming the generations to new challenges.

Elaboration by Bassetti, 2008.

GLOCALISM AND SUSTAINABILITY: WHAT REPORTS?

The listed principles of glocalism pose an interesting question to its possible relationships with the postulates which are typical of environmental, economic, and social sustainability and their political consequences.

Surely, glocalism highlights social sustainability issues arising from the new arrangements. In particular, it emphasizes the value of innovation in linking knowledge and power to create new customs and alternative values, thus characterizing the future stories of peoples. Innovation is certainly a source of opportunities, but also of threats, especially for the next generations. Indeed, innovation has caused the cancellation of distances, thanks in particular to technological development, thus affirming the prevalence of mobility on stationary habits, which characterized the previous ages.

As a result, the new society is without borders, developing a new global and local relationship in which the networks of the protagonists of society, economics, and politics appear to be dominant.

Any hypothesis on the social sustainability of these new arrangements will have to face the actual developments of the coming years. The next future will be characterized by people who, consciously or unconsciously, will be defined by glocalism (de Burgh-Woodman, 2014; Yama, 2016). Certainly, the diffusion of glocalism, which avoids the uniform standardization of customs and, therefore, stateless uniformity, should favour the transmission to new generations of styles reflecting local traditions, while compatible with globalized reality. This should make the new social arrangements more compatible with the aspirations of the advocates of sustainability.

Yet, glocalism alone will hardly solve the problem of inequalities (Lenger & Schumacher, 2015). Much will also depend on the emergence of new political powers that will be called upon to handle the dynamics in which the territorial control, as it is traditionally understood, will be less and less (Chan, 2016). In fact, new structures do not serve frontiers, citizenship, sovereignty, and subordinate localities; these concepts are more suited to a socially outdated structure. Anyhow, politics will compete for the difficult task of connecting global and local businesses, and foster the fairness of the system by avoiding undue concentration of wealth only on some territories or at a few subjects, while favoring the homogenous spread of well-being. This requires a new state of affairs in which individuals, ethnicities, and different nations can live together, and networks and territories are organized without nationalist or localist conditioning. In short, a new citizenship will be based on multimembership, with the consequent ability to feel cosmopolitan, European, Catholics, Muslims, Liberals, Socialists, Technicians, or Humanists, without losing their sense of political identity. In a glocal world, new cosmopolitan governance is indispensable to ensure environment, peace, rights, justice, and current choices compatible with the needs of future generations. Further, the apparatus of central and peripheral public administration will have to adapt, also adopting innovative forms of communication and social reporting (Ricci, 2005, 2013; Ricci, Esposito & Landi; 2010; Ricci & Fusco, 2016; Ricci & Landi, 2010; Ricci, Siboni & Nardo, 2013).

In this context, the urban reorganization of glocal cities, the pillars of a new one, is fundamental metanational status (Chan, 2016).

These new social systems are more suitable for a sustainable logic. In these systems, the enterprise that is governed by glocal markets plays a central role and operates in function networks that are interlinked according to a logic of global scale. Glocal enterprises are and will be the first protagonists of the generation of mobility flows of goods, people, and relationships that are partially disengaged from merely territorial considerations. These companies are sufficiently responsive to economically viable production processes, using resources at such a pace that they can be naturally regenerated to protect future generations. The glocalist ratio seems to be oriented towards companies responsible for this, inspired by a "sustainability management" (Truant, 2009). Also, it seems to wish for the simultaneous presence of productive units of varying size, from large corporations to smaller ones (Broccardo, Culasso & Truant, 2016; Ricci, Landi & Cillo, 2010; Truant, Broccardo & Culasso, 2015), recalling that the typologies of smaller corporations, and even their accounting, distinguish them decisively from the others (Broccardo et al., 2016; Ricci, 2011; Truant, 2014; 2015;). Sustainability and glocalism will likely induce innovative ways of communication and business reporting, also considering the new phenomena of business risk (Culasso, Broccardo, Manzi & Truant, 2016; Truant, Corazza & Scagnelli, 2017).

At the same time, however, there is a need for generalizable rules that hamper short-term speculative tendencies (Laszlo, 2013), and a need for the spread of ethical values that induce the spontaneous respect of the environment and of future generations.

In terms of environmental sustainability, glocalist principles appear less explicit than social and economic requirements. They clearly mention the ecodrams to be prevented by attributing a regulatory task to the new political institutions. Still, it would be desirable that the future update of the glocal principles indicates the role of the glocal enterprise in protecting the three classical functions that are attributed to the environment: Resource provider, waste collector, and direct source of utility, ensuring protection and renewal of natural resources and heritage. Meanwhile, the best doctrine is clear about the relationship between glocalism and natural environment (Ángeles Murga-Menoyo, 2009; Barton & Fløysand, 2010; Debarbieux & Price, 2008; Loorbach & Lijnis Huffenreuter, 2013; Spillare, 2016; Strizhakova & Coulter, 2013; Svensson, Padin & Eriksson, 2016).

TOWARDS A "GLOCAL" BUSINESS?

The articulated glocal scenario which has briefly been described above raises the need to identify glocal businesses. Can economic actors be identified and sufficiently distinguished from local and international companies? Or can the glocal only be considered a form of internationalization of unfinished business that gradually turns to more general areas, preserving its more or less pronounced roots on the territory of origin (Marino, 2005)? With reference to the glocal business, what are the parameters to be considered when defining a category on the basis of organizational and management features that make them stable forms of production?

A mere functional approach could lead to define glocal a company that has at least one global strategic function that will remain stable next to other local functions. Along with organizational processes and logic which are rooted in a specific territorial area, the globalization of the marketing function itself (or more generically marketing) profiles strategically well-known practices and doctrine, too (Foglio, 2004). Subject to its guiding principles, the glocalization seeks to preserve the individual identity within a complex system. In marketing, "glocalization" means therefore comparing the characteristics of the local product in the global market.

The same occurs to companies that, together or independently, by the globalization of supply or sales, globalize also their production process, with establishments in different localities. This is, namely, the usual multidomestic strategy based on exports or on the decentralization of production, which normally precedes a global transnational or homogeneous strategy (Porter, 1992).

Those strategies would certainly not identify a specific orientation that can qualify a business as glocal by adding it to ethnocentric, polycentric, geocentric, regiocentric (Bertoli, 2014) or other classifications that distinguish global, transactional, corporate, and multilocal companies (Bertoli, 2014; Buckley & Ghauri, 2004). A more logical and perhaps satisfactory approach would be to focus on the strategic choices that could definitely and definitively lead to define the company as glocal. In this regard, Krishnan (2008) affirmed:

Strategic management in any type of organization ... has got a new dimension today. This dimension is the all too familiar 'GLOCAL' vision. Well, what is really interesting and worth analyzing for all managers, leaders and entrepreneurs of today's progressive, knowledge-based corporations, is that this

'GLOCAL' element is now an indisputably imperative ingredient for all successful organizations – in different flavours, of course! (p. 1)

Krishnan (2008) concluded:

Hence, it may be concluded that most successful organizations leverage the 'GLOCAL' concept when it comes to mission, resources, and geographical locus and control. This is what makes any organization follow the 'GLOCAL' strategy. I have therefore formed the following acronym for 'GLOCAL': Global Long-term Objectives Customized to Assets Locally, where the explanation to each of the keywords is given in the following depiction. (p. 11).

However, this is a very vast and varied category, whereas the combination of local and international functions could be endless and with varying degrees of glocal (Svensson, 2001, 2003).

Despite these indications, the concept of "glocal business" has yet to be thoroughly investigated, even in relation to empirical studies on companies that will concretely want to adapt to this new entrepreneurial model. Anyhow, the choice to focus on strategy as an identifier of the glocal vocation seems to be the only plausible, unless the idea of delineating a glocal company other than the globalized international is deserted. This last hypothesis, however, appears to be much less likely, given the rapid development of economic and social systems towards glocalism. Scholars from different disciplines will need to better define a concept that must necessarily be made of typical aspects of internal management, but also, and especially, of the relations with the changing external scenarios of society and the economy.

WHAT MANAGEMENT FOR THE GLOCAL BUSINESS?

The varied configuration of the treated category of glocal companies naturally makes it difficult to identify specific aspects of their management (Migliaccio, 2009). It will acquire its connotations in relation to global functions, at the same time both local and global and local (and therefore glocal) as well as properly assembled by a clear and permanently glocal strategy . In this way, the glocal company's approach, which consists in a purely global marketing function, is combined with local management and eventually has characteristics that are very similar to known and cited models.

In several situations the human resources of the production process are not just employed in global outsourced production plants, but also in local businesses that have workers from different ethnic, cultural, and ethical backgrounds and that must necessarily coexist in a single production context. In this case, the logic of diversity management is more suitable than the more usual standardization (Arredondo, 1996; Cox, 1993; Cuomo & Mapelli, 2007; Kandola & Fullerton, 1998; Mauri & Visconti, 2004).

Even the combination of financial sources with the local traditional instruments available in international markets can lead to a glocal financial management which, of course, requires appropriate professional and flexible staff (Granelli, 2002; Peghin, 2008). It is, therefore, impossible to assume a priori whether a specific company management has glocal features, without priority of local, global, and glocal characteristics. What is certain is that the simultaneous presence of a comprehensive approach coexists stably with the local one. A local approach requires an open mind to innovation and tradition. This mindset inspires a dedicated organization (Beukema, 2004; Beukema & Carrillo, 2004; Gonzalez,

2006; Shi, 2007) that is looking for a difficult, but possible mediation between entrenched habits and new horizons that a global approach provides.

A natural consequence of these considerations is the expansion of categories of stakeholders who impact differently in size and importance, in relation to the degree of global and local features that are simultaneously present. There will certainly be local stakeholders, probably with more known characteristics, and global stakeholders to be equally well known for all the managerial choices involved. This effects, of course, the common institutional, commercial, financial, and more general economic and social choice.

A concluding note can be devoted in particular to the management of small and medium-sized companies.

Indeed, the smallest dimensions could make the membership of the glocal model particularly complicated, even though the described principles of glocalism defend the local productive models that, as in Italy, are often made up of a myriad of small and medium production units.

Mediation between the needs of globalization and the preservation of indigenous traditions can be found by preserving the typical management for the local contexts, relying instead on collaborative forms of presence in global environments. These experiments have already been conducted in many countries (Capaldo, 2015; Faldetta, Fasone & Provenzano, 2014; Tommaso, 2010) and therefore should only be refined in relation to the new glocal economic productive dynamics. Obviously, this implies the absolute necessity of the individual firm to abandon all egocentric attitudes, by developing a necessary spirit of cooperation that can be transformed into different legal forms, from the more traditional consortium to the most modern business networks.

WHAT COMMUNICATION FOR THE GLOCAL BUSINESS?

The preservation of local and global scope is also achieved by subjecting the above communications to serious analysis to protect individuals and groups (Migliaccio, 2009). Indeed, new technologies have the merit of universalizing information, but they often distort it, so encouraging standardized surface of language, which is a first characteristic of a culture to be preserved. Thus, a necessary feature is not mere translations, but a cultural and linguistic adaptation that has deep roots.

As to Web sites and Internet communications, first vehicle of globalization which must communicate with users through familiar speech and mode of expression, they must avoid a cultural message that is far from a segment of users with limited computer literacy and a dramatic local nature, because these people will always be those more who need the services of the Web (Bookin Blog, 2008[1] & 2008[2]).

A glocal communication should therefore consider some particular aspects:

1. The multiplicity and diversity of stakeholders with diverse local and global backgrounds.
2. The need to preserve local languages, while wanting to encourage global communication.

It is clear that mediation is difficult because globalization tends to standardize to a single language, while localization promotes the conservation of local and regional dialects. However, mediation is necessary and possible at least for many areas of corporate communication, and institutional, managerial, marketing, and financial information (Boccardelli, Marcati & Marchigiani, 2006). Institutional information refers to the multiple relationships with the public. It is of considerable importance because it contributes to the reputation of the institution which should then appear anywhere with similar features, although the details should adapt to the specific practices of each place. Unique reputation and image throughout the world, therefore, could be obtained through messages that are easily understood through different cultures. In this regard, for example, the Web site, which is the first mode of presentation, should prospectively have colors, music, and forms in line with the likely expectations of each area. Also, it should not be a single site, perhaps in multiple languages, but as many sites as the areas of interest.

Similar principles should oversee the communication management that is responsible for relations with the parties that are directly involved in the administration of the company. A need for glocal communication arises especially when the actors belong to different ethnic, cultural, and ideological matrix, regardless of the physical location of the business units. It requires a common approach to diversity management that best highlights the differences, using direct natural means adapted to the unique characteristics of each person. Surely, however, communication is more complex than that of glocal marketing. Indeed, global marketing has the delicate task of providing the perception of value to corporate supply markets, which may have very different characteristics.

The promotional mix, and especially the policies of commercial communications, must maintain a common logic, specify what to share in each field and how to communicate, and maintain consistency with other "pictures" of the company. Needless to emphasize, the importance of this form of communication is closely related to the global marketing to which it refers.

The communication that deals with economic and financial relations is less discussed and certainly needs further reflection and some specific considerations.

In conclusion, it is appropriate to emphasize the essential role of internal and external communication in a glocal company with its many and diverse stakeholders (Gramigna, 2009; Tettamanzi, Luoni & Fossati, 2009). External communication publicizes, within the various global and local areas, the different opportunities that the company offers to customers/users and, at the same time, includes the collection of information on possible improvements, proposing also different perimeters (more or less confined) of operations. Frequent managerial changes, which are typical of glocal strategies, must also be promptly expressed, also in favour of institutional reputation in the markets.

Internal communication, instead, enhances the information the company has and disseminates the priorities, which are identified by the different "sensors" of the organization. It facilitates the updating of the central and peripheral actors and the circulation of news in the glocal circuit. Thus, inside stakeholders contribute directly to pronouncements of institutional objectives. As a result, organizational changes are more easily assimilated. Internal communication becomes a tool for understanding and promoting change, fostering a common understanding of the value of work, spreading a sense of belonging, and making most persons motivated in a positive context.

In summary, then, the benefits of a careful and proper communication is amplified considerably in glocal reality.

WHAT FINANCIAL STATEMENT FOR THE GLOCAL BUSINESS?

The increase in number and characteristics of the stakeholders and the need inherent in the ethical principles of localism to preserve local languages pose fundamentally unsolvable problems to the accounting. Preliminary questions to ask and answer (Migliaccio, 2009) are: At who to address the economic and financial sheet reporting? Could the company restrict the range of the recipients of the reporting exclusively to individuals with special knowledge that should have already globalized their knowledge in this area? In this case, the adoption of a single universal language of accounting might be an easy pragmatic solution, acceptable to the glocal company willing to restrict the audience of those concerned. However, this would circumvent the need to respect the local language, which is easily understood, only marginally, but would also betray the fundamental function of the financial statement to reach all stakeholders, regardless especially of their degree of globalization and of international accounting literacy achieved. In other words, deleting possible users, such as the countless small suppliers or customers and many employees, and permitting access to the financial statement only to banks, big investors or customers/suppliers of international relevance is highly simplistic, especially in productive contexts that are characterized by a dense population of small operators related to local accounting traditions. Consequently, the general statement of international accounting standards that major economic powers impose appears to result from the logic of globalization, but is incompatible with the logic of glocalization.

On the other hand, nationalist assumptions of conservation of the viability of traditional communication collide with the needs of internationalization.

Proposing a single financial statement, which would be drafted in adherence to international accounting standards and to which financial statements reflecting the logic of local interests in the various areas of reference would be attached, is a confusing and impractical solution. The main reason is that financial statements that are prepared on the basis of a different treatment substantially differentiate incomes and consequent heterogeneous configurations of quantitative heritage.

Even the current project to forge a glocal language book, which results from a complex mediation between radically different modes of representation, is impossible, given the unbridgeable distance between the various competing approaches separated by the "Great Wall of China" (Dezzani, 2006) or "Hadrian's Wall" (Ricci, 2007). And this without considering the plausible risk of prevarication of values, just because they are more widespread in larger areas.

As to accounting, therefore, in first approximation, the problem seems unsolvable, unless the overcoming of the so-called "prism effect" of the financial statement and the creation of a class of its "prosumer" are considered, as the following section illustrates.

A note must be also devoted (Hinna, 2002; Matacena, 1984; Ricci, 2004; Rusconi, 1987; Vermiglio, 1984) to ethical and social accountability. Ethical principles, including the localism, require that ethical and social accountability is attached or subsequently added to the traditional financial statement. The main (but surmountable) difficult in its preparation is certainly the more complex identity of the company and its mission. Thus, it is completed in stages and therefore the representation of different scenarios and contexts of reference vary. Consequently, the social reporting must be more structured and elaborated. The multiplicity of stakeholders makes their effective involvement, which is already difficult in restricted areas, challenging. Samples of social reporting would be necessary, especially if stakeholders wish to be involved since the design of accountability, rather than just the mere collection of judgments and opinions.

The section on the reclassification of accounting data, however, echoes the difficulties that have been already outlined above, and therefore reflects the possible solutions.

In the end, a brief reflection on the relations between companies and public administration, also called a glocal logic, is necessary.

Can a number of "local" bodies still be defined, today? Are their characterization, their transethnic cultural background that the digitization services report, and their contingency of physical relations with the computerized world still compatible with domestic and "provincial" disputes that are often calibrated for the protection of specific and purely local interests?

Now that the cities are radically changing their appearance, is the multifaceted public, at least the public that is made aware because a notice is expected by the public bodies in general, also glocal (Baroni, 2009; Saonara, 2009)? Further, what relationship can and must be establish between glocal business communication and public administration, also called in support of economic activities?

A possible solution that seems to be outlined is the international dissemination of "integrated reporting" (IR), which proposes a single document that combines financial, environmental, social, and governance outcomes, addressing all stakeholders, illustrating the company's capacity to create value responsibly. It should lead to more sustainable decisions (Bianchi, 2013; Gesuele, 2015; Gherardi, 2014; Indelicato, 2014; Riccaboni, Quattrone & Busco, 2014; Supino & Sica, 2011). It can benefit from telecommunication technologies that can facilitate the important external communication aspect of integrated reporting. Internet technologies possess rich features and capabilities that have potentially significant application in enhancing external communication with integrated reporting stakeholders, even if there are some risks (Lodhia & Stone, 2017).

Recently, many international studies have been published on the subject, particularly after the adoption of the IR Framework by the International Integrated Reporting Council (IIRC) in December 2013 (Velte & Stawinoga, 2017). They are related to the analysis of possible relationships between integrated information disclosure and the degree of information asymmetry in firms characterized by higher/lower financial reporting quality and those located in environments defined by strong/weak investor protection (García-Sánchez & Noguera-Gámez, 2017). There are also studies on the effectiveness of a company's strategy to report on its environmental, social, and governance (ESG) activities, with regard to the extent and direction in which the firm's ESG performance is valued by investors in the capital market (Mervelskemper & Streit, 2017) and about the determinants of materiality disclosure among IIRC Pilot Program companies implementing the IIRC Framework (Fasan & Mio, 2017).

Zhou, Simnett, and Green (2017) suggest that IR is providing incrementally useful information to the capital market over existing reporting mechanisms. However, the benefits are still uncertain. Maniora (2017), for example, examined the impact of IR on the integration of ESG issues into the business model, and the related economic and performance changes. He concludes that a separate change analysis reveals that companies do not benefit from a switch from stand-alone ESG reporting to IR. Thus, his studies provide empirical evidence that contradicts the general notion of IR as a superior reporting mechanism, as the benefits of IR are driven by several factors.

Also Stacchezzini, Melloni, and Lai (2016) express some doubts. Their analysis highlights that companies not only provide limited forward-looking and quantitative disclosure of their actions to achieve sustainability outcomes, but also avoid providing information about their sustainability performance when their social and environmental results are poor. This evidence suggests pessimistic conclusions about the capability of this reporting process to encourage the integrative management of corporate sustainability.

Towards the Overcoming of the "Prism Effect" of the Financial Statement?

The discovery of the properties of the prism glass is credited to Isaac Newton: When a beam of an apparently white sunlight passes through the prism, it is decomposed in different colours, each deflected in different directions.

In international marketing, the prism effect expresses the deformation of the evaluations of potential foreign consumption caused by environmental variables that affect the positioning of the product (Valdani, 2014).

In accounting, the optical prism effect can be used to delineate the pragmatically appropriate choice to opt for a single financial statement, which must meet the different needs of the different stakeholders of a company. This financial statement should be a seamless flow of information which should play in different tones and meanings the relation to the different needs of the public. The limits for this are obvious. Indeed, it is operationally impossible to satisfy everyone in the same manner, and one or more categories of users will benefit more than others from the chosen type of communication of balance.

Over time, though companies were aware that certain users were hindered, they have always opted for a single statement, considering operationally complex to use alternative forms that would meet a wider audience of users. Nonetheless, may that choice still be retained for glocal companies, considering the expansion of categories of public stakeholders, particularly their increased and enhanced differentiation?

Limits that were tolerable before, today show the need for different and more satisfying solutions, even considering the spread of culture and economic organization and that the available technology rapidly developed on accounting data, which was previously unthinkable.

Why not reflecting on the practical feasibility of an "open" financial statement (Capaldo, 1975), with transparency as the main objective in prospectuses and many other data attached to allow free composition, adaptable to each user's needs, so far only presented as an abstract academic hypothesis?

In fact, the attached production of balance sheet and income statement of user data is already in the documents of many companies, often mandatory under domestic laws requiring more frequent and complex communication.

Nevertheless, it would be impossible to impose such a choice in the international arena and create uniform criteria for the award of full reporting, different for the main categories of users. It should be a single structure for the objective quantities, to be completed by the estimated ones, taking advantage of the additional information, also and above all in relation to the objectives of document (Amodeo, 1971; Onida, 1974).

Of course, a difficult and complex period of transition should accompany this radical innovation. It would require a gradual and difficult familiarisation from both specialist operators and information users. Thus, overcoming the prism effect of the financial statement is complicated, difficult, but possible in prospect.

A Desirable "Prosumer" of the Reporting?

The reflections resulting from the spread of the glocal can go further, with the risk that now they could appear only as utopian scenarios.

The proposal by the prism effect of the financial statement overrun with the establishment of "open" reporting. It is, in fact, a manifestation of a need for more flexibility in balance communication, as a result of the abundance and diversity of users.

This flexibility is also necessary because of the new direction of the international accounting standards IAS/IFRS for financial statements. These standards allow to adapt a balance to varied information needs, while respecting a required minimum content (Migliaccio, 2007a,2007b). It is already in practice, therefore a greater discretion in the composition of the financial statements is possible.

After years of rigid rules, this freedom of expression has initially disoriented. After adequate consideration, though, it can be transformed into an opportunity. In the future, flexibility may be required for effective communication that highlights the peculiarities of any entity in a given period and in response to their particular stakeholders' cognitive needs.

Hoping that a wider dissemination of accounting skills could glimpse the possibility, now only utopian, of statements that are agreed with the users, there will no longer be passive receivers of information, required by rule or chosen by the apical organs of the companies.

The methods of reporting met minimum conditions, which were set by Italian legislation. They could arise from a constructive and productive constant comparison between the company (companies or local authorities) and the addressees of the information naturally learned on the subject, in order to facilitate the movement and use of needs and ideas for solutions.

Thus, the stakeholder would be prosumer, "*consumattore*" (Fabris, 2008), producer and consumer of information, reporting that the actor in helping to identify interesting to reveal and sensitive data.

It would be extended to the preparation of financial statements and economic assets, too, and the active role of stakeholders already common for production manufacturing is again called for the drafting of financial statements, to avoid their social self.

FUTURE RESEARCH DIRECTIONS

The current theme and its interdisciplinary value, that involves the destiny of the peoples, left behind presuppositions for further developments that implement the growing international bibliographic production. In the broad debate that is already going on, it will be necessary, especially for business economics, to add empirical studies that can refute or confirm the assertions that this chapter contains. It will be necessary to verify, through the analysis of concrete cases, the actual glocal strategies that companies will pose and put into place, the innovative ways of communication, and, above all, how information systems will be transformed into small and medium-sized businesses with a glocal vocation. It is likely that each location will retain its typical aspects, but being shared with others by common elements that will be well focused. This will promote economic development, but also, above all, governance geared towards social, economic, and environmental sustainability, which is absolutely necessary to protect future generations.

CONCLUSION

The future evolution of society and its protagonists, especially those active in the economy, is certainly an unknown one. However, the hypotheses of a possible and permanent cohabitation between globalizing logic and the maintenance of local traditions are now consolidated.

This chapter, therefore, focuses on the characteristics of glocalism, also the forerunner of a concrete development of sustainability logic.

The nascent principles of glocalism, which will certainly need to be revised and updated later, seem to illustrate an articulated scenario in which states, public administration, businesses, families, and individuals have a different role from their present function, to foster the peaceful coexistence between structurally diverse subjects who are citizens of the world, but, at the same time, also actors of the territory in which they live.

In this changing reality, the firm maintains its indisputable centrality, which is the driving force behind producing goods and services in response to human needs. However, its management must necessarily adapt to the different stages to which it is addressed.

Thus, it is possible to synthesize some answers to the initial research questions:

RQ1: First of all, there are defining problems. What are the parameters that distinguish the glocal enterprise from others? Among the dotted hypotheses of response, it seems more convincing that a business that focuses on glocal strategies has a diversifying element, compared to other types of companies which are still crystallized in economic models and are destined to abandon.

RQ2: A glocal strategy, of course, induces all business functions to adapt to the changed reality. Consequently, its internal organization, its marketing, and its finances assume contemporary global and local characteristics. It has been said that marketing in particular must consider the different articulation of demand by trying to adapt a standardized global production to specific local needs.

RQ3: In this context, institutional and promotional glocal communication must respond to two key features at the same time: The multiplicity and diversity of stakeholders with diverse local and global backgrounds, and the need to preserve local languages while wanting to encourage global communication. Obviously, this requires a considerable investment in the training of the management and operators of each company.

RQ4: A different communication also affects the financial environment, which must also address a plurality of stages, both international and local. It's not enough, of course, to translate a company's reports into the different languages of the regions in which it works. It is also necessary to affirm financial sustainability reports, including social and environmental sustainability reports, as it has been the case in many countries for some time, now. This is the result of the gloomy relationship between glocalism and sustainability, which should also affect small-scale manufacturing companies in the production of many states, such as Italy. More generally, however, the glocal advent poses even more radical issues, such as the relationship between financial report content and its objectives, which may well be different in relation to the needs of the stakeholder who sees it. Considering the expansion of the stakeholder level, the principle of neutrality is increasingly difficult to concretise. This makes the hypothesis of an "open" budget, conditional on the objective information common to all prospects that any interested person can add to his/her purposes.

RQ5: Better. Yet, but obviously, the times will be much longer, encouraging stakeholder engagement in drafting the budget, as it is already the case for drafting social or environmental reports. These are, of course, only hypotheses for the academic momentum that comes up against the insensitivity and incompetence of many stakeholders who are involved in the process of communication and reporting. However, the future seems to have been traced: It is not possible to hypothesize the monopolistic dominance of a single stakeholder in the production of a document that would illustrate the company's prospects and structure by influencing the decisions of many other parties that are concerned with the future of the production unit.

RQ6: The principles of glocalism do not explicitly mention the logic of sustainability. However, indirectly, they mostly call for social sustainability, emphasizing the value of innovation as a moment of encounter between knowledge and the power of creating new customs and alternative values, at the same time, as new threats. Only glocalism will hardly solve the problem of inequalities. Politics will have the difficult task of connecting global and local businesses, and promoting the fairness of the economic system. In terms of environmental sustainability, the glocalist principles appear less explicit. In the future, it is therefore hoped that their update will better indicate the role of the glocal enterprise in protecting the environment.

ACKNOWLEDGMENT

This chapter is a revised, reworked, and expanded version of a paper entitled "Financial statements for glocal companies? Socioeconomic and financial communication issues for firms and agencies with a global vocation and strong ties with local contexts", which the author presented at the 2nd Annual Conference of the EuroMed Academy of Business, Salerno (Italy), 26-28 October 2009. Gratitude goes to Paolo Ricci, chair of the session, and to the participants for their thoughtful comments. However, the author's greatest thanks are addressed to Elisa Truant for her many and helpful suggestions.

REFERENCES

Amato Mangiameli, A. C. (Ed.). (2006). Persone e Stati. Le conseguenze della "glocalizzazione" e della innovazione tecnologica. Atti del Convegno (Teramo, 13-15 novembre 2003). Milano, Italy: Giuffrè.

Amodeo, D. (1971). Il bilancio delle società per azioni come strumento di informazione. In D. Amodeo (Ed.), *Argomenti di varia ragioneria* (pp. 231–260). Napoli, Italy: Giannini.

Ángeles Murga-Menoyo, M. (2009). The Earth Charter. A reference for the decade of education for sustainable development. *Review of Education*, 239–262.

Angelidou, M., Komninos, N., Leal, X., Passas, I. A., Schoina, M. S., & Sefertzi, E. (2015). Intelligent Transport Systems: Glocal Communities of Interest for technology commercialization and innovation. In NICT for Transport: Opportunities and Threats, (pp. 226-248). Northampton, MA: Edward Elgar Publishing Ltd.

Anonymous. (2013). Understanding the contemporary advertising environment: Is glocal the most effective strategy? *Strategic Direction*, *29*(2), 10–12. doi:10.1108/02580541311297994

Arnold, D. (2007). "Think global, act local": The modularization of marketing and marketing organizations. *Globe Management Review*, *1*(1), 5.

Arredondo, P. (1996). *Successful diversity management initiatives*. London: Sage.

Asprone, D., & Manfredi, G. (2015). Linking disaster resilience and urban sustainability: A glocal approach for future cities. *Disasters*, *39*(s1), s96–s111. doi:10.1111/disa.12106 PMID:25494959

Barkemeyer, R., & Figge, F. (2014). CSR in multiple environments: The impact of headquartering. *Critical Perspectives on International Business*, *10*(3), 124–151. doi:10.1108/cpoib-05-2013-0013

Baroni, V. (2009). *Glocal, vivere la città nell'era digitale*. Retrieved September 3, from http://www.comunicatoripubblici.it

Barton, J. R., & Fløysand, A. (2010). The political ecology of Chilean salmon aquaculture, 1982-2010: A trajectory from economic development to global sustainability. *Global Environmental Change*, *20*(4), 739–752. doi:10.1016/j.gloenvcha.2010.04.001

Bassetti, P. (2008). *Manifesto dei Glocalisti*. Retrieved September 3, 2009, from http://www.glocalisti.org

Bauman, Z. (2005). *Globalizzazione e glocalizzazione*. Roma, Italy: Armando.

Bertoli, G. (2014). L'impresa e le strategie internazionali. In E. Valdani & P. Bertoli (Eds.), *Mercati internazionali e marketing* (pp. 47–84). Milano, Italy: Egea.

Beukema, L. (2004). Work restructuring as ongoing glocal processes: concluding remarks. In L. Beukema & J.H. Carrillo (Eds.), Globalism/Localism at Work. Bingley, UK: Emerald. doi:10.1016/S0277-2833(04)13011-2

Beukema, L., & Carrillo, J. H. (Eds.). (2004). Globalism/Localism at Work. Bingley, UK: Emerald.

Bianchi, S. (2013). Linee guida internazionali per la redazione del report integrato. *Amministrazione & finanza, 28*(2), 13-18.

Bjerrisgaard, S. M., & Kjeldgaard, D. (2013). How Market Research Shapes Market Spatiality: A Global Governmentality Perspective. *Journal of Macromarketing*, *33*(1), 29–40. doi:10.1177/0276146712462891

Boccardelli, P., Marcati, A., & Marchigiani, L. (2006). Strategie e politiche di marketing. In F. Fontana & M. Caroli (Eds.), *Economia e gestione delle imprese* (pp. 259–334). Milano, Italy: McGraw-Hill.

Bookin Blog. (2008b). *"Glocale", il futuro linguaggio del web #1 – Dalla Cina alla Russia, i nuovi mercati turistici"*. Retrieved July 23, 2009, from: http://www.bookingblog.com

Bookin blog (2008a). *"Glocale", il futuro linguaggio del web #2 - Come cambia la comunicazione del sito dell'hotel*. Retrieved July 23, 2009, from: http://www.bookingblog.com

Broccardo, L., Culasso, F., Giacosa, E., & Truant, E. (2016). The diffusion of management control systems in Italy: A comparison between family and non-family firms. *Corporate Ownership and Control, 13*(4), 165-172.

Broccardo, L., Culasso, F., & Truant, E. (2016). Business Process Management: An Investigation In Italian Smes. *Proceedings of the 9th Annual Conference of the EuroMed-Academy-of-Business: Innovation, Entrepreneurship And Digital Ecosystems*, 366-376.

Buckley, P.J., & Ghauri Pervez, N. (2004). Globalization, economic geography and strategy of multinational enterprises. *Journal of International Business Study*, (35), 81-98.

Capaldo, A. (2015). *Strategia, reti di imprese e capacità relazionali*. Padova, Italy: Cedam.

Capaldo, P. (1975). Qualche riflessione sull'informazione esterna d'impresa. *La Rivista dei Dottori Commercialisti*, (5), 833-867.

Caporaso, S., Esposito, P., & Ricci, P. (2016). Corporate social responsibility in the North and South of Europe: a comparison between Finland and Italy. *Proceedings of the 9th Annual Conference of the EuroMed-Academy-of-Business Location: Innovation, Entrepreneurship and Digital Ecosystems*, 405-416.

Champy, J. (1997). Think globally, sell locally. *Sales & Marketing Management*, *7*(1), 24–25.

Chan, D. K.-H. (2016). City diplomacy and "glocal" governance: Revitalizing cosmopolitan democracy. *Innovation*, *29*(2), 134–160.

Cox Taylor, H. (Ed.). (1993). *Cultural diversity in organizations: theory, research and practice*. San Francisco, CA: Berrett-Koheler.

Culasso, F., Broccardo, L., Manzi, L. M., & Truant, E. (2016). Management Accounting and Enterprise Risk Management. A Potential Integration as a New Change in Managerial Systems. *Global Business and Economics Review*, *18*(3-4), 344–370. doi:10.1504/GBER.2016.076238

Cuomo, S., & Mapelli, A. (2007). *Diversity management. Gestire e valorizzare le differenze individuali nell'organizzazione che cambia*. Milano, Italy: Guerini e Associati.

D'Agostino, G. (2002). Tra locale e globale: "glocalismo". *Meridione, 2*(4), 60-68.

de Burgh-Woodman, H. C. (2014). Homogeneity, "glocalism" or somewhere in between?: A literary interpretation of identity in the era of globalization. *European Journal of Marketing*, *48*(1), 288–313. doi:10.1108/EJM-03-2011-0132

Debarbieux, B., & Price, M. F. (2008). Representing mountains: From local and national to global common good. *Geopolitics*, *13*(1), 148–168. doi:10.1080/14650040701783375

Dezzani, F. (2006). Gli Ias e la loro applicazione in Italia. In G. Migliaccio (Ed.), *Le rivoluzioni contabili di inizio millennio. Atti del Convegno di Paestum (Sa) del 14 maggio 2005* (pp. 95–135). Milano, Italy: Angeli.

Dinçer, H., & Hacioğlu, U. (2013). Global Strategies in Banking and Finance. Hershey, PA: IGI Global.

Fabris, G. (2008). *Societing. Il marketing nella società postmoderna*. Milano, Italy: Egea.

Faldetta, G., Fasone, V., & Provenzano, C. (2014). *Le reti di impresa innovative. Profili economici, aziendali, giuridici e sociali*. Roma, Italy: Aracne.

Fasan, M., & Mio, C. (2017). Fostering Stakeholder Engagement: The Role of Materiality Disclosure in Integrated Reporting. *Business Strategy and the Environment*, *26*(3), 288–305. doi:10.1002/bse.1917

Foglio, A. (2004). *Il glocal marketing. Glocalizzazione per rispondere a globalizzazione e localizzazione*. Milano, Italy: Angeli.

García-Sánchez, I.-M., & Noguera-Gámez, L. (2017). Integrated Reporting and Stakeholder Engagement: The Effect on Information Asymmetry. *Corporate Social Responsibility and Environmental Management, 24*(5), 395–413. doi:10.1002/csr.1415

Gesuele, B. (2015). Report integrato: prassi operativa. *Guida alla contabilità & bilancio*, (3), 6-10.

Gherardi, L. (2014). Il Reporting integrato come espressione della nuova impresa. *Equilibri, 52*(1), 62–70.

Gonzalez, J. (2006). Il middle management in Cina: una risorsa da gestire in un'ottica "glocal". *Sviluppo e organizzazione*, (215), 24-30.

Gramigna, A. (2009). *Ruoli, attori e competenze della comunicazione nel processo di cambiamento della P.A.* Retrieved September 5, 2009, from: www.urp.it

Granelli, M. (2002). *Glocal banking. Creare relazioni con la vendita consulenziale*. Milano, Italy: Angeli.

Grau, F. X. (2016). A short communication on glocal universities. *International Journal of Knowledge-Based Development, 7*(1), 63–74. doi:10.1504/IJKBD.2016.075442

Hartman, J. D. (2016). Glocalism: Situating global civic engagement in the local community. In R. Shin (Ed.), Convergence of Contemporary Art, Visual Culture, and Global Civic Engagement (pp. 151-169). Hershey, PA: IGI Global.

Hinna, L. (Ed.). (2002). Il bilancio sociale: scenari, settori e valenze; modelli di rendicontazione sociale; gestione responsabile e sviluppo sostenibile. Esperienze europee e casi italiani. Milano, Italy: Il Sole 24 Ore.

Hudak, K. C. (2017). Touring Pittsburgh's glocal narratives: Leveraging city brands for global and local audiences. In Advertising and Branding: Concepts, Methodologies, Tools, and Applications (pp. 430-455). Hershey, PA: IGI Global.

Indelicato, F. (2014). Report e Reporting integrato: Verso un nuovo modello di bilancio. *Equilibri, 52*(1), 9–37.

Japutra, A., Nguyen, B., & Melewar, T. C. (2015). A framework of brand strategy and the "glocalization" approach: The case of Indonesia. Alcántara-Pilar. In J.M., del Barrio-García, E., Crespo-Almendros, & L. Porcu, (Eds.), Analyzing the Cultural Diversity of Consumers in the Global Marketplace (pp. 101-125). Hershey, PA: IGI Global.

Jolliffe, L., Cave, J., & Baum, T. (2013). Lessons in tourism and souvenirs from the margins: Glocal perspectives. In Tourism and Souvenirs: Glocal Perspectives from the Margins (pp. 189-199). Bristol, UK: Channel View Publications.

Kandola, R., & Fullerton, J. (1998). *Managing the mosaic: Diversity in action*. London: Institute of Personnel Development.

Kipnis, E., Broderick, A. J., & Demangeot, C. (2014). Consumer multiculturation: Consequences of multi-cultural identification for brand knowledge. *Consumption Markets & Culture, 17*(3), 231–253. doi:10.1080/10253866.2013.778199

Kjeldgaard, D., Askegaard, S., & Eckhardt, G. M. (2015). The role of cultural capital in creating "glocal" brand relationships. In Strong Brands, Strong Relationships (pp. 48-60). Abingdon, UK: Taylor and Francis.

Krishnan, R. (2008). *"GLOCAL" Mission, Resources & Locus in Organizational Strategy*. Submitted for 11th Annual Convention of the Strategic Management Forum. Retrieved July 6, from http://www.iitk.ac.in

Laszlo, E. (2013). The optimal worldshift strategy in light of complex systems theory. *World Futures: Journal of General Evolution*, *69*(2), 61–64. doi:10.1080/02604027.2012.762190

Lenger, A., & Schumacher, F. (2015). The global configurations of inequality: Stratification, glocal inequalities, and the global social structure. In Understanding the Dynamics of Global Inequality: Social Exclusion, Power Shift, and Structural Changes (pp. 3-46). Berlin, Germany: Springer.

Levitt, T. (1983). The Globalization of Markets. *Harvard Business Review*, *61*(3), 92–102.

Levitt, T. (2006). *Ted Levitt on Marketing. Timeless Classic from the "Father of modern marketing". Including: Marketing Miopia, The Globalization of Markets, marketing Success Through Differentiation – of Anything*. Boston: A Harvard Business Review Book.

Lo Turco, A., & Maggioni, D. (2017). "Glocal" ties: Banking development and SEs' export entry. *Small Business Economics*, *48*(4), 999–1020. doi:10.100711187-016-9809-7

Lodhia, S., & Stone, G. (2017). Integrated Reporting in an Internet and Social Media Communication Environment: Conceptual Insights. *Australian Accounting Review*, *27*(1), 17–33. doi:10.1111/auar.12143

Loorbach, D. A., & Lijnis Huffenreuter, R. (2013). Exploring the economic crisis from a transition management perspective. *Environmental Innovation and Societal Transitions*, *6*, 35–46. doi:10.1016/j.eist.2013.01.003

Maniora, J. (2017). Is Integrated Reporting Really the Superior Mechanism for the Integration of Ethics into the Core Business Model? An Empirical Analysis. *Journal of Business Ethics*, *140*(4), 755–786. doi:10.100710551-015-2874-z

Marino, V. (2005). *Il governo dell'impresa nella prospettiva sistemica delle relazioni internazionali*. Milano, Italy: Angeli.

Marques, L. (2013). Constructing social landscape through events: The glocal project of 's-Hertogenbosch. In Exploring the Social Impacts of Events (pp. 84-94). Abingdon, UK: Taylor and Francis.

Matacena, A. (1984). *Impresa e ambiente. Il bilancio sociale*. Bologna, Italy: Clueb.

Matusitz, J., & Leanza, K. (2009). Wal-Mart: An Analysis of the Glocalization of the Cathedral of Consumption in China. *Globalizations*, *6*(2), 187–205. doi:10.1080/14747730902854158

Mauri, L., & Visconti, L. M. (Eds.). (2004). *Diversity management e società multiculturale. Teorie e prassi*. Milano, Italy: Angeli.

Maylor, H., & Blackmon, K. (2005). *Researching Business and Management*. New York: Palgrave MacMillan. doi:10.1007/978-1-137-11022-0

Mervelskemper, L., & Streit, D. (2017). Enhancing Market Valuation of ESG Performance: Is Integrated Reporting Keeping its Promise? *Business Strategy and the Environment*, *26*(4), 536–549. doi:10.1002/bse.1935

Migliaccio, G. (2007a). Gli schemi di rendicontazione economico-patrimoniale di imprese ed enti locali: profili evolutivi e comparativi. *Esperienze d'impresa*, (2), 79-94.

Migliaccio, G. (2007b). *Verso nuovi schemi di bilancio. Note su evoluzione e prospettive di forme e strutture del bilancio d'esercizio*. Milano, Italy: Angeli.

Migliaccio, G. (2009). Financial statements for glocal companies? Socio-economic and financial communication issues for firms and agencies with a global vocation and strong ties with local contexts. In *Proceedings of the 2nd Annual EuroMed Conference of the EuroMed-Academy-of-Business: Managerial And Entrepreneurial Developments In The Mediterranean Area*, 1087-1106.

Mourdoukoutas, P., & Ioannidis, A. (2007). The three rules of glocal corporate citizenship. *Globe Management Review*, *1*(1), 26–35.

Müller, F. (2017). IRENA as a glocal actor: Pathways towards energy governmentality. *Innovation*, *30*(3), 306–322.

Myers, M. D. (2013). *Qualitative Research in Business & Management*. London: Sage.

Nascente F. (2015). Success strategies and agri-food companies: The glocalism role. *Quality - Access to Success*, *16*(147), 80-84.

Nava, M. R. (2017). The development of intercultural competences in post-bureaucratic organizations. In Evolution of the Post-Bureaucratic Organization (pp. 401-421). Hershey, PA: IGI Global. doi:10.4018/978-1-5225-1983-6.ch019

Onida, P. (1974). *Il bilancio d'esercizio nelle imprese. Significato economico del bilancio. Problemi di valutazione*. Milano, Italy: Giuffrè.

Onkvisit, S., & Shaw, J.J. (2002). "Glocal" advertising: Think global, act local. In *AMA Educators' Conference, Proceedings* (pp. 378-379). American Marketing Association.

Papathanassis, A. (2014). Cruise Sector & 'Glocal' Corporate Citizenship: The 5th International Cruise Conference, Bremerhaven, Germany, 24-26 January 2014. *International Journal of Tourism Research*, *16*(4), 415–416. doi:10.1002/jtr.2006

Peghin, F., (2008). Antonveneta banca "glocale". *Il mattino di Padova*.

Porter, M. E. (1992). *Competizione globale*. Torino, Italy: Isedi.

Preti, P. (2006). Un'azienda glocal. *Sviluppo e organizzazione*, (213), 115-116.

Ramanau, R. (2016). Internationalization at a Distance: A Study of the Online Management Curriculum. *Journal of Management Education*, *40*(5), 545–575. doi:10.1177/1052562916647984

Riccaboni, A., Quattrone, P., & Busco, C. (2014). Al di la della rappresentazione: Il Reporting integrato come strumento di mediazione e innovazione sociale. *Equilibri*, *52*(1), 38–43.

Ricci, P. (Ed.). (2004). *La responsabilità sociale dell'impresa: il ruolo e il valore della comunicazione - Atti del convegno di Benevento del 29 gennaio 2004*. Milano, Italy: Angeli.

Ricci, P. (2005). *Enti strumentali regionali e loro accountability. Il caso Campania*. Milano, Italy: Angeli.

Ricci, P. (2007). Le immobilizzazioni materiali negli enti locali. In *Gruppo di studio e attenzione dell'Aidea, L'analisi degli effetti sul bilancio dell'introduzione dei principi contabili internazionali Ias/ Ifrs* (pp. 455–469). Roma, Italy: Rirea.

Ricci, P. (2011). Short Notes about Financial Reporting in Italian Family Business. *Review of International Comparative Management, 12*(1), 73–82.

Ricci, P. (2013). What future for social reporting and accountability in academic systems. An overview of the Italian case. *Review of International Comparative Management, 14*(2), 202–221.

Ricci, P., Esposito, P., & Landi, T. (2010). L'accountability per il fronteggiamento dello State Capture nel management delle amministrazioni pubbliche locali. *Azienda Pubblica*, (2), 205-232.

Ricci, P., & Fusco, F. (2016). Social reporting in the Italian justice system: Milan Court experience. *Public Integrity, 18*(3), 254–268. doi:10.1080/10999922.2016.1139524

Ricci, P., & Landi, T. (2010). Governance and Accountability for Italian Listed Public Utilities Companies. *Review of International Comparative Management, 11*(3), 376–388.

Ricci, P., Landi, T., & Cillo, V. (2010). The Italian SMEs in the global context: the accountability system role. *Esperienze d'impresa, 11*(1), 59-77.

Ricci, P., Siboni, B., & Nardo, M. T. (Eds.). (2013). La rendicontazione di sostenibilità. Evoluzione, linee guida ed esperienze in imprese amministrazioni pubbliche e aziende non profit. Roma, Italy: Rirea.

Rivera, M. (2017). 'Glocal' discussion as leverage. Debating urban sustainability in Bogotá. *Journal of Environmental Studies and Sciences, 7*(1), 145–151. doi:10.100713412-014-0206-8

Robertson, R. (1992). *Globalization: Social Theory and Global Culture*. London: Sage.

Robertson, R. (1994). Globalisation or Glocalisation? *Journal of International Communication, 1*(1), 33–52. doi:10.1080/13216597.1994.9751780

Robertson, R. (1995). Glocalization: time-space and homogeneity-heterogeneity. In Global Modernities. London: Sage. doi:10.4135/9781446250563.n2

Rowley, C., & Warner, M. (2013). Strategic challenges and issues for Chinese managers and management in the global economy: Conclusions. *Asia Pacific Business Review, 19*(4), 617–624. doi:10.1080/13602381.2013.832918

Rusconi, G. (1987). Il ruolo del bilancio sociale nel contesto dell'economia aziendale. *Rivista Italiana di Ragioneria e di Economia Aziendale*, (3/4), 171-187.

Salazar, N. B. (2005). Tourism and glocalization, 'Local' Tour Guiding. *Annals of Tourism Research, 32*(3), 628–646. doi:10.1016/j.annals.2004.10.012

Saonara, G. (2009). *Segnali sulla città "glocale"*. Retrieved September 3, from http://www.argomenti2000.it

Sedda, F. (Ed.). (2004). *Glocal. Sul presente a venire*. Roma, Italy: Sossella.

Shamsuddoha, M. (2008). *Globalization to Glocalization: A Conceptual Analysis*. Retrieved July 23, 2009 from http://ssrn.com/abstract=1321662

Shi, Y. (2007). The organizational factors of globalization and localization: A "travel of ideas" approach. *Globe Management Review*, *1*(1), 16–25.

Smida, L., Hrdinova, G., Sakal, P., & Syc, M. (2011). A possibility of social inclusion by responsible entrepreneurship in Slovakia. *Annals of DAAAM and Proceedings of the International DAAAM Symposium 2011: Intelligent Manufacturing and Automation: Power of Knowledge and Creativity*. Vienna, Austria: Academic Press.

Smith, B. D. (2013). Our glocal market. *Journal of Medical Marketing*, *13*(3), 133–134. doi:10.1177/1745790413500130

Sobh, R., Belk, R., & Gressel, J. (2014). Mimicry and modernity in the Middle East: Fashion invisibility and young women of the Arab Gulf. *Consumption Markets & Culture*, *17*(4), 392–412. doi:10.1080/10253866.2013.865166

Søderberg, A. (2015). Recontextualising a strategic concept within a globalising company: A case study on carlsberg's 'winning behaviours' strategy. *International Journal of Human Resource Management*, *26*(2), 231–257. doi:10.1080/09585192.2014.922358

Spillare, S. (2016). Agro-ecological consumerism between system response and glocal reflexivity: The example of organic food consumption. *Quality - Access to Success*, (17), 580-584.

Stacchezzini, R., Melloni, G., & Lai, A. (2016). Sustainability management and reporting: The role of integrated reporting for communicating corporate sustainability management. *Journal of Cleaner Production*, *136*, 102–110. doi:10.1016/j.jclepro.2016.01.109

Stahler-Sholk, R. (2010). The zapatista social movement: Innovation and sustainability. *Alternatives*, *35*(3), 269–290. doi:10.1177/030437541003500306

Strizhakova, Y., & Coulter, R. A. (2013). The "green" side of materialism in emerging BRIC and developed markets: The moderating role of global cultural identity. *International Journal of Research in Marketing*, *30*(1), 69–82. doi:10.1016/j.ijresmar.2012.08.003

Supino, S. & Sica, D., (2011). Nuovi paradigmi di rendicontazione d'impresa: il report integrato. *Esperienze d'impresa, 19*(2), 81-92.

Svensson, G. (2001). Glocalization Of Business Activities: A Glocal Strategy Approach. *Management Decision*, *39*(1), 6–14. doi:10.1108/EUM0000000005403

Svensson, G. (2003). Beyond Global Marketing And The Globalization Of Marketing Activities. *Management Decision*, *40*(6), 574–583. doi:10.1108/00251740210433963

Svensson, G., Padin, C., & Eriksson, D. (2016). Glocal business sustainability - performance beyond zero! *International Journal of Procurement Management*, *9*(1), 15–26. doi:10.1504/IJPM.2016.073385

Tai, S. H. C., & Wong, Y. H. (1998). Advertising decision making in Asia: "Glocal" versus "regcal" approach. *Journal of Managerial Issues*, *10*(3), 318–339.

Tardia, T. (2002). "Glocalizzazione", un'alternativa alla globalizzazione? *Pmi*, *8*(12), 26–30.

Tettamanzi, P., Luoni, L., & Fossati, S. (2009). *Il bilancio sociale e la comunicazione con gli stakeholder*. Torino, Italia: Pearson Education.

Thompson, C. J., & Arsel, Z. (2004). The Starbucks and Consumers' (Anticorporate) Experiences of Glocalization. *The Journal of Consumer Research*, *31*(3), 631–642. doi:10.1086/425098

Tommaso, S. (2010). *Distretti e reti di imprese. Evoluzione organizzativa, finanza innovativa, valutazione mediante rating*. Roma, Italy: Angeli.

Truant, E. (2009). Sustainability Management: a Business Model Applied to Publicly-Owned Enterprises in the Waste Sector. *Proceedings of the 2nd Annual EuroMed Conference of the EuroMed-Academy-of-Business: Managerial And Entrepreneurial Developments In The Mediterranean Area*, 1824-1837.

Truant, E. (2014). *Strumenti di pianificazione & controllo e performance aziendali. Confronto tra family e non-family firms*. Torino, Italy: Giappichelli.

Truant, E. (2015). Product and Process Innovation to Exploit new Market Opportunities and Overcome the Crisis: An Italian Family Firm Case Study. *Proceedings of the 10th European Conference on Innovation and Entrepreneurship (ECIE 2015)*, 716-723.

Truant, E., Broccardo, L., & Culasso, F. (2015). Adoption And Benefits Of Management Accounting Practices In Italian Smes: An Explorative Survey. *Proceedings of the 8th Annual Conference of the EuroMed-Academy-of-Business: Innovation, Entrepreneurship And Sustainable Value Chain In A Dynamic Environment*, 2310-2323.

Truant, E., Corazza, L., & Scagnelli, S. D. (2017). Sustainability and Risk Disclosure: An Exploratory Study on Sustainability Reports. *Sustainability*, *9*(4), 636. doi:10.3390u9040636

Vaciago, G. (2003). Le piccole imprese in un mondo "glocale". *L'imprenditore*, (10), 41-42.

Valdani, E. (2014). La politica del prodotto. In E. Valdani & P. Bertoli (Eds.), *Mercati internazionali e marketing* (pp. 315–356). Milano, Italy: Egea.

Van Wijk, J., Van der Duim, R., Lamers, M., & Sumba, D. (2015). The emergence of institutional innovations in tourism: The evolution of the African Wildlife Foundation's tourism conservation enterprises. *Journal of Sustainable Tourism*, *23*(1), 104–125. doi:10.1080/09669582.2014.927878

Velte, P., & Stawinoga, M. (2017). Integrated reporting: The current state of empirical research, limitations and future research implications. *Journal of Management Control*, *28*(3), 275–320. doi:10.100700187-016-0235-4

Vermiglio, F. (1984). *Il bilancio sociale nel quadro evolutivo del sistema d'impresa*. Messina, Italy: Grapho Editor.

Yama, H. (2016). A perspective of cross-cultural psychological studies for global business. In Information Resources Management Association (Ed.), International Business: Concepts, Methodologies, Tools, and Applications (pp. 1734-1755). Hershey, PA: IGI Global.

Yin, R. K. (1994). Applied Social Research Methods Series: Vol. 5. *Case Study Research.* Thousand Oaks, CA: Sage.

Yin, R. K. (2003). *Case Study Research: Design and Methods.* Thousand Oaks, CA: Sage.

Young, L. (2003). Ed Marra's 'glocal' marketing. *Marketing Magazine, 108*(36), 11.

Zhao, P., & Li, P. (2017). Rethinking the relationship between urban development, local health and global sustainability. *Current Opinion in Environmental Sustainability, 25*(1), 14–19. doi:10.1016/j.cosust.2017.02.009

Zhou, S., Simnett, R., & Green, W. (2017). Does Integrated Reporting Matter to the Capital Market? *Abacus, 53*(1), 94–132. doi:10.1111/abac.12104

KEY TERMS AND DEFINITIONS

Accountability: To be responsible to someone for outcome. To maintain and audit accounts and to prepare social and environmental reports of a business.

Accounting: To maintain and audit accounts and prepare financial reports on the assets, liabilities, etc. of a business.

Globalization: The process enabling economic operators to operate internationally, as a result of deregulation and improved communications.

Glocalization: A neologism that were coined to mediate the characteristics of globalization with those of the more entrenched localization.

Localization: To be local in behavior and in the main social and economic choices.

Prosumer: Economic operator that both produces and consumes a good or service.

Report: An account, normally a written one, prepared for the benefit of others that provides information.

Sustainable: Capable to maintain a steady level without exhausting or damaging environmental, economic, and social resources.

Chapter 15
Sustainable Management Accounting Systems for Small and Medium-Sized Businesses

Nuwan Gunarathne
University of Sri Jayewardenepura, Sri Lanka

Thilini Cooray
University of Sri Jayewardenepura, Sri Lanka

ABSTRACT

The purpose of this chapter is to provide an overview of environmental and sustainability management accounting (EMA) systems that can be adopted by small and medium-sized enterprises (SMEs). It presents a detailed description of how and why corporate sustainability performance is important for SMEs while placing EMA as a decision support tool to aid sustainability-related corporate strategies. Having discussed various EMA tools and techniques, the chapter also provides an integrative framework for EMA adoption which is based on the evolutionary stages of environmental management. This framework aims to guide SMEs to progress from compliance-orientation towards higher order sustainability outcomes. The chapter stresses the need for the SMEs to continuously take deliberate managerial actions with the support of EMA systems to reach the advanced stages of sustainability in an ever-changing business environment.

INTRODUCTION

The purpose of this chapter is to provide a comprehensive discussion on sustainability management accounting that can be used by Small- and medium- sized enterprises (SMEs). SMEs represent the majority of firms in the economic systems of both developed and developing countries (Perrini & Tencati, 2006). Their economic contribution is significant in any country. The role of SMEs is evident on many economic fronts such as the creation of business, provision of employment and promotion of innovation and creativity. For example, according to the European Commission (2017), SMEs represent 99% of all businesses in the European Union (EU). Similarly, in emerging economies, the formal SMEs contribute

DOI: 10.4018/978-1-5225-5267-3.ch015

to 45% of total employment and to 33% of national income (World Bank, 2015). These figures can further increase if the contribution of the informal SMEs is taken into account. SMEs act as a prominent source of generating new employment opportunities. As per Savlovschi and Robu (2011), two thirds of the newly created jobs are owned by the SME sector. Further, the costs of creating jobs in an SME are lower when than in a large-scale firm. This helps to reduce the unemployment rates and to address the demographic challenges created by population growth all over the world (Commission for Economic, Social and Territorial Affairs, 2012). Especially in developing economies, SMEs play a major role in poverty alleviation and empowering women and youth (Okpara, 2011; Tambunan, 2011). Since most of SMEs are owned by entrepreneurs, creativity and innovation are often promoted by the introduction of new products, processes, markets and/or new business models (Varis & Littunen, 2010). This helps to create new jobs and satisfy the requirements of customers by providing value-added product and services. Another important facet of SMEs is their ability to counterbalance monopolies and oligopolies by restricting the ability of large firms to dominate the market (Savlovschi & Robu, 2011). Owing to these various beneficial roles, SMEs are usually considered as the engine of economic growth in any country (Aris, 2007; Singh et al., 2008).

Despite the significant role played by these entities, what constitutes an SME is not definitive. There are numerous definitions of SMEs and they largely related to the country and/or the institution concerned. Further, depending on the economic sectors, these definitions can vary. In defining SMEs different criteria, such as number of employees, turnover, capital investment, nature of the business, production volume and net assets have been generally used (Ayyagari et al., 2007). For example, the Organization for Economic Co-operation and Development (OECD) (2005) defines SMEs as non-subsidiary, independent firms which employ less than a given number of employees while the European Union (2003) defines them based on the staff headcount and either turnover or total balance sheet value. On the other hand, the International Finance Corporation (2012) offers three levels of SMEs based on the number of employees. Accordingly, when the number of employees is less than ten those entities are recognized as micro enterprises, ten to fifty as small enterprises and fifty to three hundred as medium-scale enterprises. Among the various factors used to characterize SMEs, the number of employees can be highlighted as the most frequently used criterion (Ayyagari et al., 2007). These different definitions point to the absence of a universally accepted definition of SMEs.

Irrespective of what entities constitute an SME, no country can achieve sustainable development without their contribution. The impacts of SMEs, which, in turn, require that they consider and integrate economic, social and environmental concerns into their day-to-day operations. Usually, large- scale firms proactively engage in sustainability practices influenced by a wide range of stakeholders. However, it has been observed that SMEs generally adopt reactive sustainability strategies and tend to react only to the pressures exerted by external stakeholders (Loucks et al., 2010). It is thus evident that SMEs pay little heed to sustainability practices despite their potential to drive the sustainable development agenda of a country. A factor contributing to this situation could be their limited financial resources and their perception that involvement in sustainability activities is too complex as task (Dressen, 2009). Although the negative impact of an individual SME on the environment and society is insignificant when compared to that of a large-scale firm, their collective negative impact can be substantial. For example, the SMEs in the UK account for 60% of commercial waste and 80% of pollution incidents (Environment Agency, 2003). Similarly, in Wales, 97% of businesses represent SMEs and they contribute to 91% of the waste produced within the county (OECD, 2007). These macroeconomic indicators stress the importance of and need for SMEs adopting proper sustainable corporate practices.

There are numerous benefits that can be achieved by SMEs enhancing their sustainability performance. They can develop new methods and techniques to drive the effective use of resources with minimum wastage through their innovative spirit (Nulkar, 2014; Association of Chartered Certified Accountants, ACCA, 2012). The way can also be paved for SMEs to develop sustainability-driven niche markets by bypassing the mass market competition. Refer Illustration 1 which presents a real life example on how SMEs can avoid mass market competition by carefully selecting a market niche through its sustainability-focused operations. By engaging in various sustainability related practices, SMEs can improve their public profile in the eyes of various stakeholders. In addition to mitigating the environmental risks, a favorable public image could also bring in tax benefits such as tax credits and exemptions as well as government grants/loans to develop their businesses (Nulkar, 2014; Thorpe & Prakash-Mani, 2003). Further, SMEs have a high likelihood to attract investors who are interested in environmental and social performance when seeking funds for expansion (OECD, 2007).

Illustration 1: Maximus creating a niche market for its eco-products:

Maximus is a small-scale Sri Lankan manufacturing company which produces handmade paper and value added products using elephant dung. In addition to elephant dung, its eco-friendly production process only utilizes post-consumer raw materials and non-toxic consumables. The key competitive advantage is flexibility as Maximus has the ability to change colours, textures and thickness to suit individual customer needs. This unique production system has enabled Maximus to create a niche market for its products. Even the name of the company denotes a part of the scientific name of elephants - Elephas maximus. Maximus produces a variety of paper-based products including note books, albums, paper holders, greeting cards, jewellery and photo frames. Approximately 90% of their products are exported so that Maximus enjoys a solid international market.

Maximus has a deep concern for the elephants as they provide its main raw material. Therefore, the company has projects for elephant conservation and wildlife protection. A percentage of the earnings from its sales goes to the Millennium Elephant Foundation, an affiliated organization of the World Society for Protection of Animals (WSPA), which maintains a home for elderly and disabled elephants. Further, the company is focused on rural development via generating employment opportunities for the rural communities.

In recognition of its outstanding performance, the company has won many national and international awards for sustainable best practices including the International ARC Award, National Energy Globe Awards, Excellence in Social Responsibility Award (USA) and Presidential Gold Awards. These sustainable practices have created an opportunity for Maximum to cater to a green-conscious niche market while avoiding mass market competition.

Source: Maximus (2017)

However, in order to derive the aforementioned benefits, SMEs must follow carefully articulated sustainability practices. When SMEs engage in corporate sustainability activities, they need information to facilitate planning, decision making and control. Scagnelli et al. (2013) suggest that to become accountable for their sustainability performances, SMEs need to integrate this sustainability information into their accounts. Thus, SMEs can use sustainability accounting systems for this purpose. However, so far very little knowledge is available on sustainability accounting systems specifically focused for SMEs. Hence this chapter addresses this gap by providing a comprehensive discussion on sustainability management accounting systems for SMEs. With this objective in mind, the rest of the chapter is organized as follows. Section Two provides an overview of corporate sustainability management accounting with special focus on SMEs. Section Three provides an overview of some of the useful sustainability (environmental) management accounting tools and techniques that would deal with various sustainability aspects. Next, Section Four presents how the environmental strategy of an SME would evolve through various evolutionary environmental management stages. Section Five provides an integrative framework for the adoption of sustainability by SMEs. Finally, Section Six provides the conclusions.

SUSTAINABILITY MANAGEMENT ACCOUNTING

Section Two provides an overview of sustainability management accounting systems. Firstly, it this section highlights corporate sustainability management in the broad context of sustainable development. Next, it provides a comprehensive coverage of environmental and sustainability management accounting (EMA) by referring to the widely used integrative framework that deals with physical and monetary accounting systems. Finally, it deals with the motivations and/or drivers and challenges that SMEs face in adopting EMA systems.

Corporate Sustainability Management for SMEs

Although the term 'sustainability' is not new, it was in 1987 that worldwide attention was directed to sustainable development following its definition by the United Nations World Commission on Environment and Development (1987) as "[the] development that meets the needs of the present generation without compromising the ability of future generations to meet their own needs". Despite some of the criticisms levelled against this definition, it stresses the need to maintain inter-generational and intra-generational equity. Inter-generational equity "requires attaining a balance between meeting the consumptive demands of existing societies and ensuring that adequate resources are available for future generations to meet their needs" while intra-generational equity emphasizes "fairness in the utilization of resources among human members of present generations, both domestically and globally" (Maggio, 1997, pp. 163-164). Achievement of sustainable development has become a global challenge in the light of man-made and natural disasters such as the Fukushima nuclear disaster, Bhopal gas leak, and Indian Ocean tsunami together with other environmental and social upheavals such as climate change, deforestation, rise of global terrorism and child labour. These challenges have created many problems for countries, large corporations and particularly for SMEs. Given the contribution and the role of SMEs, as highlighted in Section One, the impact of these challenges on SMEs is greatly felt. Refer Illustration 2 that describes the problems faced by the African SMEs owing to climate change.

Illustration 2: Impact of climate change on small-scale farmers in Africa

Climate change has become a major threat to the agriculture industry in Africa. Due to the continent's very high dependence on agriculture, climate change impacts are largely felt in African countries. For

example, the agriculture industry provides employment to 65% of Africa's labour force while accounting for 32% of the continent's overall GDP. It has been identified that the temperature of the greater part of the continent has risen by 0.5 Celsius during the last century. This increase in temperature associated with a reduction in rainfall has resulted in poor agricultural productivity, which in turn demands an increase in land used for agriculture to meet the continent's growing demand for food. Small-scale cattle farmers in southern Ethiopia saw a loss of nearly half of their cattle, sheep and goats to droughts between 1995 and 1997.

Since most of the agricultural systems in this region are rain-fed, small-scale farmers become highly vulnerable to changes in precipitation and temperature. It has been identified that a rise in temperature by 1.5 Celsius by 2030 could make 40 percent of the present maize cropping areas unsuitable for cultivation in sub-Saharan Africa. This means a loss of livelihood for millions of poor small-scale farmers in addition to severe threats to food security. These climate change-related issues raise a major threat to the achievement of sustainable development goals by 2030 in this region.

Sources: The Conversation (2015), Our World (2008)

In recent years, there has been wide interest among many parties including business corporations in achieving the inter-generational and intra-generational equity implied in the concept of sustainable development. As a response, many companies around the world are committed to follow the practices and principles of sustainable development (KPMG, 2013), usually referred to as corporate sustainability management. Schaltegger and Burritt (2015) define corporate sustainability management as "all activities which design, measure, analyze and improve environmental, social and economic activities in order to firstly create a sustainable development of the organization itself, and secondly to enable the company to contribute to sustainable development of the economy and society as a whole" (p. 2). Implementation of these sustainability management practices involves not only setting-related sustainability goals, but also measurements and evaluations of the progress in achievement of those goals (Virtanen et al., 2013). In order to implement and ensure the success of these sustainability strategies there should be proper monitoring, measurements and evaluations of the progress in the achievement of those goals (Sroufe et al., 2002; Virtanen et al., 2013). According to Schaltegger et al. (2017), measurement systems and accounting are important for sustainable development since they provide information for decision makers and stakeholders of a firm to act favourably in regard to sustainability initiatives. If they are well informed about undesired environmental and social impacts, they can compare different options for dealing with their sustainability impacts. The role of every organization including SMEs is vital for contributing to sustainable development through corporate sustainability. This section next deals with SMA in detail.

Environmental and Sustainability Management Accounting (EMA) Systems

In order to support corporate sustainability management practices, managers have sought the support of accounting. In this context, a body of practices referred to as 'environmental and sustainability management accounting' (EMA)[1] has emerged. As it is an evolving discipline, it is difficult to find a universal boundary or definition for EMA (Jasch & Savage, 2005). However, it has been used widely despite the inadequate conceptualization (Schaltegger & Burritt, 2010). Although there is no universally accepted definition of EMA, it is broadly defined as the identification, collection, analysis and use of physical information on the use, flows and destinies of energy, water and materials (including wastes) and monetary information on environment-related costs, earnings and savings for internal decision making (United Nations Division for Sustainable Development, UNDSD, 2001). The above definition of EMA highlights two important aspects of EMA information. First, EMA provides information regarding various environmental domains such as energy, water, materials, carbon, waste and biodiversity. Second, EMA information on these various domains can be physical and monetary information (Burritt, Hahn, & Schaltegger, 2002; Jasch & Savage, 2005). This implies that there can be two types of EMA systems: physical EMA (PEMA) and monetary EMA (MEMA). MEMA reflects the environment- related impacts on economic systems and is expressed in monetary measurements, for instance, environmental licence fees and cost of energy. In the view of Burritt et al. (2002), MEMA systems "can be considered as a broadening of the scope of, or a further development or refinement of, conventional accounting in monetary units, as they are based on the methods of conventional accounting systems" (p. 41). PEMA systems reflect the impacts of company-related activities on the environment in physical unit terms. PEMA information entails consumption of resources and is expressed in a variety of physical measures such as kilograms, litres, cubic metres and joules. Usually, MEMA takes place when a financial value is assigned to PEMA (Gunarathne et al., 2014) (refer Illustration 3). However, MEMA can also arise without any relation to physical measures. For instance, MEMA information such as license fees and environmental fines arise purely in monetary terms without a relationship to PEMA information. Moreover, there can be some measurements that can only be expressed in physical units such as an organization's biodiversity in terms of flora and fauna. There are some approaches to monetizing these physical measurements but they have been widely criticised.

Illustration 3: Investment appraisal of a solar panel

When an SME purchases a solar panel system, there is a need to assess the financial viability of the investment. This situation provides a good example of how EMA takes place both in physical and monetary terms. Based on the capacity of the panel, climate and various other factors, the SME can calculate the electricity cost saved due to the installation of the solar panels. These electricity cost savings in units is the PEMA information. When these electricity units are valued at the existing electricity rates, the amount of money saved can be identified. This cost savings is the MEMA information.

In order to provide a broad framework for understanding EMA, Burritt et al. (2002) suggest that EMA information encompass three broad dimensions: a) time frame (i.e. whether the time period is past or future), b) length of time frame (whether the length of the period is short or long term), and c) routineness (whether the frequency of information gathering/provision is ad-hoc or routine). Combining these three dimensions of EMA with physical and monetary aspects, Burritt et al. (2002) suggest the following comprehensive framework (refer Figure 1).

Figure 1 suggests that SMEs have a wide array of EMA tools and techniques that can fall into sixteen quadrants of the framework. Refer Illustration 4 which explains simply the use of EMA information as per this framework for an environmentally-friendly investment.

Illustration 4: MEMA and PEMA for investment appraisal of a solar panel

Figure 1. Comprehensive EMA framework
Source: Burritt et al. (2002)

<table>
<tr><td colspan="2" rowspan="2"></td><td colspan="2">Monetary EMA</td><td colspan="2">Physical EMA</td></tr>
<tr><td>Short term</td><td>Long term</td><td>Short term</td><td>Long term</td></tr>
<tr><td rowspan="2">Past-oriented</td><td>Routine information</td><td></td><td></td><td></td><td></td></tr>
<tr><td>Ad-hoc information</td><td></td><td></td><td></td><td></td></tr>
<tr><td rowspan="2">Future-oriented</td><td>Routine information</td><td></td><td></td><td></td><td></td></tr>
<tr><td>Ad-hoc information</td><td></td><td></td><td></td><td></td></tr>
</table>

When evaluating the financial viability of the solar panel system discussed in Illustration 3, an SME will usually calculate the payback period to understand its recovery of the capital outlay. As this is usually done before the capital expenditure decision, it is future-oriented ad-hoc long-term MEMA information. In order to assess the realization of expected benefits, after the installation, the SME will calculate the kilowatts of electricity saved on a daily basis. This is the identification of the actual savings made from the investment. Hence, it is past-oriented routine information for short-term (perhaps for long-term) decision making.

From the discussion so far, it is clear that EMA is not another environmental management tool among others, but a broad set of principles and approaches that provide information for the successful implementation of environmental strategies (Jasch & Savage, 2005). Hence, it acts as an interface between inward focused management accounting and environmental management strategies of an organization (Bennett, Bouma, & Wolters, 2002). In essence, it can be viewed as a decision support tool that facilitates environmental management strategies of an organization (Schaltegger & Burritt, 2010). Day by day, new EMA practices are being introduced or existing practices are being adopted (Gunarathne et al., 2014). When SMEs follow EMA practices, they will encounter various drivers and challenges, which will be discussed next.

Drivers and Challenges for EMA

Various factors drive SMEs to adopt EMA practices within their organizations: legislative pressure, stakeholder pressure, green washing motives and self-regulation. Most of these factors are interrelated and mutually non-exclusive. Some of them are discussed next.

Regulations are perceived to be the most widespread stimulus for environmental improvements amongst SMEs (Baylis et al., 1998; Schaltegger & Burritt, 2010). For example, Australia, Denmark, the Netherlands, Norway, Sweden and the US have mandatory requirements for companies to report to the public on their environmental performance (Kolk et al., 1999). SMEs have to follow EMA to comply with the mandatory legal requirements for the continuation of their corporate activities. Another driver for SMEs to pursue EMA is the pressure from stakeholders. SMEs are encouraged to invest in environmental improvements by stimuli and incentives deriving from interaction with different kinds of stakeholders (Biondi et al., 2002). For example, SMEs need to focus on ethical and social performance in response to the demands of supply chain partners (Burke & Gaughran, 2007). Thus, this can be considered as another major motivator. In addition to these external drivers, internal drivers such as self-regulation can also push the SMEs to follow EMA. Self-regulation is a voluntary activity where an entity restrains its actions or commits itself to certain non-market actions (Schaltegger & Burritt, 2010). For example, companies follow eco-management and audit schemes (EMAS) and international environmental management systems (EMS) such as standard ISO 14001 mainly for self-regulation, despite the availability of other reasons. According to Petts et al. (1999), self-regulation is more supportive in terms of extending the role of regulation in influencing corporate behaviour for sustainable development. This is applicable to SMEs as well. Another driver, which does not necessarily improve the sustainability performance of SMEs, is the green washing motive. Green washing is the structuring of corporate disclosures regarding environmental matters so as to maximize perceptions of legitimacy (Roberts & Koeplin, 2011). SMEs may be encouraged to follow EMA practices for communicating and reporting purposes rather than for enhancing sustainability performance with the ultimate objective of creating a positive image among the general public (Schaltegger & Burritt, 2006).

When SMEs follow SMA practices, not only they encounter these benefits but many challenges. There can be several barriers or challenges facing SMEs in following EMA practices such as the lack of awareness, limited availability of financial and other resources, and absence of clear directions. Like in the case of drivers, these barriers or challenges are also highly interrelated.

Among the reasons that retard the adoption of EMA, lack of management awareness of the negative impacts and positive benefits is important. Most of the time, owners (or the management) of the SMEs have little understanding about the negative impacts they create on the environment and society. Hence, these impacts are perceived to be negligible at the individual level compared to large firms. Thus, SMEs are not interested in taking action to mitigate these impacts. However, given the large volume of SMEs in any country, their collective impact is significant. It has been identified that this wrong perception largely deters SMEs from adopting sustainability practices (Johnson & Schaltegger, 2015; Revell & Blackburn, 2007). Similarly, the lack of awareness of the benefits of following sustainability practices can also be considered as a barrier for SMEs to adopt EMA (Borga et al., 2009). Another major hindrance prevailing at the SME level is the lack of both financial and non-financial resources. It has been suggested that scarce financial resources discourage SMEs from following sustainability practices (Tinsley, 2002; Pimenova & van der Vorst, 2004). Usually, SMEs are run with the capital invested by a single owner (or group of owners) and this limited capital is mainly utilized to improve the main business operations. This leaves SMEs with limited funds for sustainable initiatives (Tinsley & Melton, 1997). Although there can be several non-financial resource limitations that deter SMEs from following sustainability practices, lack of human resources and required skills is uppermost (Lee, 2009; Tencati et al., 2004). Most SMEs have few employees who are responsible for more than one business function. Thus, it is difficult for these employees to find time to concentrate on sustainability practices amidst their other responsibilities (Pimenova & van der Vorst, 2004; Burke & Gaughran, 2007). Another hindrance that is interwoven with the aforementioned barriers/challenges is the absence of clear direction towards sustainability. This can be attributed to several factors such as inadequate sustainability guidelines for SMEs (Borga et al., 2009), and insufficient support from governments and other relevant authorities for promoting sustainability among SMEs (Revell & Blackburn, 2007).

As discussed already, due to the lack of awareness and absence of direction, SMEs have limited knowledge of the potential EMA tools and techniques that can be applied in their organizations. The next section discusses some of the important EMA tools and techniques.

ENVIRONMENTAL MANAGEMENT ACCOUNTING TOOLS AND TECHNIQUES

This section provides an overview of EMA tools and techniques that can be easily adopted by SMEs. They deal with various environmental domains such as energy, materials, waste, water and carbon. As such, the section presents energy accounting, water management accounting, accounting for materials and material flow cost accounting, carbon management accounting and capital budgeting. This section also discusses the sustainability balanced scorecard as an all-encompassing performance measurement tool for SMEs. These EMA tools and techniques which are developing day by day include extensions to or adaptations of conventional management accounting tools and techniques while others are newly developed (Christ & Burritt 2017; Gunarathne et al., 2014). Finally, this section briefly presents how an SME could externally report sustainability performance with the help of this EMA information generated through these tools and techniques.

Energy Accounting

For any SME energy costs form a significant portion of the cost structure. Hence, SMEs should pay special attention to effectively manage the cost of energy. This is where energy accounting can become very useful. As Bennett and James (2000) state, energy accounting is "tracking and analysis of all flows of energy into, through and out of an organization" (p. 31). This requires SMEs to identify, quantify, value, record and communicate energy information. As there is no specific method to account for energy, an SME can take the following steps towards this (Gunarathne et al., 2014).

- Maintain separate meters for energy for each significant process, product, or department. This enables the management to collect specific energy data for an organization, which will lay the foundation for subsequent analysis and decision making.
- Develop a system for regular data collection and recording. This requires assigning responsibilities to specific personnel in the organization.
- Maintain separate accounts for different sources of energy (if used by an SME) in the accounting information system. This helps an organization separate the energy-related costs to avoid pooling with the general overhead (Burritt, 2004).
- Develop energy reporting practices for the management of an SME. As Burritt et al. (2002) suggest SMEs can use a range of physical and monetary reporting formats in this regard. For example, energy-related indicators such as energy consumption per period and energy consumption per unit of production can be quite useful. Obviously, these measures should be compared against the

previous months and if possible, with industry norms or competitors to better identify the position of the SME in terms of energy consumption.

Refer Illustration 5 that presents a real example of how a small hotel in Sri Lanka uses energy accounting to improve profitability.

Illustration 5: Use of energy accounting in a small hotel

Gunarathne et al. (2015) describe how a hotel in Sri Lanka benefits from energy-related EMA practices. First, the hotel carried out a detailed analysis of its energy consumption in terms of physical units and monetary values. This analysis enabled the hotel to identify its main energy consumers. Second, having identified the A/C system as the main consumer accounting for 53% of the hotel's energy consumption, the management took several corrective measures. They included conversion of the conventional A/C process into a "chilled water system", deployment of "intelligent thermostats" and some structural changes to the hotel. The hotel used PEMA and MEMA systems for making such changes and subsequently evaluating the success of the measures taken.

Water Management Accounting (WMA)

Depending on the nature of the operations of the SME, water can be an important environmental concern. However, due to the importance of water and uncertainty surrounding water supplies, in recent years WMA has received increased attention (Christ, 2014; Christ & Burritt, 2017). According to Christ & Burritt (2017), water accounting is the measurement and accounting for water use and waste water discharges throughout the value chain. Perhaps, at the initial stages, an SME would find it difficult to keep track of water- related data of the whole value chain. Hence, they are encouraged to at least account for their own consumption of water within the boundaries of the SME. The measures suggested for energy accounting can be used for accounting for water. Accounting for energy and water can bring numerous benefits for SMEs such as identification of processes, products or departments with high usage and/or wastage of water to trigger necessary controls, identification of abnormal losses to initiate quick remedial action, and facilitation of decisions on strategies to improve energy and water efficiency, all of which will contribute to better cost management.

Material Flow Cost Accounting (MFCA)

MFCA is one of the EMA tools that have been developed to deal with efficient material usage (Schaltegger & Zvezdov, 2015). Due to the availability of the ISO standard, 14051: Material Flow Cost Accounting and other guidance, MFCA enjoys a well laid out approach to the EMA tools (Christ & Burritt, 2015; ISO, 2011; Jasch, 2008; Schaltegger & Zvezdov, 2015). MFCA can be used as a tool for the quantification of flows and stocks of materials in processes or production lines in both physical and monetary units (Kokubu et al., 2012; Strobel & Redmann, 2002). MFCA stems from the broad management concept known as "flow management" which views an enterprise as a system of material flows. Accordingly, an SME can be first understood as an entity to which different materials enter. These materials then generate desirable output (product output) and undesirable residues (non-product output) (Jasch & Savage, 2005). Refer Table 1 that presents the material flow balance for a typical organization. The non-product output

Table 1. Material flow balance (or mass balance) in a typical organization

Materials Inputs	Product Outputs
Raw and auxiliary materials	Products (including packaging)
Packaging materials	By-products (including packaging)
Merchandise	**Non-product outputs (waste and emissions)**
Operating materials	Solid waste
Water	Hazardous waste
Energy	Wastewater
	Air emissions

Source: (Jasch and Savage, 2005)

is undesirable from both environmental and economic viewpoints. MFCA quantifies material flows and stocks in a process or processes in terms of both physical and monetary units.

According to MFCA methodology, there are mainly three steps in its application. They are a) creation of the material flow model which displays the sequence and loss flows, b) physical quantification of material flows in which product and non-product output is recognized, and c) monetary quantification of material flows by assigning cost. A special feature of MFCA in costing is the assignment of full cost for the non-product output so that the losses are highlighted to trigger managerial actions for mitigation.

Carbon Management Accounting

Another EMA tool that can be useful for SMEs is the carbon management accounting. Due to the recent developments in carbon emissions trading market, corporate carbon accounting, a relatively a new area in EMA, is now receiving the attention of both academia and professionals (Gibassier & Schaltegger, 2015; Schaltegger & Csutora, 2012). Corporate carbon management requires companies not only to comply with regulations and to respond to societal pressures but also to incorporate carbon-related issues into their business on a proactive basis (Schaltegger & Csutora, 2012). Due to the various incentive schemes and the introduction of carbon markets, carbon management is now becoming economically important for many different departments and managers in an organization (Burritt et al., 2011). Despite the different meanings of carbon accounting (Stechemesser & Guenther, 2012), it can we understood in two different ways (Hespenheide et al., 2010). First, it is the measurement of direct and indirect carbon emissions and removals and retaining an ongoing inventory of operations-based emissions. Carbon accounting, which is measurement, monitoring, and reporting (can be voluntary or mandatory) but it enables firms to reduce carbon emissions, save cost or trade emission allowances. Second, it is the reflection of carbon related information arising from changed regulations or transactions in the financial statements of a company. Irrespective of the difference in the approach to carbon accounting, SMEs can benefit in numerous ways, if carbon accounting practices are appropriately adopted. Illustration 6 shows how SMEs can benefit from carbon footprint accounting by developing innovative tools.

Illustration 6: A tool to measure carbon footprint in SMEs

Moss et al. (2008) show how carbon footprint (with the support of carbon accounting) can be used as a valuable tool for environmental proactive measures in SMEs. The unsuitability of the existing carbon footprint assessment tools led them to evaluate different types of tools available for measuring carbon footprint and their appropriateness for SMEs. In calculating the carbon footprint for SMEs, they looked at three aspects: scope, assessment method and conversion factors. Moss et al. (2008) proposed a tool in the form of an online calculator capable of measuring carbon emissions in the full life cycle of a company. Further, they recommended the use of Economic Input-Output (EIO) conversion factors as well as those of the Life-Cycle Analysis (LCA). Thus, the proposed tool has the ability to provide options and advice for selecting the scope of the assessment with the suitable conversion factor and deciding on the most effective mitigation choices after the assessment.

Capital Budgeting

Capital budgeting is a traditional management accounting tool that can be quite useful for SMEs when trying to pursue various corporate sustainability management practices. Capital budgeting/investment decisions involve capital outlays in return for a stream of future benefits (Drury, 2009). Every organization, including SMEs, makes capital investment decisions for which there is a variety of capital budgeting techniques such as net present value (NPV), payback period/ discounted payback period and internal rate of return (IRR). However, these traditional capital budgeting techniques generally ignore environmental costs, cost savings and revenues (Environmental Protection Agency, EPA, 1995). Consequently, companies fail to recognize the benefits of environmentally-friendly investments. EPA (1995) therefore suggests a four-step process to integrate environmental accounting with capital budgeting decisions. They are a) quantification of environmental costs, b) allocation and projection of environmental costs and benefits, c) use of appropriate capital budgeting techniques, and d) consideration of appropriate time horizons to capture environmental benefits. This mainly implies that SMEs will have to consider and incorporate the environmental and social costs and benefits in their long-term investment decisions. If an SME has been able to successfully establish an environmental information system or procedures like the techniques mentioned previously (e.g. accounting for energy, water, waste, etc.), the identification and qualification of potential costs and benefits will be easier (Gunarathne et al., 2014). Obviously there will be some costs or benefits that are difficult to quantify, in which case, a qualitative analysis of them is necessary (EPA, 1995).

Sustainability Balanced Scorecard (SBSC)

SBSC offers the management of an SME to align and manage all corporate activities according to their strategic relevance (Figge et al., 2002). BSC has been promoted, in the recent past, as a balanced performance measurement technique that overcomes the limitations of financial bias in conventional performance measurement techniques (Drury, 2009). According to Kaplan and Norton (1992), BSC encompasses four perspectives, namely, financial, customer, internal business and learning and growth. SBSC is the modifications to the original BSC, which explicitly considers environmental, social or ethical issues (Hansen & Schaltegger, 2016). This modification or the integration of environmental and social aspects into a BSC can be done in three ways (Figge et al., 2002): a) integration of environmental and social aspects with the existing four standard perspectives, b) addition of a fifth perspective, referred to as "non-market", to consider environmental and social aspects, and c) formulation of a specific environmental and/or social scorecard. The openness of SBSC enables it to be used together with other corporate sustainability management tools described herein (Figge et al., 2002). In the context of an Austrian SME, Falle et al. (2016) show how the freedom inherent in SBSC methodology and content design enables the SBSC development process to be adapted to the requirements of SMEs. They further suggest that SBSC development is not a consecutive process as often suggested in the literature but a complex iterative process.

The following illustration presents some empirical evidence of the extent of use of these EMA tools by SMEs in Malaysia.

Illustration 7: Use of EMA amongst Malaysian SMEs

Jamil et al. (2015) identified a range of EMA practices among Malaysian small medium manufacturing firms. Table 2 shows the application of some of the above techniques described in their study.

According to Table 2, physical material and energy flow analysis is used the most while the physical and monetary environmental-related capital budgeting the least among the selected EMA techniques presented in this chapter.

External Reporting of Environmental Performance

If an SME is capable of generating sustainability information using the aforementioned tools and techniques, they can consider reporting the corporate sustainability performance externally. However, not every SME will consider external reporting of environmental and sustainability performance of their business by way of a sustainability report. There can be a host of factors that will determine whether an SME is ready to prepare a sustainability report or not. However, if they decide to do so, there will be many benefits they can gain. According to Global Reporting Initiative (GRI) (2014), the value or benefits of sustainability reporting can be of two types: internal benefits and external benefits (refer Table 3).

In order to guide the SMEs to prepare a sustainability report, GRI issued a booklet titled *Ready to Report? Introducing Sustainability Reporting for SMEs* in 2014, based on the GRI G4 standard in a five-phase GRI model for a sustainability reporting process. (Refer GRI, 2014 for more details).

Table 2. Application of EMA techniques in Malaysia

Technique	MEMA	PEMA
	Mean Value*	Mean Value*
Environmental-related capital budgeting	1.197	1.968
Material flow analysis		3.375
Energy flow assessment		3.375
Cost accounting	3.125	
Environmental-related budgeting	2.188	2.188

* Maximum score for the mean value is 5.
Source: (Jamil et al., 2015)

Table 3. Benefits of external reporting of sustainability

Internal benefits	External Benefits
Identification of Strengths and opportunities	Enhancement of reputation
Mitigation of risks	Attraction of funding
Employee motivation	Development of better dialogue with stakeholders
Improvement of internal processes	Ability to be portrayed as a sustainability leader
Development of sustainability vision and strategy	

Source: (GRI, 2014)

The application of these EMA tools and techniques by SMEs can depend on a variety of factors. Among them, their stage of development/maturity of environmental strategy is important. Hence, the next section of this chapter is devoted to explaining the environmental strategy evolution with emphasis on SMEs.

ENVIRONMENTAL STRATEGY EVOLUTION IN SMEs

This section presents how the environmental strategy of an SME would evolve according to the various evolutionary environmental management stages suggested by prominent scholars. Hence, various maturity stages ranging from compliance to realization to integration will be discussed in the light of SMEs. The purpose of this section is to highlight how SMEs could develop their environmental strategies to reap higher order strategic benefits.

Environmental Management Evolution Models

Many studies around the world have shown that organizations are at different levels of environmental management adoption. While some companies have become sustainability leaders by having advanced processes, there are companies that are still experimenting (Ormazabal et al., 2017). This situation is even common to SMEs. Therefore, it is important to identify how an SME could evolve and move to an advanced level of environmental management adoption. There are different environmental management evolution classification methods with a diversity of labels such as strategies, responses, development/ maturity stages or performance (Kolk & Mauser, 2002). The purpose of these taxonomies is to systematize the various aspects of the relationship between companies and the environment (Jabbour & Santos, 2006). Despite their diversity, many of these models are stage or phase models that describe a development in time consisting of an increasing integration of environmental concerns into business policy and strategy (Kolk & Mauser, 2002; Ormazabal et al., 2017). These models focus on how organizations integrate the environmental variable into their management activities while classifying companies according to their stage of environmental management evolution (Jabbour & Santos, 2006). Moreover, these "maturity staging models deconstruct the operating processes of a firm, with each stage representing a more effective and efficient use of the firm's resources for achieving the firm's goals" (Ormazabal et al., 2017, p. 28).

In order to explain environmental strategy evolution, we also follow the stage model concept. While there are many versions of maturity stages available (Jabbour & Santos, 2006; Kolk & Mauser, 2002;

Ormazabal et al., 2017; Ormazabal & Sarriegi, 2012; Roome, 1992) our model for SME follows a three-stage model closely linked to Jabbour and Santos (2006). These three stages are compliance, realization and integration.

Compliance Stage

The initial stage of the environmental management development of an SME is usually the compliance stage. When an SME develops its environmental management practices in response to legal or social pressures, they fall into this category (Jabbour, et al., 2010). This stage represents a passive reactive strategy for environmental management (Jabbour & Santos, 2006; Jabbour et al., 2010; Roome, 1992). Organizations in this stage only pay attention to some critical areas such as waste (Gunarathne, 2015) and do not take control of the environment (Roome, 1992). Since legislation is reactive and generally lags behind the current environmental thinking, these organizations fail to obtain any competitive advantage in their environmental strategies (Roome, 1992). Due to the limited focus on environmental management actions, these organizations develop only a limited number of EMA practices that are easy to adopt. Most often they represent accounting for energy, for water management or for waste (Gunarathne, 2015; Gunarathne & Lee, 2015).

Realization Stage

The next stage of environmental strategy is the realization stage which is a transitional stage. After pursuing a compliant strategy for a while, an organization will realize the cost saving potential of these environmental strategies (Gunarathne, 2015). Hence, an organization will integrate some of the environmental management practices into its business strategy representing a similar stage which Roome (1992) characterizes as "compliance plus". This is where an organization moves into the realization stage, which is the next stage of environmental strategy evolution. Hence, this is a stage in which an organization's involvement in environmental management increases (Jabbour et al., 2010) and represents a preventive strategy (Jabbour & Santos, 2006). However, the environmental considerations are not yet systematically integrated into the business strategy (Jabbour & Santos, 2006). In this stage, top management's willingness and support for the environmental strategies are received, which would trigger organizational changes (Roome, 1992). Consequently, from an accounting point of view, these organizations will develop better EMA systems that would encompass several environmental challenges/domains (Gunarathne, 2015; Gunarathne & Lee, 2015).

Integration Stage

If an organization develops the right systems and procedures and if the organizational changes initiated at the realization stage are effective, an SME will move on to the most desirable stage of development, i.e., the integration stage. This stage is similar to what is described as "environmental excellence" and "leading edge" stages of Roome (1992). The organizational changes that are triggered now become a part of business strategy embedding environmental values in the management's decision making and in individuals (Jabbour & Santos, 2006). Thus this stage represents a proactive strategy for environmental management (Jabbour & Santos, 2006). Hence, environmental considerations become part of the day-to-day decision making process of an organization. From an accounting point of view, this is the stage at which more sophisticated EMA tools and techniques are adopted while using that information for stakeholder communication, perhaps through a sustainability report (Gunarathne, 2015). These actions necessitate the inclusion of stakeholders in an organization's activities while covering all material environmental aspects. At this stage an organization generates competitive advantage through its noteworthy environmental management practices.

Although these stages with different labels have been discussed heavily in the academic literature in general, the role of EMA and stakeholders have not been addressed properly. The next section of this chapter presents an integrative framework for EMA that can also be adopted by SMEs.

INTEGRATIVE FRAMEWORK FOR EMA SYSTEMS

This section presents an integrative framework for SMEs to analyse the status of their EMA systems. The suggested framework combines physical and monetary accounting systems and various EMA tools and techniques with environmental management evolutionary stages. This section also discusses how SMEs can derive benefits from this integrative framework.

As the name suggests, the framework integrates different vital components for the successful adoption of an EMA system by an SME. In this paper, we follow the integrative framework suggested by Gunarathne (2015). This general framework suggested for any organization can be adopted by the SMEs as well. By considering three aspects of environmental management, this integrative framework identifies three development stages discussed in the last section (refer Figure 2).

Figure 2. Integrated framework for environmental management
Source: Adopted from Gunarathne (2015)

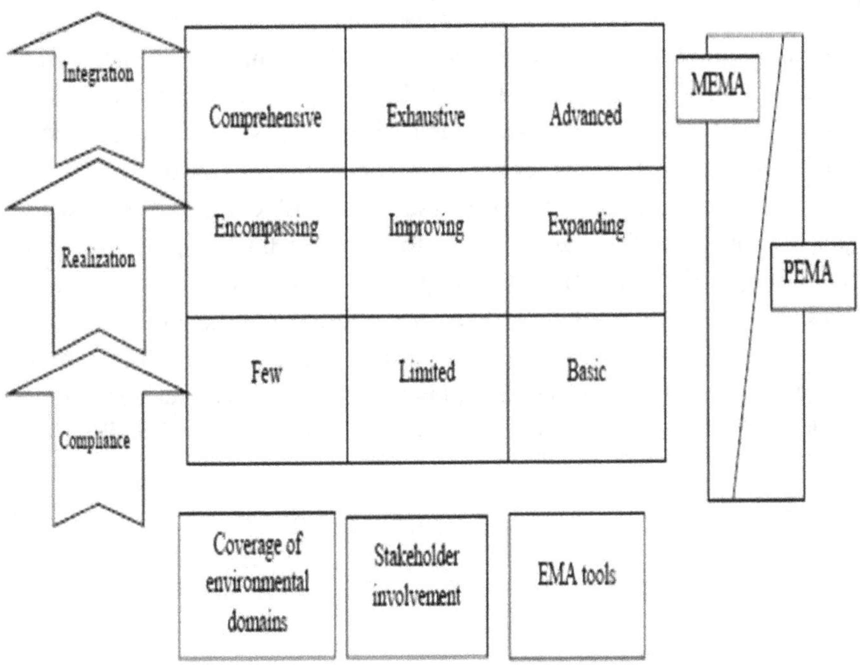

Based on a maturity stage model, this framework highlights how the key features (coverage of environmental aspects, stakeholder involvement and EMA tools) should develop when an organization gradually progresses from the compliance to the integration stage. It further highlights the focus of EMA systems in terms of PEMA and MEMA in each stage. As given in the diagram, initially there will be more PEMA practices, but when an organization progresses to higher levels of integration, there will be more MEMA practices. The arrows in the Figure imply that it is an ongoing process. Further, it should be noted that the integration stage is not the most desired final stage, but due to changes in the environment, further developments are always desirable.

A framework of this nature could offer an SME several benefits. Firstly, it enables an SME to map where they currently stand in terms of the development stages of EMA. It should be noted that an SME will display characteristics at different stages of development for different environmental aspects. For example, an SME may have a better coverage of environmental domains but little support of stakeholders and the use of EMA tools can be at a low level of development. Hence, rather than seeking a perfect mapping, an SME should strive to identify the lagging areas for future consideration. Next, this mapping could guide them to identify and focus on the key dimensions for future development. Moreover, this guides SMEs to develop an integrated sustainable environmental management programme in the light of the changing business landscapes. This is particularly important as many scholars have noted that organizations around the world have developed only fragmented EMA systems (Bartolomeo et al., 2000; Gunarathne & Lee, 2015; Lee, 2011). As suggested in this framework, it will be necessary for an SME to articulate its vision based on sustainability to progress from a lower level to an advanced level of development.

CONCLUSION

In order to contribute to the achievement of sustainable development, every business organization has to incorporate sustainability into their business operations. In this context, the role of SMEs is significant due to the crucial role they play in any country. Hence, this chapter provides an overview of EMA systems that can be adopted by small- and medium- sized enterprises (SMEs) to support corporate sustainability development. With this objective, the chapter presents a detailed description on how and why corporate sustainability performance is important for SMEs and how EMA could aid their sustainability-related corporate strategies. Having discussed various EMA tools and techniques, the chapter provides an overview of evolutionary stages of environmental management. Then it presents an integrative framework for EMA adoption by considering three aspects of environmental management. It is expected that this framework could guide SMEs to progress from compliance-orientation to the achievement of higher order sustainability outcomes. However, SMEs will have to continuously take deliberate managerial action with the support of EMA systems to reach the advanced stages of sustainability in an ever-changing business environment.

REFERENCES

Aris, N. M. (2007). SMEs: Building blocks for economic growth. Malaysia: Department of National Statistics.

Association of Chartered Certified Accountants (ACCA). (2012). *Embedding Sustainability in SMEs*. London: ACCA.

Ayyagari, M., Beck, T., & Demirguc-Kunt, A. (2007). Small and medium enterprises across the globe. *Small Business Economics*, *29*(4), 415–434. doi:10.100711187-006-9002-5

Bartolomeo, M., Bennett, M., Wolters, T., & Bouma, J. J. (2000). Environmental management accounting in Europe: Current practice and future potential. *European Accounting Review*, *9*(1), 31–52. doi:10.1080/096381800407932

Baylis, R., Connell, L., & Flynn, A. (1998). Company size, environmental regulation and ecological modernization: Further analysis at the level of the firm. *Business Strategy and the Environment*, *7*(5), 285–296. doi:

Bennett, M., Bouma, J. J., & Wolters, T. (2002). Environmental management accounting: Informational and institutional developments (Vol. 9). Netherlands: Springer Science & Business Media.

Bennett, M., & James, P. (2000). The green bottom line: environmental accounting for management: current practice and future trends (New ed.). Sheffield, UK: Greenleaf.

Biondi, V., Iraldo, F., & Meredith, S. (2002). Achieving sustainability through environmental innovation: The role of SMEs. *International Journal of Technology Management*, *24*(5-6), 612–626. doi:10.1504/IJTM.2002.003074

Borga, F., Citterio, A., Noci, G., & Pizzurno, E. (2009). Sustainability report in small enterprises: Case studies in Italian furniture companies. *Business Strategy and the Environment*, *18*(3), 162–176. doi:10.1002/bse.561

Burke, S., & Gaughran, W. F. (2006). Intelligent environmental management for SMEs in manufacturing. *Robotics and Computer-integrated Manufacturing*, *22*(5), 566–575. doi:10.1016/j.rcim.2005.11.008

Burritt, R. L. (2004). Environmental management accounting: Roadblocks on the way to the green and pleasant land. *Business Strategy and the Environment*, *13*(1), 13–32. doi:10.1002/bse.379

Burritt, R. L., Hahn, T., & Schaltegger, S. (2002). Towards a Comprehensive Framework for Environmental Management Accounting — Links Between Business Actors and Environmental Management Accounting Tools. *Australian Accounting Review*, *12*(27), 39–50. doi:10.1111/j.1835-2561.2002.tb00202.x

Burritt, R. L., Schaltegger, S., & Zvezdov, D. (2011). Carbon Management Accounting: Explaining Practice in Leading German Companies. *Australian Accounting Review*, *21*(1), 80–98. doi:10.1111/j.1835-2561.2010.00121.x

Christ, K. (2014). Water management accounting and the wine supply chain: Empirical evidence from Australia. *The British Accounting Review*, *46*(4), 379–396. doi:10.1016/j.bar.2014.10.003

Christ, K. L., & Burritt, R. L. (2015). Material flow cost accounting: a review and agenda for future research. *Journal of Cleaner Production, 108, Part B*, 1378-1389. Doi: 10.1016/j.jclepro.2014.09.005

Christ, K. L., & Burritt, R. L. (2017). Water management accounting: A framework for corporate practice. *Journal of Cleaner Production*, *152*, 379–386. doi:10.1016/j.jclepro.2017.03.147

Commission for Economic, Social and Territorial Affairs. (2012). Paper presented at the third plenary session of ARLEM, Bari, Italy.

Dreessen, E. A. (2009). *Sustainability and Business: A narrative and annotated bibliography*. E. A. J. Dreessen.

Drury, C. (2009). *Management and cost accounting*. New Delhi: Thomson Learning.

Environment Agency. (2003). *SME-Environment 2003*. Retrieved 20 May, 2017 from http://www.netregs.org.uk

Environmental Protection Agency (EPA). (1995). An introduction to environmental accounting as a business management tool: Key concepts and terms. Washington, DC: EPA.

European Commission. (2017). *What is an SME?* Retrieved 6 June, 2017 from http://ec.europa.eu/growth/smes/business-friendly-environment/sme-definition_en

European Union. (2003). Commission recommendation of 6 May 2003 concerning the definition of micro, small and medium-sized enterprises. *Official Journal of the European Union*, *46*, 36-41.

Falle, S., Rauter, R., Engert, S., & Baumgartner, R. (2016). Sustainability Management with the Sustainability Balanced Scorecard in SMEs: Findings from an Austrian Case Study. *Sustainability*, *8*(6), 545. doi:10.3390u8060545

Figge, F., Hahn, T., Schaltegger, S., & Wagner, M. (2002). The Sustainability Balanced Scorecard – linking sustainability management to business strategy. *Business Strategy and the Environment*, *11*(5), 269–284. doi:10.1002/bse.339

Gibassier, D., & Schaltegger, S. (2015). Carbon management accounting and reporting in practice: A case study on converging emergent approaches. *Sustainability Accounting, Management and Policy Journal*, *6*(3), 340–365. doi: 10.1108/SAMPJ-02-2015-0014

Global Reporting Initiative (GRI). (2014). *Ready to Report? Introducing sustainability reporting for SMEs*. Amsterdam, The Netherlands: GRI.

Gunarathne, N. (2015). Fostering the Adoption of Environmental Management with the Help of Accounting: An Integrated Framework. In M. M. Rahim & S. O. Idowu (Eds.), *Social Audit Regulation: Development, Challenges and Opportunities* (pp. 301–324). Cham: Springer International Publishing. doi:10.1007/978-3-319-15838-9_15

Gunarathne, N., & Lee, K.-H. (2015). Environmental Management Accounting (EMA) for environmental management and organizational change: An eco-control approach. *Journal of Accounting & Organizational Change*, *11*(3), 362–383. doi:10.1108/JAOC-10-2013-0078

Gunarathne, N., Peiris, S., Edirisooriya, K., & Jayasinghe, R. (2015). *Environmental management accounting in Sri Lankan enterprises. Nugegoda.* Department of Accounting, University of Sri Jayewardenepura.

Gunarathne, N., Ranasinghe, A., & Peiris, S. (2014). *Guidelines on environmental management accounting for Sri Lankan Enterprises.* Colombo: Institute of Certified Management Accountants of Sri Lanka.

Hansen, E. G., & Schaltegger, S. (2016). The Sustainability Balanced Scorecard: A Systematic Review of Architectures. *Journal of Business Ethics, 133*(2), 193–221. doi:10.100710551-014-2340-3

Hespenheide, E., Pavlovsky, K., & McElroy, M. (2010). Accounting for Sustainability Performance. *Financial Executive, 26*(2), 52-54, 57-58.

International Finance Corporation. (2012). *Interpretation Note on Small and Medium Enterprises and Environmental and Social Risk Management.* Retrieved June 12, 2017 from https://www.ifc.org/wps/wcm/connect/de7d92804a29ffe9ae04af8969adcc27/InterpretationNote_SME_2012.pdf?MOD=AJPERES

ISO. (2011). *ISO 14051:2011. Environmental Management. Material Flow Cost Accounting. General Framework.* Geneva: ISO.

Jabbour, C. J. C., & Santos, F. C. A. (2006). The evolution of environmental management within organizations: Toward a common taxonomy. *Environmental Quality Management, 16*(2), 43–59. doi:10.1002/tqem.20120

Jabbour, C. J. C., Santos, F. C. A., & Nagano, M. S. (2010). Contributions of HRM throughout the stages of environmental management: Methodological triangulation applied to companies in Brazil. *International Journal of Human Resource Management, 21*(7), 1049–1089. doi:10.1080/09585191003783512

Jamil, C. Z. M., Mohamed, R., Muhammad, F., & Ali, A. (2015). Environmental management accounting practices in small medium manufacturing firms. *Procedia: Social and Behavioral Sciences, 172*, 619–626. doi:10.1016/j.sbspro.2015.01.411

Jasch, C. (2008). Environmental and material flow cost accounting: principles and procedures (Vol. 25). Netherlands: Springer Science & Business Media.

Jasch, C., & Savage, D. (2005). International Guidance Document on environmental management accounting (EMA). International Federation of Accountants. New York: IFAC.

Johnson, M. P., & Schaltegger, S. (2016). Two decades of sustainability management tools for SMEs: How far have we come? *Journal of Small Business Management, 54*(2), 481–505. doi:10.1111/jsbm.12154

Kaplan, R. S., & Norton, D. P. (1992). The balanced scorecard: Measures that drive performance. *Harvard Business Review, 1992*(January-February), 71–79. PMID:10119714

Kokubu, K., Kitada, H., & Mouritsen, J. (2012). *Material flow cost accounting and conventional management thinking: introducing a new environmental management accounting tool into companies.* Paper presented at the IPA Conference.

Kolk, A., & Mauser, A. M. (2002). The evolution of environmental management: From stage models to performance evaluation. *Business Strategy and the Environment, 11*(1), 14–31. doi:10.1002/bse.316

Kolk, A., van der Veen, M. L., van Wateringen, S. L., van der Veldt, D., & Walhain, S. P. (1999). *KPMG International survey of environmental reporting 1999*. The Hague, The Netherlands: KPMG/WIMM.

KPMG. (2013). *International Survey of Corporate Responsibility Reporting 2013*. Amstelveen: KPMG.

Lee, K. H. (2009). Why and How to Adopt Green Management into Business Organizations? The Case Study of Korean SMEs in the Manufacturing Industry. *Management Decision*, *47*(7), 1101–1121. doi:10.1108/00251740910978322

Lee, K. H. (2011). Motivations, barriers, and incentives for adopting environmental management (cost) accounting and related guidelines: A study of the republic of Korea. *Corporate Social Responsibility and Environmental Management*, *18*(1), 39–49. doi:10.1002/csr.239

Loucks, S. E., Martens, M. L., & Cho, C. H. (2010). Engaging small-and medium-sized businesses in sustainability. *Sustainability Accounting. Management and Policy Journal*, *1*(2), 178–200. doi:10.1108/20408021011089239

Maggio, G. F. (1997). Inter/intra-generational equity: Current applications under international law for promoting the sustainable development of natural resources. *Buffalo Environmental Law Journal*, *4*(2), 161.

Maximus. (2017). *About Us*. Retrieved May 29, 2017 from http://www.ecomaximus.com/max/jm/index.php?option=com_content&view=article&id=1&Itemid=2

Moss, J., Lambert, C. G., & Rennie, A. E. (2008). SME application of LCA-based carbon footprints. *International Journal of Sustainable Engineering*, *1*(2), 132–141. doi:10.1080/19397030802332930

Nulkar, G. (2014). SMEs and environmental performance–A framework for green business strategies. *Procedia: Social and Behavioral Sciences*, *133*, 130–140. doi:10.1016/j.sbspro.2014.04.177

Okpara, J. O. (2011). Factors constraining the growth and survival of SMEs in Nigeria: Implications for poverty alleviation. *Management Research Review*, *34*(2), 156–171. doi:10.1108/01409171111102786

Organisation for Economic Co-operation and Development (OECD). (2005). *OECD SME and entrepreneurship outlook*. Paris: OECD Publishing.

Organisation for Economic Co-operation and Development (OECD). (2007). *Small Businesses and Environmental Compliance -Review and Possible Application of International Experience in Georgia*. Paris: OECD Publishing.

Ormazabal, M., Rich, E., Sarriegi, J. M., & Viles, E. (2017). Environmental Management Evolution Framework: Maturity Stages and Causal Loops. *Organization & Environment*, *30*(1), 27–50. doi:10.1177/1086026615623060

Ormazabal, M., & Sarriegi, J. M. (2012). Environmental management: Understanding its evolution through maturity states. *Environmental Quality Management*, *22*(1), 31–42. doi:10.1002/tqem.21315

Our World. (2008). *Africa and Climate Change*. Retrieved 12 May, 2017 from https://ourworld.unu.edu/en/africa-and-climate-change

Perrini, F., & Tencati, A. (2006). Sustainability and stakeholder management: The need for new corporate performance evaluation and reporting systems. *Business Strategy and the Environment, 15*(5), 296–308. doi:10.1002/bse.538

Petts, J., Herd, A., Gerrard, S., & Horne, C. (1999). The climate and culture of environmental compliance within SMEs. *Business Strategy and the Environment, 8*(1), 14–30. doi:

Pimenova, P., & Van Der Vorst, R. (2004). The role of support programmes and policies in improving SMEs environmental performance in developed and transition economies. *Journal of Cleaner Production, 12*(6), 549–559. doi:10.1016/j.jclepro.2003.07.001

Revell, A., & Blackburn, R. (2007). The business case for sustainability? An examination of small firms in the UK's construction and restaurant sectors. *Business Strategy and the Environment, 16*(6), 404–420. doi:10.1002/bse.499

Roberts, D. H., & Koeplin, J. P. (2011). Sustainability reporting practices in Portugal: Greenwashing or triple bottom line? *International Business & Economics Research Journal, 6*(9). doi:10.19030/iber.v6i9.3403

Roome, N. (1992). Developing environmental management strategies. *Business Strategy and the Environment, 1*(1), 11–24. doi:10.1002/bse.3280010104

Savlovschi, L. I., & Robu, N. R. (2011). The role of SMEs in modern economy. *Economia. Seria Management, 14*(1), 277–281.

Scagnelli, S. D., Corazza, L., & Cisi, M. (2013). How SMEs disclose their sustainability performance. Which variables influence the choice of reporting guidelines? In L. Songini, A. Pistoni, & C. Herzig (Eds.), *Accounting and control for sustainability* (pp. 77–114). Emerald Group Publishing Limited.

Schaltegger, S., & Burritt, R. (2015). Business Cases and Corporate Engagement with Sustainability: Differentiating Ethical Motivations. *Journal of Business Ethics*. doi:10.100710551-015-2938-0

Schaltegger, S., & Burritt, R. L. (2006). Corporate sustainability accounting: A nightmare or a dream coming true? *Business Strategy and the Environment, 15*(5), 293–295. doi:10.1002/bse.537

Schaltegger, S., & Burritt, R. L. (2010). Sustainability accounting for companies: Catchphrase or decision support for business leaders? *Journal of World Business, 45*(4), 375–384. doi:10.1016/j.jwb.2009.08.002

Schaltegger, S., & Csutora, M. (2012). Carbon accounting for sustainability and management. Status quo and challenges. *Journal of Cleaner Production, 36*, 1–16. doi:10.1016/j.jclepro.2012.06.024

Schaltegger, S., Etxeberria, I. Á., & Ortas, E. (2017). Innovating Corporate Accounting and Reporting for Sustainability – Attributes and Challenges. *Sustainable Development, 25*(2), 113–122. doi:10.1002d.1666

Schaltegger, S., & Zvezdov, D. (2015). Expanding material flow cost accounting. Framework, review and potentials. *Journal of Cleaner Production, 108*, 1333–1341. doi:10.1016/j.jclepro.2014.08.040

Singh, R. K., Garg, S. K., & Deshmukh, S. G. (2008). Strategy development by SMEs for competitiveness: A review. *Benchmarking: An International Journal, 15*(5), 525–547. doi:10.1108/14635770810903132

Sroufe, R., Narasimhan, R., Montabon, F., & Wang, X. (2002). Environmental management practices: a framework. *Greener Management International*, (40), 23.

Stechemesser, K., & Guenther, E. (2012). Carbon accounting: A systematic literature review. *Journal of Cleaner Production*, *36*, 17–38. doi:10.1016/j.jclepro.2012.02.021

Strobel, M., & Redmann, C. (2002). Flow Cost Accounting, an Accounting Approach Based on the Actual Flows of Materials. In M. Bennett & J. J. Bouma (Eds.), *Environmental Management Accounting: Informational and Institutional Developments* (pp. 67–82). Dordrecht: Springer Netherlands.

Tambunan, T. (2011). Development of small and medium enterprises in a developing country: The Indonesian case. *Journal of Enterprising Communities: People and Places in the Global Economy*, *5*(1), 68–82. doi:10.1108/17506201111119626

Tencati, A., Perrini, F., & Pogutz, S. (2004). New tools to foster corporate socially responsible behavior. *Journal of Business Ethics*, *53*(1), 173–190. doi:10.1023/B:BUSI.0000039407.37497.44

The Conversation. (2015). *Climate change is hitting African farmers the hardest of all*. Retrieved 12 May, 2017 from http://theconversation.com/climate-change-is-hitting-african-farmers-the-hardest-of-all-40845

Thorpe, J., & Prakash-Mani, K. (2003). Developing value: The business case for sustainability in emerging markets. *Greener Management International*, (44), 17.

Tinsley, S. (2002). EMS models for business strategy development. *Business Strategy and the Environment*, *11*(6), 376–390. doi:10.1002/bse.340

Tinsley, S. J., & Melton, K. (1997). Sustainable development and its effect on the marketing planning process. *Eco-Management and Auditing*, *4*(3), 116–126. doi:

United Nations Division for Sustainable Development (UNDSD). (2001). *Environmental management accounting: Procedures and principles*. New York: UNDSD.

United Nations World Commission on Environment and Development (UNWCED). (1987). *Report of the World Commission on Environment and Development: Our Common Future*. Oxford, UK: Oxford University Press.

Varis, M., & Littunen, H. (2010). Types of innovation, sources of information and performance in entrepreneurial SMEs. *European Journal of Innovation Management*, *13*(2), 128–154. doi:10.1108/14601061011040221

Virtanen, T., Tuomaala, M., & Pentti, E. (2013). Energy efficiency complexities: A technical and managerial investigation. *Management Accounting Research*, *24*(4), 401–416. doi:10.1016/j.mar.2013.06.002

World Bank. (2015). *BRIEF: Small and Medium Enterprises (SMEs) Finance*. Retrieved 10 June, 2017 from http://www.worldbank.org/en/topic/financialsector/brief/smes-finance

KEY TERMS AND DEFINITIONS

Capital Budgeting: The decisions involving capital outlays in return for a stream of future benefits.

Corporate Sustainability Management: All activities which design, measure, analyze, and improve environmental, social, and economic activities in order to firstly create a sustainable development of the organization itself, and secondly to enable the company to contribute to sustainable development of the economy and society as a whole.

Energy Accounting: The tracking and analysis of all flows of energy into, through, and out of an organization.

Environmental Management Accounting: The identification, collection, analysis, and use of physical information on the use, flows and destinies of energy, water and materials (including wastes) and monetary information on environment-related costs, earnings, and savings for internal decision making.

Sustainable Development: The development that meets the needs of the present generation without compromising the ability of future generations to meet their own needs.

ENDNOTE

1 Although the authors use EMA to refer to environmental and sustainability management accounting, in this chapter it is used interchangeably when referring to environmental management accounting.

Compilation of References

Aaker, D. A. (2010). *Brand Relevance: Making Competitors Irrelevant*. John Wiley & Sons.

Aarset, B., Beckmann, S., Bigne, E., Beveridge, M., Bjorndal, T., Bunting, J., ... Young, J. (2004). The European consumers' understanding and perceptions of the "organic" food regime: The case of aquaculture. *British Food Journal*, *106*(2), 93–105. doi:10.1108/00070700410516784

Abdirahman, Z.-Z., Sauvée, L., & Shiri, G. (2014). Analyzing network effects of Corporate Social Responsibility implementation in food small and medium enterprises. *Journal on Chain and Network Science*, *14*(2), 103–115. doi:10.3920/JCNS2014.x005

Abitabile, C., Giuca, S., Madau, F., & Sardone, R. (2015). Le politiche per il consumo sostenibile e il caso dei prodotti biologici. *Agriregionieuropa (Ancona)*, *11*(41), 28–32.

Acosta-Alba, I., López-Ridaura, S., van der Werf, H. M. G., Leterme, P., & Corson, M. S. (2012). Exploring sustainable farming scenarios at a regional scale: An application to dairy farms in Brittany. *Journal of Cleaner Production*, *28*, 160–167. doi:10.1016/j.jclepro.2011.11.061

Adams, C. A., & McNicholas, P. (2007). Making a difference: Sustainability reporting, accountability and organisational change. *Accounting, Auditing & Accountability Journal*, *20*(3), 382–402. doi:10.1108/09513570710748553

Adams, D., & Salois, M. (2010). Local versus organic: A turn in consumer preferences and willingness to pay. *Renewable Agriculture and Food Systems*, *25*(4), 331–341. doi:10.1017/S1742170510000219

Agostini, M., & Costa, E. (2018). Financial and Sustainability Reporting: An Empirical Investigation of Their Relationship in the Italian Context. In Sustainability and Social Responsibility: Regulation and Reporting (pp. 411-441). Singapore: Springer Nature Singapore Pte Ltd. doi:10.1007/978-981-10-4502-8_17

Agostini, M., Cordazzo, M., & Saccon, C. (2018). Historical origins and evolution of Small and Medium Practices in the Northeast of the Italian peninsula. In The Origins of Accounting Culture: The Venetian Connection. London, UK: Routledge.

Agovino, M., Crociata, A., Quaglione, D., Sacco, P., & Sarra, A. (2017). Good Taste Tastes Good. Cultural Capital as a Determinant of Organic Food Purchase by Italian Consumers: Evidence and Policy Implications. *Ecological Economics*, *141*, 66–75. doi:10.1016/j.ecolecon.2017.05.029

Ahmad, J., & Krishnan, M. (2017). Environmental Related CSR Initiatives for Business Strategy: A Case Study on Small and Medium (SME) Industries in Malaysia. In The Dynamics of Corporate Social Responsibility (pp. 305–322). Springer.

Ahrens, T., & Chapman, C. S. (2007). Management accounting as practise. *Accounting, Organizations and Society*, *32*(1-2), 1–27. doi:10.1016/j.aos.2006.09.013

Aldrich, H. E. (1979). *Organizations and environments*. Englewood Cliffs, NJ: Prentice-Hall.

Alfiero, S., Elba, F., Esposito, A., & Resce, G. (2017). The Impact of Environmental Factors on the Measurement of Managerial Efficiency in the Italian Waste Management Sector: Framework and Empirical Evidence. *International Journal of Public Administration*, 1–13.

Ali, W., Frynas, J. G., & Mahmood, Z. (2017). Determinants of Corporate Social Responsibility (CSR) Disclosure in Developed and Developing Countries: A Literature Review. *Corporate Social Responsibility and Environmental Management*, *24*(4), 273–294. doi:10.1002/csr.1410

Alrøe, H. F., & Noe, E. (2016). Sustainability assessment and complementarity. *Ecology and Society*, *21*(1), 30. doi:10.5751/ES-08220-210130

Alrøe, H. F., Sautier, M., Legun, K., Whitehead, J., Noe, E., Moller, H., & Manhire, J. (2017). Performance versus Values in Sustainability Transformation of Food Systems. *Sustainability*, *9*(3), 332. doi:10.3390u9030332

Alrøe, H., Moller, H., Læssøe, J., & Noe, E. (2016). Opportunities and challenges for multicriteria assessment of food system sustainability. *Ecology and Society*, *21*(1), art38. doi:10.5751/ES-08394-210138

Amato Mangiameli, A. C. (Ed.). (2006). Persone e Stati. Le conseguenze della "glocalizzazione" e della innovazione tecnologica. Atti del Convegno (Teramo, 13-15 novembre 2003). Milano, Italy: Giuffrè.

Amin, A. (2009). Extraordinarily ordinary: Working in the social economy. *Social Enterprise Journal*, *5*(1), 30–49. doi:10.1108/17508610910956390

Amodeo, D. (1971). Il bilancio delle società per azioni come strumento di informazione. In D. Amodeo (Ed.), *Argomenti di varia ragioneria* (pp. 231–260). Napoli, Italy: Giannini.

Anderson, R. C., & Reeb, D. M. (2003). Founding-Family Ownership and Firm Performance: Evidence from the S&P 500. *The Journal of Finance*, *58*(3), 1301–1328. doi:10.1111/1540-6261.00567

Ángeles Murga-Menoyo, M. (2009). The Earth Charter. A reference for the decade of education for sustainable development. *Review of Education*, 239–262.

Angelidou, M., Komninos, N., Leal, X., Passas, I. A., Schoina, M. S., & Sefertzi, E. (2015). Intelligent Transport Systems: Glocal Communities of Interest for technology commercialization and innovation. In NICT for Transport: Opportunities and Threats, (pp. 226-248). Northampton, MA: Edward Elgar Publishing Ltd.

Annunziata, A., & Vecchio, R. (2015). Organic farming and sustainability in food choices: An analysis of consumer preference in Southern Italy. *Agriculture and Agricultural Science Procedia*, *8*, 193–200. doi:10.1016/j.aaspro.2016.02.093

Anonymous. (2013). Understanding the contemporary advertising environment: Is glocal the most effective strategy? *Strategic Direction*, *29*(2), 10–12. doi:10.1108/02580541311297994

Araújo, A. L., Rodrigues, B. A., Telles, L. B., Vaz, M. C., & Bittencourt, J. V. (2017). A bibliometric analysis of the Scielo database: A Brazilian portfolio of the solidarity economy. *Scientometrics*, *112*(1), 1–20. doi:10.100711192-017-2382-2

Arbenz, M., Gould, D., & Stopes, C. (2016). *ORGANIC 3.0 – for truly sustainable farming and consumption. 2nd updated edition*. Bonn: IFOAM Organics International, Bonn and SOAAN.

Arbenz, M., Gould, D., & Stopes, C. (2017). ORGANIC 3.0 - the vision of the global organic movement and the need for scientific support. *Organic Agriculture*, 1–9.

Aris, N. M. (2007). SMEs: Building blocks for economic growth. Malaysia: Department of National Statistics.

Arnold, D. (2007). "Think global, act local": The modularization of marketing and marketing organizations. *Globe Management Review*, *1*(1), 5.

Arnold, S. J., & Fischer, E. (1994). Hermeneutics and consumer research. *The Journal of Consumer Research*, *21*(1), 55–70. doi:10.1086/209382

Aronoff, C. (2004). Self-Perpetuation Family Organization Built on Values: Necessary condition for long-term family business survival. *Family Business Review*, *17*(1), 55–59. doi:10.1111/j.1741-6248.2004.00003.x

Arrangle, J., Hitt, M., Sirmon, D., & Very, D. (2007). The development of organizational social capital: Attributes of family firms. *Journal of Management Studies*, *44*(1), 73–95. doi:10.1111/j.1467-6486.2007.00665.x

Arredondo, P. (1996). *Successful diversity management initiatives*. London: Sage.

Asprone, D., & Manfredi, G. (2015). Linking disaster resilience and urban sustainability: A glocal approach for future cities. *Disasters*, *39*(s1), s96–s111. doi:10.1111/disa.12106 PMID:25494959

Association of Chartered Certified Accountants (ACCA). (2012). *Embedding Sustainability in SMEs*. London: ACCA.

Astrachan, J. H., Klein, S. B., & Smyrnios, K. X. (2002). The F-PEC scale of family influence: A proposal for solving the family business definition problem1. *Family Business Review*, *15*(1), 45–58. doi:10.1111/j.1741-6248.2002.00045.x

Aureli, S., & Forlani, F. (2015). The effects of formal networks on territorial tourism offers. Current usage of network contracts in Italy. *European Journal of Tourism Research*, *10*(July), 76–94.

Autorità di Regolazione dei Trasporti. (2017, July). *Quarto Rapporto Annuale al Parlamento*. Camera dei Deputati.

Avram, D. O., & Kühne, S. (2008). Implementing responsible business behavior from a strategic management perspective: Developing a framework for Austrian SMEs. *Journal of Business Ethics*, *82*(2), 463–475. doi:10.100710551-008-9897-7

Ayyagari, M., Beck, T., & Demirguc-Kunt, A. (2007). Small and medium enterprises across the globe. *Small Business Economics*, *29*(4), 415–434. doi:10.100711187-006-9002-5

Azapagic, A. (2004). Developing a framework for sustainable development indicators for the mining and minerals industry. *Journal of Cleaner Production*, *12*(6), 639–662. doi:10.1016/S0959-6526(03)00075-1

Baden, D., Harwood, I. A., & Woodward, D. G. (2011). The effects of procurement policies on "downstream" corporate social responsibility activity. *International Small Business Journal*, *29*(3), 259–277. doi:10.1177/0266242610375770

Bagnoli, C., & Biloslavo, R. (2012). L'innovazione strategica nei piccoli e medi studi commercialistici triveneti. *Rivista Dei Dottori Commercialisti*, *63*(2), 247–273.

Baker, W. E., & Sinkula, J. M. (2009). The complementary effects of market orientation and entrepreneurial orientation on profitability in small businesses. *Journal of Small Business Management*, *47*(4), 443–464. doi:10.1111/j.1540-627X.2009.00278.x

Baldo, M. D. (2011, January). Il contratto di rete come strumento di sviluppo delle piccole e medie imprese. *Un'analisi delle prime esperienze*.

Baldo, M. D., & Aureli, S. (2012). Networks' contribution to small-sized firms' internationalization. *International Journal of Economic Behavior*, (2), 47–66.

Baldwin, R. (2004). *Better Regulation: is it Better for Business? A report on behalf of The Federation of Small Businesses*. Retrieved August 10, 2017, from http://www.fsb.org.uk/LegacySitePath/policy/assets/0952%20Better%20Regulation.pdf

Banker, R. D., Charnes, A., & Cooper, W. W. (1984). Some models for estimating technical and scale inefficiencies in data envelopment analysis. *Management Science, 30*(9), 1078–1092. doi:10.1287/mnsc.30.9.1078

Baptista, C. (2011). *Relatório de Avaliação Final-Implementação do Projecto Q3 Norte*. Porto: Federação Minha Terra.

Barabanova, Y., Zanoli, R., Schlüter, M., & Stopes, C. (2015). *Transforming Food and Farming: An Organic Vision for Europe in 2030*. Brussels: IFOAM EU.

Barbera, F., & Dagnes, J. (2016). Building Alternatives from the Bottom-up: The Case of Alternative Food Networks. *Agriculture and Agricultural Science Procedia,* (8), 324 – 331.

Barbera, F., Corsi, A., Dansero, E., Giaccaria, P., Peano, C., & Puttilli, M. (2014). Cosa c'è di alternativo negli Alternative Food Networks? Un'agenda di ricerca per un approccio interdisciplinare. *Scienze del territorio,* (2), 35 - 44.

Barbosa, F., & Romero, F. (2014). Strategy, Innovation and Internationalization in SMEs: The Implementation Issue. *Proceedings of the 9th European Conference on Entrepreneurship and Innovation.*

Barkemeyer, R., & Figge, F. (2014). CSR in multiple environments: The impact of headquartering. *Critical Perspectives on International Business, 10*(3), 124–151. doi:10.1108/cpoib-05-2013-0013

Barnett, M. L. (2007). Stakeholder influence capacity and the variability of financial returns to corporate social responsibility. *Academy of Management Review, 32*(3), 794–816. doi:10.5465/AMR.2007.25275520

Barnett, M. L., & Salomon, R. M. (2006). Beyond dichotomy: The curvilinear relationship between social responsibility and financial performance. *Strategic Management Journal, 27*(11), 1101–1156. doi:10.1002mj.557

Barney, J. (1991). Firm resources and sustained competitive advantage. *Journal of Management, 17*(1), 99–120. doi:10.1177/014920639101700108

Barómetro Europeo de la Empresa Familiar (EFB-KPMG). (2016). *Exitosa y Resilente*. Author.

Baroni, V. (2009). *Glocal, vivere la città nell'era digitale*. Retrieved September 3, from http://www.comunicatoripubblici.it

Bartolomeo, M., Bennett, M., Wolters, T., & Bouma, J. J. (2000). Environmental management accounting in Europe: Current practice and future potential. *European Accounting Review, 9*(1), 31–52. doi:10.1080/096381800407932

Barton, J. R., & Fløysand, A. (2010). The political ecology of Chilean salmon aquaculture, 1982-2010: A trajectory from economic development to global sustainability. *Global Environmental Change, 20*(4), 739–752. doi:10.1016/j.gloenvcha.2010.04.001

Basco, R. (2015). Family business and regional development-A theoretical model of regional familiness. *Journal of Family Business Strategy, 6*(4), 259–271. doi:10.1016/j.jfbs.2015.04.004

Basha, M. B., Mason, C., Shamsudin, M. F., Hussain, H. I., & Salem, M. A. (2015). Consumers attitude towards organic food. *Procedia Economics and Finance, 31*, 444–452. doi:10.1016/S2212-5671(15)01219-8

Basole, R. C. (2009). Visualization of interfirm relations in a converging mobile ecosystem. *Journal of Information Technology, 24*(2), 1–16. doi:10.1057/jit.2008.34

Bassetti, P. (2008). *Manifesto dei Glocalisti*. Retrieved September 3, 2009, from http://www.glocalisti.org

Bastida, R., Marimon, F., & Tanganelli, D. (2017). Alliance success factors and performance in social economy enterprises. *Management Decision, 55*(5), 1065–1080. doi:10.1108/MD-12-2016-0881

Battaglia, M., Bianchi, L., Frey, M., & Iraldo, F. (2010). An innovative model to promote CSR among SMEs operating in industrial clusters: Evidence from an EU project. *Corporate Social Responsibility and Environmental Management*, *17*(3), 133–141. doi:10.1002/csr.224

Battaglia, M., Testa, F., Bianchi, L., Iraldo, F., & Frey, M. (2014). Corporate social responsibility and competitiveness within SMEs of the fashion industry: Evidence from Italy and France. *Sustainability*, *6*(2), 872–893. doi:10.3390u6020872

Baumann-Pauly, D., Wickert, C., Spence, L. J., & Scherer, A. G. (2013). Organizing Corporate Social Responsibility in Small and Large Firms: Size Matters. *Journal of Business Ethics*, 1–13. doi:10.100710551-012-1502-4

Bauman, Z. (2005). *Globalizzazione e glocalizzazione*. Roma, Italy: Armando.

Baylis, R., Connell, L., & Flynn, A. (1998). Company size, environmental regulation and ecological modernization: Further analysis at the level of the firm. *Business Strategy and the Environment*, *7*(5), 285–296. doi:

Bazzani, C., & Canavari, M. (2013). Alternative agri-food networks and short food supply chains: A review of the literature. *Economia Agro-Alimentare*, *15*(2), 11–34. doi:10.3280/ECAG2013-002002

Bazzani, C., & Canavari, M. (2017). Is local a matter of food miles or food traditions? *Italian Journal of Food Science*, *29*(3), 505–517.

Bebbington, J. (2007). *Accounting for Sustainable Development Performance* (1st ed.). Burlington: CIMA Publishing.

Bebbington, J., Gray, R., Hibbitt, C., & Kirk, E. (2001). *Full cost accounting: An agenda for action*. Certified Accountants Educational Trust London.

Beck, A., Cuoco, E., Häring, A. M., Kahl, J., Koopmans, C., Micheloni, C., & Rasmussen, I. A. (2014). *Strategic Research and Innovation Agenda for Organic Food and Farming*. Brussels: Tp Organics.

Bedeian, A. G., Mossholder, K. W., Touliatos, J., & Barkman, A. J. (1986). The accountant's stereotype: An update for vocational counsellors. *Career Development Quarterly*, *35*(2), 113–122. doi:10.1002/j.2161-0045.1986.tb00771.x

Bennett, M., & James, P. (2000). The green bottom line: environmental accounting for management: current practice and future trends (New ed.). Sheffield, UK: Greenleaf.

Bennett, M., Bouma, J. J., & Wolters, T. (2002). Environmental management accounting: Informational and institutional developments (Vol. 9). Netherlands: Springer Science & Business Media.

Bennett, R. J., & Robson, P. J. A. (2004). The Role of Trust and Contract in Supply of Business Advice. *Cambridge Journal of Economics*, *28*(4), 471–488. doi:10.1093/cje/28.4.471

Benneworth, P., & Cunha, J. (2015). Universities' contributions to social innovation: Reflections in theory & practice. *European Journal of Innovation Management*, *18*(4), 508–527. doi:10.1108/EJIM-10-2013-0099

Berrone, P., Cruz, C., Gomez-Mejia, L., & Larraza-Kintana, M. (2010). Socioemotional wealth and corporate response to institutional pressures: Do family-controlled firms pollute less? *Administrative Science Quarterly*, *55*(1), 82–113. doi:10.2189/asqu.2010.55.1.82

Berry, A. J., Sweeting, R., & Goto, J. (2006). The effect of business advisors on the performance of SMEs. *Journal of Small Business and Enterprise Development*, *13*(1), 33–47. doi:10.1108/14626000610645298

Berry, E. M., Dernini, S., Burlingame, B., Meybeck, A., & Conforti, P. (2015). Food security and sustainability: Can one exist without the other? *Public Health Nutrition*, *18*(13), 2293–2302. doi:10.1017/S136898001500021X PMID:25684016

Bertoli, G. (2014). L'impresa e le strategie internazionali. In E. Valdani & P. Bertoli (Eds.), *Mercati internazionali e marketing* (pp. 47–84). Milano, Italy: Egea.

Besana, A. (2017). Animal Spirits or Engaging Spirits?: The Importance of the Not-for-Profit Economy – Coopetitiveness and Grant-Making Foundations. In A. Vlachvei, O. Notta, K. Karantininis, & N. Tsounis (Eds.), *Factors Affecting Firm Competitiveness and Performance in the Modern Business World* (pp. 223–250). Hershey, PA: IGI Global. doi:10.4018/978-1-5225-0843-4.ch008

Besser, T. L. (2012). The consequences of social responsibility for small business owners in small towns. *Business Ethics (Oxford, England), 21*(2), 129–139. doi:10.1111/j.1467-8608.2011.01649.x

Beukema, L. (2004). Work restructuring as ongoing glocal processes: concluding remarks. In L. Beukema & J.H. Carrillo (Eds.), Globalism/Localism at Work. Bingley, UK: Emerald. doi:10.1016/S0277-2833(04)13011-2

Beukema, L., & Carrillo, J. H. (Eds.). (2004). Globalism/Localism at Work. Bingley, UK: Emerald.

Bevan, S., & Wilmott, M. (2002). *The Ethical Employee*. London: The Work Future Foundation.

Bianchi, S. (2013). Linee guida internazionali per la redazione del report integrato. *Amministrazione & finanza, 28*(2), 13-18.

Biancolillo, A., Bucci, R., Magrì, A. L., Magrì, A. D., & Marini, F. (2014). Data-fusion for multiplatform characterization of an Italian craft beer aimed at its authentication. *Analytica Chimica Acta, 820*, 23–31. doi:10.1016/j.aca.2014.02.024 PMID:24745734

Bieker, T. (2002). *Sustainability management with the Balanced Scorecard.* Paper of Institute for Economy and the Environment at the University.

Bieker, T. (2002). *Managing corporate sustainability with the Balanced Scorecard: developing a Balanced Scorecard for Integrity Management.* Oikos PhD Summer Academy.

Biondi, V., Iraldo, F., & Meredith, S. (2002). Achieving sustainability through environmental innovation: The role of SMEs. *International Journal of Technology Management, 24*(5-6), 612–626. doi:10.1504/IJTM.2002.003074

Bird, B., Welsch, H., Astrachan, J. H., & Pistrui, D. (2002). Family business research: The evolution of an academic field. *Family Business Review, 15*(4), 337–350. doi:10.1111/j.1741-6248.2002.00337.x

Bjerrisgaard, S. M., & Kjeldgaard, D. (2013). How Market Research Shapes Market Spatiality: A Global Governmentality Perspective. *Journal of Macromarketing, 33*(1), 29–40. doi:10.1177/0276146712462891

Blackburn, R., Carey, P., & Tanewski, G. A. (2011). *Business Advice to SMEs. Professional Competence, Trust and Ethics*. ACCA.

Blackburn, R., & Jarvis, R. (2010). *The Role of Small and Medium Practices in Providing Business Support to Small- and Medium-sized Enterprises*. New York: International Federation of Accountants.

Blay-Palmer, A., Custot, J., & Sonnino, R. (2016). A food politics of the possible? Growing sustainable food systems through networks of knowledge. *Agriculture and Human Values, 33*(1), 27–43. doi:10.100710460-015-9592-0

Blockeel, J., Baumgart, L., Landert, J., & Schrader, C. (2016). Sustainability performance of organic and conventional farms in Ticino: How well does the SMART-Farm Tool capture the differences? *Proceedings of the 20th Conference of the Environmental and Sustainability Management Accounting Network (EMAN).*

Block, J. H. (2012). R&D investments in family and founder firms: An agency perspective. *Journal of Business Venturing, 27*(2), 248–265. doi:10.1016/j.jbusvent.2010.09.003

Boccardelli, P., Marcati, A., & Marchigiani, L. (2006). Strategie e politiche di marketing. In F. Fontana & M. Caroli (Eds.), *Economia e gestione delle imprese* (pp. 259–334). Milano, Italy: McGraw-Hill.

Bond, C. A., Thilmany, D., & Bond, J. K. (2008). What to choose? The value of label claims to fresh produce consumers. *Journal of Agricultural and Resource Economics, 33*, 402–427.

Bookin blog (2008a). *"Glocale", il futuro linguaggio del web #2 - Come cambia la comunicazione del sito dell'hotel.* Retrieved July 23, 2009, from: http://www.bookingblog.com

Bookin Blog. (2008b). *"Glocale", il futuro linguaggio del web #1 – Dalla Cina alla Russia, i nuovi mercati turistici".* Retrieved July 23, 2009, from: http://www.bookingblog.com

Borga, F., Citterio, A., Noci, G., & Pizzurno, E. (2009). Sustainability report in small enterprises: Case studies in Italian furniture companies. *Business Strategy and the Environment, 18*(3), 162–176. doi:10.1002/bse.561

Borgerson, J. L., Schroeder, J. E., Escudero Magnusson, M., & Magnusson, F. (2009). Corporate communication, ethics, and operational identity: A case study of Benetton. *Business Ethics (Oxford, England), 18*(3), 209–223. doi:10.1111/j.1467-8608.2009.01558.x

Borzaga, C., & Tortia, E. (2007). Social Economy Organisations in the Theory of the Firm. In *The Social Economy: Building Inclusive Economies*. Paris: OECD Publishing. doi:10.1787/9789264039889-3-en

Bourguignon, A. (2000). *Performance et control de gestion. In Encyclopedie de Comptabilitè, Control de gestion et Audit* (pp. 931–941). Ed. Economica.

Bouwens, J., & Abernethy, M. (2000). The consequences of customization on management accounting system design. *Accounting, Organizations and Society, 25*(3), 221–241. doi:10.1016/S0361-3682(99)00043-4

Bowlin, W. F. (1998). Measuring performance: An introduction to data envelopment analysis (DEA). *The Journal of Cost Analysis, 15*(2), 3–27. doi:10.1080/08823871.1998.10462318

Brammer, S., & Pavelin, S. (2006). Voluntary environmental disclosures by large UK companies. *Journal of Business Finance & Accounting, 33*(7-8), 1168–1188. doi:10.1111/j.1468-5957.2006.00598.x

Brinkmann, S., & Kvale, S. (2008). Ethics in qualitative psychological research. In C. Willig & W. Stainton-Rogers (Eds.), *The SAGE Handbook of Qualitative Research in Psychology* (pp. 263–279). New Delhi: Sage. doi:10.4135/9781848607927.n15

Broccardo, L., Culasso, F., & Truant, E. (2016). Business Process Management: An Investigation In Italian Smes. *Proceedings of the 9th Annual Conference of the EuroMed-Academy-of-Business: Innovation, Entrepreneurship And Digital Ecosystems*, 366-376.

Broccardo, L., Culasso, F., Giacosa, E., & Truant, E. (2016). The diffusion of management control systems in Italy: A comparison between family and non-family firms. *Corporate Ownership and Control, 13*(4), 165-172.

Broccardo, L. (2011). Family Versus Non Family Firms in the Luxury Yachts Sector: Strategy – Structure Combination to Manage the Performance. *Electronic Journal of Family Business Studies, 5*(1-2), 96–125.

Brown, J., & Fraser, M. (2006). Approaches and perspectives in social and environmental accounting: An overview of the conceptual landscape. *Business Strategy and the Environment, 15*(2), 103–117. doi:10.1002/bse.452

Brown, R. B., Saunders, M., & Bresford, R. (2006). You owe it to yourself: The financially literate manager. *Accounting Forum, 30*(2), 179–191. doi:10.1016/j.accfor.2006.03.001

Brunke, J.-C., Johansson, M., & Thollander, P. (2014). Empirical investigation of barriers and drivers to the adoption of energy conservation measures, energy management practices and energy services in the Swedish iron and steel industry. *Journal of Cleaner Production*, *84*, 509–525. doi:10.1016/j.jclepro.2014.04.078

Brunori, G., Galli, F., Barjolle, D., Van Broekhuizen, R., Colombo, L., Giampietro, M., ... de Roest, K. (2016). Are local food chains more sustainable than global food chains? considerations for assessment. *Sustainability*, *8*(5), 449. doi:10.3390u8050449

Brusa, L. (2007). *Attuare e controllare la strategia aziendale – Mappa strategica e Balanced Scorecard*. Giuffrè Editore.

Buckley, P.J., & Ghauri Pervez, N. (2004). Globalization, economic geography and strategy of multinational enterprises. *Journal of International Business Study*, (35), 81-98.

Buhmann, K. (2009). Regulating Corporate Social and Human Rights Responsibilities at the UN plane: Institutionalising new forms of law and law-making approaches? *Nordic Journal of International Law*, *78*(1), 1–52. doi:10.1163/157181009X397063

Buhmann, K. (2011). Danish CSR Reporting Requirement: Migration of CRS-Related International Norms into Companies' Self-Regulation through Company Law, The. *Eur. Company L.*, *8*, 65.

Bunse, K., Vodicka, M., Schönsleben, P., Brülhart, M., & Ernst, F. O. (2011). Integrating energy efficiency performance in production management--gap analysis between industrial needs and scientific literature. *Journal of Cleaner Production*, *19*(6), 667–679. doi:10.1016/j.jclepro.2010.11.011

Bureau of Energy Efficiency (BEE). (2010). Manual on Energy Conservation Measures in *Ceramic Industry*. Author.

Bürgi, J. (2010). A Comprehensive Model for SMEs: Measuring the Dynamic Interplay of Morality, Environment and Management Systems. Towards Continuous Improvement. In Ethics in Small and Medium Sized Enterprises (pp. 147-171). Dordrecht, The Netherlands: Springer.

Bürgi, J. (2010). A comprehensive model for SMEs: Measuring the dynamic interplay of morality, environment and management systems–Towards continuous improvement. In *Ethics in Small and Medium Sized Enterprises* (pp. 147–171). Springer. doi:10.1007/978-90-481-9331-8_9

Burke, S., & Gaughran, W. F. (2006). Intelligent environmental management for SMEs in manufacturing. *Robotics and Computer-integrated Manufacturing*, *22*(5), 566–575. doi:10.1016/j.rcim.2005.11.008

Burritt, R. (2012). Environmental performance accountability: Planet, people, profits. *Accounting, Auditing & Accountability Journal*, *25*(2), 370–405. doi:10.1108/09513571211198791

Burritt, R. L. (2004). Environmental management accounting: Roadblocks on the way to the green and pleasant land. *Business Strategy and the Environment*, *13*(1), 13–32. doi:10.1002/bse.379

Burritt, R. L., Hahn, T., & Schaltegger, S. (2002). Towards a Comprehensive Framework for Environmental Management Accounting — Links Between Business Actors and Environmental Management Accounting Tools. *Australian Accounting Review*, *12*(27), 39–50. doi:10.1111/j.1835-2561.2002.tb00202.x

Burritt, R. L., Schaltegger, S., & Zvezdov, D. (2011). Carbon Management Accounting: Explaining Practice in Leading German Companies. *Australian Accounting Review*, *21*(1), 80–98. doi:10.1111/j.1835-2561.2010.00121.x

By, R. T. (2005). Organizational Change Management : A Critical Review. *Journal of Change Management*, *5*(4), 369–380. doi:10.1080/14697010500359250

Cabras, I., Higgins, D., & Preece, D. (2016). *Brewing, Beer and Pubs: A global perspective*. Springer. doi:10.1057/9781137466181

Cacciolatti, L. A., Garcia, C. C., & Kalantzakis, M. (2015). Traditional Food Products: The Effect of Consumers' Characteristics, Product Knowledge, and Perceived Value on Actual Purchase. *Journal of International Food & Agribusiness Marketing*, *27*(3), 155–176. doi:10.1080/08974438.2013.807416

Campbell, A., Fischel, S., Bowman, N., Duffy, S., Sedler, M., & Thornton, S. (2013). Retrospective analysis of outcomes after IVF using an aneuploidy risk model derived from time-lapse imaging without PGS. *Reproductive Biomedicine Online*, *27*(2), 140–146. doi:10.1016/j.rbmo.2013.04.013 PMID:23683847

Campbell, J. L. (2007). Why would corporations behave in socially responsible ways? An institutional theory of corporate social responsibility. *Academy of Management Review*, *32*(3), 946–967. doi:10.5465/AMR.2007.25275684

Canavari, M., Bazzani, G.M., Spadoni, R., & Regazzi, D. (2002). Food safety and organic fruit demand in Italy: a survey. *British Food Journal*, *104*(3/4/5), 220–232.

Candelo, E., Casalegno, C., & Civera, C. (2014). Meanings and Implications of Corporate Social Responsibility and Branding in Grocer Retailers: A Comparative Study over Italy and the UK. In F. Musso & E. Druica (Eds.), *Handbook of Research on Retailer-Consumer Relationship Development* (pp. 351–370). IGI Global. doi:10.4018/978-1-4666-6074-8.ch019

Canfora, I. (2016). Is the short food supply chain an efficient solution for sustainability in food market? *Agriculture and Agricultural Science Procedia,* (8), 402-407.

Cantele, S., Vernizzi, S., & Ricciardi, F. (2016). The emerging wave of agility-oriented business networks in Italy: A new strategy for facing global competition. *World Review of Entrepreneurship, Management and Sustainable Development*, *12*(2/3), 270–284. doi:10.1504/WREMSD.2016.074967

Capaldo, P. (1975). Qualche riflessione sull'informazione esterna d'impresa. *La Rivista dei Dottori Commercialisti*, (5), 833-867.

Capaldo, A. (2015). *Strategia, reti di imprese e capacità relazionali*. Padova, Italy: Cedam.

Capasso, A., Gallucci, C., & Rossi, M. (2015). Standing the test of time. Does firm performance improve with age? An analysis of the wine industry. *Business History*, *57*(7), 1037–1053. doi:10.1080/00076791.2014.993614

Capehart, B. L., Turner, W. C., & Kennedy, W. J. (2006). *Guide to Energy Management* (5th ed.). Lilburn, GA: The Fairmont Press.

Capone, R., El Bilali, H., & Bottalico, F. (2016). Assessing the sustainability of typical agro-food products: Insights from Apulia region, Italy. *New Medit*, *15*(1), 28–36.

Caporaso, S., Esposito, P., & Ricci, P. (2016). Corporate social responsibility in the North and South of Europe: a comparison between Finland and Italy. *Proceedings of the 9th Annual Conference of the EuroMed-Academy-of-Business Location: Innovation, Entrepreneurship and Digital Ecosystems*, 405-416.

Caracciolo, F. F. (2012). *Il trasporto pubblico locale in Italia: stato, prospettive confronti internazionali*. Academic Press.

Cardoni, A., & Tiacci, L. (2013). The "Enterprises' Network Agreement": The Italian Way to Stimulate Reindustrialization for Entrepreneurial and Economic Development of SMEs. *The enterprises' Network Agreement,* 471–480. 10.1007/978-3-642-40543-3_50

Cardoni, A., Rossi, V., & Tiacci, L. (2011). Le reti d'impresa e la sfida per l'innovazione: un progetto di networking tra PMI nel settore della meccanica. *AUR&S Agenzia Umbria Ricerche*, 5–6.

Cardoni, A., Saetta, S., & Tiacci, L. (2010). Evaluating how potential pool of partners can join together in different types of long term collaborative networked organizations. *IFIP Advances in Information and Communication Technology, 336*, 312–321. 10.1007/978-3-642-15961-9_37

Cardoso, L., Meireles, A., & Peralta, C. (2012). Knowledge management and its critical factors in social economy organizations. *Journal of Knowledge Management*, *16*(2), 267–284. doi:10.1108/13673271211218861

Carminucci, C., & Procopio, M. (2008). *La riforma del trasporto pubblico locale nelle regioni: lo stato di attuazione e le prospettive*. Istituto Superiore di Formazione e Ricerca per i Trasporti.

Carnegie, G. D., & Napier, C. J. (2010). Traditional accountants and business professionals: Portraying the accounting profession after Enron. *Accounting, Organizations and Society*, *35*(3), 360–376. doi:10.1016/j.aos.2009.09.002

Caroli, M. (2017). *L'innovazione delle imprese leader per creare valore sociale, Terzo rapporto CERIIS sull'innovazione sociale, Studi ed esperienze sull'innovazione sociale – CERIIS*. FrancoAngeli Editore.

Carpenter, R. A. (1993). Can sustainability be measured. *Environmental Strategy*, *5*(February), 13–16.

Carpio, C. E., & Isengildina-Massa, O. (2009). Consumer willingness to pay for locally grown products: The case of South Carolina. *Agribusiness*, *25*(3), 412–426. doi:10.1002/agr.20210

Carroll, A. B. (1979). A three-dimensional conseptual model of corporate performance. *Academy of Management Review*, *4*, 4497–4530.

Carroll, A. B. (1979). A Tridimensional Conceptual Model of Corporate Social Performance. *Academy of Management Review*, *4*, 497–505.

Carroll, A. B. (1999). Corporate social responsibility: Evolution of a definitional construct. *Business & Society*, *38*(3), 268–295. doi:10.1177/000765039903800303

Carroll, A., & Buchholtz, A. (2014). *Business and society: Ethics, Sustainability, and stakeholder management*. Cengage Learning.

Carruthers, B. G. (1995). Accounting, ambiguity, and the new institutionalism. *Accounting, Organizations and Society*, *20*(4), 313–328. doi:10.1016/0361-3682(95)96795-6

Casalegno, C., & Pellicelli, M. (2008). The Human Capital Impact on the Shareholder Value Creation. *Economia Aziendale On Line 2000 Web, 1*(2/3).

Casalegno, C., & Civera, C. (2016). *Impresa e CSR: la non comunicazione di successo*. Milan, Italy: Franco Angeli.

CASES-INE. (2012). *Conta satélite da Economia Social: 2010 Resultados preliminares*. Retrieved February 6, 2017, from http://www.animar-dl.pt/index/documentacao/documentos/economia_social/ine

Casillas, J. C., Moreno, M., & Barbero, J. L. (2010). A Configurational Approach of the Relationship Between Entrepreneurial Orientation and Growth of Family Firms. *Family Business Review*, *23*(1), 27–44. doi:10.1177/0894486509345159

Castilla-Polo, F., Sánchez-Hernández, M. I., & Gallardo-Vázquez, D. (2017). Assessing the Influence of Social Responsibility on Reputation: An Empirical Case-Study in Agricultural Cooperatives in Spain. *Journal of Agricultural & Environmental Ethics*, *30*(1), 99–120. doi:10.100710806-017-9656-9

Castka, P., & Balzarova, M. A. (2008). ISO 26000 and supply chains-On the diffusion of the social responsibility standard. *International Journal of Production Economics, 111*(2), 274–286. doi:10.1016/j.ijpe.2006.10.017

Cedrola, E., & Battaglia, L. (2011). Piccole e medie imprese e internazionalità: Strategie di business, relazioni, innovazione. *Sinergie, 85*(11), 71–92.

Cerrato, S. (2016). Appunti sul contratto di rete: un modello «à la carte» dal contratto all'istituzione... e ritorno. *Rivista Di Diritto dell'Impresa*, (3), 491.

Champy, J. (1997). Think globally, sell locally. *Sales & Marketing Management, 7*(1), 24–25.

Chan, D. K.-H. (2016). City diplomacy and "glocal" governance: Revitalizing cosmopolitan democracy. *Innovation, 29*(2), 134–160.

Charnes, A., Cooper, W. W., & Rhodes, E. (1978). Measuring the efficiency of decision making units. *European Journal of Operational Research, 2*(6), 429–444. doi:10.1016/0377-2217(78)90138-8

Chaves, R., & Sajardo-Moreno, A. (2004). Social Economy Managers: Between Values and Entrenchment. *Annals of Public and Cooperative Economics, 75*(1), 139–161. doi:10.1111/j.1467-8292.2004.00246.x

Chell, E., & Baines, S. (2000). Networking, entrepreneurship and microbusiness behaviour. *Entrepreneurship and Regional Development, 12*(3), 195–215. doi:10.1080/089856200413464

Chell, E., Spence, L., Perrini, F., & Harries, J. (2016). Social Entrepreneurship and Business Ethics: Does Social Equal Ethical? *Journal of Business Ethics, 133*(4), 619–625. doi:10.100710551-014-2439-6

Chetty, S. (1996). The case study method for research in small-and medium-sized firms. *International Small Business Journal, 15*(1), 73–85. doi:10.1177/0266242696151005

Christ, K. L., & Burritt, R. L. (2015). Material flow cost accounting: a review and agenda for future research. *Journal of Cleaner Production, 108, Part B*, 1378-1389. Doi: 10.1016/j.jclepro.2014.09.005

Christ, K. (2014). Water management accounting and the wine supply chain: Empirical evidence from Australia. *The British Accounting Review, 46*(4), 379–396. doi:10.1016/j.bar.2014.10.003

Christ, K. L., & Burritt, R. L. (2017). Water management accounting: A framework for corporate practice. *Journal of Cleaner Production, 152*, 379–386. doi:10.1016/j.jclepro.2017.03.147

Christ, K., & Burritt, R. (2013). Environmental management accounting: The significance of contingent variables for adoption. *Journal of Cleaner Production, 41*(2), 163–173. doi:10.1016/j.jclepro.2012.10.007

Christman, P. (2000). Effects of Best Practises of Environmental Management on Cost Advantage: The role of Complementary Assets. *Academy of Management Journal, 43*(4), 663–680. doi:10.2307/1556360

Chryssochoidis, G. (2000). Repercussions of consumer confusion for late introduced differentiated products. *European Journal of Marketing, 34*(5/6), 705–722. doi:10.1108/03090560010321992

Chu, X., Fielding, G. J., & Lamar, B. W. (1992). Measuring transit performance using data envelopment analysis. *Transportation Research Part A, Policy and Practice, 26*(3), 223–230. doi:10.1016/0965-8564(92)90033-4

Ciliberti, F., Pontrandolfo, P., & Scozzi, B. (2008). Investigating corporate social responsibility in supply chains: A SME perspective. *Journal of Cleaner Production, 16*(15), 1579–1588. doi:10.1016/j.jclepro.2008.04.016

CIRIEC. (2012). *The Social Economy in the European Union.* Brussels: European Economic and Social Committee.

CIRIEC. (2016). *Recent evolutions of the Social Economy in the European Union*. Brussels: European Economic and Social Committee.

Claessens, S., Diankov, S., & Lang, L. H. P. (2000). The Separation of Ownership and Control in East Asian Corporations. *Journal of Financial Economics*, *58*(1-2), 81–112. doi:10.1016/S0304-405X(00)00067-2

Claessens, S., Djankov, S., Fan, J. P., & Lang, L. H. (2002). Disentangling the incentive and entrenchment effects of large shareholdings. *The Journal of Finance*, *57*(6), 2741–2771. doi:10.1111/1540-6261.00511

Clarkson, M. B. (1995). A Stakeholder Framework for Analyzing and Evaluating Corporate Social Performance. *Academy of Management Review*, *20*(1), 92–117.

Clarkson, P. M., Li, Y., Richardson, G. D., & Vasvari, F. P. (2008). Revisiting the relation between environmental performance and environmental disclosure: An empirical analysis. *Accounting, Organizations and Society*, *33*(4-5), 303–327. doi:10.1016/j.aos.2007.05.003

Clement-Jones, T. (2005). *Bottom line issue or public relations exercise. In Investing in Corporate Social Responsibility: A Guide to Best Practice, Business Planning and the UK's Leading Companies* (pp. 5–13). London: Kogan Page.

Coelli, T. (1996). *A guide to DEAP version 2.1: a data envelopment analysis (computer) program*. Centre for Efficiency and Productivity Analysis, University of New England.

Coelli, T. J., Rao, D. S. P., O'Donnell, C. J., & Battese, G. E. (2005). *An introduction to efficiency and productivity analysis*. Springer Science & Business Media.

Collis, J., & Jarvis, R. (2002). Financial information and the management of small private companies. *Journal of Small Business and Enterprise Development*, *9*(2), 100–110. doi:10.1108/14626000210427357

Colucci, F., Menegoni, P., Nocenzi, M., & Presenti, O. (2012). L'evoluzione dei modelli di consumo e degli stili alimentari tra sostenibilità e benessere. *Rivista di studi sulla sostenibilità*, *2*, 47-67.

COM. (2012). *795 final, "Plan de Acción sobre Emprendimiento 2020, Relanzar el espíritu emprendedor en Europa"*. COM.

Commission for Economic , Social and Territorial Affairs. (2012). Paper presented at the third plenary session of ARLEM, Bari, Italy.

Commission of the European Communities. (2011). *Renewed European Union Strategy for 2011-2014 on Social Responsibility*. Available at: http://eur-lex.europa.eu

Cooper, C., Coulson, A., & Taylor, P. (2011). Accounting for human rights: Toxic health and safety practices the accounting lesson from ICL. *Critical Perspectives on Accounting*, *22*(8), 738–758. doi:10.1016/j.cpa.2011.07.001

Corbetta, M., & Shulman, G. L. (2002). Control of goal-directed and stimulus-driven attention in the brain. *Nature Reviews. Neuroscience*, *3*(3), 201–215. doi:10.1038/nrn755 PMID:11994752

Corsi, A., Novelli, S., & Pettenati, G. (2014). *Alternative Food Networks in Piedmont: determinants of on-farm and off-farm direct sales by farmers*. Paper presented at the Third Congress of Italian Association of Agricultural and Applied Economics (AIEAA), Alghero, Italy.

Costa, E., & Agostini, M. (2016). Mandatory disclosure about environmental and employee matters in the reports of Italian-listed corporate groups. *Social and Environmental Accountability Journal*, *36*(1), 1–23. doi:10.1080/0969160X.2016.1144519

Costanigro, M., Kroll, S., Thilmany, D., & Bunning, M. (2014). Is it love for local/organic or hate for conventional? Asymmetric effects of information and taste on label preferences in an experimental auction. *Food Quality and Preference*, *31*, 91–105. doi:10.1016/j.foodqual.2013.08.008

Cox Taylor, H. (Ed.). (1993). *Cultural diversity in organizations: theory, research and practice*. San Francisco, CA: Berrett-Koheler.

Cramer, J. (2002). From Financial to Sustainable Profit. *Corporate Social Responsibility and Environmental Management*, *9*(2), 99–106. doi:10.1002/csr.12

Crane, A. (2010). From governance to Governance: On Blurring Boundaries. *Journal of Business Ethics*, *94*(1), 17–19. doi:10.100710551-011-0788-y

Crediop, D. (2004). *Local public companies in the 25 countries of the European Union*. Paris: Dexia.

Culasso, F., Broccardo, L., Mazzoleni, A., & Giacosa, E. (2012). Corporate Governance in Listed Italian Family Firms: Impact on Performance and Comparison with Non-Family Firms. *Journal of Management & Change*, *29*(1).

Culasso, F., Broccardo, L., Manzi, L. M., & Truant, E. (2016). Management Accounting and Enterprise Risk Management. A potential integration as a new change in managerial systems. *Global Business and Economics Review*, *18*(3-4), 344–370. doi:10.1504/GBER.2016.076238

Cummings, S., Bridgman, T., & Brown, K. G. (2016). Unfreezing change as three steps : Rethinking Kurt Lewin ' s legacy for change management. *Human Relations*, *69*(1), 33–60. doi:10.1177/0018726715577707

Cunha, J., Benneworth, P., & Oliveira, P. (2015). Social entrepreneurship and social innovation: A conceptual distinction. In L. Farinha, J. Ferreira, H. L. Smith, & S. Bagchi-Sen (Eds.), *Handbook of Research on Global Competitive Advantage through Innovation and Entrepreneurship* (pp. 616–639). Hershey, PA: IGI Global. doi:10.4018/978-1-4666-8348-8.ch033

Cuomo, S., & Mapelli, A. (2007). *Diversity management. Gestire e valorizzare le differenze individuali nell'organizzazione che cambia*. Milano, Italy: Guerini e Associati.

Curran, J., & Blackburn, R. A. (1994). *Small firms and local economic networks: The death of the local economy?* London, UK: Paul Chapman/Sage.

D'Agostino, G. (2002). Tra locale e globale: "glocalismo". *Meridione*, *2*(4), 60-68.

D'Alessio, R. (2008). *Le coalizioni aziendali: caratteri del fenomeno e forme relazionali*. G. Giappichelli.

Daily, C. M., & Thompson, S. S. (1994). Ownership structure, strategic posture, and firm growth: An empirical examination. *Family Business Review*, *7*(3), 237–249. doi:10.1111/j.1741-6248.1994.00237.x

Dansero, E., & Puttilli, M. (2014). Multiple territorialities of alternative food networks: Six cases from Piedmont, Italy. Local Environment. *The International Journal of Justice and Sustainability*, *19*(6), 626–643.

Dantas, J., & Moreira, A. C. (2011). *O Processo de Inovação*. Lisboa: Edições Lidel.

Daraio, C., Diana, M., Di Costa, F., Leporelli, C., Matteucci, G., & Nastasi, A. (2016). Efficiency and effectiveness in the urban public transport sector: A critical review with directions for future research. *European Journal of Operational Research*, *248*(1), 1–20. doi:10.1016/j.ejor.2015.05.059

Daugbjerg, C., Smed, S., Andersen, L. M., & Schvartzman, Y. (2014). Improving eco-labelling as an environmental policy instrument: Knowledge, trust and organic consumption. *Journal of Environmental Policy and Planning*, *16*(4), 559–575. doi:10.1080/1523908X.2013.879038

Davis, K. (1973). The case for and against business assumption of social responsibilities. *Academy of Management Journal*, *16*(2), 312–323. doi:10.2307/255331

Dawkins, J., & Lewis, S. (2003). CSR in stakeholder expectations: And their implication for company strategy. *Journal of Business Ethics*, *44*(2/3), 185–193. doi:10.1023/A:1023399732720

de Burgh-Woodman, H. C. (2014). Homogeneity, "glocalism" or somewhere in between?: A literary interpretation of identity in the era of globalization. *European Journal of Marketing*, *48*(1), 288–313. doi:10.1108/EJM-03-2011-0132

de Colle, S., Henriques, A., & Sarasvathy, S. (2014). The paradox of corporate social responsibility standards. *Journal of Business Ethics*, *125*(2), 177–191. doi:10.100710551-013-1912-y

De Geuser, F., Mooraj, S., & Oyon, D. (2009). Does the balanced scorecard add value? Empirical evidence on its effect on performance. *European Accounting Review*, *18*(1), 93–122. doi:10.1080/09638180802481698

De Gruyter, C., Currie, G., & Rose, G. (2016). Sustainability Measures of Urban Public Transport in Cities: A World Review and Focus on the Asia/Middle East Region. *Sustainability*, *9*(1), 43. doi:10.3390u9010043

de Jesus Pacheco, D. A., ten Caten, C. S., Jung, C. F., Ribeiro, J. L. D., Navas, H. V. G., & Cruz-Machado, V. A. (2016). Eco-innovation determinants in manufacturing SMEs: Systematic review and research directions. *Journal of Cleaner Production*, *142*. doi:10.1016/j.jclepro.2016.11.049

de los Reyes, G. Jr, Scholz, M., & Smith, N. C. (2017). Beyond the "Win-Win." *California Management Review*, *59*(2), 142–167. doi:10.1177/0008125617695286

Debarbieux, B., & Price, M. F. (2008). Representing mountains: From local and national to global common good. *Geopolitics*, *13*(1), 148–168. doi:10.1080/14650040701783375

DeCoster, D. T., & Rhode, J. G. (1971). The accountant's stereotype: Real or imagined, deserved or unwarranted. *The Accounting Review*, *46*, 651–664.

Deegan, C. (2002). The legitimising effect of social and environmental disclosures – a theoretical foundation. *Accounting, Auditing & Accountability Journal*, *15*(3), 282–311. doi:10.1108/09513570210435852

Deegan, C. (2003). *Environmental management accounting: An introduction and case studies for Australia (EMAP)*. Sydney: Institute of Chartered Accountants in Australia.

Deegan, C. (2007). Organizational legitimacy as a motive for sustainability reporting. In J. Unerman, J. Bebbington, & B. O'Dwyer (Eds.), *Sustainability Accounting and Accountability*. Abingdon, UK: Routledge. doi:10.4324/NOE0415384889.ch7

Defourny, J., & Nyssens, M. (2013). Social innovation, social economy and social enterprise: What can the European debate tell us? In F. Moulaert, D. MacCallum, A. Mehmood, & A. Hamdouch (Eds.), *International Handbook on Social Innovation. Social Innovation, Collective Action and Transdisciplinary Research* (pp. 40–52). Cheltenham, UK: Edward Elgar. doi:10.4337/9781849809993.00013

Del Baldo, M. (2016). Formal Cooperation for Developing Sustainability and Corporate Social Responsibility Among Tourism SMEs in Italy: Insights, Limits and Potentialities of the Network Contract BT - Key Initiatives in Corporate Social Responsibility: Global Dimension of CSR. Cham: Springer International Publishing; doi:10.1007/978-3-319-21641-6_5

Deng, X., Kang, J., & Low, S. (2013). Corporate social responsibility and stakeholder value maximization: Evidence from mergers. *Journal of Financial Economics*, *110*(1), 87–109. doi:10.1016/j.jfineco.2013.04.014

Déniz, M. de la C. D., & Suárez, M. K. C. (2005). Corporate social responsibility and family business in Spain. *Journal of Business Ethics*, *56*(1), 27–41. doi:10.100710551-004-3237-3

Dentchev, N. A. (2004). Corporate social performance as a business strategy. *Journal of Business Ethics*, *55*(4), 397–412. doi:10.100710551-004-1348-5

Denzin, N. K., & Lincoln, Y. S. (2017). *The Sage Handbook of qualitative research* (5th ed.). Thousand Oaks, CA: Sage Publications.

Dezzani, F. (2006). Gli Ias e la loro applicazione in Italia. In G. Migliaccio (Ed.), *Le rivoluzioni contabili di inizio millennio. Atti del Convegno di Paestum (Sa) del 14 maggio 2005* (pp. 95–135). Milano, Italy: Angeli.

Dhaliwal, D., Li, Z., Tsang, A., & Yang, Y. (2011). Voluntary nonfinancial disclosure and the cost of equity capital: The initiation of corporate social responsibility reporting. *The Accounting Review*, *86*(1), 59–100. doi:10.2308/accr.00000005

Di Maggio, P. J., & Powell, W. (1991). *The New Istitutionalism in Organizational Fields*. Chicago: University of Chicago Press.

Di Maggio, P. J., & Powell, W. W. (1983). The iron cage revisited: Collective rationality and institutional isomorphism in organizational fields. *American Sociological Review*, *48*(2), 147–160. doi:10.2307/2095101

Dias-Sardinha I, Reijnders L., (2001). Environmental performance evaluations and sustainability performance evaluation of organizations: an evolutionary framework. *The Journal of Corporate Environmental Management*, *8*(2), 71-79.

Dinçer, H., & Hacioğlu, U. (2013). Global Strategies in Banking and Finance. Hershey, PA: IGI Global.

Dittmar, A., & Mahrt-Smith, J. (2007). Corporate governance and the value of cash holdings. *Journal of Financial Economics*, *83*(3), 599–634. doi:10.1016/j.jfineco.2005.12.006

Dobni, C. B. (2010). Achieving Synergy between Strategy and Innovation: The Key to Value Creation. *International Journal of Business Science and Applied Management*, *5*(1), 48–58.

Doernberg, A., Zasada, I., Bruszewska, K., Skoczowski, B., & Piorr, A. (2016). Potentials and Limitations of Regional Organic Food Supply: A Qualitative Analysis of Two Food Chain Types in the Berlin Metropolitan Region. *Sustainability*, *8*(11), 1125. doi:10.3390u8111125

Doherty, T. L., & Horne, T. (2002). *Managing Public Services--implementing Changes: A Thoughtful Approach to the Practice of Management*. Psychology Press.

Dolan, S. V., Ramón, J., Susan, E., & Schuler, R. (2007). La gestión de los recursos humanos. Madrid: McGraw-Hill.

Dolan, C., & John, W. (1998). Defining and Describing Family Business Ownership Configurations. *Family Business Review*, *1*, 301–3101.

Donadini, G., & Porretta, S. (2017). Uncovering patterns of consumers' interest for beer: A case study with craft beers. *Food Research International*, *91*, 183–198. doi:10.1016/j.foodres.2016.11.043 PMID:28290323

Dougherty, D. (1992). Interpretive barriers to successful product innovation in large firms. *Organization Science*, *3*(2), 179–202. doi:10.1287/orsc.3.2.179

Doving, E., & Gooderham, P. N. (2008). Dynamic Capabilities as Antecedents of the Scope of Related Diversification: The Case of Small Firm Accountancy Practices. *Strategic Management Journal*, *29*(8), 841–857. doi:10.1002mj.683

Dowling, J., & Pfeffer, J. (1975). Organizational legitimacy: Social values and organizational behavior. *Pacific Sociological Review*, *18*(1), 122–136. doi:10.2307/1388226

Dragan, A., & Popa, N. (2017). Social Economy in Post-communist Romania: What Kind of Volunteering for What Type of NGOs? *Journal of Balkan & Near Eastern Studies*, *19*(3), 330–350. doi:10.1080/19448953.2017.1277088

Dreessen, E. A. (2009). *Sustainability and Business: A narrative and annotated bibliography*. E. A. J. Dreessen.

Drichoutis, A. C., Lazaridis, P., & Nayga, R. M. Jr. (2006). Consumers' use of nutritional labels: A review of research studies and issues. *Academy of Marketing Science Review*, *2006*, 1.

Drury, C. (2009). *Management and cost accounting*. New Delhi: Thomson Learning.

Durden, C. (2008). Towards a socially responsible management control system. *Accounting, Auditing & Accountability Journal*, *21*(5), 671–694. doi:10.1108/09513570810872969

Dyllick, T., & Hockerts, K. (2002). Beyond the business case for corporate sustainability. *Business Strategy and the Environment*, *11*(2), 130–141. doi:10.1002/bse.323

Edvardsson, B., Gustafsson, A., Johnson, M., & Sandém, B. (2000). *New service Development and Innovation in the New Economy*. Lund: Studentliteratur, European Commission, Retrieved December 12, 2016, from: https://ec.europa.eu/growth/sectors/social-economy_en

Eisenhardt, K. M. (1989). Building theories from case study research. *Academy of Management Review*, *14*(4), 532–550.

Eisenhardt, K. M. (1989). Building Theories From Case Study Research. *Academy of Management Review*, *14*(4), 532–550.

Eisenhardt, K. M., & Graebner, M. E. (2007). Theory Building from Cases: Opportunities and Challenges. *Academy of Management Journal*, *50*(1), 25–32. doi:10.5465/AMJ.2007.24160888

Elkington, J. (1994). Towards the sustainable corporation: Win-win-win business strategies for sustainable development. *California Management Review*, *36*(2), 90–100. doi:10.2307/41165746

Elkington, J. (1997). *Cannibals with forks: the triple bottom line of 21st century business*. Oxford, UK: Capstone.

Elo, S., Kääriäinen, M., Kanste, O., Pölkki, T., Utriainen, K., & Kyngäs, H. (2014). Qualitative Content Analysis. *SAGE Open*, *4*(1), 2158244014522633. doi:10.1177/2158244014522633

Elo, S., & Kyngäs, H. (2008). The qualitative content analysis process. *Journal of Advanced Nursing*, *62*(1), 107–115. doi:10.1111/j.1365-2648.2007.04569.x PMID:18352969

Environment Agency. (2003). *SME-Environment 2003*. Retrieved 20 May, 2017 from http://www.netregs.org.uk

Environmental Protection Agency (EPA). (1995). An introduction to environmental accounting as a business management tool: Key concepts and terms. Washington, DC: EPA.

Environmental Protection Agency. (2008). *Ensuring a Sustainable Future: An Energy Management Guidebook for Wasterwater and Water Utilities*. Washington, DC: Energy Protection Agency.

Epstein, M. J. (2008). *Making sustainability work: Best practices in managing and measuring corporate, social, environmental, and economic impacts*. San Francisco: Berret-Koehler Publishers, Inc.

Epstein, M. J. (2008). *Making Sustainability Work: Best practises in managing and measuring social and environmental impacts*. Sheffield, UK: Greenleaf.

Epstein, M. J., & Buhovac, A. R. (2014). *Making sustainability work: Best practices in managing and measuring corporate social, environmental, and economic impacts*. Berrett-Koehler Publishers.

Epstein, M. J., & Roy, M. J. (2001). Sustainability in action: Identifying and measuring the Key performance drivers. *Long Range Planning*, *34*(5), 585–604. doi:10.1016/S0024-6301(01)00084-X

Epstein, M. J., & Wisner, P. S. (2001). Using a Balanced Scorecard to implement sustainability. *Environmental Quality Management*, *11*(2), 1–10. doi:10.1002/tqem.1300

EU Commission. (2016). *2016 SBA Fact Sheet — Italy*. Retrieved from https://ec.europa.eu/docsroom/documents

European Commission (2002). *Communication: Corporate Social Responsibility: A Business Contribution to Sustainable Development*. Author.

European Commission. (2001). *Promoting a European Framework for Corporate Social Responsibility*. Green Paper, July. Author.

European Commission. (2009). *Final Report of the Group of Experts: Overview of family-business-relevant issues: research, networks, policy measures and existing studies*. Author.

European Commission. (2011). *Communication from the Commission to the European Parliament, the Council, the European Economic and Social Committee and the Committee of the Regions*. A renewed EU strategy 2011-2014 for Corporate Social Responsibility. Brussels: EC.

European Commission. (2013). *Facts and figures on organic agriculture in the European Union*. Retrieved January 10, 2017, from http://ec.europa.eu/agriculture/markets-and-prices/more-reports/pdf/organic-2013_en.pdf

European Commission. (2016). *Annual report on European SMEs 2015/2016*. .10.2873/886211

European Commission. (2016). *Annual report on European SMEs 2015/2016*. 10.2873/886211

European Commission. (2017). *What is an SME?* Retrieved 6 June, 2017 from http://ec.europa.eu/growth/smes/business-friendly-environment/sme-definition_en

European Union. (2003). Commission recommendation of 6 May 2003 concerning the definition of micro, small and medium-sized enterprises. *Official Journal of the European Union*, *46*, 36-41.

European Union. (2011). *Business Dynamics: Start-ups Business transfers and Bankruptcy*. Retrieved from http://ec.europa.eu/enterprise/policies/sme/business-environment/files/ busines_dynamics-report_en.pdf

Eurostat. (2011). *Key figures on European business - with a special feature on SMEs*. Retrieved August 10, 2017, from http://ec.europa.eu/eurostat/documents/3930297/5967534/KS-ET-11-001-EN.PDF

Exame. (2017). Conheça as 1000 melhores PME do país. *Edição Expresso*, 207.

FabraUtray, J. (2011). Sostenibilidad económica y sostenibilidad medioambiental: ¿son compatibilidad en el sector eléctrico? *Economistas*, *29*, 299-301.

Fabris, G. (2008). *Societing. Il marketing nella società postmoderna*. Milano, Italy: Egea.

Faccio, M., & Lang, L. H. P. (2002). The Ultimate Ownership of Western EuropeanCorporations. *Journal of Financial Economics*, *65*(1), 365–395. doi:10.1016/S0304-405X(02)00146-0

Faccio, M., Lang, L., & Young, L. (2001). Dividends and expropriation. *The American Economic Review*, *91*(1), 54–78. doi:10.1257/aer.91.1.54

Faldetta, G., Fasone, V., & Provenzano, C. (2014). *Le reti di impresa innovative. Profili economici, aziendali, giuridici e sociali*. Roma, Italy: Aracne.

Falle, S., Rauter, R., Engert, S., & Baumgartner, R. (2016). Sustainability Management with the Sustainability Balanced Scorecard in SMEs: Findings from an Austrian Case Study. *Sustainability*, *8*(6), 545. doi:10.3390u8060545

Fama, E., & Jensen, M. (1983). Separation of Ownership and Control. *The Journal of Law & Economics*, *26*(2), 301–325. doi:10.1086/467037

Färe, R., & Grosskopf, S. (2000). Network DEA. *Socio-Economic Planning Science, 34*, 35-49.

Farneti, F., Siboni, B., & Del Sordo, C. (2017). La misurazione della performance sociale nell'esperienza dell'Università di Bologna [The social and environmental performance measurement at the University of Bologna]. *Management Control*, *1*(1), 135–164. doi:10.3280/MACO2017-001007

Farrell, M. J. (1957). The measurement of productive efficiency. *Journal of the Royal Statistical Society. Series A (General)*, *120*(3), 253–290. doi:10.2307/2343100

Fasan, M., & Mio, C. (2017). Fostering Stakeholder Engagement: The Role of Materiality Disclosure in Integrated Reporting. *Business Strategy and the Environment*, *26*(3), 288–305. doi:10.1002/bse.1917

Fassin, Y. (2008). SMEs and the fallacy of formalising CSR. *Business Ethics (Oxford, England)*, *17*(4), 364–378. doi:10.1111/j.1467-8608.2008.00540.x

Fassin, Y., Werner, A., Van Rossem, A., Signori, S., Garriga, E., von Høivik, H. W., & Schlierer, H. J. (2015). CSR and Related Terms in SME Owner-Managers Mental Models in Six European Countries: National Context Matters. *Journal of Business Ethics*, *128*(2), 433–456. doi:10.100710551-014-2098-7

Fasterling, B. (2012). Development of Norms Through Compliance Disclosure. *Journal of Business Ethics*, *106*(1), 73–87. doi:10.100710551-011-1055-y

Fastigi, M., Esposti, R., & Viganò, E. (2015). La craft beer revolution in Italia ei birrifici agricoli: traiettorie evolutive e principali criticità. *Argomenti*, (2), 67–92.

Fekete, G., Hubai, L., Kiss, J., & Mihály, M. (2017). *Social Enterprise in Hungary.* ICSEM Working Papers, No. 47. Liege: The International Comparative Social Enterprise Models (ICSEM) Project.

Fernandez, J. L., & Camacho, J. (2016). Effective Elements to Establish an Ethical Infrastructure: An Exploratory Study of SMEs in the Madrid Region. *Journal of Business Ethics*, *138*(1), 113–131. doi:10.100710551-015-2607-3

Ferrari, C. (2010). The Italian "Network Contract" A new tool for the growth of enterprises within the framework of the "SMALL BUSINESS ACT." *Colum. J. Eur. L. Online*, *16*, 77–89.

Fethi, M. D., & Pasiouras, F. (2010). Assessing bank efficiency and performance with operational research and artificial intelligence techniques: A survey. *European Journal of Operational Research*, *204*(2), 189–198. doi:10.1016/j.ejor.2009.08.003

FiBL & IFOAM. (2016). *The world of organic agriculture. Statistics and emerging trends 2016.* Bonn, Germany: FiBL and IFOAM. Retrieved January 10, 2017, from https://shop.fibl.org/CHen/mwdownloads/download/link/id/785/?ref=1)

Fielding, G. J., Babitsky, T. T., & Brenner, M. E. (1985). Performance evaluation for bus transit. *Transportation Research Part A, General*, *19*(1), 73–82. doi:10.1016/0191-2607(85)90009-3

Fielding, G. J., Brenner, M. E., & Faust, K. (1985). Typology for bus transit. *Transportation Research Part A, General*, *19*(3), 269–278. doi:10.1016/0191-2607(85)90015-9

Figge, F., Hahn, T., Schaltegger, S., & Wagner, M. (2002). The sustainability balanced scorecard - Linking sustainability management to business strategy. *Business Strategy and the Environment*, *11*(5), 269–284. doi:10.1002/bse.339

Figgie, F., Hahn, T., Schaltegger, S., & Wagner, M. (2001). The Sustainability Balanced Scorecard – a tool for value oriented sustainability management in strategy-focused organizations. *Conference Proceedings of the 2001 eco-management and auditing conference*, 83-90.

Fiksel, J., McDaniel, J., & Mendenhall, C. (1999). Measuring progress towards sustainability: principles, process, and best practices. In Greening of industry network conference: best practise proceedings. Battelle Memorial Institute.

Financing Schemes for Sustainable Development including Energy Efficiency and Cleaner Production in MSMEs. (n.d.). *Small Industries Development Bank of India.*

Fitzgerald, M. A., Haynes, G. W., Schrank, H. L., & Danes, S. M. (2010). Socially responsible processes of small family business owners: Exploratory evidence from the national family business survey. *Journal of Small Business Management*, *48*(4), 524–551. doi:10.1111/j.1540-627X.2010.00307.x

Fleiter, T., Gruber, E., Eichhammer, W., & Worrell, E. (2012). The German energy audit program for firms-a cost-effective way to improve energy efficiency? *Energy Efficiency*, *5*(4), 447–469. doi:10.100712053-012-9157-7

Floridi, L. (2009). Network Ethics: Information and Business Ethics in a Networked Society. *Journal of Business Ethics*, *90*(S4), 649–659. doi:10.100710551-010-0598-7

Foglio, A. (2004). *Il glocal marketing. Glocalizzazione per rispondere a globalizzazione e localizzazione*. Milano, Italy: Angeli.

Food and Agriculture Organisation of the United Nations (FAO). (2013). *Sustainability Assessment of Food and Agriculture Systems (SAFA)*. FAO. Retrieved January 10, 2017, from http://www.fao.org/nr/sustainability/sustainability-assessments-safa/en/

Forssell, S., & Lankoski, L. (2015). The sustainability promise of alternative food networks: An examination through "alternative" characteristics. *Agriculture and Human Values*, *32*(1), 63–75. doi:10.100710460-014-9516-4

Fotopoulos, C., Krystallis, A., & Ness, M. (2003). Wine produced by organic grapes in Greece: Using means-end chains analysis to reveal organic buyers' purchasing motives in comparison to the non-buyers. *Food Quality and Preference*, *14*(7), 549–566. doi:10.1016/S0950-3293(02)00130-1

Frank, H., Lueger, M., Nosé, L., & Suchy, D. (2010). The concept of "Familiness". Literature review and systems theory-based reflections. *Journal of Family Business Strategy*, *1*(3), 119–130. doi:10.1016/j.jfbs.2010.08.001

Fransman, M. (2010). The new ICT ecosystem: Implications for policy and regulation. Cambridge, UK: Academic Press. doi:10.1017/CBO9780511676130

Freeman, R. E., Harrison, J. S., Wicks, A. C., Parmar, B., & de Colle, S. (2010). *Stakeholder Theory. The state of the art*. Academic Press.

Freeman, E. D., & Driver, J. (2006). Subjective appearance of ambiguous structure-from-motion can be driven by objective switches of a separate less ambiguous context. *Vision Research*, *46*(23), 4007–4023. doi:10.1016/j.visres.2006.07.008 PMID:16996558

Freeman, R. E., & Velamuri, S. R. (2006). A new approach to CSR: Company stakeholder responsibility. In *Corporate social responsibility* (pp. 9–23). Springer. doi:10.1057/9780230599574_2

Freeman, R. E., Wicks, A., Harrison, J., Parmar, B., & de Colle, S. (2010). *Stakeholder Theory: The State of The Art.* Cambridge, UK: Cambridge University Press. doi:10.1017/CBO9780511815768

Freeman, S., Edwards, R., & Schroder, B. (2006). How Smaller Born-Global Firms Use Networks and Alliances to Overcome Constraints to Rapid Internationalization. *Journal of International Marketing*, *14*(3), 33–63. doi:10.1509/jimk.14.3.33

Friedman, A. L., & Lyne, S. R. (2001). The beancounter stereotype: Towards a general model of stereotype generation. *Critical Perspectives on Accounting*, *12*(4), 423–451. doi:10.1006/cpac.2000.0451

Galbreath, J., & Galvin, P. (2008). Firm factors, industry structure and performance variation: New empirical evidence to a classic debate. *Journal of Business Research*, *61*(2), 109–117. doi:10.1016/j.jbusres.2007.06.009

Galbreath, J., & Shum, P. (2012). Do customer satisfaction and reputation mediate the CSR-FR Link? Evidence from Australia. *Australian Journal of Management*, *37*(2), 211–229. doi:10.1177/0312896211432941

Gallardo-Vázquez, D., & Sanchez-Hernandez, M. I. (2014). Measuring Corporate Social Responsibility for competitive success at a regional level. *Journal of Cleaner Production*, *72*, 14–22. doi:10.1016/j.jclepro.2014.02.051

Gallhofer, S., Haslam, J., & van der Walt, S. (2011). Accountability and transparency in relation to human rights: A critical perspective reflecting upon accounting, corporate responsibility and ways forward in the context of globalization. *Critical Perspectives on Accounting*, *22*(8), 765–780. doi:10.1016/j.cpa.2011.07.002

Gallo, M. Á. (1993). *La cultura en empresa familiar*. Publicaciones de la Cátedra de Empresa Familiar.

Garavaglia, C. (2015). *Entrepreneurship and entry of small firms into a mature industry: the case of microbreweries in Italy*. AAWE Working Paper No. 179–Economics, American Association of Wine Economists.

Garcia Sanchez, I. M. (2009). Technical and scale efficiency in Spanish urban transport: Estimating with data envelopment analysis. *Advances in Operations Research*.

García-Sánchez, I.-M., & Noguera-Gámez, L. (2017). Integrated Reporting and Stakeholder Engagement: The Effect on Information Asymmetry. *Corporate Social Responsibility and Environmental Management*, *24*(5), 395–413. doi:10.1002/csr.1415

Garengo, P., Biazzo, S., & Bititci, U. S. (2005). Performance measurement systems in SMEs: A review for a research agenda. *International Journal of Management Reviews*, *7*(1), 25–47. doi:10.1111/j.1468-2370.2005.00105.x

Garrido Palacios, J., & Villalba Salvador, B. (1999). La empresa familiar: aspectos laborales y de Seguridad Social. *Boletín del Ilustre Colegio de Abogados de Madrid*, (12), 195-198.

Gedajlovic, E., Carney, M., Chrisman, J. J., & Kellermanns, F. W. (2012). The adolescence of family firm research taking stock and planning for the future. *Journal of Management*, *38*(4), 1010–1037. doi:10.1177/0149206311429990

Gesuele, B. (2015). Report integrato: prassi operativa. *Guida alla contabilità & bilancio*, (3), 6-10.

Gherardi, L. (2014). Il Reporting integrato come espressione della nuova impresa. *Equilibri*, *52*(1), 62–70.

Ghosh, D., & Roy, J. (2011). Approach to energy efficiency among micro, small and medium enterprises in India: Results of a field survey (No. 8). Vienna: Academic Press.

Gibassier, D., & Schaltegger, S. (2015). Carbon management accounting and reporting in practice: A case study on converging emergent approaches. *Sustainability Accounting, Management and Policy Journal*, *6*(3), 340–365. doi:10.1108/SAMPJ-02-2015-0014

Girón, M. (2013). *Derecho de la Seguridad Social*. A Coruña: Netbiblo.

Giupponi, T. F. (2016, May). *Le frontiere del trasporto pubblico locale, tra competenze normative e situazioni giuridiche soggettive. Verso un "diritto alla mobilità"?* Università di Catania.

Global Reporting Initiative (GRI). (2014). *Ready to Report? Introducing sustainability reporting for SMEs*. Amsterdam, The Netherlands: GRI.

Godfray, H. C. J., Beddington, J. R., Crute, I. R., Haddad, L., Lawrence, D., Muir, J. F., ... Toulmin, C. (2010). Food Security: The Challenge of Feeding 9 Billion People. *Science*, *327*(5967), 812–818. doi:10.1126cience.1185383 PMID:20110467

Golany, B., & Roll, Y. (1989). An application procedure for DEA. *Omega*, *17*(3), 237–250. doi:10.1016/0305-0483(89)90029-7

Gomez-Mejia, L. R., Haynes, K. T., Nunez-Nickel, M., Jacobson, K. L., & Moyano-Fuentes, J. (2007). Socioemotional Wealth and business risks in family controlled firms. *Administrative Science Quarterly*, *52*(1), 106–137. doi:10.2189/asqu.52.1.106

Gond, J. P., Grubnic, S., Herzig, C., & Moon, J. (2012). Configuring management control systems: Theorizing the integration of strategy and sustainability. *Management Accounting Research*, *23*(3), 205–223. doi:10.1016/j.mar.2012.06.003

Gond, J. P., & Herrbach, O. (2006). Corporate social reporting as a learning tool? A theoretical framework. *Journal of Business Ethics*, *65*(4), 359–371. doi:10.100710551-006-6405-9

Gonzalez, J. (2006). Il middle management in Cina: una risorsa da gestire in un'ottica "glocal". *Sviluppo e organizzazione*, (215), 24-30.

Gooderham, P. N., Tobiassen, A., Doving, E., & Nordhaug, O. (2004). Accountants and Sources of Business Advice for Small Firms. *International Small Business Journal*, *22*(1), 5–22. doi:10.1177/0266242604039478

Goodman, D. (2003). The quality 'turn' and alternative food practices: Reflections and agenda. *Journal of Rural Studies*, *19*(1), 1–7. doi:10.1016/S0743-0167(02)00043-8

Goodman, D., DuPuis, E. M., & Goodman, M. K. (2012). *Alternative food networks: Knowledge, practice, and politics*. London: Routledge.

Gordić, D., Babić, M., Jovičić, N., Šušteršič, V., Končalović, D., & Jelić, D. (2010). Development of energy management system - Case study of Serbian car manufacturer. *Energy Conversion and Management*, *51*(12), 2783–2790. doi:10.1016/j.enconman.2010.06.014

Gossain, S., & Kandiah, G. (1998). Reinventing value: The new business ecosystem. *Strategy and Leadership*, *26*(5), 28–33. doi:10.1108/eb054622

Gracia, A., Barreiro-Hurlé, J., & Galán, B. L. (2014). Are local and organic claims complements or substitutes? A consumer preferences study for eggs. *Journal of Agricultural Economics*, *65*(1), 49–67. doi:10.1111/1477-9552.12036

Gramigna, A. (2009). *Ruoli, attori e competenze della comunicazione nel processo di cambiamento della P.A.* Retrieved September 5, 2009, from: www.urp.it

Granados, M. L., Mohamed, S., & Hlupic, V. (2017). Knowledge management activities in social enterprises: Lessons for small and non-profit firms. *Journal of Knowledge Management*, *21*(2), 376–396. doi:10.1108/JKM-01-2016-0026

Granelli, M. (2002). *Glocal banking. Creare relazioni con la vendita consulenziale*. Milano, Italy: Angeli.

Granleese, J., & Barrett, T. F. (1990). The social and personality characteristics of the Irish Chartered Accountant. *Personality and Individual Differences*, *11*(9), 957–964. doi:10.1016/0191-8869(90)90278-Y

Grant, R. (1996). Prospering in dynamically-competitive environments: Organizational capability as knowledge integration. *Organization Science*, *7*(4), 374–380. doi:10.1287/orsc.7.4.375

Grau, F. X. (2016). A short communication on glocal universities. *International Journal of Knowledge-Based Development*, *7*(1), 63–74. doi:10.1504/IJKBD.2016.075442

Grayson, D., & Hodges, A. (2004). *Corporate Social Opportunity! 7 Steps to Make CSR Work for Your Business. GreenLeaf.* Sheffield, UK: Google Scholar.

Greenwood, R., Suddaby, R., & Hinings, C. R. (2002). Theorizing change: The role of professional associations in the transformation of institutional fields. *Academy of Management Journal*, *45*(1), 58–80. doi:10.2307/3069285

Griggs, D., Stafford-Smith, M., Gaffney, O., Rockström, J., Öhman, M. C., Shyamsundar, P., ... Noble, I. (2013). Policy: Sustainable development goals for people and planet. *Nature*, *495*(7441), 305–307. doi:10.1038/495305a PMID:23518546

Gruère Guillaume, P. (2015). An Analysis of the Growth in Environmental Labelling and Information Schemes. *Journal of Consumer Policy*, *38*(1), 1–18. doi:10.100710603-014-9275-z

Gubitta, P., & Gianecchini, M. (2002). Governance and Flexibility in family-owned SMEs. *Family Business Review*, *15*(4), 277–297. doi:10.1111/j.1741-6248.2002.00277.x

Guercini, S., & Tunisini, A. (2017). Formalizing in business networks as a tool for industrial policy. *IMP Journal*, *11*(1), 91–108. doi:10.1108/IMP-07-2015-0040

Gunarathne, N. (2015). Fostering the Adoption of Environmental Management with the Help of Accounting: An Integrated Framework. In M. M. Rahim & S. O. Idowu (Eds.), *Social Audit Regulation: Development, Challenges and Opportunities* (pp. 301–324). Cham: Springer International Publishing. doi:10.1007/978-3-319-15838-9_15

Gunarathne, N., & Lee, K.-H. (2015). Environmental Management Accounting (EMA) for environmental management and organizational change: An eco-control approach. *Journal of Accounting & Organizational Change*, *11*(3), 362–383. doi:10.1108/JAOC-10-2013-0078

Gunarathne, N., Peiris, S., Edirisooriya, K., & Jayasinghe, R. (2015). *Environmental management accounting in Sri Lankan enterprises. Nugegoda.* Department of Accounting, University of Sri Jayewardenepura.

Gunarathne, N., Ranasinghe, A., & Peiris, S. (2014). *Guidelines on environmental management accounting for Sri Lankan Enterprises*. Colombo: Institute of Certified Management Accountants of Sri Lanka.

Haanaes, K., Balagopal, B., Arthur, D., Kong, M. T., Velken, I., Kruschwitz, N., & Hopkins, M. S. (2011). First Look: The Second Annual Sustainability & Innovation Survey. *MIT Sloan Management Review*, *52*(2), 77–83.

Habbershon, T. G., & Williams, M. L. (1999). A resource-based framework for assessing the strategic advantages of family firms. *Family Business Review*, *12*(1), 1–25. doi:10.1111/j.1741-6248.1999.00001.x

Haddoud, M. Y., Jones, P., & Newbery, R. (2017). Export promotion programmes and SMEs' performance. *Journal of Small Business and Enterprise Development*, *24*(1), 68–87. doi:10.1108/JSBED-07-2016-0116

Hadjimanolis, A. (2000). A resource-based view of innovativeness in small firms. *Technology Analysis and Strategic Management*, *12*(2), 263–281. doi:10.1080/713698465

Håkansson, H., & Snehota, I. (2006). No business is an island: The network concept of business strategy. *Scandinavian Journal of Management*, *22*(3), 256–270. doi:10.1016/j.scaman.2006.10.005

Hamilton, J. T. (1995). Pollution as news: Media and stock market reactions to the toxics release inventory data. *Journal of Environmental Economics and Management*.

Hamzaoui-Essoussi, L., & Zahaf, M. (2012). Canadian organic food consumers' profile and their willingness to pay premium prices. *Journal of International Food & Agribusiness Marketing*, *24*(1), 1–21. doi:10.1080/08974438.2011.621834

Handfield, R. B., & Melnyk, S. A. (1998). The scientific theory-building process: A primer using the case of TQM. *Journal of Operations Management*, *16*(4), 321–339. doi:10.1016/S0272-6963(98)00017-5

Hansen, E. G., & Schaltegger, S. (2016). The Sustainability Balanced Scorecard: A Systematic Review of Architectures. *Journal of Business Ethics*, *133*(2), 193–221. doi:10.100710551-014-2340-3

Harper, G. C., & Makatouni, A. (2002). Consumer perception of organic food production and farm animal welfare. *British Food Journal*, *104*(3/4/5), 287-299.

Harrison, J. S., & Wicks, A. C. (2013). Stakeholder Theory, Value, and Firm Performance. *Business Ethics Quarterly*, *23*(1), 97–124. doi:10.5840/beq20132314

Hartman, J. D. (2016). Glocalism: Situating global civic engagement in the local community. In R. Shin (Ed.), Convergence of Contemporary Art, Visual Culture, and Global Civic Engagement (pp. 151-169). Hershey, PA: IGI Global.

Hart, S. L., & Ahuja, G. (1996). Does it pay to be green? An empirical examination of the relationship between emission reduction and firm performance. *Business Strategy and the Environment*, *5*(1), 30–37. doi:

Henri, J. F. (2006). Management control systems and strategy: A resource based view. *Accounting, Organizations and Society*, *31*(6), 529–558. doi:10.1016/j.aos.2005.07.001

Henry, J. F., & Journault, M. (2009). *Revisiting the link between management control systems and strategy in contingency-based research.* Paper of the Annual Conference of the Canadian Accounting Academic Association.

Henry, J. F., & Journault, M. (2010). Eco-control: The influence of management control systems on environmental and economic performance. *Accounting, Organizations and Society*, *35*(1), 63–80. doi:10.1016/j.aos.2009.02.001

Herzig, C., & Schaltegger, S. (2006). Corporate Sustainability Reporting. In Sustainability Accounting and Reporting. Springer.

Herzig, C., Viere, T., Schaltegger, S., & Burrit, R. (2012). *Environmental Management Accounting. Case Studies of South East-Asian Companies*. London: Routledge.

Hespenheide, E., Pavlovsky, K., & McElroy, M. (2010). Accounting for Sustainability Performance. *Financial Executive, 26*(2), 52-54, 57-58.

Hill, H., & Lynchehaun, F. (2002). Organic milk: Attitudes and consumption patterns. *British Food Journal*, *104*(7), 526–542. doi:10.1108/00070700210434570

Hindy, S. (2014). *The craft beer revolution: How a band of microbrewers is transforming the world's favorite drink.* Macmillan.

Hinna, L. (Ed.). (2002). Il bilancio sociale: scenari, settori e valenze; modelli di rendicontazione sociale; gestione responsabile e sviluppo sostenibile. Esperienze europee e casi italiani. Milano, Italy: Il Sole 24 Ore.

Hirst, E., & Brown, M. (1990). Closing the efficiency gap: Barriers to the efficient use of energy. *Resources, Conservation and Recycling*, *3*(4), 267–281. doi:10.1016/0921-3449(90)90023-W

Hitt, M. A., Ireland, R. D., & Hoskinsson, R. E. (2011). *Strategic Management: Competitiveness and Globalization.* South Western Cengage Learning, Mason.

Holt, D. T., Rutherford, M. W., & Kuratko, D. F. (2010). Advancing the field of family business research: Further testing the measurement properties of the F-PEC. *Family Business Review*, *23*(1), 76–88. doi:10.1177/0894486509349943

Hopwood, A. G. (2009). Accounting and the environment. *Accounting, Organizations and Society*, *34*(3–4), 433–439. doi:10.1016/j.aos.2009.03.002

Horisch, J., Johnson, M. P., & Schaltegger, S. (2015). Implementation of Sustainability Management and Company Size: A Knowledge-Based View. *Business Strategy and the Environment*, *24*(8), 765–779. doi:10.1002/bse.1844

Horngren, C. T., Foster, G., Datar, S. M., Rajan, M., Ittner, C., & Baldwin, A. A. (2010). Cost accounting: A managerial emphasis. *Issues in Accounting Education*, *25*(4), 789–790. doi:10.2308/iace.2010.25.4.789

Hoy, F., & Verser, T. G. (1994). Emerging business, emerging field: Entrepreneurship and the family firm, *Entrepreneurship. Theory into Practice*, *19*(1), 9–24.

Hrebiniak, G. L. (2006). Obstacles to Effective Strategy Implementation. *Organizational Dynamics*, *35*(1), 12–31. doi:10.1016/j.orgdyn.2005.12.001

Hubrich, D.-K., Bund, E., Schmitz, B., & Mildenberger, G. (2012). *Comparative Case Study Report on the State of the Social Economy. A deliverable of the project: "The theoretical, empirical and policy foundations for building social innovation in Europe" (TEPSIE), European Commission – 7th Framework Programme*. Brussels: European Commission, DG Research.

Hudak, K. C. (2017). Touring Pittsburgh's glocal narratives: Leveraging city brands for global and local audiences. In Advertising and Branding: Concepts, Methodologies, Tools, and Applications (pp. 430-455). Hershey, PA: IGI Global.

Hudon, M., & Huybrechts, B. (2017). From Distant Neighbours to Bedmates: Exploring the Synergies between the Social Economy and Sustainable Development. *Annals of Public and Cooperative Economics*, *88*(2), 141–154. doi:10.1111/apce.12170

Hudson, M., Bourne, M., Lean, J., & Smart, P. A. (2000). Only just managing – no time to measure. In *Proceedings Performance Measurement – Past, Present and Future*. Craneld University.

Hughner, R. S., McDonagh, P., Prothero, A., Shultz, C. J., & Stanton, J. (2007). Who are organic food consumers? A compilation and review of why people purchase organic food. *Journal of Consumer Behaviour*, *6*(1), 1–17.

Hur, W. M., Kim, H., & Woo, J. (2014). How CSR Leads to Corporate Brand Equity: Mediating Mechanisms of Corporate Brand Credibility and Reputation. *Journal of Business Ethics*, *125*(1), 75–86. doi:10.100710551-013-1910-0

Husain, N., Abdullah, M., & Kuman, S. (2000). Evaluating public sector efficiency with data envelopment analysis (DEA): A case study in Road Transport Department, Selangor, Malaysia. *Total Quality Management*, *11*(4-6), 830–836. doi:10.1080/09544120050008282

Hyršlová, J. (2014). Sustainability reporting – a review of trends and situation in CR. *The 8th International Days of Statistics and Economics*.

Iansiti, M., & Levien, R. (2004). Strategy as Ecology. *Harvard Business Review*, 1–11. PMID:15029791

IFAC. (2008). *The Crucial Roles of Professional Accountants in Business in Mid-Sized Enterprises*. Information Paper, International Federation of Accountants.

IFAC. (2016). *The Role of SMPs in Providing Business Support to SMEs: New Evidence*. Information Paper, International Federation of Accountants.

Indelicato, F. (2014). Report e Reporting integrato: Verso un nuovo modello di bilancio. *Equilibri*, *52*(1), 9–37.

Instituto de Empresa Familiar. (2015). La Empresa Familiar en España. Madrid: Instituto de Empresa Familiar.

Instituto de la Mujer para la Igualdad de Oportunidades. (2015). *Informe Periódico*. Ministerio de Sanidad, Sevicios Sociales e Igualdad.

International Energy Agency. (2016). *CO2 Emissions from Fuel Combustion*. Paris: International Energy Agency.

International Finance Corporation. (2012). *Interpretation Note on Small and Medium Enterprises and Environmental and Social Risk Management*. Retrieved June 12, 2017 from https://www.ifc.org/wps/wcm/connect/de7d92804a29ffe-9ae04af8969adcc27/InterpretationNote_SME_2012.pdf?MOD=AJPERES

Isckia, T. (2009). Amazon's Evolving Ecosystem : A Cyber-bookstore and Application Service Provider. *Canadian Journal of Administrative Sciences*, *26*(4), 332–343. doi:10.1002/cjas.119

ISFORT. (2017, April). *Quattordicesimo Rapporto sulla Mobilità in Italia*. Rome, Italy: Author.

ISO. (2011). *ISO 14051:2011. Environmental Management. Material Flow Cost Accounting. General Framework*. Geneva: ISO.

Jabbour, C. J. C., & Santos, F. C. A. (2006). The evolution of environmental management within organizations: Toward a common taxonomy. *Environmental Quality Management*, *16*(2), 43–59. doi:10.1002/tqem.20120

Jabbour, C. J. C., Santos, F. C. A., & Nagano, M. S. (2010). Contributions of HRM throughout the stages of environmental management: Methodological triangulation applied to companies in Brazil. *International Journal of Human Resource Management*, *21*(7), 1049–1089. doi:10.1080/09585191003783512

Jain, A. (2011). *Unlocking Energy Efficiency Market in India's SME Sector: Cluster Approach and Role of ESCOs & Fiscal Incentives*. University of Southern California.

Jamali, D., Zanhour, M., & Keshishian, T. (2009). Peculiar strengths and relational attributes of SMEs in the context of CSR. *Journal of Business Ethics*, *87*(3), 355–377. doi:10.100710551-008-9925-7

Jamil, C. Z. M., Mohamed, R., Muhammad, F., & Ali, A. (2015). Environmental management accounting practices in small medium manufacturing firms. *Procedia: Social and Behavioral Sciences*, *172*, 619–626. doi:10.1016/j.sbspro.2015.01.411

Jansson, J., Nilsson, J., Modig, F., & Hed Vall, G. (2017). Commitment to Sustainability in Small and Medium-Sized Enterprises: The Influence of Strategic Orientations and Management Values. *Business Strategy and the Environment*, *26*(1), 69–83. doi:10.1002/bse.1901

Japutra, A., Nguyen, B., & Melewar, T. C. (2015). A framework of brand strategy and the "glocalization" approach: The case of Indonesia. Alcántara-Pilar. In J.M., del Barrio-García, E., Crespo-Almendros, & L. Porcu, (Eds.), Analyzing the Cultural Diversity of Consumers in the Global Marketplace (pp. 101-125). Hershey, PA: IGI Global.

Jarosz, L. (2008). The city in the country: Growing alternative food networks in Metropolitan areas. *Journal of Rural Studies*, *24*(3), 231–244. doi:10.1016/j.jrurstud.2007.10.002

Järvi, K., & Kortelainen, S. (2017). Taking stock of empirical research on business ecosystems : A literature review Samuli Kortelainen. *International Journal of Business and Systems Research*, *11*(3), 8–11. doi:10.1504/IJBSR.2017.085469

Jarvis, R., & Rigby, M. (2012). The provision of human resources and employment advice to small and medium-sized enterprises: The role of small and medium-sized practices of accountants. *International Small Business Journal*, *30*(8), 944–956. doi:10.1177/0266242612445403

Jarvis, R., & Thompson, P. (2014). *The Evolving Advisory Role of SMPs in Supporting the Internationalization of SMEs*. IFAC, International Federation of Accountants.

Jasch, C. (2008). Environmental and material flow cost accounting: principles and procedures (Vol. 25). Netherlands: Springer Science & Business Media.

Jasch, C., & Savage, D. (2005). International Guidance Document on environmental management accounting (EMA). International Federation of Accountants. New York: IFAC.

Jeacle, I. (2008). Beyond the boring grey: The construction of the colourful accountant. *Critical Perspectives on Accounting*, *19*(8), 1296–1320. doi:10.1016/j.cpa.2007.02.008

Jenkins, H. (2006). Small business champions for corporate social responsibility. *Journal of Business Ethics*, *6*(3), 241–256. doi:10.100710551-006-9182-6

Jenkins, H. (2009). A 'business opportunity' model of corporate social responsibility for small- and medium-sized enterprises. *Business Ethics (Oxford, England)*, *18*(1), 21–36. doi:10.1111/j.1467-8608.2009.01546.x

Johnson, M. (2007). *Stakeholders dialogue for sustainable service* (Doctoral Dissertation). Karlstad University Studies.

Johnson, M. P. (2013). Awareness and Application of Sustainability Management Tools in Small and Medium-Sized Enterprises. *Academy of Management Proceedings*, *2013*(1), 1–18. 10.5465/AMBPP.2013.16036abstract

Johnson, M. P. (2015). Sustainability Management and Small and Medium-Sized Enterprises: Managers' Awareness and Implementation of Innovative Tools. *Corporate Social Responsibility and Environmental Management*, *22*(5), 271–285. doi:10.1002/csr.1343

Johnson, M. P., & Schaltegger, S. (2016). Two Decades of Sustainability Management Tools for SMEs: How Far Have We Come? *Journal of Small Business Management*, *54*(2), 481–505. doi:10.1111/jsbm.12154

Johnson, S., Webber, D. J., & Thomas, W. (2007). Which SMEs use external business advice? A multivariate sub-regional study. *Environment & Planning*, *39*(8), 1981–1997. doi:10.1068/a38327

Jolliffe, L., Cave, J., & Baum, T. (2013). Lessons in tourism and souvenirs from the margins: Glocal perspectives. In Tourism and Souvenirs: Glocal Perspectives from the Margins (pp. 189-199). Bristol, UK: Channel View Publications.

Josep & Ernesto. (2005) ¿Medir la sostenibilidad? una aproximación al tema de los indicadores de sostenibilidad. *Cátedra UNESCO a la UPC de Sostenibilidad*, *5*, 140-144.

Jouzi, Z., Azadi, H., Taheri, F., Zarafshani, K., Gebrehiwot, K., Van Passel, S., & Lebailly, P. (2017). Organic farming and small-scale farmers: Main opportunities and challenges. *Ecological Economics*, *132*, 144–154. doi:10.1016/j.ecolecon.2016.10.016

Juliani, D., Silva, A., Cunha, J., & Benneworth, P. (2017). Universities' contributions to sustainable development's social challenge: A case study of a social innovation practice. *International Journal of Social Ecology and Sustainable Development*, *8*(3), 1–18. doi:10.4018/IJSESD.2017070101

Junior, F. H., Galleli, B., Gallardo-Vázquez, D., & Sánchez-Hernández, M. I. (2017). Strategic aspects in sustainability reporting in oil & gas industry: The comparative case-study of brazilian Petrobras and Spanish Repsol. *Ecological Indicators*, *72*, 203–214. doi:10.1016/j.ecolind.2016.08.007

Kandola, R., & Fullerton, J. (1998). *Managing the mosaic: Diversity in action*. London: Institute of Personnel Development.

Kannan, R., & Boie, W. (2003). Energy management practices in SME - case study of a bakery in Germany. *Energy Conversion and Management*, *44*(6), 945–959. doi:10.1016/S0196-8904(02)00079-1

Kaplan, R. S., & Norton, D. P. (1992). The balanced scorecard: Measures that drive performance. *Harvard Business Review*, *1992*(January-February), 71–79. PMID:10119714

Kaplan, R. S., & Norton, D. P. (1996). *The Balanced Scorecard*. Boston: Harvard Business School Press.

Kaplan, R. S., & Norton, D. P. (2001). *The Strategy-Focused Organization*. Boston: Harvard Business School Press.

Kaplan, R., & Norton, D. (2004). *Strategy Maps: Converting Intangible Assets into Tangible Outcomes*. Boston: Harvard Business School Press.

Kaplan, R., & Norton, D. (2006). *Alignment: Using the Balanced Scorecard to Create Corporate Synergies*. Boston: Harvard Business School Press.

Kaplan, R., & Norton, D. (2008). *Execution Premium: Linking Strategy to Operations for Competitive Advantage*. Boston: Harvard Business School Press.

Karlaftis, M., Kepaptsoglou, K., Stathopoulos, A., & Starra, A. (2004). Planning public transport networks for the 2004 Summer Olympics with decision support systems. *Transportation Research Record: Journal of the Transportation Research Board,* (1887), 71-82.

Karlaftis, M. G. (2004). A DEA approach for evaluating the efficiency and effectiveness of urban transit systems. *European Journal of Operational Research, 152*(2), 354–364. doi:10.1016/S0377-2217(03)00029-8

Karlaftis, M. G., & McCarthy, P. S. (1997). Subsidy and public transit performance: A factor analytic approach. *Transportation, 24*(3), 253–270. doi:10.1023/A:1004956532174

Keast, R., Brown, K., & Mandell, M. (2007). Getting The Right Mix: Unpacking Integration Meanings and Strategies. *International Public Management Journal, 10*(1), 9–33. doi:10.1080/10967490601185716

Keast, R., Mandell, M. P., Brown, K., & Woolcock, G. (2004). Network structures: Working differently and changing expectations. *Public Administration Review, 64*(3), 363–371. doi:10.1111/j.1540-6210.2004.00380.x

Keeble, J. J., Topiol, S., & Berkeley, S. (2003). Using indicators to measure sustainability performance at a corporate and project level. *Journal of Business Ethics, 44*(2), 149–158. doi:10.1023/A:1023343614973

Kenny, B., & Fahy, J. (2011). Network resources and international performance of high tech SMEs. *Journal of Small Business and Enterprise Development, 18*(3), 529–555. doi:10.1108/14626001111155691

Kerlinger, F. N. (1964). Foundations of Behavioral Research. New York: Holt, Reinhart, and Winston.

Kerlin, J. (2006). Social Enterprise in the United States and Europe: Understanding and Learning from the Differences. *Voluntas, 17*(3), 247–263. doi:10.100711266-006-9016-2

Keune, M., Leschke, J., & Watt, A. (Eds.). (2008). *Privatisation and liberalisation of public services in Europe. An analysis of economic and labour market impacts*. Brussels: ETUI.

Kinyuira, D. K. (2017). Pursuing social mission as part of a deliberate and managed strategy: Social performance management in Co-operatives. *Journal of Strategy and Performance Management, 5*(2), 23–41.

Kipnis, E., Broderick, A. J., & Demangeot, C. (2014). Consumer multiculturation: Consequences of multi-cultural identification for brand knowledge. *Consumption Markets & Culture, 17*(3), 231–253. doi:10.1080/10253866.2013.778199

Kirkels, Y., & Duysters, G. (2010). Brokerage in SME networks. *Research Policy, 39*(3), 375–385. doi:10.1016/j.respol.2010.01.005

Kirwan, J. (2006). The interpersonal world of direct marketing: Examining conventions of quality at UK farmers' markets. *Journal of Rural Studies, 22*(3), 301–312. doi:10.1016/j.jrurstud.2005.09.001

Kjeldgaard, D., Askegaard, S., & Eckhardt, G. M. (2015). The role of cultural capital in creating "glocal" brand relationships. In Strong Brands, Strong Relationships (pp. 48-60). Abingdon, UK: Taylor and Francis.

Klein, S. B., Astrachan, J. H., & Smyrnios, K. X. (2005). The F-PEC scale of family influence: Construction, validation, and further implication for theory. *Entrepreneurship Theory and Practice*, *29*(3), 321–339. doi:10.1111/j.1540-6520.2005.00086.x

KMPG. (2015). *The KPMG Survey of Corporate Responsibility Reporting 2015*. Retrieved August 10, 2017, from https://home.kpmg.com/xx/en/home/insights/2015/11/kpmg-international-survey-of-corporate-responsibility-reporting-2015.html

Kokubu, K., Kitada, H., & Mouritsen, J. (2012). *Material flow cost accounting and conventional management thinking: introducing a new environmental management accounting tool into companies.* Paper presented at the IPA Conference.

Kolk, A., & Mauser, A. M. (2002). The evolution of environmental management: From stage models to performance evaluation. *Business Strategy and the Environment*, *11*(1), 14–31. doi:10.1002/bse.316

Kolk, A., van der Veen, M. L., van Wateringen, S. L., van der Veldt, D., & Walhain, S. P. (1999). *KPMG International survey of environmental reporting 1999*. The Hague, The Netherlands: KPMG/WIMM.

Konar, S., & Cohen, M. (1997). Information as Regulation: The effect of community right to know laws on toxic emissions. *Journal of Enronvmental Economic and Management*, *32*(1), 109–124. doi:10.1006/jeem.1996.0955

Konsti-Laakso, S., Pihkala, T., & Kraus, S. (2012). Facilitating SME Innovation Capability through Business Networking. *Creativity and Innovation Management*, *21*(1), 93–105. doi:10.1111/j.1467-8691.2011.00623.x

KPMG. (2013). *International Survey of Corporate Responsibility Reporting 2013*. Amstelveen: KPMG.

Kraaijenbrink, J., Spender, J.-C., & Groen, A. J. (2010). The resource-based view: A review and assessment of its critiques. *Journal of Management*, *36*(1), 349–372. doi:10.1177/0149206309350775

Kraus, S., Pohjola, M., & Koponen, A. (2012). Innovation in family firms: An empirical analysis linking organizational and managerial innovation to corporate success. *Review of Managerial Science*, *6*(3), 261–270. doi:10.100711846-011-0065-6

Krippendorff, K. (1980). Validity in Content Analysis. *Computerstrategien Für Die Kommunikationsanalyse*, 69–112. Retrieved from http://repository.upenn.edu/asc_papers/291

Krishnan, R. (2008). *"GLOCAL" Mission, Resources & Locus in Organizational Strategy*. Submitted for 11th Annual Convention of the Strategic Management Forum. Retrieved July 6, from http://www.iitk.ac.in

La Porta, R., Lopez-De-Silanes, F., Shleifer, A., & Vishny, R. (1998). Law and Finance. *Journal of Political Economy*, *106*(6), 1113–1155. doi:10.1086/250042

Lai, A., Lionzo, A., Stacchezzini, R., & Rossignoli, F. (2015). *Dall'impresa al network. Profili di governance e modelli di business: Profili di governance e modelli di business*. FrancoAngeli.

Lamanna Di Salvo, D. (2004). Ragioniere e Dottore Commercialista: una storica diatriba tra differenziazione ed unificazione. *Rivista Scuola superiore dell'economia e delle finanze, 8/9*, 2.

Lambert, D., & Stock, J. (1979). The corporate energy policy: A management planning perspective. *Long Range Planning*, *12*(2), 45–51. doi:10.1016/0024-6301(79)90072-4

Lamertz, K., Foster, W. M., Coraiola, D. M., & Kroezen, J. (2016). New identities from remnants of the past: An examination of the history of beer brewing in Ontario and the recent emergence of craft breweries. *Business History*, *58*(5), 796–828. doi:10.1080/00076791.2015.1065819

Lansberg, I. (1983). Managin Human resources in family firms: The problem of institutional overlan. *Organizational Dynamics*, *12*(1), 40–42. doi:10.1016/0090-2616(83)90025-6

Laszlo, E. (2013). The optimal worldshift strategy in light of complex systems theory. *World Futures: Journal of General Evolution*, *69*(2), 61–64. doi:10.1080/02604027.2012.762190

Lau, C.-M., & Woodman, R. W. (1995). Understanding organizational change: A schematic perspective. *Academy of Management Journal*, *38*(2), 537–554. doi:10.2307/256692

Laurentiis, I., Klaer, E., & Martignetti, L. (2017). Social Economy. In D. Domanski & C. Kaletka (Eds.), *Exploring the Research Landscape of Social Innovation – A deliverable of the project Social Innovation Community (SIC)*. Dortmund: Sozialforschungsstelle.

Le Breton-Miller, D., & Miller, D. (2015). Family firms and practises of sustainability: a contingency view. *Journal of Family Business Strategy*, (7), 26-33.

Lee, H., Kelley, D., Lee, J., & Lee, S. (2012). SME survival: The impact of internationalization, technology resources, and alliances. *Journal of Small Business Management*, *50*(1), 1–19. doi:10.1111/j.1540-627X.2011.00341.x

Lee, J. (2004). The effects of family ownership and management on firm performance. *S.A.M. Advanced Management Journal*, *69*(4), 46.

Lee, K. H. (2009). Why and How to Adopt Green Management into Business Organizations? The Case Study of Korean SMEs in the Manufacturing Industry. *Management Decision*, *47*(7), 1101–1121. doi:10.1108/00251740910978322

Lee, K. H. (2011). Motivations, barriers, and incentives for adopting environmental management (cost) accounting and related guidelines: A study of the republic of Korea. *Corporate Social Responsibility and Environmental Management*, *18*(1), 39–49. doi:10.1002/csr.239

Leggett, J. K. (1996). *Climate change and the financial sector*. Gerling Akademie.

Lenger, A., & Schumacher, F. (2015). The global configurations of inequality: Stratification, glocal inequalities, and the global social structure. In Understanding the Dynamics of Global Inequality: Social Exclusion, Power Shift, and Structural Changes (pp. 3-46). Berlin, Germany: Springer.

Lepoutre, J., & Heene, A. (2006). Investigating the impact of firm size on small business social responsibility: A critical review. *Journal of Business Ethics*, *67*(3), 257–273. doi:10.100710551-006-9183-5

Levaggi, R. (1994). *Parametric and non parametric approach to efficiency: the case of urban transport in Italy*. Studi Economici.

Levison, H. (1971). Conflicts that plage family businesses. *Harvard Business Review*, 91-92.

Levitt, T. (2006). *Ted Levitt on Marketing. Timeless Classic from the "Father of modern marketing". Including: Marketing Miopia, The Globalization of Markets, marketing Success Through Differentiation – of Anything*. Boston: A Harvard Business Review Book.

Levitt, T. (1983). The Globalization of Markets. *Harvard Business Review*, *61*(3), 92–102.

Lin, C. H., Yang, H. L., & Liou, D. Y. (2009). The impact of corporate social responsibility on financial performance: Evidence from business in Taiwan. *Technology in Society*, *31*(1), 56–63. doi:10.1016/j.techsoc.2008.10.004

Lindblom, C. K. (1994). The implications of organizational legitimacy for corporate social performance and disclosure. In Critical perspectives on accounting conference (Vol. 120). New York: Academic Press.

Li, Y.-R. (2009). The technological roadmap of Cisco's business ecosystem. *Technovation*, *29*(5), 379–386. doi:10.1016/j.technovation.2009.01.007

Lo Turco, A., & Maggioni, D. (2017). "Glocal" ties: Banking development and SEs' export entry. *Small Business Economics*, *48*(4), 999–1020. doi:10.100711187-016-9809-7

Lodhia, S., & Stone, G. (2017). Integrated Reporting in an Internet and Social Media Communication Environment: Conceptual Insights. *Australian Accounting Review*, *27*(1), 17–33. doi:10.1111/auar.12143

Loorbach, D. A., & Lijnis Huffenreuter, R. (2013). Exploring the economic crisis from a transition management perspective. *Environmental Innovation and Societal Transitions*, *6*, 35–46. doi:10.1016/j.eist.2013.01.003

López-Arceiz, F. J., Bellostas, A. J., & Rivera-Torres, M. P. (2017). The Slaughtered and the Survivors: Collaboration between Social Economy Organizations as a Key to Success in Times of Financial Crisis. *Voluntas*, 1–26.

López-Cózar Navarro, C. (2014). Peculiaridades de la pequeña empresa familiar ante la responsabilidad social empresarial. *Un análisis exploratorio enla Comunidad de Madrid*, (18), 42.

Loucks, S. E., Martens, M. L., & Cho, C. H. (2010). Engaging small-and medium-sized businesses in sustainability. *Sustainability Accounting. Management and Policy Journal*, *1*(2), 178–200. doi: 10.1108/20408021011089239

Lujan Alcaraz, J. (2006). *La empresa familiar ante el Derecho del Trabajo y de la Seguridad Revista Doctrinal Aranzadi Social num.10/2006 parte Tribuna Social*. Editorial Aranzadi, S.A.U.

Lumpkin, G. T., Brigham, K. H., & Moss, T. W. (2010). Long-term orientation: Implications for the entrepreneurial orientation and performance of family businesses. *Entrepreneurship and Regional Development*, *22*(3–4), 241–264. doi:10.1080/08985621003726218

Lumpkin, G. T., & Dess, G. G. (1996). Clarifying the entrepreneurial orientation construct and linking it to performance. *Academy of Management Review*, *21*(1), 135–172.

Lynch-Wood, G., Williamson, D., & Jenkins, W. (2009). The over-reliance on self-regulation in CSR policy. *Business Ethics (Oxford, England)*, *18*(1), 52–65. doi:10.1111/j.1467-8608.2009.01548.x

MacGregor, R. C. (2004). Factors associated with formal networking in regional small business: Some findings from a study of Swedish SMEs. *Journal of Small Business and Enterprise Development*, *11*(1), 60–74. doi:10.1108/14626000410519100

Maggio, G. F. (1997). Inter/intra-generational equity: Current applications under international law for promoting the sustainable development of natural resources. *Buffalo Environmental Law Journal*, *4*(2), 161.

Magnusson, M. K., Arvola, A., Koivisto Hursti, U. K., Aberg, L., & Sjoden, P. O. (2001). Attitudes towards organic foods among Swedish consumers. *British Food Journal*, *103*(3), 209–227. doi:10.1108/00070700110386755

Maignan, I., & Ferrell, O. C. (2000). Measuring corporate citizenship in two countries: The case of the United States and France. *Journal of Business Ethics*, *23*(3), 283–297. doi:10.1023/A:1006262325211

Maignan, I., Ferrell, O. C., & Ferrell, L. (2005). A stakeholder model for implementing social responsibility in marketing. *European Journal of Marketing*, *39*(9/10), 956–977. doi:10.1108/03090560510610662

Makatouni, A. (2002). What motivates consumers to buy organic food in the UK? Results from a qualitative study. *British Food Journal*, *104*(3/4/5), 345-352.

Mandell, M. P., & Keast, R. (2008). Evaluating the effectiveness of interorganizational relations through networks. *Public Management Review*, *10*(6), 715–731. doi:10.1080/14719030802423079

Mandell, M., Keast, R., & Chamberlain, D. (2016). Collaborative networks and the need for a new management language. *Public Management Review*, *9037*(August), 1–16. doi:10.1080/14719037.2016.1209232

Maniora, J. (2017). Is Integrated Reporting Really the Superior Mechanism for the Integration of Ethics into the Core Business Model? An Empirical Analysis. *Journal of Business Ethics*, *140*(4), 755–786. doi:10.100710551-015-2874-z

Marino, V. (2005). *Il governo dell'impresa nella prospettiva sistemica delle relazioni internazionali*. Milano, Italy: Angeli.

Mark-Herbert, C., & Von Schantz, C. (2007). Communicating corporate social responsibility and brand management. *Electronic Journal of Business Ethics and Organization Studies*, *12*(2), 4–11.

Maron, I. Y. (2006). Toward a unified theory of the CSP–CFP link. *Journal of Business Ethics*, *67*(2), 191–200. doi:10.100710551-006-9023-7

Marques, L. (2013). Constructing social landscape through events: The glocal project of 's-Hertogenbosch. In Exploring the Social Impacts of Events (pp. 84-94). Abingdon, UK: Taylor and Francis.

Marriott, N., Marriott, P., Collis, J., & Son, D. D. (2008). *The Accountant and the Provision of Financial Advice to UK Smaller Companies*. British Accounting Association Annual Conference, Blackpool, UK.

Marsden, T., Banks, J., & Bristow, G. (2000). Food Supply Chain Approaches: Exploring their Role in Rural Development. *Sociologia Ruralis*, *40*(4), 424–438. doi:10.1111/1467-9523.00158

Marsden, T., & Smith, E. (2005). Ecological entrepreneurship: Sustainable development in local communities through quality food production and local branding. *Geoforum*, *36*(4), 440–451. doi:10.1016/j.geoforum.2004.07.008

Martínez Girón, J., & Arufe Varela, A. (2006). *Derecho del Trabajo*. Netbiblo SL.

Martínez Girón, J., & Arufe Varela, A. (2012). *Derecho Crítico del Trabajo*. Netbiblosl.

Matacena, A. (1984). *Impresa e ambiente. Il bilancio sociale*. Bologna, Italy: Clueb.

Matacena, R. (2016). Linking alternative food networks and urban food policy: A step forward in the transition towards a sustainable and equitable food system? *International Review of Social Research*, *6*(1), 49–58. doi:10.1515/irsr-2016-0007

Matusitz, J., & Leanza, K. (2009). Wal-Mart: An Analysis of the Glocalization of the Cathedral of Consumption in China. *Globalizations*, *6*(2), 187–205. doi:10.1080/14747730902854158

Matute-Vallejo, J., Bravo, R., & Pina, J. M. (2011). The influence of Corporate Social Responsibility and Price Fairness on Customer Behaviour: Evidence from the Financial Sector. *Corporate Social Responsibility and Environmental Management*, *18*(6), 317–331. doi:10.1002/csr.247

Mauri, L., & Visconti, L. M. (Eds.). (2004). *Diversity management e società multiculturale. Teorie e prassi*. Milano, Italy: Angeli.

Maury, B. (2006). Family ownership and firm performance: Empirical evidence from Western European corporations. *Journal of Corporate Finance*, *12*(2), 321–341. doi:10.1016/j.jcorpfin.2005.02.002

Maximus. (2017). *About Us*. Retrieved May 29, 2017 from http://www.ecomaximus.com/max/jm/index.php?option=com_content&view=article&id=1&Itemid=2

Maxwell, J. A. (2008). Designing a qualitative study. The SAGE Handbook of Applied Social Research Methods, 2, 214–253.

Maye, D., & Kirwan, J. (2010). Alternative Food Networks. *International Journal of Agricultural & Food*, *20*(3), 383–389.

Maylor, H., & Blackmon, K. (2005). *Researching Business and Management*. New York: Palgrave MacMillan. doi:10.1007/978-1-137-11022-0

Mazzola, E., & Perrone, G. (2013). A strategic needs perspective on operations outsourcing and other inter-firm relationships. *International Journal of Production Economics*, *144*(1), 256–267. doi:10.1016/j.ijpe.2013.02.012

Mazzola, E., Perrone, G., & Kamuriwo, D. S. (2016). The interaction between inter-firm and interlocking directorate networks on firm's new product development outcomes. *Journal of Business Research*, *69*(2), 672–682. doi:10.1016/j.jbusres.2015.08.033

McWilliams, A., & Siegel, A. D. (2001). Corporate Social Responsibility: A Theory of the Firm Perspective. *Academy of Management Review*, *26*(1), 117–127.

Melé, D. (2009). The Practice of Networking: An Ethical Approach. *Journal of Business Ethics*, *90*(S4), 487–503. doi:10.100710551-010-0602-2

Menguc, B., & Ozanne, L. K. (2005). Challenges of the "green imperative": A natural resource-based approach to the environmental orientation–business performance relationship. *Journal of Business Research*, *58*(4), 430–438. doi:10.1016/j.jbusres.2003.09.002

Mercati, V. (2016). Organic Agriculture as a Paradigm of Sustainability: Italian Food and its Progression in the Global Market. *Agriculture and Agricultural Science Procedia*, *8*, 798–802. doi:10.1016/j.aaspro.2016.02.071

Mervelskemper, L., & Streit, D. (2017). Enhancing Market Valuation of ESG Performance: Is Integrated Reporting Keeping its Promise? *Business Strategy and the Environment*, *26*(4), 536–549. doi:10.1002/bse.1935

Midmore, P., Naspetti, S., Sherwood, A. M., Vairo, D., Wier, M., & Zanoli, R. (2005). *Consumer attitudes to quality and safety of organic and low input foods; a review. Report of EU-funded project "Improving Quality and Safety and Reduction of Cost in the European Organic and 'Low Input' Food Supply Chains."*. Aberystwyth, UK: University of Wales.

Midttun, A. (2009). *Strategic CSR Innovation: Serving Societal and Individual Needs*. Oslo: BI Norwegian School of Management: Department of Innovation and Organizational Management.

Migliaccio, G. (2007a). Gli schemi di rendicontazione economico-patrimoniale di imprese ed enti locali: profili evolutivi e comparativi. *Esperienze d'impresa*, (2), 79-94.

Migliaccio, G. (2009). Financial statements for glocal companies? Socio-economic and financial communication issues for firms and agencies with a global vocation and strong ties with local contexts. In *Proceedings of the 2nd Annual EuroMed Conference of the EuroMed-Academy-of-Business: Managerial And Entrepreneurial Developments In The Mediterranean Area*, 1087-1106.

Migliaccio, G. (2007b). *Verso nuovi schemi di bilancio. Note su evoluzione e prospettive di forme e strutture del bilancio d'esercizio*. Milano, Italy: Angeli.

Migliore, G., Forno, F., Guccione, G. D., & Schifani, G. (2014). Food Community Networks as sustainable self-organized collective action: A case study of a solidarity purchasing group. *New Medit*, *13*(4), 54–62.

Milestad, R., Bartel-Kratochvil, R., Leitner, H., & Axmann, P. (2010). Being close: The quality of social relationships in a local organic cereal and bread network in Lower Austria. *Journal of Rural Studies*, *26*(3), 228–240. doi:10.1016/j.jrurstud.2010.01.004

Millar, R., & Hall, K. (2013). Social Return on Investment (SROI) and Performance Measurement. *Public Management Review*, *15*(6), 923–941. doi:10.1080/14719037.2012.698857

Miller, D. (1983). The correlates of entrepreneurship in three types of firms. *Management Science*, *29*(7), 770–791. doi:10.1287/mnsc.29.7.770

Milne, M. J., Tregidga, H. M., & Walton, S. (2009). Words not actions! The ideological role of sustainable development reporting. *Accounting, Auditing & Accountability Journal*, *22*(8), 1211–1257. doi:10.1108/09513570910999292

Ministero delle Infrastrutture e dei Trasporti. (2014). *Piano di Azione Nazionale sui Sistemi Intelligenti di Trasporto*. ITS.

Ministero delle Infrastrutture e dei Trasporti. (2015). *Conto Nazionale delle Infrastrutture e dei Trasporti.* Author.

Ministry of Micro Small and Medium Enterprises. (2011). Annual report 2010-11. New Delhi: Author.

Mintzberg, H. (1999). *Structure et Dynamique des Organisations*. Paris: Les Éditions d'Organisation.

Mio, C., & Venturelli, A. (2013). Non-financial Information About Sustainable Development and Environmental Policy in the Annual Reports of Listed Companies: Evidence from Italy and the UK. *Corporate Social Responsibility and Environmental Management*, *20*(6), 340–358. doi:10.1002/csr.1296

Mitnick, B. M. (1995). Systematics and CSR. *Business & Society*, *34*(1), 5–33. doi:10.1177/000765039503400102

Montemerlo, D. (2000). *Il governo delle imprese familiari: modelli e strumenti per gestire i rapporti tra proprietà e impresa*. Milano: Egea.

Montiel, I. (2008). Corporate social responsibility and corporate sustainability. *Organization & Environment*, *21*(3), 245–269. doi:10.1177/1086026608321329

Montoya Melgar, A. (Ed.). (2000). *Curso de Seguridad Social.* Servicio de Publicaciones de la Facultad de Derecho. Universidad Complutense, 2ª edición, Madrid, 2000, Capítulo XIII, págs. 299 y ss.

Monzon, J. L., & Chaves, R. (2008). The European Social Economy: Concept and Dimensions of the Third Sector. *Annals of Public and Cooperative Economics*, *79*(3/4), 549–577. doi:10.1111/j.1467-8292.2008.00370.x

Moore, H. (2015). Global Prosperity and Sustainable Development Goals. *Journal of International Development*, *27*(6), 801–815. doi:10.1002/jid.3114

Moore, J. F. (1993). Predators and Prey: A New Ecology of Competition. *Harvard Business Review*, 75–84. PMID:10126156

Moores, K., & Mula, J. (2000). The salience of market, bureaucratic, and clan controls in the management of family firm transitions: Some tentative Australian evidence. *Family Business Review*, *13*(2), 91–106. doi:10.1111/j.1741-6248.2000.00091.x

Moores, K., & Yuen, S. (2001). Management Accounting Systems and Organizational Configuration: A Life Cycle Perspective. *Accounting, Organizations and Society*, *26*(4-5), 351–389. doi:10.1016/S0361-3682(00)00040-4

Moratis, L. (2017). The (In) credible Bulk: The Role of CSR Standards in Enhancing the Credibility of Corporate CSR Claims. In *The Dynamics of Corporate Social Responsibility* (pp. 239–263). Springer. doi:10.1007/978-3-319-39089-5_13

Morck, R., Shleifer, A., & Vishny, R. (1988). Management ownership and firm value: An empirical analysis. *Journal of Financial Economics*, *20*(1), 293–315. doi:10.1016/0304-405X(88)90048-7

Morck, R., & Yeung, B. (2003). Agency problems in large family business groups. *Entrepreneurship Theory and Practice*, *27*(4), 367–382. doi:10.1111/1540-8520.t01-1-00015

Morse, W., Davis, J., & Hartgraves, A. (2003). *Management accounting: a strategic approach*. Moscove, Thomspon/South-Western.

Morsing, M., & Perrini, F. (2009). CSR in SMEs: Do SMEs matter for the CSR agenda? *Business Ethics (Oxford, England), 18*(1), 1–6. doi:10.1111/j.1467-8608.2009.01544.x

Mosca, F., Casalegno, C., & Civera, C. (2016, September). *Opportunities and Peculiarities of the Online for Communicating Corporate Social Responsibility. A cross investigation on luxury players and consumers' perceptions.* Paper presented at the meeting of the British Academy of Management (BAM), Newcastle, UK.

Moskovitz, M. (1972). Choosing Socially Respnsible stocks. *Business and Society Review*, (1): 72–75.

Moskovitz, M. (1972). Choosing Socially Responsible stocks. *Business and Society Review*, (1): 72–75.

Moss, J., Lambert, C. G., & Rennie, A. E. (2008). SME application of LCA-based carbon footprints. *International Journal of Sustainable Engineering, 1*(2), 132–141. doi:10.1080/19397030802332930

Mourdoukoutas, P., & Ioannidis, A. (2007). The three rules of glocal corporate citizenship. *Globe Management Review, 1*(1), 26–35.

Müller, F. (2017). IRENA as a glocal actor: Pathways towards energy governmentality. *Innovation, 30*(3), 306–322.

Murdoch, J., Marsden, T., & Banks, J. (2000). Quality, nature, and embeddedness: Some theoretical considerations in the context of the food sector. *Economic Geography, 76*(2), 107–125. doi:10.2307/144549

Murillo, D., & Lozano, J. (2009). Pushing forward SME CSR through a network: An account from the Catalan model. *Business Ethics (Oxford, England), 18*(1), 7–20. doi:10.1111/j.1467-8608.2009.01545.x

Murillo, D., & Lozano, J. F. (2006). SMEs and CSR: An approach to CSR in their own words. *Journal of Business Ethics, 67*(3), 227–240. doi:10.100710551-006-9181-7

Musso, T., & Drago, M. (2013). *Baladin: La birra artigianale è tutta colpa di Teo*. Feltrinelli Editore.

Myers, M. D. (2013). *Qualitative Research in Business & Management*. London: Sage.

Nascente F. (2015). Success strategies and agri-food companies: The glocalism role. *Quality - Access to Success, 16*(147), 80-84.

Naspetti, S., Lampkin, N., Nicholas, P., Stolze, M., & Zanoli, R. (2011). Organic supply chain collaboration: A case study in eight EU countries. *Journal of Food Products Marketing, 14*(2), 141–162. doi:10.1080/10454446.2011.548733

Nava, M. R. (2017). The development of intercultural competences in post-bureaucratic organizations. In Evolution of the Post-Bureaucratic Organization (pp. 401-421). Hershey, PA: IGI Global. doi:10.4018/978-1-5225-1983-6.ch019

Negueruela, V., & Luis, J. (2005). Especial Problemática de la Empresa Familiar. Actualidad Jurídica Aranzadi num.678/2005(opinión), ed. Aranzadi, page 3-4.

Neubauer, F., & Lank, A. G. (1998). *The Family Business: Its Governance for Sustainability*. London: Macmillan Business. doi:10.1007/978-1-349-14465-5

Nicholls, A., & Murdock, A. (2012). The nature of social innovation. In *Social innovation* (pp. 1–30). Springer. doi:10.1057/9780230367098_1

Nidumolo, R., Prahalad, C. K., & Rangaswami, M. R. (2009). Why sustainability is now the key driver of innovation. *Harvard Business Review, 87*(9), 56–64.

Niehm, L. S., Swinney, J., & Miller, N. J. (2008). Community social responsibility and its consequences for family business performance. *Journal of Small Business Management, 46*(3), 331–350. doi:10.1111/j.1540-627X.2008.00247.x

Noe, E., & Alrøe, H. F. (2015). Sustainable agriculture issues explained by differentiation and structural coupling using social systems analysis. *Agronomy for Sustainable Development*, *35*(1), 133–144. doi:10.100713593-014-0243-4

Nogales Lozano, F. (2007). Las culturas familiares: gestión clave para la cohesión y continuidad de las familias empresarias, en La Empresa Familiar y los nuevos retos de gestión, Coordi. Nogales Lozano, Colección EOI Empresas, págs. 241-242.

Nolan, J. F. (1996). Determinants of productive efficiency in urban transit. *Logistics and Transportation Review*, *32*(3), 319.

Noran, O. (2010). Towards an Environmental Management Approach for Collaborative Networks. *Collaborative Networks for a Sustainable World*, *336*, 17–24. doi:10.1007/978-3-642-15961-9_2

Nordheim, E., & Barrasso, G. (2007). Sustainable development indicators of the European aluminium industry. *Journal of Cleaner Production*, *15*(3), 275–279. doi:10.1016/j.jclepro.2006.02.004

Noya, A., & Clarence, E. (2007). The Social Economy. Building Inclusive Economies. Paris: OECD, Local Economic and Employment Development (LEED).

Nulkar, G. (2014). SMEs and environmental performance–A framework for green business strategies. *Procedia: Social and Behavioral Sciences*, *133*, 130–140. doi:10.1016/j.sbspro.2014.04.177

O' Connor, M. (2006). The four spheres framework for sustainability. *Ecological Complexity*, *3*(44), 285–292. doi:10.1016/j.ecocom.2007.02.002

O'Donnell, A. (2004). The nature of networking in small firms. *Qualitative Market Research*, *7*(3), 206–217. doi:10.1108/13522750410540218

O'Sullivan, D., & Dooley, L. (2009). *Applying Innovation*. London: Sage Publications.

OECD. (2005). *Oslo Manual: Guidelines for Collecting and Interpreting Innovation Data*. Organization for Economic Co-operation and Development, European Commission.

OECD. (2016). *Financing SMEs and Entrepreneurs (2016): An OECD Scoreboard*. Retrieved August 10, 2017, from http://www.keepeek.com/Digital-Asset-Management/oecd/industry-and-services/financing-smes-and-entrepreneurs-2016_fin_sme_ent-2016-en#page306

Okpara, J. O. (2011). Factors constraining the growth and survival of SMEs in Nigeria: Implications for poverty alleviation. *Management Research Review*, *34*(2), 156–171. doi:10.1108/01409171111102786

Onida, P. (1974). *Il bilancio d'esercizio nelle imprese. Significato economico del bilancio. Problemi di valutazione*. Milano, Italy: Giuffrè.

Onkvisit, S., & Shaw, J.J. (2002). "Glocal" advertising: Think global, act local. In *AMA Educators' Conference, Proceedings* (pp. 378-379). American Marketing Association.

Organisation for Economic Co-operation and Development (OECD). (2005). *OECD SME and entrepreneurship outlook*. Paris: OECD Publishing.

Organisation for Economic Co-operation and Development (OECD). (2007). *Small Businesses and Environmental Compliance -Review and Possible Application of International Experience in Georgia*. Paris: OECD Publishing.

Ormazabal, M., Rich, E., Sarriegi, J. M., & Viles, E. (2017). Environmental Management Evolution Framework: Maturity Stages and Causal Loops. *Organization & Environment*, *30*(1), 27–50. doi:10.1177/1086026615623060

Ormazabal, M., & Sarriegi, J. M. (2012). Environmental management: Understanding its evolution through maturity states. *Environmental Quality Management*, *22*(1), 31–42. doi:10.1002/tqem.21315

Osservatorio Nazionale sulle Politiche del Trasporto Locale. (2014). *Relazione Annuale al Parlamento*. Author.

Osservatorio Nazionale sulle Politiche del Trasporto Locale. (2015). *Relazione Annuale al Parlamento*. Author.

Otley, D. T. (1999). Performance management; a framework for management control system research. *Management Accounting Research*, *10*(10), 363–382. doi:10.1006/mare.1999.0115

Our World. (2008). *Africa and Climate Change*. Retrieved 12 May, 2017 from https://ourworld.unu.edu/en/africa-and-climate-change

Ozbek, M. E., de la Garza, J. M., & Triantis, K. (2009). Data envelopment analysis as a decision-making tool for transportation professionals. *Journal of Transportation Engineering*, *135*(11), 822–831. doi:10.1061/(ASCE)TE.1943-5436.0000069

Padel, S., & Foster, C. (2005). Exploring the gap between attitudes and behaviour: Understanding why consumers buy or do not buy organic food. *British Food Journal*, *107*(8), 606–625. doi:10.1108/00070700510611002

Padel, S., Röcklinsberg, H., & Schmid, O. (2009). The implementation of organic principles and values in the European Regulation for organic food. *Food Policy*, *34*(3), 245–251. doi:10.1016/j.foodpol.2009.03.008

Padel, S., Vaarst, M., & Zaralis, K. (2015). Supporting Innovation in Organic Agriculture: A European Perspective Using Experience from the SOLID Project. *Sustainable Agriculture Research*, *4*(3), 32–41. doi:10.5539ar.v4n3p32

Pais, C. A., & Parente, C. (2015). Representations of team work among organizations with a social entrepreneurship profile: A multiple case-study. *Team Performance Management*, *21*(1/2), 65–84. doi:10.1108/TPM-07-2014-0042

Panwar, R., Paul, K., Nybakk, E., Hansen, E., & Thompson, D. (2014). The legitimacy of CSR actions of publicly traded companies versus family-owned companies. *Journal of Business Ethics*, *125*(3), 481–496. doi:10.100710551-013-1933-6

Papathanassis, A. (2014). Cruise Sector & 'Glocal' Corporate Citizenship: The 5th International Cruise Conference, Bremerhaven, Germany, 24-26 January 2014. *International Journal of Tourism Research*, *16*(4), 415–416. doi:10.1002/jtr.2006

Parente, C. (2016). Social entrepreneurship in Portugal: Intervention and management models in third sector. *The International Journal of Sociology and Social Policy*, *36*(7-8), 531–546. doi:10.1108/IJSSP-01-2016-0002

Parente, C., Marcos, V., Costa, D., & Amador, C. (2013). Representações sobre empreendedorismo social. *Cooperativismo e Economía Social*, *35*, 37–65.

Parker, L. (2001). Back to the future: The broadening accounting trajectory. *The British Accounting Review*, *33*(4), 421–453. doi:10.1006/bare.2001.0173

Parker, S. C. (2008). The economics of formal business networks. *Journal of Business Venturing*, *23*(6), 627–640. doi:10.1016/j.jbusvent.2008.01.003

Passetti, E., Cinquini, L., Marelli, A., & Tenucci, A. (2014). Sustainability accounting in action: Lights and shadows in the Italian context. *The British Accounting Review*, *46*(3), 295–308. doi:10.1016/j.bar.2014.05.002

Peano, C., Migliorini, P., & Sottile, F. (2014). A methodology for the sustainability assessment of agri-food systems: An application to the Slow Food Presidia project. *Ecology and Society*, *19*(4), art24. doi:10.5751/ES-06972-190424

Peghin, F., (2008). Antonveneta banca "glocale". *Il mattino di Padova*.

Pérez Molina, Ana Isabel, Gisbert Soler, Victor (2012), La continuidad en la empresa familiar: estudio de casos, 3 Ciencias, Editada por Área de Innovación y Desarrollo, S.L., págs. 7-8.

Pérez, C., & Perdomo, J. (2017). An Alternative Financial Reporting Model: Social Economy Organizations. *Lex Social, 7*(2), 229–249.

Pérez, M. J., Basco, R., García-Tenorio, J., Giménez, J., & Sánchez, I. (2007). *Fundamentos en la dirección de la empresa familiar*. Madrid: Thomson.

Perrini, F. (2005). Building a European Portait of Corporate Social Responsibility Reporting. *European Management Journal, 23*(6), 611–627. doi:10.1016/j.emj.2005.10.008

Perrini, F. (2006). SMEs and CSR theory: Evidence and implications from an Italian perspective. *Journal of Business Ethics, 67*(3), 305–316. doi:10.100710551-006-9186-2

Perrini, F., Russo, A., & Tencati, A. (2007). CSR strategies of SMEs and large firms. Evidence from Italy. *Journal of Business Ethics, 74*(3), 285–300. doi:10.100710551-006-9235-x

Perrini, F., & Tencati, A. (2006). Sustainability and stakeholder management: The need for new corporate performance evaluation and reporting systems. *Business Strategy and the Environment, 15*(5), 296–308. doi:10.1002/bse.538

Petrescu, D. C., & Petrescu-Mag, R. M. (2015). Organic food perception: Fad, or healthy and environmentally friendly? A case on Romanian consumers. *Sustainability, 7*(9), 12017–12031. doi:10.3390u70912017

Petrescu, D. C., Petrescu-Mag, R. M., Burny, P., & Azadi, H. (2017). A new wave in Romania: Organic food. Consumers' motivations, perceptions, and habits. *Agroecology and Sustainable Food Systems, 41*(1), 46–75. doi:10.1080/21683565.2016.1243602

Petrini, C. (2012). *Slow food: le ragioni del gusto*. Gius. Laterza & Figli Spa.

Petrini, C. (2016). *Buono, pulito e giusto*. Giunti Editore.

Petts, J., Herd, A., Gerrard, S., & Horne, C. (1999). The climate and culture of environmental compliance within SMEs. *Business Strategy and the Environment, 8*(1), 14–30. doi:

Picciotti, A. (2017). Towards sustainability: The innovation paths of social enterprise. *Annals of Public and Cooperative Economics, 88*(2), 233–256. doi:10.1111/apce.12168

Pimenova, P., & Van Der Vorst, R. (2004). The role of support programmes and policies in improving SMEs environmental performance in developed and transition economies. *Journal of Cleaner Production, 12*(6), 549–559. doi:10.1016/j.jclepro.2003.07.001

Pina, V., & Torres, L. (2001). Analysis of the efficiency of local government services delivery. An application to urban public transport. *Transportation Research Part A, Policy and Practice, 35*(10), 929–944. doi:10.1016/S0965-8564(00)00033-1

Pomering, A., & Dolnicar, S. (2009). Assessing the Prerequisite of Successful CSR Implementation: Are Consumers Aware of CSR Initiatives? *Journal of Business Ethics, 85*(2), 285–301. doi:10.100710551-008-9729-9

Porter, M. E., & Kramer, M. R. (2011). The Big Idea. Creating Shared Value. *Harvard Business Review, 89*(1-2), 62-77.

Porter, M. E. (1980). *Competitive Strategy: Techniques for Analyzing Industries and Competitors*. New York, NY: The Free Press.

Porter, M. E. (1992). *Competizione globale*. Torino, Italy: Isedi.

Porter, M. E., & Kramer, M. R. (2002). The competitive advantage of corporate philanthropy. *Harvard Business Review, 80*(12), 56–68. PMID:12510538

Porter, M. E., & Kramer, M. R. (2011). The Big Idea: Creating Shared Value. *Harvard Business Review*, *89*(1), 1–2. doi:10.2469/dig.v41.n1.28

Porter, M. E., & van der Linde, C. (1995). Green and Competitive. *Harvard Business Review*, *73*(5), 120–134. doi:10.1207/S15374424JCCP3203_02

Porter, M., & Kramer, R. (2002). The Competitive Advantage of Corporate Philanthropy. *Harvard Business Review*, *80*(12), 57–68. PMID:12510538

Prencipe, A., Bar-Yosef, S., & Dekker, H. C. (2014). Accounting research in family firms: Theoretical and empirical challenges. *European Accounting Review*, *23*(3), 361–385. doi:10.1080/09638180.2014.895621

Preti, P. (2006). Un'azienda glocal. *Sviluppo e organizzazione*, (213), 115-116.

Quazi, A. M., & O'Brien, D. (2000). An empirical test of a cross-national model of corporate social responsibility. *Journal of Business Ethics*, *25*(1), 33–51. doi:10.1023/A:1006305111122

Raffestin, C., & Butler, S. A. (2012). Space, territory and territoriality. *Environment and Planning. D, Society & Space*, *30*(1), 121–141. doi:10.1068/d21311

Rahman, N. H. W. A., Zain, M. M., & Al-Haj, N. H. Y. Y. (2011). CSR disclosures and its determinants: Evidence from Malaysian government link companies. *Social Responsibility Journal*, *7*(2), 181–201. doi:10.1108/17471111111141486

Rahmann, G., Ardakani, M. R., Bàrberi, P., Boehm, H., Canalis, S., Chander, M., ... Hamm, U. (2016). Organic Agriculture 3.0 is innovation with research. *Organic Agriculture*, 1–29.

Rainero, C., & Brescia, V. (2016). Corporate Social Responsibility» and «Social Reporting»: The Model of Innovation «Piedmont Method. *International Journal Series in Multidisciplinary Research, 2*(3), 18-40.

Rainero, C., Puddu, L., & Migliavacca, A. (2016). Aziende, Amministrazione Razionale e Impatto Sociale. In *Aziende non-profit etica e responsabilità sociale* (pp. 7–26). Milan, Italy: Franco Angeli.

Ramanau, R. (2016). Internationalization at a Distance: A Study of the Online Management Curriculum. *Journal of Management Education*, *40*(5), 545–575. doi:10.1177/1052562916647984

Ranson, S., Hinings, B., & Greenwood, R. (1980). The structuring of organizational structures. *Administrative Science Quarterly*, *25*(1), 1–17. doi:10.2307/2392223

Rawls, J. (1999). *A theory of justice* (Rev. Ed.). Oxford, UK: Oxford University Press.

Reichard, C. (2008). Trend towards a more diversified institutional landscape. *Public Management Review*, *10*(5), 569–571. doi:10.1080/14719030802264176

Reid, W. V., Chen, D., Goldfarb, L., Hackmann, H., Lee, Y. T., Mokhele, K., ... Schellnhuber, H. J. (2010). Earth system science for global sustainability: Grand challenges. *Science*, *330*(6006), 916–917. doi:10.1126cience.1196263 PMID:21071651

Renting, H., Marsden, T. K., & Banks, J. (2003). Understanding Alternative Food Networks: Exploring the role of short food supply chains in rural development. *Environment and planning. Part. A*, *35*(3), 393–411.

Report of de EY y Kennesaw State University. (2014). *Staying power: How do familybusinesses create lasting success*? Author.

Revell, A., & Blackburn, R. (2007). The business case for sustainability? An examination of small firms in the UK's construction and restaurant sectors. *Business Strategy and the Environment*, *16*(6), 404–420. doi:10.1002/bse.499

Reverte, C. (2009). Determinants of corporate social responsibility disclosure ratings by Spanish listed firms. *Journal of Business Ethics, 88*(2), 351–366. doi:10.100710551-008-9968-9

Revilla, A. J., Pérez-Luño, A., & Nieto, M. J. (2016). Does family involvement in management reduce the risk of business failure? The moderating role of entrepreneurial orientation. *Family Business Review, 29*(4), 365–379. doi:10.1177/0894486516671075

Riccaboni, A., Quattrone, P., & Busco, C. (2014). Al di la della rappresentazione: Il Reporting integrato come strumento di mediazione e innovazione sociale. *Equilibri, 52*(1), 38–43.

Ricci, P., Esposito, P., & Landi, T. (2010). L'accountability per il fronteggiamento dello State Capture nel management delle amministrazioni pubbliche locali. *Azienda Pubblica*, (2), 205-232.

Ricci, P., Landi, T., & Cillo, V. (2010). The Italian SMEs in the global context: the accountability system role. *Esperienze d'impresa, 11*(1), 59-77.

Ricci, P., Siboni, B., & Nardo, M. T. (Eds.). (2013). La rendicontazione di sostenibilità. Evoluzione, linee guida ed esperienze in imprese amministrazioni pubbliche e aziende non profit. Roma, Italy: Rirea.

Ricciardi, A., Cardoni, A., & Tiacci, L. (2014). Strategic Context, Organizational Features and Network Performances: A Survey on Collaborative Networked Organizations of Italian SMEs. In *Working Conference on Virtual Enterprises* (pp. 534–545). Springer. 10.1007/978-3-662-44745-1_53

Ricci, P. (2005). *Enti strumentali regionali e loro accountability. Il caso Campania*. Milano, Italy: Angeli.

Ricci, P. (2007). Le immobilizzazioni materiali negli enti locali. In *Gruppo di studio e attenzione dell'Aidea, L'analisi degli effetti sul bilancio dell'introduzione dei principi contabili internazionali Ias/Ifrs* (pp. 455–469). Roma, Italy: Rirea.

Ricci, P. (2011). Short Notes about Financial Reporting in Italian Family Business. *Review of International Comparative Management, 12*(1), 73–82.

Ricci, P. (2013). What future for social reporting and accountability in academic systems. An overview of the Italian case. *Review of International Comparative Management, 14*(2), 202–221.

Ricci, P. (Ed.). (2004). *La responsabilità sociale dell'impresa: il ruolo e il valore della comunicazione - Atti del convegno di Benevento del 29 gennaio 2004*. Milano, Italy: Angeli.

Ricci, P., & Fusco, F. (2016). Social reporting in the Italian justice system: Milan Court experience. *Public Integrity, 18*(3), 254–268. doi:10.1080/10999922.2016.1139524

Ricci, P., & Landi, T. (2010). Governance and Accountability for Italian Listed Public Utilities Companies. *Review of International Comparative Management, 11*(3), 376–388.

Rimal, A. P., Moon, W., & Balasubramanian, S. (2005). Agro-biotechnology and organic food purchase in the United Kingdom. *British Food Journal, 107*(2), 84–97. doi:10.1108/00070700510579162

Rivera, M. (2017). 'Glocal' discussion as leverage. Debating urban sustainability in Bogotá. *Journal of Environmental Studies and Sciences, 7*(1), 145–151. doi:10.100713412-014-0206-8

Roberts, D. H., & Koeplin, J. P. (2011). Sustainability reporting practices in Portugal: Greenwashing or triple bottom line? *International Business & Economics Research Journal, 6*(9). doi:10.19030/iber.v6i9.3403

Robertson, R. (1995). Glocalization: time-space and homogeneity-heterogeneity. In Global Modernities. London: Sage. doi:10.4135/9781446250563.n2

Robertson, R. (1992). *Globalization: Social Theory and Global Culture*. London: Sage.

Robertson, R. (1994). Globalisation or Glocalisation? *Journal of International Communication*, *1*(1), 33–52. doi:10.1080/13216597.1994.9751780

Robson, P. J. A., & Bennett, R. J. (2000). SME growth: The relationship with business advice and external collaboration. *Small Business Economics*, *15*(3), 193–208. doi:10.1023/A:1008129012953

Rockström, J., Steffen, W., Noone, K., Persson, Å., Chapin, F. S. I. I. I., Lambin, E., ... Foley, J. (2009). Planetary boundaries: Exploring the safe operating space for humanity. *Ecology and Society*, *14*(2), art32. doi:10.5751/ES-03180-140232

Roddy, G., Cowan, C. A., & Hutchinson, G. (1996). Consumer attitudes and behaviour to organic foods in Ireland. *Journal of International Consumer Marketing*, *9*(2), 41–63. doi:10.1300/J046v09n02_03

Rodríguez Muñoz José Manuel. (2011). la políticas públicas de fomento de la responsabilidad social empresarial. *Aranzadi, 7*, 7.

Rodríguez Zapatero, Maribel, Rodríguez Jiménez Magdalena, la mujer en la empresa familiar, revista de empresa familiar, Volumen 1, nº 2., págs. 20-25.

Rodriguez, M. J., & Guzman, C. (2013). Innovation in social economy firms. *Management Decision*, *51*(5), 986–998. doi:10.1108/MD-08-2012-0538

Rohdin, P., & Thollander, P. (2006). Barreirs to and driving forces for energy efficiency in the non-energy intensive manufacturing industries in Sweden. *Energy*, *31*(12), 1836–1844. doi:10.1016/j.energy.2005.10.010

Roininen, K., Arvola, A., & Lähteenmäki, L. (2006). Exploring consumers' perceptions of local food with two different qualitative techniques: Laddering and word association. *Food Quality and Preference*, *17*(1), 20–30. doi:10.1016/j.foodqual.2005.04.012

Ron Latas, R. (2011). La *empresa familiar en el Derecho del Trabajo*. netbiblo.

Roome, N. (1992). Developing environmental management strategies. *Business Strategy and the Environment*, *1*(1), 11–24. doi:10.1002/bse.3280010104

Rowley, C., & Warner, M. (2013). Strategic challenges and issues for Chinese managers and management in the global economy: Conclusions. *Asia Pacific Business Review*, *19*(4), 617–624. doi:10.1080/13602381.2013.832918

Roy, W., & Yvrande-Billon, A. (2007). Ownership, contractual practices and technical efficiency: The case of urban public transport in France. *Journal of Transport Economics and Policy*, *41*(2), 257–282.

Rudberg, M., Waldemarsson, M., & Lidestam, H. (2013). Strategic perspectives on energy management: A case study in the process industry. *Applied Energy*, *104*, 487–496. doi:10.1016/j.apenergy.2012.11.027

Rumelt, R. P., Schendel, D. E., & Teece, D. J. (1991). Strategic Management and Economics. *Strategic Management Journal*, *12*(S2), 5–29. doi:10.1002mj.4250121003

Rumelt, R. P., Schendel, D. E., & Teece, D. J. (1994). *Fundamental Issues in Strategy: A Research Agenda*. Boston: Harvard Business School Press.

Rusconi, G. (1987). Il ruolo del bilancio sociale nel contesto dell'economia aziendale. *Rivista Italiana di Ragioneria e di Economia Aziendale*, (3/4), 171-187.

Russel Bernard, H. (1988). *Research methods in cultural anthropology*. Qualitative and.

Russo, A., & Perrini, F. (2010). Investigating stakeholder theory and social capital: CSR in large firms and SMEs. *Journal of Business Ethics*, *91*(2), 207–221. doi:10.100710551-009-0079-z

Russo, A., & Tencati, A. (2009). Formal vs. informal CSR strategies: Evidence from Italian micro, small, medium-sized, and large firms. *Journal of Business Ethics*, *85*(S2), 339–353. doi:10.100710551-008-9736-x

Saeidi, S. P., Sofian, S., Saeidi, P., Saeidi, S. P., & Saaeidi, S. A. (2015). How does corporate social responsibility contribute to firm financial performance? The mediating role of competitive advantage, reputation, and customer satisfaction. *Journal of Business Research*, *68*(2), 341–350. doi:10.1016/j.jbusres.2014.06.024

Sage, C. (2003). Social embeddedness and relations of regard: Alternative 'good food' networks in south-west Ireland. *Journal of Rural Studies*, *19*(1), 47–60. doi:10.1016/S0743-0167(02)00044-X

Salazar, N. B. (2005). Tourism and glocalization, 'Local' Tour Guiding. *Annals of Tourism Research*, *32*(3), 628–646. doi:10.1016/j.annals.2004.10.012

Salustri, A. & Vigano, F. (2017). *The non-profit sector as a foundation for the interaction among the social economy, the public sector and the market.* MPRA Paper No. 78113, p. 27.

Salvato, C., & Moores, K. (2010). Research on accounting in family firms: Past accomplishments and future challenges. *Family Business Review*, *23*(3), 193–215. doi:10.1177/0894486510375069

Sánchez-Hernández, M. I. (2015). Clusters as entrepreneurial ecosystems for Corporate Social Resposibility in SMEs. In L. Carvalho (Ed.), *Handbook of Research on Entrepreneurial Success and its Impact on Regional Development* (pp. 72–87). Hershey, PA: IGI Global.

Sánchez-Hernández, M. I., Bnegil-Palacios, T., & Sanguino-Galván, R. (2017). Competitive success in responsible regional ecosystems: An empirical approach in Spain focused on the firms'relationship with stakeholders. *Sustainability*, *9*(3), 449. doi:10.3390u9030449

Santana, A., Vaccaro, A., & Wood, D. J. (2009). Ethics and the Networked Business. *Journal of Business Ethics*, *90*(S4), 661–681. doi:10.100710551-010-0599-6

Sanzo-Perez, M. J., Álvarez-González, L. I., & Rey-García, M. (2015). How to encourage social innovations: A resource-based approach. *Service Industries Journal*, *35*(7/8), 430–447. doi:10.1080/02642069.2015.1015517

Saonara, G. (2009). *Segnali sulla città "glocale"*. Retrieved September 3, from http://www.argomenti2000.it

Savlovschi, L. I., & Robu, N. R. (2011). The role of SMEs in modern economy. *Economia. Seria Management*, *14*(1), 277–281.

Scagnelli, S. D., Corazza, L., & Cisi, M. (2013). How SMEs disclose their sustainability performance. Which variables influence the choice of reporting guidelines? In L. Songini, A. Pistoni, & C. Herzig (Eds.), *Accounting and control for sustainability* (pp. 77–114). Emerald Group Publishing Limited.

Scarpa, R., & Del Giudice, T. (2004). Market segmentation via mixed logit: Extra-virgin olive oil in urban Italy. *Journal of Agricultural & Food Industrial Organization*, *2*(1). doi:10.2202/1542-0485.1080

Schader, C., Baumgart, L., Landert, J., Muller, A., Ssebunya, B., Blockeel, J., ... Gerrard, C. (2016). Using the sustainability monitoring and assessment routine (smart) for the systematic analysis of trade-offs and synergies between sustainability dimensions and themes at farm level. *Sustainability*, *8*(3), 274. doi:10.3390u8030274

Schader, C., Grenz, J., Meier, M., & Stolze, M. (2014). Scope and precision of sustainability assessment approaches to food systems. *Ecology and Society*, *19*(3), 42. doi:10.5751/ES-06866-190342

Schaltegger, S., & Burrit, R. (2006). Corporate Sustainability Accounting: A Catchphrase for Compliant Corporations or a Business Decision Support for Sustainability Leaders? In Sustainability Accounting and Reporting. Springer.

Schaltegger, S., & Müller, K. (1997). Calculating the true profitability of pollution prevention. *Greener Management International*, 53–68.

Schaltegger, S., & Wegner, M. (2006). Integrative Management of Sustainability Performance Measurement and Reporting. *International Journal of Accounting and Performance Evaluation*, (3), 1-19.

Schaltegger, S., Bennett, M., & Burritt, R. (2006). *Sustainability accounting and reporting (21)*. Springer Science and Business Media. doi:10.1007/978-1-4020-4974-3

Schaltegger, S., Bennett, M., & Burritt, R. (2006). Sustainability Accounting and Reporting: Development, Linkages and Reflection. In R. B. S. Schaltegger & M. Bennett (Eds.), *Sustainability Accounting and Reporting* (pp. 1–33). Dordrecht: Springer. doi:10.1007/978-1-4020-4974-3_1

Schaltegger, S., & Burrit, R. (2000). *Contemporary environmental accounting: issues, concepts and practice*. Sheffield, UK: Greenleaf.

Schaltegger, S., & Burritt, R. (2015). Business Cases and Corporate Engagement with Sustainability: Differentiating Ethical Motivations. *Journal of Business Ethics*. doi:10.100710551-015-2938-0

Schaltegger, S., & Burritt, R. L. (2006). Corporate sustainability accounting: A nightmare or a dream coming true? *Business Strategy and the Environment*, *15*(5), 293–295. doi:10.1002/bse.537

Schaltegger, S., & Burritt, R. L. (2010). Sustainability accounting for companies: Catchphrase or decision support for business leaders? *Journal of World Business*, *45*(4), 375–384. doi:10.1016/j.jwb.2009.08.002

Schaltegger, S., Burritt, R., & Petersen, H. (2003). *An Introduction to Corporate Environmental Management: Striving for Sustainability*. Sheffield, UK: Emerald Group Publishing Limited; doi:10.1108/meq.2003.14.4.541.4

Schaltegger, S., & Csutora, M. (2012). Carbon accounting for sustainability and management. Status quo and challenges. *Journal of Cleaner Production*, *36*, 1–16. doi:10.1016/j.jclepro.2012.06.024

Schaltegger, S., Etxeberria, I. Á., & Ortas, E. (2017). Innovating Corporate Accounting and Reporting for Sustainability – Attributes and Challenges. *Sustainable Development*, *25*(2), 113–122. doi:10.1002d.1666

Schaltegger, S., Herzing, C., Kleiber, O., & Müller, J. (2002). *Sustainability management in business enterprises. Concepts and instruments for sustainable organisation development* (2nd ed.). Bonn, Germany: The Federal Ministry for the Environment, Nature Conservation and Nuclear Safety.

Schaltegger, S., Lüdeke-Freund, F., & Hansen, E. G. (2012). Business cases for sustainability: The role of business model innovation for corporate sustainability. *International Journal of Innovation and Sustainable Development*, *6*(2), 95–119. doi:10.1504/IJISD.2012.046944

Schaltegger, S., & Wagner, M. (2006). Integrative management of sustainability performance, measurement and reporting. *International Journal of Accounting, Auditing and Performance Evaluation*, *3*(1), 1–19. doi:10.1504/IJAAPE.2006.010098

Schaltegger, S., & Wagner, M. (2011). Sustainable entrepreneurship and sustainability innovation: Categories and interactions. *Business Strategy and the Environment*, *20*(4), 222–237. doi:10.1002/bse.682

Schaltegger, S., & Zvezdov, D. (2015). Expanding material flow cost accounting. Framework, review and potentials. *Journal of Cleaner Production*, *108*, 1333–1341. doi:10.1016/j.jclepro.2014.08.040

Schleenbecker, R., & Hamm, U. (2013). Consumers' Perception of Organic Product Characteristics. A Review. *Appetite*, *71*, 420–429. doi:10.1016/j.appet.2013.08.020 PMID:24012637

Schnell, S. M., & Reese, J. F. (2014). Microbreweries, place, and identity in the United States. In *The geography of beer* (pp. 167–187). Springer. doi:10.1007/978-94-007-7787-3_15

Schulze, M., Nehler, H., Ottosson, M., & Thollander, P. (2016). Energy management in industry – a systematic review of previous findings and an integrative conceptual framework. *Journal of Cleaner Production*, *112*, 3692–3708. doi:10.1016/j.jclepro.2015.06.060

Schulze, W. S., Lubatkin, M. H., Dino, R. M., & Bucholtz, A. K. (2001). Agency Relationships in Family Firms: Theory and Evidence. *Organization Science*, *12*(2), 99–116. doi:10.1287/orsc.12.2.99.10114

Schulze, W. S., Lubatkin, M. H., & Dino, R. N. (2002). Altruism, agency, and the competitiveness of family firms. *Managerial and Decision Economics*, *23*(4-5), 247–259. doi:10.1002/mde.1064

Sciascia, S., Mazzola, P., Astrachan, J. H., & Pieper, T. M. (2012). The role of family ownership in international entrepreneurship: Exploring nonlinear effects. *Small Business Economics*, *38*(1), 15–31. doi:10.100711187-010-9264-9

Searcy, C. (2012). Corporate sustainability performance measurement systems: A review and research agenda. *Journal of Business Ethics*, *107*(3), 239–253. doi:10.100710551-011-1038-z

Sebhatu, S. P. (2009). *Sustainability performance measurement for sustainable organizations: beyond compliance and reporting*. Karlstad: Service Research Centre Karlstad University.

Sedda, F. (Ed.). (2004). *Glocal. Sul presente a venire*. Roma, Italy: Sossella.

Sen, S., & Bhattacharya, C. B. (2001). Does Doing Good Always Lead to Doing Better? Consumer Reactions to Corporate Social Responsibility. *JMR, Journal of Marketing Research*, *38*(2), 225–243. doi:10.1509/jmkr.38.2.225.18838

Sethi, G., & Ghosh, A. M. (Eds.). (2008). *Towards Cleaner Technologies A process story in the Firozabad glass industry cluster*. New Delhi: The Energy and Resources Institute.

Sexton, T. R. (1986). The methodology of data envelopment analysis. *New Directions for Evaluation*, *1986*(32), 7–29. doi:10.1002/ev.1438

Seyfang, G. (2006). Ecological citizenship and sustainable consumption: Examining local organic food networks. *Journal of Rural Studies*, *22*(4), 383–395. doi:10.1016/j.jrurstud.2006.01.003

Shafie, F. A., & Rennie, D. (2012). Consumer perceptions towards organic food. *Procedia: Social and Behavioral Sciences*, *49*, 360–367. doi:10.1016/j.sbspro.2012.07.034

Shamsuddoha, M. (2008). *Globalization to Glocalization: A Conceptual Analysis*. Retrieved July 23, 2009 from http://ssrn.com/abstract=1321662

Shang, T., & Shi, Y. (2013). The emergence of the electric vehicle industry in Chinese Shandong Province: A research design for understanding business ecosystem capabilities. *Journal of Chinese Entreprenuership*, *5*(1), 61–75. doi:10.1108/17561391311297888

Shank, J. (1989). Strategic cost management: New wine or just new bottles? *Journal of Management Accounting Research*, *1*, 47–65.

Shank, J. (1996). Analysing technology investments from NPV to strategic cost management. *Management Accounting Research*, *7*(2), 185–197. doi:10.1006/mare.1996.0011

Shaw, E. (2006). Small Firm Networking: An Insight into Contents and Motivating Factors. *International Small Business Journal*, *24*(1), 5–29. doi:10.1177/0266242606059777

Shen, B., Price, L., & Lu, H. (2012). Energy audit practices in China: National and local experiences and issues. *Energy Policy*, *46*, 346–358. doi:10.1016/j.enpol.2012.03.069

Shiva, V. (2010). Earth Democracy: Beyond Dead Democracy and Killing Economies. *Capitalism, Nature, Socialism*, *21*(1), 83–95. doi:10.1080/10455751003655922

Shiva, V. (2016). *Who Really Feeds the World? The Failures of Agribusiness and the Promise of Agroecology*. North Atlantic Books.

Shi, Y. (2007). The organizational factors of globalization and localization: A "travel of ideas" approach. *Globe Management Review*, *1*(1), 16–25.

Siano, A., Vollero, A., & Siglioccolo, M. (2015). *Corporate Communication Management*. Torino, Italy: Giappichelli.

Siggelkow, N. (2007). Persuasion with case studies. *Academy of Management Journal*, *50*(1), 20–24. doi:10.5465/AMJ.2007.24160882

Simons, R. (2000). *Performance Measurement and Control Systems for Implementing Strategy: text and cases*. Englewood Cliff, NJ: Prentice Hall.

Singh, R. K., Garg, S. K., & Deshmukh, S. G. (2008). Strategy development by SMEs for competitiveness: A review. *Benchmarking: An International Journal*, *15*(5), 525–547. doi:10.1108/14635770810903132

Small, L. (2011). *Corporate Responsibility, Marketing and Economic Development in Emerging Markets*. Retrieved from http://www.accountability.org/about-us/news/accountability-1/accountability.html

Smed, S., Andersen, L. M., Kærgård, N., & Daugbjerg, C. (2013). A Matter of Trust: How Trust Influence Organic Consumption. *The Journal of Agricultural Science*, *5*(7), 91.

Smida, L., Hrdinova, G., Sakal, P., & Syc, M. (2011). A possibility of social inclusion by responsible entrepreneurship in Slovakia. *Annals of DAAAM and Proceedings of the International DAAAM Symposium 2011: Intelligent Manufacturing and Automation: Power of Knowledge and Creativity*. Vienna, Austria: Academic Press.

Smith, B. D. (2013). Our glocal market. *Journal of Medical Marketing*, *13*(3), 133–134. doi:10.1177/1745790413500130

Smith, T. (2005). Institutional and social investors find common ground. *Journal of Investing*, *14*(3), 57–65. doi:10.3905/joi.2005.580550

SOAAN-IFOAM. (2013). *Best practice guidelines for agriculture and value chains*. Retrieved November 15, 2016, from www.ifoam.bio/sites/default/files/best_practice_guideline_v1.0_ratified.pdf

Soares, C., Fialho, J. A. S., Chau, F., Gageiro, J., & Pestana, H. (2012). *A Economia Social e a sua Sustentabilidade como Fator de Inclusão Social*. Lisboa: Serga.

Sobh, R., Belk, R., & Gressel, J. (2014). Mimicry and modernity in the Middle East: Fashion invisibility and young women of the Arab Gulf. *Consumption Markets & Culture*, *17*(4), 392–412. doi:10.1080/10253866.2013.865166

Søderberg, A. (2015). Recontextualising a strategic concept within a globalising company: A case study on carlsberg's 'winning behaviours' strategy. *International Journal of Human Resource Management*, *26*(2), 231–257. doi:10.1080/09585192.2014.922358

Songini, L. (2007). The professionalization of family firms: theory and practice. In *Handbook of Research on Family Business*. Cheltenham, UK: Edward Elgar.

Songini, L., Gnan, L., & Malmi, T. (2013). The role and impact of accounting in family business. *Journal of Family Business Strategy*, *4*(2), 71–83. doi:10.1016/j.jfbs.2013.04.002

Sonnino, R., & Marsden, T. K. (2006). Beyond the divide: Rethinking relations between alternative and conventional food networks in Europe. *Journal of Economic Geography*, *6*(2), 181–199. doi:10.1093/jeg/lbi006

Spaargaren, G., Oosterveer, P., & Loeber, A. (2011). *Sustainability Transitions in Food Consumption, Retail and Production. Food practices in transition: changing food consumption, retail and production in the age of reflexive modernity.* New York, NY: Routeledge.

Spear, R. (2013). *Social economy - laying the groundwork for innovative solutions to today's challenges. European Commission*. Luxembourg: Publications Office of the European Union.

Spence, L. J. (2014). Small Business Social Responsibility: Expanding Core CSR Theory. *Business & Society*. 10.1177/0007650314523256

Spence, L. J. (2014a). Business ethics and social responsibility in small firms. In Handbook of research on small business and entrepreneurship. Northampton, MA: Edward Elgar. doi:10.4337/9781849809245.00031

Spence, L. J. (1999). Does size matter? The state of the art in small business ethics. *Business Ethics (Oxford, England)*, *8*(3), 163–174. doi:10.1111/1467-8608.00144

Spence, L. J. (2007). CSR and small business in a European policy context: The five "C" s of CSR and small business research agenda 2007. *Business and Society Review*, *112*(4), 533–552. doi:10.1111/j.1467-8594.2007.00308.x

Spence, L. J. (2014b). Small business social responsibility: Redrawing core CSR theory. *Business & Society*. doi:10.1177/0007650314523256

Spence, L. J. (2016). Small Business Social Responsibility: Expanding Core CSR Theory. *Business & Society*, *55*(1), 23–55. doi:10.1177/0007650314523256

Spence, L. J., Agyemang, G., & Rinaldi, L. (2012). *Environmental Aspects of Sustainability: SMEs and the Role of the Accountant*. London, UK: Certified Accountants Educational Trust.

Spence, L. J., Habisch, A., & Schmidpeter, R. (2004). *Responsibility and social capital: The world of small and medium sized enterprises*. Palgrave Macmillan. doi:10.1007/978-1-349-72886-2

Spence, L. J., & Rinaldi, L. (2014). Governmentality in accounting and accountability: A case study of embedding sustainability in a supply chain. *Accounting, Organizations and Society*, *39*(6), 433–452. doi:10.1016/j.aos.2012.03.003

Spence, L. J., & Rutherfoord, R. (2001). Social responsibility, profit maximisation and the small firm owner-manager. *Journal of Small Business and Enterprise Development*, *8*(2), 126–139. doi:10.1108/EUM0000000006818

Spence, L. J., & Rutherfoord, R. (2003). Small business and empirical perspectives in business ethics [editorial]. *Journal of Business Ethics*, *47*(1), 1–5. doi:10.1023/A:1026205109290

Spillare, S. (2016). Agro-ecological consumerism between system response and glocal reflexivity: The example of organic food consumption. *Quality - Access to Success*, (17), 580-584.

Spitzer, M. A. (1992). Calculating the benefits of pollution prevention. *Pollution Engineering*, *24*(15), 33–42.

Sroufe, R., Narasimhan, R., Montabon, F., & Wang, X. (2002). Environmental management practices: a framework. *Greener Management International,* (40), 23.

Stacchezzini, R., Melloni, G., & Lai, A. (2016). Sustainability management and reporting: The role of integrated reporting for communicating corporate sustainability management. *Journal of Cleaner Production, 136*, 102–110. doi:10.1016/j.jclepro.2016.01.109

Stafford, K., Duncan, K. A., Danes, S. M., & Winter, M. (1999). A research model of sustainable family businesses. *Family Business Review, 12*(3), 197–208. doi:10.1111/j.1741-6248.1999.00197.x

Stahler-Sholk, R. (2010). The zapatista social movement: Innovation and sustainability. *Alternatives, 35*(3), 269–290. doi:10.1177/030437541003500306

Stampacchia, P., Mele, C., & Russo Spena, T. (2008). Processi di governo e crescita internazionale nelle PMI familiari. Il caso Harmont&Blaine. In C. Devecchi & G. Fraquelli (Eds.), *Dinamiche di sviluppo e internazionalizzazione del family business* (pp. 501–518). Bologna: Edizione Il Mulino.

Stechemesser, K., & Guenther, E. (2012). Carbon accounting: A systematic literature review. *Journal of Cleaner Production, 36*, 17–38. doi:10.1016/j.jclepro.2012.02.021

Storey, D. J. (1994). *Understanding the Small Business Sector*. Thomson Learning Emea; doi:10.1016/0024-6301(95)90953-2

Strand, R., & Freeman, R. E. (2015). Scandinavian cooperative advantage: The theory and practice of stakeholder engagement in Scandinavia. *Journal of Business Ethics, 127*(1), 65–85. doi:10.100710551-013-1792-1

Strand, R., Freeman, R. E., & Hockerts, K. (2015). Corporate social responsibility and sustainability in Scandinavia: An overview. *Journal of Business Ethics, 127*(1), 1–15. doi:10.100710551-014-2224-6

Strauss, A., & Corbin, J. (1998). *Basics of qualitative research: Techniques and procedures for developing grounded theory*. Thousand Oaks, CA: Sage Publications.

Strizhakova, Y., & Coulter, R. A. (2013). The "green" side of materialism in emerging BRIC and developed markets: The moderating role of global cultural identity. *International Journal of Research in Marketing, 30*(1), 69–82. doi:10.1016/j.ijresmar.2012.08.003

Strobel, M., & Redmann, C. (2002). Flow Cost Accounting, an Accounting Approach Based on the Actual Flows of Materials. In M. Bennett & J. J. Bouma (Eds.), *Environmental Management Accounting: Informational and Institutional Developments* (pp. 67–82). Dordrecht: Springer Netherlands.

Stubbs, W., Higgins, C., & Milne, M. (2012). Why do companies not produce sustainability reports? *Business Strategy and the Environment, 22*(7), 456–470. doi:10.1002/bse.1756

Suchman, M. C. (1995). Managing Legitimacy: Strategic and Institutional Approaches. *Academy of Management Review, 20*(3), 571–610. doi:10.5465/AMR.1995.9508080331

Supino, S. & Sica, D., (2011). Nuovi paradigmi di rendicontazione d'impresa: il report integrato. *Esperienze d'impresa, 19*(2), 81-92.

Svensson, G. (2001). Glocalization Of Business Activities: A Glocal Strategy Approach. *Management Decision, 39*(1), 6–14. doi:10.1108/EUM0000000005403

Svensson, G. (2003). Beyond Global Marketing And The Globalization Of Marketing Activities. *Management Decision, 40*(6), 574–583. doi:10.1108/00251740210433963

Svensson, G., Padin, C., & Eriksson, D. (2016). Glocal business sustainability - performance beyond zero! *International Journal of Procurement Management*, *9*(1), 15–26. doi:10.1504/IJPM.2016.073385

Swoboda, B., Meierer, M., Foscht, T., & Morschett, D. (2011). International SME Alliances: The Impact of Alliance Building and Configurational Fit on Success. *Long Range Planning*, *44*(4), 271–288. doi:10.1016/j.lrp.2011.04.002

Symbola, U. (2010). *GreenItaly Rapporto 2010*. Academic Press.

Symbola, U. (2016). *GreenItaly Rapporto 2016*. Academic Press.

Tagiuri, R., & Davis, J. A. (1982). *Bivalent Attributes of the Family Firm*. Working paper. Harvard Business School.

Tai, S. H. C., & Wong, Y. H. (1998). Advertising decision making in Asia: "Glocal" versus "regcal" approach. *Journal of Managerial Issues*, *10*(3), 318–339.

Tambunan, T. (2011). Development of small and medium enterprises in a developing country: The Indonesian case. *Journal of Enterprising Communities: People and Places in the Global Economy*, *5*(1), 68–82. doi:10.1108/17506201111119626

Tardia, T. (2002). "Glocalizzazione", un'alternativa alla globalizzazione? *Pmi*, *8*(12), 26–30.

Tashakkori, A., & Teddlie, C. (2010). *Sage Handbook of Mixed Methods in Social & Behavioral Research*. Thousand Oaks, CA: Sage Publications. doi:10.4135/9781506335193

Taurino, T. (2015). A Cluster Reference Framework for Analyzing Sustainability of SME Clusters. *Procedia CIRP*, *30*, 132–137. doi:10.1016/j.procir.2015.02.138

Teece, D. J. (2007). Explicating dynamic capabilities: The nature and microfoundations of (sustainable) enterprise performance. *Strategic Management Journal*, *28*(13), 1319–1350. doi:10.1002mj.640

Teece, D. J., Pisano, G., & Shuen, A. (1997). Dynamic Capabilities and Strategic Management. *Strategic Management Journal*, *18*(7), 509–533. doi:

Tencati, A., Perrini, F., & Pogutz, S. (2004). New tools to foster corporate socially responsible behavior. *Journal of Business Ethics*, *53*(1), 173–190. doi:10.1023/B:BUSI.0000039407.37497.44

Teoh, S. H., Welch, I., & Wazzan, C. P. (1999). The effect of socially activist investment policies on the financial markets: Evidence from the South African boycott. *Journal of Business Ethics*, *72*(1), 35–89.

Terziev, V. (2017). *Social entrepreneurship as an opportunity to model an active social program. In Topical issues of contemporary science: Collection of scientific articles* (pp. 6–12). Valencia, Venezuela: C.E.I.M.

Testa, F., Grappio, P., Gusmerotti, N. M., Iraldo, F., & Frey, M. (2016). Examining green public procurement using content analysis: Existing difficulties for procurers and useful recommendations. *Environment, Development and Sustainability*, *18*(1), 197–219. doi:10.100710668-015-9634-1

Tettamanzi, P., Luoni, L., & Fossati, S. (2009). *Il bilancio sociale e la comunicazione con gli stakeholder*. Torino, Italia: Pearson Education.

Thanasanborrisude, J., & Phadoongsitthi, M. (2015). Firm characteristics and CSR disclosures: Case study in MAI firms. *Journal of Accounting Profession, 11*(30), 23-40. (in Thai)

Thanassoulis, E. (2001). *Introduction to the theory and application of data envelopment analysis*. Dordrecht: Kluwer Academic Publishers. doi:10.1007/978-1-4615-1407-7

The Conversation. (2015). *Climate change is hitting African farmers the hardest of all*. Retrieved 12 May, 2017 from http://theconversation.com/climate-change-is-hitting-african-farmers-the-hardest-of-all-40845

Thollander, P., & Ottosson, M. (2010). Energy management practices in Swedish energy-intensive industries. *Journal of Cleaner Production*, *18*(12), 1125–1133. doi:10.1016/j.jclepro.2010.04.011

Thompson, C. J., & Arsel, Z. (2004). The Starbucks and Consumers' (Anticorporate) Experiences of Glocalization. *The Journal of Consumer Research*, *31*(3), 631–642. doi:10.1086/425098

Thomson, I. (2014). Accounting and Sustainability: Mapping the terrain. In J. Bebbington, J. Unerman, & B. O'Dwyer (Eds.), *Sustainability accounting and accountability*. Routledge.

Thorpe, J., & Prakash-Mani, K. (2003). Developing value: The business case for sustainability in emerging markets. *Greener Management International*, (44), 17.

Thorsøe, M. H. (2015). Maintaining trust and credibility in a Continuously Evolving Organic Food System. *Journal of Agricultural & Environmental Ethics*, *28*(4), 767–787. doi:10.100710806-015-9559-6

Thorsøe, M. H., Christensen, T., & Povlsen, K. K. (2016). Organics' are good, but we don't know exactly what the term means! Trust and Knowledge in Organic Consumption. *Food, Culture, & Society*, *19*(4), 681–704. doi:10.1080/15528014.2016.1243767

Thorsøe, M. H., Kjeldsen, C., & Noe, E. (2017). It's never too late to join the revolution!–Enabling new modes of production in the contemporary Danish food system. *European Planning Studies*, *25*(7), 1166–1183. doi:10.1080/09654313.2016.1267112

Thurnell-Read, T. (2014). Craft, tangibility and affect at work in the microbrewery. *Emotion, Space and Society*, *13*, 46–54. doi:10.1016/j.emospa.2014.03.001

Tikkanen, H. (1998). The network approach in analyzing international marketing and purchasing operations: A case study of a European SME's focal net 1992-95. *Journal of Business and Industrial Marketing*, *13*(2), 109–131. doi:10.1108/08858629810213333

Tilley, F. (2000). Small firm environmental ethics: How deep do they go? *Business Ethics (Oxford, England)*, *9*(1), 31–41. doi:10.1111/1467-8608.00167

Tinsley, S. (2002). EMS models for business strategy development. *Business Strategy and the Environment*, *11*(6), 376–390. doi:10.1002/bse.340

Tinsley, S. J., & Melton, K. (1997). Sustainable development and its effect on the marketing planning process. *Eco-Management and Auditing*, *4*(3), 116–126. doi:

Tomazinis, A. R. (1977). *Study of efficiency indicators of urban public transportation systems. Final report.* Philadelphia: Transportation Studies Center. doi:10.2172/5406787

Tommaso, S. (2010). *Distretti e reti di imprese. Evoluzione organizzativa, finanza innovativa, valutazione mediante rating*. Roma, Italy: Angeli.

Tomšič, N., Bojnec, Š., & Simčič, B. (2015). Corporate sustainability and economic performance in small and medium sized enterprises. *Journal of Cleaner Production*, *108*, 603–612. doi:10.1016/j.jclepro.2015.08.106

Tone, K. (2001). A slacks-based measure of efficiency in data envelopment analysis. *European Journal of Operational Research*, *130*(3), 498–509. doi:10.1016/S0377-2217(99)00407-5

Torjusen, H., Lieblein, G., Wandel, M., & Francis, C. A. (2001). Food system orientation and quality perception among consumers and producers of organic food in Hedmark County, Norway. *Food Quality and Preference*, *12*(3), 207–216. doi:10.1016/S0950-3293(00)00047-1

Toro-González, D., McCluskey, J. J., & Mittelhammer, R. C. (2014). Beer snobs do exist: Estimation of beer demand by type. *Journal of Agricultural and Resource Economics*, *39*(2), 174–187.

Torquati, B., Viganò, E., & Taglioni, C. (2016). Construction of Alternative Food Networks for organic products: A case study of "Organized Groups of Supply and Demand". *New Medit*, *15*(4), 53–63.

Torres, L., & Pina, V. (2002). Delivering public services—mechanisms and consequences: Changes in public service delivery in the EU countries. *Public Money & Management*, *22*(4), 41–48. doi:10.1111/1467-9302.00328

Tregear, A. (2011). Progressing knowledge in alternative and local food networks: Critical reflections and a research agenda. *Journal of Rural Studies*, *27*(4), 419–430. doi:10.1016/j.jrurstud.2011.06.003

Truant, E. (2009). Sustainability Management: a Business Model Applied to Publicly-Owned Enterprises in the Waste Sector. *Proceedings of the 2nd Annual EuroMed Conference of the EuroMed-Academy-of-Business: Managerial And Entrepreneurial Developments In The Mediterranean Area*, 1824-1837.

Truant, E. (2015). Product and Process Innovation to Exploit new Market Opportunities and Overcome the Crisis: An Italian Family Firm Case Study. *Proceedings of the 10th European Conference on Innovation and Entrepreneurship (ECIE 2015)*, 716-723.

Truant, E., Broccardo, L., & Culasso, F. (2015). Adoption And Benefits Of Management Accounting Practices In Italian Smes: An Explorative Survey. *Proceedings of the 8th Annual Conference of the EuroMed-Academy-of-Business: Innovation, Entrepreneurship And Sustainable Value Chain In A Dynamic Environment*, 2310-2323.

Truant, E. (2014). *Strumenti di pianificazione & controllo e performance aziendali. Confronto tra family e non-family firms*. Torino, Italy: Giappichelli.

Truant, E., Corazza, L., & Scagnelli, S. D. (2017). Sustainability and Risk Disclosure: An Exploratory Study on Sustainability Reports. *Sustainability*, *9*(4), 636. doi:10.3390u9040636

Turner, W. C., & Doty, S. (2007). *Energy Management Handbook*. Fairmont Press.

Uhlaner, L. M., van Goor-Balk, H. J. M., & Masurel, E. (2004). Family business and corporate social responsibility in a sample of Dutch firms. *Journal of Small Business and Enterprise Development*, *11*(2), 186–194. doi:10.1108/14626000410537128

Ullman, A. (1985). Data in search of a theory: A critical examination of the relationship among social performance, social disclosure and economic performance of US firms. *Academical Management Review*, *10*, 540–557.

Unioncamere e Ufficio Studi di Mediobanca. (2016). *Le medie imprese industriali italiane*. Mediobanca Ufficio Studi.

United Nations Division for Sustainable Development (UNDSD). (2001). *Environmental management accounting: Procedures and principles*. New York: UNDSD.

United Nations World Commission on Environment and Development (UNWCED). (1987). *Report of the World Commission on Environment and Development: Our Common Future*. Oxford, UK: Oxford University Press.

Usunier, J. C., Lee, J. A., & Lee, J. (2005). *Marketing across cultures*. Pearson Education.

Vaciago, G. (2003). Le piccole imprese in un mondo "glocale". *L'imprenditore*, (10), 41-42.

Valdani, E. (2014). La politica del prodotto. In E. Valdani & P. Bertoli (Eds.), *Mercati internazionali e marketing* (pp. 315–356). Milano, Italy: Egea.

Vallaster, C., Lindgreen, A., & Maon, F. (2012). Strategically Leveraging Corporate Social Responsibility: A Corporate Brand Perspective. *California Management Review*, *54*(3), 34–60. doi:10.1525/cmr.2012.54.3.34

Vallejo Martos, M. C. (2005). Cuando definir es una necesidad. Una propuesta integradora y operativa del concepto de empresa familiar. *Investigaciones Europeas de Dirección y Economía de la Empresa, 11*(3), 151–171.

Vallejo, M. C. (2008). Is the culture of family firms really different? A value-based model for its survival through generations. *Journal of Business Ethics, 81*(2), 261–279. doi:10.100710551-007-9493-2

van de Vrande, V., de Jong, J. P. J., Vanhaverbeke, W., & de Rochemont, M. (2009). Open innovation in SMEs: Trends, motives and management challenges. *Technovation, 29*(6–7), 423–437. doi:10.1016/j.technovation.2008.10.001

Van Marrewijk, M. (2003). Concepts and Definitions of CSR and Corporate Sustainability: Between Agency and Communion. *Journal of Business Ethics, 44*(2), 95–105. doi:10.1023/A:1023331212247

Van Wijk, J., Van der Duim, R., Lamers, M., & Sumba, D. (2015). The emergence of institutional innovations in tourism: The evolution of the African Wildlife Foundation's tourism conservation enterprises. *Journal of Sustainable Tourism, 23*(1), 104–125. doi:10.1080/09669582.2014.927878

Varis, M., & Littunen, H. (2010). Types of innovation, sources of information and performance in entrepreneurial SMEs. *European Journal of Innovation Management, 13*(2), 128–154. doi:10.1108/14601061011040221

Vasudevan, S., & Higgins, B. (2004). Strategic Energy Risk Management for End Users. *Journal of Structured and Project Finance, 10*(1), 74–78. doi:10.3905/jsf.2004.74

Vázquez-Carrasco, R., & López-Pérez, M.E. (2013). Small & medium-sized enterprises and Corporate Social Responsibility: a systematic review of the literature. *Quality & Quantity, 47*(6), 3205-3218.

Vázquez-Carrasco, R., & López-Pérez, M. E. (2012). Small & medium-sized enterprises and Corporate Social Responsibility: A systematic review of the literature. *Quality & Quantity*. doi:10.100711135-012-9713-4

Veleva, V., & Ellenbecker, M. (2001). Indicators of sustainable production: Framework and methodology. *Journal of Cleaner Production, 9*(6), 519–549. doi:10.1016/S0959-6526(01)00010-5

Velte, P., & Stawinoga, M. (2017). Integrated reporting: The current state of empirical research, limitations and future research implications. *Journal of Management Control, 28*(3), 275–320. doi:10.100700187-016-0235-4

Veltmeyer, H. (2017). The social economy in Latin America as alternative development. *Canadian Journal of Development Studies*, 1–17. doi:10.1080/02255189.2017.1294052

Venturelli, A., Caputo, F., Leopizzi, R., Mastroleo, G., & Mio, C. (2017). How can CSR identity be evaluated? A pilot study using a Fuzzy Expert System. *Journal of Cleaner Production, 141*, 1000–1010. doi:10.1016/j.jclepro.2016.09.172

Vermiglio, F. (1984). *Il bilancio sociale nel quadro evolutivo del sistema d'impresa*. Messina, Italy: Grapho Editor.

Vézina, M., Malo, M.-C., & Ben Selma, M. (2017). Mature social economy enterprise and social innovation: The case of the Desjardins environment fund. *Annals of Public and Cooperative Economics, 88*(2), 257–278. doi:10.1111/apce.12169

Villalonga, B., & Amit, R. (2006). How do family ownership, control and management affect firms value? *Journal of Financial Economics, 80*(2), 385–417. doi:10.1016/j.jfineco.2004.12.005

Virtanen, T., Tuomaala, M., & Pentti, E. (2013). Energy efficiency complexities: A technical and managerial investigation. *Management Accounting Research, 24*(4), 401–416. doi:10.1016/j.mar.2013.06.002

Visser, W. (2012). *The future of CSR: Towards transformative CSR, or CSR 2.0*. Browser Download This Paper.

Visser, W. (2012). The Future of CSR: Towards Transformative CSR, or CSR 2.0. *Kaleidoscope Futures Paper Series, 1*, 1–17.

Visser, W. (2014). *CSR 2.0: Transforming corporate sustainability and responsibility*. Berlin: Springer. doi:10.1007/978-3-642-40874-8

Visser, W., & Kymal, C. (2015). Integrated value creation (IVC): Beyond corporate social responsibility (CSR) and creating shared value (CSV). *Journal of International Business Ethics*, *8*(1), 29.

Viton, P. A. (1997). Technical efficiency in multi-mode bus transit: A production frontier analysis. *Transportation Research Part B: Methodological*, *31*(1), 23–39. doi:10.1016/S0191-2615(96)00019-7

Viton, P. A. (1998). Changes in multi-mode bus transit efficiency, 1988–1992. *Transportation*, *25*(1), 1–21. doi:10.1023/A:1004906024774

Vives, A. (2006). Social and environmental responsibility in small and medium enterprises in Latin America. *Journal of Corporate Citizenship*, 21.

von Høivik, H. W., & Shankar, D. (2011). How Can SMEs in a Cluster Respond to Global Demands for Corporate Responsibility? *Journal of Business Ethics*, *101*(2), 175–195. doi:10.100710551-010-0708-6

Voss, C., Tsikriktsis, N., & Frohlich, M. (2002). Case research in operations management. *International Journal of Operations & Management Production Management*, *22*. 10.1108/01443570210414329

Vurro, C., Russo, A., & Perrini, F. (2009). Shaping Sustainable Value Chains: Network Determinants of Supply Chain Governance Models. *Journal of Business Ethics*, *90*(S4), 607–621. doi:10.100710551-010-0595-x

Vyakarnam, S., Bailey, A., Myers, A., & Burnett, D. (1997). Towards an understanding of ethical behaviour in small firms. *Journal of Business Ethics*, *16*(15), 1625–1636. doi:10.1023/A:1022452502299

Wagner, M. (2010). Corporate Social Performance and Innovation with High Social Benefits: A Quantitative Analysis. *Journal of Business Ethics*, *94*(4), 581–594. doi:10.100710551-009-0339-y

Wales, W. J., Gupta, V. K., & Mousa, F.-T. (2011). Empirical research on entrepreneurial orientation: An assessment and suggestions for future research. *International Small Business Journal*, *31*(4), 357–383. doi:10.1177/0266242611418261

Walley, N., & Whitehead, B. (1994). It's not easy being green. *Harvard Business Review*, *72*(3), 46–51. doi:10.2345/0899-8205(2007)41[336:INEBG]2.0.CO;2

Wander, M., & Bugge, A. (1997). Environmental concern in consumer evaluation of food quality. *Food Quality and Preference*, *8*(1), 19–26. doi:10.1016/S0950-3293(96)00004-3

Weber, M. (2008). The business case for corporate social responsibility: A company level measurement approach for CSR. *European Management Journal*, *26*(4), 247–261. doi:10.1016/j.emj.2008.01.006

Werther, W. B. Jr, & Chandler, B. (2005). Strategic Corporate Social Responsibility as Global Brand Insurance. *Business Horizons*, *48*(4), 317–324. doi:10.1016/j.bushor.2004.11.009

Whatmore, S., Stassart, P., & Renting, H. (2003). What's alternative about food networks? *Environment & Planning*, *35*(3), 389–391. doi:10.1068/a3621

Wheeler, A. (2009). *Designing Brand Identity: An Essential Guide for the Whole Branding Team*. New York: Wiley.

Wiengarten, F., Lo, C., & Lam, J. (2017). "How does Sustainability Leadership Affect Firm Performance? The Choices Associated with Appointing a Chief Officer of Corporate Social Responsibility". *Journal of Business Ethics*, *140*(3), 477–493. doi:10.100710551-015-2666-5

Wigginton, N. S. (2016). Evidence of an Anthropocene epoch. *Science*, *351*(6269), 134–136. doi:10.1126cience.351.6269.134-j

Willer, H., & Lernoud, J. (Eds.). (2017). *The World of Organic Agriculture. Statistics and Emerging Trends 2017. Research Institute of Organic Agriculture (FiBL)*. Frick & IFOAM – Organics International Bonn.

Williamson, D., Lynch Wood, G., & Ramsay, J. (2006). Drivers of Environmental Behaviour in Manufacturing SMEs and the Implications for CSR. *Journal of Business Ethics*, *67*(3), 317–330. doi:10.100710551-006-9187-1

Williams, S., & Schaefer, A. (2013). Small and medium-sized enterprises and sustainability: Managers' values and engagement with environmental and climate change issues. *Business Strategy and the Environment*, *22*(3), 173–186. doi:10.1002/bse.1740

Wilson, C., Williams, I., & Kemp, S. (2012). An evaluation of the impact and effectiveness of environmental legislation in small and medium-sized enterprises: Experiences from the UK. *Business Strategy and the Environment*, *21*(3), 141–156. doi:10.1002/bse.720

World Bank. (2015). *BRIEF: Small and Medium Enterprises (SMEs) Finance*. Retrieved 10 June, 2017 from http://www.worldbank.org/en/topic/financialsector/brief/smes-finance

World Business Council for Sustainable Development. (2001). *The Business Case for Sustainable Development: Making a Difference Towards the Johannesburg Summit 2002 and Beyond*. Available: http:// www. wbcsd. org

Worthington, I., Ram, M., & Jones, T. (2006). Exploring corporate social responsibility in the UK Asian small business community. *Journal of Business Ethics*, *67*(2), 201–217. doi:10.100710551-006-9024-6

Wu, J. (2009). Environmental compliance: The good, the bad, and the super green. *Journal of Environmental Management*, *90*(11), 3363–3381. doi:10.1016/j.jenvman.2009.05.017 PMID:19573979

Yama, H. (2016). A perspective of cross-cultural psychological studies for global business. In Information Resources Management Association (Ed.), International Business: Concepts, Methodologies, Tools, and Applications (pp. 1734-1755). Hershey, PA: IGI Global.

Yin, K., Wang, R., An, Q., Yao, L., & Liang, J. (2014). Using eco-efficiency as an indicator for sustainable urban development: A case study of Chinese provincial capital cities. *Ecological Indicators*, *36*, 665–671. doi:10.1016/j.ecolind.2013.09.003

Yin, R. K. (1994). Applied Social Research Methods Series: Vol. 5. *Case Study Research*. Thousand Oaks, CA: Sage.

Yin, R. K. (2003). *Case Study Research: Design and Methods*. Thousand Oaks, CA: Sage.

Yin, R. K. (2014). *Case study research: Design and methods* (5th ed.). Thousand Oaks, CA: Sage Publications.

Young, D. R., Searing, E. A. M., & Brewer, C. V. (2016). *The Social Enterprise Zoo. A Guide for Perplexed Scholars, Entrepreneurs, Philanthropists, Leaders, Investors, and Policymakers*. Cheltenham, UK: Edward Elgar Publishing.

Young, L. (2003). Ed Marra's 'glocal' marketing. *Marketing Magazine*, *108*(36), 11.

Zanoli, R., & Naspetti, S. (2001). *Values and Ethics in Organic Food Consumption*. Paper presented at the third EurSafe Congress on: "Food Quality and Food Ethics," Florence, Italy.

Zanoli, R., & Naspetti, S. (2002). Consumer motivations in the purchase of organic food: A means-end approach. *British Food Journal*, *104*(8), 643–653. doi:10.1108/00070700210425930

Zellweger, T., & Sieger, P. (2012). Entrepreneurial orientation in long-lived family firms. *Small Business Economics, 38*(1), 67–84. doi:10.100711187-010-9267-6

Zepeda, L., & Deal, D. (2009). Organic and local food consumer behaviour: Alphabet Theory. *International Journal of Consumer Studies, 33*(6), 697–705. doi:10.1111/j.1470-6431.2009.00814.x

Zepeda, L., & Reznickova, A. (2017). Innovative millennial snails: The story of Slow Food University of Wisconsin. *Agriculture and Human Values, 34*(1), 167–178. doi:10.100710460-016-9701-8

Zhao, P., & Li, P. (2017). Rethinking the relationship between urban development, local health and global sustainability. *Current Opinion in Environmental Sustainability, 25*(1), 14–19. doi:10.1016/j.cosust.2017.02.009

Zhou, S., Simnett, R., & Green, W. (2017). Does Integrated Reporting Matter to the Capital Market? *Abacus, 53*(1), 94–132. doi:10.1111/abac.12104

Zhu, Q., Geng, Y., & Lai, K. (2011). Environmental supply chain cooperation and its effect on the circular economy practice-performance relationship among Chinese manufacturers. *Journal of Industrial Ecology, 15*(3), 405–419. doi:10.1111/j.1530-9290.2011.00329.x

Zocchi, W. (2004a) Discontinuità e sinergie generazionali nell'azienda di famiglia. Un'indagine empirica nel Lazio. Luiss University Press – Pola Srl, Roma.

Zocchi, W. (2004b) Il family business. Famiglia, azienda di famiglia e il patrimonio dell'imprenditore. Il Sole 24 Ore, Milano.

About the Contributors

Luisa Carvalho holds a PhD in Management in University of Évora – Portugal. Professor of Management on Department of Management and Social Sciences – Open University - Lisbon – Portugal. Guest professor in international universities teaches in courses of master and PhDs programs. Researcher at CEFAGE (Center for Advanced Studies in Management and Economics) University of Evora – Portugal. Author of several publications in national and international journals, books and book chapters.

Elisa Truant, PhD, is Aggregate Professor in Business Administration at University of Turin, Italy. Sustainability, family business and managerial accounting represent her main research interests. She is the author of many studies on sustainability, strategic planning and management control within family business and SMEs.

* * *

Marisa Agostini is Assistant Professor of Accounting at the Department of Management of University Ca' Foscari (Venice). During her international Ph.D. in Business, she was visiting researcher at the McCombs School of Business (The University of Texas at Austin, U.S.A.). Her research interests include financial statement analysis and accounting fraud, integrated reporting and accounting history. Her research has appeared in international publications, including Accounting History and Social And Environmental Accountability Journal.

Simona Alfiero received the PhD Degree in Business and Management. She is an Assistant Professor at the Department of Management, University of Turin and the President of the Italian Business Administration Academy (AIDEA GIOVANI). Her main research topics are: corporate performance, CSR, financial disclosure, risk management and food management.

Carlo Bagnoli is Full Professor of Strategy Innovation at the Department of Management of University Ca' Foscari (Venice). His research interests include Business model innovation, Strategic fit and innovation, Intellectual capital strategic management. His research has appeared in international publications, including Journal Of Cleaner Production, Journal Of Intellectual Capital, Management Decision, Journal Of Knowledge Management, Journal Of Management And Governance, Industrial Management & Data Systems.

Fernando Barbosa is Invited Assistant at the Department of Production and Systems at Minho University, Guimarães, Portugal. He is also CEO and Founder at Focus Cooperative, a nonprofit organization, whose mission is to be the specialist in the offer of individualized life projects to individuals with global developmental delay and autism spectrum disorders. He holds a BA in Business Administration and a MSc in Industrial Engineering, concluding the Doctoral Programme in Industrial and Systems Engineering at Minho University. His research interests include Knowledge, Strategy, Innovation and Internationalization.

Shounak Basak is a doctoral student in the Operations Management area at Indian Institute of Management Calcutta.

Laura Broccardo received a Ph.D. in Business Administration in 2010. She is currently an Assistant Professor in Business Administration at the Department of Management, University of Turin, Italy. She was Erasmus Visiting Professor in some foreign universities. She teaches Management Accounting and Business Organization courses (Italian and English undergraduate) and the Business Organization and Process Management course (graduate). Her research interests are in management accounting, cost management, strategic management, governance, and the organisational and behavioural aspects of accounting, on which several international publications were focused. She's Fellow of the EuroMed Academy of Business.

Giacomo Büchi is full professor in management at University of Turin, Department of Management.

Massimo Cane received his Ph.D. in Business Administration in 2003. He is currently an Assistant Professor in Business Administration at the Department of Management of the University of Turin, where he teaches Financial Accounting and IT Management. His research interests, discussed in many international publications, involve food management, accounting and financial analysis, gender diversity, CSR, risk management and Integrated Reporting. He is a member of National and International Academies.

Cecilia Casalegno took her Master degree in International Management at the Faculty of Economics, University of Turin, in 2003. She has a PhD degree in business administration and from the 2008 she has been researcher and lecturer at the Department of Management, University of Turin and she is visiting professor at Universitad Autonoma del Barcelona. Her main fields of research concern the integrated marketing communication, the strategic human resource management, the leadership development strategy. She is author of national and international publications (books and papers).

Maurizio Cisi is Associate Professor Management at the Department of Management, University of Turin. His research focuses on Corporate Social Responsibility, SMEs' financial disclosure and business networking and cooperation. Responsible of the local CPAs' study group on business networks.

Chiara Civera is Research Fellow at the University of Turin, Department of Management and Ph.D. in Business and Management. She is visiting researcher at London South Bank University in London (UK) and at Darden Business School, University of Virginia, United States and is lecturer of Business Ethics at Abat Oliba CEU (Barcelona, Spain). The main subjects of interest and current researches are: corporate social responsibility, stakeholder theory, sustainability, communication, common goods. She is currently lecturer of Marketing Management, Business Strategy and Business Ethics.

Thilini Cooray is a Lecturer at the Department of Accounting, University of Sri Jayewardenepura, Sri Lanka. Thilini is interested in research topics related to corporate sustainability, sustainability reporting, and accounting education.

Laura Corazza, Ph.D., is Research Fellow at the Department of Management, University of Turin (UniTo), Italy. She is visiting researcher at Laurea University of Applied Science (Helsinki - Finland). She is the editor of the Sustainability Reporting of UniTo. Her teaching and research area are: Social Accounting, Corporate Social Responsibility, Universities Social Responsibility. Her research has appeared in international publications, including Corporate Social Responsibility and Environmental Management, Sustainability and Information Resources Management Journal.

Damiano Cortese is Research Fellow at the Department of Management, University of Turin in Italy and Ph.D. in Business and Management. He teaches Business Administration at the Department of Foreign Languages, Literatures and Modern Cultures. He is visiting lecturer at University of Gastronomic Sciences and visiting researcher at Darden School of Business, University of Virginia. His research interests are in food, tourism management, culture management and history of accounting.

Ericka Costa (PhD in Business Economics, University of Udine, Italy) is Assistant Professor of Accounting, University of Trento. She is International Associate for Italy in the Centre for Social and Environmental Accounting Research (CSEAR) networks. Her research interests are aimed at investigating Sustainability Accounting and Corporate Social Responsibility both for profit and non-profit organisations. She has written a number of chapters in books and articles and papers that have been accepted for national and international journals and conferences. Her research has appeared in international publications, including: Accounting and Business Research, Social and Environmental Accountability Journal, Sustainability Accounting and Management Policy Journal, Journal of Business Ethics, Voluntas and Service Business.

Francesca Culasso is Professor in Business Administration at the University of Turin, Italy. Her research interests are in management accounting, cost management, strategic management, governance, risk management, and the organisational and behavioural aspects of accounting. She teaches the Management Accounting (Italian and English undergraduate) and Business Organization and Process Management courses (graduate).

Jorge Cunha is Assistant Professor at the Department of Production and Systems, Engineering School, University of Minho, Portugal, and is a researcher on ALGORITMI Research Centre, Portugal. He holds a degree in Economics (1996), a MSc in Financial Economics (1999), both from Faculty of Economics, University of Coimbra, and a PhD in Production and Systems Engineering (2005) from University of Minho, Portugal. His recent research interests are on the social innovation process, economic impact studies, energy finance, and strategic investment decisions. He is the author and co-author of several scientific papers published in international journals. Recently, he has been involved in a project for the evaluation of the economic impact of Polytechnic Institutes in Portugal.

Paola De Bernardi is an Assistant Professor currently working at the Department of Management, University of Torino, Italy, in the Business Administration Division. Her teaching and research focuses in the field of Business and Management with a special focus on Managerial Accounting, Performance Measurement and Control System, Corporate Social Responsibility, as well as Integrated Thinking and Reporting . She has been visiting professor at Lethbridge University, Canada. She is currently working on and supervising two national funded projects on Industry 4.0, named "Food Digital Monitoring" and "Hierarchy Open Manufacturing Europe".

Ruggiero Doronzo. Since 2015 Ph.D. student in Business and Management at the Department of Management of the University of Turin. His research project and interests involve Integrated Reporting, board diversity and accounting and financial analysis.

Alfredo Esposito. Since 2014 Ph.D. student in Business and Management at the Department of Management of the University of Turin. His research project and interests involve Integrated Reporting, board diversity and accounting and financial analysis.

Simona Fiandrino is a Ph.D. Candidate in Business and Management at the University of Turin, Department of Management in Italy. The main subjects of interest are Business Ethics, Corporate Social Responsibility and Social Finance.

Irina Gavancha is a manager corporate clients in the Corporate Recovery Department at Caixa Geral de Depósitos, Portugal with a degree in business management from the Polytechnic Institute of Santarém and a specialization in accounting and taxation of Lusófona University of Humanities and Technology. She has authored a per-reviewed paper about credit risk analysis in mortgage loans. Her major research interests include credit risk analysis and the relation between accounting and sustainability.

Nuwan Gunarathne is a Senior Lecturer at the Department of Accounting, University of Sri Jayewardenepura, Sri Lanka. Nuwan is a committee member of the Environmental and Sustainability Management Accounting Network (EMAN) Asia Pacific (AP) and country representative of the Sri Lanka Chapter of EMAN-AP. Nuwan is interested in research topics related to corporate sustainability, integrated and sustainability reporting, sustainability and accounting education.

Mª Asunción López-Arranz is a Professor and researcher in the area of labor law and social security. Specialist in labor relations, sustainability, employment, training and gender.

Sara Giovanna Mauro is a Resarch Fellow at the Department of Management, University of Turin (Italy). She holds an international PhD in Management and has spent research periods in several countries. Her primary research interests are in accounting and management, with a special focus on public sector.

Fabrizio Mosca is Bachelor of Business Management (University of Torino, Italy), MBA (University of Torino, Italy) and took a Ph.D. in Economics and Business Administration at Luigi Bocconi University, Milano, Italy. Fabrizio Mosca has written several articles and books on Strategic Luxury Management and Luxury Marketing. This topic is the main field of his research. Fabrizio Mosca is, presently, a professor at the Business Management Department of University of Torino, where he teaches Marketing, Marketing Advanced and Strategic Management. He is also involved in many different postgraduate and International Master programs, in the Luxury Master of Il Sole24Ore and in the doctoral program. He is also part of the Scuola di Amministrazione Aziendale, the Turin Business School of Management.

Inna Sousa Paiva (PhD) Auxiliary Professor of Accounting at the Lisbon University Institute (ISCTE-IUL). She has considerable academic experience in programs in financial accounting area. Her research interests are the implementation of International Financial Reporting Standards, Accounting Quality and Family Firms. She is the author of several communications in international scientific conferences, published articles and book chapters.

Christian Rainero is associate professor in Business administration at University of Turin, Department of Management; He currently holds positions as a Professor of public accounting courses in undergraduated, postgraduated and master courses. He is a member of several groups of study on accounting and management of public, private and no-profit entities.

Fernando Romero holds an MA in Technology Policy and Innovation Management from the University of Maastricht (NL), and a Ph.D. in Science and Technology Studies from the University of Manchester (UK). He is at the Production and Systems Department, and at the ALGORITMI Research Centre, at the University of Minho. He lectures and publishes regularly in the area of innovation systems and innovation management, with main interests on university relations with society, technology transfer, research and technology management, and the determinants of innovation. He has been involved in several international research projects and hold several middle and high-level university management responsibilities.

Kushal Saha is a doctoral student in the Management Information Systems area at Indian Institute of Management Calcutta.

Simone Domenico Scagnelli, PhD, is Associate Professor of Business Administration at the Department of Management, University of Torino, Italy. His teaching and research focuses in the areas of Sustainability Reporting and Corporate Social Responsibility, International Accounting and Innovation Management.

Sudhanshu Shekhar is a doctoral student in the Organizational Behavioral area at Indian Institute of Management Calcutta.

Lia Tirabeni, PhD in Sociology, is Research Fellow at the Department of Cultures, Politics, and Society and Adjunct Professor at the Department of Psychology (University of Turin). She has been Visiting Research Fellow at the Department of Management Science & Technology, Athens University of Economics & Business, (Athens, Greece). Her research concerns economic sociology and organization studies. She is particularly interested in family business dynamics and the ways technology affects work practices and organizations.

Paola Vola, PhD, is Aggregate Professor in Business Administration at University of Eastern Piedmont. Family business and managerial accounting represent her main research interests. She is the author of many studies on strategic planning and managerial accounting within family business and SMEs.

Index

G

H

I

K

L

M

N

O

P

R

S

T

U

V

www.ingramcontent.com/pod-product-compliance
Lightning Source LLC
LaVergne TN
LVHW080534300926
849162LV00007B/1606